THE

NORTH

ATLANTIC,

1775

SCOTLAND

North Sea

IRELAND

ENGLAND

London

Plymouth

Dunkirk

English Channel

Paris

Brest

l'Orient

FRANCE

El Ferrol

Azores

PORTUGAL

Madrid

SPAIN

Cadiz

Strait Of Gibraltar

Madeira

AFRICA

Canary
Islands

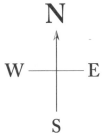

N

W — E

S

Cape Verde
Islands

MILES

0   500

GIVE ME A FAST SHIP

★ ★ ★

ALSO BY TIM McGRATH

John Barry: An American Hero in the Age of Sail

GIVE ME
A FAST SHIP

★ ★ ★

The Continental Navy
and America's Revolution at Sea

TIM McGRATH

NAL
CALIBER

NAL Caliber
Published by the Penguin Group
Penguin Group (USA) LLC, 375 Hudson Street,
New York, New York 10014

USA | Canada | UK | Ireland | Australia | New Zealand | India | South Africa | China

penguin.com
A Penguin Random House Company

First published by NAL Caliber, an imprint of New American Library,
a division of Penguin Group (USA) LLC

First Printing, July 2014

LIBRARY OF CONGRESS CATALOGING-IN-PUBLICATION DATA:
McGrath, Tim, 1951–
Give me a fast ship: the Continental Navy and America's Revolution at sea/Tim McGrath.
p. cm.
Includes bibliographical references and index.
ISBN 978-0-451-41610-0
1. United States—History—Revolution, 1775–1783—Naval operations.
2. United States. Continental Navy—History.   3. United States. Navy—History—
Revolution, 1775–1783.   I. Title.   II.Title: Continental Navy and America's Revolution at sea.
E271.M445 2014
973.3'5—dc23   2014008295

Printed in the United States of America
3   5   7   9   10   8   6   4   2

Set in Adobe Caslon Pro   •   Designed by Elke Sigal

To Ted and Courtney

I wish to have no connection with any ship that does not sail fast;
for I intend to go in harm's way.

—JOHN PAUL JONES

CONTENTS

✯   ✯   ✯

MAPS

★ ★ ★

GIVE ME A FAST SHIP

CHAPTER ONE

★　★　★

"REBELLIOUS FANATICKS"

What can we do—if united? We only want a navy to give law to the world, and we have it in our power to get it.

—MAJOR ADAM STEPHENS TO RICHARD HENRY LEE, 1775[1]

To begin with, they paid hardly any taxes.

But it was not the amount that angered these New Englanders. It was the idea of the tax itself; the act of a governing body demanding revenue from fellow countrymen who, because they lived an ocean away, did not possess the right to be represented among the lawmakers who levied the tax.

At dusk on Thursday, December 16, 1773, dozens of them stood along Griffin's Wharf in Boston, huddled together against the wind and rain, a band of men and boys handpicked by Samuel Adams and the other leaders of the Sons of Liberty, a society of patriots united in their resistance to the policies of King George III and Parliament. The gang at the wharf ranged in notoriety from the well-known silversmith and sometime propagandist Paul Revere to fifteen-year-old Joshua Wyeth, a blacksmith's apprentice. Most of them were dressed as Indians, wrapped in blankets and carrying hatchets. Their faces had been smudged with burnt cork by Mrs. James Bruce, whose husband was one of the ringleaders.[2]

Some blocks away on Boylston Street, inside Old South Church, the most vocal faction of the town's resistance to British taxation took turns addressing a crowd that filled the pews, packed the aisles, and spilled outside into the streets. Old South was a perfect venue for such a revolutionary meeting; one of its earlier members, Samuel Sewall, was among the first Americans that railed against the practice of slavery and later advocated women's rights.

For weeks, American ports had been abuzz over the latest affront from Parliament: a tax on tea. For ten years, Parliament had passed a series of taxes levied at the American colonies as part of its efforts to pay for the defense of the colonies. Each measure, from the Sugar Act and the Stamp Act through the Townshend Acts, was aimed at paying down this debt, and each one was vehemently resisted by many colonists. They were led by the merchants, who viewed any tax, even those ordained to pay for the victory over their French and Indian enemies, as an attack on their rights—or lack of them—by the Crown. Their resistance consistently bore fruit, for measure after measure was repealed.

But the Tea Act was naked in its lack of any connection to colonial self-interest. Its purpose was to bolster the sagging fortunes of the East India Company, a pillar of the British economy whose stock had recently plummeted from £280 to £160 per share. Deeming "John Company" as too big to fail, Parliament, in passing the Tea Act, hoped to give it a virtual monopoly on the most popular drink in the British Empire. The East India Company could undersell everyone, including American merchants who smuggled the profitable leaves outright.[3]

Those colonial merchants designated as agents of the East India Company anticipated a financial windfall, but quickly discovered that their appointments were more curse than blessing. Once news reached America of this latest tax, resistance quickly spread, growing from outcry to physical intimidation, especially when the ships bearing the tea—many of them owned by the agents themselves— entered port roadsteads from Boston to Charleston. By December news reached Massachusetts of the broadside delivered to Delaware River pilots, signed by "the Committee for Tarring and Feathering" and informing them of what awaited anyone who dared bring a tea ship into Philadelphia. One captain named Ayres did sail his ship, the *Polly*, into port, and was soon brought to the State House (later known as Independence Hall) by a crowd of hundreds while the "committee" got their tar ready. After Ayres assured one and all that he would sail back to England with the next tide, they joyfully dispersed. Among them was John Barry, a young merchant captain who, at six feet four, was easy to spot. He went home that evening to regale his wife with the most recent events. The next morning he stood downriver aboard his merchantman, bound for the island of St. Eustatius, the *Polly* sailing just ahead.[4]

Thus inspired, the speakers at Old South had made their plans days before they took turns at the pulpit on this dreary afternoon.

Word of Philadelphia's planned tea party also reached the home of the Massachusetts governor, Thomas Hutchinson, whose two sons were among the agents awaiting tea shipments. Tension mounted daily as, one by one, the merchantmen, loaded down with hundreds of chests full of tea, made their way up the King's Roadstead to Boston harbor. The first ship, the *Dartmouth*, dropped anchor on November 17, followed by the *Eleanor* and the *Beaver*. By law, no cargo could be unloaded for thirty days. If the Sons of Liberty were to act, they had until tonight to do so—hence this meeting inside Old South Church.

Throughout the late afternoon, speakers urged Bostonians to stand united in opposition to Crown policy. Their oratory was a delaying action. Earlier, the Sons of Liberty sent the *Dartmouth*'s owner, Francis Rotch, to see Governor Hutchinson with a request to let the ship depart unloaded, and thus defuse the situation. Everyone in the church awaited Rotch's arrival and word of Hutchinson's decision.

Shortly after six o'clock Rotch entered the church, jostling his way through the throng until he reached the altar railing, where he told Sam Adams of Hutchinson's verdict: the *Dartmouth* would remain in port, to be unloaded in the morning.

As everyone hushed, Adams again ascended the pulpit. Gazing over the crowd, in a clear, ringing voice, he said, "This meeting can do nothing more to save the country." The sentence, simply read, smacks of hyperbole, but it was not overblown oratory: it was a prearranged signal. Once he uttered the words, the shrill cry of a boatswain's (bosun's) whistle blew outside, calling the "Indians" at Griffin's Wharf to action.

The rain was tapering off as they manned three longboats, each assigned a commander and a bosun. Following orders from Adams and Revere, the men rowed to their designated ship, scrambled over the sides, and went to work with surety and speed. Carrying lanterns, several went below to the ship's hold. With block and tackle, they brought the tea chests on deck, where their comrades attacked them with hatchets. Then the tea was poured overboard, followed by the empty chests. One of the hoists snapped violently and a chest struck one of the men, a carpenter, upside his head. His companions, believing him dead, rowed him to shore.

At first, the tea leaves lapped against the hulls. But the tide was so low that, as the tea piled higher and higher, it began to spill over the gunwales. Sweeping it back as best they could, the "Indians" kept at their task until each chest was destroyed. Soon more than 90,000 pounds of tea floated in Boston harbor. By this time most of the Old South crowd had made their way down Mill Street to the docks, joyfully watching their fellow New Englanders at work.[5]

Not all of the witnesses were amused. From a nearby house, Admiral James Montagu watched helplessly, later reporting to the British Admiralty that any intervention by his men to stop this destruction would have "endangered the Lives of innocent People."[6]

Two hours after the fake Indians boarded the ships, those "brave and resolute men," as the *Boston Gazette* called them, finished their work. Years later, Joshua Wyeth (whose descendants include three generations of distinguished American painters) would chuckle about "making so large a cup of tea for the fishes." As the tide rose it carried the tea from one end of the harbor to the other. The following morning, Montagu asked onlookers rhetorically, "Who is to pay the fiddler now?" and later informed the Admiralty that "the Devil is in this people."[7]

In the ensuing months other cities followed the example of Boston and Philadelphia, holding tea parties from New York to Charleston. In Annapolis, a mob forced agents to use the tea chests as kindling to burn the *Peggy Stewart*. In Charleston, demonstrators led by Christopher Gadsden, a former Royal Navy officer, escorted the agents aboard ship, handed them hatchets, and oversaw the pouring of tea leaves as "an oblation to Neptune." Leave it to southerners to have owners destroy their own property, an eighteenth-century reversal of the time-honored tourist trap warning *You bought it, you break it* . . . and burn it for good measure.[8]

The participants in the tea parties were an odd mix of backgrounds and vocations. They were doctors, lawyers, and merchants; politicians, carpenters, and laborers. A great number of them were sailors.

That, as we shall see, was only fitting.

One Bostonian did not partake in his town's revelry but was nevertheless so captivated that he called it "the most magnificent Moment of all." By 1773 John Adams was well-known as a lawyer consumed with the pursuit of justice, regardless of partisanship. In 1769, he was the hero of the hour after successfully defending several American sailors for slaying a British naval officer whose press gang boarded their ship looking for "recruits" to pad his muster rolls. One year later, Adams was villainy personified—at least to his cousin Sam's followers—when his skillful defense won acquittal for the "Lobsterbacks" who killed five members of a mob in what was immediately called the Boston Massacre.[9]

By the spring of 1775, much had changed for John Adams, just as much had changed for the thirteen colonies. The increasing hard-heartedness of king and Parliament, culminating in the closing of the port of Boston until every tea leaf tossed in the harbor was paid for, succeeded in radicalizing Adams and thousands of other colonists. Adams was now making his second pilgrimage to Philadelphia, to act as a delegate from Massachusetts to the second Continental Congress, just as he had served in the first. The lawyer who had championed reason while abhorring his cousin's less dignified approach now led the open opposition to George III and his latest prime minister, Frederick, Lord North. Adams saw his personal rebellion as an extension of his devotion to justice. For him, these times were an "age of trial," and he was determined to play a part regardless of the financial and emotional cost to both himself and his family.[10] The world had not yet turned upside down, but Adams's life certainly had.

When he arrived in Philadelphia for the first Congress, he was fascinated by the largest city of the colonies, home to 30,000 souls. A century earlier, William Penn designed the city as a giant grid, each even, spacious, squared-off street a replica of the ones adjoining it. The redbrick houses of the rich frequently stood within a few feet of the modest homes of fellow Philadelphians—artisans, shopkeepers, printers, and the booming merchant class, whose work ethic was visible to all—aspiring to join them in wealth and position. Rich merchants and their wives, dressed in colorful clothes, presented a marked contrast to the dull black or gray cloth suits of the Quakers.[11]

It was a bustling city. There were churches of every denomination and taverns for every taste. The waterfront hummed with the sounds of windlasses and stevedores weighed down with cargo from and for ships of all sizes. Blocks away, wagon after wagon carried fresh food along High Street, known to all as Market. Printing presses turned out more newspapers than were in London. Philadelphia was noisy and filthy, and reeking from the permeating stench of a tannery behind Carpenters' Hall, the small jewel of a building off Chestnut Street that hosted the first Continental Congress in 1774. The city offered its distinguished visitors everything from the intellectual pursuits of the American Philosophical Society, created by Benjamin Franklin, to the new hospital on the outskirts of town (also founded by Franklin), where Adams discovered a former client locked in the "lunatick" ward. Other delegates found Philadelphia disconcerting. Adams admired it.[12]

He was not so complimentary of the first Congress. After spending the fall of 1774 debating their proposals, Adams was "wearied to death." New Englanders in particular sought decisive measures against the Crown, but as this session of Congress neared adjournment, the calmer and more conservative members held the upper hand. When Paul Revere galloped into Philadelphia with news that citizens of Suffolk County, Massachusetts, had issued a set of resolves declaring "no obedience" to the latest acts of Parliament, Adams and the other firebrands passed a series of economic sanctions against England. No goods would be imported from the British Isles and her West Indies territories after December 1. Beginning May 1, 1775, no goods would be exported from the colonies to the mother country.[13]

In late spring, congressmen began returning to Philadelphia. Weeks earlier, when news reached Adams at his Braintree farm that Minutemen and Redcoats had murdered one another at nearby Lexington and Concord, he rode out to see the carnage firsthand. Talk of rebellion had become rebellion; threats of bloodshed were now a terrible reality.

Adams soon departed for Philadelphia. Earlier he had written, "We have not men fit for the times." The first Congress left him skeptical about his colleagues and their collective willingness to find common ground and unify. With each mile of his journey, he carried the knowledge that he had left his wife and children without an income and within reach of the British, too. That truth never left his mind. In fact, it would stoke each proposal he made. Francis Bacon called one's family "hostages to fortune" in wartime. Adams understood that all too well.[14]

Most of the delegates were returnees, though there were three notable exceptions. The diminutive John Hancock was now a member of the Massachusetts delegation. Well-known as he was for his patriotic zeal, he also suffered from the ignominious nickname "king of smugglers" for his success as a businessman and the enmity he aroused from British authorities for his political views. Virginia's representatives now included a young red-haired lawyer, Thomas Jefferson, so silent during the sessions that he was conspicuous only for his height.

And the most famous American in the world, Benjamin Franklin, had returned home to Philadelphia after years of serving in England as Pennsylvania's agent. When his involvement in some backroom intrigue over the political impasse in Massachusetts became public knowledge, Franklin was summoned to "the cockpit," the well of Parliament's chamber, where he was berated, mocked, and threatened by its members. Franklin subsequently sailed home to Philadelphia and arrived on May 6, greeted as one onlooker recalled, "to the satisfaction of friends and the lovers of Liberty."[15]

Adams found Philadelphia caught up with martial fervor. News of Lexington and Concord reached Philadelphia on April 23, St. George's Day, where a party of notable Philadelphians was celebrating the birthday of the king's namesake at the City Tavern. The renowned merchant Robert Morris was raising his glass to toast George III when a rider burst through the door with the news. As the celebrants scrambled outside, overturning tables and chairs, Morris, now alone in the room, toasted the Massachusetts rebels, and drained his glass. From that day forward, Penn's peaceful city took on a martial aura: sounds of fife and drum wafted through the streets while various regiments and militia, organized by politician and well-endowed private citizen alike, drilled before the State House on Fifth and Chestnut Streets.[16]

Congress had a new venue, having moved from Carpenters' Hall to the more spacious State House. Its block-long redbrick walls and six-story bell tower dominated the Philadelphia landscape. Two Philadelphians had submitted plans for its design in 1732. The winning draft came from the hand of attorney Andrew Hamilton, who successfully defended New York newspaperman Peter Zenger against an accusation of libeling the royal governor. The loser was the designer of Christ Church, Dr. John Kearsley, whose nephew would be arrested for treason shortly after Congress learned of his plan to raise an army of 5,000 Loyalists to keep Philadelphia in Tory hands.[17]

Adams and his colleagues set up shop in the Assembly Room on the first floor, where the high, broad windows, spaced between the gray-painted walls, were open to the spring breezes. Each colony's representatives sat on round-backed chairs at tables covered with green cloth that added a touch of somberness to a room that was 40 feet, 4 inches long and 38 feet, 6 inches wide, about one-third the length of a frigate and just slightly wider than her beam.[18]

For the next six months, in this room, ninety miles from the Atlantic Ocean, John Adams—whose only sailing experience had been a fishing trip near Cohasset Rocks, fifteen miles off Boston—would serve as midwife in the birth of the first American navy.[19]

The Second Continental Congress moved slowly. Dispatches from the colonies, particularly those from the New England army that now had Gage's forces penned in Boston, were devoured and debated, if not always acted upon. In a move to unify the southern delegates with their northern colleagues, John Adams nominated Virginian George Washington to take command of the newly christened American Continental Army facing Boston. Working relationships were established with each colony's government—that is, those represented by American politicians who were unfettered by Crown loyalty.

Ironically, two giant issues were rarely mentioned. Independence from Great Britain was one. An American navy was the other. Those representatives who yearned, openly or privately, for reconciliation with the Crown viewed the creation of the latter as guaranteeing the former. The colonies they called home began in New York and ran south to Georgia; the war had yet to visit their territory. As far as the New England delegations were concerned, sentiments for reconciliation had long since vanished.

That summer, John Adams proposed the idea of an American navy. In Christopher Gadsden, he found a willing ally among the reluctant southerners. Gadsden believed the British fleet stationed off the coast "is not so formidable to America as we fear." Further, Adams recounted to his fellow New Englander Elbridge Gerry that Gadsden believed

> We can easily take their Sloops, schooners, and Cutters, on board of whom are all their best Seamen, and with these We can easily take their large Ships, on board of whom are all their impress'd and discontented Men [who] would certainly kill their own officers.

Adams concurred: "It is a different Thing, to fight the French or Spaniards from what it is to fight british Americans," he wrote, and was as hopeful as his new friend Gadsden that "We may get a Fleet of our own."[20] The conservative bloc in Congress, led by Pennsylvanian John Dickinson, dismissed the idea out of hand. Dickinson engineered a peace feeler to George III, known as "the Olive Branch Petition." A bitter Adams wrote his friend James Warren, whose brother Joseph—Adams's friend and physician—had recently been killed at Bunker Hill:

> We ought to have had in our Hands a month ago the whole Legislative, executive and judicial of the whole Continent . . . to have raised a naval Power, and opened our Ports wide; to have arrested every Friend to Government on the Continent and held them as Hostages for the poor victims in Boston, and then opened the Door as wide as possible for Peace and Reconciliation.[21]

In his letter Adams called Dickinson "a piddling genius." He believed this epithet would be kept in confidence, only to find his letter intercepted by the

British, whose gleeful publishing of it in Loyalist newspapers caused Adams embarrassment and provoked enmity from the more peaceable members of Congress.[22] Dickinson's faction did throw a bone to the war hawks in Congress, approving a resolution that each colony "at their own expence" purchase or build enough vessels "for the protection of their harbours and navigation on their sea coasts" from the Royal Navy.[23] Congress adjourned until September.

The fates, or at least events, were kinder to Adams's cause. When Congress reconvened that fall, he found new allies and foes. Back in Boston, he had one man serve him in both capacities: Vice Admiral Samuel Graves.

Graves was the senior British naval officer in America. At sixty-two, he was still a formidable presence on deck or in a salon, with a lifetime of action at sea behind him. By appearance and experience, he seemed every bit the perfect warrior to end this uprising. That was certainly his goal after Lexington and Concord; afterwards, he informed the Admiralty that his ships kept the rebels "in awe" while assuring the Lords of "heartily co-operating" with General Gage and "giving him every assistance in my power."[24]

But Graves's strong words were not followed by strong actions. No sooner had those Redcoats retreating from Concord returned to Boston than Yankee sailors, not wanting to be left out of the action, manned dozen of whaleboats and struck out for the islands around Boston. With their innate knowledge of tides, currents, and shoals, they went on a binge of destruction, burning lighthouses and hay bales and seizing livestock to keep the food-on-the-hoof out of reach of British foraging parties. Graves sent out longboats in pursuit, but they were easily outdistanced by the lighter, swifter whaleboats. By mid-May such unpunished activity had Graves feeling like Gulliver, bound by Lilliputians, especially when he learned that "it is forbidden under pain of death by the Rebels" to supply British forces. When asked by the royal governor of Virginia—John Murray, Lord Dunmore—for naval support, Graves initially refused; as "a numerous and well appointed [rebel] Army is assembled which without the protection of the Kings Ships can utterly destroy this Town and the Troops pent up in it."[25]

The actions of Graves's captains towards the colonists did little to win them over to the British side. "The depredations of the once formidable navy of Britain [are] now degraded to a level with the corsairs of Barbary," James Warren's wife, Mercy, wrote John Adams, although not all of their "pirattically plundering" went unanswered. British captain John Linzee took his sloop, the *Falcon*, into Buzzard's Bay below Cape Cod and seized a timber ship, her hold full of ballast. When her captain informed Linzee that a merchantman laden with West Indies goods was heading that way, Linzee set off in pursuit, capturing her as well. He soon learned that New Bedford sailors were as feisty as their Boston counterparts; they fitted out a sloop, chased the "royal pirates," and recaptured both of Linzee's prizes, sending him back to Boston empty-handed.[26]

But it was off the coast of Maine—then the eastern district of Massachusetts—where American sailors emulated the Minutemen of Lexington and Concord. Ichabod Jones, a Loyalist businessman admired by Graves for having "exerted himself in Supplying this Garrison" of Redcoats, proposed an expedition from Boston north to Machias, where its "New Settlers" had just survived a horrific winter. Jones offered to bring supplies to this coastland outpost, situated between New Brunswick and Mount Desert Island. With Graves's blessing, he took two timber ships, the *Unity* and the *Polly*, carrying twenty barrels each of pork and flour to be exchanged for Machias lumber. To guarantee the mission's success, Graves sent along a consort, the armed schooner *Margaretta*, under command of a young midshipman named James Moore. Jones saw the venture as a win-win-win: food for the Machias settlers, lumber for the Royal Navy, and a handsome profit for himself. He set sail in May and arrived on June 2.[27]

Jones's plans of success did not go immediately awry when his ship anchored off Machias that evening. After a good night's sleep, he went ashore to find the settlers neither glad to see him nor simpatico with his Tory mission. Weeks earlier, when news of Lexington and Concord had reached Machias, it was not received so much as embraced. Walking into town, Jones spied a "liberty pole" in the public square, a flagstaff topped by a replica of the Phrygian cap worn by freemen in ancient Rome, and erected by the local Sons of Liberty as a symbol of local sympathies. From the start, negotiations between Jones and the townsfolk were acrimonious, but after a bitter debate, his offer of goods for wood was put to a vote. The result barely went his way.[28]

His victory did not put Jones in a magnanimous mood. He brought the *Unity* and *Polly* to the wharf and began distributing the foodstuffs and goods only to residents who voted for his proposal. Then the "aggrieved party," as one eyewitness reported, "determined to take Capt. Jones [and] put a final stop to his supplying the King's troops with any thing." A chosen band of kidnappers attempted to seize Jones at the church service, but he and Midshipman Moore were alerted by the minister's servant. They escaped through a side window and fled into the woods. Once back aboard his ship Moore, already seething at the sight of the liberty pole, raised his sovereign's colors, letting it be known that "if the people presumed to stop Capt. Jones' vessels, he would burn the Town."[29]

The villagers called Moore's bluff. Some seized the *Unity* and "went directly to stripping the sloop," while others attacked the *Polly*, manned her guns, and began firing on the *Margaretta*. Moore sailed his schooner downriver. At dusk, he saw a fleet of rowboats and canoes approaching. Once "within hail of the ship," Moore seized his speaking trumpet, demanding to know what they wanted. They wanted Jones. Moore refused. The men of Machias raised their muskets and pistols. "Fire and be damn'd," he roared. "Brisk fire from the [*Margaretta's*] Swivels" sent the Americans hurriedly rowing out of range.[30]

At sunrise Moore could make out the *Unity* and *Polly*, manned to the gunwales with armed rebels. Determining that discretion was the order of the moment—if not, as we shall see, the day—Moore sailed the *Margaretta* to the harbor's entrance. As the ship came about, her boom and gaff were carried away. Moore now sent his crippled ship over to a sloop in the harbor, a neutral observer of the fray. British tars boarded her and confiscated two spars to replace their damaged ones, while the Americans changed course and made straight for the *Margaretta*.

As the Americans got closer and closer to the schooner, it occurred to them that they had not appointed a leader. While some maintained their course and others constructed makeshift breastworks from the timber in the ships' holds, they chose Jeremiah O'Brien, whose five brothers were also among the attacking force. Once they got close enough to the *Margaretta*, O'Brien ordered the British to "strike to the Sons of Liberty."

Moore had eyes; he could see his position was hopeless. But whether he was overcome by anger or devotion to king and country, he "luffed the Vessel too [*sic*]" and brought her into the wind, unleashing as strong a broadside as swivels, muskets, and pistols could fire. His men "threw some Hand grenades" at the Americans for good measure, while O'Brien sent his two ships on either side of the *Margaretta*. "At that instant," Moore's pilot later recalled, "Mr. Moore received two Balls, one in his right Breast, the other in his Belly." When the smoke cleared, nine British tars and fourteen Americans had been killed or wounded. The *Margaretta* struck her colors, the first British ship to surrender to Americans.

Fatally wounded, Moore was transported back to Machias, unrepentant of his decision to fight. Shortly after gasping that "he preferred Death before yielding to such a sett of Villains," he died. The exultant townspeople rewarded O'Brien with command of the *Unity*, armed her with the *Margaretta's* guns, and renamed her the *Machias Liberty*. "The naval Lexington," as historian Nathan Miller called it, had been fought and won.[31]

While O'Brien was still flush with success, another opportunity for twisting the British lion's tail dropped into his lap, or at least into the harbor. The schooner *Diligent* and the tender *Tattamagouche* were sent there not for revenge but to take soundings of the harbor for accurate chart making. O'Brien seized both without firing a shot. The small village of Machias now had something Congress did not—a navy.[32]

Farther south, General George Washington had arrived on July 2 to assume command of the rebel army that encircled Boston by land. "A good Soldier and a Man of sence," one official recalled, while Abigail Adams wrote her husband how "the Gentleman and Soldier look agreeably blended in him." As always, Washington had made a nearly universal good first impression, with the exception of one sentry who wrote, "Nothing happening extroderly" that day.[33]

But Washington's implacable countenance concealed deep anxieties over his new command. The army ranged from trained Rhode Islanders under the magnetic Nathanael Greene to undisciplined locals known as "the 8 month army" for their term of enlistment. Their only semblance of professionalism was found in John Glover's 21st Massachusetts Regiment from Marblehead, almost all of them sailors with a lifetime of practice in obeying and understanding orders. But Washington's real problem was not manpower as much as it was supplies, especially gunpowder.[34]

What made this crisis more vexing for Washington was what he saw through his spyglass: British transports arriving in Boston harbor, with half barrel after half barrel of gunpowder unloaded among the other supplies for Gage's Redcoats. Washington dispatched countless appeals to Congress, asking that each colony send him what he could "only lament the want of." For the rest of the summer he awaited overland caravans of the precious necessity, or at least the hope of word of any imminent arrivals. Meager supplies of it drifted in. He bore the lack of gunpowder stoically, but when Franklin related the novel, money-saving idea of replacing muskets with bows and arrows, Washington must have been torn between rolling his eyes heavenward or sheer frustration: it did not seem likely that Gage would agree to a battle for Boston using the weapons of Crécy and Agincourt.[35]

From his first day in camp, Washington insisted that American resistance be conducted on land and land only. When the Massachusetts Congress approved a mission sending the Machias "fleet" to raid Nova Scotia, he vociferously objected; while he applauded the sailors' "Spirit and Zeal," he cited everything from "our Weakness and the Enemy's Strength at Sea" to his main argument: "Our

Situation as to Ammunition absolutely forbids our Sending a Single Ounce [of powder] out of the Camp at present." But by September he changed his mind. Seeing that the answer to his problem was encamped alongside him, Washington turned to Glover and his "Webfoots."[36]

Before the war, Glover was a successful merchant who had a reputation as a rum trader with his own schooner, the *Hannah*, named for his wife. He fought in the French and Indian War. Since the Stamp Act he had been a leader in resistance to Crown policies; after Lexington and Concord he organized the Marblehead Regiment, comprising the coastal town's sailors and fishermen. He had a broad forehead, wide-set eyes, and a rounded, firm chin. Glover, his men, and his ship were the obvious choice for Washington to start his own navy.[37]

The cautious Washington did not buy the *Hannah*. He rented her for "ONE Dollar pr. Ton pr. Month." Glover picked officers and a crew from his Webfooters and placed Nicholas Broughton, an experienced merchant captain, in charge. Washington gave Broughton page after page of explicit orders: to "Cruise against such Vessels as may be found on the High Seas" carrying "Soldiers, Arms, Ammunition, or Provisions," to treat any prisoners "with Kindness and Humanity," and "to avoid any Engagement with any armed Vessel of the Enemy." And, last but not least, "to be extremely careful and frugal with your Ammunition" and "by no Means to waste any of it in Salutes."[38]

The *Hannah* was refitted as best as possible for wartime service, her bulwarks pierced for four 6-pounders. She sailed out of Gloucester under perfect conditions on September 5, flying a flag at her masthead with the words "Appeal to Heaven." Among her crew was Glover's son, John Junior. By late afternoon Broughton encountered the enemy, "two ships of War [that] gave me Chace." Over the next twenty-four hours the cruisers pursed the *Hannah*. Using his knowledge of the waters and shoals, Broughton eluded them. His first two attempts at leaving Gloucester were thwarted, but he finally slipped out at sunset and headed south.[39]

The next morning Broughton saw a ship under the *Hannah*'s lee quarter— the ship's side away from the wind. Finding her a ship of no force, Broughton pursued her, hailing her once she came within range of his guns. She was the *Unity*, bound for Boston, her hold full of supplies for Gage's army (not the *Unity* from Machias). The *Hannah* escorted her back to Gloucester. Broughton and his crew were ecstatic. They could feel the prize money Washington promised jingling in their pockets.

But their joy was short-lived; days earlier, the *Unity* had been taken by the

British as a prize and hastily put into the king's service. She was the property of New Hampshire congressman John Langdon. Once the ship was in port, Washington ordered her returned to Langdon. The *Hannah*'s crew, in a state of rebellion against the British, now rebelled against their general. Three dozen of them mutinied, forcing Washington to send troops to Gloucester with orders to bring them back to camp, where he intended "to bestow a different kind of reward for their behavior." A court-martial convicted them and sentenced them to the lash. Just before the sentence was to be carried out, Washington changed his mind: only the ringleader was flogged.

With just one ship, Washington had started an unofficial American navy, settled a dispute with a congressman, and quelled a mutiny that provided him an opportunity to administer both discipline and mercy. That said, it was one instance where Washington might have, on the whole, wished he was back in Philadelphia.[40]

While he would later complain about "rascally privateersmen," Washington nevertheless sought more ships to be armed and manned by soldiers in an effort to seize powder and supplies for his needy army. Over the next three months, the *Hannah* was joined by other schooners, manned by other "Webfooters," their actions giving the general an equal amount of success and exasperation.[41]

They also brought apoplexy to Vice Admiral Graves. In truth, the admiral lacked sufficient ships for his needs. He had twenty-four at the outbreak of hostilities, with a coastline from Canada to Florida to cover. That summer he was criticized both to his face and behind his back for his lack of action against Machias and Falmouth, where Henry Mowat, commander of the ship *Canceaux*, was captured by rebels shortly after being warmly received by the town Loyalists. Mowat escaped. From Boston, Major General John Burgoyne complained to Lord George Germain in London, "What is the Admiral doing?" He provided the answer in the next sentence: "I can only say what he is <u>not</u> doing."[42]

As summer ended, Graves decided to answer the American rebels in the harshest terms possible. Soon he and they would discover that the Royal Navy had just the right officers for such dirty work.[43]

By the time Broughton captured the *Unity*, Congressman Langdon was back in Philadelphia and Congress was back in session after a monthlong hiatus. There was much to do, and its members were beginning to discover they possessed powers that had been utterly beyond their comprehension just weeks earlier. They issued two million dollars in credit to run affairs; they began direct negotiations with the Native American tribes; they established a postal service. Delegates were now lawmakers.[44]

As a humid Philadelphia summer rolled into a cooler-than-usual autumn, John Adams returned to his favorite topic: an American navy. Events in their backyards—and along their coastline—continued to move the New England faction further towards an out-and-out break with Great Britain, and Adams began to personalize his arguments. He had every reason to. Letters from his wife, Abigail, contained thorough reports on the latest military actions around Boston. Adams had sent his family to their farm in Braintree, twelve miles outside of the city limits but along the main road into the town. From there, his wife told how she and their young children had American

> Soldiers comeing in for lodging, for Breakfast, for Supper, for Drink . . . refugees from Boston tierd and fatigued, seek an assilum for a Day or Night, a week—you can hardly imagine how we live.[45]

The Adams family first heard and then witnessed the Battle of Bunker Hill from Braintree, later giving water to the beaten, exhausted, and wounded New Englanders as they limped past the farm. When a British man-of-war anchored nearby, Abigail wrote her husband how "it occurred an alarm in this Town and we were up all night." Most delegates learned of the fighting around Boston through official dispatches. Adams read firsthand reports from an eyewitness, the mother of his children, and it fueled his desire for an escalation of all things military. He had lost his first battle to create a navy, but with his family in mind as much as his beloved Massachusetts, the landlubber lawyer made a new case for maritime armament that October.[46]

Adams also found in Congress both a formidable ally and a fearsome antagonist, each with a physical presence that dwarfed his own, and practically everyone else's: Stephen Hopkins of Rhode Island and Samuel Chase of Maryland.

Hopkins came from a prominent Quaker family from Providence. He did not tie his hair back—it hung alongside his broad, open face. He was as bulky as he was tall, and always wore clothes of gray broadcloth and a felt hat that were positively drab compared to the clothing worn by his congressional colleagues, especially the youngest, Edward Rutledge of South Carolina, whose colorful dress Adams compared to a peacock. At sixty-eight, with a long political career behind him, Hopkins was senior to every delegate but Franklin. He had served as both governor and chief justice of Rhode Island and was an ardent abolitionist, although one younger brother, Esek, still dabbled in the slave trade.

Samuel Chase always believed himself to be the better man in any confrontation. He, too, cut an intimidating figure. Standing over six feet, he threw his weight around along with his words. A lawyer, he possessed a vicious tongue, and he relished using it. Chase was an ardent patriot; ten years earlier, during the Stamp Act controversy, he had admittedly burned both the stamps and their agent—the latter, fortunately, in effigy.[47]

Thus far, the greater Boston area had borne the brunt of British army operations, but no colony's coastline had witnessed more depredations by the Royal Navy than Rhode Island, and for good reason. Rhode Islanders had tried to start the Revolution three years before Lexington and Concord. On June 10, 1772, a British schooner, the *Gaspee*, was in chase of a packet suspected of smuggling. The Rhode Islanders made for the shoals of Narragansett Bay, where the pursuing *Gaspee* ran aground. That night, men from Providence, led by Abraham Whipple, attacked the British crew, shot their commander, ransacked the *Gaspee*, and set her afire. Minutes later, she blew up.[48]

Parliament offered a £1,000 reward for the leader of this outrage against the Crown, but no Rhode Islander was greedy enough—or fool enough—to turn in the popular Whipple. It would be two years before retribution was exacted, coming from His Majesty's frigate *Rose* and her captain, James Wallace.

Years before Banastre Tarleton and Walter Butler personified British villainy, James Wallace set the mark. Once his frigate reached the Rhode Island coast, he was determined to use every measure and each of his ship's twenty guns to establish the king's laws over these disloyal colonists. Sharing Wallace's enthusiasm for punishing the Americans, Admiral Graves ordered him to "prevent all Supplies going to Providence" and to "seize Provisions and send them to Boston." In Wallace, Graves had a most willing officer. Wallace embarked on a binge of seizures of both merchantmen and merchant men, arousing alarm and adding to the already bitter feelings between colony and king. Learning of Whipple's role in the *Gaspee* affair, Wallace publicly declared he would hang Whipple "from the *Rose*'s yard arm." The rascally Whipple sent Wallace a note: "Sir, always catch a man before you hang him." Once hostilities broke out in 1775, Whipple had the first laugh aboard ship as well; as captain of the sloop *Katy*, fitted out by the Rhode Island Congress for the protection of the colony's merchantmen, he captured the *Rose*'s tender after a brief but furious exchange of cannon fire.[49]

Congress was still in summer recess when Wallace, "in One of his mad Fits," as Rhode Island officials put it in a letter to Hopkins, "drew up all three of the Men of War before the town of Newport and swore with the most bitter imprecations that he would burn it." That was more than enough for the Rhode Island Assembly. Exasperated by Congress's lack of leadership, they passed a resolution declaring "that the building and equipping of an American fleet" was necessary for "the preservation of the lives, liberty and property of the good people of these Colonies." They sent Hopkins and their other representatives a directive: use any and every political measure in getting a national fleet to sea, and get Congress to pay for it. Once Hopkins made their resolution known, John Adams went to work to make sure their wishes—and those of their fellow New Englanders—would become a reality.[50]

Adams, Hopkins, and the rest of the New England delegates faced opposition from members of every other colony from New York to South Carolina, especially the peace-loving Quakers and rebellious southerners who shared the viewpoint that a national navy was the latest in a series of actions designed not only to defend New England but to increase that region's influence. Southern congressmen, with the exception of South Carolina's Christopher Gadsden and Joseph Hewes of North Carolina, were adamant in their opposition. They were led by Samuel Chase.

Adams and Hopkins did not make a frontal assault on behalf of their cause. They spent September letting events play out. Upon their return to Philadelphia, the representatives were invited to inspect the row galleys being built at shipyards along the waterfront. When completed, twenty oars and two lateen sails propelled each of them across the water. Every galley carried a large cannon at the bow. The Pennsylvania Committee of Safety had appointed engineer Louis Nicola to come up with a plan to defend the Delaware, and he saw the galleys as an integral part in his strategy to repel what he called "an Insult by water" by British warships. The galleys made a favorable impression on Congress in general and Adams in particular.[51]

From Boston, Washington's dispatches arrived on a regular basis. The general interspersed his pleas for powder and arms with news of the comings and goings of enemy ships, along with reports of the *Hannah* and the other "rented" ships serving as his army's navy. In September he had issued a permit to Rhode Island merchants to sail "at their own Risque" for the West Indies and buy "what gunpowder they could find."[52]

By the fall, Graves and his captains were no longer restricting their punitive actions to New England. Word soon reached Congress that, after the New York Provincial Congress ordered cannons removed from a New York City port battery for use by rebel forces, musket fire was exchanged between colonists and the ship-of-the-line *Asia*, moored in New York harbor. Her captain, Captain George Vandeput, directed a three-hour bombardment against the battery and the surrounding homes. Afterwards, Vandeput informed the city's mayor that, if New Yorkers persisted in further rebellious acts, "the Mischiefs that may arise must lie at their Doors, and not mine."[53]

Several southern royal governors, fearing for their safety and that of their families, fled their palatial homes for the confined creature comforts and maximum security found aboard British warships. First and foremost of these new exiles was John Murray, Lord Dunmore. After hearing the news of Lexington and Concord, the ruddy-faced Virginia governor, bowlegged after years of fox hunting with the local gentry (including Washington), had ordered the removal of gunpowder stores from the Williamsburg arsenal while abolishing Virginia's House of Burgesses. When a band of patriots led by Patrick Henry seized the powder before Dunmore's men could do so, Dunmore and family took refuge aboard the HMS *Fowey*, a twenty-gun frigate. Throughout the summer, he and Captain George Montagu raided Virginia's coastline, using the ship, her men, and a new force meant to instill fear among white Virginians: armed runaway slaves whom Dunmore called his "Ethiopian Regiment."[54]

The Royal Navy's actions gave Adams the chance to resurrect his cause, and on October 3, he renewed his advocacy for sending Americans to war at sea on October 3. It nearly ended before it began. When Hopkins and Samuel Ward (an old Rhode Island foe of Hopkins until the rebellion) presented Congress with their colony's proposal it was immediately tabled. But the delay lasted only two days, thanks, in part, to reports given to Congress by Philadelphia's best-known sea captain.[55]

Days before, John Barry had returned from London aboard the *Black Prince*, the finest ship yet built in the colonies. Due to sluggish weather it had been a tedious voyage, save for one twenty-four-hour period when a gale and Barry's expert seamanship sent the *Black Prince* flying over 237 miles, the fastest known sailing day in the eighteenth century. Upon his return, Barry presented his boss, Robert Morris, with the latest London newspapers and reports from Morris's agents: news that "Eight men of war, from forty to fifty guns each, are ordered for the American station" and that five more British regiments were heading to

America. Barry also brought word that two other ships bound for Canada were "loaded with Arms and powder" but without armed escort.[56]

Such tidings did not bring joy, nor tip the balance of votes Adams's way, but they did reignite debate. Already convinced of the "daring intrepidity of our seamen," Adams argued that "if they were once let loose upon the ocean they would contribute greatly to the relief of our wants as well to the distress of the enemy." John Langdon concurred, as did Connecticut's Silas Deane.

Opposition was, as Adams put it, "very loud and vehement," but his most vocal critic that day was not Samuel Chase; it was Edward Rutledge. While Adams marveled at how "some of my colleagues appeared greatly alarmed" about even the idea of a navy, Rutledge was carried away with both his argument and himself. "Rutledge never displayed so much eloquence," Adams acerbically recalled, convinced the twenty-six-year-old had been coached "out-of-doors" by the opposition. Comparing the idea of a navy to "an infant, taking a mad bull by his horns," Rutledge concluded, "It would ruin the character, and corrupt the morals of our seamen. It would make them selfish, piratical, mercenary, bent wholly on plunder." In short, an American navy would turn its sailors into their British counterparts—although some thought his descriptions of potential avarice drew comparison to American merchants. Rutledge had succeeded in switching the argument from having a navy to *not* having a navy.

Rutledge received an answer from his fellow South Carolinian Christopher Gadsden. The bald, hawk-faced old sailor reasoned that if there were no means to defend American ports, they should be closed. "The [British] Navy can stop our Harbours and distress our Trade," he declared. "Therefore it is impracticable to open our Ports." The sun was setting outside when Adams and his backers passed a resolution for a three-man committee to prepare a plan for intercepting the Canadian-bound vessels. The three? Adams, Silas Deane, and John Langdon.[57]

Congress returned to the State House the next morning, reviewing military expenditures, permitting each colony to arrest any citizen "whose going at large may, in their opinion, endanger the safety of the colony, or the liberties of America." They took action to fortify the Hudson River. They discussed the recommendations of Adams's committee that Washington use two Massachusetts armed ships, the *Machias Liberty* and the *Unity*, to intercept the two British supply ships. Before Congress adjourned for the day, they heard at last from Samuel Chase.

Citing the "hostilities" committed by Lord Dunmore, Chase delivered a sarcastic harangue: "I don't think the Resolution goes far enough," he bellowed. "Have the Committee any naval Force?" Calling the resolution "a mere Piece of Paper," he lobbed question after question at his worthy colleagues like so many mortar shells: "Is there a Power in the Committee to raise and pay for a naval Force? Is it to be done at the Expence of the Continent[?] Have they Ships or Men?" To Chase the answer was clear—a government fights with the forces they have. Congress decided to take up debate on the Rhode Island Resolution the next day.[58]

The sun was shining on Saturday, October 7, as Adams joined his colleagues inside the State House. There was an air of anticipation among the representatives. Surely this would be the day when Adams would square off against Chase.[59]

It was not as pleasant in Bristol, Rhode Island, twelve miles southeast of Providence. "Little Wind and Hazy," James Wallace entered in the *Rose*'s log. Wallace had brought with him a sizable squadron: four warships, four tenders, two transports, three schooners, and three sloops—sixteen vessels in all, making for Bristol. Later that morning he sent a lieutenant into town, demanding supplies that included three hundred sheep. The townsfolk refused. Almost biblically, the sky blackened and a soaking rain began to fall.

The lieutenant's longboat no sooner bumped along the *Rose*'s hull than the guns were run out from each warship, and Wallace began bombarding the town. For more than an hour cannonballs slammed into homes, shops, stables, even the town church. The Newport *Mercury* would later report how women and children "in great distress" fled the town to "seek shelter in the adjacent county." Samuel Chase was right the day before: the Rhode Island Resolution did not go far enough—especially, on this day, for Rhode Islanders.[60]

Three hundred miles south, Adams and Chase faced each other from across the assembly chamber. Adams was as steadfast as ever. Days earlier he had interviewed John McPherson, an old privateer captain from the French and Indian War whom Adams considered "well skilled in naval affairs." He found McPherson "sanguine, confident, positive, that he can torch or burn every Man of War in America." While the Philadelphia press deemed the old salt "eccentric," Adams saw him as a visionary whose confidence fed the fire in the congressman's belly for his cause.[61]

But once again, it was Chase who carried the day. "It is the maddest Idea in the World," he shouted, "to think of building an American fleet." He did not relinquish the floor until he was certain he had decimated the opposition. To build a navy, the derisive Chase concluded, "We should mortgage the whole Continent."

It was the long-nosed Silas Deane, not Adams, who took on Chase's argument. "I wish [a navy] may be seriously debated. I don't think it romantic at all." Hopkins, seeing that Chase's opinion still held sway, had no objections to another delay. Further debate was scheduled for October 16.[62]

Fortunately for Adams and his pro-navy contingent, the reports that reached Philadelphia over the next nine days began tipping the scales in their favor. News that Parliament was sending thousands of Scottish Highlanders and Irish Roman Catholic soldiers to augment British forces in America was enough to sway Thomas Jefferson that Adams's viewpoint had merit. Dispatches regarding Wallace's bombardment of Bristol forced many representatives to rethink their earlier belief that state navies would be an adequate defense. Adams began recounting votes.[63]

On October 12, he presented Congress with a detailed proposal for procuring gunpowder from West Indies ports, citing where it could be found, how large a supply was last noted, and the size of any enemy garrison American sailors might encounter. After all, "as the british Ministry have taken Every Step that human Nature could provide" to keep Americans from each and every half barrel of the stuff, then American captains and their crews should take it "wherever they can get it." He also solicited information from his Boston friends about the Royal Navy's activities: any news of captured American merchantmen, the treatment of their crews, and the financial worth taken from their holds. "Nothing will contribute so much to facilitate Reprisals, as an expert Account of our Losses and Damages," he wrote James Warren.[64]

On Friday the thirteenth, an agreement was made between the citizens of Newport and James Wallace. In exchange for the supplies of "Beef Beer &c necessarys for his Ships" he promised "he would not fire upon the Town without giving the Inhabitants sufficient warning." In Virginia, colonists learned that Lord Dunmore had received reinforcements from St. Augustine, Florida. And in Philadelphia, John Hancock read a dispatch from Washington: General Gage had been recalled, to be replaced by General William Howe; a new fleet, including six ships-of-the-line, was sailing from England; "5 Regiments and 1000 Marines" were "expected to join Howe in Boston in 3 or 4 weeks," and that

A Fleet consisting of a 64 & 20 Gun Ship, 2 Sloops of 18 Guns, 2 Transports with 600 Men were to sail from Boston . . . They took on Board two Mortars, four Howitzers, and other Artillery calculated for the Bombardment of a Town. Their Destination was kept a profound Secret.

One other thing: Washington learned that Lord North was "determined to push the War to the utmost." The British Empire was striking back.[65]

In doing so it did Adams and his supporters a favor. The day before, Adams sought detailed reports of actual British attacks. But Washington's letter, with its list of what was to come from the enemy both near and far, gave Adams something he had not counted on to sway Congress to his cause: fear. Fear of the future, fear of what might come to pass. Not even the argumentative Chase had a rejoinder. That more ships and more men were crossing the Atlantic was one thing. But that a fleet of Washington's description was heading up or down the coast to shell some defenseless American town only heightened Congress's collective anxiety.

With single-minded swiftness, Congress overwhelmingly

> *Resolved,* That a swift sailing vessel, to carry ten carriage guns, and proportionate number of swivels, with eighty men, be fitted with all possible dispatch, for a cruise of three months . . . That a Committee of three be appointed to prepare an estimate for expence, and lay the same before Congress, and to contract with proper persons to fit out the vessel . . . That another vessel be fitted out for the same purposes [and] a committee [be] appointed to bring in regulations for [a] navy.[66]

The Continental Navy was born.

The three representatives chosen for the Naval Committee were Deane, Langdon, and Gadsden. Adams did not mind being omitted. Gadsden added a southerner's presence, and Adams was now free to find ships, supplies, and men to take his dream from the State House to the Atlantic. An ebullient Adams wrote James Warren back in Boston: "We begin to feel a little of a Seafaring Inclination here," adding that

> We must excite by Policy that kind of exalted Courage, which is ever victorious by seas and land—which is irresistible. The Saracens had it— the Knights of Malta—the Assassins—Cromwell's soldiers and sailors. Nay, N[ew] England men have ever had it hitherto. They never failed in an Attempt of any Kind.

Adams and his colleagues could be satisfied with their efforts this day. What they could not do was learn where that British fleet Washington had mentioned was heading. [67]

That same day squalls from the northwest struck Falmouth, Massachusetts, a sea town eighty miles up the coast from Boston, in Casco Bay (now Portland, Maine). Through the wind and the rain, the village minister, Reverend Jacob Bailey, watched as a British squadron sailed past the bay, alarming the townsfolk.[68] Three days later, the ships entered the harbor, literally blown in by the still prevailing northwest winds. As they approached, a committee of patriots, whom Bailey described as "tradesmen and persons of no property," stood at the wharf while their fellow citizens, like a Greek chorus, watched from the nearby houses and street corners. It was Lieutenant Mowat's squadron.

The next day Mowat sent a longboat from the *Canceaux*, with a junior officer carrying a statement informing the town of his intentions: "After so many premeditated Attacks on the legal Prerogatives of the best of Sovereigns" in general and "the most unpardonable Rebellion" of the citizens of Falmouth in particular, Mowat carried "orders to execute a just Punishment on the Town." A "Red pendant will be hoisted at the Maintopgallant Masthead" to signal the start of bombarding the town.

Mowat's declaration had the desired results; after hearing it, Reverend Bailey saw that "every heart was seized with terror." Frantic negotiations commenced. As daylight waned, Mowat agreed to hold off his bombardment. After all, he felt "not a little for the Innocent" in the village; all the committee need do was "surrender their cannon and musketry and give hostages for their future good behaviour," as Bailey put it, and Mowat would delay bombardment until he heard from Admiral Graves. That evening a rowboat approached the *Canceaux*. The Americans aboard delivered a substantially smaller arsenal to Mowat than he expected: a handful of muskets and pistols. Mowat would wait until morning to reply to this insult.

By this time word of the fleet's arrival and its intentions had reached the countryside. That night the town was overrun by militia comprising the local Sons of Liberty. Under lit bonfires—easily seen from the *Canceaux*'s quarterdeck— the militia threatened the more peaceable villagers that it would be they, and not Mowat, who would burn the town to ashes if they acquiesced.[69]

The weather cleared on Wednesday. Streets leading out of town were jammed with villagers, their wagons and carts overflowing with furniture, clothes, and china. Mowat's ships were a-row in the harbor, their guns loaded and run out. The wind was still; only inconsequentially small waves lapped against the hulls of Mowat's ships. One long minute passed, then another. Finally, at nine forty, Mowat ordered the red pennant raised.

For the fleeing villagers, puffs of smoke and the roar of broadsides were followed by the deadly *whoosh* of cannonballs overhead before they slammed into earth and building. To cause the greatest panic, Mowat fired over the fleeing Americans, their screams adding to the cacophony. Many of the oxen towing carts broke from their yokes and stampeded through the crowded streets.

Minutes later, Mowat ordered his gunners to fire hot shot on the town. Winds spread the fire from house to house. Soon flames were licking at the town hall and the church. Looking through his spyglass, Mowat watched as "a brisk fire was keeped up by all the squadron." He kept his guns firing into the afternoon. "The whole town," Bailey later reported, "was involved in smoak and combustion."

By three o'clock only the buildings on the south end of town near the docks stood untouched, and Mowat sent a longboat loaded with sailors and marines to burn them. As they reached land they drew fire from the Sons of Liberty who were still in town, killing one jack tar and wounding several others before being driven off. Two hours later, his guns blazing hot, Mowat ceased firing. With the town destroyed, he gave orders to make sail. As the British departed, small-arms fire peppered the squadron but did no damage. Under darkness and a heavy rain, the British ships left Casco Bay, mission accomplished.

In the hills above Falmouth, Reverend Bailey watched in horror as his church disappeared into ashes, along with the homes of his flock. Another eyewitness, fifteen-year-old Daniel Tucker, later recalled how an uncommonly early winter set in almost immediately, forcing his neighbors to find shelter inland "among a people as poor as themselves." Shortly afterwards young Tucker went to sea to fight in three different engagements against the navy that had destroyed his home.[70]

News of Falmouth soon reached Portsmouth, where a courier immediately rode south to General Washington, who sent a rider posthaste to Philadelphia with a dispatch to Hancock. Calling the bombardment a "horrid Procedure," Washington warned Congress that "the same Desolation is meditated upon all the Towns on the Coast." He sent a detachment of soldiers to Portsmouth, where he believed Mowat might strike next.[71]

For the next two weeks, more congressmen went on record supporting Adams's campaign for armed ships. "Why should not America have a navy?" Virginian George Wythe asked his colleagues, citing Rome's sudden construction of one when at war with Carthage. Even Samuel Chase chimed in. Without a navy to defend merchantmen and ports, "we must submit." By the end of October Congress doubled the proposed navy from two ships to four, and added four new members to the committee responsible for coming up with ships, ordnance, supplies, and sailors: Stephen Hopkins, Richard Henry Lee of Virginia, Joseph Hewes of North Carolina, and John Adams, who "procured a room in a public house"—Tun Tavern—for dinner and the business of creating a navy.[72]

Persistent in adversity, Adams proved positively zealous in victory. While he found it odd for someone who "never thought much of old Ocean" to be in the forefront of this endeavor, it was now "my fate and my Duty" to learn about ship design and construction, refitting existing merchantmen, proving ordnance, and regulations. Like a sponge, he soaked up anything and everything that would enable him to get his ideas from paper to the docks and thence to sea.

To James Warren and Elbridge Gerry in Boston he sent letter upon letter, inquiring what ships were available for purchase or loan to Congress, who among the "Whalemen, Codfishers, and other Seamen" might "be inlisted into the service of the Continent," and "the Names, Ages, Places of Abode and Characters" who might serve as officers in this new enterprise.[73]

He soon learned that he did not need to find ships, for there were several available down the street, nestled against Philadelphia docks. And he need not have sought nominees for captains. Adams and his fellow committee members were about to be played like a string section in a small orchestra by the smartest politician among them, Stephen Hopkins.

Each evening after Congress adjourned the seven made their way to Tun Tavern on the Philadelphia waterfront—not nearly as ostentatious as the City Tavern two blocks west, but not as frequented by their cronies. The ninety-year-old tavern was owned by Robert Mullan, a convivial host whose passion for the rebellion made him known citywide as a rabid patriot.[74]

After a sumptuous meal and more than enough rum, Hopkins held court. He also held his colleagues in the palm of his hand. To Adams, the committee was composed of "sensible Men and very cheerful," but it was the ancient mariner from Rhode Island who enthralled them all with his sailor's knowledge and storytelling. Usually the business at hand concluded by eight, but that was just when Hopkins got started. Consuming round after round of "Jamaica Spirits," Hopkins regaled his colleagues with sea tales, ancient history, and poetry. Instead of Hopkins's rum consumption making him drunk, Adams later recalled, it was immediately converted "into Wit, Sense, Knowledge, and good humour" that miraculously "inspired in Us all with similar qualities."

To the committee, Hopkins was mentor, sage, and raconteur, but he saw the committee differently. Thus far, there were four captain's berths in the Continental Navy, and Hopkins had a family to look out for.[75]

Small wonder, then, as Adams busied himself with writing the voluminous *Rules of the Regulations of the Navy of the United Colonies* (borrowing liberally from the Royal Navy's Articles of War), Hopkins put into practice another time-honored Admiralty practice: nepotism. He began by suggesting a commodore for the Continental "fleet": his younger brother, Esek. The committee heartily approved, and he wrote the new commodore that they "have pitched upon you to take command." Promising Esek that the "Pay and Perquisites will be such as you will have no Reason to complain of," the older brother cast his net over the waters of Rhode Island for more relatives.[76]

He ceded two captaincies to other colonies. Silas Deane solicited his brother-in-law, Dudley Saltonstall, to be senior captain. Pennsylvania congressman Edward Biddle had the honor of informing his younger brother, Nicholas, that he, too, would be among the navy's first commanders. That left two remaining posts, and Hopkins filled them with an in-law, Abraham Whipple, and then tapped his nephew (and Esek's son) John.[77]

Congress gave shipwright John Wharton £100,000 to "fitt for Sea the first fleet." The first ship purchased was Robert Morris's *Black Prince*. Lacking congressional connections, her captain, John Barry, was not even considered for a commission despite his reputation as a peerless mariner. Instead, he was appointed to the triumvirate assigned to speedily refit the *Black Prince* into a ship of war, along with another Philadelphia captain, Nathaniel Falconer, and a young shipwright, decades away from revolutionizing naval warfare with his brilliance: Wharton's protégé, Joshua Humphreys, soon to be disowned by the Quakers for his military efforts.[78]

The next ship acquired was the ship *Sally*, built by Humphreys for the merchant firm of Conyngham and Nesbitt and given the more adventurous name *Columbus* for her new role as a warship. The Anglican Conynghams were originally from County Donegal in Ireland; one of the younger members, Gustavus, was a merchant captain who had just embarked for Europe on another of the firm's vessels, the *Charming Peggy*. Gustavus was on a mission for Congress "to

procure powder, salt-peter, arms, medecins & every thing Necessary for War."
When his attempt at passing himself off as an Irish merchant captain failed to fill
his hold in Holland, he made for Dunkirk on the French coast and the beginning
of years of adventures and misadventures both nautical and political.[79]

The *Black Prince* soon had company at Wharton's shipyard, four ships altogether, being refitted and renamed, but let John Adams explain:

> The first we renamed *Alfred* in honor of the founder of the greatest Navy
> that ever existed. The second *Columbus* after the Discover[er] of this quarter
> of the Globe. The third *Cabot* for the Discoverer of this northern Part
> of the Continent. The fourth *Andrew Doria* in memory of the Great
> Genovese Admiral.[80]

A fifth soon arrived from Rhode Island, the sloop *Katy*, bearing her captain,
Abraham Whipple. She was renamed the *Providence*.[81]

The trio of Barry, Falconer, and Humphreys worked tirelessly day and night.
Beginning with the *Black Prince/Alfred*, carpenters busied themselves piercing
her bulwark for gun ports and reinforcing her hull. Mile after mile of rope, thousands of planks and boards, and countless buckets of paint and tar arrived daily.
As Humphreys's carpenters and sawyers kept at their tasks from the keelsons to
the quarterdecks, Barry's riggers, working like a troupe of high-wire acrobats,
adjusted stays and shrouds, blackening the standing rigging—and themselves—
with pitch and tar. Wending their way between the two groups were Falconer's
men, stevedores carrying bales, yards of sailcloth, hoisting cannons over the rails
with block and tackle, and toting what half barrels of precious gunpowder came
their way. Miraculously, the ships were ready for their new role as a naval fleet by
December. Soon two schooners, the *Wasp* and the *Fly*, were added to the fleet,
along with another sloop, the *Hornet*. Nearly giddy with such visible evidence of
their resolve, Congress resolved to build no fewer than thirteen frigates, each
carrying between twenty-four and thirty-two guns, to be constructed, launched,
and battle-ready within four months, and budgeted at $866,666.67. They would
find their deadlines delayed not by weeks but years, and their projected cost off by
millions.[82]

At another dinner at Tun Tavern, Adams, Hopkins et al. discussed adding a
contingent of marines to their naval needs. Their subsequent resolution "That
two Battalions of marines be raised" was approved by Congress, which gave the

first captain's commission to a Philadelphia Quaker, Samuel Nicholas, a fox-hunting crony of Robert Morris and Charles Biddle. Known for his fearlessness, Nicholas was soon joined in this venture by another captain, his friend and Tun Tavern proprietor, Robert Mullan. Using his tavern and its reputation for quality ale, Mullan went immediately to work as the Continental Marine Corps' first recruiter.[83]

As November's winds ushered in December and winter, Adams's naval manual was completed and approved. Most of the navy's officers had arrived in Philadelphia, with the notable exception of their "Commander-in-Chief," Esek Hopkins.

Sunday, December 3, was cold and clear, giving no hint of how soon true winter weather would arrive. Sometime after church services, a crowd of Phila-delphians and their congressional guests gathered at the docks to watch the first act of the Continental Navy.[84]

The senior lieutenant aboard the *Alfred* was a small Scotsman. Still in his twenties, he had made a name for himself as a successful merchant captain in the West Indies trade, but after killing one of his sailors during an argument over wages in 1773 he fled to his brother's adopted home, Fredericksburg, Virginia, with just fifty pounds in his pocket. Once ashore, he learned that his brother had died. Lacking both money and connections, he used his Freemason's membership as a way to advance himself.

Virginians quickly learned that he lacked riches but not confidence. Soon he was competing with a firebrand lawyer for the affections of Dorothea Dandridge, Martha Washington's cousin. After sizing up her suitors, she opted for the lawyer and became Mrs. Patrick Henry. But Congressman Hewes, a fellow Mason, saw merit in the young mariner. Hearing of the new navy, he headed to Philadelphia, where Hewes pulled some strings on his behalf. The captaincy of the sloop *Prov-idence* was offered him, but lacking experience commanding a fore-and-aft rigged vessel, he declined, accepting a lieutenant's commission instead.

Now he officiated at a small ceremony aboard the *Alfred*. After a short burst of song from a fife and drum band, probably playing "The British Grenadiers"— now known in patriotic circles as "Washington at War"—the lieutenant raised the symbol of American rebellion, the Grand Union flag: thirteen stripes of red and white, with the British ensign in the canton. After a call for three cheers was raised, the crowd departed.[85]

It is not known whether John Adams attended. By then, his mind had moved on to other things. Describing himself as "Worn down with long and uninterrupted Labor," he was granted permission to visit his family, his long battle to create a navy having been won. For the rest of his life, he would call these days "the pleasantest part of my Labors" in Congress. He departed for Massachusetts on December 8.[86]

The day before, December 7, the *Alfred*'s lieutenant was officially sworn in as an officer in the Continental Navy. His real name was not on his commission; killing that sailor had forced him to add a common alias to it. The name his father gave him, John Paul, belonged to the Old World. The commission was made out to John Paul Jones.

As much as any man, Adams had given birth to this American navy. Its learning to sail—and fight—would be up to Jones, Hopkins, and other officers.

CHAPTER TWO

★ ★ ★

"IF THE REBELS SHOULD
PAY US A VISIT . . ."

On my arrival at Balt[imore] I found the whole country had taken
up arms against the Injustice of England, my heart soon caught
the flame.

—JOSHUA BARNEY, LIEUTENANT, CONTINENTAL SLOOP *HORNET*[1]

On a cold December day in 1775, Robert Mullan stepped out the front
door of Tun Tavern. He had work to do.

At three stories, Mullan's tavern was one of the taller structures on the waterfront, with a handsome porch facing the Delaware River. A long bar occupied
the first floor, with drawing rooms on the second floor and bedrooms for lodgers
on the third. Mullan's mother, Peggy, had been Tun's proprietress for thirty
years, establishing it as a fine place for beefsteak and oysters, with an endless
supply of fine spirits and ale.[2]

As second-in-command of the newly created Continental Marine Corps,
Mullan saw it as his duty to find the right men, fit for him to command. Dressed
in his best clothes with a sheathed sword strapped to his side and accompanied by
a fifer and a drummer, he marched down the streets of the waterfront. Bystanders
were taken with an image he had painted on the drumhead: a coiled rattlesnake
above the words "Don't Tread on Me." Like the Pied Piper, he soon had a curious
throng following him back to Tun Tavern. Then Mullan—or one of his musi-
cians, if he had the better voice—belted out freshly written words to the familiar
tune "The British Grenadier":

All you that have bad masters,
And cannot get your due,

Come, come my brave boys,
And join with our ship's crew.

Though Mullan may have been unaccustomed to public speaking, he was certainly accustomed to speaking in public houses. Clearing his throat, he made a stem-winding speech, exhorting the men and boys in the crowd to join him in the fight for both their God-given rights as free Englishmen and the glory and prize shares awaiting them. Then he welcomed them inside, where ale and rum flowed freely until enough new recruits added their names or marks to his enlistment sheets.[3]

Some blocks west of Dock Street, Samuel Nicholas, Mullan's superior, was doing the same thing at his own rendezvous point, *his* family's watering hole, the Conestoga Wagon. Thanks to the efforts of Nicholas and Mullan, the Continental Navy quickly recruited enough marines for each ship in Esek Hopkins's squadron. Hopkins's captains had a much more challenging time recruiting sailors—but then none of the captains owned a tavern.

To solve this problem, Hopkins sought the Pennsylvania Committee of Safety's permission to enlist sailors already committed to the row galleys of the Pennsylvania Navy. Aware that these tars had signed on to serve at a generous five dollars a month, Hopkins had already received permission from Congress to offer eight dollars. He also made it known that food and rum rations were ampler aboard Continental ships. Soon his muster rolls were full (Hopkins did not know how lucky he was; as we will see, the navy would be plagued with manpower shortages for the rest of the war).[4]

The glowing fire of an inn hearth and a tempting mug of hot buttered rum were the closest things to warmth the Continental Navy possessed as 1776 began. Philadelphia was in the midst of a bleak, bitterly cold winter that threatened to keep the little fleet from departing. The delay also gave Hopkins time to mull over his orders from Congress. While the congressmen had appointed him "Commander-in-Chief of the Fleet of the United Colonies," they never deemed him equal in rank to Washington, whom they acknowledged as "Commander-in-Chief of the Continental Forces in America" to make sure Hopkins got their drift. They addressed him as "Commodore," but the title was an honorary one, given to the head of any squadron. It never occurred to them to bestow upon him the rank that mattered: Admiral.[5]

Born in 1718, Esek Hopkins was ten years younger than his brother, Stephen. He had followed the family's maritime tradition and established himself as a merchant captain with years of successful voyages from Providence to Surinam and the West Indies. Marriage to the daughter of a wealthy Newport merchant changed both his address and his financial status. During the French and Indian War he served as a privateer, and was a good one. By war's end he was famous and richer. In 1775 both his political clout and his waistline had substantially increased. The moon-faced Hopkins was in charge of Rhode Island's armed forces, with the rank of brigadier general, when his elder brother wangled his appointment from Congress. At fifty-seven, he was old by colonial standards.[6]

By the New Year all of Hopkins's captains were in Philadelphia, including Dudley Saltonstall of the *Alfred*. There was a mad scramble to get the ships ready for sea, in terms of both supplies and officers. It fell to the Pennsylvania Committee of Safety to supply sufficient powder, arms, and ammunition. Miraculously, it did—though it was a nearly endless list, indeed: thousands of pounds of grapeshot, cannonballs, and musket balls; 150 muskets and bayonets; and 128 full and half barrels of gunpowder.[7]

Officer vacancies were summarily filled. Among the marine lieutenants stood Matthew Parke, scion of a military family from England whose grandfather had been an aide to Winston Churchill's ancestor, the Duke of Marlborough, at the Battle of Blenheim. With wide-set eyes and a hook nose, he looked like a human hawk. He would fight in some of the most famous sea battles of the war. Naval lieutenants included the *Cabot*'s Hoysted Hacker, whose career would be marred with bad luck, and the *Andrew Doria*'s James Josiah, a ruddy-faced young man personally selected by the ship's captain (and Josiah's good friend) Nicholas Biddle.[8]

But the forbidding weather conditions soon turned the brio of Congress and their commodore into trepidation. The Delaware River was icing over. A snowstorm had blanketed Philadelphia on Christmas Day, and northern gales swept downriver, sending armadas of ice floes past the city. In a frenetic effort to get the ships under way, dockhands slipped on the ice and slush that coated gangway and pier alike, lugging supplies aboard the ships as fast as wagons and carts brought them dockside. Sailors, now living aboard ship, were so cold they fell asleep to the chattering of their own teeth, prompting Philadelphia's best-known physician, Benjamin Rush, to beg the Committee of Safety that blankets be donated by each Philadelphia family for the freezing recruits.

Congress had hoped to have the fleet out by the end of the year. Now, thanks to Mother Nature, they might not get to sea until the spring thaw. Accordingly, on January 4, the Naval Committee ordered all naval personnel to "immediately repair on board their respective Ships" and get to sea before the ice hemmed them in port. Those who missed the boat would be labeled deserters. All the next morning, rowboats of every type departed Robert Morris's wharf, carrying the enlistees to their designated vessels. That afternoon Nicholas Biddle, standing on his quarterdeck, gave orders to Lieutenant Josiah to cast off. Aboard each ship, the bosuns bellowed orders to get under way and sailors weighed anchor and made sail. Soon the *Andrew Doria*, *Alfred*, *Cabot*, and *Columbus* were standing downriver with the cheers from a crowd of congressmen, merchants, and Philadelphians ringing in sailors' ears.

Some among the throng were not patriotic well-wishers. A few Loyalists were present who afterwards sent detailed reports to the British describing the ships' sizes, colors, and guns, while guessing the departed fleet's destination: perhaps to convoy merchantmen, to sail to neutral European ports for gunpowder, or to seek and fight the British.

The ships made an impressive sight as the *Alfred* took the lead; as the fleet shrank in the distance the crowd could still identify Hopkins's flagship by her black and yellow colors. Light winds and heavy ice soon slowed their progress. At dusk they reached Mud Island, now renamed Liberty and home to an unfinished fort designed by British army engineer John Montresor.[9]

Hopkins intended to continue down the Delaware the next morning, but awoke to find the river completely frozen. His ships remained at Liberty Island for twelve days. The enforced ennui—along with the bitterly cold conditions—took its toll on a few tars and landsmen. Quite a few jumped ship, compelling Hopkins to post notices back in Philadelphia offering a reward for information leading to their arrest. One broadside offered the grand sum of two dollars to help nab

PETER M'TEGART, born in Ireland, about thirty years of age, five feet seven inches high, smooth faced, brownish complexion, short dark brown hair. Had on a light brown coat, white cloth jacket and breeches, blue stockings and new shoes.

All one need do was deliver the said deserter to the sheriff's office to claim the reward (as the broadside was published throughout the month it's unknown if Mr. "M'Tegart" ever returned to duty). Hopkins's letter-book for February 2 would not indicate whether he saw his shadow from the quarterdeck, but the commodore had six more weeks of winter coming.[10]

While the ships were stuck at Liberty Island, Congress sent Hopkins his orders—a well-crafted synthesis of military, political, and practical matters. It made no sense to send Hopkins north in the dead of winter; it was too late weather-wise for the new navy to assist Washington in his siege of Boston. In fact, the general was enjoying a successful few weeks with his own navy, thanks in no small part to John Manley, a former Royal Navy bosun's mate, now a middle-aged sea captain from Marblehead who, commanding the armed schooner *Lee*, captured the British ordnance vessel *Nancy*. Washington could not have asked for a better present. The *Nancy*'s hold contained 2,000 muskets, 30,000 cannonballs, more than 30 tons of musket shot, and a 13-inch mortar—a short, stocky piece of ordnance with a large bore that could lob shells at a high arc—the very weapon for a siege. In Boston, General Howe lamented the *Nancy*'s loss as "rather unfortunate." Washington, on the other hand, could barely contain his glee. Manley was made commodore of Washington's "little fleet" and given command of the *Hannah*.[11]

Word of Manley's success no sooner reached Congress in Philadelphia than news from the south determined the plans for the Continental fleet. For months, dispatches about Lord Dunmore's raids along the Virginia coastline had been sent to the colony's congressional representatives. By the end of 1775, Dunmore's "Ethiopian Regiment" had grown to nearly five hundred men, thanks in part to his issuing the first emancipation proclamation in American history in November. In it, Dunmore declared

All indentured Servants, Negroes, or others (appertaining to Rebels) free that are able and willing to bear Arms, they joining His Majesty's Troop as soon as may be, for the more speedily reducing this Colony to a proper Sense of their Duty.[12]

As Lincoln would do four score and eight years later, Dunmore only freed slaves whose masters were in open rebellion. His proclamation set in motion the same fear that would shake white Virginians fifty-six years later during Nat Turner's uprising: that of armed blacks fighting for freedom from their masters and revenge for generations of slavery. It also sent neutral-minded Virginians dashing pell-mell into the Patriot fold.[13]

Earlier, in September, forces from Dunmore's ships had landed in Norfolk and seized the town's printing press, as its patriotic owner was "poisoning the minds of the People." Dunmore used that same press to print his proclamation.

To counter his offer of freedom, plantation owners mounted their own propaganda campaign, telling slaves that the offer was a trick to fill Dunmore's coffers with the money he would make selling them to West Indies sugar barons. Meanwhile, rebel forces converged on Norfolk. In a fierce battle that their commander, William Woodford, called "a second Bunker Hill," Americans overran Dunmore's British sailors, Loyalist allies, and the Ethiopian Regiment.[14]

After Dunmore returned to his ship, his request for water and supplies from Norfolk was denied, and he promised "fire and sword." On New Year's Day all Norfolk was aflame. It was Falmouth all over again—but as much from patriot torches as from Dunmore's cannons.[15]

The next day in Philadelphia, Esek Hopkins broke the seals of two dispatches from the Naval Committee. The shorter of the two contained his orders and directions regarding his leadership and conduct, a long list including maritime discipline, correspondence with Congress on a regular basis, directions on sending any captured prizes into American ports under command of a carefully chosen officer, the feeding and care for his men, humane treatment of any prisoners, and providing signals and contingency orders for his captains should they become separated from the squadron by storms.[16]

The longer missive, after saluting Hopkins's "Valour, Skill, and diligence," got to the essence of his mission:

> Proceed directly to the Chesapeak Bay in Virginia . . . to gain intelligence of the Enemies Situation and Strength—if by such intelligence you find that they are not greatly superiour to your own you are immediately to Enter the said bay, search out and attack, take or destroy all the Naval forces of our Enemies that you may find there.

Simple enough. And, if Hopkins were successful in Virginia, he was to "proceed immediately to the Southward and make yourself Master of such forces as the Enemy may have both in North and South Carolina." And that was not all. Once Hopkins completed that task, he was "to proceed Northward directly to Rhode Island" and rid his home waters of James Wallace and his ilk, without mention of the refitting or repairing of his ships, or of the possibility of any casualties. To Congress, the entire American coastline was Hopkins's oyster.

The salty old tar never lacked confidence in his ability to do anything, but these orders were daunting enough to make Don Quixote wince. Fortunately, at the end of this to-do list, Hopkins found an escape clause: "If bad Winds, or

Stormy Weather, or any other unforeseen accident or disaster disable you so to do You are then to follow such Courses as your best Judgement shall Suggest."[17]

Now all Hopkins had to do was clear the Delaware of ice, train his merchant sailors in the art of warfare, and boldly go to war at sea with a fistful of hastily converted merchantmen against the finest navy the world had ever seen.

While ice kept the American ships bottled up in the Delaware, two profound changes took place in British leadership that would have a significant impact on the war.

In England, George III and his prime minister, Lord North, sought a man who shared their ardor to vanquish the American rebels while possessing the one thing they lacked: military experience. Since Lexington and Concord they had been bombarded with complaints from their generals about Admiral Graves's ineffective management while the liberal Whigs in Parliament eloquently railed against their policies. The Irishman Edmund Burke would be a thorn in the king's side throughout the war; when Lord North appointed a special secretary of state to direct American affairs, joining the Crown's two existing secretaries of the northern and southern departments, Burke chortled, "The two secretaries [were] doing nothing, so a third was appointed to help them." Thanks to Burke's leadership, opposition to Crown policy grew. "The spirit of America," Burke marveled, "is incalculable."[18]

In November 1775, King George dismissed Lord Dartmouth, whose efforts on His Majesty's behalf seemed to some—especially the king—to be halfhearted at best. To succeed him the king appointed the Viscount George Sackville, Lord Germain, who had grown up in a palace with 365 rooms (one for each day) and a fifty-two-step staircase (one for each week of the year). The place was cold and forbidding, as was he. A soldier in his younger days, Sackville maintained an air of disdain for those beneath him—which was, in his mind, pretty much everyone else. In 1770 he inherited the expansive Germain estate and assumed the title Lord Germain. A political ally of Lord North, he was an easy choice for the king to make, believing as he did that the American population consisted of "peasants." A contemporary engraver etched a profile of his likeness: a bulging-eyed old man (he was nearly sixty at the time of his appointment) with a weak chin and an impossibly long nose.[19]

Germain immediately got off on the wrong foot with First Lord of the Admiralty John Montagu, Earl of Sandwich. Once he assumed the position of secretary for the Americas, Germain waded through each report, from general and admiral alike, and concluded that Sandwich and not Graves was responsible for the Royal Navy's poor showing thus far in the war. The only thing the two men shared was a hearty dislike of America and Americans, who Sandwich believed were the "most worthless race of men on earth." Sandwich boasted that the more Americans joined the rebellion, the easier it would be for the king's men to vanquish them.[20]

In actuality, Sandwich did possess the organizational skills to run the Admiralty, as well as the savvy politician's gifts of infighting and survival; all he lacked was popularity. He wore such a look of perpetual grimness that Charles Churchill derided him as one who had been "half-hanged" and "cut down by mistake." The second change went hand in hand with the first. Months earlier, General Gage had been replaced by General William Howe as senior commander in America. Now came Graves's turn. Tired of the litany of complaints, Sandwich replaced Graves with Vice Admiral Molyneux Shuldham. Confounded by rebel resourcefulness as much as the demands on him from generals and royal governors, Graves seemed to welcome his removal. In a letter to his favorite captain, James Wallace, he commiserated about the "arduous task" of enforcing the king's insistence "to render the Colonies to obedience." Graves truly believed he had done his best, but after his orders reduced towns to ashes he realized that he—or probably any commander—could not suppress the Americans' hydra-like unwillingness to admit defeat.

Shuldham arrived in America with lengthy orders that could be distilled into three words: subjugate, subjugate, subjugate. For decades he had fought for his country on the high seas. Now his own body seemed at war with itself: piercing eyes losing a battle with his drooping eyelids; wide shoulders sloping southward, a potbelly relentlessly escaping the bounds of his greatcoat.

As much as to any Englishmen, it would fall to these three—Germain, Sandwich, and Shuldham—to end American resistance before year's end.[21]

By January 18, two weeks after the four original Continental ships sailed from Philadelphia only to become ice-bound at Liberty Island, Congress added new tasks to Hopkins's to-do list. Word had reached Philadelphia that three southern royal governors, aboard two sloops and one cutter (a speedy single-mast vessel, fore-and-aft rigged like a schooner) were en route to Savannah, Georgia, "to seduce that Province" into joining the king's side of the fighting. Therefore, once Hopkins had disposed of Lord Dunmore's fleet, he was to make for Savannah and subdue the three Loyalist ships, making it "very probable you may have three Governors to dine with you on board your own ship." If the ice did not clear soon, Congress might decide to send Hopkins to London to capture George III.[22]

By now Hopkins would have gladly clapped on all sail, but the cold front showed no signs of departing; therefore, neither could Hopkins. Nine days later, he informed the Naval Committee that the Delaware had "froze so much that the Pilots will not undertake to carry us from here." Not until February 11 were conditions permissible for the fleet to stand downriver, a pilot at each helm. Pilots were indispensable in getting ships in and out of ports. Their knowledge of shallows, currents, and potential dangers made all the difference between a smooth passage and a disastrous one. Since the outbreak of hostilities, conditions on the Delaware were much more hazardous, thanks to defensive precautions taken by the Pennsylvania Committee of Safety.

The committee had implemented a combination of defenses and alarms that allowed Philadelphians to know within a few hours if British warships were approaching the two capes—Cape May in New Jersey and Cape Henlopen in Delaware. Once a man-of-war entered the bay, a designated rider was sent galloping ten miles to the next way station, where another rider charged north to the next one, until the last courier reached Philadelphia with the dispatch about the number of ships and their sizes—a forerunner to the Pony Express. As a safeguard against any rider being captured by Loyalist partisans, a small cannon would be fired from each station until the last gun's echo reached Philadelphia.

The river was also booby-trapped with chevaux-de-frise, wooden spikes more than thirty feet long with sharp iron tips cross-cut and secured in fifty tons of crushed stone, then placed in the river. Unsuspecting captains, unaware of the spikes, got a rude surprise when a shocking jolt, accompanied by a loud crunching sound, informed them of a punctured hull. The effectiveness of the maneuver was proven when a merchantman's captain neglected to hire a patriotic pilot with knowledge of the chevaux locations; the ship, her hold full of West Indies goods, struck a chevaux and sank immediately.[23]

River pilots prided themselves on their abilities to bring a ship of any draft safely into port. Rarely did a captain's log record a mishap (although when it did, it usually included saltier language than the rest of the journal: when one of his ships was run aground by a wayward pilot, John Barry called him a "dammed Raskill" for posterity). Once ships were at sea, it fell to captain, mates, and crew—all hands aboard ship—to keep the vessel afloat and on course. But the man who got her to sea, and brought her safely into port—that was a pilot.[24]

Once hostilities commenced, the Committee of Safety notified the Delaware pilots that, due to the booby-trapping of the Delaware, their services would not be needed for the duration of the war. This meant economic disaster for all of them, and also doubly stung the patriots among them: their own credibility was being questioned, if not disbelieved outright. Furthermore, it placed pro-American ships in peril. Upset that the committee was taking "the Bread out of their mouths," they chose as spokesperson the intrepid Henry Fisher, who protested that their patriotism was equal to that of any politician. Relenting, the committee approved ten pilots whom Fisher recommended. Throughout the war they served not only as pilots but as scouts of the waterway, sending dispatches of enemy activities on the coast. Fisher was one of the unsung heroes of the Revolution, as were the other pilots who risked their lives from Massachusetts to Georgia.[25]

Freed from ice, the ships reached Cape Henlopen with only one incident, and that on land. They no sooner dropped anchor when they were joined by the schooner *Wasp* and the sloop *Hornet* from Maryland. By then, weeks of boredom and ice had cooled if not frozen the warm patriotic glow of more than a few sailors. The sea town of Lewes provided the first chance to jump ship, and a few did just that. They were quickly nabbed by the local militia and returned to their respective ships, but those from the *Andrew Doria* were put in the Lewes jail. Their leader was William Green, a hulking malcontent from the Pennsylvania Navy, which was likely glad to be rid of him. He convinced the others to overcome their guards, and soon the jail became their fortress. They barred the door and armed themselves.

Captain Biddle sent an officer and a small detachment of marines ashore to put an end to Green's rebellion. They returned empty-handed. Taking a midshipman along, Biddle decided to quell the mutiny himself.

He found the jail surrounded by militia and curious townsfolk, while Green and the other sailors inside welcomed anyone to come and get them. "Oh, damn," Biddle swore, and stood before the door. "Green! Come out of there," he demanded. "Open the door or we will break it in."

Green remained defiant. "I'll not come out, and I'll shoot you if you try to come in," he replied.

Biddle sent the militia to find a log strong enough for use as a battering ram. The irresistible force of the log slammed into the immovable object of the door until, with a noisy crack, it snapped off its hinges. Biddle stepped across the threshold to find the muzzle of Green's musket pointed right at him. Holding a cocked pistol in one hand, Biddle said in a calm, unwavering voice, "Now Green, if you do not take good aim, you are a dead man."

Whether it was that Biddle's show of courage cowed Green or that Green was not as good a shot as he was a bully may not be clear, but the next sound from the jail was the clatter his musket made as it fell to the floor, followed by those of his comrades.

Word of Biddle's bravado jumped from ship to ship: here was a captain not to be trifled with. To Biddle it was all in a day's work; he downplayed it in a letter to his sister Lydia, promising another missive would be forthcoming "when I can find Something worth telling." The crew of the *Andrew Doria* was the first in the fleet to learn what kind of man they had for a captain. Once they put to sea, Biddle and the other officers began learning what kind of sailors *they* had.[26]

Few careers held more danger than the lot of sailors in the wooden world. Any given day saw any man's life dependent on the seaman next to him. Storms swept men overboard. Too much grog, and a tipsy sailor aloft could miss a line or put his foot wrong and fall into the sea, or land on deck with a sickening thud. Tainted food or the wrong fish at mess could send him into writhing intestinal agony. Tedium went hand in hand with danger. Aboard ship, there were so many ways to die.

If one were a landsman—a farm boy, street urchin, or runaway apprentice who had never been to sea—the first challenge was to win his sea legs, and that happened only after days of total incapacitation. Seasickness came with the constant rolling and pitching of the ship, whose motion was decidedly more prevalent up front in the forecastle ("fo'c'sle") where the sailors lived. Landsmen, Horatio Nelson wrote, were usually "in the low scuppers, floating in a most wretched state of sea-sickness."[27]

Once a newcomer got his stomach under control, he joined the other hands in what seemed to be an eternity of boredom, work, and sleep. A twenty-four-hour day began at noon, broken into seven watches: five of four hours and two "dog watches," a schedule that ensured that a man never served consecutive days on the same watch. The hours were marked by a ship's bell, eight bells per four-hour watch. Crews were usually divided in half; off duty they slept below deck in hammocks within inches of each other, swaying in unison to the rhythm of the ocean.

Landsmen "learned the ropes" with the assistance of the seasoned hands and with the insistence of the bosun. If they were too dense to pick something up quickly, they learned it with the aid of a rope's end, which the bosun always carried. Some ropes were part of the standing rigging, tarred black and stiff, that supported the masts and was secured by pierced pieces of elm or ash called deadeyes. Those fore and aft of the masts were called stays; those alongside were shrouds; smaller strips of tarred rope, called ratlines, ran across them, serving as ladders for going aloft.

Other ropes made up the running rigging, running through block and tackle to adjust sails and spars (called "yards") in a system that allowed the hands to change a sail's direction and respond to any shift in the wind. Halyards were the lines that raised and lowered the yards, while those called braces set the sails in position. Block and tackle took the weight off the sailors' hands and backs, and was secured on deck by a belaying pin, resembling a short baseball bat, set into a pin rail with a figure-eight knot that could easily be opened in battle or storm.

The most dangerous part of the workday was going aloft, climbing the ratlines to the tops, where a landsman learned the most important rule of all: never let go of one line until your other hand firmly grasped another. To reef (shorten) or furl a sail, one carried gaskets and walked parallel to the yard on footropes—the slender lines just a few feet beneath the yard, always approaching from the windward side of the canvas, with the wind blowing one into the sail, not away from it. Landsmen were drilled in this under the calmest conditions; aloft in a storm there was no margin for error. Each sailor's skill and nerve increased the safety of the men around him. Each man's ignorance and fear added to their peril.[28]

On-deck duties, while less daunting, were repetitive chores. Sailors were constantly repairing spars, splicing rope, and mending sail. And there was the endless drudgery of scrubbing the decks. Using a holystone (called, fittingly, a "prayer book"), one got on hands and knees and cleaned the deck, which was then finished with a swab—a mop made up of bits of rope.

Little respite was found below deck, where the creature comforts of eating and sleeping took place in dark, damp, and smelly quarters. Bilge water, livestock, unwashed bodies, smoke, and tar created an odor that defied description.

Congress had passed a "Mess Bill" providing each hand with a pound of bread, beef or pork, potatoes or turnips, and a half pint of rum. Butter and cheese were meted out Tuesdays and Fridays. Wednesday was "banyon day," following the Royal Navy's custom of bread, butter, cheese, and rice for meals. Six sailors shared a pint and a half of vinegar a week. For bread, there was "ship's biscuit"—a recipe of salt, flour, and water that more than lived up to its name and also became the home of choice for weevils. Every so often the ship's cook made "lobscouse" out of potato skins, soaked salted beef, beans, and hardtack, which, unappetizing as it sounds, was a sailor's favorite. To combat the ravages of scurvy, undiluted lime juice was offered.[29]

Then there was grog. This mixture of rum, lime juice, and water was ladled out two or three times a day, beginning with "the nooner," the first measure passed out once the sun was over the foreyard. Grog was mother's milk to most sailors, giving many a tipsy feeling while hopefully not causing any fights or thickheaded execution of performing one's duties.[30]

The jibboom extended beyond the bowsprit, where one found the head—a plank with a hole cut in the center and used by the crew to relieve themselves efficiently if not comfortably. Rows of cannons ran down both sides of the ships, starting with two bow chasers that pointed ahead from the bow, used in pursuit of a fleeing enemy. The ship's bell was mounted by the mainmast on a wooden belfry. Directly behind the fo'c'sle was the ship's waist, where hatches covered by gratings led to stairways to go below. Lashed beneath the gunwales (the rails atop the ship's sides) were spare masts and spars. Secured above them were the ship's boats, usually a longboat, a cutter, and a captain's gig, their sails stored inside. Livestock was kept in pens along the waist to provide occasional rations of fresh meat.

Astern of the waist rose the captain's domain, the quarterdeck, whose height gave the officers a clear view of the deck. It also served as a tangible reminder of the difference in status between sailor and officer (larger ships had another level above that, called the "poop deck," rarely found on a ship smaller than a frigate).[31]

Rank aboard ship increased the farther aft one walked below deck, beginning past the fo'c'sle with the wardroom, where the command and warrant officers had mess. For Hopkins's fleet, this included the lieutenants, the marine captain, his lieutenant, and the warrant officers: the sailing master, responsible for the ship's navigation; the surgeon, gunner, purser (responsible for the ship's accounting and supplies), and the bosun, the top seaman responsible for on-deck activities and chores. His piercing whistle piped all hands.[32]

Compared to a lieutenant's berth, the captain's cabin was palatial. Like the British frigates that the *Alfred* vainly tried to resemble, Hopkins's cabin contained at least two cannons, one large table, several heavy chairs, a washbowl, and a cot. A settee was built in just below the stern widows.

The lowest deck, the orlop, contained the quarters for midshipmen and the master's and surgeon's mates. Large as the room was, it rarely exceeded five feet in height; it also served as the surgeon's domain during battle, with the large eating table cleared for surgery. Though midshipmen were frequently boys not yet in their teens, they had plenty of clout; one complaint by a midshipman about a sailor's behavior could get the man flogged or put in irons. They were, on the whole, careful not to abuse their authority, for their own misconduct would likely find them bent over a gun and given "a taste of the colt." More often, they were "mast-headed"—sent aloft to the highest crosstrees for hours at a time.[33]

While merchantmen carried a cannon or two for protection against pirates, it was a guessing game for Hopkins at this stage as to how his new sailors would fight against a real navy. Under his orders, the captains held constant gunnery practice. Only Biddle had served in the Royal Navy, and he worked his crew day and night exercising the guns.

Cannons were classified by the weight of the ball they fired. The largest guns among Hopkins's fleet were 9-pounders, which weighed 1,500 pounds. They could fire a cannonball up to 1,800 yards, but their accuracy at that distance was haphazard at best. In fact, the preferred distance to commence firing by British captains was much closer, usually "within pistol shot"—50 yards or less.[34]

Gunnery practice typically began with the captain's order "Beat to Quarters." As a marine drummer played a sustained, rapid roll, the men flew to their battle stations. Any fires aboard ship were doused, as the gunner went from cannon to cannon to ensure that each gun crew had their equipment ready.

Mounted on wooden carriages, the guns were held in place by two sets of rope, block and tackle attached to ringbolts driven into the bulwarks (and a spare set of ringbolts in place, in case the first set was yanked out of the bulwark by the gun's recoil). Several sailors made up a gun crew; each had assigned duties and stations. The equipment included a rammer/sponger (a broomstick-like rod several feet long with a butt end and a stiff sponge on the other end), a bucket of water, a crowbar, a handspike to set the gun in place, and a quoin—a notched wooden wedge that elevated the gun. Balls and powder charges were brought to the gun by ship's boys, not yet called "powder monkeys." But for Hopkins's fleet, the drills were carried out without a cannonball in the muzzle, except for the last practice round. Powder was too scarce to use for practice.

Gunnery exercises aboard the *Alfred* were under the direction of Lieutenant John Paul Jones, who began the sessions with a series of orders. "Cast off your guns," he bellowed, and the tars removed the muzzle lashings that secured their cannons. "Level your guns," he cried, and the men set the guns parallel to the deck. "Take out your tompions," and the stoppers that kept any seawater from entering the muzzle were removed. "Load with cartridge" came next, and the men pantomimed the act of sending a wad and powder down the muzzle. "Shot your guns," Jones continued, and they pretended to run a cannonball down the gun. "Run out your guns," and the men, using the block and tackle, sent the gun through the opening pierced through the bulwark.

At "Prime," gunpowder would be poured from a powder horn into the touchhole. "Point your guns," Jones commanded, and each cannon was set in position by the quoin, while the gunner blew on the slow match in his hand to keep it lit. At "Elevate" the gun was aimed. Finally, on the ship's up-roll, Jones yelled, "Fire!" and, if this was the last practice round and the gun was actually loaded, there was a spark from the touchhole, followed by a deafening roar from the cannon. The act sent the cannon recoiling several feet; only the lines secured by the ringbolt kept it from flying dangerously across the deck, where it could shatter a man's leg with its thrust.

After the recoil—real or pantomimed—Jones ordered, "Sponge your guns," and the wet sponge end of the rammer was run down the muzzle, extinguishing any sparks or burning remnants of the powder bag. If this was the last round, the gun was "wormed" with a long-handled corkscrew that cleared it of any debris.

Aboard the *Andrew Doria*, Nicholas Biddle worked his men tirelessly at the guns to reach the Royal Navy's goal: that every gun crew aboard could discharge a round within two minutes, firing the guns in unison and with accuracy. Each and every time his men exercised the guns his objective was simple: be faster.

Like the British vessels, Hopkins's ships carried a deadly variety of projectiles to fire at the enemy, based on both battle conditions and distance. Two halves of a cannonball connected by a twelve-inch iron bar ("bar-shot") or chain ("chain-shot") could easily cut rigging or sailor into pieces. Grapeshot (consisting of iron balls set in a round wooden frame) and canister (scrap metal and musket balls wrapped in paper) were deadlier versions of buckshot when fired at close range. Swivel guns, set along the gunwales, were larger versions of shotguns.

But the most dangerous weapon to a crew was their own ship when struck by enemy gunfire. Nothing was deadlier than long, jagged splinters, ripped from the bulwarks and sent flying across the deck after a cannonball's impact. Add the risk of masts, spars, and rigging hurtling to the deck after being shot away, and it became terrifyingly easy for a sailor to realize that the workings of his ship could both save and end his life, depending on split-second luck, good or bad.

The captain's order "Clear the decks for action" was also a call for the marines to go aloft. With their muskets slung over their shoulders, they climbed the ratlines to the fighting tops—the small platforms above the spars. If they had any coehorns—small mortars embedded in a wooden stand—they were hoisted up to the tops where their shells could be lobbed onto the enemy's decks. While some marines owned rifles, most carried muskets, which, like cannons, were smooth-bored and thus not as accurate as a rifle, whose barrel was grooved to enhance both accuracy and range. Marines also carried "grenadoes," forerunners of hand grenades. Lighting the fuse once the ship had closed in on the enemy, they hurled them down to the enemy's deck.

When two opposing ships drew close enough, a captain sometimes gave orders to board the enemy. Grappling hooks—iron claws attached to long ropes—were thrown across the water, sinking into the enemy ship's bulwarks and allowing his men to pull the ships closer. Once a ship was boarded, the fighting became hand-to-hand combat. Boarding parties carried muskets with bayonets, pistols, cutlasses, pikes, axes, even boat hooks—anything that could inflict maximum harm on the enemy.

As Hopkins's little fleet made its way to the Virginia coast, the drills increased, and his officers assessed each hand's capabilities as best they could to see who among them would take up arms and who would best serve the ship by sailing her.[35]

Prior to departing Cape Henlopen, Hopkins ordered his red pennant raised on the ensign staff—the signal calling for a captains' council aboard the *Alfred*. Once they were aboard and had entered the commodore's cabin, the door was closed and guarded by two armed marines to ensure privacy. The officers made an interesting group, most of them, including Hopkins, speaking in New England accents.[36]

As Nicholas Biddle took his seat at the great table in Hopkins's cabin he acknowledged each captain with a short greeting or a simple nod. He did not know Marylander Henry Hallock of the *Wasp* but thought William Stone of the *Hornet*, a Bermudian by birth, to be "A Very Stout and Very Good kind of Man." In a letter to his sister Lydia, he shared his opinions of some fellow officers, calling John Hopkins "a Good Natured Man" and Hoysted Hacker "an Active Smart Seaman." He considered John Hazard "a Stout Man Very Vain and Ignorant" with "as much low cunning as Capacity," and declared Dudley Saltonstall "Sensible" and "indefatigable" but "Morose." Biddle was "Very happy in haveing Sam Nicholas in the Fleet" as captain of the marines, and lightheartedly judged himself as "a Mighty Good Young Man." He did not reveal to his sister any judgment of Abraham Whipple or of his commodore.[37]

Hopkins opened the meeting by handing out a thorough set of signals he had painstakingly put together. Saying that a signal book was invaluable was an understatement: it would be their main communication source in fair weather or foul, of such importance to their success that each captain knew his book was to be destroyed if there was any chance of his being captured. Signals, a combination of other countries' flags and different colored pennants flown from various masts, gave the captains specific instructions, from changing course to engaging (or not engaging) enemy ships. They were to learn the signals thoroughly, for the wrong interpretation could turn victory into defeat, or tragedy in a storm.[38]

Next, Hopkins shared his plans with his captains without confiding in them about his decision not to carry out Congress's orders. Reports and rumors that Dunmore's fleet was reinforced had confirmed in his own mind that this jury-rigged American fleet was no match for men-of-war belonging to the finest navy in the world. British ships were built for war from the keelson to the main topgallants, its captains expertly trained in the deadly art of naval combat, their crews having mastered their gunnery skills with live ammunition. Weeks of being trapped in ice had given Hopkins time to think, and the more he reviewed Congress's grandiose orders—and subsequent instructions—the more he was convinced that the Americans should not make their debut on the seas in such engagements, and he wisely decided that they would not.

Instead, Hopkins took advantage of the loophole in his original orders, deciding that "bad weather or any other unforeseen accident" let him arbitrarily change them. Substituting ice for "bad Weather" and an outbreak of smallpox filling his sick bays for "unforeseen accidents," he determined that his squadron was "not in a condition to keep on a cold coast." Seeking an alternate destination worth making for, he told his captains to "Make the best of your Way to the Southern part of Abaco"—one of the Bahama Islands. Directing them "to keep Company with me if possible and truly Observe the Signals given by the Ship I am in," Hopkins made sure that, even if "Separated in a Gale of Wind or Otherwise" they were not to miss their rendezvous point.[39]

Hopkins's new plan testified to his political skills as well as knowing when and when not to fight. He had a hunch that the British forts in the Bahamas held the one thing Washington and Congress lusted after more than victories at sea: gunpowder. With the blessing of Congress to "follow such Courses as your best

Judgement shall Suggest," Hopkins was off and sailing. The meeting over, the captains were rowed back to their ships.[40]

Final preparations proceeded as the little fleet rocked at anchor offshore. Taking quill in hand, Biddle wrote one last letter that reflected both his enthusiasm for the cruise and his matter-of-fact approach to its dangers. "Fare you well My Dear Brother," he wrote to James Biddle, adding,

> I well know the Glorious Cause I am engaged in. And if ever I disgrace it May My Kind father who gave me being instantly Blast me in mercy to me. I mean not to be de[s]perate beyond measure. But to do my duty to the utmost of My Ability. If in spite of my best endeavour I should be taken, If Fortune Should frown upon me I hope I shall bear up against it with that Fortitude Patience and Resignation which I usually found Myself Possessed of . . . And Never in my Life was better pleased with a trip I was going to take than I am with this . . . I beg you to give my Sincere Love to My dear Sister Fanny to My Mother and all the Family.[41]

On February 18, under clear skies and with a fair breeze touching his cheek, Hopkins stood on the *Alfred*'s quarterdeck and ordered Saltonstall to "loose the foretopsail and Sheet it home"—the signal for the fleet to weigh anchor and make sail. Wind captured canvas with a pleasant groaning sound as each ship got under way at a fair clip. The townsfolk of Lewes, not used to seeing such an array of vessels sail together, found them a memorable sight as they made for the Atlantic. The masts of the square-riggers seemed to reach for the heavens while the fore-and-aft-rigged schooners and sloops easily kept up with them. Gradually they shrank in size until all of them, even the sluggish *Hornet*, "crossed the bar," slipping out of sight over the horizon.[42]

The fleet was just two days below Cape Henlopen when a brutal storm struck, separating the *Hornet* and *Fly* from the squadron that evening. A sunny morning followed, giving Hopkins ten days of smooth sailing. Pleasant conditions allowed the captains to repair any damages to their ships from the storm and continue their seemingly endless gunnery practice. The men, too, got to know one another. For each friendship formed, some distances were kept. A wide berth was usually given to any salt with a predilection for bullying or fighting.

Just as captains used this shakedown cruise as a chance to see the officers and men at work, the leadership style of each captain began to emerge. Thirty-eight-year-old Dudley Saltonstall, commanding the *Alfred*, had served in privateers during the French and Indian War. He possessed a snobbish manner that guaranteed unpopularity with both his officers and his men; Lieutenant Jones found him "ill mannered and narrow minded." Aboard the *Columbus*, the wizened Abraham Whipple issued his orders with blunt directness. Whipple had nerve, but his tendency to act without considering consequences was not yet evident to his sailors. John Hopkins of the *Cabot* was deferential to both his father and his peers.[43]

The most unpopular captain was John Hazard, the man who got the *Providence* after Jones declined command. Earlier, when the fleet was iced in at Reedy Island, he was accused of failing to deliver a supply of wood to the *Fly* that Hopkins had ordered. Minor as it sounds, it was the beginning of Hazard's poor relationship with practically everyone. Overweight but handsome, William Stone had a reputation as a good skipper whose sailing talents became evident after successfully getting both the *Wasp* and the *Hornet* out of the Chesapeake, eluding Lord Dunmore's fleet. Stone also benefited from having decent officers aboard, including Joshua Barney, his master's mate. Barely old enough to shave, Barney was embarking on what would be a forty-year habit of fighting the British.[44]

Aboard the *Wasp*, William Hallock was an experienced sea captain disposed to both caution and prayer, frequently seeking the advice of the Almighty as much as—if not more than—that of his superiors. Hoysted Hacker was not Hopkins's first choice to take over the *Fly*, but once again Jones had declined an offer to command. Misfortune would sail hand in hand with Hacker throughout the war; blessed throughout the conflict with offers to command several ships, he had the bad luck to accept each one of them. If there was a Jonah in the Continental Navy, it was Hacker.[45]

Of all the senior officers, it was Biddle whose star shone brightest. Only twenty-five, he was already a skilled sailor, a respected captain, and a Royal Navy veteran. He possessed enough courage to supply the fleet.

Both his talent and his drive had been honed by necessity. Biddle came from prestigious stock, but his family frequently found themselves on both sides of the coin where fate was involved. His great-grandfather had served bravely under Cromwell in the English Civil War, but his battlefield experiences turned him into a pacifist. He joined the Society of Friends just when the Restoration began persecuting Quakers. After a stint in hellish Newgate Prison, he immigrated to New Jersey and soon owned nearly 1,000 acres of farmland on both sides of the

Delaware. Upon his death the land became his son's property and was in turn meted out to his six children upon his death. One of them, Nicholas's father, William, used his share of the estate and his family connections to go into business in Philadelphia after marrying Mary Scull, the fetching daughter of the city's surveyor. Upon his marriage William joined the Church of England.[46]

As his family grew, William established a reputation as a true gentleman whose trusting personality dovetailed with a decided lack of business acumen. The Biddle family fortune rescued his first complete financial failure, but there was no deus ex machina a second time. "I had nine children, one at my breast," his wife, Mary, later recalled, when William informed her that he had ruined them. Forced to sell his lands to pay off his astronomical debt, he could not look at his family without weeping over what he had done to them. When he died five years later of a lingering illness, he and his were penniless; even his in-laws' money was spent to keep the family out of debtors' prison. Mary was forced to follow in her father's footsteps, taking work as a surveyor.[47]

Her older children joined their mother in an effort to recover the family's reputation, scrambling to make money as best they could. By the time Nicholas was fourteen, in 1764, his elder siblings were lawyers, merchants, and in the military. Charles, then eighteen, was a sailor, and the sea called Nicholas as well. He signed on as ship's boy aboard a snow—a two-masted square-rigged vessel ideally suited for the West Indies trade. His first voyage exposed to him to every aspect of a sailor's lot: pleasant days of progress mixed with gales and terrific storms; idyllic islands fraught with blackguards and thieves. With pluck and ambition he earned a mate's rank, surviving a shipwreck for good measure. At twenty he had grown to five feet nine, handsome and unassuming—as long as he was not crossed.[48]

Rumors of war with Spain over the Falkland Islands were the talk of Philadelphia in 1770. Nicholas saw this as an opportunity to further his maritime career by joining the Royal Navy. Putting his family's contacts to use, he wangled letters from Robert Morris's partner Thomas Willing and Pennsylvania Assembly leader Joseph Galloway that recommended him to Benjamin Franklin, the colony's agent in England. Galloway's letter described young Biddle's "Good Character and Esteem," adding, "his laudable Ambition leads him to pursue some Thing more honourable." Thus armed, Biddle booked passage to England, where he found Franklin full of "good advice and encouragement" and a midshipman's warrant aboard the HMS *Seaford*, twenty guns.

The *Seaford* was off the Isle of Wight in the English Channel when Biddle learned there would be no war with Spain. He transferred to the *Portland*, a fifty-gun two-decker bound for the West Indies. Then he was back to England, where he wrote his sister Lydia that the navy had not changed him much, if at all: not only had the affable Nicholas made many friends in the service, but "I wear my own hair . . . lodge in London and sleep in a bed."[49]

While ashore, Biddle learned that the king and the Earl of Sandwich had approved the Royal Society's proposal "for an expedition to try how far navigation was practicable towards the North Pole." Two bomb-ketches, the *Carcass* and the *Racehorse* (two-masted vessels usually armed with mortars), were in dry dock, their hulls being reinforced to withstand ice. Here was an adventure young Biddle could not pass up, but the berths for command and warrant officers were already filled by other applicants with political connections. Undeterred, Biddle volunteered as an able seaman. He was assigned to the *Carcass*. One of the midshipmen was a teenager who, like Biddle, was the very model of a future captain, mature and confident beyond his years: Horatio Nelson. The ships departed in June.[50]

Biddle found the voyage exhilarating and character-building. Almost immediately he was promoted to coxswain, in charge of the captain's launch. The two ships made their way to Spitsbergen Island, north of the Arctic Ocean's deepest point—more than 18,000 feet. Under the long daylight summer hours, the two ships entered the ice-bound channels, making progress by the yard; "ice clogging us on every side" was one log entry. A shipmate described the setting sun's rays "of bright blue, like sapphire, and sometimes like the variable colours of a prism, exceeding in luster the richest gems of the world." Biddle later recalled "the Sun[']s not setting for two months."

Throughout the passage, Biddle and the others beheld "Whales spitting their fountains towards the skies"; when polar bears fearlessly approached the ships they were frequently shot and skinned. Conditions baffled and alarmed captain and crew alike—on one side of the *Carcass* the sun beat so warmly one day that the captain noted how the tar was running off the standing rigging, while on the other side, where ice had just been removed, the water was instantly freezing over.

By August the ships were ensnared in the ice from a western cold front. Without an easterly wind to send them to open water, the men would be trapped until the spring thaw. Their only hope of escape was to haul the ships' boats over the ice, heading east during the day, walk back to the two ships for a night's rest, and repeat the same arduous task until the boats had been carried to running water—all the while hoping for a change of wind. On the morning of August 7 all the boats were lowered, with Biddle in charge of the *Carcass*'s launch and young Nelson commanding her four-oared cutter. Working with deliberate caution they painstakingly hauled the boats eastward. By sunset they had made only four miles. Exhausted and cold to the bone, they trudged back to the ships. On the second day they returned to find that the ice had broken sufficiently for the rest of the men to make sail and slowly inch the ships towards safety. On August 10 the ships finally reached the boats, and they were hoisted back aboard. A strong northeast wind sent the *Carcass* and *Racehorse* slamming into ice floes; only their strengthened hulls kept them from being ripped apart. In the afternoon they broke through to the open sea. Their mission a failure, the crew shouted with joy. After another six weeks of rough seas, they made it home.

Nothing is more telling about Biddle's character than the letter he wrote to Lydia about this ordeal. With tongue in cheek, he told her "my hand shakes as I write." But "what astounds, confounds, and frightens me most of all is that during the whole voyage, I did not apprehend danger." He was planning on volunteering for a similar expedition to the "Southern Ocean" by naturalist Sir Joseph Banks when word of the Boston Tea Party reached London. Seeing what the future held, Biddle returned his midshipman's warrant and booked passage home.[51]

Upon arriving, Biddle sailed a snow to Santo Domingo, officially for molasses but actually for gunpowder. Stowing the half barrels of powder in the hold behind a row of large barrels of molasses, he sailed homeward. He picked up a pilot off Cape Henlopen, who informed him that a British warship was upriver, stopping and searching American vessels and seizing any smuggled "contraband." The cagey Biddle ran up French colors, boldly sailed past the king's ship, and docked in Philadelphia. Soon afterwards he accepted the command of a Pennsylvania row galley, the *Franklin*. The ink on his commission was barely dry when the Continental Navy was born.[52]

These were the first Americans to sail under John Adams's Articles of War, a long list of commandments intended to maintain discipline and keep each ship well run and, hopefully, happy. Before drafting them, Adams devoured the Royal Navy's articles. His new bylaws were influenced by both the British code and the Age of Enlightenment:

> Commanders . . . are strictly required to shew themselves as a good example of honor and virtue to their officers and men . . . No Commander

shall inflict any punishment upon a seaman beyond twelve lashes upon his bare back, with a cat of nine tails; if the fault shall deserve a greater punishment, he is to apply to the Commander in Chief of the Navy never by his own authority to discharge a commission or warrant officer, nor to punish or strike him . . . any [person] who shall utter any words of sedition or mutiny . . . shall suffer such punishment as a court-martial shall inflict.

In copying nearly verbatim many of the articles, the puritanically minded Adams found that many reflected his New England abhorrence of the human frailties he found sinful:

The Commanders . . . are to take care that divine service shall be performed twice a day on board, and a Sermon preached on Sundays, unless bad weather or other extraordinary accidents prevent it. If any shall be heard to swear, curse, or blaspheme the name of God, the Commander is strictly enjoined to punish them for every offence, by causing them to wear a wooden collar, or some other badge of distinction . . . He who is guilty of drunkenness, if a seaman, shall be put in irons until he is sober, but if he is an officer, he shall forfeit two days pay.[53]

★   ★   ★

On Friday, March 1, Hopkins's fleet reached the island of Abaco, east of Grand Bahama Island. The ships dropped anchor off Hole-in-the-Wall, the treacherous southern end of the island still dangerous for mariners to this day.[54]

The Bahamas, a chain of islands that stretches gracefully north to southeast in the Atlantic Ocean, were the colonies' gateway to the Caribbean. The southeast part of Abaco, where Hopkins now waited, hoping for the arrival of the *Hornet* and the *Fly*, is separated by the Northeast Providence Channel from the island of New Providence, where Nassau, the Bahaman capital, lies. Almost immediately the fleet captured two Bahaman sloops and their pilots, who informed Hopkins that the two old forts guarding New Providence—Montague on the east, Nassau on the west—both had working cannons and sizable supplies of gunpowder: just what Hopkins came for, just what Washington needed. Further, the forts were manned by an inconsequential force, mostly armed citizens instead of seasoned troops. Hopkins dispatched a midshipman and some longboats to resupply the fleet with freshwater and signaled his captains to convene for a council of war.[55]

One of the *Cabot*'s lieutenants, Thomas Weaver, was familiar with the islands and their soundings. With his help, Hopkins concocted a plan: he would place sailors and marines aboard the captured sloops and sail them straight towards Fort Nassau to surprise and subdue the garrison before they had time to defend themselves, while the fleet remained out of sight but within striking distance. The plan sounded brilliant—in theory. It required trusting the captured pilots to safely navigate the sloops through the passage, with the fleet keeping out of sight of the fort's lookouts as the sloops sailed boldly into the harbor. His captains approved, and returned to their ships.

Hopkins made sail on March 2. At first he had his ships right where he wanted them, the two sloops making straight for the fort while his squadron tarried behind. But whether he forgot to order his captains to remain out of sight, or was himself caught up in seeing his stratagem carried out firsthand, the entire fleet was soon close behind the sloops and easily visible to everyone in the fort. All hope of surprise ended when, from the *Alfred*'s quarterdeck, Hopkins saw one puff of white smoke from the fort's walls, then another. Seconds later he and his men heard a cannon's roar, followed by a cannonball humming towards them. It splashed harmlessly in the water, as did the ones that followed. No ships were hit by the meager cannonade. Hopkins signaled the sloops to wear ship—turn through the wind, and follow the fleet out of the harbor. There would be no victory for the Continental Navy this day.[56]

From Fort Nassau, Bahaman governor Montford Browne watched the Americans retreat. Even though British forces had abandoned New Providence, Browne and the volunteer garrison, having sent the Americans out of the harbor, "thought Ourselves secure with our own internal Strength and Defence."[57]

Meanwhile, in the *Alfred*'s cabin, Hopkins and company discussed another attack, this time on Fort Montague but still requiring Weaver and the captured pilots to get the ships safely within striking distance. Years later, John Paul Jones would insist that the idea was his, colorfully describing how he ascended the foretopmast head "where he could see every danger" while guiding the ships to safety. A great story, but untrue: Jones, unlike Weaver, had never been to the Bahamas.[58]

On Sunday, March 3, the fleet's marines were once again transferred to the two captured sloops along with the *Providence* and the *Wasp*. Then, with Biddle's speedy *Andrew Doria* in the lead, they sailed eastward to Rose Island, a tiny spit of land just north of Fort Montague. By ten o'clock the ships had assembled and dropped anchor, while the four carrying the marines and about two hundred sailors stood for shore. Once they reached the shallows, the longboats were lowered and rowed to shore, packed tight with marines. As soon the boats touched bottom, Captain Samuel Nicholas and the marines vaulted over the sides, their shoes splashing in the water. The tradition citing "the shores of Tripoli" actually began on the beach of Nassau.

As they hit the beach, the guns of the *Providence* and the *Wasp* were run out. The marines soon found themselves on a cart road that wound the two miles up to the fort. At first, the islanders on the shore thought they were being attacked by Spaniards, but as the Americans closed in they were "soon undeceived," as Captain Nicholas later recalled. As he formed his men into marching order he was confronted by a messenger from Governor Browne, asking his intentions, and Nicholas made them plain: take possession of the "war-like" stores while not harming anyone or their property unless provoked. His message delivered, Nicholas marched the marines up the road to the fort.

The marines had neither the time nor the inclination to take in the beautiful view. The road curved around a deep cove, while the leeward side was covered by thick undergrowth. The Americans could be clearly seen from the fort's ramparts. The garrison was outnumbered but not outgunned: sixteen cannon in all, ranging from 12-pounders to 32-pounders.

Fortunately, they were not manned by seasoned British gunners, nor were the defenders as itching for a fight as were the advancing marines. Nonetheless, they fired three of the 12-pounders at the Americans and, while they hit no one, at least stopped the marines in their tracks. Nicholas held a hurried consult with his officers and approached the fort under a flag of truce, reiterating what he had just told the townsfolk below. To Nicholas's surprise, the garrison's commander replied that he had fired on the Americans because the governor had ordered him to do so, while behind him the gun crews busied themselves spiking the guns— driving spikes through the touchholes and rendering them useless. Then the defenders fled into town. By three o'clock, the fort was flying American colors. When his men informed Nicholas that the guns were not badly damaged by the garrison's hasty sabotage, he decided to remain in Fort Montague and give his men a decent night's rest as reward for their efforts, sending word to Governor Browne that he would meet him in the morning.[59]

As the exhausted Americans slept, Browne met with the town council, the militia officers, and the island's more prominent citizens to determine if this "sudden and unexpected Attack" could be repelled by defending Fort Nassau. Earlier, he had sent out a call to arms among the New Providence citizenry, offering the "Reward of a Pistole to every free Negroe" who "would immediately enter the Fort" and help defend it. Few, if any, took Browne up on his offer. Now, with the sun setting behind them and the Grand Union flying before them, the principal inhabitants and Browne's other guests decided resistance was futile.

If he could not defend his town, Browne could at least deprive its invaders of what they had come for. He gave orders to remove the gunpowder from Fort Nassau's magazine, load it onto a merchant's sloop and sail to St. Augustine, Britain's Florida stronghold. The Bahamans removed 160 of the 182 half barrels of powder after Browne decided that "sending away the whole of it might enrage a disappointed enemy, & induce them to burn the Town, & commit other depredations."[60]

The sloop was escorted by the *St. John*, a British schooner in disrepair. Any hopes Browne had of rallying his fellow British subjects to return to Fort Nassau and duty sailed with the sloop: she no sooner weighed anchor and sailed than "three fourths of the Men and Negroes" disappeared into the shadowy streets to the safety of their homes, leaving the disgusted governor alone with his principles.[61]

Even in the dark of night, the sloop and her sluggish escort would have been easy prey for Hopkins's ships had he done what any British squadron leader would have: blockaded the harbor. The sloop rode low in the water, thanks to a hold full of gunpowder. Nevertheless, the unarmed sloop and her barely seaworthy escort of eight guns and thirty men easily slipped through Hopkins's fingers.[62]

The following morning Nicholas marched his marines and sailors across town to Fort Nassau, where the British colors were struck without a shot fired. From the ramparts the Americans could see their fleet sail into the harbor, then turn and watch Governor Browne pacing the piazza at his mansion with his council and servants in tow. With Nicholas's permission, an enthusiastic junior officer and a small detachment of marines were sent to escort the governor to the fort. The indignant Browne insisted he would leave only "By force of arms" and was assured that would be the case. Once Hopkins got ashore and learned of Browne's defiance, he placed him under arrest.

Hopkins made his way to Fort Nassau under the bright sunshine and the pleasant breezes that have lured people to the Bahamas for centuries: even the water has an otherworldly sparkle there. The commodore was master of all he surveyed. The war against Britain was not yet a year old; weeks earlier, the Continental Navy did not even exist. Hopkins did not know it, but at that moment his career reached its zenith.[63]

The cache of stores in the fort was wondrous to behold: no less than seventy-one cannons, fifteen mortars, thousands upon thousands of round shot, and other ordnance supplies—and those twenty-two half barrels of powder. For two long weeks sailors and marines unloaded ballast from their ships and dismantled the fort. When the ships' holds were packed, Hopkins requisitioned a Bermuda sloop, lading her hold full while promising to send her back to New Providence. The sailors also found a puncheon of rum. After endless trips carrying massive guns, the cask was deemed too heavy to bring aboard ship. Lightening it helped them celebrate their victory, and also made them too drunk for work. Among the itemized list of supplies, Hopkins entered "Part of a Cask [of] Spirit[s]," if less gunpowder than he might have captured had he been more vigilant.[64]

Those tars down with alcohol poisoning soon had company as one American after another came down with fever as well as some cases of smallpox. The captains had no experience aboard ships with such large crews—merchantmen usually sailed with "skeleton crews" to minimize overhead and maximize profits. They lacked any understanding of how to maintain a healthy albeit crowded ship. Only Biddle, with his Royal Navy pedigree, possessed such knowledge. In fact, the *Andrew Doria* boasted the only crew inoculated for smallpox; thus she became the first, though unofficial, hospital ship in an American navy. Even Biddle handed his bed over to an ailing sailor, sleeping atop his lockers for the duration. Soon even his men were prostrate with "tropical fever," although they escaped the ravages of the pox.[65]

On March 18, under "Clear Weather" and "a fresh Sea Breese," Hopkins led his fleet north. While there was no stirring victory, his New Providence venture had been a success, his ships weighed down with munitions and supplies.[66]

Not every American was glad to be returning; aboard the *Wasp*, Captain Hallock noted that one seaman literally jumped ship and swam to shore. Hopkins had three guests aboard the *Alfred* who probably wished they, too, were good swimmers: Governor Browne; British army officer James Babbidge; and Thomas Irving, a South Carolina Loyalist and His Majesty's Inspector General of Customs for the thirteen colonies. "I have been tore away from my family at a moment's notice" and "cruelly treated," a distressed Browne wrote to Lord Dartmouth.[67]

Once past Abaco, Hopkins sent each captain orders to keep up with the *Alfred* if possible but, "Should you Separate by accident you are to make the best of your way to Block Island Channel" just off the Rhode Island coast. Hopkins was heading home. In his later reports to Congress he would take care to mention that he considered making for Georgia and ridding that colony's coast of British warships, but this is doubtful. Surviving logs and correspondence show that his men were getting sicker by the hour, his captains stopping for burials at sea. Over the next two weeks they sailed past Georgia, South Carolina, and Virginia—as much a part of Hopkins's ordered destinations now as they were before. The return trip encountered the same stormy weather as when the ships left Cape Henlopen, even losing the *Wasp* in a storm.

En route home, as Biddle returned to exercising his men at the guns, the American ships frequently gave chase to sighted sails that proved to be American or neutral. One day they "spoke" a Frenchman out of Connecticut (hailing its captain across the water), who informed them that the Redcoats had abandoned Boston the same day they had departed New Providence. For the most part, the fleet dealt with medical and meteorological conditions. Hard gales forced the captains to reef sails and man the pumps, while the sick lists mounted. The ships' bottoms were foul, as were the dispositions of their captains. A beleaguered Hallock, trying to catch up with Hopkins, spoke for his peers when he wrote in his log, "We are in a bad Setuation."[68]

Hopkins ordered the fleet to make for Rhode Island, passing the Delaware Bay and thereby Congress, awaiting his return to Philadelphia. In so doing, Hopkins also eluded capture. A British squadron was lying in wait for him there, led by Captain Andrew Snape Hamond, a proud, talented sea warrior who daily anticipated the Americans' arrival. By April 4 the Continental ships were off Montauk Point on Long Island, where the *Columbus* captured the *Hawke*, a schooner serving as tender to James Wallace's squadron. She struck her colors without a fight, the first Royal Navy ship taken by the Continental Navy. Tenders, used by larger ships for supplies and carrying dispatches—the *Hawke* carried just six guns and eight swivels—seemed the perfect prey to Hopkins, who soon had all his ships scouring the horizon for others.[69]

The next day, Hopkins led the entire fleet in capturing another ship from the despised Wallace's squadron: the *Bolton*, a bomb brig used for mortar shelling. Her crew was dispersed among the fleet, including seven African slaves of the British officers. Rather than being set free, they were added to the ships' muster rolls. Hopkins now had a fleet of a dozen ships.[70]

As they continued towards Block Island, another Continental ship was departing Philadelphia.

John Barry had spent months seeing to it that merchantmen were successfully converted into ships of war, only to watch Congress hand them over to other captains. Barry waited, somewhat patiently, for his turn.[71]

It came in March, when the Maryland brigantine *Wild Duck* docked in Philadelphia after a harrowing voyage from St. Eustatius, her hold containing 2,000 pounds of gunpowder and other wartime supplies. While sailing past Virginia she was chased by HMS *Edward*, a sloop acting as tender to Lord Dunmore's fleet and under the command of young Richard Boger, who already had one prize under his belt. The Americans barely escaped, and then eluded Hamond's squadron off the Delaware Capes. While the *Wild Duck*'s stores were unloaded, Congress purchased her for the navy, renamed her *Lexington*, and offered command of her to John Barry. "With a determined resolution of distressing the enemy as much as in my power," Barry accepted.[72]

The ebullient Irishman had her ready for sea in just two weeks. Along with her "square-tuck Stern painted yellow, and a low, rounded stem painted lead colors, black sides and yellow moldings," as one Loyalist spy reported, she carried sixteen 4-pounders and twelve swivels—a bee with a potent sting for her diminutive size. Barry strode tirelessly from shipyard to storehouse to statehouse to obtain munitions, supplies, and men. He was inadvertently aided by Henry Fisher's latest dispatch from the capes: an enemy sloop was heading upriver. News of such imminent danger shortened the pilot's letter; instead of the typical signoff "I am Sirs, your obedient Servant, etc.," Fisher simply wrote, "Yours in haste."[73]

His urgent message went a long way in getting Barry's supply of small arms up the gangplank and stowed aboard while Philadelphia slept one evening—up until then, the only small arm aboard was a pistol Barry himself had bought. He hoped for at least a hundred hands from the rendezvous held by his lieutenant, a free spirit named Luke Matthewman, but got only seventy-five—plus a slave Barry purchased for the cruise. With a Grand Union ensign flying above her quarterdeck (purchased by the captain for seven pounds), the *Lexington* stood down the Delaware, silently gliding past sleeping Philadelphia on March 28.[74]

Fisher's message compelled the Pennsylvania Committee of Safety to order four row galleys to accompany the *Lexington* downriver under Barry's command and "Take and destroy all such Vessels of the Enemy." Twenty miles below Philadelphia, Barry was hailed by Fisher at Reedy Island, a spit of land on the Delaware side of the river near the fishing village of Port Penn: the British ship was not a sloop but Hamond's forty-four-gun frigate, the *Roebuck*. Leaving the row galleys at Reedy Island, Barry went on alone, exercising his men at the guns in the same fashion as Biddle and Jones had done.

While Hamond awaited an answer to his request for a land force to accompany his passage up the Delaware, his ships stood off Cape May. On March 28 he came down with "an inflammation in my Bowels" so severe that he turned command over to one Lieutenant Leak, who unsuccessfully pursued the leaky *Hornet* as she approached the bay.

Three days later, a recovering Hamond spied the *Lexington* for the first—but not the last—time, off Cape May. Lowering his spyglass, he ordered his helmsman to change course and pursue at the same time. The sun was just coming up when Barry viewed the *Roebuck* for the first—but not the last—time. For sixteen years, the thirty-one-year-old Irishman had plied his trade with the Delaware River as his route to and from the Atlantic; he knew her twists and turns, her depths and shallows, as well as the savviest pilot. Seeing the *Roebuck* plowing the waves, heading straight at him, Barry changed course and headed for the Overfalls, the treacherous shoals that encircle Cape May. The *Lexington*'s shallow draft allowed Barry to enter the shoals, while the *Roebuck*'s deeper draft made her pursuit more perilous the faster she neared the Overfalls, whose depths can change from thirty feet to three feet in a matter of a few yards.

Hamond, with more than twenty years of service in the navy, was smart enough to order his leadman to swing his line—a rope long enough to reach a depth of twenty-five fathoms with a ten-pound lead weight, hollowed out at its end and tallowed, allowing it to bring back a sample of the bottom. Slowly and methodically, the sailor made circular revolutions with the line, each revolution accompanied by a deep *whoosh*, audible to the crew. Then he released it into the water. Soon he struck ground shallow enough to imperil the frigate, forcing Hamond to break off the chase and, even more vexing for Hamond, with Barry's brigantine out of the range of the *Roebuck*'s bow chasers. The *Lexington* sped past Cape May, heading north.[75]

Fisher's reports convinced Congress that, as William Whipple wrote to Josiah Bartlett, "The Coast is much infested with pirates"—that is, British warships. But Barry found no evidence of them after two days of sailing north along the Jersey coast; he only found signs that they had been there (including a British raiding party that had terrorized an Absecon family, taking "even the clothes off the children's backs"). After overtaking a sloop of dubious origins and sending her to Philadelphia, Barry changed course. Congress wanted Lord Dunmore's depredations addressed, and Barry was determined to oblige as best he and his little ship could.[76]

Hamond, too, was after bigger game, convinced that the "Philadelphia Squadron," as he called Hopkins's fleet, was close by. Therefore he "took care to place my Ship in the best manner I could to intercept them," unaware that the Americans were already past the Delaware Bay.[77]

Just after midnight on Saturday, April 6, the *Andrew Doria*'s lookout "Saw two Sail, to the ESE." Roused from his slumber, Biddle ordered a light placed on the ensign staff and lit two "false Fires"—the night signal for sighting a strange sail. The *Andrew Doria* gave chase. One hour later, the *Cabot* was alongside her with the *Alfred* right behind. They were after the HMS *Glasgow*, twenty guns, and her tender, the *Nautilus*. Biddle cried, "Beat to Quarters!" Immediately the drummer pounded out the frantic rhythm as the crew hastened smartly to their battle stations. Seconds later, the drummer's endless *rat-a-tat* was echoed across the water by his counterparts aboard the other Continental ships.

The *Glasgow* was commanded by Tyringham Howe. Originally part of Wallace's squadron, Howe was heading south to Virginia with dispatches for Dunmore from Admiral Shuldham. Now he changed course—not to run, but to fight. With the wind blowing south, Howe headed NNW to come across the *Cabot*. By then the Americans had been joined by the *Columbus* and the *Providence*. All of Hopkins's original ships were ready to engage, five against one. From his quarterdeck, the commodore could taste another victory.[78]

In February Hopkins had believed that his ships, captains, sailors—perhaps even he himself—were not ready to do battle at sea. He would soon learn if he was right.

CHAPTER THREE

✯ ✯ ✯

"I FEAR NOTHING"

I have the pleasure to acquaint you that all our people behaved
with much courage.

—CAPTAIN JOHN BARRY TO THE CONTINENTAL MARINE COMMITTEE[1]

The *Glasgow* came through the north wind, making for the *Cabot* on a port tack. From the *Andrew Doria*'s quarterdeck, Nicholas Biddle kept a weather eye on the coming confrontation while glancing towards the *Alfred*, expecting Hopkins's signal to "Fire a gun and light as many false fires as there is Ships in the fleet." But no gun was fired, and no fires were set.[2]

Thanks to his years in the Royal Navy, Biddle realized that if the *Glasgow* was part of Wallace's squadron, the rest of the British ships were not far off. He wondered if Hopkins would follow the Royal Navy practice of forming his ships into a line of battle; one ship behind another, one broadside after another. Other American captains may not have been looking for this, but Biddle was.

Again, no signal from Hopkins. Disgusted, Biddle watched as the American ships "all went Helter Skelter, one flying here and another there to cut of[f] the retreat of a fellow who did not fear us."[3]

Indeed, "the fellow" in question, Tyringham Howe, showed no fear of superior numbers and firepower. He made for the Americans with an assurance that must have seemed foolhardy. There was such stillness aboard the ships that Biddle could hear Howe's voice as the Englishman hailed John Hopkins with his speaking trumpet: "Who are you? What ships are these?"

With as much bravado as he could muster, young Hopkins replied, "The *Cabot* and *Alfred*, a twenty-gun frigate."

Conversation abruptly ceased when a marine from the *Cabot*'s fighting tops threw a grenade at the *Glasgow* that exploded on her deck. Howe answered it with a broadside, and the battle was joined.

Howe's fearlessness was justified. The *Cabot* was outgunned; her 6-pounders, manned by overanxious gun crews, were no match for their British counterparts and their 9-pounders. Reloading with a speed incomprehensible to the Americans, they poured round after round into the *Cabot*, their marksmanship unerring and deadly. Standing on the *Alfred*'s quarterdeck next to Captain Saltonstall, the commodore watched the battle between his son's ship and the *Glasgow*, masking as best he could any anxieties father had for son. But his self-control was tested with each British broadside. Soon the brig was disabled, her rigging in tatters, and four were dead on deck, including Charles Seymour, the sailing master. To Hopkins's muted horror, the next broadside struck John down, one of seven wounded from the *Glasgow*'s onslaught.

The *Cabot* sheered off, heading west through the wind to let the *Alfred* pick up the fight. But as the flagship closed in, she came perilously close to ramming the *Andrew Doria*. Biddle roared orders to his men to tack to port. Hastily manning the braces and preparing to change course, the ship just missed being fouled by the limping *Cabot*. The *Andrew Doria* slid past her unharmed, but the maneuver carried her away from the fight. The *Alfred* faced the *Glasgow* alone. With her twenty 9-pounders and her ten 6-pounders she was more than a match for Howe's frigate—on paper.

One American officer had his men ready. "Stationed between decks to command the *Alfred*'s first battery" and with cool deliberation, Lieutenant John Paul Jones recited the orders he had hammered into his gun crews. The two ships exchanged broadsides as they sailed past each other. Few, if any, of Jones's men had seen battle before. Smoke stung their eyes and their ears rang from the din of their cannons, but his gun crews obediently ran out their reloaded guns. What they lacked in accuracy they made up for with steadfast obedience to their lieutenant. Through the gun ports Jones could see the results of his endless drilling: the *Glasgow* was taking damage. This night, no Americans were better led.[4]

Above deck in her fighting tops, the *Glasgow*'s marines fired volley after volley, first at the sailors on the *Alfred*'s deck, then taking aim at the American marines aloft. One shot missed marine captain Samuel Nicholas, but struck the officer next to him in the head; Nicholas knew he was dead as soon as he saw him hit. No time to mourn now. Nicholas ordered his marines to return fire.[5]

For half an hour, the two ships pounded away at each other. Then an "unlucky shot," as Jones called it, "carried away our Wheel Block & Ropes"—the helmsman could no longer steer the ship effectively. Suddenly the *Alfred* "broached to"—veering sharply to windward and putting her at the mercy of both nature and the enemy. Until the crew could jury-rig a repair, the ship was helpless.

Seeing his foe crippled, Howe tacked through the wind and came across the *Alfred*'s bow—"crossing the T." At that moment, the *Glasgow* was invincible, and the *Alfred* indefensible. Howe's gunners made the best of these precious seconds. British cannonballs slammed into the *Alfred*'s mainmast, shredded her rigging, breached her hull below the waterline, and killed four, one a young British midshipman confined to the cockpit. They were outnumbered and outgunned, but Howe's crew were seasoned warriors, and they fought that way. What was the King's Navy made of? This.[6]

Hopkins and Saltonstall had the *Alfred*'s steering working again when Biddle arrived, bringing the *Andrew Doria* up behind the *Glasgow* as the frigate sailed past the *Alfred*, heading northeast. Soon Hopkins was coming up on the *Glasgow*'s port side, just as the missing Whipple brought the *Columbus* up on her starboard quarter. "The whole fleet," it seemed to Howe, was "within Musket shot, on pourt quarters and Stern." Throughout the battle, Whipple had tried to get the *Columbus* into the fight, while John Hazard kept the speedy *Providence* out of harm's way. Two hours had passed before three American ships were in a position to fight in unison.

For the moment, the outcome looked to be in Hopkins's hands. American guns raked the *Glasgow* and kept up a continual fire. Seeing the momentum of the battle swinging against him, Howe sent his clerk to the captain's cabin, where he took Howe's dispatches and signal book, placed them in a bag weighted down with round shot and heaved it overboard so as not to be seized.

But luck, like everything else that night, was with Howe. The wind unexpectedly changed from the north to the northwest, and the *Glasgow* "bore away" like a weary stag pursued by exhausted hounds. Howe made for Newport. American bow chasers kept blasting at the fleeing *Glasgow*; Howe ordered his stern chasers run out through his cabin windows to return fire. From the east, daylight began stretching across the horizon, filling the ocean with sunlight.

With dawn came a harsh realization for Hopkins: Howe was not fleeing—he was leading the Americans straight to James Wallace's squadron and his crack gunners. Caught up in the chase as he was, Hopkins needed only look at his battered flagship to envision the consequences of further pursuit. At six thirty, gazing back from his taffrail, Tyringham Howe watched as the Americans changed course and broke off the chase. Three hours later, the *Glasgow* was safely in Newport. Howe's casualties: one dead and three wounded, all coming from the musket fire of Nicholas's marines, but American broadsides did their share of damage. Howe's lower masts were pockmarked from cannonballs, and most of his standing and running rigging was shot away.[7]

Hopkins's decision not to encounter Wallace was the soundest he ever made as commander-in-chief of the Continental Navy. It would have been slaughter to send his sluggish, damaged ships against seasoned captains and sailors. Instead, the Americans inched their way northward through a front of fog and rain, arriving off New London, Connecticut, on April 7.[8]

That same front of fog surrounded HMS *Roebuck* off Cape Henlopen, where Captain Andrew Snape Hamond anxiously awaited Hopkins's fleet. The *Roebuck* did not ride idly at anchor. Hamond continued terrorizing Philadelphia shipping, capturing half a dozen small vessels whose cargoes were so inconsequential he burned them. They were all he would get for now; Hopkins's fleet had passed him days earlier.[9]

Two hundred miles south, the ship that had eluded Hamond the week before was cruising under clearer skies. John Barry's *Lexington* had reached the Virginia Capes, where, in accordance with his orders, he began searching for the ships of Lord Dunmore's navy. The brigantine's gun ports were closed when the lookout spotted a sail to the southwest. Peering through his spyglass Barry saw a sloop of war, a fair fight by size and a chance to test his men—and himself—in combat.

As the sloop sailed closer, the hands from the *Lexington*'s days as the *Wild Duck* recognized her as the *Edward*, the same ship that had chased them a month ago. Barry ordered his men to their battle stations. With his 4-pounders loaded, but not run out, he sent the *Lexington* fleeing eastward, hoping the *Edward* would follow. She did.

Stripped to their waists to lessen the chance of being burned in the coming fight, the gun crews bent over their weapons. Only Barry's calm exhortations were heard over the sounds of wind breathing into canvas and waves making way for the brigantine's hull.

Aboard the *Edward*, Lieutenant Richard Boger already had his 3-pounders

GLASGOW against Continental Fleet
off Block Island, April 6, 1776

HMS *Glasgow*   *Alfred*   *Columbus*   *Cabot*   *Andrew Doria*   *Providence*
FRIGATE

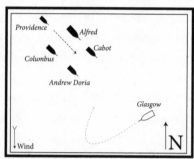

1:00 A.M.: After sighting Continental ships, *Glasgow* changes course and stands for them.

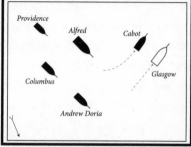

1:30 A.M.: *Glasgow* engages *Cabot* and disables her. *Alfred* and *Andrew Doria* endeavor to engage.

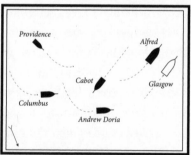

1:45 A.M.: *Alfred* engages *Glasgow*. In her withdrawal, *Cabot* interferes with *Andrew Doria*.

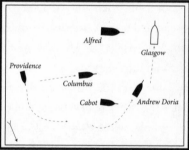

2:15 A.M.: After *Alfred*'s steering is damaged, *Andrew Doria* moves into action against *Glasgow*. *Columbus* attempts to enter the battle.

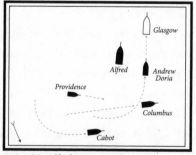

2:45 A.M.: *Alfred* returns to the engagement as *Columbus* attempts to come up on *Glasgow*'s stern.

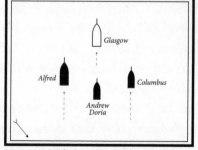

3:00 A.M.: With the wind shifting NW, *Glasgow* makes for Newport with three Continental ships in pursuit.

loaded and run out. Now he fired a warning shot at his prey. The cannon's echo had died when Boger's sloop came alongside the brigantine. Speaking trumpet in hand, Boger cried, "Heave to!"—ordering the brigantine brought into the wind, and her captain to identify himself.

Barry obliged in part: "Continental brig *Lexington*," he replied through his speaking trumpet. Then, turning to his men, he ordered the Grand Union run up and his guns run out. "Fire!" he roared, and the port battery's 4-pounders spewed fire and iron at the enemy. The damage to the *Edward* was negligible, but the very act of being fired on forced a change in Boger's strategy. He reversed course, hoping to lead the *Lexington* on a chase back towards the Chesapeake Bay and Dunmore's ships, but in coming through the wind, the *Edward* was exposed to another broadside.

It was now both race and battle as the ships bore WSW. As the *Lexington* came alongside the *Edward*, Boger's little 3-pounders fired on the uproll. His gunners' experience and accuracy were telling. Their cannonballs killed two Americans and wounded another.

But not even the sight of their three stricken comrades deterred the *Lexington*'s crew from their duties. Everyone aboard, including Barry's slave, kept to their assigned tasks. American gunners began hitting their target, shattering the *Edward*'s bulwarks "in a terrible manner." Before long the damages to the sloop's rigging and sails slowed her to a crawl. At one point, the *Lexington*'s speed looked to carry her past the *Edward* when Barry suddenly tacked behind her stern and "crossed the T." The last broadside of the battle killed one British tar and left a gaping hole below Boger's cabin, and water started pouring into the *Edward*. Lacking enough hands to sail the ship, plug the open wound in her stern, and continue the fight, Boger lowered his colors. Barry placed a prize crew aboard her and sent her back to Philadelphia.[10]

The town of New London greeted Hopkins's fleet like conquering heroes, with good reason: had they not safely sailed along the American coastline, captured two British forts, and returned with their holds full of munitions, stores, and valuable ordnance? As litters bore more than two hundred wounded or sick sailors off their battle-scarred and barnacle-infested ships, the moved townsfolk opened both their hearts and their homes. All of New London became a hospital.

Once the wounded were settled, Hopkins issued a flurry of dispatches to Congress, to his cronies in Rhode Island, and to General Washington. They were mostly detailed reports that maximized his successes while minimizing the setbacks due to his leadership, such as not following his original orders or telling the whole truth about the *Glasgow* battle. He praised his fleet's officers, especially those under his wounded son's command. But, as before, he disregarded his new orders from Congress. Instead, he offered the captured cannons from the Bahaman forts to the governors of Connecticut and Rhode Island for their protection.[11]

Initially, the hyperbole surrounding the fleet's success spread from ship to dock to tavern, from New London to New England. It was not superior British seamanship and fighting skills that kept the *Glasgow* from Hopkins's clutches, the Newport *Mercury* reported, but the "precious cargo" in the fleet's holds that "were the sole cause of Mrs. *Glasgow* making her escape." Other newspapers followed suit. Hopkins was the hero of the hour. Congressmen showered praise on him, and Washington loaned him two hundred troops from Boston to replace his sick and injured sailors. A poem written in his honor happily concluded that Neptune had turned over his trident and crown to "Gallant Hopkins."[12]

The officers soon found their heroics were not admired by just the men of Connecticut. The ladies sought their company as well, especially young, unmarried ones. Nicholas Biddle so enjoyed his dalliances with two Connecticut girls that he confided to his sister about his dilemma as to "which I love most," and summed New London up for all the officers: "There never was a more free sociable set of dear Creatures got together in any one place as in this."[13]

John Adams shared the initial stories of Hopkins's successes with everyone, while crowing to his wife, Abigail, "I have Vanity enough to take to myself, a share in the Merit of the American Navy . . . my Heart was much engaged in, and I pursued it, for a long Time, against the Wind and the Tide."

But the euphoria over Hopkins's return was short-lived.[14] The first crack in the veneer of the commodore's luster came from his sailors, beginning with the *Cabot*'s crew. A day after docking in New London, fifty of them signed a round-robin—a document signed in a circular configuration, giving equality to each petitioner and also eliminating the identity of the ringleaders. Stating their devotion to duty and citing "the Usual Custom observed in board Vessels of War," they requested that Hopkins advance them enough money to "procure them what's necessary for their Health & preservation." Simple enough; but lacking both the money and the authority to advance it, Hopkins refused. They were the first sailors of the Continental Navy to go unpaid. They would not be the last.[15]

And they were not happy about it. They had exposed themselves to storms, disease, and enemy fire, but now their grumbling joined the growing talk in the taverns and coffeehouses that Hopkins's account of the *Glasgow* affair was not, perhaps, the unvarnished truth.

The sailors' inquietude was shortly corroborated by some officers who at first publicly supported Hopkins's actions. In one letter, John Paul Jones tactfully assured Congressman Joseph Hewes that Hopkins was "respected thro' the fleet." Nicholas Biddle was less circumspect. Writing to his brother Charles, he decried Hopkins's leadership during the battle as "Shameful," adding, "A more ill conducted Affair never happened."[16]

Nor was Hopkins the only commanding officer whose conduct became a not-so-secret topic. The lack of action by Captains Hazard and Whipple was also publicly questioned. Whipple, hero of the *Gaspee* incident that preceded Lexington and Concord by three years, could not bear to walk down the town's cobblestone streets. "All the People at New London look on me with Contempt," he told Hopkins, insisting that only a court-martial could clear his name. Writing in the privacy of his cabin, Jones bitterly denounced the "Rude ungentle treatment" dispensed with relish by Dudley Saltonstall upon his junior officers. But rancor for John Hazard's bullying, embezzlement, and lack of fight commanding the *Providence* topped them all: "We are used like dogs," Hazard's crew bravely wrote to Hopkins.[17]

News of Hopkins's arrival in New London reached Congress on April 11, the same day the battered *Edward*, flying American colors, came up the Delaware, to the cheers of a large crowd. It was Philadelphia's first tangible sight of a victory from their armed forces, and a happy Congress congratulated Barry, promising that shares for "the officers and Crew shall be deposited in the hands of your Agents" in no time. Barry's prize joined another ship, the *Molly*, as the latest additions to the navy's roster, with new names: the *Edward* called the *Sachem*, the *Molly* called the *Reprisal* and turned over to a Marylander, Lambert Wickes.[18]

As the *Edward* underwent repairs at Wharton and Humphreys shipyard, the revisionist reports of Hopkins's cruise and conduct began trickling into Philadelphia. Upon hearing that the battle with the *Glasgow* took three glasses to fight (about ninety minutes), Biddle derisively wrote, "They must mean half-Minute Glasses." Word that Hopkins sent the captured cannons to Rhode Island and Connecticut instead of to Washington or Congress did little to help his growing public relations problem. In New London, Biddle returned from a short cruise convoying merchantmen, bringing back a British prize and news that Wallace's squadron had departed the waters off Newport.

Washington wrote Hopkins. He wanted his loaned soldiers back, but Hopkins had other plans. He needed their numbers to get his ships out to sea— not back to Philadelphia and Congress, but back to Rhode Island and home— home for Hopkins, that is. After issuing orders to Biddle to careen the foul *Andrew Doria* and then escort a convoy of Connecticut merchantmen, Hopkins set sail for Rhode Island, reaching Providence on May 1. Eager to get to sea again, and get the bitter taste of the *Glasgow* out of his mouth, Biddle put all hands to work at one of the dirtiest and most necessary of tasks, careening the brig.[19]

Once the *Andrew Doria* was emptied of all guns and stores, Biddle sent her to the shallow end of the harbor, placing his strongest hands at the "heaving down post," weighted down with crushed stone. Three fresh cables crossed the brig's deck, then ran through the capstan and around the post. Under Biddle's watchful eye, his men slowly brought the *Andrew Doria* onto one side. They were too strong; their last heave put her gunwale into the water, and the ship started to go under, forcing his men to ever so slowly release her to the proper pitch to begin work. The crew spent several days atop the hull. With kerchiefs tied across their faces to lessen the foul odor of the hull, they scraped the side, checking for holes from the infamous teredo: the long, wormlike mollusk that feasted on wooden ships, eating right through the planks. Rotting wood was replaced before the final step of the process—applying a fierce-smelling treatment of oil, tallow, and brimstone that coated the hull and keel. Many of the Royal Navy's ships had copper-sheathed hulls that required careening but extended a ship's life by years. But copper was expensive, and this noxious brew was the best defense the Americans could afford. Once one side was done, the process was reversed (in this case, Biddle's men made the same mistake of over-heaving), and the ship returned to her usual appearance. One week later she put out to sea, a faster, better sailer.[20]

Hopkins reached Providence on April 26 to learn that Congress had ordered two of the thirteen frigates built there, and that they wanted his captured guns divided up and sent to Philadelphia and Boston. They also wanted the fleet refitted and sent to sea. Before complying, Hopkins also had some careening to do—with his officers.

The first court-martial was held aboard the *Alfred* on May 6. That morning, twelve of the fleet's officers, led by Dudley Saltonstall, sat at the great table in Hopkins's cabin. Abraham Whipple was called in; after entering, the door was closed and guarded by two armed marines. The officers spent the day in a back-and-forth exchange with Whipple, who argued that "Want of Wind" kept him from sailing into the fight until the very end. His peers decided his lack of action was due to "Errors in Judgment and not for Cowardice," and he was exonerated.[21]

John Hazard was not. Two days later, the same officers reviewed the allegations against Hazard, who declared himself innocent of all charges and that even his embezzling was a "Mear Triffle." After reviewing his crew's accusations of being beaten with a rope's end and "a stick with bullets" on a daily basis, the court questioned everything from his honesty to his courage. Hazard was unanimously found guilty on every charge, and ordered to return his commission. He protested the verdict and wrote Hopkins, requesting and fully expecting to have his command restored.[22]

Hopkins refused, having already decided on a new commander. Two days after Hazard's court-martial, the commodore summoned John Paul Jones to his cabin, offering the *Providence* to him a second time. The lieutenant who had been wary of the fore-and-aft-rigged sloop back in December was no more; after five months under the overbearing Saltonstall, Jones needed no convincing to command the sloop. His first assignment, taking Washington's men to his new encampment in New York, provided a perfect opportunity. Jones had been seeking a way to escape Saltonstall. As it turned out, he need only have looked to *Providence*.[23]

In Philadelphia, Congress put Hopkins's actions and inactions aside, having a bigger issue to deal with. The city faced invasion, from Andrew Snape Hamond.

For weeks, Hamond had sailed the *Roebuck* between the Delaware Capes, sometimes solo, sometimes leading other warships. On the surface, his cruising was eminently successful, sending countless prizes up to Sandy Hook or down to Virginia. But he had yet to capture one Continental vessel.

Hamond frequently chased Continental ships into shallows where his frigate dared not go. No one vexed him more than John Barry. Calling him "the Master" of the bay, Hamond vented his frustrations to Lord Dunmore: "I have chased him several times but can never draw him into the Sea." The *Lexington* was entering the bay on May 4 after a southern cruise during which Barry dogged a fleet of British merchantmen before leading the frigate *Solebay* on a fruitless eight-hour chase. As the *Lexington* rounded Cape Henlopen, Hamond sent the *Roebuck* in pursuit with her studding sails set to grab every inch of the wind, only to lose Barry again as he took his brigantine into the shallows. Before giving up the chase, a frustrated Hamond discharged a lone gun, its cannonball splashing far short of the *Lexington*. Barry returned the compliment, the bemused Irishman firing one of his 4-pounders before heading up the bay to a hero's welcome in Philadelphia.[24]

Thanks to his successes, Barry had an easy rendezvous for new hands, with a full complement of 110 names on his muster rolls. The only unhappy man was the slave he had purchased before leaving Philadelphia in March. Barry was no sooner back ashore than he resold the man, whose pay and prize shares were paid to Barry, as his master. The slave, whose name is unknown to history, appealed to the Pennsylvania Committee of Safety. He was not looking to buy new slops or spend the money in taverns and brothels—what he wanted to purchase was his freedom. After fighting against the *Edward* with the same degree of courage the rest of the crew displayed, would the committee intervene on his behalf?

They could not and would not. Countless slaves—including those owned by congressmen—saw action at sea aboard Continental ships. All of them, including this man, saw their wages and prize shares go to their masters. Many of them jumped ship upon their return to port. Their captains called their act desertion; their owners called it "running off." The slaves called it freedom.[25]

On May 7, Congress was deliberating on pay scales for naval officers and new parameters for privateers when the booming echoes of Henry Fisher's cannons were heard, followed by a courier stopping his lathered horse outside the State House and running inside to give John Hancock a message from Fisher himself: the British were coming, by sea. The *Roebuck* was leading a small squadron of ships upriver, including one tender, the schooner *Betsey*, and the frigate *Liverpool*, Captain Henry Bellew, twenty-eight guns.[26]

In truth, Hamond had no intention of sailing into Philadelphia: his water barrels were empty. He brought the ships into the Delaware to resupply "and reconnoitre the enemys force of the River." His only interruption in filling his casks came when the *Wasp* sailed by, heading for Philadelphia. Miraculously, she evaded capture and continued upriver, dropping anchor near Wilmington.

News of his approach threw some Philadelphians into a panic, while fellow citizens prepared to defend their city. With the fort on Liberty Island still unfinished, protecting Philadelphia fell to the Pennsylvania Navy's row galleys. The *Lexington* was being refitted, so Robert Morris, vice president of the Marine Committee and Barry's old boss, ordered the brigantine's crew to board one of the galleys, and Wickes to take the *Reprisal* downriver with them.

Rain and wind delayed Hamond's progress, and he anchored off Wilmington for the night. In Philadelphia, Ben Franklin's son-in-law Richard Bache was sure that "We are ready to receive them," but most Philadelphians got little, if any, rest.[27]

Wednesday, May 8, broke with light breezes and a haze covering the river. The first act between the antagonists was a peaceful one. Captain Bellew was not only a happily married man but a considerate one. At daybreak he sent William Budden, an American captain whose ship Bellew had recently captured, with a dispatch to Hancock. Bellew's wife was aboard the *Liverpool*, and he requested safe conduct for her to visit friends in Marblehead, hopefully escorted by his friend and Congress's prisoner, Richard Boger.[28]

On shore, as Bellew and Hamond waited for Hancock's reply and the arrival of the American row galleys, Nicholas Biddle's brother Charles set off in the early morning in a chair—a small horse-drawn carriage—with one Mrs. Gibbs, a widow whose relationship with Biddle he tactfully described as "intimate." The widow's carriage led a large crowd of sightseers making their way south along the riverbank to watch the coming fight. The Widow Gibbs believed she was being squired by her lover, but Biddle had other plans. Once the galleys came within sight, he planned to hail one, get onboard, and join the fray. Biddle had not confided in Mrs. Gibbs, as she was rooting for the other side. Besides, it was her carriage. Thanks to Biddle's switch, the widow's horses made a fast pace.[29]

Lack of wind kept the row galleys from arriving until one in the afternoon. From his quarterdeck, Hamond counted thirteen of them, "each carrying a Gun, from 32 Pounders to Eighteen, a Floating Battery of 10 Eighteen Pounders and a Sloop fitted as a fire ship." The tide and Hamond's lack of knowledge of the river compelled him to "Meet them under Sail," putting the British "under the disadvantage of being obliged to engage them at a distance they chose to fix on . . . scarcely within point blank shot." Hamond was fighting the battle on his opponent's terms. Thanks to Barry, this was getting to be a habit.

By this time thousands of Americans had gathered along the riverbanks. British gunners were usually expert marksmen, but the row galleys were so small they could not hit them at first. Even the two accompanying ships, the *Montgomery* and the *Reprisal*, were spared. The Americans aboard the row galleys returned fire, but like their British counterparts, they could not hit the *Roebuck*. For the first hour, the only damage was to the Widow Gibbs's chair. Frantically trying to get closer to the fray and carry out his plan, Biddle pushed the carriage so hard that the shaft broke. Both widow and driver fell to the ground. After securing the horses, Biddle made a mad dash for the riverbank near Marcus

Hook, but he arrived too late; the battle was under way. The only broadside he faced came when Mrs. Gibbs arrived, her carriage repaired, shall we say, in a jury-rigged style.[30]

By the time the *Liverpool* caught up with the *Roebuck* (about two o'clock) the wind had died. Using the current, Hamond and Bellew swung their vessels around so that their full array of guns on their port sides could rake the row galleys. The sounds of the battle echoed along the Philadelphia waterfront, where cries of "To arms!" accompanied the furious beating of drummer boys. Shop owners, servants, and other noncombatants joined carpenters, stevedores, and chandlers at the shipyards, manning rowboats, skiffs, and shallops. Armed with muskets or pistols, they rowed and sailed to the sound of the guns: Philadelphia was their home, too.

Biddle paced back and forth near a grove of trees while watching the battle. Cannonballs roared overhead, crashing into and above the riverbank and sending the sightseers running—all except old, gout-ridden Colonel Turbutt Francis, a retired British army officer and friend of Biddle's family. Francis remained seated in a small chair. Biddle offered to help him move to safety, but Francis would have none of it.[31]

By four p.m. the British gunners were finding their range, forcing the row galleys to withdraw into the shallows on the Jersey side of the river. Aboard the *Roebuck*, Hamond's composure barely masked his urge to finish off the row galleys. That required bringing the frigate closer to shore. The captain whose forbearance had kept him from running aground in his earlier pursuits of the rebels now sent the *Roebuck* towards the enemy. From the quarterdeck of the *Liverpool*, Bellew watched as the *Roebuck*'s sails filled and the frigate made headway before coming to a lurching stop. There was a loud, crunching sound as she struck fast on a sandbar. Bellew, seeing he had no choice but to come to Hamond's rescue, sent his leadman forward to take soundings. Slowly, cautiously, Bellew came to the aid of his superior.[32]

Watching from the *Wasp*, Charles Alexander saw the chance to really make Hamond gnash his teeth. "Man the sweeps," he ordered, and the schooner made straight for the *Betsey*. As Hamond watched helplessly from his impotent ship, the *Wasp* took a new prize.

The *Roebuck* might be stuck in the mud, but she still had her teeth, and with the *Liverpool* soon beside her the row galleys dared not close in. From the *Montgomery*, Captain Read gave orders to keep out of range. With dusk approaching, they would resume the fight in the morning. The spectators departed for home, including the Widow Gibbs. Biddle drove slower this time, lectured all the way by the widow for abandoning her.[33]

Hamond waited for the tide to drop before sending his carpenter onto the sandbar to check the damage, which was minimal. While Bellew's men formed a ring of longboats around the frigates, the Roebucks passed cables and ropes over to the *Liverpool*, whose crew secured them in the best possible manner to provide both leverage and support. Promising both ample rewards for their efforts while assuring that the merest neglect of duty would be punished, Hamond put the crews to the arduous task of freeing the massive frigate. Around two a.m., the last cry of "Heave!" came from the *Liverpool*, and one last tug on the lines freed the *Roebuck*. Both frigates returned to the middle of the river, but none aboard slept that night, as Hamond waited for the attack in the dark from the row galleys, which he would have ordered, had he commanded them.[34]

Fog blocked the sunrise the following morning as the two captains aboard the *Montgomery* sent dispatches to Philadelphia. Read formed a line of battle with the row galleys. "All we want is men," he scribbled in a report to the Committee of Safety, thought a second, and added, "Ammunition." Barry's report to Robert Morris urged that the *Lexington* be sent down, "for the More thare is the Better." Read did not have his friend Barry's recent battle experience, but as he was in charge, Barry deferred to Read's leadership.

Back in Philadelphia, Congress formed a committee to a resolve Bellew's request for a proper chaperone to escort his wife to Marblehead. Then they waited silently in the State House for the sound of the guns. Fog kept them silent until the afternoon. By then the throngs of onlookers had reappeared, and the row galleys were back along the Pennsylvania riverbank.[35]

The *Wasp* became the first American vessel to find the *Roebuck* free of the sandbar. Alexander was heading upriver from Wilmington when a sudden breeze began clearing the fog, and he saw the two frigates right ahead of him. He was surprised; Hamond was ready. A fierce barrage of gunfire sent the *Wasp* across the river to the row galleys, who covered her with their own cannonade. Round two had commenced.

Once the *Liverpool* caught up to the *Roebuck*, Hamond called over to Bellew: he had "reconnoitred" enough this trip, and if they headed south and the row galleys followed, they could turn and fight where the river was wider, and take the Americans one vessel at a time. Bellew agreed.

Almost immediately the wind picked up force to near-gale strength—perfect for Hamond's plan. The frigates made an easy sail downriver, with the American ships, now twenty-two in number, blasting away from a safe distance. For two hours, the Americans kept up a smart fire but did not close in; Read and company could see what Hamond was up to. By nightfall the firing was sporadic; the *Roebuck* and the *Liverpool* anchored off Wilmington, and the Americans sailed home.[36]

The third day's hostilities were confined to Bellew's cabin. That morning, a rowboat flying a flag of truce brought Captain Walter Stewart of Pennsylvania's Third Battalion alongside the *Liverpool*. Once in Bellew's cabin, Stewart extended Congress's offer to provide an escort for Mrs. Bellew. But her husband's heart had hardened, and he would not let her go—not after the rebels' "damned gondolas" had treated him so roughly these past two days. Any chance of further diplomatic pleasantries vanished. Bellew chastised the Americans for their "deceit, rancour, & Malice" and would not risk his wife's safety to anyone, with the possible exceptions of *Mrs.* Hancock and Lieutenant Boger. After a few choice words of his own, Stewart returned to Philadelphia, leaving Mrs. Bellew without an escort, just like the Widow Gibbs. The first battle for the Delaware was over.[37]

Philadelphians welcomed the news of Hamond's departure with mixed emotions of euphoria and dread. Hancock wrote Washington that Hamond had returned to the capes, while John Adams informed Abigail how the battle "diminished, in the minds of the People . . . the Terror of a Man of War." All the same, a perceptible number of Philadelphians began leaving town. Hamond, on the other hand, realized how lucky he was. "Had the commanders of the row-galleys acted with as much judgment as they did courage," he later remarked, the Americans would have taken his ship.[38]

The battle also showed Congress the need to crack down on Esek Hopkins. Already peeved that he had given those Bahaman guns away—Congress's property, after all—it reiterated previous orders that Hopkins send them to Philadelphia without delay.

In Providence, Hopkins busied himself with getting what ships he could back out to sea. He was sending the *Andrew Doria* and *Cabot* on a cruise, with Nicholas Biddle as senior captain, to be followed by another joint cruise of the *Columbus* and the *Providence*. That left Hopkins, Saltonstall, and the *Alfred* with just a few sailors and officers. The unrelenting "Malignant Fever" kept adding to Hopkins's sick list, while frightening the few recruits who considered enlisting, and Washington's men were departing. Last, but not least, the lucrative money offered by privateers made Congress's penurious pay scale (one-third of the take distributed to the crews for prize shares, paid in near worthless Continental scrip) a laughingstock among sailors. Why did Congress allow this? Because many congressmen invested in privateers.[39]

By this time Nicholas Biddle was nearly stir-crazy from inactivity. "Good God of Heaven I am out of all patience with being kept so long in port," he sputtered to his brother James in Congress. Wallace's squadron had been replaced by HMS *Cerberus*, the frigate that had earlier brought to Boston the three major generals: William Howe; Charles, Lord Cornwallis; and "Gentleman Johnny" Burgoyne. Unlike during his stay in New London, Biddle paid no attention to the admiring ladies of Providence. At long last, Hopkins ordered Biddle to sail forth and "annoy the Enemy." To accompany him, Hopkins sent the *Cabot*, replacing his wounded son with forty-four-year-old Elisha Hinman. With Biddle as senior officer, the two brigs headed out to sea.[40]

For a week they cruised under calm conditions; then, on May 19, they sighted the *Cerberus* off the island named No Mans Land. Signaling Hinman to split up, the Americans parted company. Both successfully eluded the frigate. Two days later Biddle's brig was off Nantucket when another sail was sighted and chased: the *Two Friends*, bound for Nova Scotia from the Virgin Islands, her hold full of rum, sugar, and salt. Her captain made all sail to escape, but the freshly careened *Andrew Doria* easily overtook her. "So ends the day," a contented Biddle entered in his log.[41]

After sending his prize back to Newport, Biddle headed north to Nova Scotia, hoping to intercept what troop passports might be heading that way from England. A series of squalls from the east sent the *Andrew Doria* bobbing precariously on huge swells like a toy boat in the surf. The gales were so strong they tore the brig's barge off its chocks, nearly killing a sailor sleeping underneath while taking the brig hundreds of miles off course.

At four a.m. on May 29, the mastheader hailed the quarterdeck—two ships to the northward. Roused from his slumber, Biddle came on deck and immediately gave orders to pursue. The *Andrew Doria* sped over the water; by sunrise she was on top of the first ship, her sixteen guns run out. Biddle hailed the British captain: "Heave to or be Sunk!" The man obeyed. In the growing daylight the Americans saw that the ship's "guns" were actually painted logs.

She was the Scottish transport *Oxford* out of Glasgow, with a hundred Scottish Highlanders aboard. Soon Biddle took the other one, too: the *Crawford*, another transport carrying Highlanders, officers, and their wives. The ships were part of a fleet of thirty transports bound for Boston. Biddle made his captures without firing a gun, writing Charles that "I took them with the Speaking Trumpet."

Pleased as he was with his captures, they created a logistics problem for Biddle: he had eighty-two men to divide among three ships and watch over more than three times that many prisoners, along with so many ladies that Marine Lieutenant Trevett could not count them all. Biddle transferred all arms and every British sailor to the *Andrew Doria*. He placed all the enemy soldiers aboard the *Oxford* with nine Americans under Third Lieutenant John McDougall along with Trevett. He turned the *Crawford* over to the capable Lieutenant James Josiah, along with four of his best sailors. The transferring went well enough until a heavy blow came up and swamped one boat, but no one was lost. The three ships set sail for Newport.[42]

The ships sailed together without incident until June 11. They were off Martha's Vineyard when five large sail were sighted from the northeast, heading their way. As with the *Cabot*, Biddle split the ships up, sending the *Oxford* westward, the *Crawford* southeast, and the *Andrew Doria* eastward. He could not know that he was flying from the HMS *Merlin*, a sloop acting as convoy to four merchantmen. Biddle easily got away, but in doing so he lost sight of his prizes. He reached Newport two days later, finding Hopkins there as well. The captured supplies in the *Andrew Doria*'s hold included everything a Highlander needed for fighting, from muskets to bagpipes.

As days passed, Biddle gave up hopes of seeing his prizes again. What befell Lieutenants McDougall and Josiah was not atypical of the times, and adds an ironic coda to this cruise. Once the southeast-bound *Oxford* went over the horizon, the Highlanders saw their chance and overcame their captors, an action Lieutenant Trevett understood; he would have done the same. Lacking a navigator among them, the Scotsmen did their best to make for Hampton Roads and Lord Dunmore.

Remarkably, they succeeded, reaching the Virginia Capes two days later, where two boats approached them. Believing their visitors to be Loyalist pilots, they asked of Dunmore's whereabouts and were told he was just up the James River. The Highlanders became delirious with joy: their odyssey was over. They continued upriver, where they were happily met by ships and sailors of the Virginia Navy, every man jack a rebel. Lord Dunmore was forty miles away. After some tedious negotiations with Congress over paying their way, McDougall, Trevett, and company headed home to Philadelphia.[43]

The *Crawford* was also back in British hands, but with a different twist, chased and taken by the *Cerberus* on June 12. Captain John Symons put Josiah and his four sailors aboard his frigate and sent the *Crawford* to Sandy Hook, New Jersey, a nautical way station for the Royal Navy throughout the war. She did not get far; on June 19, she was intercepted by one of Washington's sloops, the *Schuyler*, off Fire Island. Her supplies were now the property of the Continental Army, just as Biddle intended.[44]

Josiah and his men were not as lucky as the Americans aboard the *Oxford*. For several months, they remained prisoners aboard the *Cerberus*, where Symons treated them brutally—especially Josiah. They were eventually transferred to the *Whitby*, a prison ship anchored in New York harbor. Enraged at the news of his friend's treatment, Biddle fired off two letters: one to the Marine Committee, exhorting them to arrange an exchange for Josiah, the second a vociferous protest to Lord Admiral Howe. Biddle and other American captains treated their prisoners humanely, and as a former Royal Navy officer he expected the same for his comrade. As we will see, that would hardly be the case.[45]

In Newport, Biddle made his official report to Hopkins, and a long, personal one to his brother Charles. He opened this letter with the sentence that has been felt by every serviceman: "It is with the greatest Pleasure imaginable I Received letters from home as it convinces me that I am not intirely forgot." He humorously regaled Charles with his latest adventures. After praying that Hopkins would "not send me to that out of the way Place, Providence," instead of another cruise, Biddle inquired of his friends in the Pennsylvania Navy. Then he added a postscript—a rare, serious statement about himself, obvious by now to anyone who had seen Nicholas in action:

> I fear Nothing but what I ought to fear. I am much more Afraid of doing a foolish Action than loosing My Life. I aim for a Character of Conduct as well as courage And hope never to throw away the Vessel and Crew merely to convince the <u>world</u> I have Courage. No one has dar[e]d to impeach it yet. If any should I will not leave them a Moment to doubt.[46]

As Biddle's deeds sent his stock skyrocketing with both Congress and the public, Esek Hopkins's reputation was sinking daily. Following the *Andrew Doria*'s return, the *Cabot* brought another prize into port, but the accomplishments of

Biddle and Hinman could not offset the growing accusations made against their commodore. When Congress considered Hopkins's disregard of their initial orders (and, as southern congressmen saw it, disregarding their colonies' needs), it was easy to see why southern representatives saw the new navy just as they had feared they would: as a New England enterprise for New England, paid for by all thirteen colonies.

The old tar defended himself in endless letters to Washington, Hancock, John Adams, and anybody he could sway. He did not infect his sailors; he did not set up the miserly pay scale for his officers and men. Yes, he gave the guns to New England sea towns, but it was they who needed them in April, not Philadelphia. And, as disastrous as the *Glasgow* affair was, it proved Hopkins correct in his original assumption that any engagement by the Continentals against the Royal Navy was pure stupidity, regardless of the locale—be it off Rhode Island, Virginia, or South Carolina. Add to this the envy and ambition exhibited by his captains in "getting higher Stations in the new Ships"—those thirteen frigates—and Hopkins requested his brother Stephen to replace him. "Get a good Man in my Room," he begged.

While awaiting Stephen's reply, Hopkins continued sending out his ships on convoy assignments. On June 18, the *Columbus* had just cleared Newport when she was pounced on by the *Cerberus*. Watching from town, Hopkins sent the *Andrew Doria* and *Providence* down to assist Whipple. The ships were scarcely under way when their captains saw the *Cerberus* break off the engagement; a strong flood tide was running towards the harbor, pushing the frigate toward the nearby reefs. Biddle's subsequent cruise brought more misfortune, capturing a prize only to lose her to the *Cerberus* again.[47]

Days later, Hopkins's letters were answered, not by Stephen but by Hancock. Hopkins, Saltonstall, and Whipple were ordered to Philadelphia. "Come prepared to answer for your general Conduct," the President of Congress added. Hancock was less tactful to Washington, complaining about "the shameful Inactivity of our Fleet." Before departing, Hopkins turned command over temporarily to the senior officer, Nicholas Biddle.[48]

Except for Charles Alexander, the Continental captains present during the repulse of the *Roebuck* and *Liverpool* were spectators in that encounter, but they were now about to reenter the fray. Their ships—John Barry's *Lexington*, Lambert Wickes's *Reprisal*, Alexander's *Wasp*, and William Hallock's *Hornet*—were under orders from the Marine Committee to escort merchantmen safely through the

Delaware Capes. The *Roebuck* had departed for Virginia, leaving the *Liverpool* as chief watchdog of the Royal Navy.

And Captain Bellew, with or without his wife, was more than up for the assignment, capturing merchantmen and pursuing the smaller Continental vessels. It was a hazy morning on May 27 when Bellew sighted the *Lexington*, *Reprisal*, and *Wasp*, fresh from one of their escort services. Clapping on all sail, he sent his frigate boldly after them. Three hours later, Barry ordered his ships to heave to, and they stopped dead in the wind. Seeing this, Bellew ran out his guns and began thinking of how to successfully take these rebels. For a half hour, Barry waited, waited, and waited, until the ships were within range of the *Liverpool*'s bow chasers. A gale started blowing when he ordered the ships to make way for the Overfalls, his favorite refuge.

To Barry's pleasant surprise, the *Liverpool* kept coming. She was inside the shoals when Bellew's leadman cried from the bow—the ship was in less than three fathoms of water—about eighteen feet. "Wear Ship!" Bellew roared, changing course seconds before she would have run aground, and been taken as a prize herself. The *Liverpool* made for Cape Henlopen. She soon sailed for New York, but the cat-and-mouse game would continue with the next British ships assigned the task of keeping watch over Delaware Bay.[49]

By the end of June, a dozen merchantmen were inside Cape May, awaiting escort. Barry was reluctant to take them out, since two new warships now prowled the bay's entrance—the frigate *Orpheus*, Captain Charles Hudson, and the sloop-of-war *Kingfisher*, Captain Alexander Graeme. Barry was not afraid, just cautious. He preferred convoying his charges out when fog or bad weather came his way. On June 28, another challenge presented itself.[50]

That morning, the *Orpheus* was anchored off Cape Henlopen when two sail were sighted in chase. Hudson recognized the pursuer as the *Kingfisher*, coming fast after an American brigantine. She was the *Nancy*, Captain Hugh Montgomery, an old friend of Barry's. Her hold was full of gunpowder from St. Croix, and Congress was anxiously awaiting her arrival. Hudson instantly joined in the chase. Montgomery was in his home waters now, and he made for the Overfalls. Barry's mastheader saw them as they came up by Cape May. The *Lexington* was with the *Reprisal* and the *Wasp* (the *Hornet* was being refitted in Philadelphia), waiting for an opportune time to get the merchantmen out and to provide any assistance in bringing the *Nancy* safely into Philadelphia. At dusk, Barry signaled for Wickes and Hallock to join him for a council of war.

Inside his lantern-lit cabin Barry and the other officers reviewed their options. They decided to send their barges around the cape in the morning, to reinforce Montgomery's crew and get the gunpowder ashore. Barry would assume command of the action. The *Wasp*'s barge was placed under the teenage Lieutenant Joshua Barney while, with reluctance, Wickes bowed to the pleas of his young brother Richard to command the *Reprisal*'s barge. Unbeknownst to them all, Montgomery was making their coming task easier. Once in the shoals, he sailed above Cape May to the oddly named Turtle Gut Inlet, just as his pursuers anchored safely off the cape.

A fine mist and gray skies greeted the adversaries on Saturday, June 29. The three American barges started up the Jersey shoreline, with the *Reprisal* in the lead. Before weighing anchor to resume pursuit, Hudson called all hands aboard the *Orpheus* to witness punishment (Hudson frequently let the cat out of the bag). Then he joined Graeme in pursuing the *Nancy*. It was now a race to see who would reach her first. As Graeme and Hudson kept their ships out of the shallows, the *Nancy* remained anchored outside Turtle Gut Inlet.

Richard Wickes reached the *Nancy* first. After relaying Barry's plans to Montgomery, they cut the *Nancy*'s hawser (the stout anchor rope) and sailed the brigantine into the inlet. Just before running her onto shore, Montgomery turned the ship so that her port guns faced the inlet's entrance. The other barges joined them shortly.

Once aboard, Barry immediately took command, sending the *Lexington*'s gunners to man the 3-pounders, while those marines brought by the barges waited behind the bulwark, reloading their muskets with dry powder. Barry then ordered the rest of the men to start unloading the gunpowder. Working like a bucket brigade, they passed the first half barrel out of the hold, up the hatch, over the side, and into one of the *Nancy*'s boats. One unloaded, 385 to go.

The *Kingfisher*, her draft lighter than that of the *Orpheus*, led the tenders to the inlet's entrance, turning as the *Nancy* did to line up their broadside for maximum effect. As soon as the guns were run out, Graeme yelled "Fire!" and British iron flew over the *Nancy*, the cannonballs thudding into the dry sand beyond her. Graeme ordered marines and his best fighting sailors into his longboats. Within minutes they were lowered. Sailors bent their backs and pulled strongly in unison, heading into the inlet and straight for the *Nancy*. During the initial onslaught Barry kept the *Nancy*'s guns silent. But once the longboats came in range, the Americans let fly with an accurate broadside, damaging one boat beyond repair and driving the British back to their ship. They reached the *Liverpool* just as the *Orpheus* joined the fighting. With the frigate's longer guns for cover, Graeme sent the *Kingfisher* and the tenders in another three hundred yards. In half an hour the British gunners found their range. With each broadside, the *Nancy* was being blasted to bits, but miraculously, no American had been killed. The Lexingtons fired back, the *Nancy*'s 3-pounders spitting defiantly at the enemy.

There were 121 half barrels left when the bombardment became too much for Barry to ignore, and he sent all hands to the boats. As they went over the side, Barry and Montgomery set several half barrels in the captain's cabin, filled a spare sail with gunpowder, and ran it between the hold and the cabin as a makeshift fuse. Barry lit it with a hot coal, and the two captains climbed down to the boats. They were just pushing off when someone noticed the *Nancy*'s colors still flying aboard. Suddenly, a "daring but foolhardy seaman" named John Hancock scaled the ship's side, snatched the colors off the staff, and jumped overboard. The boats rowed smartly for the beach, where their comrades had hurriedly built a breastwork of wood and sand, and put at least two swivel guns in place.

While they abandoned ship, British longboats from both the *Orpheus* and the *Liverpool* were again rowing furiously towards the brigantine for a second attack. The Americans on the beach fired unremittingly at them, while the British rowers briefly slowed their boats, allowing the marines to balance themselves, stand, raise their muskets, and fire back at the rebels. When the Americans fired another volley of muskets and swivel guns, some marines and sailors fell into their boats or over the side and into the shallow water.

Finally, one of the longboats reached the *Nancy*. Immediately the men climbed hand over hand up the side. Seeing them reach the deck, their comrades watching from the ships gave a loud cheer. That very second, as their exultant cry was still in their throats, the burning fuse reached both cabin and hold. With a deafening roar that could be heard in Philadelphia, the *Nancy* exploded.

Both American and Englishman watched dumbstruck as debris and bodies flew more than a hundred feet into the air. Even when the smoke from the blast cleared, the sky was still raining down remains of ship and man: "Eleven bodies, two laced hats, and a leg with a white spattered dash" fell among the plummeting wood that had once been a ship. The men on both sides, their ears ringing and mouths agape, watched in silent horror until this most unnatural cloudburst subsided.

For a few seconds Turtle Gut Inlet was deathly quiet, and then a monstrous cannonade roared from the British ships. Suddenly the beach was all flying sand and iron. Only one American was hit, a cannonball taking half his chest away just as more men from the *Reprisal* showed up, led by Lambert Wickes. The crowd kneeling around the mortally wounded man parted; Wickes arrived just in time to watch the man die. It was his brother Richard.

Seeing any further resistance as futile, Barry ordered the men into the woods behind the beach. Lambert Wickes helped carry his younger brother's body away from the battle in which Richard had so desperately wanted to participate. As the Americans brought their valuable cargo inland, Barry posted a rear guard to ward off another British attack. He did not have to. The enemy ships soon departed. Neither side had any fight left in them that morning.

The next day—Sunday—American sailors bore Richard Wickes's coffin into the Cold Spring Meetinghouse. After the parson's simple, heartfelt sermon, they shuffled past the wooden pews and out to the cemetery. Under the same misty skies as the day before, they buried their comrade.

Richard's death haunted his brother. Like Barry, Biddle, and Jones, Lambert was young, confident, and patriotic. He hailed from Maryland's Eastern Shore, already legendary for supplying the colonies with hearty sailing stock. No portraits or descriptions of Lambert exist. By eighteen he was already a ship's master, and he proved his patriotism in 1774 when he refused to carry a cargo of tea ordered by his Loyalist-leaning bosses. When Congress chose him to command the *Reprisal*, he was a proven master whose courage and patriotism set an example for his crew—and also his brother Richard.

After Richard's burial, Lambert faced the sad task of informing his family back home of the tragic news, writing about the desperate battle and saving the news of the death of "a dear Brother & good officer" for the end. Wickes enclosed the letter to his family with a bag of captured coffee, placing the items with his and Barry's dispatches on July 2.[51]

Congress busied itself that day as well. Hopkins, Saltonstall, and Whipple had reached Philadelphia, and the Marine Committee was ordered "to enquire into the complaints exhibited against them." They sent Barry back to sea. And they resolved "that these United Colonies are, and, of right, ought to be, Free and Independent States."[52]

The debate over the Declaration of Independence was a long one, with many similarities to the earlier one concerning the creation of the Continental Navy. Initially, New England congressmen were nearly unanimous in favor of independence, the mid-Atlantic colonies were split evenly, and most southerners—with the exception of Virginians—were opposed to the idea. As with the navy, it was

John Adams who led the charge, until finally the combination of his passion, Thomas Jefferson's eloquent words, and Benjamin Franklin's behind-the-scenes orchestration carried the day.

But the euphoria of crying, "We are independent!" was short-lived, and with good reason. In April, the Continental Army had arrived in New York City. Morale was high, Washington's forces having just ejected the Lobsterbacks from Boston after a prolonged siege. Following the reading of the Declaration on July 8 in New York, a boisterous mob of soldiers and civilians took down the lead statue of a mounted George III, under the disapproving gaze of the many Loyalists in town. The deposed statue was melted into musket balls. The army's swagger was not shared by its commander-in-chief, who daily looked for the British armada he knew was coming. Already more than one hundred ships were massing off Sandy Hook.[53]

Congress daily awaited news from South Carolina, where forces under General Sir Henry Clinton and a fleet commanded by Rear Admiral Sir Peter Parker attempted to gain entry to Charleston harbor by attacking Forts Sullivan and Jones. Clinton had been assured that upon his arrival, southern Tories would rally and help defeat their rebellious neighbors, but a spirited defense by patriot forces—Christopher Gadsden among them—resulted in utter defeat for the British.[54]

Back in Philadelphia, Gadsden's colleagues returned to naval matters the week after independence was declared. They had already assigned commanders to the thirteen frigates being built from Massachusetts to Maryland. Now they sent out orders, requisitions, and requests to procure supplies, ordnance, and manpower. They approved the recommendations of sailor-turned-soldier Benedict Arnold to build a fleet of schooners and row galleys on Lake Champlain, where Arnold expected an attack by a British fleet from the St. Lawrence River in the coming weeks.[55]

The Marine Committee began its inquiries into the accusations leveled against Hopkins, Saltonstall, and Whipple. After exhaustive testimony from their subordinate officers present in Philadelphia, the committee ruled in favor of Saltonstall and Whipple, warning the latter to "cultivate harmony with his officers." They delayed Hopkins's inquiry for a month. The postponement did nothing for Hopkins's cause; his daily appearances on the streets of Philadelphia only added to the growing anti–New England sentiment in Congress. Southerners recalled his unwillingness to sail to their rescue in the spring, the middle-states' representatives still begrudged their missing cannon, and New Yorkers fretted as daily dispatches arrived, listing more and more British ships arriving off Sandy Hook.

The Marine Committee finally summoned Hopkins on August 12. His opening statement was read, a perfect example of humble pugnacity: "The Reputation of the Navey has Not Sufford by aney misconduct of myne" in the carrying out, or *not* carrying out, of his "odors." Then the grilling began. Saltonstall and Whipple, still in town, were called in to defend their commodore. Standing and sweating before the committee, Hopkins never swayed from his already documented defense pertaining to his inactions along the southern coastline. Then Hopkins was excused, and the debate over his future began.

Once again, John Adams rose to speak for New England in general and Hopkins in particular. "The Commodore was pursued and persecuted by that Anti New England Spirit" which Adams found in countless congressional arguments, whether the sentiment was there or not. In this case, it was. Ever his region's champion, Adams became Hopkins's knight-errant, exerting "all the Talents and Eloquence I had, in justifying him where he was justifiable, and excusing him where he was excusable." Defending Hopkins as if in a courtroom, Adams admitted the man's "Experience and Skill might have been deficient . . . But where could We find greater Experience or Skill?"

Adams finished his defense, and Congress postponed the decision. Afterwards, William Ellery of Rhode Island, as strong a naval advocate as Adams, told his colleague, "You have made the Old Man your Friend for Life." That was true; more to the point, so was Jefferson's opinion of the argument: the objection to Hopkins's conduct was not over "an honest discretion in departing from his [instructions] but that he never did intend to obey them." On August 16, Congress censured Hopkins, the first in a series of humiliations for the commodore.[56]

While Hopkins sweated out both his hearing and the Philadelphia humidity, his latest promotion sailed into town. John Paul Jones arrived with several colliers (strong round-bowed and broad-sterned coal-bearing ships) that he had been assigned to convoy from Boston, arriving on August 1, several days after John Barry's latest prize, one of Lord Dunmore's privateers, nuzzled against a Philadelphia dock. Aboard her was a young man who had joined the Virginia Navy as a lieutenant, only to be captured by this privateer. Rather than go to prison, Richard Dale joined the Loyalists. Seeing merit in the lad, Barry persuaded him to change sides again, making him a midshipman. Sailing home, the *Lexington* ran into a thunderstorm. The new recruit was on deck when lightning struck and knocked him senseless. Barry and the Lexingtons anxiously gathered around him, greatly relieved when Dale was "providentially restored" to consciousness. His remarkable career would be entwined with Barry and Jones for another thirty years.[57]

The Continental Navy was less than a year old, but that was enough time to show everyone from congressman to commodore all the personality traits contained inside the diminutive John Paul Jones. Only five feet five, he was handsome, some thought, to the point of prettiness: chestnut hair, hazel eyes, high cheekbones, a slender, hawkish nose, and a strong jaw ending with a cleft chin. He rarely smiled. Sloping shoulders were still broad enough to carry the chip that never fell from them. He looked every part the young, dour Scotsman.[58]

There was much in the vessel that was John Paul Jones: ambition, pettiness, courage, and vanity. He was born in 1747 on a prosperous laird's estate on the Firth of Solway, a body of water that has forever been trying to cleave Scotland from England. He was the fourth child of the gardener, John Paul, and his wife, Mary, the housekeeper. The estate, Arbigland, ranged over 1,400 acres with beautiful gardens, thanks to John Senior's talents. They adorned the palatial home for the laird, William Craik, who rewarded Paul's services with a cottage that still stands today and can best be described as "charming." Young John roamed through the gardens that sprang from his father's fertile mind. They looked like something from a fairy tale, leading to both deep woods and a cliff overlooking the firth.

Craik was rich and overbearing, a "king's man" who held no loyalty for the Jacobites who loved Bonnie Prince Charlie despite his losing the Battle of Culloden the year before John's birth. Craik also had a reputation in the neighboring town of Kirkbean as an unfaithful husband; one of his illegitimate sons grew up to become George Washington's physician, and rumors circulated that the laird, not the gardener, was father to John Junior—gossip that only fueled the simmering hostility John Senior barely kept under control when dealing with his master.[59]

The family cottage faced the firth, where young John watched merchantmen sail for the Irish Sea and thence to ports near and far. He was intelligent, particularly in mathematics (his childhood copy of *Euclid's Elements* still exists). He was also bossy and contentious, rounding up the other children on the estate to reenact the adventures of Admiral Hawke defeating the French. John, of course, played Hawke. From childhood he longed to join the King's Navy, but his humble origins were not enough to warrant a midshipman's berth, and Craik was not inclined to pull any strings for the boy. The best that young Master Paul could get was a seven-year apprenticeship to John Young, owner of the brig *Friendship* out of Whitehaven—a port the boy would revisit years later.

Over the years he mastered everything about sailing, with the exception of developing a taste for rum. He would not abide any spirits, anything or anyone that distracted him from his tasks. When Young died in 1764, he was released from his contract. He rose in abilities and rank, becoming third mate on the ship *King George* out of Whitehaven. Few ships could be identified by smell, but the *King George* was one of them. She was a "black birder"—a slave ship—carrying seventy-seven Africans, chained together in the ship's small hold. Throughout his life Jones wrote endlessly about his deeds and himself, never at a loss for words. But he wrote only once about his duties aboard the *King George*, which included the loathsome practice of "weeding": unchaining the corpses found each morning in the reeking hold, then throwing them overboard as if they were nothing more than rotting cargo. Paul called the slave trade "abominable," but kept at it for three years.

He was twenty-one when he was made captain of the *John*, a ship he had successfully brought home after the previous captain and first mate died at sea. As master, he was hard on careless sailors; halfhearted efforts reflected poorly on his leadership. He was no stranger to the brothels of West Indies ports, but spent most of his shore time reading Shakespeare and beginning a lifelong hobby of writing poetry, all the while trying to lose his Scottish burr. He did not suffer fools, or the slipshod in anyone, especially himself.[60]

Life for John Paul seemed to be a series of stories with one moral: connections matter. No one in the British Empire was more determined to better himself socially, only to have those above him in class—meaning caste—remind him of where they thought he belonged. On one voyage from the *John*'s home port of Kirkudbright, Paul's crew included Mungo Maxwell, carpenter's mate—an insubordinate malingerer from an influential family. A squall between the two was inevitable, and Jones had him flogged. When the *John* reached Tobago, Maxwell filed charges, showing the Admiralty court the welts on his back. To Paul's relief, the court ruled in his favor—a victory of his authority over Maxwell's sense of entitlement. Maxwell took another ship home. Weeks later, the *John*'s hold bursting with rum, sugar, cotton, and ginger, Paul sailed for home.

The ship had no sooner docked in Kirkudbright than the sheriff hauled Paul to "the Tollbooth"—the town jail. In between his protests, Paul learned that Maxwell had died at sea. His grieving and vengeful father believed the flogging caused his death. Paul also discovered that William Craik was in town, to offer his support—to Maxwell's father. It was days before Paul could post bail. He sailed back to Tobago to collect the court records and affidavits proving his innocence. It took a full year to clear his name. He did not live long enough to forgive Craik's coldhearted act. Years later he would repay it.[61]

The Maxwell affair slowed Paul's ascent but did not stop it. Three years later he was master of the *Betsy*, a 300-ton three-masted merchantman sailing from London to Tobago. He wangled part ownership in the ship, and two years later he had earned £2,500—a handsome sum. Layovers in her home port gave Jones a taste of life in the world's largest city, a chance to hobnob with Royal Navy officers (who rarely considered a merchant captain the equal of a lowly midshipman), and dalliance with the "Court Garden ladies," especially one Miss Drew. Somewhere along the way he became a Freemason.[62]

Sailors are not meant for calm seas, and certainly John Paul was not. Beginning a voyage to Tobago in January 1773, the *Betsy* proved "so very Leaky" that her pumps were manned day and night, forcing Jones to put into Cork, Ireland, for repairs. While waiting for word from his insurance underwriters he was stricken with fever. The *Betsy* did not leave Cork until June.

Once in Tobago he was obsessed with selling his goods, restocking his hold with Caribbean merchandise, and getting back to London: time was money, and Paul did not have enough, telling the crew they would not be paid until they reached London. Some hands grumbled. Some did more than that, taking direction from a giant whom Paul later would call "the Ringleader" in a letter he wrote to Benjamin Franklin. The ringleader and his followers demanded their pay; they had earned it, and the Tobago taverns and brothels beckoned.

Paul refused. Cursing and spitting threats, the ringleader grabbed a bludgeon and raised it over his head. He never finished the blow. Paul ran him through with his sword, and the ringleader fell, mortally wounded.

The other sailors carried their dead comrade away, and Paul immediately went into town to report the incident to the first magistrate he could find. He was not arrested, but his act, while in self-defense, nevertheless required a trial. The judge told Paul that an Admiralty Court gave him the best chance to be found innocent, while a civil procedure would as likely side with the crew as the master. It was Christmastide, and no Admiralty court was scheduled to sit for months. Jones's presence in a port full of sailors made him a marked man, for the ringleader was an Islander, whose friends might decide to take Jones's fate into their own hands. Seeing that leaving the island was the only way to stay safe, Paul fled. He would forever call the incident his "Great Misfortune."[63]

For a year he traveled "incog," then arrived in Fredericksburg, Virginia, where his brother William lived. He came ashore with £50 in his pocket and a new last name, Jones. His welcome was not what he expected. William was dead. Years earlier he had separated from his wife, leaving his estate to a sister in Scotland and leaving his brother completely on his own in the New World.

The resourceful Jones now made the most of being a Mason, befriending every member he encountered, from young Thomas Jefferson to Joseph Hewes, a prominent North Carolina merchant with political aspirations. Jones took particular advantage of another new acquaintance, Dr. John Read, a fellow Scotsman and nephew of Benjamin Franklin. Read put Jones up at his country estate, where the two spent "Many sentimental hours" discussing literature, poetry, the Enlightenment, and the growing estrangement between the colonies and England. Like Washington and John Adams, Jones was smitten with Joseph Addison's play *Cato*. The line "We cannot insure success, but we can deserve it" were words Jones was already living by.

He also set his sights on a wife: the beautiful nineteen-year-old Dorothea Dandridge, whose favors were coveted by sea captain and country squire alike. She was the granddaughter of the beloved former governor of Virginia Alexander Spotswood and a cousin to Martha Washington. Dorothea was also way beyond Jones's reach. How far he got in his wooing we do not know; Jones was in the Continental Navy years later when Dr. Read informed him that she had chosen a husband. Earlier, Patrick Henry had famously declared, "Give me liberty or give me death." Mr. Dandridge gave him Dorothea.[64]

Late in April 1775, word reached Virginia of Lexington and Concord. That was all the news Jones needed to hear to forget his heartache. He headed for Philadelphia and the Continental Navy.[65]

By August 6, 1776, Congress had learned that 32,000 enemy soldiers—more than the population of Philadelphia—were disembarking from the countless British transports that glutted New York City's harbor. Anxious to get its own navy out to sea, the Marine Committee issued Jones the orders he had been lusting after: a "Cruise against our Enemies . . . in & about the latitude of Bermuda" to "Seize, take, Sink, Burn or Destroy" enemy shipping. Jones had made the most of his time in Philadelphia. Joseph Hewes had introduced him to the rest of the committee, including the member who signed his captain's commission, John Hancock, and the man who would become his greatest champion, Robert Morris.[66]

Jones wasted little time loading provisions and munitions aboard. His crew of seventy-three included three boys (one fifer and two drummers), a master's mate who had earlier deserted the *Andrew Doria*, and seventeen Philadelphia "landsmen." Jones later called this hearty band the finest crew he ever commanded. Not even a duel between a marine lieutenant and the sailing master, fought just before the sloop departed, could diminish the esprit de corps Jones established between captain and crew.[67]

Most Continental officers, like Barry and Biddle, had sailed sloops and schooners in their merchant days, but Jones was a square-rigged sailor from the first. Months of running errands between Rhode Island and Boston, New York, and Philadelphia gave him time to acclimate himself to the merits and foibles of the *Providence*. By now he was so enamored with her that he turned down the chance to command a captured brig, the *Hampden* (subsequently given to Hoysted Hacker).

The *Providence* was 70 feet long, with a 20-foot beam and an 84-foot mainmast. Her bowsprit and jibboom extended another 39 feet. Her mainsail was monstrous, and she could carry a square sail above the main, along with course and studding sails ("stuns'ls"). The favorite of pirate and smuggler alike, sloops were built for speed, but were unforgiving during a sudden or unexpected jibe—a change of direction running before the wind that brought the long boom flying across the deck, causing her to "broach"—veer to windward and roll on her side; amateur sailors racing any boat from a Sunfish to a yawl can attest to such hazards. But master a sloop, and a captain can outrace a frigate. By August, Jones had mastered the *Providence*.[68]

One week after she had cleared the Delaware Capes, the mastheader sighted five ships, one so large Jones could not determine if she was an "Old Indiaman" or a "Jamaica three decker." She was neither.[69]

✯ ✯ ✯

CHAPTER FOUR

"THAT REBEL IS MY BROTHER"

The impartial World will Judge between us, whether a Salute de-
liberately returned by a Dutch Fort to the Rebel Brigantine *Andrew
Doria* . . . be, or not, a Partiality in Favour of those Rebels and a
flagrant Indignity offered to His Majesty's Flag.

—GOVERNOR CRAISTER GREATHEAD TO GOVERNOR JOHANNES DE GRAAF[1]

The ship was the British frigate *Solebay*. Her captain, Thomas Symonds,
was escorting four merchantmen, his journal filled with names of captured ships—although he, like Hamond, had failed to capture Barry's *Lexington*.
Upon sighting the *Providence*, Symonds left his convoy and stood for the sloop.
In that instant, the *Providence* went from predator to prey; she was no match
against a twenty-eight-gun frigate.

Heavy air and cross seas sent high waves undulating across the ocean, conditions the *Solebay* handled better than the smaller, less forgiving *Providence*. Even
so, John Paul Jones did not lose his nerve. The mere possibility of battle—and
battle itself—lightened his mood. He found combat exhilarating. As his crew
watched the enemy run out their guns, Jones took the *Solebay* on a stern chase.
Four hours passed before the frigate got within musket shot (about two hundred
yards) of the sloop's stern quarter. Cannonballs from the *Solebay*'s bow chasers
splashed alongside the speedy *Providence*; if possible, Symonds hoped to capture
the rebel sloop undamaged.

Throughout the chase, neither captain flew his colors—they sailed uniden-
tified to each other. Now Jones ordered the Grand Union raised while his gunners
fired their little 4-pounders, a terrier against a wolfhound. Symonds also flew
American colors, but Jones laughed at the ruse—"the bait would not take," he

later joked. Once the *Solebay* was within fifty yards, Symonds ordered his marines aloft to the fighting tops. Suddenly, Jones ordered his helmsman to bear away before the wind. His topmen set the sloop's studding sails while other hands let the mainsail fly. Furious, Symonds watched from his quarterdeck as the nimble *Providence* flew out of reach of the *Solebay*'s guns. Jones happily reported that "Our 'Hairs breadth Scape' & the Saucy manner of making it must have mortified [Symonds] not a little."

Jones's good fortune was just beginning. One week later he had his first prize, the brigantine *Sea Nymph*, from Barbados to London, her hold packed tight with West Indies goods, a sea turtle, and the "best particular London Market Madeira Wine." A prize crew took her back to Philadelphia. It was September 4, and the hurricane season was nigh. After a few days of cruising, Jones made for Nova Scotia to attack the fishing fleet.

Before making sail, Jones sent an official report to the Marine Committee and a letter to Robert Morris, picking up where his correspondence with Hewes had left off—a thorough account of events, conditions, thinly veiled appeals to raise his station (he had learned that his commission was postdated and therefore put him behind later appointments), and his opinions of both the navy and how to run it. He included cogent suggestions as to how to improve the selection of officers, borrowing from any egalitarian aspects of the Royal Navy's selection process while being careful not to dwell on another practice, promotion based on family and class connections as means of ascent—obviously not of use to Jones.

Congress wanted regular reports from its captains. Some, like Barry, rarely wrote at all, often due to their lack of formal education. But Jones loved to write, viewing every addressee as a potential pen pal. After mentioning that the *Sea Nymph*'s turtle was earmarked for Morris's dinner table "with Great Esteem," Jones sailed up the Gulf Stream.[2]

Three days after Jones sent Morris's turtle to Philadelphia, a man-made turtle made history.

David Bushnell was a Connecticut farmer who decided to try college at age thirty-one, attending Yale in 1771. Many of his classmates were half his age. Bushnell aspired to be a great inventor like his hero, Benjamin Franklin. Water was Bushnell's element and laboratory. While at Yale he made news, proving that gunpowder "could take fire underwater" (i.e., explode). With witnesses looking on, he attached a wooden pipe to a hogshead filled with gunpowder and stones,

sank it in a pond, and dropped a match into the pipe. The ensuing explosion surprised everyone but Bushnell.

Five years later, the arrival of the British army and navy in New York harbor
gave Bushnell the chance to test his greatest invention, his "Submarine Vessel,"
which

> Bore some resemblance to two upper tortoise shells of equal size, joined
> together . . . the opening, made by the swell of the shells . . . the inside
> capable of containing the Operator, and air, sufficient to supply him,
> thirty minutes . . . a quantity of lead for ballast . . . an oar, for rowing . . .
> a rudder for steering . . . two brass pumps . . . A Watergage . . . determined
> the depth of descent . . . a compass . . . & a ventilator.[3]

Bushnell called his invention the *Turtle*. The entrance to the submarine was
so narrow that only a small man could get inside. Three round doors let in air
while the sub was on the surface, and small glass windows admitted light. A
compass marked with phosphorous allowed Bushnell to read it when the con-
traption was submerged. Iron hoops, tar, and caulk sealed it. The *Turtle* submerged when a valve at his feet let in water and rose when a pump flushed her
out; a tiller controlled the rudder, and cranks operated the paddles that sent her
up and down, back and forth. She was pure Yankee ingenuity.

What's more, the *Turtle* carried a mine. It consisted of a wooden shell, loaded
with 150 pounds of gunpowder, attached to the sub's rear by a long bolt. Once
the submerged *Turtle* got close enough to an enemy's hull, the operator released
the bolt, which activated a clocklike timer. A long wood screw ran atop the sub,
with a stout rope connecting it to the mine. A rod inside the sub drove the wood
screw into the planks of the enemy's hull. The timer gave Bushnell up to twelve
hours to set for an explosion. Simply detach the screw, let it bring the mine to
the hull, fasten it, and paddle like hell away from the ships, and boom! Submarine warfare.[4]

General Washington first met Bushnell during the siege of Boston. Calling
him "a man of great Mechanical powers," Washington gave him money and assistance, only to watch as one mishap after another foiled the inventor. By September 1776, Bushnell had set off enough successful explosions that he deemed
his invention ready to face enemy ships in New York harbor.[5]

Being small of stature was not enough to do the job well. The frail Bushnell, lacking the stamina for the dangerous task, handed it over to his brother Ezra. But as the appointed date drew near, Ezra was struck with the "indisposition" ravaging Washington's army at the time. Bushnell turned to another Ezra: a volunteer, Sergeant Ezra Lee, and gave him a crash course in operating the sub.[6]

Shortly after midnight on September 7, with the moon "about two hours high," two whaleboats towed the *Turtle* from Manhattan towards the British fleet at anchor off Staten Island. Just before the whaleboats reached a point where they could be spotted they cast off the *Turtle*'s lines, and Lee was all alone.

Immediately things went awry. The tide was running stronger than Lee and Bushnell had anticipated, sweeping the *Turtle* past the British ships and forcing Lee to keep the sub on the surface, paddling for nearly three hours before he reached his target. The *Eagle*, a sixty-four-gun ship-of-the-line, was Lord Howe's flagship. Lee calculated it was about an hour until dawn; "I could see the men on the deck, & hear them talk," he recalled. After submerging the *Turtle*, he turned the screw as hard as he could, but it would not penetrate the hull. Lee made several more attempts, with no success. When he surfaced before his last attempt, he found himself three feet from the ship, easy to spot by a British sailor on deck. Lee "thought the best generalship was to retreat," and paddled as fast as he could towards the safety of Manhattan. He had four miles to go.

Unable to read his compass, Lee had to rise every few minutes to make sure he was heading in the right direction. His crooked route attracted the attention of hundreds of British soldiers standing on the parapets of Governor's Island. Dozens of them jumped on a barge and began chasing him. Had he escaped the British flagship and the surrounding fleet, only to be caught by a barge? Not Lee: when his pursuers got within fifty yards of the *Turtle*, he released the mine, hoping they would pick it up, "and then we should all be blown up together."

Seeing the makeshift mine, the soldiers panicked, rowing back to the island as fast as they had come. Eventually, Lee reached the rendezvous point, where a whaleboat towed him to safety. Minutes later, the mine exploded, throwing up a large waterspout. Watching the fleeing barge from his headquarters, General Israel Putnam cried out, "God's curse 'em, that'll do it for them."

Submarine warfare would have to wait for another war.[7]

As fall followed summer in Philadelphia that year, it seemed that the only good news regarding the war effort came from the Continental Navy. On land, the New York campaign was a series of disasters. After a thorough thrashing by the British on Long Island, Washington's army was spared capture in toto by his daring plan to ferry his men across the East River, from Brooklyn to Manhattan, in the dead of night. It would not have succeeded but for John Glover and his Marblehead "Webfooters," rowing boats tirelessly all night long, back and forth across the East River. Once on Manhattan, Washington and his men were again routed in battle.[8]

Farther west, at Lake Champlain, General Benedict Arnold hastily built a fleet of schooners, row galleys, and gondolas to stave off a British attack of superior ships and numbers, part of General Burgoyne's offensive to take control of the Hudson River. On October 11 and 12, Arnold led a valiant action against the British. He lost fifteen of his nineteen vessels, but bought precious time, stalling the grand British invasion of New York and New England for nearly a year.[9]

Admiral Richard, Lord Howe, called "Black Dick" by his men, once derided his cousin George III's "intractable obstinacy" regarding his rebellious subjects. He possessed genuine affection for America and Americans. King George named the brothers Howe "King's Commissioners for restoring Peace to his Majesty's Colonies," and they took this title seriously. The admiral was particularly interested in finding a way to bring the rebels—who he truly believed were fellow Englishmen—back into the fold.

After General William Howe's victories in New York, Richard clung to the hope that his peace feelers would bear fruit. They did not: a trio of congressmen—Benjamin Franklin, John Adams, and Edward Rutledge—met the Howes in New York to discuss terms, but they could not negotiate with the "Independent States" of America. Days later, Washington's departing Continentals put New York to the torch. Longboats from Howe's fleet, including James Wallace's *Rose*, were sent ashore to fight the blaze.[10]

Offsetting such grim tidings from New York came dispatches delivered by naval officers, usually after docking their captains' prizes along Philadelphia's wharves. Continental captains succeeded in a series of independent cruises. Isaiah Robinson, commanding the sloop *Sachem*—Barry's first prize, the *Edward*—captured the brig *Three Friends*, brought in by Joshua Barney. Among the captured goods was a large turtle with Lord North's name on its back (yes, it was given to Robert Morris). Two more prizes from Barry and the *Lexington* arrived in port; among the captured goods were eight African slaves, resold on the auction block of the Philadelphia Coffeehouse, with the proceeds going towards the *Lexington*'s prize shares. Elisha Hinman and the *Cabot* made several captures, one carrying "a woman of Caractor" aboard, while Abraham Whipple's cruise aboard the *Columbus* captured no less than five British vessels.[11]

Lambert Wickes brought the *Reprisal* into Philadelphia after completing a successful cruise to Martinique ("Martinico" in the day) for gunpowder, picking off three prizes during the voyage. He also took part in an international incident that added to the escalating distrust between England and France. Earlier in 1776 a French frigate captain delivered orders from the government of King Louis XVI to his West Indies governors. While the French king did not intend to "favor openly the Americans," his officials were to give "all possible assistance" to American ships and their captains, even though France was not in the war.

The governor of Martinique wasted no time in obeying. On August 1, the *Reprisal* was docked in St. Pierre's harbor when Lambert Wickes accepted a challenge to combat from British captain John Chapman of the sloop-of-war *Shark*, the first battle between ships from the two navies in foreign waters. The *Reprisal* sailed out to meet her foe, her guns run out and her crew armed. A throng of dignitaries and islanders, including William Bingham, America's newly appointed agent for the island, gathered on the beach to watch. The crowd openly rooted for the *Reprisal*.

For two hours, the ships hammered each other, angling for position. After that, reports diverged—depending on whose reports one believed—as to who broke off the engagement. In any event, as the *Reprisal* made for the harbor, French guns from the fort fired a supporting salvo at the *Shark*, sending her out of range and sending Chapman into a rage over such a blatant act by a supposed "neutral."

The following day, Chapman came into port to protest the belligerent act. But the governor, le Comte d'Argout, did not agree: Wickes had "claimed his protection," and had gotten it. Once Wickes put to sea, the governor tactfully added, he was on his own. Upon hearing of such a flagrant breach of neutrality, the British Admiralty was furious. "We shall now be very much pestered," Vice Admiral Young complained to Philip Stephens, the Admiralty's secretary.[12]

On September 17, Nicholas Biddle sailed the *Andrew Doria* up the Delaware, the last leg of his final cruise commanding the brig. Despite being so shorthanded that he had to sign on British and Loyalist sailors from his earlier prizes, this was Biddle's most successful cruise, capturing six ships (typically for the *Andrew Doria*, one was recaptured by the *Cerberus* off Block Island, although this time Biddle's prize crew escaped capture by reaching the island and rowing to Newport the next day). Two of the vessels belonged to Dunmore's fleet, their holds empty but for ballast. They carried passengers, Virginia Loyalists bound for Bermuda. Biddle let both ships continue on their way, allowing the Tories to keep their furniture and chests of clothes. All he took was their property of value—their slaves.

Biddle sailed back to Philadelphia in September with a vastly depleted crew. All his best hands were manning prizes, making their way to friendly ports, while he had scores of prisoners below deck, along with more than a few untrustworthy tars among his few faithful hands. With only two officers left on board, Biddle never left the quarterdeck, sleeping with his blanket covering the loaded pistol he kept in his hand. On the seventeenth, the *Andrew Doria* came in sight of Philadelphia, where a crowd waited at the waterfront to give him a hero's welcome. All in all, it had been a good run by the navy's captains.[13]

But John Paul Jones topped them all.

Sailing northward to Nova Scotia, the *Providence* was caught in a storm so fierce that Jones had to store his guns below deck. By September 19 he was off Cape Sable. Supplies were low. Jones had just given his men permission to fish when the mastheader sighted two sail, a British merchantman and her consort, the frigate *Milford*, Captain Burr, twenty-eight guns. Burr immediately made for the *Providence*. As with the *Solebay*, Jones waited until she was within pistol shot and then changed course, leading the *Milford* on an eight-hour "Wild Goose Chace," Burr firing his bow chasers all the way despite the *Providence*'s staying out of range. Knowing he was "dished," Burr turned his ship through the wind and fired a useless broadside at Jones, who responded by ordering a marine to return fire with a lone musket. The chase ended when "Night, with her sable curtains" descended (an early example of Jones's florid prose). Burr's pursuit took the *Providence* a hundred miles above Halifax.[14]

Risky as it was, the Providences preferred Jones's approach to command after months of John Hazard's mean-spirited caution. The lieutenant who earlier did not trust himself with a sloop was now a captain daring to the point of foolhardiness. Jones was a moth to danger's flame.

On September 21, he captured a shallop off Canso whose crew informed him that a Jersey fishing fleet lay docked in the harbors of Île Madame, a small nearby island. That night, Jones sailed into Canso to find three English schooners. He took one, burned one, and sank the other. After loading his prize with the fish from the other two, he recruited some friendly sailors to join in his visit to Île Madame. That night he sent the well-armed shallop into the harbor of Arichat (which he called "Narrowshock") while he sailed the *Providence* into Petitgrat (to Jones, "Peter the Great"). The islanders were so shocked at the sudden appearance of the American raiders that they made no resistance. In turn, Jones promised to leave enough vessels to carry the fishermen back to Jersey and wrote a safe conduct for them in case they encountered an American privateer. He was justifiably proud of this triumph: "Never was a Bloodless Victory more compleat," he crowed.

Jones could outrun enemy frigates, but not nature. He had no sooner sailed out of Arichat than a violent gale struck the ships. He needed both his anchors to secure the *Providence*. Two prizes were lost: one, which carried a valuable supply of oil, run ashore, the other a schooner driven so hard against the rocks that her crew abandoned ship, scrambling onto a makeshift raft as the storm raged. Shorthanded because of his prizes, his supplies low, and being in the winter quarters of British warships, Jones made for home. "The Fishery at Canso and Madame is effectually destroyed," he reported. He had captured sixteen vessels: six accompanied him up Narragansett Bay, the others were sunk, burned, or retaken en route home by the British. Jones had repaid the depredations of Mowat and Wallace, as much an officer as they, more a gentleman than both.[15]

That fall, Jones and the other captains returned to various ports to learn that Congress was paying more attention to naval matters. It passed laws guaranteeing half pay to all personnel should they suffer disability while serving their country. It issued uniforms: blue coats with red lapels, flat yellow buttons, blue britches, red waistcoats for the captains, with less ostentatious variations for the junior officers; and green coats with white cuffs, waistcoats, and britches for marine officers. Jones and other captains detested the uniform. In fact, Jones later adopted the blue coat and white waistcoat and breeches of the Royal Navy, yet another way to make use of the *ruse de guerre*. Being short in stature, Jones also added epaulets, giving height to his shoulders.[16]

But dissatisfaction with the new uniform was nothing compared to the vitriol produced over the third bit of news from Congress—the rank of captains, and their assigned ships:

1. James Nicholson, Maryland Frigate *Virginia* (28 guns)
2. John Manley, Massachusetts Frigate *Hancock* (32)
3. Hector McNeill, Massachusetts Frigate *Boston* (24)
4. Dudley Saltonstall, Massachusetts Frigate *Trumbull* (28)
5. Nicholas Biddle, Pennsylvania Frigate *Randolph* (32)
6. Thomas Thompson, New Hampshire Frigate *Raleigh* (32)
7. John Barry, Pennsylvania Frigate *Effingham* (28)
8. Thomas Read, Pennsylvania Frigate *Washington* (32)
9. Thomas Grinnell, New York Frigate *Congress* (28)

10. Charles Alexander, Pennsylvania Frigate *Delaware* (24)
11. Lambert Wickes, Pennsylvania Sloop-of-War *Reprisal* (16)
12. Abraham Whipple, Rhode Island Frigate *Providence* (28)
13. John B. Hopkins, Rhode Island Frigate *Warren* (32)
14. John Hodge, New York Frigate *Montgomery* (24)
15. William Hallock, Maryland Brigantine *Lexington* (16)
16. Hoysted Hacker, Rhode Island Brig *Hampden*
17. Isaiah Robinson, Pennsylvania Brig *Andrew Doria* (14)
18. John Paul Jones, Virginia Sloop *Providence* (12)
19. James Josiah, Pennsylvania
20. Elisha Hinman, Connecticut Ship *Alfred* (28)
21. James Olney, Rhode Island Brig *Cabot* (16)
22. James Robinson, Pennsylvania Sloop *Sachem* (10)
23. John Young, Pennsylvania Sloop *Independence* (10)
24. Elisha Warner, Pennsylvania Schooner *Fly* (8)

Practically every major port north of Virginia was assigned at least one frigate to build (Philadelphia led with four); consequently captains were needed from each area. The list had most of the veterans from the navy's first year scratching their heads. Jones was easily the angriest about the men ahead of them. Manley and McNeill, for example, had served in Washington's navy, but the only official navy James Nicholson, number 1 on the Captains List, had served in was George III's in the French and Indian War. Hopkins's captains, along with Barry, were also assigned new frigates. In a scenario straight from Greek mythology, Jones had completed the most successful cruise yet by any Continental captain, just as the Marine Committee was drawing up the plum assignments. Had the committee considered results and not politics, Biddle, Jones, Barry, and Wickes would have topped the list. Jones would live another sixteen years, not long enough for such a proud, thin-skinned man to get over such a snub.[17]

The thirteen new frigates were in various stages of completion—the *Randolph* was launched in July, while Biddle was at sea. He returned home to find his new ship off the ways and in the latter stages of completion. He also learned that his brother Charles had been captured off Jamaica, sailing a merchantman bearing flour for Haiti. Once in Kingston he was brought before the fleet admiral, Clark Gayton, just as the Englishman was reading a Philadelphia paper extolling Nicholas's deeds.

"Any relation to this rebel?" Gayton haughtily inquired.

Charles grinned. "That rebel," he replied, "is my brother." Gayton responded by clapping Charles in irons (after several unsuccessful attempts to escape Jamaica, including one dressed "in the style of a mulatto girl," Charles was smuggled by friends on the island aboard a merchantman bound for New Bern, North Carolina, where he would meet his wife).[18]

Back in Philadelphia, Nicholas Biddle hurried to finish and man his frigate. He had company along the shipyards: Thomas Read was hard at it with the *Washington*, while John Barry readied the *Effingham* for her October launching. Most of the Continental ships were in port when Hopkins gave Jones new orders and a new command: the *Alfred*. With the *Hampden* for company, Jones was to sail back to Nova Scotia and destroy all the colliers (coal ships) he encountered, then make for New Breton, where a number of American sailors were prisoners, laboring in the coal pits. After that was accomplished, he was to sail south and harass the transports coming into New York from England.[19]

"All my humanity was Awakened and called up to Action by this Laudable Proposal," Jones wrote Robert Morris. All that was holding him back was manpower, as "Privateers entice [sailors] Away as fast as they receive their Months Pay," he complained. As common seamen were "Actuated by no nobler principle than that of Self Interest," Jones believed the only solution lay in substantially raising the "Private Emolument" paid to sailors. He compared Congress's paltry wages to "the Old Vulgar Proverb 'Penny Wise and Pound Foolish.'"

Jones's argument was correct. If he had only known that Morris, like many of his congressional colleagues, was financing privateers. When the *Hampden* struck a sunken ledge in Newport's waters, Jones commandeered enough men off her and the *Providence* to get the *Alfred* to sea on October 30. "Without a Respectable Navy—Alas America!" Jones bewailed before setting off to make America's navy as respectable as one captain could.[20]

The *Reprisal* was being refitted in Philadelphia when Lambert Wickes received orders from Congress's Committee of Secret Correspondence on October 24. Wickes was number 11 on the Captains List, with peers before and after his rank given frigate assignments, but he had no time to pout over it. He was to sail immediately for France with two items of utmost importance: a large supply of indigo and one seventy-year-old congressman.

Secret discussions had been going on for more than a year between Congress and the French government, both realizing they had something to offer each other. By the fall of 1776, most congressmen wanted French arms, money, and her fleet. France wanted America's tobacco trade. Initially, the aid in arms was covert, thanks to the slave trade. French slavers sailed out of Nantes, a French port in the northern part of the Bay of Biscay. The French "black birders" were as heavily armed as their American counterparts, making it easy to let them do double duty as gunrunners, joining American ships in crossing the Atlantic with powder and arms.[21]

In the spring, John Barry had escorted Silas Deane's ship the *Betsy* out of the Delaware. She made it safely to France, where Deane had spent the last eight months as Congress's representative to the court of Louis XVI. The son of a blacksmith, Deane was a seasoned politician in colonial affairs, but proved to be hopelessly out of his league at Versailles. He spoke no French, seemed oblivious to the customs of the court, and carped about how news from home reached everyone else in Paris before he heard it. Even his copy of the Declaration arrived months after all of Europe had read it. British spies became so good at dogging him that they knew what he was going to eat for dinner before he did.[22]

He did, however, see a golden opportunity for the Cause, advocating the recruitment of privateers and even naval officers to take the fight to this side of the Atlantic. Deane pleaded for a number of blank privateering commissions, adding how "little vessels" (i.e., schooners and cutters) could make "great reprisals." After all, "the armed vessel increases your navy and the prize supplies the country."[23]

Now Congress was sending its most famous member on a task nearly as herculean as Washington's—to get money, arms, munitions, and especially an alliance with Britain's traditional archenemy. Lambert Wickes was to pay utmost attention to Benjamin Franklin's needs, and refrain from any prize-taking or combat. Nothing was more important than getting Franklin safely to France. After that, "Let Old England See how they like to have an active Enemy at their own Door, they have Sent Fire and Sword to ours."[24]

Franklin's mission was secret, but how to keep it so, as Philadelphia teemed with Tory spies? Wickes and Franklin did the best they could. On October 27, the *Reprisal* stood down the Delaware, stopping at Marcus Hook. The next day, Franklin and his grandsons, Benjamin Franklin Bache and William Temple Franklin, took a coach to nearby Chester and spent the night. The morning coach carried them down to Marcus Hook. Few paid much attention when a tall, stout gentleman wearing a coonskin cap and a greatcoat over his broad swimmer's shoulders climbed gingerly up the *Reprisal*'s gangway on two gouty legs, two youngsters right behind him. Once aboard, they passed an array of marines, standing at attention in their new green uniforms. Resplendent in his own blue and red attire, Wickes gave the orders to cast off, and the *Reprisal* made sail for France.

Franklin's cover had been blown outside the State House weeks earlier, when merchant and patriot Reese Meredith loudly asked his friend Robert Morris, "Is Franklin really going to Paris?" Spies sent word to General Howe that Franklin had departed, seeking "the Interposition of the French Court & its assistance," but by then the *Reprisal* was sailing the Atlantic.[25]

The weather turned cold early that fall. At the shipyards, carpenters, chandlers, and rope men blew on their hands as they toiled aboard the *Randolph* and the other three frigates. Philadelphia was second to none at shipbuilding in the New World, and these four ships were the largest yet built in America. They loomed over the waterfront like monstrous, hulking giants, daily drawing crowds that got as close to the ways as the marines patrolling the perimeter of the yard would let them.

People openly marveled at their colossal size and graceful lines. The *Randolph* was already in the water, her hull painted a rich blue, her gun ports and bow a burnished yellow. When the *Alfred* was launched as the *Black Prince* in 1774 she was the largest ship built in Philadelphia, at 91 feet, 5 inches, with a 26-foot beam. The *Randolph* was 60 feet longer and 8 feet wider. Her bowsprit and boom added another 40 feet to her length. Her mainmast rose 150 feet above the deck. Nicholas Biddle—and Congress—could not wait to get her out to sea.[26]

The latest reports from Washington and his officers were as bitter as the weather. Having lost New York, the general had constructed Fort Washington outside of New York City and Fort Lee across the river in New Jersey to defend his evacuation of New York. By November 20, both had fallen, their garrisons now prisoners of war. To make matters worse for Washington, the brothers Howe came up with a brilliant ploy. On November 30, they guaranteed "a full and free Pardon of all Treason" to any soldier, sailor, or rebel sympathizer as long as they "disband themselves and return to their Dwelling, there to remain in a peaceable and Quiet Manner." As General Howe marched south through New Jersey, his campsites were invaded daily by thousands of former rebels, all happy to pledge their loyalty to England once again. At Sandy Hook, other penitent patriots did the same, boat after boat taking them out to British warships.

Three days after Howe's proclamation, General Charles Lee, who under-mined Washington with every letter and saw the general's array of defeats as his best chance to succeed him, was captured while dawdling at a New Jersey tavern. Six months earlier, Washington began the New York campaign with 20,000 men. On his retreat down New Jersey roads towards Philadelphia, he had fewer than 3,500. "Their Army is a wretched Plight indeed," one Loyalist happily wrote to Lord Dartmouth, adding, "Most of them have no other covering than a Rifle-man's Frock of Canvas over their shirt . . . diseased and covered with Vermin to a loathsome degree." From New York harbor, Admiral Howe sent fifteen ships—half his fleet—heading towards Rhode Island to establish winter quarters and blockade Hopkins's ships. One, a fifty-gun two-decker, the *Experiment*, had re-cently been given to James Wallace as a reward for his activities off Rhode Island these past two years. From the Delaware Bay, Henry Fisher reported that the two capes "are Lin'd with w[it]h Men of War," including the *Roebuck*.[27]

In the face of such peril, high-ranking patriots made public appeals to their fellow citizens. At a rally by the State House, two famous Philadelphians, David Rittenhouse of the Committee of Safety and Quartermaster General Thomas Mifflin of the Continental Army, beseeched the crowd to take up arms and aid Washington. More than 2,000 volunteers joined the hastily organized Phila-delphia Brigade. The navy's captains, eager to do their part, called on the Marine Committee. Biddle, Barry, Read, Alexander, and John Nicholson of the *Hornet* offered to place themselves, their sailors, and their guns under the army's orders. The committee sent Biddle and Nicholson to their ships with orders to prepare for departure, and took the other three up on their offer, placing them under General John Cadwalader, commanding the Pennsylvania "Associators." The captains re-turned to the shipyards, rounding up every sailor, carpenter, or rigger willing to join the coming fight. The navy was joining the army.[28]

And they were not the only sailors to volunteer. Seeing the need for every available fighting man to get to Philadelphia, Samuel Chase sent a courier to Baltimore with a request that the navy's top captain bring "a Body of Seamen and Marines" to help get the frigates out to sea or fight with Washington. "I shall make the best of my way," James Nicholson wrote, and he did.[29]

After Cadwalader gave Read command of a battery and put Barry and Alex-ander on his personal staff, he marched his men north to Bristol, where they could rendezvous with Washington's bedraggled soldiers. Looking back as they departed their city, Barry and Read saw hundreds of Philadelphians preparing to leave, clogging the streets with wagons and carts overloaded with furniture and household goods. Congressmen, ordered south to Baltimore, led the way. Soon only one representative remained—Robert Morris.[30]

Morris always took his responsibilities on the Marine Committee seriously, but now he *was* the Marine Committee. That week, Washington sent one of his trusted generals, Israel Putnam, to assume command of Philadelphia's defenses. With Howe's forces marching ever closer to Philadelphia, "Old Put" asked and received Congress's approval to burn the frigates. Morris immediately dismissed Putnam's proposal out of hand. "I have presumed to go one Step farther in this Navy business," he informed Hancock, adding he would continue doing so during this crisis whether Congress approved or not. Seeing Alexander delayed in getting the *Delaware* completed, Morris found enough shipyard hands remaining in town and sent them to work, promising Hancock that the *Delaware*'s "Sails will be bent, Anchors to the Bows, Stores on b[oar]d and everything in some forwardness." His efforts bore quick results; learning that the *Delaware* was nearly ready for sea, he sent for Alexander.[31]

His own frigate supplied and armed, Biddle held a rendezvous that was a complete waste of time. Practically every able hand not already on board had joined Cadwalader's forces. Before their exodus, Congress offered a twenty-dollar advance to each sailor who signed the *Randolph*'s muster rolls. When that notion also flopped, Congress permitted Biddle on December 7 to free any sailors in the city jails and prison. Five days later, it offered him an incredible enticement—especially for Congress—a ten-thousand-dollar bonus, providing that Biddle and what meager crew he could muster got the *Randolph* safely out to sea. Then Congress fled for Baltimore.[32]

Biddle went to the Walnut Street Prison to see what sailors were among the felons, vagrants, and British prisoners (many of the third group from his last cruise on the *Andrew Doria*) languishing behind bars, knowing their loyalty would be truly discerned only when the *Randolph* faced an enemy ship. There were few. Biddle arbitrarily pressed into service those inmates who did not volunteer but had the required skills. Fully manned, a frigate carried upwards of four hundred men; these, plus a few recently signed landsmen, gave Biddle barely two hundred. On December 14, his orders from Morris in hand, he sent the *Randolph* downriver, with the *Hornet* in the lead.[33]

They were barely under way when one of Henry Fisher's couriers galloped into Philadelphia with an urgent message: the *Roebuck* was off the Cape Henlopen lighthouse, and the frigate *Pearl*, Captain Thomas Wilkinson, thirty-two guns, was anchored near the Brandywine River. Morris sent word to Biddle: turn around. He did, anchoring at Liberty Island, now called "Fort Island," with construction under way to complete the defenses designed by Captain John Montresor, now Howe's chief engineer. While there, Biddle received a plea from an invalid widow with no support except for her son, now one of Biddle's pressed recruits. After his release, she promised to pray "that the great god Will Pour down his Blessings on Your Honor and Family whilst Alive.[34]

While the *Roebuck* rode at anchor near the lighthouse, Hamond was visited by a rowboat carrying townsfolk from Lewes and flying a white flag. They assured him their neighbors were all loyal to king and country—news that did not prevent Hamond and Wilkinson from a windfall of prize-taking, especially one: the *Lexington*, captured off the Delaware coast by the *Pearl* on December 20, a cold, extremely windy day. William Hallock was not John Barry. Despite her close-reefed sails, the *Pearl* overtook the *Lexington*. Conditions were so tempestuous that one of the *Pearl*'s boats stove in; Wilkinson could remove only Hallock and nine others before placing a similar number aboard as a prize crew and sending the *Lexington* south to Virginia.[35]

Such grim news worried Morris. "My labours appear to be lost & sorry I am for the disappointment," he wrote to Hancock. Adding to his woes, he learned that the British army was reportedly less than ten miles away. Morris had every reason to be distressed.[36]

But two days later, on December 23, he happily informed Hancock that the *Andrew Doria* was heading up the Delaware, back from St. Eustatius. There she received one of the first salutes fired in honor of American colors in a foreign port, cause for yet another diplomatic flap, this time between England and Holland. Shortly after Isaiah Robinson's departure from St. Eustatius its governor, Johannes de Graaf, received a scathing letter from British governor Craister Greathead of St. Christopher's, questioning how de Graaf's salute "is reconcilable with the Treaties" between England and Holland.[37]

Three weeks later Robinson's men fought a sharp battle above the West Indies against the sloop *Racehorse*, wounding William Jones, who "has the King's Commission as Master and Commander." After the *Andrew Doria* shredded the sloop's rigging and sails, Jones surrendered. Perhaps the most amazing part of Robinson's cruise came when he slipped past the *Roebuck* and the other British warships prowling about Delaware Bay. After a litany of letters to Hancock, Washington, and others in which he stoically reported the gloom descending on Philadelphia, Morris now shared with them his renewed optimism, declaring, "We ought to hazard everything to get the ships out."[38]

Across the Atlantic that same month, the *Reprisal* was on top of the coast of France. It had been a rough passage, and while the storms she encountered did no damage to the bales of indigo, they wreaked havoc on the oldest member of Congress. Benjamin Franklin spent the entire voyage so seasick he could barely stand. Whenever possible, Lambert Wickes clapped on all sail, sending the *Reprisal* to France as quickly as possible, for a speedy if not smooth passage. Franklin had often quoted Samuel Johnson's witticism that a ship at sea was like a jail without the comforts of a jail. He no longer found the line humorous.

The *Reprisal* was approaching Quiberon Bay when her mastheader cried, "Sail ho!" The desire to pursue, usually second nature to Wickes, was tempered by his orders to avoid a chase. Wickes went to Franklin's cabin and asked his advice. Ill as he was, Franklin deliberated over what to do, using what he called "moral algebra" and weighing the issue—aware of the risk, but yet, what better way to show France a potential ally's resolve than by sailing into port with a prize? Franklin made his decision. He had seen Wickes's orders; now, recalling Congress's final exhortation—*Let Old England See how they like to have an active Enemy at their own Door*—he gave his blessing.

Wickes pursued, and soon had a prize: the brigantine *George* out of Cork, Ireland, bound for home with a hold containing building materials and thirty-five hogsheads of Bordeaux claret. Just hours later, another brigantine was sighted, chased, and taken—*La Vigne*, whose hold carried more wine as well as casks of cognac. Welcome to France, Mr. Wickes; *Bienvenue en France, Monsieur Franklin.*[39]

Poor Franklin: rough seas kept the *Reprisal* off Nantes for three stormy days. Wickes was forced to flag a fishing boat to take Franklin and his healthier grandsons to shore and a waiting carriage for Paris. There Franklin would find adulation, intrigue, and betrayal, and begin to make the old enemy of thirteen British colonies the best friend of thirteen united states.

Back in Pennsylvania on Christmas Day, Washington wrote Robert Morris a long letter touching on several subjects. He would appeal to two New England regiments, whose terms of enlistment were up, that they reenlist as sailors under Biddle to get his frigate properly manned and out to sea. He informed Morris that he had written Admiral Howe, proposing an exchange of Barry's prisoner, Richard Boger of the *Edward*, for James Josiah of the *Andrew Doria*. And despite learning that the British intended to cross the Delaware and attack once the ice had sufficiently hardened, Washington clung to the hope "that some Lucky Chance might turn up in our Favour." His letter finished, he went back to his plans for the evening: cross the Delaware and attack the Hessian mercenaries camped at Trenton—before they attacked him.[40]

That night, a nor'easter set in, adding to the desperation of Washington's gamble. He gave the signal for Henry Glover's men to begin rowing what was left of the Continental Army across the Delaware to New Jersey. Using "Durham boats"—sixty-foot-long, pointed barges that transported pig iron downriver from Reading to Philadelphia—the "Webfooters" manned the eighteen-foot-long oars and began ferrying Washington's meager forces across the Delaware.

Glover's sailors had served as the first American navy in the war; they had saved Washington's army from capture in New York. Now, beset with ice floes, bitter winds, and snow, they were sure that nature itself was against them. With each stroke of their oars, they bore their fellow warriors—and their young country—towards Washington's aptly chosen password this night: *Victory or Death*.[41]

On January 11, 1777, a day he described as full of "dark Rainey W[eath]r," Andrew Snape Hamond sent the *Roebuck* in pursuit of a brig heading back from the West Indies. Four hours and several warning shots later, she became the latest of the many prizes Hamond had snatched off the Delaware Capes since returning in December.

Just before Christmas he had written that Washington's army was finished, with Cornwallis "chasing the Enemy every where before him." With the British army impeded by hordes of Americans anxious to sign the Howe brothers' clemency offer, and Congress having fled Philadelphia, the American rebellion looked to be over, a veritable Christmas present for the Howes to present their cousin and king.[42]

On December 26 Robert Morris was at his office when a courier from General Cadwalader burst in with the news. It was Charles Alexander, whom Morris had summoned to bring back the "few Tradesmen necessary" to complete work on the *Delaware*. Alexander bore tidings of great joy: a thorough victory over the 1,400 Hessians at Trenton, with 300 prisoners being marched back to Philadelphia. "General Washington is now Master of that place," Morris gratefully informed Hancock in Baltimore.[43]

One week later, Washington did it again at Princeton, this time against British soldiers from Cornwallis's army. After the battle, Cornwallis moved his forces up to New Brunswick, while Washington's rejuvenated (and reenlisted) troops made winter camp in Morristown.

The sailors of the Continental Navy missed the fighting at Trenton. Cadwalader's volunteers did not cross the Delaware until the twenty-sixth, and were ordered back to Pennsylvania. They saw plenty of action at Princeton, where they fought alongside Brigadier General Hugh Mercer's "Blue Hens." When a British counterattack threatened the American line, it was Cadwalader's men, manning naval guns from the unfinished frigates, that held the Redcoats back until Washington, mounted on a white horse, personally took command. The night before the battle, Cornwallis had bragged to his officers that they would "bag the fox" the next day. Once the British began retreating, leaving muskets, canteens, and knapsacks in their wake, Washington led the pursuit, crying, "It's a fine fox hunt, my boys."[44]

Washington's victories infused new life into the Cause. On a minor note, they also changed the tone of Hamond's reports. Sitting in the *Roebuck*'s cabin, as the ocean winds swept rain and snow onto the quarterdeck above, he duly noted the recent reversal of fortune for the British. Even as he called the published accounts of the British defeats "much embellished," he admitted it "was not greatly exaggerated."[45]

The contribution of the navy's sailors was cited in reports from the front. James Nicholson marveled at the jolt it gave sailor and soldier alike: "This affair has given such amazing spirit to the people, that you might do any thing, or go anywhere with them," he wrote back to Baltimore. The esprit de corps of the sailors made the papers:

> The captains of the frigates of Philadelphia, with their brave tars and a number of pieces of cannon . . . were willing to beat the enemy by land as well as by sea, provided the General would let them be commanded by their own officers, and fight their cannon their own way, whose request was granted, and they swear they will never flinch while the General finds them in Rum, Beef, and Biscuit.[46]

Nor were the "brave tars" the only sailors who distinguished themselves in the days that tried men's souls. From Baltimore, an ecstatic Hancock informed Morris that the *Lexington* was once again an American ship. When bad weather cut short the transfer of a larger prize crew than the *Pearl*'s Captain Williams intended, he sent the captured brigantine on her way, concerned as to whether the British hands aboard her could both sail the ship through the gale and keep the American prisoners confined below deck. His worries proved justified. The ships lost sight of each other in the storm when the Americans, led by Barry's convert to the Cause, Richard Dale, overpowered their captors and sailed for Baltimore, where they found Congress waiting for them. Having fled Philadelphia when every event took them one step closer to the hangman's noose, the representatives were thrilled beyond measure to see a favorite ship returned—not just with her crew, but with her hold full of powder and arms. Hancock could barely contain his joy.[47]

In Philadelphia, a happily determined Morris yearned to get every available Continental ship out of port and out to sea, but the enemy and nature blockaded his plans. Ice so choked the Delaware that the *Randolph* and *Hornet* were held fast off Fort Island. Captains Barry and Read returned to find that nothing had been done with their unfinished frigates *Effingham* and *Washington*. British ships maintained a stranglehold on the Rhode Island coast, hemming in Hopkins and no fewer than five Continental ships. In Boston, the only naval action came from the growing acrimony between the captains of the frigates *Hancock* and *Boston*, John Manley and Hector McNeill. In Portsmouth, New Hampshire, Thomas Thompson faced the same daunting challenges as his peers did: lack of cannons and the crew to man them.

His vision of Continental ships wreaking havoc on the high seas dashed, Morris turned his attention to the exchange of prisoners. On New Year's Eve he received a letter from Hamond. Knowing that British sailors and officers were well treated by their rebel captors, Hamond had given "immediate orders that every Prisoner now on board the Ships under my Command Shall be Set at liberty without delay." He put them ashore at Cape Henlopen. The vigilant Henry Fisher was the first American to greet those freed by "His Majesty's Pyrates." Morris arranged for those British tars in Philadelphia to be sent there in exchange. Hamond saw his act as a chance to show his humanity. He was the rebels' enemy, but also a gentleman.[48]

The same could not be said, however, for many of Hamond's fellow officers, who strictly obeyed Lord North's instructions about prisoners. While waiting for a winter thaw, Nicholas Biddle received a letter from Margaret Tarras, James Josiah's sister. Josiah had been able to write her and his father long paragraphs detailing the abuse he endured in the waist of the *Cerberus*. Now, "obligd to Smother that grief For fear of more distressing an aged father," Margaret begged Biddle to continue to intercede with the British on her brother's behalf.[49]

Morris and Biddle had long heard about mistreatment aboard British prison ships, not just for Continental sailors but also

> Masters, supercargoes, &c. of merchant vessels, with Indians, Mulattoes, and Negroe slaves, are all put together between decks . . . As to their provisions, the allowance is very small, and the quality unwholesome . . . the miserable prisoners must eat [the meat] raw . . . Butter and cheese they have none . . . they have oil, so rank they cannot eat it . . . They are often twelve or sixteen hours without a drop of fresh water . . . the prison ship had on board no less than two hundred and sixty unfortunate men . . . this prison ship had neither Doctor or medicine chest.[50]

An incensed Morris wrote Washington that "our poor Soldiers and Sailors are perishing for want of food, fresh Air and Cleanliness, whilst theirs in our possession are feasting on the fat of this Land." He urged the general to "remonstrate to Genl Howe and L[or]d Howe against the base treatment our people meet with," or face "immediate retaliation . . . if they did not alter their conduct."

Prisoner exchanges were also agreed upon in Rhode Island between Esek Hopkins and Admiral Peter Parker "by Order of Lord Howe." Washington responded to Morris's letter and made Congress's sentiments known, but for American sailors, prison conditions only worsened.[51]

As 1777—called "the Year of the Hangman" for its three 7s—dawned, most Continental captains were at work getting their ships to sea. But not even Jones and Biddle were more desperate to see action than their commodore was.

Esek Hopkins was well aware of how far his stock had dropped with both Congress and the public. Whereas Jones and Biddle enjoyed soaring popularity among congressman and citizen alike, Hopkins had fallen so low he was even being criticized from the pulpit. When the Reverend Samuel Hopkins of Newport laid the wanton habits of American sailors at Hopkins's feet in his sermon "Complaints of the Morals of the Navy," the commodore could only commiserate about "the depravity of the Times." Neptune may have given Hopkins his trident, but the God of Hopkins's fathers was relegating a pitchfork to him—or at least the Reverend Hopkins was, perhaps to prove publicly that he was no relation to the unpopular commodore.[52]

Imagine Hopkins's excitement when he learned that the British frigate *Di-*

amond, Captain Charles Fielding, had run aground in Narragansett Bay between Newport and Providence. She was part of the British blockade, and had recently captured a privateer sloop. Fielding celebrated the New Year by sending his longboats over to Patience Island, looking for remnants of a rebel stronghold, only to find the island abandoned. The boats returned at dark just as it began to rain.

That night a marine entered Fielding's cabin and roused him from his slumber. Two of the American prisoners had cut away the longboat secured at the stern and made their escape. Despite the darkness and lack of a pilot, Fielding ordered the men to make sail and hunt down the escapees. The wind began a vicious blow from the southwest, and Fielding "veered his cable"—dragging his anchor to drift—but when the wind changed direction, the *Diamond* ran aground and began listing to port.

At dawn the two American sailors reached the shore and made for the encampment of General William West, who sent word immediately to Hopkins. From his headquarters West could see the stranded *Diamond* keening hard to port, but with enough water running beneath her to keep from totally careening and allowing her starboard guns to be tilted and loaded.

Hopkins was ecstatic. Here was his chance, at long last, to cut the albatross of the *Glasgow* off his neck. He had transferred his broad pennant to the frigate *Warren*, but he sent neither her nor her sister frigate *Providence* downriver to confront the paralyzed *Diamond*, and for good reason: the shallows that trapped the British ship were just as treacherous for deep-draft American frigates. Instead he took two dozen hands off the *Warren*, added them to the crew of the sloop *Providence*, and summoned Abraham Whipple, the very man who had destroyed the *Gaspee* in similar conditions years ago. With Rhode Island's toughest old salt and a nimble sloop to sail in the most familiar of waters, Hopkins headed downriver to victory. What could possibly go wrong?

Since it was Hopkins, everything.

Initially he was right about his choice of ship. The wind, blowing exceedingly hard from the west, would have prevented the larger ships from getting downriver in time. When the *Providence* arrived to give battle (around three p.m.), Fielding had already made one attempt to heave off the bar. And help was on the way from the tender *Centurion*, Captain Richard Braithwaite, who sent his barge and longboat ahead to assist the *Diamond*. Through his spyglass Hopkins could see a large two-decker coming up fast, a mile and a half away: the hated James Wallace's *Experiment*.

By this time the local militia was getting into position to fire on the *Diamond* from nearby Warwick Island. Hopkins had the *Providence*'s boat take him there, and immediately assumed total command of the action.

Once ashore, he found militiamen throwing up breastworks while they waited for two 18-pounders, all the better to batter the *Diamond* with. After conferring with their colonel, Hopkins returned to the sloop, sending her close to the *Diamond*'s stern before he ordered his men to open fire. Fielding returned the broadside with his bow chasers, while the two guns on the island fired two dozen rounds at the frigate, damaging her hull. At that moment, the colonel signaled Hopkins to return to the island.

Once the commodore returned, the colonel informed him that they were out of ammunition. Hopkins could offer them powder and wads, but lacked the proper shot for guns this size. He sent men to Providence for more ammunition and climbed back into the longboat as darkness set in.

He had just scaled the sloop's gangway when the colonel signaled him again. "Lower away," Hopkins roared, and was rowed back to Warwick Island a third time. The colonel wanted bread—his men needed sustenance. A furious Hopkins wheeled around towards his longboat. It was gone: his men had not tied the boat properly. It was drifting away, too far out in the freezing-cold water to be retrieved. Hopkins was marooned. Shortly thereafter, the *Experiment* arrived. Unlike the *Gaspee*, the fortunate *Diamond* escaped.[53]

The whole affair made Hopkins look a fool, not so much unsuccessful as inept. It was worse than the *Glasgow*—at least she could fight back effectively. Despite his avowed empathy for the Reverend Hopkins, the commodore could not help himself, cursing like the sailor he was all the way back to Providence.

For many congressmen, getting rid of Hopkins now seemed easy. Keeping their newest hero happy was something else.

In November 1776, Hopkins sent John Paul Jones on that risky mission to Nova Scotia to take or destroy the enemy's colliers, then rescue the American prisoners toiling in the New Breton coal pits. Already smarting from his low rank on the Captains List, Jones was determined to complete his mission before winter storms and ice prevented him from doing so. In his hold he carried 583 barrels of rum, enough to keep both his crew and any rescued tars warm on the voyage home.[54]

The *Alfred* and *Providence* were sailing east near Tarpaulin Cove when a privateer, the schooner *Eagle*, was spotted. As both ships were undermanned, and suspecting that a Rhode Island privateer was likely to have deserted Continentals on the muster roll, Jones sent both ships' barges over to inspect the crew. Marine Lieutenant John Trevett, back from his adventures with Biddle, commanded the *Providence*'s barge, while Lieutenant John Peck Rathbun of the *Alfred* led the other, his men dressed as Indians in an attempt to hide their identities from their fellow Rhode Islanders.

Once aboard, the men used the time-tested way of seeking hiding sailors by stabbing the bags below deck with their cutlasses. They found four. The *Eagle*'s captain, Isaac Field, thought the inspection was over. It was not: Rathbun and Trevett took twenty-four hands from the privateer, abusing Field's men with enough cursing to make Hopkins proud. Before departing, Rathbun cut the mainsheet (the long rope that controlled the mainsail) and ordered the bulkhead smashed. Once his barges were raised, Jones was off and sailing; later, Field would have his revenge.[55]

It took ten days for Jones to reach Cape Breton, his mastheaders searching for prizes throughout the passage. The North Atlantic was getting rough; green water crashed over the gunwales and ran down the hatches, soaking every hand to the bone. On November 11 Jones took the brigantine *Active*, the goods in her hold worth £600 sterling. The next morning, Jones hit the jackpot, capturing the *Mellish*, her hold stuffed with thousands of uniforms for Burgoyne's army. Jones deemed her the most valuable ship yet taken by privateer or naval vessel. Writing his patron Joseph Hewes and his agent, Robert Smith, Jones chortled, "This will make Burgoyne 'Shake a Cloth in the wind' and check his progress on the Lakes."[56]

On the sixteenth, the *Alfred* and *Providence* took another prize, the snow *Kitty* from London, carrying oil and fish. Her captain informed Jones that the Nova Scotia harbors were already frozen over. News travels fast from ship to ship, and bad news festers in the fo'c'sle. The crew of the *Providence* began grumbling openly about tarrying any longer this far north. Thanks to the rough conditions, both ships were leaking badly. Each day the temperatures dropped by degrees. Hacker told Jones that the very hearties who had served Jones so well when he commanded the *Providence* were now cold, wet, fearful, and rebellious. They wanted to go home.

Without hesitation, Jones ordered the *Alfred*'s gig lowered and had himself rowed to the *Providence*. He called all hands on deck and faced his old shipmates, raising his voice above the howling winds, doing his best to emulate Henry V and rally his men to "relieve our Captive ill treated Brethren from the Coal Mines." He returned to the *Alfred*, believing he had silenced the "Unacceptable murmuring" aboard the *Providence*.

He had not. The "Epidemical discontent" returned as soon as he climbed into the gig. That night, Hacker, cowed by the mood before the mast, slipped away for Rhode Island. The absence of the *Providence* did two things: it steeled an angry Jones's resolve to complete his mission, while his crew, aware of why the Providences had slipped their cable and concerned over their own ship's condition, began muttering themselves.[57]

The sailors' worries were justified. Generations of mariners had learned to abandon the North Atlantic in wintertime. It was dangerous enough to climb the ratlines and inch along footropes in the fairest weather; rolling seas, strong, bitter winds, and ice-covered lines made routine labors death-defying. Nonetheless, Jones made for Canso again, sailing through a blizzard that literally blew the *Alfred* to Cape Sable.

Once off Canso, he sent his longboats into the harbor under cover of darkness, where they burned both a transport laden with Irish stores and an oil warehouse. Before departing, he seized a schooner to replace the *Providence*, and learned from an islander that three frigates had been searching for him ever since his earlier expedition commanding the *Providence*. Other captains would have heeded such a warning; Jones took it as a compliment.

Fog slowed his progress when, on the twenty-fourth, Jones found himself surrounded by three ships. Believing them to be the frigates that were after his hide, he determined "to sell my liberty as dearly as possible" and stood for the nearest one. They were colliers, the very coal ships Hopkins had ordered captured or destroyed. Jones took all three. Luckily, he was not spotted by their escort, the HMS *Flora*, a thirty-two-gun frigate.

One of his prisoners approached Jones: the American prisoners he had been ordered to rescue were gone, conscripted into the Royal Navy. Despite ice, dreadful storms, and a disappearing sloop, Jones had been unwavering in his quest to complete his mission as long as it stood even the slimmest chance of success. Now, with no one to rescue, 140 prisoners below deck, dwindling supplies, a disheartened crew, and horrific weather, it was time to go.[58]

Before departure he caught one more valuable prize, the ten-gun privateer *John*. With four frigates now hunting for him, he turned the *John* over to his friend John Rathbun and sent out orders detailing his signals for the other four vessels, telling the prize-masters to make for the most convenient port if separated. Rathbun was to keep the *John* within three cable lengths of the *Alfred*; if it came to a fight, the leaky flagship would need help.[59]

Remarkably, Jones kept his squadron together until December 7, sailing through strong gales as they reached the Massachusetts coast. A stiff wind filled every sail when the *Alfred*'s mastheader spied a large ship on the horizon twelve miles distant. She was the *Milford*, the same frigate Jones had eluded on his last cruise. Keeping the *John* alongside, Jones signaled the other ships to crack on every sail and flee. Deciding he wanted Rathbun with him on his quarterdeck, he sent Lieutenant Robert Saunders to command the *John*. Looking through his spyglass, Jones watched the *Milford*'s captain, John Burr, set his fore and mizzen topsail, run out his guns to give chase to the *Alfred* and *John*—exactly what Jones wanted. As night set in, Jones mounted a lantern aloft and led the *Milford* away from the fleeing prizes. The ruse worked. Burr believed the ships now to be the *Flora* and the very colliers now slipping through his fingers.[60]

The next morning Jones signaled Saunders. The *Alfred*'s lethargic condition prevented Jones from sailing too close to the *Milford*, not knowing her strength. He sent the *John* to windward of the frigate and signaled "if She was of Superiour or Inferiour Force," thereby to know whether to fight or flee. The clear skies were disappearing behind a line of storms when Saunders signaled Jones: *Superiour Force*.

Superior or not, Jones ordered his guns run out. Once the *Milford* was in range, he let loose a broadside, hoping to give Saunders every available second to sail away. Then, with the *Milford* following, Jones "drove the *Alfred* Seven and Eight Knots under two Courses to a point from the Wind"—an incredible bit of sailing for a ship in such poor condition. At nightfall, Burr changed course; Jones presumed he took off after the *John*, confident that he had taken the frigate far enough off course to keep his prize safe.

But the *John* did not escape. When he spotted her, Burr made such a straight beeline that he overtook her in thirty minutes. Lieutenant Saunders struck his colors, believing Jones had abandoned him.[61]

Five days later another snowstorm struck the *Alfred*, damaging her sailing abilities to the point that Jones had to forsake Boston for the trickier harbor at Plymouth, running his ship aground in the process. It would be days before the *Alfred* limped into Boston harbor. His arrival in port matched his mood: for all he had accomplished, Jones considered his cruise a failure. It weighed heavily on his conscience. "My success hath indeed fallen far short of my wishes," he wrote to the Marine Committee.[62]

Once he arrived in Boston, Jones's disappointment in himself turned into anger at practically everyone else. He was no sooner on dry land than he learned he was being sued by the owners of the privateer *Eagle* over his seizure of her crew and the vandalism of Rathbun's "Indians." The owners openly accused Jones of an act of piracy, demanding £10,000 in restitution.[63]

While his fellow captains in Philadelphia were preparing their ships for sea or joining Washington's campaign, Jones took a room at a Boston waterfront tavern, where he interrupted his fits of pacing with a prodigious outpouring of letters. Before departing for Nova Scotia, he made a stirring proposal to Robert Morris, calling it "An expedition of Importance." He would take part of the navy's original fleet, sail to the African coast, and strike a blow where the British least expected. His proposal was not answered.

With snow whipping along the Boston docks, Jones needed enemies to fight. He found them in his own navy. His first target was John Manley, number two on the infamous list and Washington's favorite, named commodore of "the General's Fleet" months earlier. Manley, Jones wrote, kept the other captains at "an Awful distance" while haughtily flying a commodore's broad blue pennant atop his frigate, the *Hancock*. Just the sight of this ship, which the British later called "the finest frigate in the world," was enough to send Jones into a jealous pique: with her beautiful lines and an exact replica of the president of Congress as her figurehead, resplendent in yellow breeches, white stirrups, and a blue coat with yellow buttonhooks. Manley, like Nicholas Biddle, was a veteran of the British navy. Unlike Biddle, he made sure everyone knew it. Jones called him "a Stick Officer"—a derisive term for a bosun's mate, which was as far as Manley had ascended in the king's service.

Manley's overbearing attitude had already alienated him from the captain of the other frigate in the harbor, Hector McNeill of the *Boston*. Both being Scots, Jones and McNeill struck up a friendship that would last throughout the war. Like McNeill, Jones believed Manley to be "a Despicable Character" who had no business in their navy. Having endured the snobbery of British officers before the war, Jones was not about to tolerate the same from an American captain. "The Navy is in a wretched Condition," he moaned to Morris.[64]

To complicate Jones's Christmas affairs further, Esek Hopkins got involved, writing from Providence how glad he was to hear that Jones, and thus Hopkins's son Esek (a midshipman under Jones), was safe. Then Hopkins lowered the boom: Jones was losing the *Alfred*. She had been given to Elisha Hinman on the

Captains List, and Jones was back to commanding the sloop *Providence*. In closing, Hopkins mentioned the *Eagle* lawsuit, believing the "great Noise" over it would amount to nothing.

Once again, Hopkins was wrong. And while he pledged to deter the suit from going anywhere, he had not informed the *Eagle's* owners that Jones had seized the men on Hopkins's orders. Jones believed Hopkins was not defending him at all, let alone acknowledging that Jones's deeds as a captain far outshone those of practically everyone above him. He accused Hopkins of "Smoking his pipe at home" while others—Jones in particular—risked their lives at sea.[65]

All of this, of course, reached Hopkins, who rose—or was it lowered?—to the occasion. He sent a dolorous letter to the Marine Committee, reporting that he had received several complaints from Jones's officers and crew (including a letter from the imprisoned Lieutenant Saunders).

The committee saw things differently. Hopkins's attacks on Jones seemed the latest in a long series of lamentations from the commodore. Hopkins was right that lack of manpower, money, and even luck had contributed to his precipitous drop in prestige, but now he was grousing about an officer who did what Hopkins did not do: succeed. To Morris, Jones was "a fine fellow and shou'd be constantly employed," and Hancock agreed. He admired "the spirited conduct of little Jones," perhaps seeing in the Scotsman a maritime version of his diminutive self. "Send him out again," he ordered Morris.[66]

Morris was also impressed with Jones's vision and insight. Here was a pragmatic captain who saw what the navy needed and dreamed of what it could accomplish. The fact that both the ideal officer needed to make the necessary changes and the one required to lead these bold missions were both named John Paul Jones did not matter to Morris. Jones wanted to fight.

Accordingly, Morris sent him a belated Christmas present, a long letter whose contents gave Jones exactly what he wanted to read. Morris acknowledged Jones's deeds ("Congress . . . never doubted that your Active Genius would find usefull employment for the Ships you command") and ideas ("Your letters [are] always entertaining & in many parts useful"). While it was too late to attempt Jones's suggested cruise to Africa, Morris now ordered him to "take the *Alfred*, *Cabot*, *Ham*[*p*]*den* & Sloop *Providence*" and wreak havoc on British islands and shipping from the Virgin Islands to Mexico.

For Jones, this was too good to be true. Unfortunately, thanks to the weather, the British blockade of Rhode Island, the abject conditions of the assigned ships, and Hopkins's obfuscations upon hearing of Jones's mission, it was. After weeks of pleading and arguing with Hopkins, Jones gave up. Determined to make his case for a fit command in person, Jones mounted a horse and rode through snow and mud around the British in New York, arriving in Philadelphia in late March. By then, Biddle was out to sea, Manley and McNeill were trying to man their frigates for a cruise, and James Nicholson was back overseeing the needs of his frigate in Baltimore.[67]

Before Jones reached Philadelphia, Hopkins's own officers filed a formal grievance to Congressman Robert Treat Paine. The *Diamond* debacle was one embarrassment too many. They branded Hopkins as "a man that ridicules religion," who called Congress "a pack of damm'd fools," treated prisoners "in the most inhuman and barbarous manner," became an "effectual obstacle" in getting the frigates manned and, finally, conducted himself "in a very blamable manner" against the *Diamond*. He also cursed.[68]

After composing a similar complaint to the Marine Committee, they sent Marine Lieutenant John Grannis to Philadelphia to personally deliver their damning statements. There were already more than enough congressmen who were tired of Hopkins's excuses and complaints, so there was more than a whiff of politics in what came next. James Nicholson's appointment as top captain was originally a sop to the southern states to placate their justified resentment of the overt New England influence on the navy and its New England–bred commodore. The officers' grievances were exactly what Congress needed to ensure that there was only one number one. Ordered to testify before the Marine Committee, Grannis augmented the accusations of his peers. One sentence sealed Hopkins's fate: sailors "would not join or reenlist in the navy so long as Commodore Hopkins had command in it."[69]

This time not even John Adams rose to defend the old mariner, and Congress suspended Hopkins from his command on March 26. Hancock sent the resolution to him personally, barring him "in any way whatsoever to exercise in Act or Authority or Command over any of the Vessels" of the United States. America's Neptune had lost both crown and trident.

The future of the navy was now in the hands of the commanders on that damned list, along with a barely known Irish American merchant captain languishing in France who would become, in King George's opinion, the most terrorizing Continental Navy captain of them all.[70]

✦ ✦ ✦

CHAPTER FIVE

"HEAVEN HAS SUCCEEDED
OUR ADVENTURES"

The Facts then really are, That an American purchased a Vessel in England, took in Warlike Stores at Dunkirk Armed his Vessel at Sea, & having a Commission from the United States made Two prizes.

—SILAS DEANE[1]

ustavus Conyngham was born in the British Isles, in Ireland like John Barry, but a Protestant like John Paul Jones. While not overly wealthy, the Conynghams were landowners, far better off in both finances and status than either the Barrys or the Pauls. One of Gustavus's cousins was the wife of the lord chancellor of Ireland.

At the time of his birth in 1744, the Conynghams lived in County Donegal in northeast Ireland. He was sixteen when his father took the family to Philadelphia, where a cousin, Redmond, ran a thriving mercantile business with James Nesbitt. Redmond gave Gustavus a seaman's apprenticeship under one Captain Henderson, the firm's top sailor, who made several voyages a year to the West Indies. In Gustavus, Henderson found a quick study, who soon became a top hand and skilled navigator. Henderson was a good example for any aspiring youth, and Gustavus made the most of the years sailing under his supervision.[2]

Henderson's main destination was Antigua, one of the Leeward Islands. The British saw the islands as a chain of sentries guarding the Caribbean Sea. As early as 1671, Sir Charles Walker hoped that the Royal Navy would seize both Antigua and the opportunity it provided. "'Tis as large as Barbados & the best land in the West Indies," he reported. Its two harbors, divided by only a neck of land, put them out of the path of most hurricanes. The navy took Walker's advice.

By the time Gustavus first saw Antigua, its native peoples had been decimated by disease and slavery, replaced in numbers by so many African-born slaves for the island's sugar plantations that the population ratio was ten slaves to every free man. Only the British military presence and a history of hanging runaway slaves prevented a general rebellion.[3]

Some years after the French and Indian War, Redmond Conyngham returned to Ireland. He left his share of the business to his son Daniel, who made his cousin one of the firm's captains. Gustavus was an instant success, and was soon invited to join the Society for the Relief of Poor, Aged & Infirmed Masters of Ships, & their Widows and Children, better known to Philadelphians as the Sea-Captains Club. Their sumptuous dinners at the City Tavern gave him the chance to rub elbows with the Biddles and John Barry, among others.[4]

In 1773, Gustavus married Anne Hockley, daughter of another successful merchant. A miniature portrait of Conyngham shows a slender man of indeterminate height with reddish hair, sad but penetrating eyes, and a thin nose above a small mouth. His uncertain expression seems to ask the painter, "What next?"

During the 1770s Conyngham & Nesbitt grew in both financial success and political activism. After war broke out, the firm made two significant contributions to the cause: selling the brig *Sally* to Congress (renamed *Columbus*) and sending another ship, the brigantine *Charming Peggy*, on a risky mission under Conyngham's command. With orders to return with "powder, salt petre, arms, medecins, and every thing Necessary for War," Conyngham departed Philadelphia in August 1775.[5]

The *Charming Peggy* crossed the Atlantic in just three weeks. Conyngham's first stop was Londonderry in Northern Ireland, a ploy to throw off any suspicions from British authorities about his true mission. After making it clear he was taking on "Irish Spirits" to sell in England, he set sail—for Dunkirk, already legendary for harboring colorful characters.

Lying six miles below Belgium, Dunkirk was named after an abbey built in the coastal dunes, and had withstood Viking raids well before a wall was built around the city. For centuries it had changed hands during European wars, conquered by Dutch, Spanish, English, and French armies until King Charles II sold it to France for £320,000. French privateers made it their bastion under Louis XIV. When the Treaty of Utrecht ended the War of the Spanish Succession, it included a clause forbidding the use of Dunkirk by the enemies of either France or England. The Treaty of Paris, which ended the French and

Indian War, forbade the French government from using the old port in any future wars with England (because of its close proximity). But its reputation for harboring pirates and smugglers kept British naval and political officials stationed there forever wary.[6]

The *Charming Peggy* reached Dunkirk on November 11. She was moored in front of the port's powder magazine, alongside a British transport that had run aground and was now under repair. Conyngham had an obvious problem: how to fill his hold with half barrels of gunpowder with an enemy captain as his next-door neighbor? At nighttime, of course. Yet the British captain was not easily fooled. His suspicions aroused, he met with the British consul, Andrew Frazer, whose protests soon reached the ears of England's ambassador to France: David Murray, Lord Stormont.

Stormont was a rotund, dark-eyed, imposing character, a distant relative of Lord Dunmore. His diplomatic talents were dwarfed by his size and his eternal suspicions that every American ship and shipmaster in France wanted to smuggle munitions and stir up trouble. He knew—he just knew—that France would help the rebels behind his broad back. When Stormont learned of Conyngham and the *Charming Peggy*, he demanded action from the Comte de Vergennes, France's foreign minister. This "vessel purporting to be Irish" was being filled to the gunwales with gunpowder. Stormont wanted it stopped.[7]

On December 3, a cadre of French Admiralty officers ascended the *Charming Peggy*'s gangway, carrying iron pokers. As Conyngham protested their presence, the Frenchmen went below, jabbing their pokers into the bales and barrels: no gunpowder. How Conyngham was tipped off, and unloaded his ship so quickly, one can only guess. Thwarted in Dunkirk, Conyngham decided to try his luck in Holland.

The *Charming Peggy* was sailing through fog in the English Channel when the mist lifted and she was spotted, chased, and taken by a British frigate. Her captain, convinced he had captured a rebel smuggler despite Conyngham's vehement protests and false documents from Londonderry, placed a small prize crew aboard with orders to sail the *Charming Peggy* to Plymouth. Once the ships lost sight of each other, Conyngham and his men successfully subdued the few British sailors aboard and continued north to Holland.[8]

Conyngham soon brought the brigantine into Dutch waters, anchoring off Texel Island, a large island in the Amsterdam roadstead. Amsterdam, like Dunkirk, was a freewheeling port, and like Philadelphia, its bustling waterfront was a mélange of shipyards, taverns, warehouses, and brothels. Conyngham hoped his luck would change here. He wasted no time in filling his hold with gunpowder, weapons, flints, and musket balls—sixteen tons of gunpowder alone.[9]

But his second attempt at getting out to sea brought even more misfortune than the first. One of his crew, an Irishman named Brackinridge who had signed on in Londonderry, jumped ship and went straight to the British consul at the nearby town of Ostend, informing him of the contraband being stored in the *Charming Peggy*. Conyngham and his men were arrested, with a detachment of British marines sent aboard to guard them. As before, Conyngham waited until the opportunity presented itself to overpower his captors, and did so. Conyngham sent the *Charming Peggy* around Texel Island and made for the open sea, but a severe gale forced him to turn into Nieuport Channel. The Americans were safe from the storm, but soon trapped by a British cutter, the *Wells*, on March 16. The Americans abandoned ship, manned their boats, and rowed back to Texel Island.

Conyngham decided to sell the *Charming Peggy* and pay off his crew, only to run afoul of the town burgomaster's chicaneries. While the Americans were ashore, Dutch fishermen looted the ship's stores, stealing the goods unguarded by the British marines. Conyngham had failed. He made his way back to France.[10]

For months, Conyngham languished in France, a captain without a ship from a country not yet recognized. By March 1777, he had been away from home and family for eighteen months. Philadelphians assumed the *Charming Peggy* had been lost at sea and that Conyngham had drowned. He hoped desperately for a second chance.

His deus ex machina was Benjamin Franklin. To the bitter dismay of Lord Stormont, the new American minister had been most graciously received by the court of Louis XVI. If Britain's ambassador had only known what Franklin had in mind—not just for Conyngham, but for Lambert Wickes and other American captains as well—Stormont would have been more than dismayed.[11]

From the second he assented to letting Lambert Wickes capture those ships in French waters, Franklin wanted to unleash America's fighting sail in England's backyard. He was impressed enough to fill in a blank captain's commission, signed by John Hancock, with Conyngham's name, promising his fellow Philadelphian a ship.[12]

Franklin knew full well that seizing British merchantmen in European waters was not only justifiable retribution for the same being done by the British to American ships but also a potential weapon for the Cause. This would send shock waves throughout England, compel the Admiralty to keep more ships on its own side of the Atlantic, force insurance rates to soar, and add to the level of British dissension over the war. It would be as if the Vikings had returned.[13]

The first captain to literally test the waters was Lambert Wickes. After setting Franklin ashore, Wickes learned from French officials in Quiberon that selling his prizes in a French port was against France's treaty with Britain. Nor was there an American Admiralty in France to libel and condemn them. However, Wickes learned that the merchants of Quiberon were more than willing to buy them at a low price while assuming the consequences of the purchase. They were sold at night, while the two ships were still officially "at sea." Once he disposed of them, Wickes sailed the *Reprisal* up the Loire River for refitting. By Christmas Eve he informed Franklin in Paris that he was "ready to sail at half-hour's warning," but the Loire had frozen over, preventing his departure.

In January, the ice began breaking up. Wickes set out on a short cruise in the perpetually stormy Bay of Biscay and the calmer English Channel, where in just three weeks he captured four merchantmen. On February 5 the *Reprisal* fought and bested the British packet *Swallow*, sixteen guns, in a hard-fought battle. The *Reprisal* took a shot to the hull and was leaking badly when Wickes closed in. After ordering "Grappling hooks away!" he led his men over the rails, and in close combat took the packet. With his ship still taking water and most of his men manning prize crews, Wickes sailed back to France, arriving on February 13.[14]

Franklin's plans for Conyngham began taking shape with the arrival in France of William Hodge, a Philadelphia merchant arrived from Martinique "after a long Passage & was near being starved." Franklin, Silas Deane, and Arthur Lee—the third American commissioner—got him fed and sent him to Dunkirk. By this time, there were four Continental captains in France: Wickes, Conyngham, William Johnson of the *Lexington*, and Samuel Nicholson, James's younger brother, fresh from London and, like Conyngham, seeking a ship. Hodge combed the French sea towns, looking to purchase luggers or cutters, small, swift sailing vessels, the favorites of smugglers for their speed and seaworthiness.[15]

He found one, ironically, in Dover, England. The *Peacock* was a lugger known in France as a *chasse-marée*—a "tide chaser." Hodge bought her under an assumed name and turned her over to John Beach, another Irishman by birth, believed loyal to the British but in actuality another Philadelphia patriot. His official destination as master of the *Peacock* was the Faroe Islands, which lie between Scotland and Iceland. Once Beach cleared Dover, he made straight for Dunkirk, but anchored offshore.[16]

In the dark of night on May 1, a shallop manned by mostly American sailors came alongside the *Peacock*. They immediately began transferring small cannons and swivel guns, followed by ammunition and supplies. While they labored at their tasks, John Beach turned over command of the *Peacock* to Gustavus Conyngham, who made Beach his first officer and renamed her *Surprise*. Then he sailed off in search of mischief.[17]

Philadelphia was free from invasion, thanks to General Washington and his bold army of veterans, volunteers, and sailors. The year 1777 began with the American and British armies huddled at their respective winter quarters. The Continental schooner *Georgia Packet* slipped between the Delaware Capes, her captain informing Robert Morris that they were now clear of enemy ships. Only ice prevented the *Randolph* and *Delaware* from getting to sea.[18]

The *Randolph* was still at Fort Island when Nicholas Biddle had a visitor— his old lieutenant, James Josiah, recently exchanged by the British. Washington had exerted what influence he possessed as rebel commander-in-chief to free him. After months spent toiling in the *Cerberus*, Josiah had been transferred to the prison ship *Whitby* in New York harbor. "Grateful" was not a strong enough word to describe Josiah's feelings after being released.

The lieutenant he was exchanged for had been freed by the Americans ten days before Josiah was discharged from the *Whitby*. When Josiah asked to be put ashore in New Jersey, he was dropped off in Connecticut without a safe-conduct pass, to make his way home as best he could. Before visiting Biddle he called on Morris, who informed him of his rank on the Captains List (number 18—one behind Jones). True, he was the only one on the list not given a command (due to his imprisonment), but the fact that Congress ranked him while he was a captive says much about James Josiah.[19]

After his visitor left, Biddle placed a double guard of marines aboard the *Randolph*. The long wait for the ice to thaw took its toll on the frigate's already small muster rolls. Boredom and ice bred restlessness in the confines of a ship, even the grandest yet built in Philadelphia. If enlisted Americans got the urge to jump ships, what about Biddle's English "volunteers"? After a spate of desertions, he posted a £5 reward for information leading to their arrest, with a £35 bonus if the informant's tips bagged the lot of them. One deserter, "stout built" and "pitted with the small pox," was American-born. The rest, the broadside concluded, "are Irishmen."[20]

The frozen river annoyed Morris as well. A four-month-old letter from Silas Deane sat on his desk, informing Morris that he had arranged for a huge quantity of supplies earmarked for Washington to be shipped from Martinique, including 20,000 uniforms, 200 brass cannon, and 100 tons of gunpowder. "The Delaware continues too full of Ice for Ships to sail," he wrote Hancock, "as Capt. Biddle has now 200 Men on b[oar]d the *Randolph* and is ready to push out at the first opening." Philadelphians have long believed the adage "If you do not like the weather, just wait, it will change." Miraculously, it did—in forty hours. "Our River is now clear of Ice, and I propose pushing out Captain Bidd[le]," Morris informed Congress. "We cannot employ him & the small Vessells better than to send them to Martinico for the Stores mentioned in Mr. D's letter."[21]

After waiting for the ice to break up, Biddle saw this retrieval of supplies by the first American frigate to get to sea as nothing more than a grocer's errand. The *Randolph* was built for a fight, not freight. He went to Philadelphia to ask, convince, and argue with Morris and get his orders changed. When he reached Morris's office he found that the congressman had already had a change of heart—thanks, ironically, to Esek Hopkins, who was still commodore of the fleet. From Baltimore, the Marine Committee had ordered Hopkins to send the *Warren* and *Providence* on a cruise to Virginia and take, burn, sink, or destroy any British ships they encountered. Realizing that such orders were what frigates were built for in the first place, Morris gave Biddle similar instructions, with the warning that he avoid two-deckers like the *Roebuck*.

Before departing, Morris received Biddle's signals in the event new orders needed to be given again: the *Randolph* would be recognized by "a White Jack at the fore top mast and a Pendant over it." Biddle headed back to Fort Island to get his frigate ready for departure. On February 3 one final contingent of British prisoners was delivered to the *Randolph*'s bosun, bringing the number aboard to 240 officers and men.[22]

Biddle had one last task to complete before sailing. The Marine Committee wanted each captain to guarantee that any marine or sailor wanting to make a will before leaving port could do so. No fewer than eight of Biddle's hands had taken lodging at Jane How's boardinghouse on the waterfront. They had been "on the beach" so long they had run out of money and were promising to pay her when the *Randolph* returned. Mrs. How had heard this line before, but whether she was being patriotic or just a savvy businesswoman, she had a solution that would get her paid one way or another. One by one, her boarders were summoned to Biddle's cabin, where he and his officers witnessed each man's signature or mark on their last will and testament, naming Jane How "Friend & Executrix" of their respective estate, large or small—most likely small.[23]

On February 4, the *Randolph* stood down the Delaware accompanied by the *Hornet*, the *Fly*, and several merchantmen under their convoy. Although the weather was clear, the pilot mixed his expertise with a heightened dose of caution—no pilot had ever sent an American frigate down Whorekiln Road before, and he wanted no mishaps.

One can see Philadelphia from Fort Island, but just south of it the river bends to the right and soon even the mastheader loses sight of the city. Biddle was not the kind of man to look back anyway, nor did his line of work allow him to think about the friends and family he was once again leaving behind. The *Randolph* continued southward, Biddle looking ahead.[24]

He left the merchantmen and smaller naval vessels at Reedy Island and took the *Randolph* on a quick shakedown cruise, sailing past the capes and into the open sea. For several days he sent his men up and down the ratlines, running the frigate with all sails set and then trimming her canvas, observing her handling in both light and heavy winds, and how she answered her helm. Without saying so, he was also testing his crew, giving the landsmen their sea legs and beginning their evolution from lubbers to sailors. Patience was at a premium in wartime— what knots and duties they did not learn the first time were subsequently taught by a bosun mate's rope's end. Gunnery practice not only provided training for the crew but also allowed Biddle to see how the *Randolph* handled the shock of a broadside. And he paid particular attention to the British "recruits," not so much regarding their capabilities (almost all were able seamen), but their attitudes. Biddle and his officers remained ever vigilant.[25]

After a few days of sailing back and forth along Cape Henlopen, Biddle believed the *Randolph* "the very Best Vessel for Sailing that ever I knew." His practice sessions were observed not just by the lighthouse keeper and Henry Fisher's pilots. Three Loyalist officers, recent escapees from the Baltimore jail and sheltered by sympathetic Lewes Tories, paid particular attention to the *Randolph*, certain that so beautiful a frigate must be British. They made plans to abscond with a small boat, row out to the frigate, and report for duty. Just before making their getaway they were informed by their Tory friends of the ship's true nationality.[26]

Biddle soon returned to the Delaware to convoy the tobacco ships to the Atlantic. Three days later, as the merchantmen headed out to sea, one captain watched as the *Randolph* changed course—heading not south but north.[27]

Morris had hoped that "Biddle will send us a *Galatea*, a *Pearl*, or a *Camilla*"—
any of the frigates that had bedeviled American shipping. Biddle had the same
idea, but a definite frigate in mind: the *Milford*. She had been as much a thorn in
the navy's side as the aforementioned ships. Before this week, no Continental
vessel stood a chance one-on-one with any British frigate. Now America possessed a ship of equal might, commanded by a captain looking for action.[28]

In heading towards New England, Biddle missed dispatches from Morris—
the Marine Committee had agreed with his original orders sending Biddle to
Martinique. The long-anticipated supplies were too valuable to risk in a merchantman's hold. Morris sent word to Elisha Warner to take the *Fly* and find
Biddle. Poor Warner cruised the waters off the Delaware Bay for two weeks
before giving up and returning the dispatches to Morris.[29]

Biddle meanwhile headed to the waters off Rhode Island, sure that the *Randolph* would pay her first compliment to the *Milford* there. Along the way, the
mastheader spotted a sail too small for a frigate. Biddle gave chase, only to find
her to be a Frenchman. He sent a boarding party under Lieutenant Panatiere de
la Falconiere across the water to inspect her papers. Falconiere returned to the
frigate with a large jug of wine taken from the ship's master. To Biddle's disgust,
Falconiere sold the wine to his shipmates for a dollar a bottle. It was the first
crack in the esprit de corps that Biddle was constantly at pains to maintain. More
cracks were forthcoming as the *Randolph* continued northward.[30]

She did not get far: without warning, her foremast sprang. Held tenuously in
place by stays and shrouds, Biddle had barely enough time to send his topmen
aloft to remove the yards and topmast to keep it from cracking and going over the
side. Once they finished, Biddle ordered the mast stepped back in place. It could
not be done—the base was rotten. Biddle would have to jury-rig a replacement,
using the longest spar available.

Bad luck now sailed with bad workmanship. As a gale pitched the *Randolph*
through high seas, a loud crack was heard from bow to stern, topgallant to
keelson. This time it was the mainmast, the same one that had loomed over Philadelphia at Humphrey's shipyard. Sheared clean through right at the deck, it
now staggered from side to side with each wave, held in place only by the rigging.
To Biddle it was "as unpleasant a sight as ever I wish to behold." The high winds
and waves turned the mainmast into a pile-driver, threatening to sink the *Randolph*.

This time Biddle ordered the carpenter's mates and topmen to cut it free of
the ship. With deliberate swings of hatchets and axes, the carpenters severed line

after line until the mast went over the side. In a split second, the navy's pride and joy was a derelict, now at the mercy of nature and the enemy.

Biddle sent the mastheader to climb the mizzen—the only mast left—and scan the horizon for any sail, while the carpenter's mates made two jury-rigged masts. Biddle and ship's carpenter Richard Fordham inspected the stump of wood that had been the mainmast and found that it was thoroughly rotten. One of the hands, a Philadelphian, told Biddle he knew the frigate's spars and masts had spent eighteen years lying in water at the mast yard—one of the first instances of shoddy supplies and chicanery in the American defense industry.

As the carpenters and other hands removed the stub and finished their makeshift replacements, Biddle went to his cabin. Until proper masts were stepped, the *Randolph* could not fight even a shallop effectively. But where to sail for repairs? The Atlantic was infested with British cruisers from Providence to Newport News, and possibly well south of Virginia as well. He decided to make for Charleston. The only ships Biddle wanted to meet were fellow frigates *Warren* and *Providence*, his orders having mentioned that they would also be cruising those waters. But there was no rendezvous—not because of the ocean's vastness, but because the frigates had never left Newport: Sir Peter Parker's fleet had them bottled up nicely.[31]

As the *Randolph* headed south, Biddle sensed that the British sailors would try to take the ship somehow, someday. His intuition was correct. One clear day several of them gave three cheers near the quarterdeck—a prearranged signal to revolt. But Biddle's officers and marines were ready, and subdued the mutineers in no time.

Biddle did not clap the ringleaders in irons to await a court-martial. Instead, he ordered the marines to stand armed guard over them and put the *Randolph* into the wind. She came to a complete stop. "All hands to witness punishment!" cried First Lieutenant William Barnes, while the bosun's mates took one of the hatch gratings and secured it to the gangway. The crew took their place on deck, with Biddle and his officers on the windward side, the breeze at their back.

At the order "Rig the grating!" the first of the mutineers was stripped of his shirt and trussed up, his bare back exposed for all to see. "Ship's company: off hats!" Barnes bellowed. Seconds later, Biddle read the punishment for mutiny from the Articles of War, which were posted below deck for every man jack to read. One of the bosun's mates approached the grating carrying a red baize bag. Inside it was a cat-o'-nine-tails. As the cat came out of the bag, Barnes said, "Do your duty." The mate shook the nine tails free, their ends tied to bits of cut iron or nails. He took his stance several feet from the grating and brought his arm back waist high. Then he sent the cat forward. It whistled in the air for a half second, then everyone heard the violent slap as the first "stripe" laid open the mutineer's back. The mate brought the cat back in the same motion for the second stripe, the beginning of a slow, unrelenting rhythm.

Unless he had been flogged before, the impact of the cat came as a horrific shock to the mutineer. One victim recalled how it "stung me to the heart, as if a knife had gone through my body . . . the time between each stroke seemed so long to be agonizing, and yet the next came too soon." Another recipient of the lash said the pain in his lungs was far worse than the pain of his flesh being ripped off his back. Many had the wind knocked out of them.[32]

The bosun's mate worked methodically, producing a rhythm interrupted only when he wiped bits of skin off the metal ends of the cat. Twelve lashes were the official limit in the Continental Navy's Articles, but mutiny was afoot, and Biddle paid no mind to the rules this day. Finally he said, "That's enough," and the man was cut away from the grating, to be replaced by the next mutineer. Once Biddle sensed that the British hands had seen enough to deter them from making another attempt to seize the ship, he dismissed the men.

As the rest of the crew returned somberly to their duty, marines took the mutineers below deck to the surgeon, Thomas Hore, whoses ministrations were nearly as painful as the flogging. After Hore washed their backs in brine and applied salt packs, the marines clapped the mutineers in irons.[33]

Biddle's sailing master, Robert Johnson, got the *Randolph* under way, a daunting task with her two smaller and weak masts. Once turned into the wind, the *Randolph* was "in irons"—lying dead still in the water (sometimes a ship even began sailing backwards). The helmsman had to trim her through the wind skillfully enough to let the sails catch the breeze and propel her forward with enough speed to allow her to resume her course, and then it was on to Charleston.[34]

Luckily, she got there, sailing through high seas all the way and without being spotted by any British warships. But that was the extent of Biddle's luck. While still at sea, a deadly fever swept the ship. Surgeon Hore labored round the clock, fighting to contain the disease while trying to make the sick as comfortable as possible as the frigate rolled over contentious waters. At least fifteen hands perished over two weeks. Neither Biddle nor Hore described the symptoms, but the contagion was likely brought aboard by one of the prisoners, infested with lice from his cell. It was called "jail fever" in Biddle's day. Another name for it is typhus.[35]

On March 10, the *Randolph* was off Sullivan's Island, site of the previous year's American victory and gateway to Charleston harbor and its high sandbar. A storm prevented a pilot from guiding the frigate into port until the following day.

None of the South Carolinians knew the woeful condition of ship and crew as the *Randolph* entered the harbor. Only the experienced eye spotted her makeshift masts until she sailed closer. Most of Charleston was anxious about the city's dwindling defenses, especially Brigadier General William Moultrie of the Continental Army. The troops that had repulsed the British a year earlier were now in North Carolina and Georgia. The *Randolph* might be dismasted and fever-ridden, but that was not what Moultrie and many others saw. In beholding Biddle's damaged frigate "their fears were a little subsided, looking upon her to be a great additional strength to our batteries and protection to the harbor," Moultrie declared.

With everything Biddle had contended with, the levelheaded captain was more relieved than frustrated at sighting Charleston. He informed his brother James that this had been "one of the most disagreeable Passages that ever I experienced." Once in port, he sent his sick men to a hospital and got his ship to the careening posts. There he removed the *Randolph*'s guns and stores, thoroughly cleaned her from stem to stern, burned gunpowder and washed her between decks with vinegar, the eighteenth-century approach to sterilization.[36]

To Biddle, this was all part of his job. Unlike Jones, he did not dwell on his setbacks. Having "been very Healthy Myself," he wrote to his brother James, and happy to have learned in Charleston that their brother Charles had escaped the British in Jamaica, he closed his letter sending love to the family and full of optimism for both a recovered crew and a repaired ship: "I hope soon to be out in Her again."[37]

For all his difficulties, at least Biddle got the *Randolph* to sea. As of the spring of 1777, she was the only frigate to sail.

Just getting a frigate built and launched was a painstakingly slow process. From the creation of the navy through the end of the Revolution, Congress sanctioned the construction of more than three dozen ships. When the thirteen frigates were ordered, it was believed they would all see action in 1776. None of them did.

Such a daunting demand from Congress alone kept shipyards busy during the war years. Once a yard received the detailed draft of the ship's design (as much a work of art as a blueprint), crews of sawyers, carpenters, joiners, caulkers, painters, and chandlers went to work—that is, once the supplies of live oak, hardwood, pine, and fir that were needed to construct the various parts of the ship reached the yard. Each ship required vast amounts of wood, a couple of acres' worth for one frigate alone.[38]

Laying the keel came first. If available, live oak was used for the ship's "skeleton," being long enough, thick enough, and bent enough for a strong frame. Live oak still dominated America's coastline from Virginia to the Gulf of Mexico, but transporting it to the northern shipyards was well nigh impossible during the war. White oak was more frequently used. The frame was supported by "knees," stout L-shaped pieces that connected the beams to the timbers. Then planking the hull began. There were two layers of planking—inner and outer—with inner planking secured fast by treenails, wooden pegs that shrank over time, letting in water and incurring the risk of rot. Once the hull was planked, the decks were added and caulked. Since the funds to sheathe the hull in copper, as the British and French did, were lacking, an acrid-smelling tallow composite used after careening was applied, after which the master carpenters and their apprentices finished the fine work along with any filigreed designs and figureheads. Then the ship was ready for launching. The work took anywhere from months to years to complete.[39]

On May 21, 1776, the frigate *Raleigh* was launched in Portsmouth, New Hampshire, one of the first of the thirteen to have her coming-out party. Thousands of people came to the waterfront, perched precariously on rooftops, overflowing in the nearby streets, and in overcrowded small boats. A frigate's launching was a major entertainment event, and the *Raleigh*'s was no exception.

It was also a dangerous one. The *Raleigh* stood high above the Piscataqua riverfront on her sloping ways—two giant rails of wood, tallowed with wax. The frigate rested on keel blocks. Her masts had not yet been stepped; to add to the festive aura of the day, Captain Thomas Thompson had festooned the gunwales with pennants and flags. Two anchors were sunk in the ground in front of the ship, with the cables run through the hawseholes in the bow. Other cables ran through the capstan, securing her fore and aft.

Some two dozen laborers, brandishing large mallets, were stationed beneath the ways, along the path of the ship's descent into the river. Their task was so dangerous that prisoners were often enlisted and promised freedom if they were successful in hammering out the blocks, as the ship slid towards the water, inches over their heads. All that was needed was high tide, the safest time to send the *Raleigh*'s 697 tons hurtling towards the river. Thompson and his officers came aboard to supervise.

When the tide was about to peak, the signal was given, and the men beneath the ways drove out the blocks, the cables were eased, and the giant frigate descended, picking up speed as she slid down the tallowed ways and into the water, creating giant waves on either side of her that sent small boats in the river bobbing furiously. The multitude of onlookers cheered loudly.

Once the *Raleigh* was securely docked, the festivities began, with a meal presented to the shipyard workers, naval officers, and town dignitaries (as much as fifty dollars had been designated for the *Warren*'s launch in Rhode Island).

Small in numbers compared to those of England and France, the Continental ships were more than equal to the Europeans in design, ingenuity, and craftsmanship. Their seaworthiness was admired by enemy and ally alike. While Joshua Humphreys is still renowned for his talent and vision (thanks in great part to his 1790s "super frigates" like the *Constitution*), there were others, such as Jedidiah Willets and the Hackett brothers, whose innovations were admired across the Atlantic, especially when one of their ships came in view.[40]

Masts, spars, and rigging did not come cheap, but at last they came to Portsmouth. What did not come were guns. In fact, the *Raleigh* got hardly any at all. There were more than enough foundries in the thirteen states, but only Pennsylvania, New Jersey, and Massachusetts had both iron foundries and iron itself. Getting the guns to other states' harbors was a rare accomplishment during the war. Add to this the demand for iron by the army, privateers, state navies, and states themselves for defense, and one can see why the *Raleigh* would go to sea practically unarmed.

The proving of guns also slowed down deliveries. Guns were "proved" by loading them with an extra charge of powder and double shot. American ironworkers were inexperienced in casting cannons, and many of them cracked or burst. Most captains attended a proving session when they could, often refusing guns outright if the one beside it had failed. It was better to wait for a shipment of quality than risk the chance of a gun bursting in battle, frequently maiming its crew. Throughout his career John Barry was fastidious about proving guns, writing one politician that many sailors "were [more] afraid of their own Guns than they are of their Enemies."[41]

The *Raleigh*'s and *Randolph*'s sister frigates were all idle that spring, for various reasons. The *Delaware*, *Effingham*, *Washington*, *Montgomery*, and *Congress* were unfinished; the *Hancock* and *Boston* lacked sailors; the *Warren* and *Providence* were bottled up by British cruisers; and the *Trumbull* and *Virginia* had their own particular issues.

The *Trumbull* had been built in Connecticut without any delays and launched flawlessly. Her captain, Dudley Saltonstall, sailed her to the mouth of the Connecticut River, where it became obvious that everyone from Saltonstall to the Marine Committee had forgotten to check one technicality—her draft. The frigate drew too much water to get over the sandbar at the Connecticut's mouth. That spring, British forces were getting close to where the *Trumbull* lay defenseless, hoping to burn her.

One experienced mariner came up with a solution. He suggested stripping her of everything unnecessary and using "lighters" (large, empty barrels lashed to her hull to add buoyancy) to take her safely over the bar and down to New London, where she could be reunited with her guns, supplies, and the rest of her crew, and sail into the war. The sailor had made many suggestions during the war, as many ignored as heeded. Once again Benedict Arnold's know-how was disregarded, even after he led the counterattack that drove the British away from the *Trumbull*. Saltonstall's frigate would remain trapped by mud and bureaucracy for another two years.[42]

The failure of the *Virginia* to get to sea rested as much with her captain as with the British ships prowling the Virginia Capes. Once James Nicholson returned from Philadelphia after Trenton and Princeton, John Hancock grew adamant about getting the frigate and the navy's top captain into action as soon as possible. Like the other captains, Nicholson lacked sailors, supplies, and guns, but Hancock, seeing the political as well as the military necessity, was determined to get everything needed for the *Virginia*—from the frigates in Philadelphia. He went so far as to order Robert Morris to send the anchors, cables, and rigging for the Philadelphia ships to Baltimore, as Morris could find replacements easier in Philadelphia than Hancock could in Baltimore.

The Marine Committee wanted Nicholson to sail to Martinique for those supplies from France that Biddle could not retrieve. All Nicholson lacked now was the usual: manpower. Bowing to Hancock's pressure, Nicholson decided that, as senior captain of the navy, it was time he exerted some authority, and he began pressing sailors. He grabbed men from the jails, sailors from the Maryland state navy, and anyone else his press gangs found in Baltimore who even remotely looked like a seaman.[43]

In doing so he lost an ally. Maryland's governor, Thomas Johnson, had so admired Nicholson's services to the Maryland Navy while commanding the *Defence* at the war's outset that he lobbied hard for the gallant officer's appointment to the top of the Captains List. But with Nicholson's recent actions "wrong to the Individuals" and "injurious to this town," Johnson now warned Nicholson that he would not be an idle spectator to such depredations.[44]

Nicholson responded immediately. While he would not dispute Johnson's authority, he assured the governor that impressments were practiced every day in Philadelphia, and that he flattered himself of his right to continue the practice. After all, every man jack he pressed was both "a proper person to serve his Country" and "Unmarried." Now the Maryland Council weighed in, demanding that every pressed Marylander be discharged or, if Nicholson refused, that he be dismissed from the navy.[45]

Congress complied, but Nicholson did not—initially. It ordered Nicholson to return the men in question and "not to depart with the frigate until further orders." While he did not hold his breath until he turned blue, he did not discharge his reluctant recruits until May 31, when a justice of the peace (at Congress's behest) ascertained that they were set free.[46]

Nicholson did not forget this affront to his station. Nor did he fail to obey, for the next ten months, Congress's orders "not to depart."

Of the original Continental ships, only the *Cabot* had sailed in early 1777, departing in March with as many men as Joseph Olney, her new commander, could sign. She was accompanied by two armed brigs from the Massachusetts Navy, the *Massachusetts* and the *Tyrannicide*. Once at sea they were sighted and pursued for two days up to Nova Scotia. Convinced that he could not shake the British warship, Olney sent the state's ships southward. Then he jettisoned his guns, his water barrels, his firewood, and his bower anchor in an effort to lighten the *Cabot* enough to shake his pursuer. Finally he ordered the gunwales to be sawed down, all to no avail. The *Cabot* became the first of the original Continental ships to be captured, taken as a prize by the dreaded *Milford*.[47]

News of the *Cabot*'s capture made quite a splash in the London newspapers, the *Chronicle* dutifully reporting that, while the *Cabot* "fell a sacrifice to the *Milford*," the *Massachusetts* and *Tyrannicide* seized two British ships en route to France. The Englishmen, freed as the ships neared their homeland, informed the *Chronicle* that the muskets and cutlasses aboard the two American vessels were French made—just another sign of France's sympathy for the rebels.[48]

It took most of the night of April 30 and a good bit of the morning of May 1 for the carriage and swivel guns Gustavus Conyngham had brought with him for the *Surprise* to be mounted and set in place. The former *Peacock* was not a ship of war, but once Conyngham was satisfied with the placement of the guns, he made all sail, heading for the English Channel and the Low Countries, looking for prizes.

At sunset on May 2 a sail was sighted. She was the *Prince of Orange*, a mail packet on her return run between Harwich (a small port fifty miles northeast of London) and Hellevoetsluis (about eighty miles southwest of Amsterdam). She was larger than the *Surprise*. Rather than run out his new guns, Conyngham turned on his charm (everyone who knew Conyngham said he possessed the Irish "gift of the gab"). He hailed the packet's captain, William Story, and engaged him in a pleasant conversation across the water, asking if he was familiar with these waters, "how the Land bore," and the packet's destination. Story replied in kind, one British master "speaking" to another, while Conyngham continued the badinage, all the while assessing the *Prince*'s fighting capacity.

Convinced that the packet could be outfought, Conyngham sent the *Surprise* ever closer to her, coming up on the *Prince*'s starboard side. Alarmed, Story called for him to sheer off; instead, Conyngham raised the Grand Union and called on Story "to surrender to the Congress of America." Story did. As a boarding party led by John Beach climbed aboard, a passenger—"one of His Majesty's Messengers"—pretended to become violently ill. Beach let him return below deck, where he quickly threw his dispatches overboard. After an attempt by Story's men to overcome the Americans failed, Beach took Story's papers and letters, transferred ten of the British sailors to the *Surprise*, and placed the rest under armed guard.

The next morning the two ships encountered a Dutch *schuyt*, a flat-bottomed fishing boat. In an effort to make it clear that he was no pirate, Conyngham placed all of his prisoners aboard the Dutch craft, ascertaining that all of their clothing, jewelry, and other belongings were given to them. As they made sail, Conyngham paid them another nautical courtesy, firing a salute from the *Surprise*'s guns. The *Prince of Orange* had little in her hold, but according to the London papers, she was to have carried £50,000 in specie and a large quantity of diamonds that were not shipped, as the packet sailed on a "Jew[ish] Holiday." What she did give Conyngham was an escort: the packet was perfect for fast raids.[49]

On May 3 another prize sailed into Conyngham's lap—the *Joseph*, Captain Robert Kelly, bound for Hamburg, Germany, with her hold full of wine. Conyngham repeated exactly the previous day's events, hailing a Dutch fishing boat bound for Nieuport, putting the *Joseph*'s officers and crew aboard her, and sending them to Holland while he made for Dunkirk with his prizes.

As the three ships approached the harbor they were met by two British ketches—sturdy two-masted vessels that the Royal Navy used for tenders. To Conyngham's amazement, they brazenly collided repeatedly with his three ships, striking them hard and severely damaging their hulls. They were picking a fight, but Conyngham knew this was not the place to respond; he would file his protests once he was ashore, and insist that the British pay for the damages to the *Surprise* and his prizes.

He never got the chance. The subterfuge regarding the acquisition of the *Peacock/Surprise* was no longer secret. The English Channel was not an ocean; news of his seizures became known in England the very next day. The Admiralty wasted no time in sending the warship *Ceres* into the channel to capture Conyngham. In France, the usually bad-tempered Stormont was positively volcanic, raging at Comte Vergennes that the Treaty of Utrecht in 1713 forbade Dunkirk from having anything to do with Conyngham's activities. Stormont wanted him arrested—if not hung outright. Franklin and Deane rose to the captain's defense, but Stormont won the French over: "There are some things too glaring to be winked at," he insisted.

Stormont had won this round. Vergennes had no alternative but to return the prizes (the quick-thinking William Hodge did take Story's documents from Conyngham, and then headed directly to Paris). As a further official sign of French displeasure with their American guests, Conyngham and his crew were thrown in the Dunkirk jail, Vergennes ordered Conyngham's commission seized by French authorties.[50]

The *Surprise*'s cruise had been to sea just a few days. Two small prizes were taken, then returned. No Englishman was killed, and the Americans involved were now behind bars. Any single victory by Biddle, Jones, Barry, Wickes, and others had cost the British government far more than Conyngham's foray. But none of these warriors' deeds yet matched the ramifications of the *Surprise*'s brief cruise. Why? Location.

The unwitting Conyngham did not realize that Dunkirk was the last port in the world to operate from, let alone return to with British prizes, being so curtailed by treaties (in many ways Dunkirk was run as much by the British as the

French). Benjamin Franklin categorized Conyngham's naiveté as "imprudent," while Vergennes simply called it *"stupide."* But it also showed British citizens that their government's claims that the war was being won were not altogether true. One newspaper, the London *Public Advertiser*, said it best, excoriating the Admiralty's Lord Sandwich in the process with a nickname he detested:

> The Capture of the *Orange* Packet is a complete Refutation of what we have been told so often concerning the reduced state of the Americans. They have hitherto kept us in sufficient Play on their *own* Coasts, and now, in their Turn, they even venture to assail *ours*. Old *Twitcher* may blush *for once* at having suffered such an *Insult* so near our very Doors, after such *repeated* but *impudent Boasts* about the Number and Readiness of his Ships. But his Fleets seem to be literally *Fleets of Observation* only.[51]

Fear of another sortie by Conyngham or another American raider also hit England in the pocketbook. Insurance rates for shipping soared. For the first time since King Alfred, British merchants turned to merchantmen of other countries—including the hated French—to ship their goods and avoid the ravages of the American navy and privateers. "For God's sake be carefull of your Packets," one British spy in Paris warned William Eden, head of Britain's intelligence service.[52]

And, while assurances were given to Stormont that such a breach of amity between France and England would never happen again, George III was not fooled. Writing to Lord North that Conyngham was in jail and the American ships were sailing home by orders of the government of Louis XVI, the king saw through the facade. Finding this "proof that the Court of Versailles mean to keep appearances," he wanted North to inform Parliament. "The news deserves a place in the Speech You will make," he decided. The king and his government were suspicious, and nothing fanned the flame of suspicion better than their spies in France.[53]

Great Britain, France, and the United States had spies operating in all three countries. Some, like Nathan Hale and John André, are well-known, mainly because they got caught. William Eden had a vast network of spies and double agents in France, including Edward Bancroft, Franklin's personal secretary, who sent his reports in invisible ink concealed with letters to an imaginary lover. Franklin never suspected. When American ships were seized after departing

France—and many were—it was in no small part thanks to Bancroft or, unintentionally, Franklin for trusting him. The Royal Navy found many a report from the commissioners to Congress to read along with ship's manifests.[54]

By 1777 the American commissioners in Paris were plainly tired of their dispatches being read by the enemy and not Congress. That January they decided to purchase a packet to deliver their mail, just as England did. On the recommendation of Lambert Wickes, they reached out to Samuel Nicholson to find one.

In addition to being James Nicholson's younger brother, Samuel was also a distant relative of Wickes and also another in the long line of successful merchant captains before the rebellion. Business at the war's outset sent Nicholson to London, leaving him, in Wickes's words, "Idle for Want of Employment." He was not actually *that* idle, as he kept a mistress in the city, one Elizabeth Carter of Portland Street. Her neighbors called Nicholson "Mr. Carter," and he did his best to act the part.

Nicholson met with the commissioners in Paris that month. Wickes's high standing with Franklin guaranteed Nicholson's appointment, and the commissioners sent Nicholson to comb the French ports to find a fast ship. If he had no luck in France, he was to go to Dover to possibly (and stealthily) purchase a ship there. He was also to contact Captain Joseph Hynson, another Marylander in England and Wickes's stepbrother. With letters of credit in his bag, Nicholson took the coach for Calais on January 29.[55]

Weighing this mission for his country against his love life, Nicholson tried to satisfy both. After spending at least five minutes in Calais scouting possible sails, he booked passage on the Dover packet. Once there, neither the legendary white cliffs nor any maritime bargains held his attention; after a cursory stroll along the waterfront he boarded the coach for London. Before long "Mr. Carter" was in the arms of Mrs. Carter. With no documented flings by Nicholson in Calais or Dover, he may be proof that not all sailors have a girl in every port.[56]

Eventually, duty won out over rapture, and Nicholson sent a not-so-secret missive to Hynson:

> D[ea]r Joe
> I came to Town 12. O clock last Night, my Business are of
> Such A Nature, wont bare putt[in]g to Paper, Shall Say
> nothing more but expect to see you Immediately, I Shall leave
> Town early on the Morrow Morning, therefore begg You will

not loose A Minute time in Coming here, as I have business of
Importance for you w[hi]ch must be Transacted this day,

     Yr Friend and Country Man
     Sam Nicholson

P.S. I begg my Name or my being in Town may not be known
to any one, to prevent w[hi]ch I shall not Stur Out of the
House this Day, Pray take Coach & come off to
me Imediately.[57]

"Joe" Hynson first encountered the Continental Navy in Nassau, where he
sold some of his cargo to Esek Hopkins to defray expenses in repairing his merchantman while Hopkins was taking New Providence. Described as "a lusty and
black looking Man," Hynson was also labeled by one of Eden's spies as "one of
the most stupid but at the same time conceited fellows living." He certainly
merited the adjective "lusty" in his relationship with young Isabella Cleghorn,
who resided at the same London boardinghouse at Stepney Street, run by Elizabeth Jump.[58]

Hynson had barely entered Mrs. Carter's house when Nicholson announced
that Franklin wanted him to command the new ship. Now all Nicholson and
Hynson had to do was buy it. A mission of such importance demanded secrecy,
and Hynson kept mum about it until he reached Mrs. Jump's. But modesty was
not one of his attributes. He immediately regaled her and Miss Cleghorn with
details of his mission, his country's plans, and his importance. The two ladies
expressed their congratulations; whether they exhibited enough fawning for
Hynson cannot be determined more than two hundred years later.

In any event, they were better actors than Joe Hynson. Once he left their
company, they panicked. Here was a man under their roof, sharing a bed with
one and jeopardizing them both, not by his furtiveness but by virtue of his big
mouth. Deciding that it would be better to inform than to be implicated, they
headed to Downing Street to see John Vardill, the twenty-five-year-old former
assistant rector of New York's Trinity Church.

Vardill had gone to London to be ordained just as war broke out; being a
Loyalist, he elected to stay there. He wrote letters to his contacts in America,
urging them to repent their treasonous ways. Among the addressees were Gouverneur Morris and a young man he once tutored—Washington's stepson, John
Parke Custis.

Promised £200 a year and a chair at Trinity College if he would spy on his fellow Americans in London, Vardill was the perfect man of the cloth to hear Mrs. Jump's confession. Her home was a favorite hostel for American seafarers; Vardill had cultivated this friendship. She poured out her heart about Hynson and her fears that his being under her roof could mean jail, or worse. Vardill allayed her fears and escorted her home.[59]

Once there, Vardill confronted Hynson with a wondrous performance as accuser, "brother" confessor, and dealmaker. Vardill "expostulated with Him & found him disposed to be made of any use that might be expedient." Vardill had played Hynson perfectly; he did not blame his lack of discretion for getting him into trouble. Given the choice between prison or the noose for his treason and an ego-inflating job for the king, Hynson jumped sides quicker than he ever changed course, and handed over Nicholson's letter.

The next day, in a meeting conducted in Vardill's coach, Hynson was given his first mission as double agent: he was to accompany Nicholson and purchase a ship, sail her to France, obtain the commissioner's dispatches, inform a British agent in France of his departure, and finally, sail into the waiting arms of a British cruiser. He took his mission so seriously that he actually obeyed Vardill's instructions and kept his mouth shut in Mrs. Jump's house.[60]

Hynson returned to Dover with "Mr. and Mrs. Carter," and found a suitable cutter, the *Rochefort*. Hynson sent Isabella a good-bye letter. She replied, "Tomorrow is Valentine Day. You Are mine. I have chuse you among the rest, the reason is I love you best." She gave it to Vardill to post; he took it to Eden and Lord North instead. The young minister was one step closer to that Trinity chair.

Nicholson had been called to France, so it fell to Hynson to finish the transaction. To make sure he did things properly, Vardill and a lieutenant under Eden's command met him at Mr. Harvey's Ship Tavern on the waterfront with Hynson's final instructions.

No fewer than seven British warships would be waiting in the channel for the *Rochefort*, now called the *Dolphin*. "Hynson will pretend to be a passenger, and will answer his name," their captains were informed. He was to be taken below, his letter bag confiscated, along with the dozens of gunpowder barrels laid in the hold. Once in England, Eden's plan included letting Hynson "escape" to France, and do it all over again with other dispatches and another ship. At Le Havre, a northern French port, Hynson had the dispatches and a crew, with a trap waiting for him in the English Channel. One spy reported he was "at least as eager to betray his Sloop [*sic*] & Dispatches as we were to take them."[61]

With all the machinations and characters in this tale it was ironic that a British king of German descent should be foiled by his German mercenaries—for that is how the plot unraveled. Just before the *Dolphin's* departure, a schooner arrived from Baltimore "with News of the Hessian Misfortune" at Trenton and Princeton. The elated commissioners immediately sent a courier to Le Havre to retrieve their dispatches and postpone Hynson's voyage for another month, to gauge France's reaction to such heartening news.[62]

Over the coming months the British hoped to have more use for Hynson. But while Wickes continued to champion his stepbrother, suspicions grew about him in both Downing Street and Passy. Before long even King George "doubted whether any trust could be reposed in Hynson," and concluded that Deane and Franklin fed him false information. While that was not true, the commissioners grew both wary and weary of Hynson. Deane summed him up best: "It is fortunate he knows nothing, but this will not prevent his pretensions to know everything."[63]

In April 1777 John Paul Jones returned to Boston. He had gone to Philadelphia to right the wrongs cast his way by Esek Hopkins, have his seniority rectified by John Hancock, and wangle a command befitting a man of his accomplishments. But his mission was a failure: Hancock asked Jones to bring his commission with him, promising to move his appointment from August 10 to the correct date of May 10. He also asked Jones to propose suggestions to improving the Continental Navy.

Jones dove headlong into this assignment, producing a detailed vision of a well-run, serviceable navy. It was never acted upon. The day before he left for Boston he went to Hancock to get his corrected commission. It was revised, all right—to October 10, with the number "18" written across it. When Jones demanded the original, Hancock claimed it was mislaid. Jones took justifiable umbrage, which Hancock viewed as petulance. The captain let Morris know he had added Hancock to his enemies list; he was already convinced that Hopkins and other captains "who lately Envied me the Command of a Fleet" would now "Exult when they See me return to the Eastward to command a Single Sloop of War." The Marine Committee sought to assuage Jones's bruised ego, promising him the pick of the ships soon to be purchased in Boston. Jones returned there with no command, his commission befouled, and his future bleak.[64]

It had been a year since the British abandoned Boston, but the city had not recovered from hosting General Gage's army. Redcoats had cut down nearly every tree for firewood; a forlorn stump was all that remained of the beloved Liberty Tree. Once the last British ship stood down the King's Roadstead—called Nantasket after the British departure—Bostonians had returned en masse to find their homes vandalized. Hancock's private wine cellar was empty. British officers and their prostitutes had destroyed houses; fires set along the waterfront had gutted warehouses. The docks that had carried the aroma of spices and fine wood now reeked of mold and rot. Within days the returning townsfolk were plagued by an epidemic of smallpox, another Lobsterback souvenir. With the exception of privateers, the Charles River was idle; few merchantmen ventured out to the capes lest they be pounced on by waiting enemy warships.[65]

Towering over this sad town were the high masts of the frigates *Hancock* and *Boston*, rising 160 feet above the decks. Bostonians were impatient to see the ships stand down Nantasket Road, escort the idle merchantmen, and return with prizes (and the much-needed supplies in their holds). As Captains John Manley and Hector McNeill blamed Congress for the lack of hands and money, the Eastern Navy Board, which reported to the Marine Committee, accused the captains. "There is Blame Somewhere," the Reverend Samuel Cooper opined. In truth, there was blame practically everywhere.[66]

Manley and McNeill were trying everything possible to get their frigates out of Boston. They went heavily into debt to cover wages and supply expenses when the Navy Board had no funds. Sending their ships in harm's way was a shared goal.

What they did not possess was the least bit of respect for each other. Friends? Not a chance. Throughout the war there were constant instances of dislike between the Continental captains. Jones did not like Saltonstall; Barry did not like Samuel Nicholson; no one liked John Hazard, and James Nicholson did not like anybody. But the loathing that Manley and McNeill felt for each other topped them all.

Hector McNeill had been raised in Boston but was living in Quebec when the Revolution started. He went over to the American rebels and fought in the noble but doomed expedition to Quebec, winning plaudits from General Benedict Arnold for his courage. Before the war he had an enviable record as a merchant captain. Like every true Scot, he was a devout Presbyterian.[67]

He also disliked Manley intensely. The enmity between the two captains was obvious to all. "Like the Jews and Samaritans," James Warren told John Adams, Manley and McNeill "will have no intercourse . . . they will not sail together." But sail together they did. After months of proving guns, raising crews, paying for slops and bonuses to sailors out of their own pockets, both men sent their frigates down Nantasket Roadstead on May 21, leading seven privateers assigned to them as a squadron. The frigates dwarfed the smaller privateers as they sailed away to the cheers of a midday crowd. "Farewell, to the sleepy Agents, dishearten'd Tradesmen and distress'd Seamen who frequent the Streets of Boston," McNeill wrote the Marine Committee.[68]

The *Boston* and the other ships picked up speed as the city receded in the distance, the crew following a series of orders McNeill gave from the quarterdeck. "Set topsails," McNeill said in a calm voice. Standing beside him, Lieutenant John Brown relayed the orders through his speaking trumpet for all hands to hear, as they rushed to their duties. At "Topmen lay aloft and loose topsails!" the topmen ascended the ratlines to the second top, then walked along the footropes to the middle of the sails and untied them. "Man the topsail sheets and halyards!" and other sailors grasped the lines controlling the sails. "Throw off the buntlines and ease the clew lines!" and the lines that helped unfurl the sails were loosened. "Sheet home!" and the lines controlling the sail's direction were set to best fill the sail with wind. At "Run away with the topsail halyards!" the sailors manning the lines walked aft, lifting the yards (spars) and making them taut. Square-rigged ships usually left port with just the topsails and jibs set, letting the vessel stand downriver under controlled conditions.[69]

Aboard the *Boston*, McNeill was like a proud papa watching his child take her very first steps. At this moment, all of the headaches, frustrations, and financial stress in getting to sea vanished. Not even Manley's presence on the nearby *Hancock*'s quarterdeck could dampen his mood.

In a nutshell, the squadron's mission was to sweep the New England seas of the British menace. Lord Admiral Howe, with many of his ships in repair, feared that a squadron of this size, at this time, could tip the balance of power in the rebels' favor. He need not have worried. To entice the privateers to obey Manley's signals and orders, Congress had paid their insurance costs. But a privateer's success was based on individual initiative. Sailing alone, one privateer could chase down all the merchantmen encountered until prize crews created a manpower shortage aboard ship, but a fleet of them—plus two large frigates—would send every merchantman sighted scurrying away. The squadron's very existence was based on fighting the Royal Navy, and no privateer went to sea for that reason.

Small wonder, then, that after a stormy night off Cape Ann just two days after leaving Boston, the privateers began deserting the frigates, beginning with the *Sturdy Beggar*—a common name for ships in those days. On May 25, another departed, her crew infested with smallpox. More storms battered the ships. This being the frigates' shakedown cruise, McNeill wrote down every flaw, including how "the gundeck Leak'd so that most of the people were wet below as well as the officers." This storm gave the remaining privateers their chance to go their freebooting ways. "Parted with the fleet all but one and that is the Commodore," Midshipman Benjamin Crowninshield wrote from his dripping wardroom.[70]

The cruise of the Continental Navy's odd couple officially began on May 29 when the frigates captured the *Patty*, a London brig loaded with iron, coal, and duck—part of a fleet of sixteen vessels escorted by the HMS *Mercury* and *Somerset*, the latter a sixty-four-gun ship-of-the-line well-known to Bostonians from the early days of the rebellion. Perhaps the frigates could trail the convoy and pick off some other prizes.[71]

At four a.m. the next morning, the *Boston*'s mastheader saw four large sail to windward. McNeill recognized one as the *Somerset* and the others as three transports under her escort—too big to challenge, in his eyes. Manley thought otherwise, and sent the *Boston* and *Patty* southward as he stood athwart the British ships' course, almost begging for a fight. As the *Somerset* made straight for the *Hancock*, firing her bow chasers in the process, Manley realized his error. British cannonballs splashed harmlessly on either side of the *Hancock* as she, too, headed southward.[72]

With the *Somerset* thus occupied, McNeill set the *Boston* after the transports in an effort to divert the *Somerset* from overtaking the *Hancock*. The ruse worked. Once the *Somerset*'s captain saw the *Boston* closing in on her charges, he tacked and made for McNeill, who took him on a six-hour chase before nightfall put an end to the pursuit. "The *Hancock*'s heels," McNeill recalled, "saved [Manley's] Bacon"—thanks also to McNeill.

His cunning and daring did not go unnoticed by the commodore. "Capt. Manley came and dined with me," McNeill wrote in his journal. "He told me he long'd to kiss me Friday last for my conduct regarding the *Somerset*—a great fav[o]r." Manley's newfound affection did not last long, however.[73]

The two frigates sailed northward, seeking prey that was more valuable than the fishing boats they encountered. They were off the Great Banks between Nova Scotia and Newfoundland when, at dawn on June 7, a more formidable ship was sighted: the *Fox*, a twenty-eight-gun British frigate. Being closer, the *Hancock* exchanged broadsides while McNeill sent his men aloft, making all sail in such haste that one topman, James Taylor, fell to his death. Seconds later, the *Fox* sheered off, desperately trying to escape the two Americans, both of them in hot pursuit, with the *Hancock* in the lead.

By midday the *Boston* was closing in, and fighting between the other two ships had resumed in what McNeill called a "Spitefull Short Action," resulting in damage and casualties to both sides. Once the *Boston* got in range, McNeill unleashed a devastating broadside. Suddenly he took up his speaking trumpet—not to call for surrender but to warn the *Fox*'s captain, Patrick Fatheringham. A burning wad from an American gun was lodged in the *Fox*'s rigging chains; it could easily start a fire if not doused. Whether McNeill did this out of gallantry or in hopes that a potential prize would not burn, he did wait until the fire was extinguished before resuming the fight. Minutes later, Fatheringham struck his colors.

McNeill might have been late to the ball, but he wasted no time claiming the dance, sending Lieutenant Browne to the *Fox* as prize-master. Seeing this, Manley lost any newfound regard for his rescuer from the *Somerset*. He had lost eight men in the fight; McNeill later reported the *Fox* had "Pegg'd [the *Hancock*'s] ribs so well" that Manley had his pumps going afterwards day and night. While McNeill despised Manley's predilections for "titles and honors," his own blatant reach for victory's laurels more than evened the score for hubris.[74]

The battle over, both ships flew English colors to entice the large fishing boats to come out. They did, accompanied by another brig which Manley took for a cartel, to carry his prisoners back to Newfoundland under a flag of truce, to be exchanged for a similar number of captured Yankee tars. June 8 brought squalls and high seas; the change in the weather and the nagging concern that the *Somerset* could tip other British cruisers off about the two frigates prompted McNeill to suggest to Manley that they abandon the North Atlantic and join up with Nicholas Biddle and the *Randolph* in Charleston. At first, Manley agreed, provided that *his* lieutenant assumed command of the *Fox*. For the sake of peace, McNeill agreed.[75]

Over the next two weeks, sighted sails invariably proved to be French or Spanish. Manley also changed his mind and course: he wanted to return to Boston. McNeill disagreed, but followed "as the Jackall does the Lyon, without Grumbling except in my Gizard." His habit of following the *Hancock* instead of sailing alongside her also nettled Manley. After the frigates narrowly missed ramming each other on a foggy night, each captain accused the other of not making the proper signals. Manley snapped. Angered at their near miss, he sarcastically offered to sail behind his junior captain. The *Fox* sailed close enough to the *Hancock* that Manley could make out her bell from his hammock every evening—why couldn't McNeill do the same? By June 29, both captains were befouled: McNeill with a bad leg from a fall and Manley "upon my beam ends," so sick he could "drink neither, Punch, Wine, nor Grog." The three ships continued towards Boston.[76]

Fog so cloaked the ships off Cape Sable, Nova Scotia, that the captains fired rockets to give each other an idea of their whereabouts. The sky was a brilliant blue on July 6, when the *Hancock* took a coal sloop, which Manley decided to tow. Later that day, the *Fox*'s mastheader saw two sails standing straight for them: the frigate *Rainbow*, a forty-four-gun two-decker (similar to the *Roebuck*) and the brig *Victor*, eighteen guns. They were under the command of Commodore Sir George Collier. Surprisingly, their looming presence on the horizon did not deter Manley from continuing to tow the sloop, forcing both the *Boston* and the *Fox* to shorten sail.

At sunrise on July 7 another ship appeared over the horizon, the frigate *Flora*, thirty-two guns, Captain John Brisbane, sailing right for Manley's squadron. Realizing his folly, Manley had the coal ship burned and signaled *Prepare to engage*. All three frigates stood for the *Rainbow*. By this time the *Rainbow* and the *Victor* were only five miles off. One of Collier's men, recently held prisoner in Boston, recognized the *Hancock* by her bright blue and yellow colors, and told his captain that her commander was Commodore Manley. Collier, a proven warrior, never needed an incentive to fight, but here were two good reasons nonetheless. He raised St. George's colors and tacked, making all sail as his gun crews ran to their stations.[77]

The *Boston* and *Flora* were the first to exchange broadsides. As usual, the British gunners were unerringly accurate, their cannonballs passing through the *Boston*'s hull at the waterline. McNeill had to temporarily sheer away to plug the holes. Believing the *Boston* too damaged to sail away, Brisbane headed straight for the *Fox*. At the same time, Manley could see the *Rainbow* closing in. Her high poop deck led Manley to believed she was a ship-of-the-line—a very fast ship-of-the-line—and he decided once again to show his heels. He ordered some men to go below and shift the ship's water barrels forward, hoping that would increase his speed. The *Rainbow* and *Victor* made for the *Hancock*, pursuing her throughout the night.

Manley's first error was continuing to tow that sloop. His second proved to be shifting his water casks forward, for it had the opposite effect, slowing the

Hancock's speed precipitously. By four a.m., shots from the *Rainbow's* bow chasers were just missing the *Hancock's* stern. Four hours later, Collier was close enough to fire a deadly broadside, but first he hailed the rebel frigate: Manley could expect quarter, but only if he surrendered immediately. When Manley made one last try at flight, Collier unleashed a salvo at the *Hancock*. Manley struck his colors, ending the thirty-nine-hour chase.[78]

If everything does happen in threes, Manley's last mistake became obvious when he boarded the *Rainbow* and found she was not a ship-of-the-line but a two-decker, which he might have beaten had he decided to fight earlier and not flee. "Manley seemed much chagrined" at this discovery, Collier reported to the Admiralty, adding that capturing Washington's commodore "will be entirely dispiriting to the Rebels." But Collier waxed poetic over his prize. "The *Hancock* is exceedingly fit in every Respect for His Majesty's Service," he informed Admiral Howe. Congress had intended her to be a terror of the seas, and she would be—as the HMS *Iris*, she would plague American shipping for years.[79]

While the *Rainbow* spent the night overtaking the *Hancock*, the *Flora* pursued the *Fox*, her bow chasers peppering her throughout the chase. Once she came alongside, a short action settled the account in Brisbane's favor. With no ship nipping at the *Boston's* heels, McNeill sailed her away from the action, although he and his crew could hear the sound of the guns into the night.

Casualties aboard the *Boston* had been light: one sailor killed outright while Quartermaster Henry Green suffered a badly wounded leg. Surgeon Joseph Linn did the best he could to save it, but that evening it became obvious it would have to come off. Green was brought to "the cockpit," the surgeon's dark, cramped room located on the lowest deck—the orlop. After Linn gave him a pannikin or two of rum, several of Green's strongest shipmates held him down on Linn's operating table: a raised platform covered by a bloodstained canvas.[80]

There was not enough rum aboard to dull the agony Green went through once Linn made two swift cuts through the leg with his amputation knife, a scimitar-like blade. Immediately he sawed through Green's leg before shock could set in and kill Green on the table. Linn did everything he could to stop the bleeding, dressing the wound with bandages and lint. Green never made it home.[81]

Once McNeill sighted Maine, he sailed the *Boston* up the Sheepscott River. Shortly thereafter, several British ships appeared at the river's mouth, waiting for McNeill to come out. Hearing of his arrival, the *Raleigh's* captain, Thomas

Thompson, sent a letter overland to him. Thompson had two reasons to write: one, to congratulate McNeill on his safe arrival and two, to ask if McNeill could spare any hands for the *Raleigh*. [82]

Reading this, McNeill thought of his own situation. Because of the *Fox*, he had sixty fewer hands than when he had departed Boston, and now scurvy plagued his crew. He continued reading Thompson's letter. "Mrs. McNeal & family is well," Thompson reported, and one more thing: "Jones is here[,] Commands the Ship *Ranger*."

CHAPTER SIX

"THE GANG OF PYRATES"

Nothing can be more humiliating to those once Proud Lords of the Ocean than the Insults they receive on their own Coasts from those they so lately despised.

—SILAS DEANE TO ROBERT MORRIS[1]

I t was not a perfect day for a wedding.

Three days earlier—July 4, 1777—the weather had been wondrous in Philadelphia. The first anniversary of American independence was celebrated from sunrise to sunset, with a parade of armed ships and row galleys, decorated with flags and streamers and firing a thirteen-gun salute. Afterwards, a lavish meal was spread for congressmen and military officials, while the citizenry feasted on barbecued foods and ices provided by street vendors. The revelries concluded at nightfall, as bells pealed from every church tower, houses were illuminated, and a grand display of fireworks enthralled everyone.[2]

On July 7, wedding guests entered Christ Church under threatening skies. The church's spire had been struck by lightning in June; as the guests arrived, the roofers and carpenters stopped hammering and sawing long enough to allow for a peaceful ceremony. William White, not yet a bishop and well-known for his patriotic sympathies, took his place at the altar beside the famous "Wine Glass Pulpit."

The bride—the beautiful Sarah Austin, just twenty-three—wore a colorful dress and was escorted down the aisle by her older brother William. He managed the family business, the Arch Street Ferry, which stretched between the Philadelphia and Camden, New Jersey, waterfronts. The family owned a nearby mansion and two blocks of houses and shops, as well as their own pew at the church. Their younger brother, Isaac, a watchmaker, had fought at Trenton and Princeton. But William was a king's man. Sarah was part of a sewing circle at Gloria Dei Church that included seamstress and upholsterer Betsy Ross. They made flags for the Continental Army and Navy.

The bridegroom stood at the altar, resplendent in his Continental Navy uniform of blue and red. The charming Sarah had been one of the most pursued girls in Philadelphia. In minutes she would become Mrs. John Barry.[3]

The lot of a sailor's lady has always been marked by excessive absences of her man with far too little time at home between voyages. John Barry's first wife died while he was at sea; in six years of marriage they were together only six months. While husbands were away, wives kept the house, raised the children single-handedly, and managed a most frugal budget. Fail to do that, and a mariner often returned to find his family in debtors' prison.

Many naval officers were already married, like Hector McNeill; some, like Esek Hopkins, were older husbands with sons serving under them. But many more were single. Being in their twenties and thirties, they often pursued relationships while ashore.

Independence Day 1777 found another naval officer in love. During the *Randolph*'s layover in Charleston, South Carolina, Nicholas Biddle had been introduced to Richard Baker, an army officer and scion of an old southern family whose plantation, Archdale Hall, lay up the Ashley River. Like most of Charleston society, Baker's invalid father wanted to meet the *Randolph*'s heroic captain, and Biddle happily obliged. He, Baker, and a few of Biddle's sailors took the *Randolph*'s barge upriver.

Archdale Hall was the epitome of the southern plantation, spacious and grand; live oaks shaded the gravel path that led from the dock to the mansion. There, among the fishponds and beautiful gardens, Nicholas was introduced to Richard's eighteen-year-old sister, Elizabeth.

Biddle had enjoyed romantic flings in Philadelphia, London, Providence, and New London, but now he was smitten. He began escorting Elizabeth to dinners, balls, and Charleston's grand celebration of the Fourth. The young captain showed her his latest addition to the *Randolph*—a lightning rod atop her mainmast. That evening the couple attended a dinner hosted by John Rutledge, president and commander-in-chief of South Carolina. A fine meal was followed by thirteen toasts, which Biddle, a teetotaler, observed with water, as thirteen guns outside the mansion fired salutes. The final toast was the nearest to Biddle's heart: "The American Army and Navy—may they be victorious and invincible." Then Biddle took Elizabeth home.[4]

Earlier that year, Lieutenant William Grinnell had written his old shipmate John Paul Jones from Providence. Having recently ended his bachelor days, he sent word to Jones of his good fortune, along with a newlywed's advice that a bachelor "might think [it] strange" to be taking a wife in these hard times. "I assure you it is a Grand Choyce," he continued, adding that Mrs. Grinnell "will Give you Letters to Some Ladys that She is Sartain will be very aGreable to you and them."[5]

Mrs. Grinnell's earnest offer to act as matchmaker for Jones was not necessary. He was as adept at courting women as he was at chasing prizes. Upon his recent return to Boston, he had sought out the companionship of other Scotsmen at St. Andrew's Lodge, other Masons (including Paul Revere) at the Dragon Tavern, and the company of women wherever he found them. The fiery warrior and patriot was quite a ladies' man ashore. In the spring of 1777, he had grown captivated by an ex-slave, Phillis Wheatley.

She was born in West Africa in 1753 and sold into slavery as a child, surviving the transatlantic voyage of the schooner *Phillis*. She was bought on the Boston auction block by Susann Wheatley, whose husband, John, was a well-to-do tailor and merchant. The family named her after the slaver. Within two years she was speaking and reading English as well as any adult and soon mastered Latin as well. By her teens, she was writing poems, and they were soon published, including an elegy for the martyrs of the Boston Massacre. Her growing celebrity was greeted with great skepticism among the "learned" Bostonians: how could such small masterpieces of language spring from the mind of an African slave girl?

Accordingly, a meeting was arranged for the pillars of Boston society—eighteen white men—to meet the teenager. The assemblage included Governor Thomas Hutchinson, Reverend Samuel Mather (son of Cotton), and John Hancock. This inquiry—"inquisition" is a better word—would determine if Wheatley's poems *were* Wheatley's poems. When they finished their grilling, they declared her the true author. Her fame skyrocketed.[6]

Wheatley had already written a paean to Washington; another, "To a Gentleman of the Navy," was penned before she met Jones, who was captivated by both her talent and her presence. Evan Thomas, Jones's biographer, called their relationship "cordial and may have been flirtatious or romantic." Either way, she left enough of a mark on Jones that he wrote poems for her in 1777, enclosing one in a letter to his friend Hector McNeill when Jones was out of town, requesting that he deliver it to "the celebrated Phillis the African favourite." Throughout his career, Jones spent his time ashore torn between getting a command and falling for the lady who most recently had captured his heart. For him, duty always won out, and it did so in Boston.[7]

In May, Congress ordered Jones to Portsmouth, New Hampshire, where he was to board the thirty-two-gun Frenchman *Amphitrite* and share command with her French captain. They were to sail to Charleston and thence to France, where Jones was told the American commissioners would find a French frigate for him. A joyous Jones went to Portsmouth, only to have his hopes dashed yet again: the Frenchman refused to share command of a French warship with an American. Jones returned to Boston.[8]

His spirits were raised when he received word of an American command. On June 14, Congress declared "That the flag of the thirteen United States be thirteen stripes, alternate red and white: that the union be thirteen stars, white in a blue field, representing a new constellation." Then they declared that Jones be appointed to command the *Ranger*, sail her to France, and assume command of that much-promised frigate, with the *Ranger* to serve as consort. The slings and arrows of Hopkins and Hancock were set aside, if not forgotten, and Jones happily returned to Portsmouth.[9]

The sloop-of-war that Jones was to command was actually a square-rigged vessel, launched in 1776. She was 97 feet long with a 29-foot beam, displacing 308 tons. To Jones's dismay he found her "Scarcely half-Rigged" and well behind schedule. The *Ranger* had black topsides and a broad yellow stripe, her figurehead a tribute to Rogers's Rangers of the French and Indian War. With her sharp bow and rakish lines, even a farmboy could tell she was built for speed.[10]

Jones plunged into both his work and the social life at Portsmouth. He immediately printed a broadside to recruit hands, promising an advance of forty dollars to able seamen and half of that to any adventure-minded landsman. For four long months he begged for both guns and experienced gunners, arguing with John Langdon, the ship's builder and Congress's agent, over everything from mast placement to a bosun's whistle, all the while sending the Marine Committee detailed complaints of his difficulties. He also returned to his favorite grievance, reminding Robert Morris of his place on the Captains List while eliciting the congressman's support in purchasing property in Virginia. He designed his own coat of arms, and joined his friend Hector McNeill in flirting with the ladies while McNeill was in town with the *Boston*. In many ways Boston and Portsmouth were no different to Jones, with one exception—in Portsmouth he had a ship to sail to France, and the promise of a frigate for him. Even Jones's own demons could not deter him now.[11]

Unbeknownst to John Paul Jones—or anyone else in America—the naval war was being taken to George III's backyard, and by the Continental Navy, to boot.

Gustavus Conyngham and his men were still languishing in the Dunkirk jail in May 1777 when Lambert Wickes embarked on the navy's most ambitious cruise yet, and with the smallest of ships for a squadron. For months, Wickes had adroitly delayed French government orders to leave France—orders meant to assuage the ever-offended Lord Stormont. He had the approval of Franklin and Deane to do something big, but he needed more than just the *Reprisal* to do it. The *Dolphin* was now in Samuel Nicholson's hands, but Wickes wanted one more ship for company.[12]

That problem was solved on April 9, when the *Lexington* arrived in Bordeaux, bringing three prizes into port. As a bonus, Captain Henry Johnson immediately boarded a coach to Paris, taking with him not only the latest dispatches from Congress but also the blank Continental commissions and letters of marque that Deane craved so desperately.

The first suggested destination for Wickes and company was the Baltic Sea, which Wickes politely dismissed as too risky: none of his officers knew those waters, and it would be fairly easy to get trapped there. The second suggestion was the Guinea coast, which, while a safer bet, required more water and supplies than the small ships could carry. But the third idea was the charm: a cruise into the Irish Sea.[13]

Refitting was carried out at l'Orient, the French naval base on the Bay of Biscay in Brittany. Originally known as Port-Louis, it was well fortified and had been the home base of the French East India Company since the 1600s. Yet before the ships were ready, Wickes's sailors mutinied. They had served with him since he took command of the *Reprisal* and sailed from Philadelphia the year before, and fought the British at Turtle Gut Inlet, Martinique, and in European waters—all without pay. Wickes did succeed in getting his men some back pay just as word reached them of Conyngham's cruise with the *Surprise*, and his being thrown in jail for his efforts.[14]

With orders to report any prize taken as "An American Vessel" to minimize diplomatic problems between France and England, the little squadron departed on May 28. Their crews consisted of Americans, Frenchmen, Spaniards, Irishmen, and Scots. After two years of the mighty Royal Navy's preying on American merchantmen in American waters, three diminutive Continental vessels set off to turn the tables.[15]

Wickes intended to clear the Bay of Biscay and make straight for the Irish Sea, but the northwest winds slowed the ships' progress. Two days later they were forty leagues west of Belle Isle, where they were spotted by the HMS *Burford*, seventy-four guns, Captain George Bowyer. He took up the chase but was easily outdistanced by the Americans. Bowyer never got within range for his guns, but was able to provide descriptions of the *Reprisal* ("Her Stern painted Black & Yellow") and the *Lexington* ("Square Tuck is painted Yellow . . . Black Sides and yellow Moldings"). While he neglected to mention the *Dolphin's* green stern and black top, Bowyer mentioned how all three ships carried new sails, set among the older ones.

For the next two days the ships encountered the harsh winds and high seas the Bay of Biscay has been forever famous for. The *Reprisal* and *Lexington* weathered the storms well, but the *Dolphin* did not. The storms did show, however, that Sam Nicholson, for all his peccadilloes, was a true mariner. During one gale the *Dolphin* sprung her mast, but came through thanks to Nicholson's skillful handling. Although she was a "Foulkestone Cutter"—built by that region's master shipwrights and carpenters, and highly regarded by the Royal Navy— she was useful as a packet, but that was all. "She is only a pick pocket," Wickes reported.[16]

Thwarted by the winds in his attempt to sail north into the Irish Sea, Wickes decided to enter by the opposite direction. He sent the ships northwest into the North Sea, sailing around Ireland's west coast with the game *Dolphin* doing her best to keep up. The ships rounded Cape Clear, the southernmost tip of Ireland, and headed northward, the lookouts ever watchful for signs of British cruisers. They sailed around the island, arriving at the North Channel on June 18, then headed south, with Scotland to port and Ireland to starboard, and the Scottish shipping lanes dead ahead.

Wickes did not know it, but coming from the north was extremely fortuitous. While British warships patrolled the southern entrance of the Irish Sea, there was no significant naval presence in the north. No one had any idea that the Americans were there. On June 19, they were off the Mull of Kintyre, the tip of a Scottish peninsula. Wickes spread his ships across the channel like three trawlers waiting for the schools of fish to come. Flying false colors, the Americans had no problem sidling up to passing merchantmen, taking them completely unaware. Four ships were seized that day.

Over the next week, the Americans captured another fourteen ships: everything from a Scottish smuggler to a brig bound for Norway loaded down with "deals"—valuable planks of pine for shipbuilding. Merchantmen from Jamaica were taken, their holds full of the usual West Indies goods of rum and sugar. Three captured colliers were sent to the bottom within eyesight of Dublin. By the time they reached south Ireland, Wickes barely had enough sailors to sail his original three ships for all the hands needed on his prizes, which he ordered to the first French port they could reach.[17]

One thing Wickes made sure of was that proper care was given to the captured British sailors. Before departing for France he used one of his prizes as a cartel for exchange. Once ashore, the prisoners told the British press "in the warmest terms of the humane treatment they met from the commander of the *Reprisal* and *Lexington*, both of whom endeavoured to make the situation of their prisoners as easy as their unhappy circumstances would permit."[18]

On June 26, the Americans were off the island of Ushant, forty miles west of Brest, one of the main ports in France. Known for its high coasts, Ushant lies at the entrance of the English Channel above the Bay of Biscay and served as a rendezvous point for both the British and the French navies. Just before reaching the island, Wickes's squadron captured their eighteenth prize, the *Friendship*, a snow that he placed under Second Mate Henry Lawrence's command.[19]

A sail came into view as they raised the island. To Wickes it looked to be the fitting end of their cruise: a ship that large, sailing alone, had to be an English East Indiaman. He signaled Johnson and Nicholas to stand for her just as some sailors noticed their prey had changed course and was coming straight for them.

Two hours later, Wickes could see why his prey was so foolhardy—she was the *Burford*, the ship-of-the-line that had originally pursued them on their departure from Nantes. With every sail available raised to speed her pursuit, the *Burford* looked to the Americans like a tower of canvas, touching the clouds as she bore down on them. Wickes may have misjudged her identity, but Captain Bowyer immediately recognized her from a month earlier, despite her now flying British colors. The race was on.[20]

Wickes ordered the four ships to separate, expecting the *Burford* to make straight for the *Reprisal*, the largest of the American ships. He was right. The *Lexington* easily escaped. As for the *Dolphin*, Nicholson watched the *Burford* fly past her without a glance. The courageous moment came from the *Friendship*. Seeing the giant warship running over the lapping water, ever closer to the *Reprisal*, Henry Lawrence changed course, cutting suddenly into the *Burford*'s path in an effort to slow her down. Had his ploy succeeded, Lawrence and his men would have been easily captured; Bowyer later called it "a willing Sacrifice." But he would not be denied the *Reprisal*, and shifted the *Burford* past the *Friendship*, leaving Lawrence's gallantry and the other three rebel ships in the *Burford*'s wake.[21]

Farther and farther the two ships flew, with Bowyer gaining by the hour. Wickes sailed due east, edging towards the coast of France. At four p.m. British bow chasers came into play with several shots slamming into the *Reprisal*'s stern. Wickes ordered his guns overboard so he could pick up speed. As his best sailors manned the sheets and braces, playing with them as subtly as possible to keep the sails full, the gun crews hastily removed the cannons from the breeching rope and tackle that secured them. The men heaved them into the sea, each splash giving the *Reprisal* less weight and more speed—but not enough.[22]

Soon the *Burford* was within musket shot, her forward guns peppering the *Reprisal*. Seeing both the proximity of the enemy and the accuracy of her gunners, Wickes sailed his ship directly before the *Burford*, a master mariner's trick that kept his ship as small a target as possible. From his high poop deck Bowyer saw the rebels heaving barrels, chests over the side—getting rid of anything of weight to speed them along.

It was past eight p.m.; dusk was giving way to darkness. The coast of Brittany beckoned, and there was enough daylight to make out storm clouds approaching. Just then, Wickes struck his British ensign—not to surrender, but to raise his Grand Union on a ship now defenseless, save for the captain's will, and one last act of cunning left in him.

As some Reprisals kept one eye on their labors and another on the mammoth ship on their heels, they heard an odd sound from below—the sawing of wood. Wickes had ordered the carpenter and his mates to saw through several of the ship's beams. This lessened their resistance to the sea, enabling her to sail a knot or two faster, but it also imperiled her: if the coming squall was strong she would break apart and sink within sight of the land she had been racing toward for these twelve hours.[23]

One last time the *Reprisal* shot ahead of the *Burford*. To the great relief of the Americans and Frenchmen aboard, the *Burford* changed course. The ships were already close to shore and the *Burford* had no pilot aboard: the risk of the coming storm and dangerous rocks was not worth the prize. Bowyers saw no choice but "to relinquish the certain prospect" of taking the *Reprisal*.[24]

Wickes nursed his frail ship along the coast until morning, when he met with Nicholson. The *Dolphin* had escaped the *Burford* only to run into an armed snow that chased her for four hours before Nicholson lost her. The two ships put into Saint-Malo in Brittany, twenty miles east of Mt. Saint-Michel. For centuries, Saint-Malo had been a haven for French privateersmen; seeing two American ships made the town's residents forget they were at peace with England. "We are received by [the] Governor and all the Officers of this port with open arms," a jubilant Nicholson wrote Jonathan Williams, Jr., Franklin's grandnephew and America's agent at Nantes. French sailors were blasé at this outpouring of camaraderie, but the American sailors were taken aback by such a welcome. Nicholson and Wickes soon learned that Johnson had safely arrived in Morlaix, eighty miles to the east. Wickes's circumnavigation of Ireland had been a rousing success, having sailed into the British lion's den and returned safely. Further, he had not only twisted the lion's tail, but in the personification of the immense *Burford*, he had escaped the lion itself.[25]

And, while Wickes had captured prizes and put the fear of rebel ships in the hearts and minds of everyone in Great Britain from coastal villagers to insurance brokers to King George himself, where he really succeeded was in tearing down the flimsy curtain of neutrality between France and England, something he and the American commissioners—particularly Franklin—had sought to do in the first place. Wickes left a sea of consternation in his wake. As with Conyngham, insurance rates soared: up 28 percent by year's end, the highest increase since the French and Indian War.[26]

An incensed Lord Weymouth wrote to Lord Stormont in France of their king's great displeasure over France's routine assurances of neutrality while supplying—and now manning—American ships. Desirous as George III was to "maintain the present Harmony subsisting between the two Crowns," France's pledge of neutrality while providing the rebels with shelter, supplies, and quick sales of their prizes was galling. "Scarcely more could be done if there was an avowed Alliance betwixt France and them, and that We were in a state of War with that kingdom," Weymouth concluded.[27]

From Ireland came word that the "Linen Fleet" required convoy out of Dublin. The linen traders were losing money daily, and the great fair at Chester, a staple of their revenue, had been canceled. Lord Sandwich was forced to redirect naval cruisers to protect the Irish coast. British warships now began hovering off French ports. On July 8, Stormont made the king's feelings known to the Comte de Vergennes, coming as close as one diplomat can to calling another a liar without using the word.[28]

The implacable Vergennes replied that nothing was closer to him than the desire to maintain peaceful relations with England. His subsequent actions sought to prove this: he ordered the sequestration of all Continental ships and privateers in all French ports. He lectured the three American commissioners that Wickes's activity "affects the king, my master" and "offends the neutrality which his majesty professes." Franklin and Deane promised that the ships in question would return immediately to America.[29]

King George was pleased; upset as he was over Wickes's exploits, he now believed "the gang of Pyrates will soon be driven off." Stormont remained skeptical, convinced that there was a "Clear Contradiction" in everything Vergennes said and did, certain that the Frenchman was lying.[30]

And Stormont was right.

By the summer of 1777, Vergennes was sure that entering the conflict on America's side was in the best interests of France. But France—that is, Vergennes—needed time to make preparations; thus he continued his crackdown on Americans while letting them do what they and he wanted in the first place, even if it meant getting into hot water with Stormont. On July 23, he wrote secretly to King Louis: France must either abandon America or "aid her courageously and effectively." After all, the British were already certain that France was on America's side, and after Wickes's cruise, Vergennes saw war as not only inevitable but winnable. Lambert Wickes had succeeded even better in the drawing rooms of Paris than in the Irish Sea.

As Wickes, Johnson, and Nicholson sailed from France on their remarkable cruise, Gustavus Conyngham and his men were walking the streets of Dunkirk, just released from jail.

As before, William Hodge was looking for a ship for Conyngham. Before long he had one: a cutter, the *Greyhound*. Cutters were built as much for speed as endurance, and she was no exception: more than 100 tons, 64 feet long with a 23-foot beam. She carried square and fore-and-aft sails, including a great mainsail for her single mast. She was black all over save for her yellow markings.[31]

Hodge went to work getting her guns and supplies while Conyngham, needing more hands than he did for the smaller *Surprise*, sought sailors of any nationality in Dunkirk to ship with him. British spies soon saw him at the local foundry, proving guns.[32]

News that Conyngham and Hodge were in cahoots again reached Stormont with gale-force swiftness, and he added this information to his lengthening list of complaints to Vergennes. The Admiralty also sent word to the cruisers in the channel: the "Dunkirk Pirate" was looking to make a comeback, with the *Greyhound* manned "by a gang of desperadoes." From Dunkirk, British captain Andrew Frazer wrote Lord Weymouth that Conyngham's crew were "about entirely English & Irish outlawed Smugglers" save one from Ipswich, whom Frazer intended to enlist in the king's service as a spy.[33]

The game of duplicity between the Americans and the French, along with the one played between the French and the British, continued on July 3, when Frazer watched Conyngham's guns brought aboard, but stowed in the hold. At the same time, Hodge was assuring the French that "no Depredations shall be committed by his Vessel on the high seas." As a further sign of compliance, Hodge sold the *Surprise*. She was returning to the smuggling business under her new owner, a French widow. But not all went peacefully that week: Conyngham's crew got into a donnybrook with some British tars at a Dunkirk tavern. They resolved to finish it with cutlasses the next morning and met to do so, but Dunkirk gendarmes stopped that brawl.[34]

With the *Greyhound* under so much scrutiny from both English and French officials, it looked impossible to get her and her captain out to sea. The solution was simple—a reprise of the *Surprise*. Hodge gave it an additional wrinkle by selling the *Greyhound* to one Richard Allen, who also received a privateer's commission to command her. Allen renamed her *Pegasus*. The only issue with this deal was that there *was* no Richard Allen. That would be Gustavus Conyngham.[35]

In the meantime, Vergennes sent word to Dunkirk officials that the *Greyhound* was not to sail, as Franklin and Deane were lobbying hard in Paris for exactly the opposite. She would sail, they promised, straight for America, and sent orders to Conyngham to do just that. "The smuggling vessel of Mr. Hodge" left Dunkirk with the evening tide on July 17, escorted out of the harbor by two French ships. Prior to her departure, a French official wrote Vergennes that he found no Frenchmen aboard but, he added, "if in the country, or the coast, or in the dunes during the night any Frenchman has been hidden"—well, "that is impossible for me to anticipate or prevent": music to Vergennes's ears.[36]

Once clear of the harbor, "Richard Allen" came aboard, had the carriage guns mounted, the bulwarks pierced, and the gun rings and bolts secured. Then he headed north, with 66 Frenchmen among his crew of 106, most of the others being veterans of the *Surprise*. The *Greyhound*, he told them, was not the *Pegasus* but the *Revenge*, and their destination was the mouth of the Thames River—the entryway to London. Conyngham was ordered not to attack a British ship, but if he was attacked, then he was "at Liberty" to "Burn—Sink & destroy the Enemy." That was music to *his* ears.[37]

He had learned there were transports of Hessians heading downriver for the North Sea and, from there, to America and Howe's army. Fate intervened in the form of a British frigate. Although armed to the teeth, the *Revenge* was no match for this confrontation. Instead, Conyngham sent the cutter flying, allowing her to show off her speed and excellent sailing capabilities.

For several days, British warships of all sizes sighted, chased, and lost the *Revenge*. They also prevented Conyngham from "a Glorious Opportunity" of capturing a host of German-speaking mercenaries. His next challenge came from his French sailors. The *Revenge* was soon in one of the great shipping lanes of the world, but Conyngham began bypassing British merchantmen, still hoping to play possum until those transports showed up. The French tars complained; they had not signed on to watch easy prey glide by on a daily basis. Soon their disgruntled attitude spread to the American sailors as well. British intelligence was correct: they *were* a gang of desperadoes. Conyngham called his officers into his cabin to discuss options. In reality, he had none—bucking his crew could lead to mutiny, or worse. The next day, Conyngham informed the crew of a change in plans. Since they had been chased by the enemy, they were, therefore, attacked by the enemy. The *Revenge* was about to live up to her name.[38]

Her first prize was a Scottish smuggler loaded with grain; Conyngham had her goods and crew transferred to the *Revenge* before burning her. Next came the merchant brig *Northampton*, loaded down with timber. Conyngham identified himself to the brig's master as "Captain Allen" and his ship as "the *Pegasus*" before turning her over to one of his officers, Benjamin Bailey, with orders to make for Bilbao, a port in northern Spain. Twenty-one sailors made up her prize crew, sixteen of them French. The ships split up, the *Revenge* heading north for more action, the *Northampton* ostensibly for Spain.[39]

She never got there. A change of heart overcame Bailey and some of his men. He decided to head for Lynn, England, and return the *Northampton*, attesting to officials that he was "Enforced, through Necessity" to act in so piratical a fashion, while actually being "Leije Subjects" of King George. Once in British hands,

Bailey turned in his orders from Conyngham. The British now knew the "Dunkirk Pirate" was prowling the waters again, and that Allen and Conyngham were one and the same. As for Bailey's crew, just listening to them speak told the British how many were French.[40]

Unaware of Bailey's betrayal, Conyngham chased two more ships, the *Maria* and the *Patty*, and captured them both. He burned the *Maria*, as she was in ballast. The *Revenge* no sooner overtook the *Patty* than a British warship came over the horizon. Conyngham was not about to let her go; nor could he escape this cruiser with the *Patty* in tow. Instead, he ransomed her for six hundred guineas, placed his prisoners aboard and sent her as a cartel back to England with orders to remit the ransom to the American commissioners in Paris.

After escaping his pursuer, Conyngham sailed up the North Sea, turned east at Scotland, and headed south towards Ireland without sighting a potential prize all that way; Wickes's earlier cruise had been so successful that British merchants refused to send their ships out of harbor. Instead, they were loading their goods into the holds of French and Dutch ships, much to the embarrassment of Parliament and Lord North's government. Conyngham's next prize came on August 4, off northern Ireland: the whaler *Venus*, which he sent across the Atlantic to Martinique.

The *Revenge* headed into Broadhaven Bay in northwestern Ireland so Conyngham could refill his water casks, repair his damaged bowsprit, and drop off the captured whalers. He docked in the small fishing village of Kinehead. The apparent calm among the villagers belied a deep panic: here was the dreaded Conyngham, walking free on their streets. But their fellow Irishman had no intention of firing on the town or mistreating its residents. Instead, he paid their price for supplies and kept his men from committing any untoward acts. Then he set sail for America. Orders were orders, after all.[41]

Once in the Atlantic, the *Revenge* was buffeted by a terrific gale, damaging her rigging and masthead. Conyngham took his bearings: the ship was injured, her bottom was foul, and supplies were low. He decided to make for Spain instead. Just before entering the port of El Ferrol, the *Revenge* took the British brig *Black Prince* and sent her on ahead. The next day, as the *Revenge* approached land, she was met by another British warship. Conyngham sent his cutter towards El Ferrol as fast as she could sail, the enemy right on his heels. The British captain fired several shots at the mouth of the harbor and then sheered off, lest he—and not Conyngham, for a change—create an international incident.[42]

Conyngham soon learned that his reputation as well as his prizes had preceded him into El Ferrol. The Spanish government was neutral regarding the Revolution; and unlike France, Spain meant it. But on this day, the Spaniards of El Ferrol were not so inclined. Their celebration at Conyngham's arrival was led by the provincial governor, Don Felix O'Neille. One British observer wrote Lord Weymouth that Conyngham not only received "the kindest reception" but was allowed to purchase any supplies—except "warlike stores" within El Ferrol or the nearby port of La Coruña.[43]

But supplies were not the reason Conyngham paid his first visit to La Coruña. He went to claim a deserter, James Macgrath, an Irishman who had jumped ship in El Ferrol and sought the protection in La Coruña of Herman Katencamp, the British consul there. Conyngham confronted Katencamp with papers from O'Neille's office; as Macgrath had signed articles in Dunkirk to sail with Conyngham, Katencamp's offer of sanctuary to Macgrath was in violation of Spain's neutrality. Katencamp watched Spanish soldiers escort Macgrath to jail. The next day, Conyngham had Macgrath released, another example of his willingness to take the high road in diplomatic situations.[44]

For the next four months, O'Neille did what he could to assist Conyngham in refitting the *Revenge* and arranging the sale of the American's prizes. Conyngham still had to deal with keeping his crew, whose enlistments were coming to an end.

The political storm clouds that broke after Wickes's cruise were nothing compared to the maelstrom in both England and France created by Conyngham's recent adventures. Seeing Stormont even more apoplectic than usual, Vergennes realized that his mild platitudes would not be enough this time. A scapegoat was required—preferably American. With Conyngham in another country, Vergennes seized the perfect sacrificial lamb. On August 11, William Hodge was arrested and sent to the Bastille.

So many more English merchants joined their colleagues already shipping their goods in the "neutral bottoms" of French, Dutch, and now Spanish vessels that Arthur Lee happily wrote Sam Adams that this alone "will prevent [England] from continuing the war." In just two months, Gustavus Conyngham, in his 64-foot ship, had become the most feared man among Englishmen—and the most hated, because he wounded their pride.

While the small ships *Reprisal*, *Lexington*, *Dolphin*, and *Revenge* sent the mighty British Empire into fits of temper and hand-wringing, their larger sister ships, the Continental frigates, did little of note during the summer of '77.

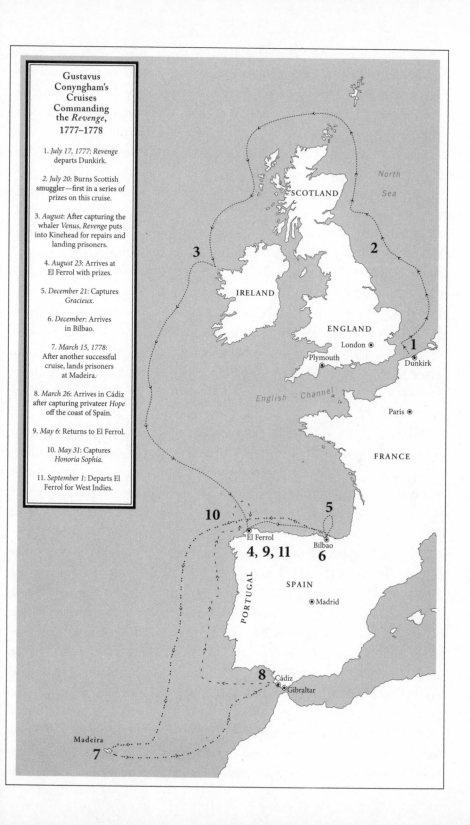

Gustavus Conyngham's Cruises Commanding the *Revenge*, 1777–1778

1. *July 17, 1777*: *Revenge* departs Dunkirk.

2. *July 20*: Burns Scottish smuggler—first in a series of prizes on this cruise.

3. *August*: After capturing the whaler *Venus*, *Revenge* puts into Kinehead for repairs and landing prisoners.

4. *August 23*: Arrives at El Ferrol with prizes.

5. *December 21*: Captures *Gracieux*.

6. *December*: Arrives in Bilbao.

7. *March 15, 1778*: After another successful cruise, lands prisoners at Madeira.

8. *March 26*: Arrives in Cádiz after capturing privateer *Hope* off the coast of Spain.

9. *May 6*: Returns to El Ferrol.

10. *May 31*: Captures *Honoria Sophia*.

11. *September 1*: Departs El Ferrol for West Indies.

As summer ended, the *Boston* had returned to her home port, where Captain Hector McNeill found himself under a darkening cloud of suspicion similar to the one that hung over Abraham Whipple after the *Gaspee* affair. Most Bostonians blamed McNeill for the capture of John Manley, the *Hancock*, and her crew—Manley might have been unpopular with his fellow captains, but he was a hero in New England. "I find my Self included in a chain of difficultys by [Manley's] blunders & misconduct," McNeill wrote to the Marine Committee in August. Weeks later, he requested a court of inquiry to review his role in the *Hancock*'s loss.[45]

In Baltimore, James Nicholson had smoothed (somewhat) his ruffled feathers after his failed attempt to impress Maryland sailors had sullied the captain's reputation with politician and mariner alike. In truth, Nicholson had so many hands to man the idle *Virginia* that shorthanded captains sarcastically asked to borrow them. He interrupted his demands for more men and money to do something rare, for him. Under brilliant blue skies, with fresh breezes filling his sails, Nicholson sailed his frigate out of Baltimore and down the Patuxent, accompanied by two galleys and a brig. By July 4 they were in the York River, just miles from the Virginia Capes, and entering at long last the war the frigate had been built for.

Nicholson never made it. Blocking the Chesapeake was the HMS *Thames*, a frigate commanded by Tyringham Howe, hero of the *Glasgow*. He watched the *Virginia* and company reach the mouth of the York, while the *Thames* still rocked at anchor. The skies darkened; Howe waited to see if the American captain would enter the bay and fire a gun to leeward, the time-honored challenge for a sea fight.

Instead, Nicholson dawdled at the river's mouth for one day, then another. At dawn on the sixth day, Howe sailed through the mist and found a few schooners, but no frigate remaining to accept his challenge: "Suppos'd Her to have gone up the River," he noted in his log. Nicholson had departed for Baltimore. He may not have intended to fight, but one of the galley captains, John David, did: "If Captain Nicholson gives me as many hands as I want I will go and attack the frigate," he wrote Governor Johnson. Nicholson returned to Baltimore, resumed asking for more men and money, and soon had a new nickname: "the Commodore snug in the harbor."[46]

In Philadelphia, no fewer than three frigates were in the Delaware. All were launched in 1776, but only one, the *Delaware*, was finished. The *Raleigh* and the *Washington* still lacked cordage and guns. Their captains, John Barry and Thomas

Read, were kept busy presiding over one court-martial after another, including one trying some lieutenants who refused to report to duty until their grievances (mostly over lack of pay) were addressed. They were all found guilty and ordered to be dismissed from the service. Once the verdict was read, Barry and Read convinced the lieutenants that an apology would reinstate them. Most did so.[47]

On July 31, the Navy Board of the Eastern District ordered the two captains to conduct a scavenger hunt along the waterfront for all available rigging and canvas. Everyone in Philadelphia correctly assumed the Howe brothers were coming—they just did not know when.[48]

Word reached Congress that General Howe's forces had combined with Admiral Howe's fleet in New York and were heading south. Originally, Howe was to join forces with General Burgoyne's army in New York for an offensive to cut New England off from the other states, but Howe wanted Philadelphia. On July 22, Henry Fisher's couriers galloped to Philadelphia, alerting Congress that Howe's fleet—267 ships in all—was off the Delaware Capes. Then, in a blink, they were gone, not to be seen again until August 22 after sailing up the Chesapeake to the Head of Elk, where General Howe's army disembarked and marched into Chester County, Philadelphia's back door. As before, the brothers Howe promised a pardon to any Continental soldiers and sailors who voluntarily surrendered.[49]

In an attempt to steel patriotic resolve and cow Philadelphia Loyalists, Washington marched his army through the city streets, his men jauntily wearing sprigs of evergreen in their hats. They headed south to meet Howe's army at Brandywine Creek on September 11. It was another resounding defeat for the Americans. After the battle, Washington sent his young aide Colonel Alexander Hamilton galloping back to Philadelphia with a note to John Hancock: Congress should leave the city. "Chased like a covey of partridges," as John Adams put it, congressmen fled Philadelphia for Trenton, rode from there to Lancaster, Pennsylvania, and from there to nearby York. This time no sailors marched with the army—they were now charged with defending the city from an attack by Admiral Howe on the Delaware. News of his brother's victory reached the British fleet by a message written on a beaten drumhead by the army's chief engineer, Captain John Montresor, who sent it to Andrew Snape Hamond aboard the *Roebuck*.[50]

As senior navy captain in Philadelphia, Barry was a visible choice to command the combined Continental and Pennsylvania navy forces. Instead, the task was given to his old "Sea Captains' Club" colleague John Hazelwood, who was already leading the Pennsylvania Navy. To their anger and dismay, Barry and Read were not ordered to serve under Hazelwood but to go away; since their frigates remained unfinished, they were sent upriver to Bordentown, accompanied by every vessel that could float but not fight, manned by "invalids"—sailors too hurt or too old to be of use. Only the *Delaware*, under Charles Alexander, was sufficiently armed and manned to take part in the coming fight.[51]

The *Effingham* and the *Washington* sailed upriver, leaving panic behind them. The streets were clogged with wagons, carts, and patriotic families, all looking to leave Philadelphia before Howe's Lobsterbacks took it over. On the morning of September 26, General Charles, Lord Cornwallis, marched 3,000 British and Hessian troops into the city, the first wave of nearly 20,000 Redcoats, German mercenaries, sailors, and marines who would occupy the American capital. They paraded past the cheering Loyalists and other residents who did not leave town. The most impressive marchers were the Hessian grenadiers, with their tall, brass-fronted miter caps and drooping mustaches, who took the hands of frightened children and reassured them in their broken English.[52]

In a meeting with city Loyalists led by the Quaker Joseph Galloway, Cornwallis charged Barry's brother-in-law, William Austin, with ensuring that no valuable goods left town via the Arch Street Ferry and organizing a ring of fire-watchers to guard against arson by departing rebels. Cornwallis also sent John Montresor to scout the best sites along the waterfront for battery emplacements to defend the American city against American ships and the guns of "the mud fort," now called Fort Mifflin. Years earlier, Montresor had designed the fort. Now he planned its destruction.[53]

Hazelwood realized that something had to be done. He sent the *Delaware*, the Pennsylvania warship *Montgomery*, and several row galleys to bombard Montresor's sites before they were fully armed and manned, putting Alexander in charge of the attack. Alexander's squadron came within five hundred yards of Dock Street, running out their guns as a longboat took an officer to see Cornwallis. He carried a message from Alexander: any attempts to man defenses or "annoy" any American ships and Alexander would fire on and destroy the city. The blood of women and children, he promised, would be on Cornwallis's hands, not his.[54]

At the south end of town, on Carpenter's Island, Captain Francis Dowman of the Royal Artillery stood by his battery of two 12-pounders and two howitzers. Dowman was downright uneasy—his was one of the last batteries erected by Montresor, and it was completely exposed to fire from rebel ships and the fort.

To add to his anxiety, he had been specifically ordered not to fire unless fired upon. Looking through his spyglass, he watched Alexander's longboat return. Seconds later, the American colors were raised to the top of both ships' main-masts, and the bombardment began.

A British artilleryman did not rise to a captaincy unless he had earned it, and Dowman was about to show that the gold epaulet on his right shoulder was merited. From the first rebel broadside Dowman realized the Americans were well trained at their guns. The rebels "fired many good shots though fortunately they did no harm," he later reported. Round after round came flying at the British defenses Montresor had skillfully placed, the fire returned by Dowman and his comrades. It was the beginning of a prolonged deafening roar that would not end for seven weeks.[55]

The winds now became a factor, forcing Alexander to change course, tacking to port, to starboard, and back again. Seeing that his gunners were accurate but not as effective as they could be, Alexander sent the *Delaware* closer to shore: four hundred yards . . . then three hundred, leaving the other vessels behind and thereby focusing British firepower on his frigate alone. Fool's courage.

When the *Delaware* got close enough, some British gunners switched to grape and canister that struck down officer and sailor alike and cut the frig-ate's rigging to pieces. A round shot from one of the farther batteries—maybe Dowman's—slammed through the ship's caboose (her galley), starting a fire. Just then a nearby British gun burst as the *Delaware*'s bowsprit came close by, starting another fire. With the ship burning and the accuracy of the British guns so deadly at close range, Alexander temporarily lost his bearings. A sudden, loud lurch stopped the *Delaware* cold. She was aground.

A few more rounds from the British batteries convinced Alexander to strike his colors. A British boarding party put out the fire. Upon surrendering, no less than fifty American sailors offered to fight for the British rather than become prisoners, and would later find themselves serving on the *Roebuck*. British artil-lerymen now directed their fire at the *Montgomery* and the row galleys, which soon departed. The city would not be destroyed by the *Delaware* after all.[56]

Farther upriver, the *Effingham* and *Washington* led the other ships towards Bordentown, the echoes of the fighting south of them ringing in their ears. This retreat was maddening; for most of them Philadelphia was home.

To add insult to injury, a rowboat approached the *Effingham* to port, bearing a visitor for Barry. Once in his cabin, the man presented the captain with an offer from Lord Howe himself: twelve thousand guineas and a captain's commission in the Royal Navy if Barry would turn his coat. For a second, the Irishman was dumbfounded. Then he hurled a tirade of insults at Howe's emissary. Having "Spurned the eydee of being a Traitor," Barry sent the messenger back to his rowboat. He never revealed the man's identity.[57]

The day after the *Delaware*'s loss, Lieutenant Colonel Samuel Smith inspected Fort Mifflin to see if the defenses and meager garrison were prepared for the coming fight. They were not, and he appealed to Washington that more men and guns were essential for an adequate defense. The general sent reinforcements along with a French engineer, Major Francis Louis de Fleury, to get the fort ready. It would be the center of the American attempt to hold the Delaware, along with Fort Mercer in nearby Billingsport, New Jersey, the maze of chevaux-de-frise, and the fleet of row galleys under Hazelwood. The Continental ships *Andrew Doria*, *Hornet*, *Wasp*, and *Fly* would be unleashed to fight at the appropriate time.

On September 28, the *Roebuck* led the British fleet upriver for the coming assault. Among the ships was Captain Sir James Wallace's two-decker, the *Experiment*. For two weeks both sides jockeyed for position, as the British ships avoided the chevaux-de-frise, angling for the best spot where their guns could be brought to bear on the forts. Meanwhile, Washington led an attack on Howe's army northwest of Philadelphia, only to be stopped at Germantown.[58]

The battles were fierce, bloody, and continuous. An attack by 1,200 Hessians on Fort Mercer was so convincingly repulsed by the American defenders that General Howe aborted a similar advance on Fort Mifflin. On October 23, during the ferocious fighting between the two navies, the HMS *Augusta*, a sixty-four-gun ship-of-the-line, blew up—the largest ship lost by the Royal Navy in an American war.

The garrison at Fort Mifflin withstood incessant bombardment for weeks; low on ammunition, soldiers bravely ran into the fort's plaza to retrieve British cannonballs and fire them back. Samuel Smith was severely wounded and removed from the fort (he not only survived, but later would command American defenses at Baltimore during the War of 1812, including Fort McHenry). "The Fire of the Enemy will never take the Fort," de Fleury wrote in his journal. But despite all the heroics of American sailor and soldier alike, slowly but surely the tide of battle was turning inexorably towards the British.[59]

On November 15, at a signal from British headquarters, every battery and warship opened fire on Fort Mifflin. Its walls were soon demolished, the barracks burning from hot shot fired by the nearby batteries. The largest bombardment of the war was "a glorious sight" to Captain Dowman. Inside the fort's remains, Private Joseph Plumb Martin described the island as "completely ploughed as a field" by the hundreds of cannonballs. That night, under cover of darkness, the garrison slipped across the river to Fort Mercer. That fort, now totally at the enemy's mercy, was also abandoned.[60]

One domino of the rebel defense fell after another. After the fall of the forts, Hazelwood had no choice but to get what row galleys he could up the Delaware to White Hill and Bordentown. Some made it past the British batteries, but many more did not. But the greatest symbol of American defeat was not the loss of the forts, or the row galleys, or even the city. That dubious honor went to the first ships of the Continental Navy.

Trapped between advancing British warships and the shore batteries, they attempted to follow Hazelwood's vessels upriver on November 21, keeping to the Jersey side of the Delaware. But there were no forts to cover their escape, and soon no wind to speed them to safety. Each captain ordered his crew to gather combustibles and set the ships afire.

As the sailors rowed to shore, each ship slowly began to burn, starting below deck, moving to the waist, then fore and aft to the quarterdeck and fo'c'sle, the fire finally licking the masts. Like in Viking funerals, the ships were consumed by the flames before disappearing into the Delaware, a short sail from where patriotic cheers and cold winter winds had first sent them to sea two years ago.[61]

Three hundred bedraggled sailors and marines slunk into Bordentown, New Jersey, where they found the Navy Board officials, the "invalids" that had brought up the frigates *Effingham* and *Washington*, and the ships that accompanied the frigates. What they did not see was the frigates.

On October 27, after learning from "An intelligent Lad from Philadelphia" that the British were contemplating sending a force upriver to capture the two frigates, General Washington sent orders to the Navy Board to sink them. Francis Hopkinson, as de facto head of the board, was more than willing to comply with Washington's orders, but Captains Barry and Read were not. Already angry at being exiled from their hometown in its hour of greatest need, they insisted that the ships could be adequately defended with the men and guns available; if proven wrong, they would burn the ships before letting them fall into British hands.

Hopkinson took umbrage. These men were questioning Washington's judgment, and therefore, his as well. He was especially angry with Barry, whom Hopkinson deemed beneath him in both rank and class. When the tall Irishman told the little lawyer that only the Marine Committee could order such an action, and that he knew more about the situation "than General Washington and the Navy Board together," Hopkinson became apoplectic with rage. To show Barry his place, he would personally supervise the sinking of the *Effingham*.[62]

Odd as it sounds, sinking the ships made some sense. If they were sunk as the tide came in, they would heel towards the shoreline, and might actually be raised after the British left Philadelphia. Sinking them was a dangerous undertaking, especially for the volunteers who went below, mallets in hand, to drive out the plugs along the keelson. The second they were out, powerful jets of water would shoot up as high as twenty feet through the openings, while the ensuing vortex could suck the sailors under while the ship flooded.[63]

On November 2, Hopkinson climbed up the *Effingham*'s gangway to oversee her sinking. Once he reached the quarterdeck, a seething Barry silently stepped aside. Hopkinson was a brilliant maritime lawyer, but no sailor; nor did he bring a tide table with him that day. As a shocked Read watched from the *Washington*, Hopkinson ordered the plugs hammered out while the tide was going out, not in. The *Effingham* immediately took in water, but began heeling towards the middle of the Delaware so quickly that she looked in danger of "turtling"— turning completely upside down. In one of the more slapstick scenes of the war, Hopkinson—known as one of Philadelphia's finest salon dancers—moved with alacrity to abandon ship, while Barry ordered his men on deck and to their boats as the *Effingham* came to rest on her beam ends. Read later sank the *Washington* at the appropriate time of day.[64]

The rancor between Barry and Hopkinson only worsened after Barry's three attempts to raise the frigate failed. The last one ended in a shouting match between the two. Hopkinson reported the affair to Washington, blaming nature and not his poor judgment for the catastrophe. Barry simply called Hopkinson a liar. Weeks later, the captain received permission from the Marine Committee to visit his wife and in-laws in nearby Reading, but first went to see Washington at Valley Forge. He had a plan that required the general's approval. Hopkinson viewed Barry's departure as "French Leave," and made plans to bring Barry to account for his insubordination.[65]

On November 23, after two years of trying, Hamond became the first Royal Navy captain to dock his ship in Philadelphia since the war began. The brothers Howe were in full possession of the rebel capital, but in abandoning Burgoyne in upstate New York for their Philadelphia campaign, they had lost his army, defeated weeks earlier at Saratoga by Continental forces under General Horatio

Gates (and inspired by Benedict Arnold's heroics). Despite their twin approach of olive branch and cannonball, they had failed to win the peace. Commodore Collier, recently arrived from New England waters, believed the Americans would not admit defeat "during this generation," while a troubled Cornwallis wrote after hearing of Burgoyne's surrender, "God only knows how this business will end." Both Howes soon asked to be relieved of their commands.[66]

In Charleston, Nicholas Biddle busied himself with refitting his ship and leaning on John Rutledge, president and commander-in-chief of South Carolina, to offer any able-bodied seaman a twenty-dollar bonus to sign on the *Randolph*'s muster rolls. Summer was nearly over. More than a few of Biddle's crew had deserted, signing on privateers. Some actually wound up in Nantes, where Sam Nicholson encountered them but "had no place to confine them in." Had he had all of his men, Biddle moaned to Robert Morris, he would be cruising for the enemy.[67]

Biddle was impatient to get sailing. He never met up with the *Warren* and the *Providence*, due to the British blockade of Newport, and plans to join up with the *Hancock* and the *Boston* ended when Manley sailed off to be captured. Once Rutledge approved the bounty, Biddle had enough men to sail. He stood down Rebellion Road in late August, with his third mainmast stepped in place.

The *Randolph* was under way when Biddle spied one of the privateers that had absconded with four of his sailors. He sent his barge across the water to pick the men up, but the privateer sailed blithely by. "Determined to sink him," Biddle fired a warning shot dreadfully close to the ship's bow, stopping her dead in the water. Two of his men were on a prize crew, but the captain gladly relinquished the other pair.

Just then, the skies darkened, the winds blew, and splashes of rain covered the frigate's deck. Lightning and thunder followed. In seconds, the *Randolph* belied the cliché that lightning never strikes twice. It struck three times where the *Randolph* was concerned, splintering the new mainmast despite its lightning rod. Not knowing whether to laugh or cry, Biddle sailed back to Charleston.

While waiting for the latest repair, Biddle's officers requested that he remove the French-born Marine Lieutenant de la Falconiere from the ship, being "Most Effectually hated and despised by every one on Board." Once Biddle learned of his most recent embarrassing act, striking a Continental soldier, his fate was sealed. The *Randolph*'s repairs complete, a pilot took her over the sandbar and then escorted de la Falconiere back to Charleston. The *Randolph* headed south.[68]

By September 3 she was twenty leagues off St. Augustine, Florida, having sailed through three days of storms, and still possessing her new mainmast. At dusk the lookout cried, "Sail ho!"

"Where away?" Biddle replied from the quarterdeck. There were five ships, sailing northward, directly ahead of the *Randolph*. Biddle decided to pursue. He ordered the ship's lights doused, and told his helmsman to steer by the lantern lights of the five ships, which became easier to see the darker it became. Biddle believed they were merchantmen; if he was wrong, then the *Randolph* would have to show her heels.

By dawn the frigate had closed the distance significantly. Peering through his spyglass, Biddle could make out his prey: two ships, two brigs, and one sloop. He ordered his men to battle stations, ran out his guns, raised the Grand Union, and maintained his speedy course. Seeing the *Randolph*'s ensign, two of the vessels began firing at her—pointless at that distance—while the others clapped on more sail. Biddle's friend, tall, reed-thin Marine Captain Samuel Shaw, frequently joked about being too skinny for British shot to hit him. Standing next to Biddle on the quarterdeck, he heard a harsh whistling sound fly past him—it was a cannonball, cutting a mizzen shroud right behind him.

Other shots soon found their mark, but Biddle held his fire. Two jagged splinters struck Midshipman John McPherson in his leg and groin. Biddle sent him below to Surgeon Hore. A squall began blowing; still no order to open fire from Biddle.

Despite his young years, Biddle possessed as much foresight as courage. Believing the ships more valuable as prizes if undamaged, and realizing he would have to yaw to fire at this point in the chase—and perhaps lose all the ships once he changed course—he continued to withhold the order. He wanted to reach the ships as quickly as possible and then take them whole. Once in their midst, he had one of his little 6-pounders fired. The nearest ship struck her colors. Although the sloop got away, he was soon in possession of the other three.[69]

One brig was a Frenchman, captured by the larger British ship. Aware of the efforts to win France over to the American side, Biddle "thought it would be most agreeable to Congress to give her up," so he freed her officers and men, and sent them on their way. The British ships were laden with West Indies goods, including 702 puncheons of rum for the British army. With prize crews taking most of his men off the *Randolph*, Biddle sent his prizes to Charleston.

Few crews in the Revolutionary War were in better humor than these hearties: three days of sailing, three valuable prizes. They were back in Charleston two days later where, to their continued joy, Continental agent John Dorsius immediately prepared the prizes legally for sale, sold them, and converted their prize shares into cash. Their subsequent celebration became the stuff of legend. Decked in the latest finery, the sailors were seen at all hours along the waterfront; newspapers reported them escorting "females ridiculously ornamented with jewelry." One sailor bought a horse and tack, only to prove as an equestrian that he was one hell of a sailor. The authorities found him dead drunk, carrying his new saddle and bridle. Slurring his words, he explained he "had lost his ship" but "saved his rigging."[70]

News of Biddle's swift success spread north, where an elated Congress congratulated him and sent new orders to sail for France. Biddle promised he would "be Ready to execute any Orders you may send," telling Robert Morris: "My Officers have on every Occasion given me the greatest satisfaction."[71]

These weeks ashore gave Biddle time for numerous visits to Archdale Hall, where he resumed his wooing of Elizabeth. By year's end they were engaged. The dashing young captain had much to look forward to.

When Congress voted to approve the Declaration of Independence on July 2, 1776, it passed by a vote of 12 to 0, with one abstention—New York. It had been a year since that vote, and New York City was now in British hands, the inhumane prison ships in the East River keeping thousands of American sailors in squalor.

In nearby Poughkeepsie, work continued on the Continental frigates *Congress* and *Montgomery*. For more than a year, sawyers, carpenters, and other craftsmen labored between the high hills that acted as nature's guardians over their work. Both ships were launched in 1776 (the *Congress* was the last of the original thirteen to slide down the ways). But the high hopes patriotic New Yorkers once held were nonexistent by the fall of '77. The New York Council of Safety bewailed the lack of cannon and supplies. And as for sailors, "it would be utterly impossible to procure seamen enough to man a single galley," they reported.[72]

By summer's end the ships were sent downriver to aid in the defense of Forts Montgomery and Clinton. British forces arrived on October 6. With another Redcoat victory assured, New Yorkers burned both frigates.[73]

The bright promise envisioned by Bostonians as they watched Captains Manley and McNeill sail their frigates down Nantasket Road had also dimmed long before Manley and the *Hancock* were captured, due in part to the rancor the two men shared for each other. McNeill reached Boston in August, and with his frigate in poor condition and Manley in a British prison ship, the only people McNeill could fight with were his own officers.

For weeks, McNeill's side of the story regarding the loss of the *Hancock* was the only one heard. Now his officers turned on him, telling the Navy Board in Boston that had McNeill "followed Manley's orders we might have had not only the *Fox*, but the *Flora* and *Rainbow*." To add to the navy's woes in Boston, James Warren informed John Adams in Philadelphia, "[W]e are destitute . . . Sums of Money are now wanted." By the time Warren's letter reached Adams, Congress was fleeing Philadelphia, "sums of money" for the navy being the last thing on their minds.[74]

Things were just as bleak in Rhode Island, where the frigates *Warren* and *Providence* spent the entire year bottled up in Narragansett Bay. The only Continental ship to elude the British blockade was the sloop *Providence*, under Lieutenant Jonathan Pitcher, in the dead of one late-February night. Her lights doused so as not to be seen and her crew maintaining a deathly silence, the *Providence* glided so close by a British vessel that the Americans could hear the British watch's conversations. Once past the blockade, Pitcher headed north and encountered the *Lucy*, a brig from Cork bound for Quebec. Just as broadsides were exchanged the wind died. The two small ships pounded at each other for two hours, and Pitcher was severely wounded. The battle ended when the *Providence*'s gunners shot down the *Lucy*'s mainmast.

The *Providence*'s marine lieutenant was John Trevett of the *Andrew Doria*. Sent across the water to accept the brig's surrender, Trevett came aboard to a blood-soaked deck so crowded with enemy wounded "you could scarcely find room for your foot." Their cries gave away their nationality: "Some of them are Irish as they cried out 'for Jesus sake,'" begging Trevett to spare their lives. The *Providence* sailed to New Bedford, Massachusetts, where the brave Pitcher turned over command to another of Esek Hopkins's officers, John Peck Rathbun.[75]

The sloop's new captain quickly resupplied the ship as she was being refitted. Shorthanded, Rathbun sent Trevett to visit the waterfront taverns and brothels to press any non-volunteers. Then he was off, soon prowling the waters off New York and northern New Jersey. The *Providence* was off Sandy Hook when four British sails were sighted: one ship, one brig, one schooner, and one sloop. Rathbun made for the ship, the *Mary*, flying her Pendant Jack and British ensign at the mizzen peak. The other three ships were close by to windward of the coming action.

Like Jones, Rathbun found the *Providence* a fast sailer; he was soon on top of the *Mary* and gave her a broadside, hoping for a quick prize. Instead, he got a fight. The *Mary* returned fire with a terrible accuracy: shot slammed into the *Providence*'s starboard quarter, where the sweeps (the long oars used to row the sloop when becalmed) were stored behind the bulwarks. Another round from the ship sliced through the *Providence*'s rigging. Three sailors were wounded; the sloop's sailing master, George Sinkens, lay dead on deck.[76]

Rathbun kept both his nerve and his wits. He sent the *Providence* ahead of the four ships, but not to escape. He ordered some hands to repair the rigging, a couple of men to get the wounded below, and others to dump Sinkens's body overboard. If his men thought they would continue their flight they were mistaken; once the ship's rigging was repaired enough to sail, Rathbun returned to the fight.

The sun was setting when the fight recommenced. Again Rathbun made straight for the *Mary*, convinced that if he could defeat her the other three would surrender as well. To his dismay, those British ships "played their part so well we gave it up"; only the schooner was captured on this long, hard day. Rathbun had fought in the *Glasgow* battle. If he still had a bad taste in his mouth from it, he cleansed his palate this day.[77]

Before returning to New Bedford, the *Providence* made for the Gulf Stream for a short cruise that included one of the eerier events of the war. The mast-header sighted a ship on the horizon at noon one day, sailing as if the helmsman was asleep or drunk. As the sloop closed in, the Americans could see that she was under full sail, all sheeted home. After midnight, the *Providence* was close enough to fire warning shots to slow her haphazard course: no reply. Rathbun sent over a boarding party with Trevett in command. Under the nighttime stars, they came alongside her stern.

Holding his lantern high, Trevett saw her rudder was gone. He hailed the ship once, then twice, with nary a reply. Upon boarding her they found only one inhabitant, a dog. The captain's cabin was jammed with chests full of ladies' silk gowns, shoes, and accessories, along with men's shirts, "all ruffles in the French style." The hold was in ballast. With no rudder to steer her by, Trevett loaded what goods would fit in the longboat, took the dog, and left the ghost ship. She was put to the torch, burning clear down to the water's edge. Trevett surmised that "she must have got on Cape Hatteras Shoals, and the crew and passengers abandoned her." The ship's secret remained with the dog.[78]

In Portsmouth that summer, Thomas Thompson and John Paul Jones were doing everything possible to get their ships ready to sail. Jones had posted a broadside to recruit sailors for the *Ranger,* and his reputation for captures stood him in good stead. He soon had a strong crew of Massachusetts and New Hampshire men, calling them "the best disposed one in the world."[79]

He was also enjoying Portsmouth social life, taking a room at the home of Sarah Purcell, a sea captain's wife and the niece of Benning Wentworth, the old royal governor of New Hampshire. She introduced Jones to the "right people" in town. He cut a dashing figure in his personally designed, pseudo–Royal Navy uniform of blue and white. He also developed a flirtatious relationship with the daughter of John Wendell, a local merchant whose son, David, entered aboard the *Ranger* as a midshipman.[80]

Jones had also made a new friend, Continental Army major John Gizzard Frazer, who wanted to sail to France with Jones and hoped to bring with him his field beds, two Windsor chairs, one case of Jamaica rum, a backgammon table, and a young girl with whom he was infatuated.

What Jones did not have was a good relationship with local navy power brokers. He did not like John Langdon, the *Ranger*'s builder. He believed Langdon was paying more attention—and providing better matériel—to the privateers in which he had ownership interests. A good captain takes keen interest in his ship under construction, and Jones paid particular attention to the *Ranger*'s completion, something Langdon did not like at all. "He thinks himself my master," Jones carped to John Brown, Robert Morris's able assistant. Langdon was as disdainful of Jones's meddling as John Bradford was in Boston. Bradford's opinion of Jones was shared by Langdon and many a New Englander: "He does not improve on acquaintance."[81]

Langdon got the last move in their stormy association with the appointment of Jones's officers. He and Congressman William Whipple, working in partnership, palmed off two men guaranteed to give Jones fits. First Lieutenant Thomas Simpson, Langdon's brother-in-law, and Second Lieutenant Elijah Hall, although seasoned merchant officers, had not served on a ship of war. Neither was a patch on John Rathbun. Jones had better luck with his marine captain, Mathew Parke, and surgeon Ezra Green; their sense of duty outweighed any misgivings about serving under a non–New Englander.[82]

As a native New Englander, Thomas Thompson had no parochial problems; his challenges were mathematical. The *Raleigh* was pierced for thirty-two guns; Thompson despaired of getting any. By summertime he had just six. The Marine

Committee came up with a novel, if risky, solution, ordering Thompson to sail to France and get his guns there. If he actually made it to France, he was to temper his desperate situation with Yankee parsimony, and not pay top dollar for even one cannon. Congress believed that in addition to courage and leadership, "Frugality is an absolutely necessary [quality] in all men that are connected with the American Revenue." For company, Thompson was given Elijah Hinman and the *Alfred*.

Thompson did not have enough hands to man his frigate until August 22, when the two ships at last sailed down the Piscataqua, leaving Jones and the unfinished *Ranger* behind. They were embarking on one of the more intriguing voyages of the war.[83]

The *Raleigh* and the *Alfred* were three days at sea when they captured a schooner bound for Halifax whose meager stores in the hold did include contraband as yet untaken by the Continental Navy: $4,390 in counterfeit American money. "I shall commit to the flames," Thompson later reported, "after saving a Sample." On September 2 the Americans captured the *Nanny*, a snow from the West Indies; she was part of the Windward Islands fleet, under escort by Commodore William C. Finch of the *Camel*, along with the warships *Druid*, *Weazel*, and *Grasshopper*. Among the captured captain's personal effects were Finch's signals for the fleet. Thompson sent the *Nanny* to Portsmouth. He and Hinman would follow the fleet.[84]

Few ships afloat could match the breathtaking sailing abilities of the *Raleigh*. The *Alfred* could not keep up with her. Thompson described his mood as "vexed" over the *Alfred*'s plodding, unaware that Hinman was equally vexed over Thompson's unwillingness for them to sail together. The *Raleigh* would speed along, her bow slicing through the water, only to slow to a crawl to wait for the *Alfred*. The two ships headed east, the beautiful, fast frigate and the slow, dowdy ex-merchantman, in joint pursuit of a huge fleet, convoyed by four well-armed enemy ships.

On the afternoon of September 3 they found them, sailing through a hard, driving rain: no less than sixty sails, with the nearest escort being the sloop *Druid*, Captain Peter Carteret. Thompson wanted to make a joint attack, but the contrary winds and the *Alfred*'s sluggishness prevented that. With six cannon mounted behind thirty-two gun ports, the *Raleigh* stood into the fleet alone.

Taking the captured signal book, Thompson dispatched a false message to the fleet that the *Raleigh* was just another British frigate, sending her gliding past the unsuspecting merchantmen until she came alongside the *Druid*. Then

Thompson ran up his country's colors, ordered all three of his port guns run out, and hailed Carteret "to Strike to the Honour of the Congresses Colours." Thompson's three port guns fired a broadside as deadly as if they had been a full complement, wounding Carteret in the thigh and killing his sailing master. Lieutenant John Bouchier took command, and immediately signaled for assistance. The *Camel* changed course, fighting the same winds as the *Alfred*, but from the opposite direction.

Had the *Raleigh* been fully armed, the battle would have been over in minutes, but the frigate's firepower was barely equal to the *Druid*'s. Young Bouchier rose to the grim occasion, both in fighting and in sailing. Try as he might, Thompson could not "cross the T" to rake the *Druid*. Bouchier continually edged to leeward, thereby keeping the *Raleigh* on the sloop's bow, firing her guns at the frigate all the while. Thompson ordered his gunners to switch from round shot to grape. For another half hour, under nearly blinding rain, the two ships continued trying to outmaneuver each other while the *Camel* and the other British warships closed in.

Thompson realized this was too much for the *Raleigh* to take on. He sheered off and returned to the *Alfred* while Finch set off to round up his dispersed charges. Bouchier sent his battle-weary men to repair his ship's shredded rigging and man the pumps: the *Druid* took in ten feet of water over the next twenty-four hours. The morning after the battle with the *Raleigh*, Carteret died of his wound. He was one of nine fatalities aboard; the *Druid* had paid a high price for not surrendering to the honor of Congress's flag.[85]

Thompson believed that if the *Alfred* had been able to come up, the Americans could have bagged the whole fleet. For days the two ships nipped at Finch's heels, then gave up and made for France. "O! for another good ship," Thompson wailed in a letter to John Langdon. Hinman was embarrassed that the *Alfred* could not come to the *Raleigh*'s aid in the fight. On their return voyage home, the tables would be reversed.[86]

The *Raleigh* and the *Alfred* entered l'Orient just as other American ships were following Vergennes's orders to leave France. From Saint-Malo, Lambert Wickes wrote Henry Johnson, glad to hear Johnson had "liberty to depart" France, hoping the two of them would be sailing home together along with the still-leaking *Dolphin*. She would soon be another captain's problem: the commissioners had purchased the frigate *Lyon*, renamed her the *Deane*, and turned her over to Sam Nicholson. The *Dolphin* went to Francis Brown.[87]

Wickes was fed up with the French Admiralty, which refused his requests for gunpowder while attempting to confiscate his guns and even his rudder to ensure that he would not attack from a French port. He demanded to know from Franklin et al. whether he was sailing home or not. He was, and continued overseeing repairs to the *Reprisal*, including replacement of his sawed-through beams.[88]

Logistics prevented the *Lexington* from joining him. Before raising sail to depart Saint-Malo on September 14, Wickes sent Johnson one last letter, telling him the *Reprisal* would swing by Morlaix before heading out to the open sea. If fate did not permit them to sail together, then he hoped to meet Johnson in Portsmouth, where "I hope to have the Pleasure of Seeing you If not Sooner."[89]

His letter finished, Wickes dropped some candle wax on the letter's fold and turned it over for delivery. The *Reprisal* and the *Dolphin* waited off Morlaix for several hours: no sign of the *Lexington*. Wickes was anxious to avoid another diplomatic imbroglio, so he sailed away.

By the time the ships reached Ushant it was obvious the *Dolphin* could not survive the voyage. Wickes put his French pilot aboard her and sent her back to France. After wishing Brown well, Wickes made for the English Channel, the first leg in the long voyage home.[90]

The *Lexington* departed Morlaix three days later, her pilot sending her into the channel under clear skies and fine winds. Johnson, too, looked forward to getting home. His muster rolls carried more French names than either he or the French government liked; in fact, most of them had learned their destination was *les États-Unis* once the brigantine made the channel—and they were none too happy about it. As if in answer to their discontent, the winds died.[91]

It took two days for the *Lexington* to reach Ushant, where her mastheader spied a small sail on the horizon in the early hours of September 19: a cutter, the *Alert*, Captain John Bazeley. The *Lexington* was larger and had the cutter outgunned. Nonetheless, the *Alert* made straight for her. Within two hours they were abreast of each other, both flying British colors. Bazeley, convinced he had caught a smuggler, fired a small gun to bring her to, and asked where she was from.

"Guernsey," Johnson replied before hauling down his false colors, raising the Grand Union, and opening his gun ports. A withering broadside shook the *Alert*, but instead of being cowed and sheering off, Bazeley returned fire.

The cutter was faster, and had one more advantage over the *Lexington*: her hull was sheathed in copper, while the brigantine's bottom badly needed cleaning. For the next two hours the ships exchanged broadsides, damaging each other's rigging as they jockeyed for position in the still water. This was not the fight Johnson had anticipated; several of his men were dead, including Marine Lieutenant John Connelly and Jeremiah Holden, who had been the *Lexington*'s sailing master since John Barry's days as captain.

Further damage to his ship and more casualties would only make it harder to sail out of British waters, so Johnson ordered the sweeps manned. Rowing fiercely, the Lexingtons took their ship out of the fight. By ten a.m. they were out of range, and Johnson set his men to repairing the rigging.

Aboard the *Alert*, Bazeley ordered the gun crews to join their shipmates in repairing the cutter's rigging. A florid-faced young man with a double chin, Bazeley was not ready to give up the fight. Once the rigging was sufficiently operational, he cried, "After them!" and the *Alert* gave chase.

The cutter was still far behind two hours later when Johnson's luck changed. The wind returned, a veritable gale bringing rain and the *Alert* down on the *Lexington*. Soon the fighting resumed. Johnson was a fearless man; whether he was low on ammunition or his French hands refused to fight on, we do not know. With inordinately high casualties, he decided further resistance was futile, and struck his colors to the smaller ship.[92]

Seven of his men were dead, and a handful of his wounded required amputation of their shattered limbs. The storm's winds propelled both ships to Dover, where Johnson and his men were hauled off to Mill Prison. Among them was Richard Dale, the young officer captured by Goodrich's navy, then by John Barry, and now the British again. They arrived just as the new "Black Hole" was finished. Another American sailor, William Ford, became its first occupant.[93]

News of the *Lexington*'s capture was hailed throughout England. "The *Lexington* appears to be one of the three which did the Mischief in the Irish Seas," the London *Daily Advertiser* proclaimed, adding how she struck to "the Supreme Valour of the Dover Boys." The Admiralty sent word to Dover officials: find out how many of her crew were French, and get the tally to Stormont.[94]

Americans in Paris took the news hard, finding solace that with just forty-eight Americans among "such a Motley Crew"—a not-so-subtle swipe at the brigantine's Frenchmen—Johnson "made so Gallant a Resistance." At least the *Reprisal* was heading home.[95]

On November 3, a French ship was passing the Newfoundland Banks when the crew spotted some debris far off in the water. Taking up his spyglass, the captain saw it was a gangway ladder, with a man floating on top of it. He immediately sent his ship to save the castaway—if he was still alive.

The poor wretch, a fellow Frenchman, had been clinging to the ladder for three days, not knowing if he would ever see another ship or soul again. Through sunburned, cracked lips, in a barely audible croak, he told his rescuers that a horrific storm had overtaken his vessel, and three titanic waves "pooped" the ship—crashing over the stern and filling her with green water, each one further breaking the already weakened ship apart. The third wave carried her and all hands underwater.

Only he and another seaman made it back to the surface, where the gangway ladder became their life raft. For two days they shared it until the other man's strength failed, and he slid silently into the watery abyss. The Frenchman was the only survivor. When asked his name and that of his ship, he whispered: Nathan Jaquays . . . ship's cook . . . Continental ship *Reprisal*.[96]

Days before that storm sank the *Reprisal* it had been howling down the entire New England coast. Ship departures were postponed, but most captains wisely accepted the delays as part of a seaman's life.

But this nor'easter did not bring out the best in John Paul Jones. Months earlier, when he had arrived in Portsmouth to take command of the *Ranger*, he anticipated sailing in the summertime. Now winter was just weeks away, and he was nearly stir-crazy to get to sea. Unlike earlier setbacks, this time his mood was not the result of his innate restlessness or desire for action. Nor had his orders changed; he was still bound for France. But he had recently been given an added task: to be "the welcome Messenger at Paris of the Joyful and important news of Burgoyne's Surrender" at Saratoga. Jones knew full well that such tidings would go a long way towards making France an open ally to America.[97]

In the face of Washington's twin defeats at Brandywine and Germantown and the loss of Philadelphia, Congress became so anxious to ensure that France learn of this momentous news that every ship bound there was given detailed reports of Gates's victory for delivery to the American commissioners. Jones, being Jones, wanted to be the first to deliver the news, even though he had but one set of sails aboard. Nevertheless, he assured the Marine Committee that he would "go out of my Course" to make the speediest way to France, "Unless I see a fair Opportunity of distressing the Enemy."[98]

Before leaving Portsmouth, Jones wrote letters to Robert Morris and Joseph

Hewes. Both dispatches interspersed his difficulties in obtaining supplies between near-paranoid passages regarding the humiliation of being superseded in rank by captains beneath him in both patriotism and ability, while informing them he had made them executors of his will. Good weather had returned on November 1, and the *Ranger* stood down the Piscataqua. As she departed, Jones had his fife-and-drum band play a tune for the onlookers at the docks while he doffed his hat to the ladies in the crowd. With "one suite of sails" and "less than thirty gal[lons] of Rum for the whole crew," Jones was finally back in his element.[99]

Storms beset the *Ranger*, giving Jones the chance to confirm his suspicion that she was over-masted (she was) and carried too many guns (how Thomas Thompson would have loved that problem!). The combination of the two made the *Ranger* "crank"—she heeled far to one side in heavy weather. Rolling over high seas in one gale, the ship's tiller rope broke. Unable to steer her until repairs were made, the helmsman and other hands grappled with the wheel as the *Ranger* threatened to "broach to"—putting her on her beam ends as the ship veered to windward. Days later, a sailor was washed overboard, then saved when his comrades threw him a rope and hauled him up the side. Jones also found his new best friend, Major Frazer, "different from what I thought him," often intoxicated and "utterly incompatible" with Jones's vision of a proper officer.[100]

Three weeks into the voyage Jones captured his first prizes: two brigantines, part of the Gibraltar fleet. On November 26 he gave chase to another, only to come into view of the *Invincible*, a seventy-four-gun ship-of-the-line. His crew's lust for another prize turned to alarm; Jones used the situation to show his men what he was made of. Shouting orders across the water to his prize-masters to follow his lead, the three ships brazenly joined the convoy. The *Invincible*'s captain determined they were part of his fleet, and the Americans sailed with the enemy until nightfall.

One of Jones's sailors wrote home about this display of cool audacity, calling Jones "a Gentleman of COURAGE and CONDUCT," and "deserving of the best Ship in America." Three days later another gale propelled the *Ranger* into the Bay of Biscay. She dropped anchor in Nantes on December 2, where Jones learned that a Massachusetts brigantine had beaten him to France with the news of Burgoyne's surrender—by just one day.[101]

Word of Saratoga thrilled Americans both stationed in Europe and imprisoned in Europe. Franklin's grandson, Temple, wrote that Frenchmen celebrated the victory as if Frenchmen had won it; one lady of the king's court composed a march to be played when Burgoyne rode off into captivity. In Mill Prison, American sailors were stealthily digging a tunnel for their escape when they learned that Philadelphia had fallen. The guards discovered their burrowing on November 28, but the punishment for their attempted escape was offset by the hope given them ten days later when they, too, learned about Saratoga.[102]

"The Year of the Hangman" ended with the Continental Army freezing in Valley Forge, Philadelphia in British hands, and the Continental Navy in disarray. Of the original thirteen frigates, two were sunk, two were burned, two were captured, and four were still bottled up in harbor. Three captains were prisoners, two faced losing their commissions, and one intrepid hero lay at the bottom of the sea. And yet, for all that, glory lay ahead—glory mixed with farce and tragedy.

CHAPTER SEVEN

★ ★ ★

"UNDER THE VAULT OF HEAVEN"

The account they gave of themselves was this—that they were quartered in the captain's cabin, and thrown into the water without receiving any hurt. But they could give no account by what accident the ship blew up.

—BROADSIDE, "ENGAGEMENT BETWEEN CONTINENTAL
NAVY FRIGATE *RANDOLPH* AND H.M.S. *YARMOUTH*"[1]

While the news about the victory at Saratoga was greeted rapturously by the American commissioners in Paris, it was equally welcomed by one Frenchman, the Comte de Vergennes.

Throughout the war, he had been assiduously rebuilding a French navy that had been decimated by the French and Indian War. By the end of 1777, there were more than 250 ships in Louis XVI's navy, including 50 ships-of-the-line. Like his king, Vergennes held no love for France's ancient enemy across the English Channel. He saw Burgoyne's surrender not just as a perfect opportunity for an alliance with the Americans, but also as a chance for France to recoup her losses from the last war—in the New World and around the globe. Vergennes even dreamed of the fleur-de-lis flying over India.[2]

In Nantes, all John Paul Jones wanted was the ship that had been promised him upon his arrival in France: *l'Indien*, a Dutch frigate under construction at Amsterdam, recently purchased by the French. Upon learning that word of Saratoga was already speeding its way to Paris, Jones awaited a formal invitation from the American commissioners, busying himself in making the *Ranger* a better sailer. He wanted to shorten her masts, lighten her deck by removing two guns, add more ballast to her hold, and clean her foul bottom—changes that would both stabilize her and increase her speed. To amuse himself, he set out to purchase the French goods he had promised Mrs. William Whipple.[3]

He was pleased to discover that he had an acquaintance in Nantes, John Young, captain of the sloop *Independence*. They had met during the summer of '76 in Philadelphia. Jones not only got to know Young's family but also enjoyed a brief romance with a friend of theirs. Young possessed skill, pluck, and at number 23 on the Captains List, an even lower rank than Jones: he was the perfect captain for Jones to cruise with.[4]

Jones put work and pleasantries aside once the commissioners summoned him to Paris, unaware that he was not at the top of the officers' list of the American commissioners that Christmastide. Franklin spent the holiday with Charles-Henri, Comte d'Estaing, one of France's ablest admirals, whose hatred of the British was legendary.[5]

No port of call, or even London itself, could have prepared Jones for the extremes that awaited him in Paris. The majesty of the Champs-Élysées and its endless rows of elm trees were blocks away from some of the worst slums on earth. Nôtre-Dame, the Louvre, and the Palace of Versailles—beautiful monuments that dazzled the eyes—were mixed with an assault on a visitor's sense of smell. "The sewers of every city on earth meet in Paris," one visitor wrote. The streets and the Seine were filthy. Coachmen heedlessly ran down child and adult alike.[6]

Once in Paris, Jones headed to Passy, a neighborhood of estates where the commissioners lived. Their headquarters was the Hôtel Valentinois, owned by Jacques-Donatien Leray de Chaumont, a Benjamin Franklin look-alike and former slave trader. A novel's worth of characters lived under the hotel's roof: diplomats, mercenaries, mistresses, and spies, including Franklin's own secretary, Edward Bancroft. The son of a New England tavern keeper, he had a flair for self-promotion and an insatiable desire to rise in society—someone Jones could easily relate to, if one exchanged patriotism for espionage. Whereas the captain's maritime skills provided his means of social ascent, Bancroft used his talents in science, including experiments with electric eels.

Franklin promised Jones a taste of the French high life, dining in a hotel *chambre* decorated with paintings by Rembrandt and Rubens and featuring the best meats, vegetables, fruits, and exotic desserts, washed down with fine wine and champagne, interrupted by conversations either indirectly or directly concerning sex, all spoken in French. Jones did not understand the language, but he easily understood the gestures that accompanied the bantering. From l'Orient, Thomas Thompson wrote Jones, hoping he would "Enjoy much Satisfaction in the pleasantries which paris afourds." Doubtless Jones did.[7]

By the time Franklin met Jones, he had his routine as frontier rustic/ diplomatic genius honed to perfection. Surrounded by the most effete culture of dress, Franklin's drab Quaker clothes and coonskin cap were an anomaly in King Louis's court. Jones was instantly beguiled by the old man's wisdom and unpretentiousness. Franklin could work a room just by standing in it. Their mutual love of Scottish reels cemented their relationship; as we shall see, Franklin would become a Henry IV–type father figure to Jones's Prince Hal.[8]

In joining Franklin's admirers Jones automatically made an enemy out of Arthur Lee, whose detestation of all things Franklin led to envious backstabbing and subterfuge. In Lee's mind, one was either on his side or on Franklin's. Seeing Jones fall under the old man's spell secured Lee's enmity. Suspicious of everyone, Lee always had room for one more vendetta. Better-born and -educated than Franklin (he was both a doctor and a lawyer), Lee treated people beneath him— which, to him, included just about everyone—with disdain.[9]

Jones soon learned that *l'Indien* was not to be his after all. Word of this proposal had reached Lord Stormont from Bancroft, who wrote his message in invisible ink (a washing agent made the text reappear), and Stormont raised enough diplomatic hell to keep the Dutch from selling her. As 1778 dawned, Stormont was completely convinced that the Franco-American alliance was a fait accompli. "The Treaty between this Court and the Rebels . . . is actually signed," he informed Lord Weymouth.[10]

L'Indien might not be Jones's, but that did not stop Lieutenant Simpson from expecting the *Ranger* to be his. Simpson sent word to Jones that although the men had colds and "were infested with Vermin," Simpson kept their spirits high, thanks to a gill of brandy served at breakfast and dinner. But soon there was not enough liquor aboard to take the men's minds off the pestilential lice, the bitter cold, the snow coating the deck, and the ice floes running down the Loire, banging into the *Ranger*'s hull while French aristocracy wined and dined their captain. Jones was rumored to have even taken a mistress: his host Chaumont's wife, Thérèse. The gills of brandy were accompanied by Simpson's own invective against the *Ranger*'s captain. A Scotsman was as foreign to his fellow New Englanders as a Frenchman—or their British enemies, for that matter.[11]

In fairness, Jones was not simply living the good life and making love to Madame de Chaumont. His mind, as always, was burning with plans—not just to annoy the British but to strike fear into them. But first he had to provide for his men, and protect his command and authority from Simpson's plotting. As best as Jones could, he managed both. First he informed the commissioners that, for him "to Strike a Stroke upon the Enemy," his crew needed to be paid. All Congress gave him was assurances that it would recommend a "generous Gratification"— *after* their next cruise.[12]

Jones also received new orders, vague in their objectives but specifically naming him commander of the *Ranger*. The orders were signed by Franklin and Deane. Lee would not sign them—the first indication that something was amiss with the third commissioner. Jones arrived in Nantes with funds from Chaumont to refit his ship, only to be greeted by surly officers and men. The former presented their captain with a petition requesting the removal of Marine Captain Mathew Parke from the ship. Their official reason was that "no Captain of marines is allow'd to any Ship or Vessell, under twenty Guns." The real reason was money: Parke's mere presence cut into their prize shares. To everyone's surprise— especially Parke's—Jones acquiesced "for the Harmony of the Service," finding Parke a berth aboard the *Deane*.[13]

The *Ranger* was ready to sail when Jones learned that Howe's ships in Philadelphia were unsupported by any cruisers guarding the Delaware Capes. It occurred to Jones that a dozen French ships-of-the-line and a few frigates could cross the Atlantic, sail up the Delaware, and not only trap the British warships in Philadelphia, but also retake Philadelphia and, with the help of Washington's army, bag Howe's forces. He shared his plan with the commissioners. "Whoever can surprise well must Conquer," he concluded. When his letter arrived at Passy, Silas Deane broke the wax seal, read it, and pitched Jones's plan to the French Court as his own brilliant idea. If good politicians, like good poets, borrow, great politicians, like great poets, steal. Deane was already on his way out of France under suspicion of embezzlement. King Louis loved the idea, ordering d'Estaing to get his fleet ready and presenting Deane with a "portrait of his majesty on a gold box set with diamonds." It was months before d'Estaing sailed. Three years later, a different French fleet would do exactly what Jones suggested, bottling up Cornwallis at Yorktown.[14]

The sun was shining and the breezes favorable on February 13, when the *Ranger* stood down the Loire for Quiberon Bay, the wind filling her new sails and speeding her along (her old sails from Portsmouth were sold to a bakery for bread bags). On Saturday, February 14, the *Ranger* accompanied the Continental sloop *Independence* out to sea, but not before passing a French admiral and his squadron. Jones ordered the American ships to fire thirteen-gun salutes; the admiral replied with nine. Jones was not pleased with the number, but his flag, one of the first "Stars and Stripes" flown above a Continental ship, had been saluted.[15]

Outside Philadelphia, the seamstress of the *Ranger*'s flag was desperately trying to hold her world together.

After the American defeat at Brandywine, Sarah Barry bade farewell to her husband, John, as he sailed his frigate, the *Effingham*, up the Delaware. Leaving her Loyalist brother, William Austin, in town, Sarah took her pregnant half sister Christiana Keen and Christiana's seven children to the Austin summer home in nearby Reading. While her husband was fighting with Francis Hopkinson, Sarah assisted Christiana in delivering her eighth child.[16]

John Barry arrived in Reading shortly before Christmas after paying a call to General Washington at Valley Forge. As the general's aides were setting up his headquarters, Barry presented his plan to harass the British below Philadelphia using the navy's barges in Bordentown. Once Washington approved, Barry headed to Reading, expecting a sympathetic ear from his bride about his troubles with Francis Hopkinson. He did not get it.[17]

Shortly after giving birth that fall, Christiana Keen died, leaving Sarah with the burden of tending to eight children while their father was assisting her brother William with his Tory assignments in Philadelphia. Word got out regarding their undertakings, and the Pennsylvania Assembly charged both men with treason, confiscating their estates. They wanted Sarah and the children out of the house. To make matters worse, Barry received notification from Congress to appear before them and answer Hopkinson's charges of insubordination.[18]

His career hanging in the balance, Barry rode off to York after New Year's, determined to vindicate himself. He soon learned that he had help: John Brown, an old friend and Robert Morris's assistant. A lawyer, Brown helped Barry draft his rebuttal to Hopkinson's well-worded complaint. Morris was busy behind the scenes as well—he had no desire to see a man of Barry's caliber lost to the Cause as a result of Hopkinson's superciliousness.[19]

In Bordentown, Hopkinson was also reviewing schemes to aggravate the British in Philadelphia. He supported two plans of the French major de Fleury, one of Fort Mifflin's heroes, to send twelve fireships downriver, but this scheme did not pass a test run. De Fleury also sought volunteers to take shirts packed with sulfur across the frozen Delaware and set them afire once close enough to the *Roebuck* or her consorts. No volunteers came forward. One plan Hopkinson loved came from the fertile mind of David Bushnell, whose submarine the *Turtle* was tested in New York harbor. Bushnell wanted to float underwater mines, buoyed by kegs, down the Delaware. The kegs were sent downriver. Not a British warship was hit. However, the attempt was not a total failure; Hopkinson did write a humorous poem, "The Battle of the Kegs," about this misadventure.[20]

On January 29, Congress debated Barry's case, and the motion was made to remove him. The vote ended in a tie, meaning, as only Congress could say, "it passed in the negative." The tally was barely finished when the Marine Committee approved Barry's plan, sending him posthaste to Bordentown to get his barges in the water, taking what sailors were willing to volunteer for such a risky mission. To Barry's bemusement, Hopkinson was ordered to give Barry whatever the captain needed to get under way.[21]

Barry returned to Bordentown to find that only two of the barges were serviceable. And while he quickly had three junior officers volunteer (including Luke Matthewman from their *Lexington* days), only two dozen sailors stepped forward. It had been a bitter winter from the onset, and the men were poorly clad for such a mission on the icy Delaware. Barry found fifteen volunteers from the army detachment Washington had given John Hazelwood months earlier. In Bordentown, Hazelwood told Barry that four of the Pennsylvania Navy's row galleys had been taken overland for just such a mission. Barry would take his barges by the usual route.[22]

On a moonless night in mid-February, two barges with muffled oars rowed past occupied Philadelphia, keeping to the Jersey side of the Delaware, with their single gun placed at the bow and loaded. The Americans could make out the sentries under the streetlights along the waterfront and their counterparts standing guard on the *Roebuck* and other warships. By dawn they were in one of the streams near Wilmington, Delaware.[23]

Once in Wilmington, Barry sought out Brigadier General William Smallwood, commander of the Continental Army forces there. A week later, they had company: the four Pennsylvania Navy barges along with three hundred soldiers from Valley Forge under Brigadier General Anthony Wayne. Washington had ordered Wayne to cross the Delaware to New Jersey, where he was to purchase, confiscate, or requisition all the cattle he could find and bring them back to Valley Forge. It was Wayne's first mission since his men had been attacked in the Paoli Massacre, where dozens of Americans had been bayoneted to death. This was Wayne's chance for vindication, just as it was Barry's. With no British ships this far below Philadelphia to spot them, the barges crossed in broad daylight on February 19.[24]

Four days later, Wayne had several hundred head of cattle. All he had to do was figure out how to get them to Pennsylvania. The British had learned through spies about the roundup, but Barry's attempt at loading the cattle into the barges did not go well—not even Noah could have succeeded. Knowing that the British would be looking to intercept them somewhere, Barry and Wayne decided to split up: Wayne took the cattle north, to cross the river above Philadelphia, while Barry took his barges south, making stops at each creek to burn every haystack he could find, hopefully drawing the British forces toward him.[25]

The deception worked. Aboard the *Roebuck*, Andrew Snape Hamond saw the growing pillars of fire through his spyglass and sent boatloads of Redcoats across the Delaware to catch the hay burners. After a second day of their bluff, Barry's men narrowly escaped in the dead of night, reaching Port Penn, a small fishing village on the Delaware shore near Reedy Island. Wayne brought his beef-on-the-hoof safely into Valley Forge. He and Barry would remain friends for the rest of their lives.[26]

Ice covered the Delaware for a week, but thawed by March 7. That day, a lookout Barry posted at the southern tip of the island made out two transports heading upriver in the fog, followed by an armed schooner. Barry's men were lodged in the homes of sympathetic villagers; the shrill cry of a bosun's whistle let them know they were wanted at the dock.

The transports were just abreast of Reedy Island when Barry's barges burst out of the mist, their bow guns loaded, each man armed to the teeth. Within minutes they had taken the transports, the *Kitty* and the *Mermaid*, both loaded with hay for the British dragoons in Philadelphia. Barry sent the transports and barges straight at the schooner. She was well armed, and more than fully manned, but she struck her colors instantly. Barry's boarding party found her carrying thirty-three sailors, a host of mechanics, and the reason for her quick surrender: three officers' wives were aboard.

She was the *Alert*, carrying "eight Double fortified four-pounders and twelve four pound howitzers"—the ideal ship, in Barry's estimation, to carry out further depredations against the British. To his continued delight, an American sailor came up the hatchway to tell him the pantry contained a large cheese and a jar of pickled oysters. The captain's cabin held the private papers of Lieutenant General Baron Wilhelm von Knyphausen, commander of the Hessians, and those of chief engineer John Montresor, while her hold was full of Montresor's engineering tools. Barry could not believe his good fortune. He sent the officers' wives under escort to Philadelphia with Knyphausen's and Montresor's correspondence, making arrangements for Montresor's tools to be sent overland to Valley Forge. He had something special planned for the cheese and oysters.[27]

The next day, the lookout sighted several sail approaching—fighting sail, to be exact. Barry's three prizes were part of a convoy that had sailed ahead of their escorts. The captain in charge of the convoy was heading upriver with his squadron of four ships—one frigate, two sloops, and his own two-decker, the fifty-gun *Experiment*. Sir James Wallace was not happy to have lost his three charges the day before, and he wanted them back.

Wallace had not changed at all since his days aboard the *Rose*; punishing rebels and their ships was his job, and he was good enough to be knighted for it. The Loyalist pilot bringing him upriver gave him the bearings of Reedy Island— that the water between the island and Port Penn was excessively shallow at low tide, and also ran shallow north and east of the island. Wallace was ruthless, but also thorough, and he planned his attack accordingly. He would attack Reedy Island the next day.[28]

Wallace's opponent also possessed that combination of aggression and prudence. Leaving the hay on board, Barry moved the 4-pounders from the transports, placing them on the Port Penn docks behind some makeshift breastworks. The *Alert* was anchored northeast of them, ready for Barry's getaway. By dusk, the winds began blowing from the northeast—a storm was coming. Everything was prepared to greet Wallace's entourage.[29]

A genuine nor'easter came howling in on the afternoon of March 9. Wallace was delaying his attack for high tide; Barry was in the *Alert*'s cabin, calmly penning correspondence. He had already requested that Congress purchase the *Alert*, "a most Excellent Vessel for our purpose." Now he took quill in hand to write Washington:

> Tis with the Greatest Satisfaction Imaginable I inform you of Capturing two Ships and a Schooner of the Enemy . . . [There] are a number of Engineering tools . . . by the Bearer Mr. John Chelten have Sent You a Cheese together with a Jar of Pickled Oysters which Crave Your Acceptance.[30]

British cannon fire interrupted his thoughts. Hastily concluding his letter, he gave it to Mr. Chelten for delivery, and stepped out into the storm.

With the tide running high, Wallace put his chess pieces in play, sending the frigate and sloops up the west side of Reedy Island. He had commandeered another sloop, sending her around the island to head off any possible retreat. Wallace had read Barry's mind well: knowing that the *Alert* was Barry's best chance of escape, he sailed the *Experiment* straight upriver, her long 18-pounders easily able to fire over the island to Port Penn and the captured ships. If Barry fled north in the *Alert*, Wallace would be waiting for him.

Stiff winds blew sleet and snow without prejudice on Englishman and American alike, as Barry's men fired the small 4-pounders back at the British ships. Seeing the fight going against him, Barry ordered the *Kitty* and *Mermaid* burnt—an easy enough task despite the storm, with all that hay on board. Then he sent his men to their assigned vessels. While some sailors hastily made sail with the *Alert*, others took the barges and rowed north, then east. Barry hoped the enemy would chase him, allowing the barges to reach New Jersey.[31]

Watching the *Alert* make her escape, Wallace ordered his gunners to open fire. There was a deafening roar from the *Experiment*'s long guns and a harsh whistling noise as the cannonballs flew over Reedy Island before splashing precariously close to the *Alert*. Some of Barry's men panicked and ran to the longboat. Barry left his spot by the ship's wheel, physically stopping them from flight.

Soon the British gunners were finding their targets, splintering the *Alert*'s stern just as she had reached the shallows north of the island. Barry turned to see that the barges were escaping to New Jersey. If Wallace had been correct in guessing Barry's plan, Barry also guessed right: Wallace was coming for him. Having "maintained an obstinate fight" for more than two hours, Barry sent the *Alert* into the shallows, running her aground. After he ordered "Abandon ship!" his men manned the longboat, rowing to the Delaware shore and safety as the last British barrage soared over their heads.[32]

Good news was hard to come by in March of 1778, and the *Pennsylvania Gazette*'s report that "Captain Barry has distinguished himself exceedingly on the river" soon spread to New England and down to the Carolinas. But the best praise of all came from Washington himself, congratulating Barry "on the Success that has crowned your Gallantry" and "the degree of Glory which you have acquired"—and thanking him for the oysters.[33]

Barry hoped to repeat his success, but Andrew Snape Hamond put a stop to that idea. British ships and barges patrolled the river daily for the next two months, capturing the sailors who escaped from Wallace's clutches on March 9, and making any further attempts at interrupting British shipping impossible. By

May 8, General Howe had turned the British army over to Lieutenant General Sir Henry Clinton. Certain that America's French allies were sending at least one fleet across the Atlantic, Clinton did not want to be caught in Philadelphia (Jones had the right idea). On this day, he sent troops up to White Hill and Bordentown to destroy the Continental Navy supplies remaining there.

The Redcoats not only burned the stores, spiked the cannons, and put the carcasses of fifty-four ships (including the half-sunk *Effingham*) to the torch, but they almost captured Barry as well. He had stopped at White Hill en route to Reading, and was staying as a guest of Captain Read's wife—Read had gone to Baltimore to take command of a Continental brig—when a detachment of British troops came to her front door. She went to warn Barry and found him shaving. As he dressed and headed out the back door, Mrs. Read politely received the soldiers at the front, informing them that Barry was no longer there. She was serving them rum and breakfast as Barry saddled his horse and galloped off to Sarah.[34]

Admiral Howe's fleet soon departed Philadelphia The transports that brought his brother's troops to Philadelphia had new passengers: the many Philadelphia Loyalists, including William Austin, who were now exiles.[35]

Wallace, who viewed his encounter with Barry as a blot on his record, was soon cruising with the *Experiment* off Boston. Fate, and the Marine Committee, would send Barry there shortly.[36]

One representative who missed the Barry-Hopkinson imbroglio was the navy's foremost champion in Congress. John Adams had gone home to Braintree, Massachusetts, in November 1777, hoping to return to his law practice and reacquaint himself with his young family.

But Congress had other ideas, selecting Adams to replace Silas Deane in France. It seemed an odd decision, since Adams was not known for tact or sensitivity. Now he was being sent to that diplomatic minefield, the court of Louis XVI, just as Benjamin Franklin was doing his utmost to cement an alliance "the French Way"—acting on the surface as if that did not matter at all.

Adams was trying a case when Congress's dispatch reached his home. Abigail read it first. As nightmarish as a midwinter Atlantic crossing was, that must have seemed becalmed in Adams's mind when he confronted the storm awaiting him at home that evening. Abigail had already noted that these were "times that tried women's souls as well as men's."[37]

Congress wanted the frigate *Boston* to take Adams to France. By this time

Hector McNeill had been replaced by Samuel Tucker, another Marblehead veteran of "Washington's Navy." The Eastern Navy Board ordered Tucker to keep Adams safe, but feel free to take or destroy enemy ships—and make sure, for God's sake, to conceal his guns once in French waters.[38]

On Friday, February 13, Tucker dined with Adams and his ten-year-old son, John Quincy, before boarding the *Boston*'s barge in Quincy Bay (there were too many spies in Boston to board the frigate there). The water was churning and the winds strong—but thanks to "a Quantity of Hay in the Bottom of the Boat, and good Watch Coats," the two future presidents boarded the *Boston* "tolerably warm and dry," a phrase he would not use again for the rest of the voyage.[39]

While young John found two boys of similar age on board (the sons of William Vernon of the Navy Board and Silas Deane), his father made friends with Tucker, First Lieutenant William Barron of Virginia, and Ship's Surgeon Nicholas Nöel, one of thirty-six Frenchmen aboard. Adams saw Barron as the epitome of an American naval officer, possessing "Qualities much needed in our Navy." He had also seen Tucker's orders, calling for the captain to consult with Adams on practically everything.[40]

Four days of howling winds and blinding snow kept the *Boston* in Quincy Bay, much to Adams's consternation. While he found Tucker "an able Seaman, and a brave, active vigilant officer," he questioned both Tucker's intelligence and judgment, wondering why he did not put to sea, or why the crew—mostly landsmen—were not being exercised at the guns, unaware that gunnery practice at anchor and in a snowstorm was pointless.

All this time, Tucker was besieged by "Mothers, Wives, [and] Sisters" who came on board, begging for leave for their "Sons, Husbands, and brothers." Tucker wisely refused most requests; when he fired a gun signaling his absent officers to return to ship, none of them showed up, forcing him to send the marines for them.[41]

Once the *Boston* set sail under sunny skies on the seventeenth, Adams became deathly seasick, keeping him temporarily out of Tucker's hair. The frigate eluded two British cruisers, taking advantage of a "Prosperous gale WNW" that sent her flying over the Atlantic and escaping their clutches.[42]

Ever the documenter, Adams entered in his diary thoughts on seasickness, taking into account not just the rolling seas but the ship's condition as well:

The Mal de Mer, Seems to be merely the Effect of Agitation. The Smoke and Smell of Seacoal, the Smell of Stagnant, putrid Water, the Smell of the Ship where the Sailors lay, or any other offensive Smell, will increase the Qualminess, but do not occasion it.[43]

On February 22 the *Boston* sailed into a tumultuous storm. Winds shredded canvas while mountainous green waves washed over the ship, running down the covered hatches and forcing Tucker to man the pumps constantly. Minute by exacting minute, Tucker sailed under "bare poles," all the while expecting to be dismasted. His fears were nearly realized when lightning struck down the mainmast, injuring several men, and another bolt struck a shipmate in the head, leaving a hole the size of a large coin. The man was raving mad for three days before he died. "Pray God Protect Us and Cary us through our Various troubles," Tucker wrote in his journal. The storm dogged the *Boston* for two full days.[44]

One week later, Adams made a telling entry in his diary, bemoaning the landsman's lot at sea, the politician's shock at waste, and the puritan's abhorrence of everything un-puritan:

> As the main Deck was almost constantly under Water . . . We were obliged to keep the Hat[ch]ways down—Wherby the Air became So hot and dry in the 'Tween decks . . . I could not breathe, or live there . . .
>
> The *Boston* is over metalled,—Her Number of Guns and the Weight . . . is too great for her Tonnage . . . There is the Same general Inattention, I find on Board the Navy to Economy that there is in the Army . . .
>
> There is the same Inattention to the Cleanliness of the Ship and the Persons & Health of the Sailors . . . The practice of Cursing and Swearing, So Silly as well as detestable . . . it is indulged and connived at by the officers . . . there is no Kind of Check against it.[45]

Tucker never had to wonder what was on Adams's mind. "I am Constantly giving Hints to the Captain," he wrote. When Tucker ordered the hammocks aired and the ship cleaned—commonsense chores that every captain saw as routine—Adams decided it was done "in Pursuance of Advice I gave him." Poor Tucker! Nöel busied himself teaching John Quincy French; Tucker may have wished it was a family lesson. But his ship was in the midst of a fairly smart passage, off the Grand Banks by early March. Adams was disconcerted by another idiosyncrasy of the crew: superstition. "They Say the Ship has been So unfortunate that they really believe there is Some Woman on board." After all,

Adams added, "Women are the unluckiest Creatures in the World at Sea." Adams, for the most part, remained nauseous and bored.[46]

Eventually he adjusted to the rolling deck and soon enjoyed those days where a "fine easy Breeze" lulled him to a slumber "as quietly and as Soundly as in my own Bed at home." On March 6, Adams found the *Boston* "all in an uproar with laughter" as the landsmen were subjected to a rite of hazing. This "Frolick" involved two dozen raw hands, bound together and soaked to the skin, all done "to conjure up a Prize." The next day Tucker was all business, assembling all hands to hear the Articles of War (that Adams had written in 1775), followed by gunnery practice. "They seemed tolerably expert," Adams marveled. Switching moods again, Tucker ordered a "Dance, upon the Main Deck." Adams and his son watched as "all Hands, Negroes, Boys and Men were obliged to dance," followed by another hazing where "the Men were powdered over, with Flour, and wet again to the Skin." Adams did not know if this was "to wash away vermin" or not; on the whole, the somewhat repressed congressman felt it "a humour of the coarsest Kind."[47]

There was little humor aboard the *Boston* on March 11, when the mastheader sighted a sail flying British colors. In obedience to his orders, Tucker sought Adams's permission to give chase. He got it. As they bore down, Tucker made her out to be a privateer or well-armed merchantman looking for action. Seeing her guns run out, Tucker ordered Adams to take the boys below. Adams refused, telling Tucker he "would Chuse to Stand the Deck."

Tucker fired a warning shot, hoping the smaller ship would strike, but by coming straight at his foe he prevented his opponent from making out the number of the *Boston*'s guns. The privateer returned fire, her shots cutting into the *Boston*'s rigging and carrying away her mizzen yard while another cannonball whizzed over Adams's head. Tucker did not return fire, telling his men "he wanted the Egg without breaking the Shell." Seconds later, his opponent realized he was engaging a ship of superior force, and "did not think himself able to get his colours down soon enough."[48]

The fight over, Tucker noticed someone standing by his marines, musket in hand. It was Adams. "I ought to do my share of the fighting," he told Tucker, who would ever after praise Adams for his courage.[49]

Tucker's prize was a good one: the letter of marque *Martha*, bound from London to New York with more than £80,000 of goods in her hold. Tucker turned her over to Hezekiah Welch, one of the oldest lieutenants in the navy.

After Adams handed Welch a letter for the Navy Board assuring them that Adams was safe, Tucker sent the *Martha* to Boston. She was recaptured en route.[50]

The upbeat mood aboard the *Boston* came to an abrupt end three days later. Another ship was sighted, and Tucker ordered Lieutenant Barron to fire a signal gun. It blew up as it fired, shattering Barron's right leg. Adams and Tucker carried the young man below, where Surgeon Nöel amputated the leg "in a Masterly manner" while Adams held him down. Barron spent several days in writhing agony. Before he died, a heartsick Adams promised to insist that the government care for his children. Barron was buried at sea, in a chest weighted down with the fragments of the very gun that had killed him.[51]

The *Boston* plowed northward to Bordeaux, where she passed the Tower of Cordouan and anchored in the Gironde River on April 1. Tucker and Adams enjoyed an elegant nine-course dinner aboard a merchantman bound for Santo Domingo. The *Boston* served as a great conversation piece, the foreigners marveling at her beautiful lines. "One would think they never saw a ship before," Tucker later wrote, adding playfully, "but it is all on account of being a Boston frigate."

By the time Adams and his young charges were ashore he was convinced that Tucker was "as sociable as any Marblehead man"—quite a compliment from a resident of nearby Braintree. For all the details in Adams's diary about the voyage, it was his son who best summed up the six-week odyssey: "I hope I shall never forget the goodness of God in preserving us through all the dangers we have been exposed to." Before departing for Paris, Adams learned that Franklin had been received by King Louis "in great Pomp" and the alliance signed, and all of France "expect War, every Moment."[52]

Heading to Bordeaux, the *Boston* sailed past the coast of Portugal, completely unaware that Gustavus Conyngham, the American whom George III detested most, was using that neutral country as a base for his continued mischief against British shipping as well as His Majesty's nervous system.

By the end of 1777, the warm welcome Conyngham had first received in Spain was wearing thin. Unlike France, Spain took her neutrality seriously, and once British officials got wind of Conyngham's presence they besieged the Spanish government with protests. When the governor of El Ferrol sent Conyngham away in October, he returned to La Coruña, capturing four more prizes on the way, including a British transport, the *Two Brothers*. Her captain, Nicholas

Kelly, swore the ship was actually the *St. John Evangelist*, out of Portugal. Conyngham kept poking holes in Kelly's story until a Spanish hand of Kelly's told the Americans to search the ballast, where Kelly's British colors were found. From La Coruña, Herman Katencamp, the British consul, raged that "this Pirate" Conyngham was sailing the *Revenge* out of Spain wherever and whenever he pleased.[53]

However, the Conde de Floridablanca, the Spanish minister of state, was not as cowed by British threats. He assured Lord Grantham, England's minister to Spain, that the *Two Brothers/St. John Evangelist* was not being sold per Conyngham's request but merely disarmed and riding at anchor in La Coruña—for the present. Then he protested "the Insults which the Spanish Flag suffers in the American Seas" as well as the seizure and inspection of Spanish ships right under the guns of Spanish forts. As long as Conyngham was only pulling the British lion's tail, he was tolerated, if not welcome, in Spain.[54]

Conyngham was also assisted by two Spanish merchant firms that had long done business with their American counterparts. They quietly sold Conyngham's prizes, allowing him to pay his men, refit the *Revenge*, and send funds to the American commissioners in Paris to buy munitions and supplies for Washington's army.[55]

Conyngham's tenuous relationship with the Spaniards looked to be at an end in December, when the *Revenge* left La Coruña and sailed east to Bilbao. Cruising near St. Sebastián on the twenty-first, she overtook the brig *Gracieux*, heading from London to Spain with her hold packed tight with woolen goods, all made in Britain. The only problem was that both the ship and her crew were French. The British merchants who owned the goods had placed them in a "neutral bottom" out of fear that a British merchantman carrying them would be captured by "the Pirate Conyngham."

Throughout the war, British cruisers had plundered neutral ships to seize any American goods they carried, so Conyngham saw no issue in returning the favor. As the *Gracieux* rocked atop the water, Conyngham and her commander dickered over the American's action. When he offered to sail the brig to Nantes as an American prize, Conyngham insisted that the *Gracieux* sail to Bilbao. As she was poorly manned—only seven hands—Conyngham put a prize crew aboard and sent her to his new base of operations.[56]

While Conyngham's agents were thrilled—the "valuable Bale goods" would sell quickly and at a good price—the seizure of the brig was a diplomatic catastrophe for both Conyngham and the commissioners in Paris. The paranoid

Arthur Lee, whose dislike of Deane extended to Deane favorites, particularly Conyngham, chastised him. Conyngham had given "great Offence to our [French] friends, and should be desisted in the future." Deane, ironically, was even angrier: "Your idea that you are at Liberty to seize English Property, on board of French or other Neutral Vessels is wrong." Deane pointed out that "every such Adventure gives our Enemies an Advantage against us by representing us as Persons who regard not the Laws of Nations." As to Conyngham's claim to the *Gracieux*, Deane was clear: drop it.[57]

The harshest fury did not come from the commissioners, the French, or even the British—it came from the Spanish. Once the *Gracieux* reached St. Sebastián, Conyngham's men were thrown in jail and Spanish officials confiscated the brig. Leaving the *Ranger* in Bilbao, Conyngham headed to St. Sebastián to get both his men and his prize released. For weeks he argued and pleaded his case with anyone who might help him. Even his old ally William Hodge, recently freed from the Bastille and sent to Bilbao to assist Conyngham, could not change the Spanish government's decision. The Conde de Floridablanca guaranteed the British that Conyngham "is not permitted to enter any of the ports of the Kingdom [of Spain], after it was perceived that he wished to abuse them." The Spanish also seized funds being held from the sale of Conyngham's prizes.[58]

All this would have taken the wind out of any captain's sails, but not Conyngham's. He apologized to Deane that *l'Affaire Gracieux* did so much diplomatic damage, adding that he "would Drop the claime as you have Requested." But he let fly at Lee, first for calling the *Revenge* a ship instead of a cutter, then regarding the *Gracieux*. If the Royal Navy could confiscate American goods out of neutral holds, the Continental Navy should do the same. "Have we not a right to retaliate?" Conyngham pointedly asked.[59]

The answer was no.

By March 1778, Conyngham had more pressing problems. In 1777 he had arrived in Spain with a polyglot crew of a hundred Americans, Frenchmen, and Spaniards. Now he had considerably fewer, a situation that forced him to recruit prisoners to adequately man the *Revenge*. He wrote a forlorn letter to his old first mate, John Beach, now in France: "Since I left you I have nothing but trouble from one thing to Another." Conyngham departed Bilbao on March 6, with fifty-seven men including William Hodge, ostensibly to sail for Martinique.[60]

Once at sea, he picked up where he had left off, capturing three British merchantmen, their holds laden with fruit. He dispatched the ships to Massachusetts; then, with an eye to padding his muster rolls, he set the captured officers ashore at Madeira (west of the Barbary Coast of Africa) while offering freedom to their sailors—as long as they joined the *Revenge*. Most did. Conyngham now headed to Gibraltar, to see what mischief could be found there.[61]

On March 20, the *Revenge* captured and burned a tender of the British frigate *Enterprize*. The next day, the *Enterprize* sailed over the horizon, hell-bent on taking the rebel cutter. Conyngham was about to take her on a wild-goose chase when the wind died. "Man the sweeps!" he ordered, and the *Revenge* was rowed to safety, the becalmed frigate unable to follow. Three days later another sail was spied as the sun set. She was coming fast, her guns run out. Taking her for a privateer, Conyngham let her come, instructing his gun crews to load their weapons but keep the gun ports closed. His pursuer believed the *Revenge* would be easy pickings; as the privateer closed in, he ordered a warning shot fired as the ship came abreast of the *Revenge*. "Run out your guns," Conyngham cried, then "Fire!" and the cutter's broadside took down the privateer's captain and one of the ship's boys. After a second broadside, the privateer, named *Hope*, struck her colors (she was later retaken by the *Enterprize*).

Conyngham put into Cádiz, the nearest Spanish port just above Gibraltar, for cleaning and refitting. Any thought that the Spanish would turn away the *Revenge* was settled right before the enemy's eyes. As British consul Joseph Hardy watched aghast from the waterfront, as did the captain of HMS *Monarch* from his quarterdeck, Conyngham "came swaggering in with his thirteen stripes, saluted the Spanish admiral, had it returned." When the Spanish dockhands began carrying freshwater, fruit, and other provisions aboard to "an Outlawed Smuggler" just two cable lengths away, it became too much for them to behold: the *Monarch*'s captain longed for the day when a British fleet would "chastise our natural and insolent enemies."[62]

As in northern Spanish ports, Conyngham received assistance in refitting the *Revenge* from sympathetic merchants who had American connections. One day, a Frenchman informed Conyngham that the British planned to set the *Revenge* on fire. The French consul, now an official ally, offered assistance, and the Spanish admiral offered the protection of a ship-of-the-line. Conyngham, not wanting his crew to be involved in another international incident, declined any help. That night a longboat carrying a gang of British tars with torches came near, only to find more than enough well-armed and menacing men from the *Revenge* to persuade them to return to the *Monarch*.

Remarkably, the *Revenge* sailed safely out of Cádiz, even though two British frigates were waiting to pounce on her. Fearful that spies knew of his West Indies destination, Conyngham received new orders: keep cruising off Spain and Portugal. Conyngham cruised the Canary Islands, capturing or burning several more ships despite being chased several times by British frigates. By May, the ship needed cleaning and supplies. With two "British Cruzers" dogging him with orders to follow the Revenge into any harbor and sink her, and well aware that Spanish ports were officially to turn him away, Conyngham raced for the closest port: La Coruña.[63]

To his surprise, Coruñans gave him a warm reception, while the frigates remained outside the harbor. Glad as Governor O'Neille was to see Conyngham personally, he warned the captain that "British influence at Court & infamous representations of their Consuls" compelled O'Neille to send the Revenge on her way as soon as she was ready. To add to Conyngham's woes, the crew demanded their pay—their enlistment was up, and they would not re-sign without coin in their pockets. Forbidden to recruit hands in Spain, Conyngham had no choice but to pay them. The Revenge departed La Coruña on May 20.[64]

Eleven days passed before they sighted a sail that Conyngham pursued and captured. She was the Honoria Sophia, a Swedish brig bearing dry goods to Tenerife in the Canary Islands for the British. It was the Gracieux all over again, but Conyngham was not succumbing to the thrill of a capture. Not a second time.

But that did not matter—his crew more than made up for his lack of lust, demanding that she be taken. Conyngham had no ally aboard—John Beach was gone, and William Hodge was no help in this instance. Refusal invited mutiny or worse, so Conyngham insisted that they write an attestation absolving him of their action. Thirty-six sailors signed their names or made their marks. The Honoria Sophia became the Revenge's last prize in European waters.[65]

To landlubber politicians and noblemen, the paper did nothing but show that Conyngham could not control his men—a fear that lay just beneath the surface of every captain's skin. The Spanish banished him for good; Vergennes disowned him in public as "an American corsair," and Franklin promised he "will certainly be punished." Conyngham's protestations of innocence were drowned in the storm he was trapped in, with no way to sail out of it but to sail out of Europe.

In an eighteen-month period, Conyngham and his little cutter had captured or burned sixty ships, a total not approached by any other Continental captain. Those prizes that made it to port went a long way towards financing the American war effort. For all his diplomatic naiveté, no officer, army or navy, did more to bring the French into the war. With European ports closed to him, he sailed at last for Martinique.[66]

In Maryland, the Continental Navy's Hamlet, James Nicholson, was asking himself: To sail, or not to sail? That was the question. The answer from Congress was sail. Sail now.

The naval war was being fought at sea from Nova Scotia to the Spanish Main and from the beaches of America to the shores of Europe, and Congress's top captain was missing in action—by choice. After his attempt to press Maryland sailors into service in the spring of '77—a public relations blunder if there ever was one—Nicholson remained in Baltimore, continuing his pleas and harangues to an exasperated Congress for more money and men. He had offered to assist in defending Philadelphia during the British invasion, but would not attempt to run the gauntlet of British warships at the mouth of the Chesapeake. From time to time, the windows of the governor's mansion rattled from the roar of the *Virginia*'s gunnery exercises, but that was all. That autumn, the Marine Committee ordered Nicholson to convoy the growing number of merchantmen awaiting escort out of the Virginia Capes. He did not budge.[67]

Finally Congress had had enough. "Wearied of the long delay of the Frigate *Virginia* under your command in port," it ordered him to sea. In answer to his request for another officer, they sent him a good one, Joshua Barney, one of the heroes of Turtle Gut Inlet, recently exchanged after being captured, and more than happy to serve under the navy's senior officer.[68]

Weeks later, the Marine Committee found it necessary to remind Nicholson of his orders. On December 19, the committee suggested that the *Virginia* be used to deliver some tobacco—a veiled insult to both Nicholson's sense of duty and his courage. The next day, they sent orders for him to escort a French two-decker up the Chesapeake. It had reached the point where Congress no longer cared why he sailed, just that he sailed.[69]

To practically everyone's surprise, the *Virginia*—with Nicholson aboard—stood down the Patuxent, only to find two British frigates, the *Emerald* and the *Richmond*, waiting for him in Hampton Roads. Nicholson wore ship and showed the *Virginia*'s heels, proving her a fast sailer as she left the British ships in her wake—a move that not even his harshest critics could fault. Even the Marine Committee was impressed, writing him on the twenty-eighth and rewarding his effort, promising a bounty to induce more sailors to enlist, sending some of the sailors at Bordentown down to Baltimore to serve under him, and allowing him to purchase a tender for the frigate. They expected to see Nicholson sailing the Atlantic in February.[70]

It is doubtful that they were surprised at writing him five weeks later, on March 4, promising him more money (again) and hoping to "wipe off any malicious reflections" on Nicholson's character, once his ship was in the damn ocean.[71]

At long last, on March 30, under extremely favorable conditions, the *Virginia* made for the capes. She was a handsome sight, slicing through the water past Annapolis, following a brig steered by a Chesapeake pilot. Night fell. The *Virginia*'s helmsman stayed behind the brig, guided by a stern lantern hanging off the quarterdeck. In the darkness, Lieutenant Joshua Barney could make out the lights of the two British frigates. They were still—proof that they had not spotted the *Virginia*.

Suddenly, around three a.m., a sickening, grinding sound was followed by a violent lurch. Whether it was too dark or the pilot did not consider the *Virginia*'s great draft is not known. The frigate had run aground. Nicholson's men dropped anchor to avoid more damage in the dark of night. For more than a year, Nicholson would not move. Now, he could not move.

The *Virginia* was easily spotted by the British as the sun rose, her tall masts silhouetted against the brightening sky. The wrenching impact had knocked off her rudder; even if the tide rose before enemy ships saw her, she would be unable to escape. Captain Benjamin Caldwell of the *Emerald* spied her first, and steered his frigate carefully towards her as the tide came in. An hour passed before the *Virginia* came within range.

Once Caldwell opened his gun ports, the *Virginia*'s crew learned what their captain was made of. Without explanation to Barney or his other officers, Nicholson ordered his barge lowered, clambered down the side, got in, and ordered his men to row hastily to shore. Barney was furious. He was also determined that the British would not take the *Virginia*. After raising the colors, he rounded up the other officers and proposed cutting the anchor cable, steering the frigate as best they could towards Cape Henry and burning her. If the British got close enough, he would fight.

The other officers, older and wiser if not as brave, would have none of it. Their rudderless frigate could wind up heading out to sea in a fickle wind, and then what? Better to wait for the British boarding parties. They approached just after a warning shot from the *Emerald* prompted a sailor to haul down the *Virginia*'s flag. Seeing the total breakdown in authority, and watching the British longboats close in, the crew made the most of their remaining minutes of freedom. They broke into the spirit room and got as drunk as time and supplies permitted.[72]

The next day, as British hands labored to refloat their prize and assess the damages, the captive Barney watched from the *Emerald* as a barge approached under a white flag. It was Nicholson. With deliberate coolness he climbed up the gangway, asking for Caldwell. In his haste to depart his ship, Nicholson had left his papers and belongings in his cabin: might he have them? Of course he could have his personal effects, Caldwell replied, but his orders, journal, and signal book were now the property of the King's Navy. Nicholson went below to get his things, but not before getting the tongue-lashing of his life from his teenage lieutenant, who hurled invective at his captain like a mortar lobbing shells. What was Nicholson going to do—flog him?

It was April Fool's Day.

Later, Nicholson reported that he had not abandoned ship in the face of the enemy. Rather, he had escaped, along with "such of my crew as was inclined to run the risque of getting on shore." Congress swallowed his story whole, and exonerated him in the loss of the *Virginia*. After all, he had finally sailed.[73]

In South Carolina that winter, two of the officers from Esek Hopkins's original squadron were determined to meet the enemy.

Two years earlier, Nicholas Biddle was captain of the *Andrew Doria* and John Peck Rathbun was a lieutenant aboard the *Providence*. As 1777 closed, Biddle was occupied with getting the *Randolph* refitted, with the possibility of leading ships from the South Carolina Navy in a cruise against the British ships lurking off Charleston. Rathbun, commander of the sloop *Providence*, was also planning something big.

The *Providence* was making for Charleston in December when she encountered a sloop, the *Governour Tonyn*. In a short, deadly engagement, Rathbun's men outfought the enemy and freed eight African American prisoners.[74]

No portraits or descriptions survive to give us an idea of what Rathbun looked like, but we know he possessed excellent sailing skills, great courage, and enough nerve for a fleet of captains. He was a farmer's son, born in Rhode Island in 1746. Rathbun's love of the sea came from his mother's side; her great-uncle fought in the battle off Ocracoke Inlet in 1720 that killed Blackbeard. Young Rathbun went to sea in Boston, living ashore with an uncle whose haberdashery shop was a stone's throw from the site of the Boston Massacre. This uncle also participated in the Boston Tea Party, by which time Rathbun had become a successful merchant captain, married to the daughter of a prominent Loyalist. They later moved to Rhode Island, where Rathbun received his lieutenant's commission.[75]

As the *Providence* underwent repairs from her recent battle, Rathbun received an intriguing Christmas present—information that the *Mary*, the ship his sloop had fought off Sandy Hook in August, was in New Providence being repaired after being severely damaged in a storm and stripped of her guns. The thought of sailing into New Providence was tempting, and Rathbun decided to make the attempt. Two years earlier, the *Providence* was part of Hopkins's squadron that had taken the town. Rathbun now decided to do it with just his sloop and his seventy-five men. As a courtesy, Rathbun and Marine Captain John Trevett went to see Biddle at a Charleston coffeehouse to get his approval.[76]

Initially, Biddle thought the plan preposterous, and openly asked Trevett to rejoin him and his approaching cruise. But neither Rathbun nor Trevett could be deterred: the reward was more than worth the risk. Biddle could understand that. As to allowing Trevett to rejoin Biddle, Rathbun was polite but firm: he wanted Trevett. Biddle could understand that, too. Their meeting concluded, Biddle rose from his chair and shook Trevett's hand. "I am so very sorry," he said, "for I never shall see you anymore." Days later, the *Providence* made sail for Nassau.[77]

Once at sea, the Americans were pursued by three British cruisers. They had the weather gauge—allowing them to easily overtake the *Providence* and also control any possible engagement. Try as he might, Rathbun could not shake them. He jettisoned his water casks, threw his supplies overboard, but his three pursuers merely grew larger against the horizon. As a moonless night set in, it seemed to be only a matter of time before the *Providence* became another Royal Navy prize.

Once it was completely dark, Rathbun told his crew to douse all lights and lower their sails as quietly as possible. Working in the dark and without a sound, his men did as ordered. Sometime that night, three British ships sailed past the possum called the *Providence*. Once Rathbun was sure they were long past his ship, he simply said, "Make sail," and they headed for Abaco.

Rathbun spent two days there, resupplying the *Providence* before making for New Providence, sailing into Nassau harbor the night of January 27. Once again he ordered the sails lowered, while Trevett's marines assisted the carpenter in building a scaling ladder. By midnight the sloop was a mile from Fort Nassau.

One of the twenty-six "lambs" that Trevett had handpicked for this action approached him. The marine had recently gone lame from some mishap at sea. Worried that he might endanger the mission, he told Trevett, "I can't run." Trevett lifted the man's spirits. "You are the Man I would choose," he said, and sent him into the longboat. With muffled oars, the Americans rowed to the beach. The failure or success of this venture was in their hands now.

Once ashore, they made their way up through the thickets towards the fort, where they came to a high picket fence. Trevett recalled it well; he had removed some of the pickets two years earlier. He found it just as he had left it, and led his men through to an embrasure where they could hear British sentries chatting along the ramparts. Suddenly one of the guards cried, "All's well," soon echoed by the sentinel aboard the *Mary*. For what seemed an interminable length of time, Trevett's men waited until the sentries had moved farther down the walls. Taking their ladder, they scaled the wall.

They were just inside the fort when Trevett bumped into a guard. Seizing him by the collar, Trevett shoved him into a barracks doorway. "For God's sake," the startled man cried, "what have I done?" After he told Trevett that there was only one other sentry, Trevett pushed him inside and went after the other one, who informed him that while they were the only two guards, five hundred men were just a holler away. The marines passed by one loaded 18-pounder, and long, lighted matches, their burning ends easy to see in the darkness. While one marine took up the call "All is well" on the half hour (answered blithely by the *Mary*'s sentinel), Trevett sent some marines to the powder magazine to fill powder cartridges while others pointed the guns towards the streets and the nearby ships in the harbor.

To the amazement of the townsfolk, sunrise found the American flag flying over Fort Nassau, her guns all manned by green-coated American marines. Trevett sent a flag of truce—not to the governor's mansion but to the home of James Gould, a merchant and resident of Rhode Island. Recognizing Trevett, Gould immediately began peppering him with questions about the size of the American fleet and its whereabouts. Trevett answered his questions directly and disingenuously: Biddle's Charleston fleet was lying off Abaco; the *Providence* was in Nassau harbor to take the *Mary* and her goods; and Trevett's marines needed breakfast.

His bluff worked. Gould sent enough bread, bacon, and coffee to feed a garrison. Trevett sent two marines to see the commandant of Fort Montague and inform him that 230 Americans (204 more than the truth) were in possession of

Fort Nassau. He, too, surrendered. A detachment of marines was sent to spike the fort's guns and throw its powder into the harbor. When the *Mary's* second officer—the captain was ill—refused to admit Trevett's boarding party to board, he got as coarse and threatening as a marine can get. This, coupled with a slew of 18-pounders looking down at the ship, changed the officer's mind.

The only thing missing in this great military bluff was the *Providence*— nowhere to be seen. Contrary winds sent her out of sight of the fort during the night. Her absence might have alarmed another officer, but not Trevett. Instead, he asked that a turtle lunch be provided his men. It was. As they ate, the *Providence* sailed into the harbor just ahead of a large British privateer, the *Gayton*, Captain William Chambers—more than a match for Rathbun's little sloop. But the intrepid Trevett was ready, and he fired a salvo at the British ship. One cannonball struck her, sending Chambers into full retreat.

Two days passed before the *Mary* and two other ships were ready to depart with the *Providence*. When word reached Rathbun that Chambers was landing his men to make a night attack, he decided to leave before his luck ran out. The marines spiked Fort Nassau's guns, those ships not going with Rathbun were burnt, and Trevett finished his work on the island with one last gesture. Taking three unopened casks of rice from the fort, he ordered it distributed to the poor. Scores of indigent residents came with baskets and bags, while a laughing Trevett informed them it was Banyon Day—the meatless weekday for sailors.

As Trevett climbed into the *Providence's* barge with the other marines, a messenger from Captain Chambers asked if he would join the captain at Mrs. Bunches Tavern on the waterfront, with the promise of "no mischief." Mischief having described Trevett's stay, he declined; if the captain "would Come over the Bar and take the Sloop *Providence* then I would take Some Punch with Him," Trevett replied. Then he was off.[78]

With his prizes sailing alongside and his crew near giddy over their success, Rathbun headed for New England, after accomplishing a feat that would have been totally unbelievable were it a piece of fiction.[79]

As the *Providence* departed on its uncertain enterprise, Nicholas Biddle returned to his chores regarding the *Randolph*. He and South Carolina president John Rutledge had decided what ships of the state navy would sail with his frigate: the *General Moultrie*, the *Notre Dame*, the *Fair American*, and the *Polly*. They would clear the coast of British warships and privateers that were picking off merchantmen with no concern for repercussions. Men from two of these ships, the frigates *Carrysfort* and *Perseus*, frequently snuck into town to be sheltered by the sizable contingent of Loyalists, who fed them both a home-cooked meal and the latest military information before they stealthily returned to their ships before sunrise.[80]

Biddle saw the mission as a chance to command a squadron similar in size to Esek Hopkins's two years earlier. The similarities did not stop there, thanks to a family connection—the *General Moultrie*'s captain was his brother, Charles. Nicholas was becoming as attached to Charleston as he was to Philadelphia, not only because of his fiancée, Elizabeth Baker, but also because of the way the townsfolk had adopted both Biddle and his crew. He saw clearing the coast of British warships as an opportunity to repay them for their kindness.[81]

The day after meeting with Rathbun and Trevett, Biddle visited an attorney to make out his will. Recent cruises had made the young captain fairly rich, and his approaching wedding was enough for him to consider getting his affairs in order. In November he was stricken with a fever "that laid Violent hands upon me" at the same time the *Randolph* was being careened. Typically, he "felt much more concern on account of the Ship than for My own Safety." The will provided £25,000 pounds for Elizabeth, and the remainder of his estate to his mother. Now he was ready to face the British.[82]

However, the *Randolph* was the only ship in readiness; it would be weeks—"the next spring Tides" was the latest deadline—before her consorts were able to sail. The delay forced a change in captains. Charles had been offered command of a privateer sailing out of New Bern, North Carolina, ready to embark immediately. Younger brother consented, and command of the *General Moultrie* was given to Philip Sullivan.

Charles had not yet departed on January 15, when he was roused from sleep at four a.m. by screaming and church bells. Charleston was afire, the blaze set by British sailors and their Tory friends in a backhouse or kitchen near the waterfront. Strong winds carried the flames from house to house until all southwest Charleston was burning. Charles ran into the street to the sight of a woman engulfed in flames. Sailors from the *Randolph* joined the soldiers and citizenry in trying to put out the fire, but there was not enough water—unlike Philadelphia, Charleston did not have enough fire engines. More than 250 homes and businesses were destroyed. The fire was not extinguished until the following evening. It was so cold that the water thrown on the roofs of the remaining homes formed icicles along the eaves.[83]

Days later, Charles took "an affectionate leave" of Nicholas, and headed north, while Nicholas led his squadron down Rebellion Road. To add to his contingent of marines, he signed on members of the South Carolina First Regiment, a dashing lot in their black uniforms. Well-wishers crowded the docks. Standing with them was Richard Fordham, the *Randolph*'s carpenter, whose injured leg had not healed; Biddle sent him ashore, to rejoin the frigate on her next cruise.[84]

Once in the Atlantic, Biddle began searching for the enemy. They were nowhere to be found; after a binge of prize-taking and weeks at sea they were in need of repairs. They also had the makings of an epidemic aboard the *Carysfort*. When Tory spies informed their senior captain, Robert Fanshawe, that Biddle's squadron was putting to sea to fight them, he made for St. Augustine.[85]

Rather than return to port, Biddle decided to sail to the West Indies, picking up one prize before reaching Bermuda. Thus far, Biddle's name was a double-edged sword: his successes were rewarded with enough manpower, but word that he was coming with such a force soon reached the Windward Islands, causing British merchantmen to scatter or stay in port, leaving only Dutch and French ships for Biddle to catch and release.[86]

The squadron was sixty leagues off Barbados on Saturday, March 7, sailing under clear skies; if the wind had been blowing a bit stronger, conditions would have been perfect. Around one p.m., the *Randolph*'s mastheader saw a sail four points off the starboard bow. Even with his spyglass, Biddle had a hard time making her out—was she a large merchantman or a frigate? As usual, the best way for Biddle to find out was to make straight for her. He signaled the other captains to follow.[87]

Light winds slowed their progress. Since it was late winter, visibility began fading by late afternoon, when the sun rides low by dusk before being swallowed up by the horizon. Biddle was partly correct: she was a Royal Navy vessel, HMS *Yarmouth*. Her captain, Nicholas Vincent, did not spot the squadron until five p.m. Vincent made out six sail standing to the southward, and decided to stand for them. Seeing the *Yarmouth* come through the wind and head his way, Biddle knew he would have a fight on his hands; how much of one he would know when he got close enough to count her guns.[88]

Biddle had spent half his life in two navies, mastering his sailing skills and developing an approach to leadership that was both fearless and fair. That his men obeyed and admired him was evident the second the drummer began his incessant rhythm: *Beat to Quarters. Beat to Quarters.*

By seven p.m. the only light was a quarter moon, yet to ascend to the roof of the sky. Earlier, Biddle had signaled the ships to heave to and await the approaching *Yarmouth*, now just a black shape closing in on them, making straight for the *Randolph*. While the *General Moultrie* and the *Notre Dame* were astern the frigate, the *Polly*, the *Fair American*, and the captured schooner were now downwind, far to the west of the *Randolph*. Biddle laid his mizzen topsail to the mast, allowing the frigate to turn to windward and wait for the enemy. The *General Moultrie* did the same, but only after she shot ahead of the *Randolph*.[89]

Shortly after nine p.m., the *Yarmouth* came alongside the *General Moultrie*. Taking up his speaking trumpet, Vincent hailed Captain Sullivan to identify himself and his ship.

"The *Polly*," he lied.

"Where from?" Vincent demanded.

"New York," Sullivan replied, in hopes of making Vincent think the ships were Loyalist.

Seeing the *Randolph* dead ahead, Vincent sent the *Yarmouth* past Sullivan's ship. For the first time that day, the *Yarmouth* could be easily identified. "My God," a marine gasped aboard the *General Moultrie*. "A two-decker!"

The *Yarmouth* was a third-rate ship-of-the-line, sixty-four guns, exactly twice the *Randolph*'s firepower, many of them 18-pounders. She was less than two hundred feet away when she came alongside Biddle's frigate. "Who are you?" Vincent demanded. "Answer, or we fire!"

Biddle nodded to Lieutenant William Barnes to answer. "Continental frigate *Randolph*," Barnes replied, as Biddle ordered the Grand Union raised, and his starboard guns opened fire.[90]

Few Continental ships carried gun crews that equaled those of the Royal Navy, but the *Randolph* did—Biddle had seen to that. Their first broadsides slammed hard and accurately into the *Yarmouth*. Vincent ordered his men to aim at the flashes from the *Randolph*'s guns and return fire. By this time, the *Notre Dame* had crossed the *Yarmouth*'s stern, discharging an accurate but light barrage from her little 4-pounders, while Sullivan fired indiscriminately at both ships until he was told that most of his shots were striking the *Randolph*. The *Fair American* and the *Polly*, far from the fray, tacked their way closer.[91]

Vincent could dismiss the effect of the *Notre Dame*'s small guns, but he was in the fight of his life as much as Biddle was because of the speed and accuracy of the *Randolph*'s gunners. Eyewitnesses recalled that they fired four broadsides to the *Yarmouth*'s one. The fight was only minutes old, and Vincent's rigging and sails were already shot to pieces, his bowsprit and mizzen topmast useless from American round shot.[92]

The ships were now so close that American and British marines could lob their grenades across the water onto their enemy's deck. Sharpshooters from the *Randolph*'s fighting tops fired volley after volley at the *Yarmouth*'s sailors, while others loaded and fired the four coehorns, lobbing their shells over the water onto the giant ship's deck. From his high poop deck, Vincent assessed the situation: five dead and twelve wounded, his ship-of-the-line being destroyed by a frigate.[93]

Biddle was directing the fight from his quarterdeck with his usual quiet assurance when suddenly he went down, blood spurting from his thigh as his officers rushed to him. Lieutenant Barnes called for hands to carry the captain below. Biddle would not hear of it. Realizing that he could not stand, he rose to a sitting position, telling his officers it was "a slight touch" and commanding a sailor to get a surgeon's mate and a chair from his cabin. His wound would be dressed on the quarterdeck. Biddle was not going anywhere.[94]

Taking heart by their captain's refusal to go below, Biddle's officers resumed their duties—there was a battle to be won. The marines maintained their hellish fire from the tops; unarmed sailors manned the sheets and braces, fearlessly adjusting them under fire to keep the wind in their favor; the gun crews, sweating from the heat of the guns despite the cool night air, their eyes smarting from smoke, loading, firing, and reloading their guns. As the surgeon's mate dressed Biddle's wound—from either a musket ball or a flying splinter—he sat in his chair, calmly directing the action.[95]

Aboard the *Yarmouth* British tars and marines were playing their parts with the same courageous deliberation. Vincent's gunners were taking a quick glance at the *Randolph*'s starboard cannon flashes to adjust their aim, when a sudden, deafening explosion detonated in front of them. Instantly, fire and smoke filled the air. Time seemed to stop; the fire seemed to extinguish itself as the smoke cleared in the light breeze.

The *Randolph* and her 305 men were gone.

Sailors from all the ships were stunned from what they had seen as much as from the blast. Suddenly debris from the vanished frigate rained down on the *Yarmouth*: shattered beams, grisly remains, even a rolled-up American flag, not so much as singed. A six-foot piece of timber crashed down on the poop deck, just missing Vincent and his officers, while another pierced the foretopgallant sail. Vincent realized how lucky he was, being windward of the frigate—had he been on her port side, the impact of the blast could have destroyed the *Yarmouth* as well.[96]

Reactions aboard Biddle's squadron ranged from coolheadedness to panic.

RANDOLPH and Squadron against *YARMOUTH* off Barbados, March 7, 1778

| HMS *Yarmouth* **SHIP-OF-THE-LINE** | *Randolph* | *General Moultrie* | *Notre Dame* | *Polly* | *Fair American* |

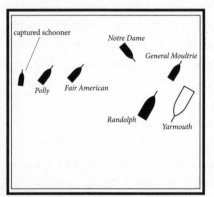

AFTERNOON OF MARCH 7: Ship-of-the-line *Yarmouth*, heading northward, sights Biddle's squadron and wears ship to pursue. Biddle turns the *Randolph* through the wind to investigate *Yarmouth*.

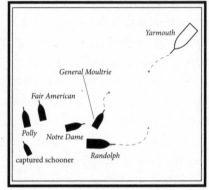

EVENING OF MARCH 7: *General Moultrie* sails ahead of *Randolph* with *Notre Dame* to windward. *Polly*, *Fair American*, and schooner tack too far westward.

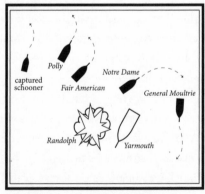

7 P.M.: *Yarmouth* fires broadside at *General Moultrie*, passing her to engage *Randolph*. *Notre Dame*, *Polly*, and *Fair American* endeavor to get on *Yarmouth*'s stern.

7:15 P.M.: After fifteen-minute engagement, *Randolph* explodes. Biddle's squadron scatters.

Aboard the *General Moultrie*, Sullivan ordered his colors struck, only to be stopped by Captain John Blake of the First South Carolina, in charge of the marines: this was not the time to surrender, Blake insisted, but to sail away—the *Yarmouth* was badly damaged, and could not catch them. One by one, the other ships followed the *General Moultrie*'s example and sailed into the darkness. The *Yarmouth* did give chase, but only for a short while; it was dark, the ship was in bad shape, and, perhaps, no one wanted to go back to fighting after what they had just witnessed.[97]

Vincent spent the better part of Sunday getting the *Yarmouth* repaired well enough to begin searching for the other American ships. For several days he scoured the seas with no sign of the rebel vessels. In the wee hours of March 12, the mastheader sighted a sail to westward. Vincent gave orders to make chase. While in pursuit, he came upon a sight he called "something very remarkable," telling his admiral

> We discovered a piece of wood with four Men on it waving. We hauled up to it, got a boat out, and brought them on board; they prov'd to be four Men who had been in the Ship when she blew up,—and who had nothing to subsist on from that time, but by sucking the rain Water that fell on a piece of Blanket, which they luckily had picked up. They informed us the Ship was called the *Randolph*.[98]

The quartet of survivors was "a Scotchman, a Frenchman, a Spaniard and a Dane." Alexander Robinson, Bartholomew Bourdeau, John Carew, and Hans Workman had been manning a gun in Biddle's cabin when the ship exploded. For some reason, the blast threw them out of the cabin into the sea and not up to their Maker. Somehow they pieced together a makeshift raft out of the *Randolph*'s floating debris. For four days and nights they survived on the open sea, "buried alive," one newspaper reported, "under the vault of heaven."[99]

Another report described them as "young and hardy," not appearing "much discomposed." All they asked their captors for was "a bason of tea" and "a hammock to each," to restore their health; soon only their swollen feet remained an issue. They had no idea why, or how, the *Randolph* blew up. Vincent gave up his search for the American ships that survived the *Randolph* after saving the *Randolph*'s survivors, and headed for Barbados for repairs.[100]

News of the *Randolph* tragedy shocked Americans. "Our little fleet," the Marine Committee wrote, "is much diminished." The new President of South

Carolina, Rawlins Lowndes, mourned "the very promising Youths of this Country who have thus immaturely fallen in their Countrys Service," while Simon Fanning, the young midshipman that Biddle placed in charge of the captured schooner, possessed "all the gallantry of the bravest officer."

The news struck Charles Biddle particularly hard; upon hearing it, he left New Bern for Charleston: "During the journey I had many melancholy reflections; it was different from my last, when I went to see and enjoy the company of a much loved brother." Elizabeth Baker could not be consoled.[101]

Not yet twenty-eight when he died, Nicholas Biddle had survived a shipwreck, almost being marooned by a sea of ice near the North Pole, an armed gang of mutineers, and endless rounds of shot and musket ball with an assured courage other men marveled at or downright envied. He was right, two years earlier, when he matter-of-factly wrote, "I fear nothing." It took an explosion to kill Nicholas Biddle.

As Captain Vincent brought the battered *Yarmouth* into Bridgetown, Barbados, he found two warships, the *Ceres* and the *Ariadne*, in port with a prize: "a very Stout Privateer called the *Alfred*."

The *Raleigh* and the *Alfred* had sailed from l'Orient on December 29, 1777, bound for the West Indies after a cruise along the African coast. Thomas Thompson's *Raleigh* now boasted a full complement of thirty-two guns; Elisha Hinman's *Alfred* was just as slow as she had been on the voyage to France, forcing Thompson to shorten sail and wait for the original Continental flagship.[102]

The African leg of their cruise was unproductive, and they were nearing the Windward Islands when the *Ceres* and *Ariadne* appeared over the horizon. The *Raleigh* had as many guns as the two smaller British ships, but she was farther away. The *Ariadne* reached the *Alfred* first, and Hinman engaged. Soon the *Ceres* came up and began firing. Hinman looked towards the *Raleigh*: what was Thompson waiting for?[103]

"I had not yet determin'd in my own mind what was best to be done," Thompson honestly recalled later. He watched as the *Alfred* tried to outfight or escape the enemy. She could do neither. Seeing her situation as hopeless, Thompson lowered his sails, hoping to draw at least one of them towards the *Raleigh*. When neither British captain fell for his ruse, Hinman struck his colors.

Now the British ships pursued the biggest dog in the fight. On the voyage across the Atlantic to France, Thompson had brazenly sailed into a British fleet with but six cannon on deck, but now he changed course. Over the next nineteen hours he fled, throwing everything he could think of overboard to lighten his ship—except his new French guns. Had it come to a fight, the *Raleigh* had every advantage, except in leadership.[104]

Once the British gave up the chase Thompson made for Boston, where, to his dismay, he learned that news of the *Alfred*'s capture had beat him there. He was a pariah, "Condemned by every One." The Marine Committee suspended him from command. As a result of John Barry's daring escapades on the Delaware, he was appointed captain.[105]

Two more ships joined the *Randolph*, the *Virginia*, and the *Alfred* in the loss column that spring. In Providence, Rhode Island, Hoysted Hacker was ordered by the Marine Committee to break out of the British blockade and sail the *Columbus* to New London, Connecticut. Earlier, John Hopkins had sailed the frigate *Warren* past the enemy's ships, despite their being tipped off by a Rhode Island Loyalist to expect the attempt. Hopkins succeeded "One Very Dark Knight," one militiaman stated; he was doing sentry duty on a nearby beach when a "black cloud" passed him by. It was the *Warren*. She eluded the British ships, including the detested *Somerset* from Lexington and Concord days, and was soon in Boston.[106]

Now came Hacker's turn. Ordered to sail "on the first opportunity of Wind & Weather," Hacker made his run on March 27, escorting a merchantman in the bargain. She made a poor convoy, having been stripped of all her guns but her swivels. She was spotted and recognized by two British frigates and trapped before she got past Port Judith. The next morning, Hacker's men and some militiamen turned back a British boarding party, but before the day was out, they abandoned the last of the original Continental ships. The British promptly burned her.[107]

That March, on the Atlantic Ocean, John Young was sailing the sloop *Independence* home from France after departing Nantes with John Paul Jones and the *Ranger*. Jones had suggested that Young make for the Carolinas, and he was doing just that. Upon reaching the North Carolina coast, Young picked up a pilot to get his ship over the Ocracoke bar. Instead, the *Independence* was wrecked on the bar. While Young managed to save most of his guns and supplies, it was suspected that the pilot had sabotaged him. The *Independence* was the fifth Continental ship lost in three months.[108]

Despite Rathbun's Nassau expedition, Barry's Delaware adventure, and Tucker's safe escort of John Adams, the Continental Navy was off to a sad start in 1778.

Even a cartel bringing captured sailors back to Boston brought more misery: the men were stricken with smallpox that spread so quickly through Boston that widespread "anoculation" was ordered. Looking back to 1775, one Boston official wrote to Colonel Timothy Pickering, "We should have bin in Much happier Sucumstances." Pickering agreed. "Our Naval affairs have been conducted shockingly," he replied.[109]

Who was going to turn this tide?

CHAPTER EIGHT

✮ ✮ ✮

"HER TEETH WERE TOO MANY"

I had the *Ranger* in disguise at Camaret but I have now pulled off
[the] Masque as the face of Affairs are altered.

—JOHN PAUL JONES TO SILAS DEANE[1]

For more than a month, John Paul Jones had been sailing the *Ranger* off the French coast, tinkering with the masts and sails, dealing with a sickly and nearly mutinous crew, and abiding the backstabbing of his senior officers, led by Lieutenant Simpson. With loyal sailors coming down with smallpox, disgruntled ones jumping ship (taking the *Ranger*'s cutter and abandoning it on the rocks offshore), and his ship's still crank condition, Jones returned to Brest on March 8.[2]

While in port, Jones finished his renovations, reducing the yards and sails and ordering lighter steering and topsails. He dispatched several letters to the American commissioners and agents, all mentioning, hinting, or outright begging for the frigate *l'Indien*. Earlier he had begun his refitting with a "Masque"—a red cloth draped over his gun ports to hide the *Ranger*'s belligerent status—but that was no longer necessary. Lord Stormont had returned to England. Louis XVI had instructed that his ambassador to George III inform the British monarch that the United States had made an offer of alliance that the French could not refuse. Next, Louis sent notification to his "Very Dear, Great Friends, and Allies" that the French army and navy were now on their side. As Louis dictated this, Comte d'Estaing was preparing his fleet to cross the Atlantic.

Knowing this, Jones removed his ship's red camouflage. Unlike Wickes, Conyngham et al., he was unencumbered by diplomatic games. He was also the guest of Admiral Louis Guillouet, the Comte d'Orvilliers, commander of the French fleet at Brest, aboard his hundred-and-ten-gun flagship *Le Bretagne*. The admiral's great cabin was more a palatial chamber than officer's quarters. That Jones was treated like an admiral by d'Orvilliers was gratifying enough for his ego, but when the admiral promised to intercede on Jones's behalf about *l'Indien*—well, that was even more to his liking.[3]

By this time, news of Lord North's changes in both personnel and policy had reached France. Admiral Howe was to be replaced by Vice Admiral James Gambier—not nearly as popular as "Black Dick"—while General Howe was to be succeeded by Sir Henry Clinton. But the big news lay in new orders from Lord North's government. As First Lord of the Admiralty, the Earl of Sandwich gave a grave assessment of the condition of the King's Navy: in a word, alarming. The French navy alone, he believed, would tip the scales in America's favor. Lord Germain's orders to Clinton stressed a drastic change from the Howes' "olive branch and musket" approach:

> Relinquish the Idea of carrying on offensive Operations against the Rebels within Land, and as soon as the Season will permit, to embark such a Body of Troops as can be spared . . . on board of transports under the Conduct of a proper number of the King's Ships, with Orders to attack the Ports on the Coast, from New York to Nova Scotia, and to Seize or destroy every Ship or Vessel . . . destroy all Wharfs and Stores, and Materials for Ship-building . . . [and establish] a Post upon the Delaware River.

Germain also directed that once New England and the mid-Atlantic ports were occupied or destroyed, "it is the King's Intention that an Attack should be made on the Southern Colonies with a View to the Conquest and Possession of Georgia & South Carolina." The Howe brothers' gentlemanly approach to the rebellion was coming home with the Howes.[4]

Since Jones's arrival in France, he had shared his ideas as to how the Continental Navy should be employed with the American commissioners, just as he had at home with Robert Morris and Joseph Hewes. Now he was about to put his theories into action, not against Nova Scotia fishing villages but in the British Empire's front yard. Jones was in Philadelphia in 1775 when news reached Congress of the burning of American towns by the British in Massachusetts and Rhode Island. He wanted to pay them back in kind—not by destroying civilian homes but "by making a good fire in England of *shipping*," he declared. Ever cocksure—at least in public—he wrote John Ross, American agent at Nantes, "the world lays all before me." He sailed on April 8.[5]

One week later, foul weather greeted Jones on his return to St. George's Channel—waters he knew well from his merchant days. He had big plans for his return to home waters: ship burnings, coastal raids, and a kidnapping.

The *Ranger* was making for Whitehaven, the very town Jones first shipped from as a boy. It remained a bustling port; scores of ships—perhaps over a hundred—might be in the harbor for Jones to torch. The last time a British seaport had been raided was in 1667 by Dutch admiral Willem Joseph van Ghent during the Second Anglo-Dutch War.

From Whitehaven, Jones would cross the Mull of Solway to Kirkudbright, where he had been ignominiously jailed over the Mungo Maxwell affair. Jones intended to kidnap the local laird, the Earl of Selkirk, a friend of William Craik and the Maxwells. His ransom would not be demanded in coin but in the release of American sailors, imprisoned at Mill Prison and Forten Prison in England. Jones saw his plans as the perfect combination of patriotic risk and retribution. Young John Paul was not deemed worthy enough for the Royal Navy; John Paul Jones wanted to show them otherwise.[6]

The peril of being in enemy waters did not concern Jones nearly as much as the tempest swirling below deck. Sometime during this brief passage, Lieutenant Jean Meijer, a Swede who had signed on this cruise in search of adventure, asked to see Jones in private. Meijer had learned from a fellow Swedish sailor that a cadre of officers and men planned to seize Jones and either clap him in irons or throw him overboard. After turning command of the *Ranger* over to Simpson, they would make for Portsmouth. At a prearranged signal, the ship's sailing master, David Cullam, a hulking brute, would subdue Jones when other officers uninvolved in the plot were scattered about the ship.

At the appointed time, the conspiring officers went below, leaving Jones alone on the quarterdeck as Cullam came up the steps. Jones greeted him with a loaded pistol and pointed it at his head. The hands on deck did not hear what Jones said, but they saw Cullam back down the stairs.

We may find it shocking that Jones did not clap Cullam in irons. In fact, Cullam was not even relieved of his position. Jones really had no choice. Other than Meijer he had no ally among the officers, and he was well aware that the crew was in Simpson's pocket. Should the *Ranger* get in a fight, Jones would have to keep one eye on the enemy before him and the other on the New Englanders behind him.

In truth, much of the blame rested upon Jones's shoulders. Unlike Barry and Biddle, he established little connection with his men. All they wanted was to survive and be paid; Jones wanted glory first and foremost. He had been weeks in Paris, and the void at the top had been filled by Simpson, the man Jones abhorred. Had this been HMS *Ranger*, Cullam would surely have been executed along with his coconspirators. But the Continental Navy was not so established. Its sailors and officers were for the most part poorly trained, frequently poorly led, and almost always poorly paid—when they were paid at all. At this moment, Jones needed a prize more than a cat-o'-nine-tails.[7]

On April 15, the *Ranger* captured the brigantine *Dolphin*, carrying flaxseed to Wexford. While the cargo was of little worth, Jones took the crew prisoner and sank her. Then came a true prize, the *Lord Chatham*, a 350-ton merchantman, her hold full of English porter, ironically bound for Dublin, the world's capital of stout. Jones put a prize crew aboard her and sent her to Brest. Two days later the *Ranger* was well up the Firth of Solway, past the Isle of Man. Soon she was off Whitehaven.

Jones rounded up thirty volunteers to man the *Ranger*'s boats; they would row into town at ten that night. The *Ranger*'s lights were doused and the boats lowered when suddenly the wind kicked up, the seas rose too high, and Jones aborted the mission. The *Ranger* sailed away.[8]

On the nineteenth, the Americans were again off the Isle of Man when they were spotted by a revenue cutter, the *Hussar*, Captain Gurley, eight guns. Suspecting that the *Ranger* was a large smuggler, Gurley made straight for her. Through his spyglass, Gurley saw her captain "dressed in white with a large hat"—a French army captain's uniform. As the *Hussar* approached, Jones ordered Cullam to take his speaking trumpet and ask Gurley for a pilot—a shopworn ruse to take hostage first, ship later. Gurley demanded that Cullam identify himself. "*Molly* of Glasgow," he replied.

The delay gave Jones time to size the *Hussar* up as easy pickings. Enough of the charade: Jones ordered Gurley to heave to or be sunk, running out his guns and running up the American flag.

But Gurley was not cowed. Just as he gave Jones the same orders, Cullam traded his speaking trumpet for his musket and fired at Gurley a split second before the *Ranger* opened fire. Cullam missed. Seeing his ship outgunned,

Gurley sheered off, taking Jones on a chase he would have been proud of had he been commanding the cutter. Despite Jones's "warm attempt" to take her, the *Hussar* got away.[9]

The cutter's escape only added to the disgruntled mood of the *Ranger*'s crew. Even the temperate Dr. Green was angry: "had the Captain have permitted the Marines to fire," the Americans "might have taken her with great Ease," he wrote in his diary. Not only that, but the *Ranger*'s cover was blown—Gurley would spread word that another rebel ship was following the route of the *Reprisal, Lexington,* and *Revenge.* Jones headed west, and sank two small ships to prevent further word of his presence getting out. He soon learned from his newest captives that a fleet of twelve merchantmen was nearby, but a hard squall ended Jones's hopes of taking them.[10]

The *Ranger* was off northeast Ireland near Carrickfergus (just above Belfast) when another fishing boat captain told Jones about a twenty-gun warship, the *Drake,* anchored there. En route, Jones developed a plan to sail into the harbor, cross the ship's bow, have his marines cover the enemy deck with musket fire, throw his grappling hooks over, and board her. He took one of the fishermen to serve as pilot.

Once more the weather and his crew befouled his plans. The *Ranger* glided silently into the harbor, her gun ports closed. The *Drake*'s watch suspected nothing. As the *Ranger* closed in, Jones ordered the anchor dropped to bring his ship right alongside the *Drake.* Had the mate in charge been sober the plan might have worked. But Jones believed the man "had too much brandy"—a gift from Simpson?—and the *Ranger* slid right past the *Drake,* forcing Jones to cut the anchor cable. Intent on another attempt, Jones wore ship, but a fierce gale began howling down the roadstead, sending the *Ranger* towards the lee shore and perilously close to the lighthouse. Curiously, Jones and his fisherman-pilot avoided running aground near the lighthouse, making it out of the harbor unscathed and undetected.[11]

The following morning, under perfect sailing conditions, Jones beheld a sight he had not seen for years: "the Three Kingdoms." The coasts of England, Scotland, and Ireland lay before him, covered in white from an overnight snowfall "as far as the Eye could reach." Jones summoned all hands.[12]

Once the crew was assembled, Jones informed them of his plan. "I am resolved once more to attempt Whitehaven," he declared. Two boats would enter the harbor that evening and take the two forts by surprise. While one party spiked the guns, another would burn the merchantmen in port before escaping to the *Ranger* before sunup. The tides would be in their favor: high in the evening, when the forts would be taken, and so low later on that the ships in port would be sitting in a foot of water or less, making it easier to burn them. Jones would lead the enterprise. Who would accompany him?

Instead of being overwhelmed with volunteers, Jones was inundated with dismissive comments and barbed questions. First to announce their lack of support were Lieutenants Simpson and Hall, citing fatigue. They were sailors, they insisted, not arsonists (Jones later stated they preferred "gain over honor"). Then Surgeon Green spoke up. Jones had considered him an ally on board; to his surprise, Green was vehemently against the raid. Believing that Jones would burn the town as well as the ships—which Green took to mean the villagers' fishing boats as well—Green remonstrated with Jones: "Nothing could be got by burning poor people's property," he scolded. There was a murmur of approval from the crew. His denunciation shocked and angered Jones.[13]

Remarkably, he kept his famous temper in check. He had no intention of burning anyone's home. His idea of striking fear into the British with this raid was being compromised by his officers, whose collective vision did not extend to Buckingham Palace, Parliament, or Lloyd's of London, as Jones's did. They saw this raid as risk with no reward. Their towns had not been bombarded nor their homes burned; they had no desire for revenge. They deemed Jones's mission as beneath them, just as Simpson did. Had Jones's crew been from Falmouth and not Portsmouth, they might have been more supportive.

But by nightfall he again had thirty volunteers. His shoulders draped by his dark blue coat, Jones stepped into the *Ranger*'s cutter while Marine Lieutenant Samuel Wallingford took charge of the jolly boat. Lieutenant Meijer came with Jones. Armed with cutlasses, pistols, and pikes, and "candles"—pinecones covered with canvas and soaked in brimstone—the volunteers lowered the boats at midnight, well behind Jones's schedule.[14]

Typical for Jones's luck on this cruise, the wind soon died. The men began their long row to Whitehaven, reaching the stone quay just before dawn; so much for taking advantage of the cover of darkness. Once the boats were secured, Jones led his party to the first fort, leaving a detail under Meijer behind with the boats. He sent Wallingford's men to the merchantmen, literally stuck in the mud of low tide. Unlike Trevett at New Providence, Jones had no scaling ladders; he and his men ascended the wall by climbing atop their comrades' shoulders. Jones was the first man over the ramparts.

It was a cold morning, and with no thought or fear of invasion or a surprise inspection by the officer of the watch, the sentries were all in the guardhouse. Brandishing their cutlasses and pistols, Jones's men burst through the door, taking them without a fight. Next, Jones led his men to the fort's three dozen guns. Within minutes they were spiked; the captain next led the Rangers in a pell-mell run to the southern battery of the fort to do the same. Looking over the wall, Jones saw scores of merchantmen, all of them two hundred tons and over, "laying side by side aground, unsurrounded by Water." Dozens more were visible on the south side of the fort, but not a sign of Wallingford's men; where there is no smoke, there is no fire.

For while Jones's men were following his orders with exactitude, Wallingford's were throwing a party. Instead of making for the idle ships, they had hustled to the nearest pub. In seconds, the tavern's liquor was the property of the Continental Navy; in minutes, Wallingford's sailors and marines were drunk. The bad news for Jones was that these volunteers had not followed his plan; the good news was that they had not followed theirs, which was to abandon their captain in Whitehaven. Meijer and his guards prevented them from taking the boats.[15]

Now betrayal was added to the mayhem and mutiny planned by the New Englanders. An Irishman named David Smith had signed on in Portsmouth, ostensibly to sail for the Cause but actually to return home. Whitehaven was close enough. As American sailors captured a fort and a tavern, Smith—in reality David Freeman—became a horseless Paul Revere, running through the streets, pounding on doors and rousing sleeping Scots, spreading the news that their ships were going to be burned. Thus alarmed, villagers left their homes, many in just nightshirts and armed with everything from muskets to carving knives, heading to the docks to repel the rebel invaders.[16]

By now it was five a.m., and daylight was breaking. Jones confronted some of Wallingford's detachment, demanding to know why they had disobeyed orders. Slurring their words, they told him their lanterns had gone out, and they had nothing to ignite their "candles." A growing noise from the streets caught Jones's ear, and soon he saw scores of Scotsmen, their eyes afire, determined to take Jones's American pirates.

Thinking quickly, Jones posted guards by the docks, then sent a sailor into a house for matches. There was a collier near the quay; if Jones could put her to the torch the fire might spread to the other ships nearby. Jones threw one of the candles on her. Nothing. Some Americans came up the pier with a barrel of tar, and Jones sent it aboard the collier, to be taken below and set on fire. Soon flames shot out of the ship's hatchways, just as the waterfront became overrun with townsfolk. Brandishing his pistol, Jones approached them, putting himself between the crowd and the burning collier, and ordered them to disperse. They withdrew, just as the flames "caught the rigging and ascended the mainmast."[17]

Jones ordered his men to their boats. "The sun was a full hour's march above the horizon," he later reported. For another minute he remained alone on the pier, taking in the panic and cacophony he had caused. Then he climbed into the cutter and the two boats rowed apace for the *Ranger* just as some of the Scotsmen retrieved a couple of dismantled, unspiked cannons. Once in place, they fired them aimlessly at the departing rebels, who discharged their muskets and pistols in a sardonic salute. There had been no casualties.[18]

Aboard the *Ranger*, the rest of Jones's crew spent the night and the early morning looking ashore, waiting for pillars of smoke to rise from Whitehaven and the ships in port. Now they "began to fear that Our People had fallen into the Enemies Hands," Ezra Green wrote in his diary. Suddenly, they could make out the *Ranger's* boats heading towards them. While the crew was glad to see their shipmates returning, Simpson and Hall, recognizing Jones by his dark hat and white uniform, fell glum. If Jones's plan had gone awry for the most part, his very presence was proof that theirs had failed abysmally.[19]

While Jones was angry that the Whitehaven raid had fallen so far short of his expectations, he kept this to himself. Had he landed sooner, or had he the crew from the *Providence*, he later wrote, "not a single Ship out of more than Two hundred could possibly have escaped; and all the World would not have been able to save the Town." He later took heart that his exploit showed "that not all their boasted Navy can protect their own Coasts, and that the Scenes of distress which they have occasioned in America may soon be brought to their own doors."[20]

For now, Jones was on borrowed time. Between the *Hussar's* escape and his Whitehaven incursion it would not be long before the enemy would be combing the Irish Sea and the North Channel looking for "the Pirate Jones," as he was soon to be called. He still had two more "scheems" to carry out, and he was already off on the next one. The *Ranger* was soon under full sail, heading to Kircudbright. They reached St. Mary's Isle and were below the Selkirk castle before noon.[21]

St. Mary's Isle is actually a peninsula that barely juts into the Firth of Solway, and the Selkirk "castle" a brick mansion situated on a hundred wooded acres. Jones assumed Lord Selkirk to be of such importance and influence that kidnapping him would guarantee both the freeing of American prisoners and give further luster to Jones's reputation. Again, he got it wrong; Selkirk was a peer of the realm with very little influence, political or otherwise. He was also not nearly as malevolent as old Craik, possessing a reputation for generosity and civic duty.[22]

The channel to St. Mary's Isle has its hazards, but Jones knew these waters from his boyhood. Acting as his own pilot, he took the *Ranger* past Torr's Point and the endless array of blooming trees of Clauchcandolly, below Criffel, the looming snowcapped peak that had looked down on Jones's activities as a child. He was home. For the second time that day, the cutter was lowered, and Jones headed off to kidnap a lord.[23]

To accompany him and the volunteers Jones brought two officers, Wallingford and Cullam. As they made their way up the steep, wooded path they came upon Selkirk's gardener. Jones informed him that this gang of toughs was a press gang, seeking to add some landsmen to the Royal Navy's "recruits." Not wanting to be taken himself, the gardener fled, but not before telling Jones that Selkirk was away.

For Jones, such news was the perfect end to the day. As far as he was concerned, there was no reason to proceed to the mansion, and he began the long walk back to the cutter. The mission was pointless. But his officers stopped him cold: the mansion was right through the clearing ahead, unprotected, with most of the men on the estate fleeing to hide from Jones's "press gang." Riches awaited them inside: jewelry, gold, and silver, along with fine food, drink, and women.

Jones could understand this coming from Cullam, a mutineer. But he was shocked that Wallingford was equally game. Ironically, they used Jones's own rationale for burning Whitehaven against him. Unlike Simpson and Hall, they did have friends in Falmouth, and knew other civilians who had suffered under British hands. Jones was right, they said. It was time for retribution, and what better place than a lord's estate? The men echoed their sentiments.[24]

Jones had been—and would be—in hard places, but never in a circumstance like this. What his men proposed to do—and more—was way off Jones's moral compass. But oppose them, and he could be killed right on this footpath. Wash his hands of them, and his reputation, more valuable to him than his life, would never recover. He had seconds to defuse this situation.

He did it. The men would accompany Wallingford and Cullam to the front door, but not go in. The officers were to request—not simply seize—the Selkirk silver. They were to be on their best behavior—they were representing the United States Navy—and take only what was given them and return without one match being lit, one servant being struck, and one woman touched. The men agreed.

Embarrassed that his grand, if odd, plan for freeing imprisoned sailors had become a thief's errand, Jones remained where he stood. In insisting that his men do their duty, Jones was in dereliction of his. He waited on the path.[25]

The vacuum of moral authority that Jones had created was filled once his officers knocked at the Selkirk front door. The butler let the officers in and went for Lady Selkirk, who was breakfasting with guests. There was a press gang at the door, he explained, adding that the gardeners had all fled. Peering through a window, she saw a band of "horrid wretches" outside, sent the females in the house to the third floor, and went to confront the brigands at her door.

In the grand foyer she encountered a "younger officer in [a] Green uniform" with a "vile blackguard" in a blue coat. Wallingford and Cullam found themselves facing a very pregnant lady who swept into the room like a galleon, the perfect combination of manners and courage.

Told by Wallingford that "we are masters of this house and everything in it," Lady Selkirk showed neither rage nor fear. "I am sensible of that," she answered. Exuding more discomfort than his hostess, Wallingford demanded the silver. Lady Selkirk sent the butler to retrieve it, along with some bags to carry it in. She showed the men into the parlor and gave them each a glass of wine.

The butler did not bring down enough of it for Cullam. "Where is the teapot and the coffee pot?" he asked derisively. These were also brought to the parlor, still warm from breakfast. Lady Selkirk asked for a receipt; the uncomfortable Wallingford began writing one, but Cullam stopped him: it was time to leave.

Somehow during this escapade Jones's name came up. This John Paul Jones was really "One John Paul born at Arbigland, who once commanded a Kircudbright vessel," Lady Selkirk wrote her husband, and "as great a villain ever born," recounting his run-ins with the law as a Scottish mariner. As for the officers, she remarked that they "behaved with great civility."[26]

Jones could hear his men coming down the path before he saw them. The whole affair had taken but twenty minutes, but each one was a lifetime for the captain, pacing constantly and half expecting that the mansion and his reputation would soon be up in smoke. The men clambered into the cutter. As his men rowed Jones and their loot back to the *Ranger*, word spread from the runaway gardeners among the villagers. Soon it was mixed with news from Whitehaven, and the entire population along the Firth of Solway was alarmed. A few determined souls manned a decrepit cannon and fired it at the cutter, but fear was the prevalent emotion. Shops closed. People hid in their homes.

Jones had burned neither town nor ship (the collier was saved after he departed), and had failed miserably in his brief career as a kidnapper. But he had done what he set out to do: strike terror in British hearts. It was as if the Vikings had returned.[27]

And the day was not over. Once aboard the *Ranger*, he informed the crew that they were heading back to Carrickfergus—and the *Drake*. His men, in Surgeon Green's words, showed "great unwillingness to make the attempt." Enough was enough. Jones had been victimized by his crew twice this day, as they stepped on the line dividing sullen insubordination and mutinous betrayal. There would not be a third. Even Simpson's mutinous remarks would not deter Jones from returning to France with a British prize, flying the American flag atop British colors, the time-honored sign of a capture.[28]

By sunrise on April 24 the *Ranger* was sailing through Belfast Lough, heading straight for the Carrickfergus harbor and the *Drake*. Although it seemed impossible to Green, "the Tide & what little wind there was, had imperceptibly carry'd us in so far that there was very little chance for an Escape"—even nature was finally bowing to Jones's "determination to go in." To make the situation even better, the *Drake* was making sail, preparing to come out and confront the strange ship heading into the harbor. Looking through his spyglass, Captain Burden, an older officer whose life was spent in the Royal Navy, thought he was looking at a merchantman flying British colors, her master in a British uniform. He sent the launch to board her and investigate as his men continued readying the *Drake*.

It was noon when the launch came alongside the *Ranger*. As the midshipman in charge came aboard, he was greeted by the *Ranger*'s captain, who informed him that he and his men were now prisoners. To Jones's surprise, this easy capture had "an exhilarating effect" on his crew. Seeing the *Drake* now standing for them, followed by some pleasure boats manned by curious townsfolk, the Rangers caught Jones's spirit. They were spoiling for a fight.

Burden fired a gun to signal his men to return; Jones ran out his guns. Seeing that the coming action was not going to be a lark, the boats with curiosity seekers returned to port. Just then, the shoreline was lit up with bonfires, the centuries-old method of warning sea towns of an enemy ship since the Spanish Armada. The tide was coming in, slowing the *Drake*'s progress; all the while, Jones sailed the *Ranger* back and forth, laying his main topsail to the mast, waiting anxiously in mid-channel for the *Drake*.[29]

On the surface, the two ships seemed evenly matched, the *Ranger*'s eighteen 6-pounders against the *Drake*'s twenty 4-pounders. Burden had a significant edge in both manpower and experience; with 150 men he had forty more than Jones, and they were battle-tested. The Americans were not—particularly Jones's lieutenants. As the *Drake* neared, Jones sent Wallingford and his marines aloft and the Stars and Stripes raised: no need for pretense now.

It was near sundown when Jones cried, "Wear Ship!" As the *Drake* closed within pistol shot, Jones noticed her figurehead, nearly identical to that of his old command, the *Alfred*. The image never left him.[30]

Taking his speaking trumpet, Burden hailed the Americans: "What ship is this?" Cullam answered, "The American Continental ship *Ranger*" just as Jones "ordered the helm up," crossed the *Drake*'s bow, and let fly. He had the guns loaded with grapeshot for this broadside, which whistled through the air, ripping through the *Drake*'s rigging and striking down British tars.

"The Action was warm, close and obstinate," Jones later reported. The *Ranger* had "crossed the T," and now came the *Drake*'s turn as she came across the rebel's stern. But Jones suddenly ordered the helmsman, Thomas Taylor, to send the *Ranger* through the light wind, bringing the ships broadside to broadside. Nevertheless, the British gunners were unerringly accurate, as were their marines in the fighting tops. Taylor felt a burning sensation on his hand, followed by excruciating pain: a musket ball had sheared off his little finger.

Jones's courage was as natural to him as breathing. Pure warrior, he devoted his full attention to directing the battle and paid no heed to personal danger. He kept his gun crews firing at the *Drake*'s deck and rigging. After half an hour, Burden's ship was incapable of effectively sailing. His fore and main topsail yards were "cut away down to the cap"—the thick block of wood that held the long pieces of the mast together. The *Drake*'s flag had been shot away. Burden had another hoisted, only to see that one shot off as well.

Burden's gunners were hammering at the *Ranger*'s hull in an effort to sink her while British marines took deadly aim at the rebels. Aboard the *Ranger*, Midshipman Pierce Powers lost his right hand and nearly his left. Seaman John Dangle was cut in two by a double-headed cannon shot. From the *Drake*'s fighting tops a British marine took aim at a green-coated rebel counterpart across the water and fired. The ball struck Lieutenant Wallingford in the head. He fell lifeless to the deck below.

By seven p.m. it was dark. Damaged as the *Ranger*'s hull was, she could still maneuver. Jones ordered another broadside fired. This one struck down both Captain Burden and his second-in-command, Lieutenant Dobbs, leaving the

Drake's sailing master in command. By now the ship's jib was hanging in the water, and her hull was perforated. Jones's gunners learned their trade this day.

Seeing the futility of maintaining the fight when the *Drake* could no longer sail, her sailing master called for quarter. Jones sent some marines—in the *Drake*'s own launch—to inspect the prize and bring back the commanding officer. The Americans found the deck running with a grisly combination of blood and rum; one of Burden's officers had brought a keg on deck, in anticipation of celebrating victory over the rebels. A cannonball had smashed it to pieces.

The following day, Jones transferred his prisoners to the *Ranger*—133 in all, along with the cook's wife (possible proof that the *Boston*'s sailors' suspicions about women aboard were correct). Jones ordered the masts and rigging repaired as quickly and thoroughly as possible—the Irish Sea was no place for dawdling. The *Ranger* had lost three men, with five wounded; the *Drake* had four killed—including Captain Burden and Lieutenant Dobbs—and nineteen wounded. Jones ordered all buried with full honors. That afternoon, he freed the Irish fishermen captured days before, giving them a boat and "the last Guineas in my Possession to defray their traveling Expences" to Dublin. They in turn gave Jones "three Huzzahs" as they rowed away. He might be a brigand to Lady Selkirk, but he was Robin Hood to these Irishmen.[31]

One last time Jones tried to mollify Simpson, giving him command of the *Drake*. "Contrary winds" forced Jones around northern Ireland, sailing south off the island's west coast with the *Drake* in tow. On May 5, a sail was sighted. Jones, looking for another prize, ordered Simpson to cast off and sail "a Cable's length" from the *Ranger*. Instead of releasing the hawser, Simpson had it severed; as the *Ranger* pursued the sail, the *Drake* disappeared over the horizon. It took a day to catch her.

Over the next two days Jones spotted several potential prizes but passed up pursuit lest he lose Simpson—who would have sailed the wounded *Drake* back to America if he could only give Jones the slip. Both ships reached Brest on May 7, with the *Drake* sailing under American colors over an inverted British flag, just as Jones had envisioned. Once ashore he immediately placed Simpson under arrest for disobeying written orders.[32]

Jones expected a hero's welcome, but the crowd waiting for him in the old French port was sparse. This disappointing reception was soon overshadowed by the lack of acknowledgment of his arrival by the American commissioners in Paris. Jones was no sooner on dry land than he sent them report after report of his cruise, his two hundred prisoners, the open war with Simpson, and his un-dying desire for *l'Indien*. He also informed them that he had drawn 24,000 livres on the commissioners' account to feed, clothe, and pay his men. For days he heard nothing from Paris.[33]

Then a tidal wave of correspondence arrived: a letter from Arthur Lee, de-manding more detailed reports from Jones about his cruise and expenses, and denying a court-martial for Simpson, due to the dearth of American officers to make up a board of inquiry. Lee's solution was simple: send Simpson home.[34]

Jones also began one of the oddest correspondences of the war. It commenced with a letter to Lady Selkirk, written from the *Ranger*'s cabin on May 8. In it he explained that his attempted kidnapping of her husband was motivated by Jones's desire to end "the horrors of hopeless captivity" suffered by the Americans in English prisons. Nor did he consider himself a Scotsman or American but "a Citizen of the World" who had given up a life of "calm Contemplation and poetic ease" to fight for universal freedom. He ended this long-winded attempt at as-suring "the feelings of your gentle Bosom" by guaranteeing that, when the Selkirk silver was put up for sale, he would buy and return it.[35]

Lady Selkirk did not answer the letter. Her husband did: a long, polite rebuke of Jones's stem-winder to his wife. Sorry as Selkirk was about the rebellion, Jones's kidnapping of the earl would not have led to the freedom of American sailors. Further, "had any of my Family suffered outrage murder or violence, no Quarter of the Globe should have secured you." After expressing the Selkirks' sorrow at hearing of Wallingford's death, his lordship insisted that the proceeds of his sil-ver's sale be given to the rebels left outside Selkirk's door "as an incouragement for their good behaviour." Selkirk gave the letter to the British postmaster, who re-fused to deliver it to "Such a rascal" as Jones.[36]

If Jones was disappointed in his voyage he hid it well. In fact, anger was his ruling emotion, especially when justifying his arrest of the recalcitrant Simpson. But news soon reached Brest of the British reaction to Jones's escapades. Not content to have sloops-of-war hunt down this most recent rebel celebrity, the Admiralty dispatched the frigate *Thetis* to capture him.

Even as Jones's cruise shows the frustrations of an American captain re-garding malevolent junior officers and sailors—as well as the unexpected bad luck that dogs even the best-laid plans—the British press showed the rewards of Jones's persistence. While some London newspapers, citing the brazen White-haven raid, called for the Earl of Sandwich's head, others reported that the loss of the *Drake* at least came at the hands of rebels who were once "our own

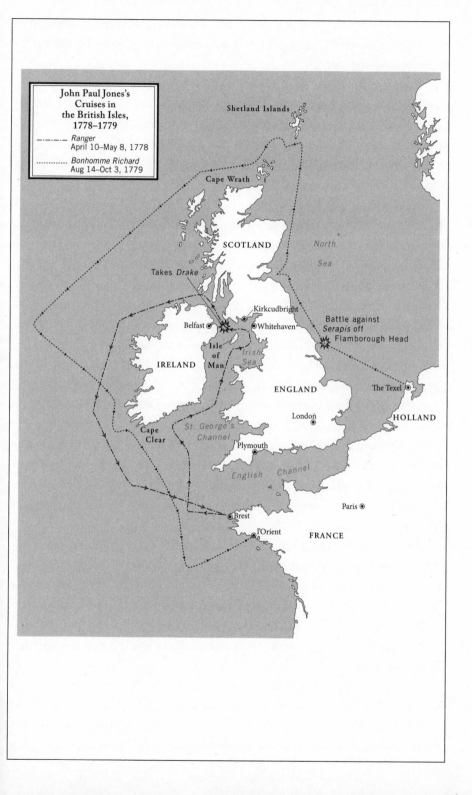

John Paul Jones's
Cruises in
the British Isles,
1778–1779

—·—·— *Ranger*
April 10–May 8, 1778
·············· *Bonhomme Richard*
Aug 14–Oct 3, 1779

Shetland Islands

Cape Wrath

SCOTLAND

North
Sea

Takes *Drake*

Kirkcudbright

Belfast ◉ ● Whitehaven

Battle against
Serapis off
Flamborough Head

Isle
of
Man

Irish
Sea

IRELAND

ENGLAND

The Texel ◉

London ◉

HOLLAND

Cape
Clear

St. George's
Channel

Plymouth ◉

English Channel

Paris ◉

◉ Brest

l'Orient ◉

FRANCE

countrymen." The diminutive Jones of real life was transformed by the British illustrators into a hulking giant, a bewhiskered buccaneer rivaling Blackbeard by their ferocious depiction.[37]

When Jones planned this return home he anticipated being seen as the commoner with a noble heart; instead he was portrayed as an eighteenth-century terrorist. Jones never returned to Scotland. It took him seven years to keep his promise to return the Selkirk silver. When the silver was delivered to the earl at last, the tea leaves from that eventful morning's breakfast were still in the teapot.[38]

On April 13, Admiral d'Estaing sailed for America with a fleet that included eleven ships-of-the-line and more than four thousand men. On the surface, that did not seem a strong enough force to cause great alarm for the British. After all, Admiral Howe (still awaiting his successor, Admiral James Gambier) had ninety-two ships off the American coast. But half of them were protecting British forces in Rhode Island, New York, and Philadelphia, while the others were split between convoys, carrying dispatches, and blockading rebel ports. Howe's ships, from the smallest tender to his flagship, were all in various states of disrepair. He knew d'Estaing was coming, but did not know where d'Estaing was heading.[39]

On May 23, General Howe sailed for England aboard HMS *Andromeda*. So many Philadelphia Loyalists boarded the transports that had brought the Redcoats to Pennsylvania that Clinton had to march his army through New Jersey for New York. Admiral Howe was left with eight ships-of-the-line and four two-deckers. He had them assembled off Sandy Hook by June 29, the day after Washington's Continentals held their own against Clinton during the Battle of Monmouth.[40]

While Congress viewed frigates as flagships for its still toddling navy, they were used by European navies as scouts—the eyes and ears of a fleet. In that capacity, Andrew Snape Hamond sailed the *Roebuck* out of Delaware Bay and up the rebel coast, where he learned that another frigate, HMS *Mermaid*, had spotted d'Estaing off Virginia, heading north. With his usual professional dispatch, Hamond made for Sandy Hook, where Howe's ships were transporting Clinton's army to Manhattan.

From London, Lord North ordered a hastily refitted fleet to sail for America under Admiral John Byron (uncle of the famed poet). Byron, known as "Foul Weather Jack," lived up (or is it down?) to his nickname. Storms hammered his fleet the second it reached the Atlantic; before long the ships were strewn across the ocean, victims of a shortage of quality masts and spars—supplies the Admiralty once had in abundance from the American colonies. Howe would have to confront d'Estaing alone.

Just the news of d'Estaing's imminent arrival, and his possibly linking up with Washington's forces, sent shudders through Parliament. While the Earl of Sandwich boasted that "our navy is more than a match for the whole House of Bourbon," the Earl of Chatham declared the situation "truly perilous." On July 11, the French fleet was sighted off Sandy Hook.[41]

Howe found himself in a position the Continental Navy knew all too well: being severely shorthanded, he called for volunteers from the army and Loyalists. Outnumbered and outgunned, Howe took stock of his assets, the principal one being geography: the sandbar at Sandy Hook, a roadblock of nature. He set one ship-of-the-line and two frigates ahead of the bar to give the French some trouble, with his other large ships placed broadside to broadside along with shore batteries inside the bar.

General Washington had reached White Plains above New York City, and sent his French-speaking aide John Laurens to join d'Estaing aboard the admiral's flagship, *Languedoc*, and let him know how happy Washington would be to assist in taking the city lost to Howe two years earlier. But the admiral could see the brilliance of Howe's defense—d'Estaing could only enter the harbor one ship at a time. After staring down each other for eleven days, d'Estaing departed.[42]

Guessing that d'Estaing's next move would be for Rhode Island, Howe took what seaworthy ships he had and made for Narragansett Bay, still under British control by General Sir Robert Pigot's six-thousand-man army and the ongoing naval blockade. D'Estaing hoped to link up with the Continental forces under Major General John Sullivan. Hopes were high among the American general and the French admiral for a decisive victory, which could lead to a quick end of the war.

Once again, Howe thwarted a Franco-American offensive. Not wanting to fight in the confines of Narragansett Bay, d'Estaing made for the open sea. Despite the odds against him, Howe followed. It looked like there would be a battle for sure on August 11. Both sides angled for the weather gauge while the weather turned foul. By nightfall high seas and vicious winds sent French and English ships in various directions. The storm took ships apart indiscriminately; the *Languedoc* was dismasted and lost her rudder. Both fleets made for safe harbors— Howe's to New York, and d'Estaing's to Boston. Sullivan accused d'Estaing of abandoning him in Rhode Island.

The missed opportunities for an allied attack on Philadelphia, New York, or Newport gnawed at Washington; while he wrote flowery missives to d'Estaing for his efforts, he believed the French to be "old in war." Howe's actions that summer—a blend of sailing skills, courage, bluff, and luck—had restored parity to the chessboard. He soon returned to England, his last efforts on his king's behalf unsung and unappreciated, for they did not end with a victory at sea.[43]

After John Rathbun's amazing success in New Providence, New Englanders longed for word of another victory by one of their own that summer. In the fall of '77, Elisha Warner, at number 24 the low man on Congress's Captains List, had successfully escaped the Delaware with the *Fly* before Howe's fleet closed it off completely, but Warner turned the schooner over to a Marylander, James Robinson. That same year, Samuel Chew, a Connecticut merchant captain, was given command of the ten-gun brigantine *Resistance*. Chew enjoyed moderate success with his first cruise down to South Carolina, capturing a Scottish merchantman and a British privateer.[44]

After refitting his ship, Chew sailed for the West Indies and again made some initial captures. On March 4, the *Resistance* encountered HM packet *Grenville*, Captain Kempthorne. Her twenty guns proved to be too powerful to trade broadsides with, but rather than sheer off, Chew sent the *Resistance* closer, determined to board her. His men armed for hand-to-hand combat, Chew was about to lead them in the attack when he was felled by musket fire. Shortly afterward both ships broke off the engagement. Lieutenant William Leeds took the *Resistance* back to Boston.[45]

Command of the *Resistance* was offered to Daniel Waters, captured aboard the *Hancock* and recently freed. He declined the offer and was scolded by the Marine Committee, who threatened dismissal should he reject another offer. The committee turned to William Burke, another old lieutenant of Manley's who had also been captured. Burke was officially paroled but insisted he had escaped a British prison ship. Rumors spread from the Boston taverns to Congress in York, Pennsylvania, that Burke had been way too admiring of his captors, while other officers like James Josiah had borne their sufferings heroically. But Sam Adams liked Burke, and he received his captain's commission on May 1.[46]

In August the Eastern Navy Board ordered Burke to sail the *Resistance* off Cape Cod. Anticipating d'Estaing's fleet any day, the board wanted Burke to guide the French into Boston harbor. Somehow he missed them, but did manage to run smack into Howe's fleet. Once again a prisoner, Burke related his mission to his captors. He was paroled in October. Although a court-martial exonerated him, he was finished in the navy, and became a privateer.[47]

The naval inquiries in Boston were being held aboard the *Raleigh*, and were a veritable who's who of Continental captains. John Manley had been paroled on April 21 and could not wait to have his day in court. He wanted revenge, but not against the British. He was after Hector McNeill.

And he got him. For Manley to be exonerated for his poor judgment regarding the loss of the *Hancock*, McNeill would have to be found guilty for abandoning him while commanding the *Boston*—and that is exactly how the two decisions went. Manley immediately began pursuing another Continental ship to command. It took him four years, during which time he turned privateer. McNeill appealed his decision, to no avail, and was dismissed from the navy. He also turned privateer. After these two trials, the inquiry over Hoysted Hacker's loss of the *Columbus* was anticlimactic. Hacker was cleared of any wrongdoing.[48]

One other star-crossed New Englander was briefly on the Continental muster rolls. Like most of the others, John Skimmer had served in "Washington's Navy," commanding the schooners *Franklin* and *Lee* in '76. In 1778 he was cited by the Marine Committee as "a Gentleman every way well qualified for a command in our navy," and made captain of the brigantine *Industrious Bee*, recently purchased by Congress and being refitted as a warship in Boston. She was also given the more warlike name *General Gates*. That summer, Skimmer put to sea after bidding farewell to his wife and ten of his children. His oldest, John Junior, came with him to serve as cabin boy.[49]

Unlike the real General Gates, the *General Gates* made a terrific first impression; like Samuel Chew, Skimmer made two fast captures as soon as he got to sea, seizing two brigs and 2,070 quintals of fish that he sent home to feed d'Estaing's sailors. Even Congress was impressed. Days later, Skimmer's lookout spotted two sail. The *General Gates* made chase.[50]

They proved to be a schooner, the *Polly*, and a British privateer, the *Montague*, which immediately ran out her guns. Skimmer decided to engage. Over the next hour, the ships had one at another. The *Montague* was running out of ammunition, but her captain would not yet surrender. Instead, he ordered every piece of iron they could lay their hands on rammed into the muzzles. After crowbars, hammers, and iron rings were used, the men reached into their pockets for their jackknives while the captain rolled up his brass speaking trumpet for one last broadside. Among the Americans hit was Skimmer, who died in the presence of his young son as the *Montague* finally surrendered.[51]

As the Eastern Navy Board once again offered Waters a command (this time he accepted), Skimmer's champion, John Bradford, sought a pension for his widow and eleven children. Declaring Skimmer a "brave and worthy officer," Congress approved a $400 annual pension for three years. Other navy widows were not as fortunate.[52]

After the brutal storm that sent British and French ships akimbo, d'Estaing's fleet limped en masse into Boston harbor on August 28. Despite their forlorn appearance, the Boston batteries fired welcoming salutes and Bostonians cheered their new allies. John Hancock, now governor of Massachusetts, held a magnificent dinner in d'Estaing's honor, with those Continental Navy captains who were in port among the guests.[53]

One American captain did his best to conceal his disappointment at d'Estaing's arrival. For three months, John Barry had been in Boston, trying to get his latest command, the frigate *Raleigh*, to sea. Others may have been dismayed at the sight of d'Estaing's damaged fleet, but happy to see visible proof of French support. Barry's emotions were also mixed. The fleet was a godsend, but its arrival would only further delay his departure from Boston, and he was eager to leave.

The *Raleigh* was Congress's reward to Barry for his daring adventures in the Delaware, succeeding Thomas Thompson after his disastrous retreat from the British ships that had captured the *Alfred*. Thompson had yet to have his day in court, but public opinion had convicted him even before he brought the *Raleigh* into Boston. Barry was given a letter to present to the Eastern Navy Board from the Marine Committee, informing the board of his appointment, anticipating its cooperation in getting the frigate to sea, and reminding the parochial-minded New Englanders that Barry was "a brave Active Officer . . . very attentive to his duty." He left Philadelphia for Boston on June 1.[54]

He found a ship with few guns and no crew aboard—just naval officers, presiding over the courts-martial of Manley, McNeill, and Hacker. John Deshon and James Warren headed up the Navy Board, and they treated Barry with polite aloofness. There were four other Continental ships in the harbor, including the *Warren* and the *Resistance*, and two arrivals from France: the *Deane*, under Sam Nicholson's command, and the *Queen of France*, captained by an old friend of Barry's from his merchant days, John Green. With that many ships to choose from, Barry lobbied hard to get Deshon and Warren to transfer the inquiries, as Congress wanted the *Raleigh* out to sea as much as Barry did. By July 4, Barry had won over both politicians with his earnestness, hard work, and charm, and they began assisting him with his needs—which were many.[55]

He found the frigate beautifully designed but in disrepair. She was more than 131 feet long, with a figurehead of Sir Walter himself, sword in hand. Her rounded bow, similar to those of British frigates, gave sailors more room in the fo'c'sle. Her handsome stern was decorated with carved vines, and she carried a lateen sail (similar in size to a modern Sunfish) set on the ensign staff past the spanker to steady her in strong winds. But her bottom was foul, and most of her supplies had been stolen.[56]

Over the next three months Barry exhausted himself getting her seaworthy, with the help of $524,000 sent to the Navy Board for its ships' needs. He watched in frustration as new guns arrived (to replace the ones Thompson had thrown overboard), only to burst when being proved. When a rendezvous failed to enlist even a hundred hands (most were *Raleigh* veterans), Barry sought sailors from the perpetually idle *Trumbull*. He even looked into borrowing some French sailors from d'Estaing, but was turned down.

By the end of August he finally had enough hands to sail. Keeping only Marine Captain George Osborne from Thompson's officers, he signed on David Phipps as first lieutenant, and three new midshipmen: Matthew Clarkson, who had accompanied Barry on those Delaware barges; David Porter, whose family would supply the American navy with officers for generations to come; and young and untried Jesse Jeacocks. With no marines to speak of, Barry resorted to a risky solution and signed on British infantrymen, now lying in Boston's jail after being captured at Saratoga.[57]

During this summer Congress sent Barry orders to sail off Virginia and North Carolina to resume his earlier actions against Goodrich's navy, leading a squadron that would include all five Continental ships. But over the weeks the *Warren*, *Deane*, and *Resistance* had sailed on orders from the Navy Board. Barry informed Robert Morris of the French fleet's battered condition, begging his old employer to let him sail once the last wagonload of ordnance was unloaded. When those supplies were finally trundled down the waterfront's cobblestone streets, an elated Barry paid for the guns out of his pocket, treating the wagon drivers to plenty of rum to show his appreciation. The *Raleigh* stood down Nantasket Road the next day. Lack of wind kept her from departing the Massachusetts capes until September 25, accompanied by a brig and a sloop.[58]

Now working with a decent breeze, Barry marveled at the *Raleigh*'s smooth sailing as she sliced through the water. Once she reached the mouth of the bay, he sent a lookout aloft; it was common knowledge that Royal Navy cruisers and Loyalist privateers were prowling these waters. The ships were about ten leagues north of Cape Cod when the mastheader called down from his perch: two sail, bearing southeast. Pulling out his spyglass, Barry took them to be fishing schooners.

Then a second hail came from above: two more ships standing south by southeast, eight to ten leagues away. Barry could tell these were not fishermen. They were British warships, which stood for the *Raleigh* and her consorts as soon as they spied the three American vessels. He signaled the two captains to keep up with the frigate as best they could. Unable to head south as per his orders, Barry headed north, clapping on every inch of canvas the *Raleigh* could carry. He soon outdistanced the other Americans. This was a fight Barry did not want; much as he hated leaving the smaller ships behind, he knew full well that the last thing Congress wanted was one more captured Continental frigate.[59]

For the rest of the day the *Raleigh* took the two enemy ships on a long northward race, losing them in the dark, but not before the smaller one fired several shots from her bow chasers. The next morning they reappeared, along with a schooner he took to be a tender for one of his pursuers, and the American brig he had left in the *Raleigh*'s wake. Barry did not know what ships were chasing him, but upon the brig's capture their captains learned who they were after. The smaller ship stalking the *Raleigh* was the frigate *Unicorn*, Captain John Ford, twenty-two guns. The larger ship was the two-decker *Experiment*, Captain Sir James Wallace—the very man Barry had bested in the Delaware six months earlier; the same captain whose name was anathema to New Englanders from his days tormenting Rhode Island.[60]

Once again, the chase was on. In his merchant career, Barry had made few voyages north from Philadelphia. Completely unfamiliar with the shoreline, he sought the advice of Lieutenant Phipps, who suggested they make for Portsmouth. Barry agreed. Once again, the *Raleigh* showed off her wondrous sailing skills, making eleven knots throughout the day. By late afternoon, the British ships were long out of sight. The southern horizon was clear of ships. Barry changed course to east by northeast, and then changed direction again at midnight to east by southeast. As he had done so many times with the *Lexington*, Barry had eluded pursuit. The British captains must have given up, just as Hamond, Symonds, and the others did whenever Barry had eluded them. "They had quitted chasing of us," he believed.[61]

After sunrise the next day—September 27—Barry sent the *Raleigh* on a southward course under full sail, hoping to use the morning's prime sailing conditions to make up for two lost days. The *Raleigh* responded marvelously. As she increased in speed she made a sound well-known to sailors since wind first captured canvas—that low, insistent "hum" along the water—sometimes barely perceptible, but always a joy to hear.

Barry's happy mood did not last the morning. At nine thirty the mastheader alerted the quarterdeck: two ships on the horizon, sailing south by southwest, on a course that would soon intersect the *Raleigh*'s. Barry did not need his spyglass to identify them. He could also see that they had the weather gauge, controlling the coming chase. Outnumbered, outmaneuvered, and outthought, Barry had no choice but to wear ship and fly northward. The *Raleigh* did not carry royal yards for a fourth sail at the top of each mast; the topgallant sails were the highest. Barry had her studding sails ("stuns'ls") set immediately on her fore and mainmast, and a four-and-a-half-hour chase northward began.[62]

By two p.m. the *Raleigh* was approaching the coast of Maine, with the *Unicorn* coming up very fast and the *Experiment* making better headway than during the previous day's chase, thanks to the more favorable wind. As before, the *Raleigh* was making eleven knots, but once she neared the coast the wind lessened. The *Unicorn* now seemed to be flying towards her. As the land came into better view, Barry saw a series of islands to westward, not a shoreline at all. He inquired if anyone aboard knew these waters—and these islands.

Not a man aboard had a clue.

Hiding any alarm, Barry sent the *Raleigh* north by northwest to maintain some speed and get a closer look at the islands. Soon he could make them out as barren, rocky masses, "and not a tree on them." The coast itself looked to be another twelve leagues to the west. Rocky islands and unknown waters were not an inviting alternative to a fight. Still, Barry "thought it most Prudent to Tack to the Southward in hopes to get to the Westward and make a harbour before the ships could come up."

Once more the *Raleigh* came through the wind, the masts groaning as she slowed through the tack before picking up speed again. Barry had little time to sail back down the coast without running into the *Unicorn* and, eventually, the *Experiment*. But if he could get past these islands before the enemy caught up with him . . .

He could not. The two hours he found after changing course were not enough. At four o'clock he tacked again, but an hour later the *Unicorn* was in range. Barry had studied how she sailed, counted her gun ports, and decided he had one last option: take her on, capture or disable her, and escape the *Experiment* before she had time to enter the fight. He ordered a gun fired to leeward, challenging the *Unicorn*. The *Raleigh's* guns were run out, and Captain Ford accepted the challenge.

Barry ran up his colors, ran out his guns, and sent his British-born marines aloft, hoping they would do their duty as he saw fit. But it was Ford, who "threw up St. George's Ensign and gave us a Broadside," that got the battle started. The Raleighs returned fire. Both opening rounds were negligibly effective, the exchange occurring at a quarter mile range.

Suddenly, Ford brought the *Unicorn* under the *Raleigh's* lee quarter, catching Barry by surprise—Ford's frigate was right in Barry's westward path. A second broadside slammed into the *Raleigh* just as Barry tried to change course. Whether what happened next was a result of British guns or Barry's hard turn—Barry called it "some unforeseen accident"—a loud cracking sound came from above the deck. The foretopmast snapped. Barry cried a warning to the starboard gun crews, but it was too late. The long projectile of tangled wood, rope, and canvas crashed to the deck, taking the main topgallant mast, jib, and fore staysail along with it. Men were stunned, wounded, or worse; guns were dislodged from their carriages; sails covered the deck and hung into the water, slowing the *Raleigh* to a crawl. Ford immediately sent another broadside flying at the crippled ship.

Barry sent for axes and ordered the wreckage cleared away—as long as the *Unicorn* was on the *Raleigh's* cluttered starboard she could not fight back. His damaged ship could no longer escape. As the fo'c'sle hands were heaving the wreckage overboard, another broadside from the *Unicorn* struck many of them down. The *Raleigh's* deck was a slaughter pen.[63]

Barry now had one last chance at turning this gruesome bad luck around: close in on the *Unicorn*, board her, and take her before the *Experiment* came up. After ordering the helmsman to change course again—putting the *Raleigh* to windward while sending her straight at the *Unicorn*—Barry called for hands to join him in boarding the British frigate. With the wind at their backs, the smoke from the battle would be in English eyes, not American. His guns loaded with grapeshot, Barry waited for the *Raleigh* to get close enough to throw his grappling hooks into the *Unicorn's* bulwarks and bring the fight aboard the British ship.

Once again, Ford thwarted Barry's hopes by abruptly changing course. The

Unicorn sheered off, maintaining her distance while the *Experiment* continued her approach. After discharging his round of grapeshot, Barry returned to solid iron; now it was the American gunners' turn to take over the fight. Within minutes, Yankee broadsides hammered the *Unicorn*'s waterline while also severely damaging her masts and rigging. Even in the dark, Barry could tell by the *Unicorn*'s increasing listing that she was "waterlogg'd." For four more hours the two ships limped northward, unable to deliver a knockout blow. From the *Unicorn*'s quarterdeck, Ford fired a distress signal into the chilly night air.[64]

The *Experiment*'s guns were finally in range at midnight. Aboard the *Raleigh*, Barry held a hasty meeting with his officers, informing them they would run the frigate aground on one of the islands, burn her, and get the men to the coast in the *Raleigh*'s boats. By this time the *Experiment* was alongside the *Unicorn*. As soon as Wallace passed Ford's lame frigate, he would blast away at the *Raleigh*.[65]

But before the *Experiment*'s 18-pounders were fired, a broadside from the *Raleigh* came slamming into the two-decker. Wallace returned fire—the first of three broadsides fired back at the *Raleigh* in the next five minutes. For all the damage they did, Barry's gunners returned fire "with redoubled vigor." Remarkably, the *Raleigh* began pulling away; soon she was far enough ahead that only her stern chasers could be fired back at the enemy ships. A cluster of craggy islands, lacking only Odysseus's Sirens, now beckoned. Barry sailed straight for the center one, beaching the wounded ship.[66]

If his men thought Barry would strike his colors they soon learned otherwise. As he had done at Turtle Gut Inlet, Barry kept his gunners at their stations. Two more broadsides struck the *Raleigh* from Wallace's two-decker. After the second one, Barry saw that the *Experiment* would have to tack or risk running aground too. Now Barry shouted, "Fire!" and his gunners raked the enemy ship. For fifteen minutes the Americans fired at will at both British ships with such fierce accuracy that the *Experiment* also sheered off, "being close to the Rocks" as well as being pounded by the wounded *Raleigh*. Wallace would wait until daylight to finish off the rebels.

But Barry was not waiting until morning to surrender, and quickly issued orders. He and Marine Captain Osborne would take two boats, load them with the ship's wounded, and get them ashore. Lieutenant Phipps would get the men off the ship with orders to hide in the crevices until Barry and Osborne returned. Jesse Jeacocks, Barry's young midshipman, would remain on board the *Raleigh* with the sailing master and twenty sailors, keep the ship's lanterns lit through the night as a decoy while amassing enough combustibles to burn the ship at daylight, then row the third longboat to the mainland.[67]

Two days earlier, Barry had miscalculated the enemy's whereabouts. Now he erred about both the distance to the shore and in his choice of officers. While it is not fair to fault him, lacking any knowledge of the Maine coast, it turned out that he was more than twenty miles from shore. It took three hours for his weary men to bring the boats in. Once on land, he got his wounded taken care of, and learned the name of the little island his men were trapped on: Wooden Ball.[68]

All morning Barry paced the beach, peering through his spyglass to search for the smoke from the burning *Raleigh*. There was no sign of a fire. In two hours the third longboat came into view. Upon landing, the sailing master told Barry the men had done what he ordered, then he and the men manned the boat, waiting for Jeacocks to set the ship afire.

From the *Unicorn* Ford saw rebel sailors scrambling for cover on the west part of Wooden Ball. He sent all of his boats towards the *Raleigh*, his men heavily armed but under a flag of truce to offer terms.

Seeing the British boats approaching, the sailing master called for Jeacocks to start his fire and abandon ship. Instead of going aboard to complete the mission, the sailing master set off for the shore. Whether young Jeacocks lost his nerve or turned traitor we do not know, but when Wallace fired several shots the *Raleigh*'s way, Jeacocks hauled down Barry's colors. Barry sent the three longboats back to Wooden Ball as fast as his weary tars could row them. When they got there at nightfall, only thirteen Americans remained to be saved. Phipps and the 122 others had surrendered to the British.[69]

While the *Unicorn* was finished as a serviceable frigate, Wallace got the damaged *Raleigh* afloat and repaired her. She was "taken into the British service." Having "Saved 85 in number," Barry took those who could travel with him on the long row back to Boston, hugging the coastline all the way. By the time they reached Boston, Barry knew it well.[70]

It was a motley-looking crew that returned to that port. A court of inquiry commended Barry for his actions; the Eastern Navy Board reported to Congress "perhaps no ship was ever better defended." Washington himself praised Barry's "gallant resistance." Some naval historians consider the court's findings a whitewash, but compared to the recent actions or inactions of his peers, it is easy to see why officials stressed Barry's fighting spirit over his misreading of both

Wallace and young Jeacocks, especially when, at Turtle Gut Inlet, Barry saw fit to torch the *Nancy* himself.[71]

But for all the praise, two facts were plainly clear. The Continental Navy had lost another frigate to the British, and one of their best captains was now "on the beach," without a ship.

The loss of the *Raleigh* was at least partially offset by the actions of another new name in naval activities—Silas Talbot.

He had been an adventurer his whole life. The ninth of fourteen children, Talbot was born in Massachusetts but raised in Rhode Island, where he went to sea as a cabin boy. He was one of the first commissioned officers in the Rhode Island regiments when war broke out and had been one of the two hundred Continental Army "volunteers" Washington had loaned Esek Hopkins after the *Glasgow* debacle. When Admiral Howe's armada sailed into New York harbor, Talbot volunteered to command the fireship sent down the Hudson to torch the ship-of-the-line *Asia*. Talbot ordered his men not to set fire to the combustibles aboard—turpentine and tar barrels—until he had sailed the ship close enough to foul the *Asia*.

As British cannonballs slammed into his vessel, Talbot ordered the gunpowder fuses lit and sent his men over the side. The last to abandon ship, he was caught as a change in the wind blew the flames towards him, and he was severely burned and blinded. The *Asia* narrowly missed catching fire.

Once ashore in the woods below New York City, Talbot's men could find no one in the cabins dotting the riverbank who would care for him; being so horribly disfigured, he frightened the children. Eventually they found a widow who took him in until he recovered his eyesight, after which he returned to his regiment and was promoted to major. In Philadelphia he was twice wounded during the siege of Fort Mifflin and given leave to return to Providence, where he served under Major General Sullivan, who anxiously awaited the arrival of d'Estaing's fleet and the chance to take Newport back from General Pigot's Redcoats. Talbot was as disappointed as Sullivan when the French sailed away.[72]

There was more bad news coming Sullivan's way. When Admiral Howe followed the Frenchman out to sea, Clinton no longer had enough naval support to drive Sullivan out of Rhode Island or possibly capture him and his army, which would have decimated the rebel cause. So Clinton vented his anger on nearby Massachusetts, sending a force under Major General Charles Grey (the author of the infamous Paoli Massacre) in a combined operation with Royal Navy ships under Captain Robert Fanshawe of the *Carysfort.*

By this time, Howe's replacement, Rear Admiral James Gambier, had arrived in America. Like Clinton, Gambier was more than willing to comply with Lord Sandwich's plans to destroy ports and commerce—eighty-five years before another military man, William Tecumseh Sherman, carried out the same practice against Georgia in the Civil War.

Talbot learned that Fanshawe had forty-five vessels at his disposal along with Grey's four thousand infantrymen. On September 4 and 5 they set upon Buzzard's Bay, Martha's Vineyard, New Bedford, Fair Haven, and Holmes's Hole, burning ships, homes, and stores. When dispatches of Fanshawe's destruction reached the Admiralty, Lord Germain's secretary chortled that Gambier had done "more to subdue the Rebellion than his lordship [Howe] during the whole of his command." Next, Gambier and Clinton set their sights on Egg Harbor, New Jersey.[73]

Back in Rhode Island, Pigot sent a schooner—named after himself—into the Sakonnet River, the eastern passageway to the mainland. Small as she was even compared to a sloop-of-war, the *Pigot* was heavily armed, with eight 12-pounders and ten swivels. Netting had been run along her sides to prevent any boarding parties from effectively getting aboard.

Talbot saw the *Pigot* not as an insurmountable foe but as an opportunity to strike back at the enemy. After familiarizing himself with the schooner, he wanted to take a small sloop, the *Hawk,* sail her downriver, and capture the *Pigot.* It took some convincing, but Sullivan approved Talbot's scheme.

He found sixty volunteers among Sullivan's men to man the *Hawk.* She was armed only with two 3-pounders, but Talbot was not looking for the coming engagement to be a slugfest. For his plan to work, he mounted a kedge anchor at the *Hawk's* bow—a small anchor mostly used to warp a ship—moving her along when becalmed by some hands who dropped it from a longboat, then pulled on the hawser until the ship reached the anchor.[74]

On the night of October 28, the *Hawk* drifted silently downriver under bare poles—Talbot let the current do the work until he passed some British batteries along Fogland Ferry. Once clear, Talbot ordered the mainsail raised, and stood straight for the *Pigot,* now visible in the distance. As the *Hawk* closed in, the British sentries hailed her. Talbot maintained silence. They fired their muskets. Still no sound from the sloop.

Just as the *Hawk* approached the *Pigot,* Talbot ordered his helmsman to hit the schooner. As the sloop bumped alongside, the kedge anchor shredded the netting, making a large hole starting at the *Pigot*'s bow. "Grappling hooks away!" Talbot ordered, and his men tossed them across, pulling them close enough for Talbot and his men to board.

The shocked British sailors were driven below deck—all except their commander, Lieutenant Dunlop, who was technically out of uniform and actually in his nightshirt. Once surrounded, he surrendered. Talbot took his prize to nearby Stonington, Connecticut, and then marched his prisoners back to Providence, presumably giving Dunlop the opportunity to dress for the occasion. For his victory Talbot received a promotion, a citation from the president of the Congress, Henry Laurens, a ceremonial sword from the Rhode Island Assembly, and the moniker "arch rebel" from the British. He was also made a captain in the Continental Navy.[75]

As naval affairs seesawed between victories and defeats off the American coast, William Bingham was still in Martinique, getting acquainted with Gustavus Conyngham.

Both Philadelphians, they had briefly met before the war. While Conyngham was making his mark as a mariner, Bingham, the son of a well-to-do family, graduated from the College of Philadelphia (now the University of Pennsylvania) at sixteen, and soon after displayed an astute head for business in the merchant trade. No less an expert than Robert Morris saw much of himself in the boy. "He has abilities & merit," he believed, "both in the Political and Commercial Line." At twenty-four Bingham was secretary of Congress's Committee of Secret Correspondence. The young man shunned wigs, tying his light-colored hair in a queue. Under long, dark eyebrows, his deep-set brown eyes missed nothing: not a detail in a contract, a suspicious face in a crowd, or a distant ship on a horizon.[76]

Morris sent Bingham to Martinique in 1776, where he quickly established friendly relations with the French officials there. By the end of 1778 he had made several missions to France. He also added to the family fortune with a series of shrewd investments in privateers. Now he was back in Martinique; Conyngham was the most recent Continental captain to arrive there in the fall of '78. Under the shadows of the high inland mountains, the two men made plans for the *Revenge* to cruise from St. Pierre, Bingham being one of the American agents trusted by Morris to issue orders to navy captains.[77]

On October 26, Bingham ordered Conyngham—so successful at capturing

British shipping in European waters—to try his hand in the Western Hemisphere, while making a point to remind the captain not to anger their French hosts. After Bingham gave him a letter for d'Estaing in the hopes that the *Revenge* might meet the admiral on his voyage to the West Indies from Boston, Conyngham departed St. Pierre to cruise the West Indies for British merchantmen and transports. For two weeks the *Revenge* sailed north against the winds without sighting a sail, but on the morning of November 13, the cutter's lookout spotted a ship off St. Eustatius.[78]

She was a sloop, the *Two Friends*. Fast as she was, the *Revenge* easily overtook her. She carried freshwater for British troops; Conyngham sent her back to Martinique (like a number of his prizes, she was retaken by a British privateer the same day). Shortly afterwards the *Revenge* captured two schooners whose prize crews got them back to St. Pierre. In the late afternoon, another schooner was spotted—a privateer, the *Admiral Barrington*, Captain Pelham, six guns. After a short chase a broadside from the *Revenge* convinced Pelham to lower his flag. Conyngham had his fourth prize as the sun set. Not a bad day. He returned to St. Pierre.

He was back at sea on November 16, again ordered to cruise for ships while keeping a weather eye out for d'Estaing. Five days later he was back with another privateer, the aptly named *Loyalist*, Captain Morris, mounting twelve 3-pounders and fourteen swivels. Morris put up a fight, but Conyngham's gunners made it a short one. By the time he departed on a third venture on November 29, Bingham had received the French fleet's signals, passing them along to Conyngham to use if he did encounter the long-awaited d'Estaing. They were in French; ironically, for all his time there, Conyngham never learned more than a few rudimentary phrases. "Take care to have them interpreted," Bingham stressed, "by those such Persons on board that you may repose unlimited Confidence in."[79]

After capturing the brig *Lukey* off St. Lucia, Conyngham did intercept d'Estaing's fleet. A French-speaking sailor made the correct signals, and the *Revenge* joined the fleet in a two-week cruise in the Caribbean, where they encountered a British squadron escorting fifty-nine transports carrying five thousand Redcoats from Sandy Hook, sent to capture St. Lucia. D'Estaing engaged, but Conyngham kept his distance—this was no battle for a cutter. The *Revenge* sailed into St. Pierre on January 2, 1779.[80]

The New Year looked promising for Conyngham. He had returned to what he did better than anyone—seizing British ships and giving the Admiralty fits in the process. And he was unencumbered by diplomatic sidestepping, thanks to the French alliance (and being an ocean away from France and Spain). News of his Caribbean exploits filled patriotic newspapers in America. "The Pirate Cunningham" of the British press was now "the celebrated Cunningham," even though American papers perpetually repeated their English counterparts in misspelling his name. Conyngham summed up his western hemisphere adventures with typical understatement: "Kept the British privateers in Good order in those seas, captured two of them." Enough said.[81]

Imagine his happiness, then, when Bingham ordered him to take fifty chests of weapons to Philadelphia. After more than three years away from his family, he was going home. The *Revenge* left St. Pierre on February 5; just sixteen days later she was sailing up the Delaware.

If he expected a hero's welcome similar to those he received in Europe, he was disappointed. What he did get was the same headache he thought he had left behind across the Atlantic: complaints from former sailors and politicians alike. Several Americans who once served aboard the *Revenge* had returned to Philadelphia months before. Led by Conyngham's former surgeon, Josiah Smith, they accused him of not paying their wages and prize shares, taking their grievances to Congress. The Marine Committee summoned him to present his side of the story. It was Lee, Deane, and Franklin all over again: be successful at sea, but do not expect us to support you if your success puts us in hot water.

What Conyngham did not know was that he had been embroiled in the scandals surrounding Silas Deane; Arthur Lee had seen to that. Lee had sent reports linking the two in Deane's scurrilous financial dealings to his brother, Richard Henry Lee—now chair of the Marine Committee, including the activities of the *Surprise* and the *Revenge*. As Deane's friend, William Hodge, had bought the ships, Deane must have profited handsomely from their cruises, and so too Conyngham. It would not be the first time Lee would add two plus two and come up with *cinq*, but Congress had not yet caught on to Lee's vituperative paranoia.[82]

Conyngham possessed neither Jones's gift for self-promotion nor Biddle's innate assurance, but he rose to the occasion, presenting a detailed list of captures and defending his actions with logic and vigor. In the end, he laid the lack of pay for his men where it belonged—with Congress, the American commissioners in Paris, and the American agents in French and Spanish ports. As Conyngham's European cruises took place during the years of France's feigned neutrality, he had to disguise his prizes in unconventional (and often illegal) ways with the approval of the diplomats before the act—if rarely afterwards.

Once Conyngham finished defending himself, the Marine Committee sent letters to the European agents, asking for any papers regarding the captain's prizes. Conyngham was willing to die for his country, but he was not about to fall on his cutlass for Arthur Lee—or Congress, for that matter. He believed he had vindicated himself.[83]

But there is no clear horizon in politics, and once again Conyngham did not see what was coming. Having been jailed in France and exiled by both the French and the Spanish for his efforts on behalf of his country, he now had the deck of his ship pulled out from under him. With no money in its coffers (and inflation running almost 100 percent), Richard Henry Lee ordered the *Revenge* decommissioned and sold at public auction. The sale would take place at the London Coffeehouse on St. Patrick's Day.[84]

There was a sizable crowd at Front and High Streets that morning, not just curious onlookers, but a host of potential buyers—the *Revenge*'s reputation saw to that. Even the Pennsylvania Assembly dispatched an agent to buy her for the state navy. The bidding was fierce until the firm Conyngham & Nesbitt raised the price well past the cutter's worth. They believed they had the ideal captain for the *Revenge*. With no Continental ship available, and Congress's assurance that he would not lose his commission (technically the French had already done that), Gustavus accepted. He turned privateer.[85]

It took a few weeks to refit the *Revenge*, but the combination of Conyngham's reputation and the quick pay sailors received from serving in a privateer made for a successful rendezvous. It would be a short cruise; after a sweet farewell with Anne and his children, Conyngham sailed down the Delaware, bound for New York waters. After three years of risk mixed with political chicanery, he would be cruising in American waters with no diplomatic tempests awaiting his return.

On April 27, the Marine Committee, still wading through the morass of paperwork regarding Conyngham, wrote the American commissioners in Paris and their agents in France and Spain, chastising them for being "at a loss for want of [the *Revenge*'s] accounts and the many Prizes she took in the European Seas." Further, when advances were paid to naval officers, Congress expected to be informed of what was paid and to whom. This included monies loaned to those sailors who had escaped to France from Mill and Forten Prisons in England.[86]

That same day, Conyngham "went round to New York," he wrote, and "laid in the roads"—the shipping lanes to New York City. He sent a lookout aloft, scanning the horizon for potential prizes. Pick off one or two merchantmen or a privateer, and Conyngham and his men could sail home considerably richer men than when they departed. Suddenly the lookout alerted Conyngham of two sails that appeared to be Loyalist privateers. After trying every nautical trick but failing to lure the ships closer to the *Revenge*, Conyngham gave chase.[87]

The ships were fast. For once, the *Revenge* could not close the gap. Nonetheless, Conyngham was confident of overtaking them and maintained pursuit. Then, suddenly, the unthinkable happened: another sail was sighted—a large and foreboding one. "As the devil would have it," Conyngham reported, the two privateers "led me into the teeth" of a British frigate. She was under full sail, making straight for the *Revenge*. The master of trickery at sea had been tricked himself.

She was the HMS *Galatea*, Thomas Jordan, one of the most feared and despised British warships on the American coast—the very frigate that Robert Morris had wanted Biddle and the *Randolph* to capture two years earlier. Quickly, Conyngham ordered, "Wear Ship!" and the *Revenge* turned through the wind, the hunter now the hunted. Necessary as the turn was, it only gave the *Galatea* more time to close the distance between the two ships. Soon the *Revenge* was within range of Jordan's bow chasers, manned by expert gunners of the King's Navy—better than a privateer's gun crew, to be sure. The low, vicious song of cannonballs whirred through the air until they splashed perilously close to the *Revenge*.

For the first time, Conyngham was beaten, and he knew it. "I made every effort to escape, but in vain," he reported. "Her teeth were too many." His crew, still stunned at his sailing into a trap, watched in disbelief as Conyngham did the unthinkable: haul down his colors. A British boarding party brought him to the *Galatea*.[88]

Captain Jordan had spent most of the war in the western hemisphere, but his ears pricked up when he heard his prisoner state his name. Every man jack in the Royal Navy knew who Gustavus Conyngham was. Jordan asked for his papers, and Conyngham presented everything except what he did not have—his captain's commission, signed by Hancock, given him by Franklin, now pigeonholed in some clerk's desk in France. Conyngham was sent below and put in irons.

Once in New York, his men were transferred to one of the rotting prison ships on the East River. Conyngham was taken to the provost's prison, where he was weighted down with fifty-five pounds of chains, fastened to his ankles, his wrists, and by a solid iron ring about his neck. When the turnkey finished shackling him, Conyngham tried to walk to the prison door, and found it an impossible task. Only by dragging one foot and then another could he move—barely.

For weeks he was given filthy water and "Went without the least Morsel of Bread from the Jailer." His two fellow prisoners—one accused of being a thief, the other a spy—slipped him bits of rotten food through the keyhole.

He was brought before Commodore Sir George Collier, the officer who had captured Manley and the *Hancock*. Collier decided Conyngham was nothing more than a pirate, and suggested he prepare for the end that awaited all captured freebooters. Conyngham would later describe Collier as "that tyrant." He was returned to his cell, not knowing what would happen next and convinced that all he could expect from his captors was "Nothing but Deceit and falsehood."

One morning he was roused from his cell, taken out into the yard, and ordered to climb—as best he could—into what was called "the hangman's cart." It was led by "A Negro called George Washington, decorated as usual with ropes [for] taking deserters & others to the gallows and executed." As a fife and drum played "The Hangman's March," a detail of Hessians plodded alongside the cart. In broken English, one of them told Conyngham, *"You vill go next."*

Instead he was trundled to the waterfront, subjected to the insults and garbage thrown his way by jeering Loyalists. At the docks he was pulled from the cart, put in a longboat, and transferred to a packet bound for London. Collier gave orders to confine Conyngham in "the coal hole"—the dark, filthy space where coal was stored. King George did not want Conyngham hanged in New York, Collier told him.

He would be hanged in London.[89]

CHAPTER NINE

"IN HARM'S WAY"

A tale could be told that would if possible for the heardend rocks to
hear would Melt them Asunder.

—GUSTAVUS CONYNGHAM[1]

Before the *Sandwich* packet raised sail and departed New York on June 12,
Captain Bull gave Gustavus Conyngham permission to write his wife,
Anne. After weeks of inhumane confinement, he was filthy, lousy with vermin,
and starving. For a man so used to being in charge of ship and crew to write the
following words must have been as heartbreaking as they were humiliating:

> Sorry I am to inform you that I am on board [the *Sandwich*]
> and to be sent to England. I have in part lost my health and
> cannot live long in this manner. If it pleases God to call me to
> himself out of this troublesome World, I live in hopes to meet
> you in Paradise. I am not able to write more. If possible rest
> contented. I would leave this western world easy if I had you
> with me. I must once more for the last time to recommend you
> to God, and live as contented as possible.
>
> Your loving affectionate husband 'till Death,
> Gustavus Conyngham[2]

Convinced that he had just written a farewell to his wife, Conyngham turned
the letter over to Captain Bull, and the *Sandwich* stood down the East River, the

first leg in her long voyage to England: home to many of her crew, and hell to her famous prisoner. Once at sea, Bull released Conyngham from the coal pit in disobedience to Collier's orders. "Had he not, I must have perished," Conyngham believed. Although kept in his burdensome irons, he was at least allowed to occasionally see daylight. Several weeks passed before the *Sandwich* docked in Falmouth, the deepest harbor in all Europe, at the southwest tip of Cornwall, midway between Plymouth and Penzance.[3]

Once word reached the docks of the packet's prisoner, a crowd of curiosity seekers gathered as the debilitated Conyngham, limping under the weight of his irons, was transferred to a cart that took him to Pendennis Castle: the massive, stone-walled construction featuring a wide circular tower. Built in 1539 by Henry VIII to protect the Cornwall Roads and Falmouth from the French and Spanish, it now served as fortress, barracks, and prison. The Admiralty's plans for Conyngham were simple—keep him at Pendennis until he was tried (and certainly convicted) of piracy.

Before departing Falmouth, Captain Bull called on Conyngham "and very politely asked if I wanted money, or any thing," the prisoner wrote. Conyngham said no—there was nothing Bull had the power to give him that he wanted.[4]

For the most part Captain Thomas Tidd, commandant of Pendennis, followed Collier's written orders to the letter. Conyngham bore his punishment bravely. Some days he was relieved of his irons only to be placed back in them at nighttime. His cell was so confining that he begged for the door to be left open. Remarkably, the jailer agreed, as long as Conyngham remained in chains. One visitor's offer of books brought Conyngham to tears. Others passing by the cell would inquire, "Is that the pirate?" and were abusive to him. Slowly, Conyngham's mental state was beginning to deteriorate along with his physical condition.

Tidd began gathering evidence against Conyngham for his trial as some of the prison's visitors were converted to "witnesses." One British sailor attested that Conyngham was with John Paul Jones at Whitehaven. But false testimony was at this point only a secondary problem for Conyngham. "My room being so full of fleas it is really a torture to lay down," he wrote, "my hands confined [I] cannot rub or scratch."[5]

Several weeks after his confinement in Pendennis the turnkey opened Conyngham's cell door, and a British officer informed him that he was being transferred to Mill Prison. Much had happened on his behalf an ocean away, thanks to Anne.

First to act on his behalf was actually the Marine Committee. Its members had learned of Conyngham's capture in May; Silas Deane and William Carmichael provided them with affidavits certifying that Conyngham "was duly commissionated" to command the *Surprise* and the *Revenge*. Thus armed, they ordered Commissary General for Prisoners John Beatty (a former prisoner himself) to notify his British counterpart that Conyngham was, in fact, a Continental captain. Further, if he was being mistreated, a captured British officer would face the same dire hardships. Weeks passed before Beatty learned of Conyngham's dastardly treatment and his being taken to England; warnings of unspecified reprisals were not enough to tell George III the rebel he loathed most was not to be hung.[6]

On the morning of July 17, Anne Conyngham arrived at the State House on Chestnut Street. A nearby pit dug by the Redcoats during Philadelphia's occupation used for garbage and animal carcasses had been filled in for over a year, but a faint stench still caused congressmen to keep the doors closed, especially on an airless summer day. Anne carried with her a letter to John Jay, the president of Congress. It was a brilliantly written combination of a wife's heartache and a stirring call to action:

> As these Extraordinary and (in the present Stage of War between Britain & America) Singular Cruelties exercised upon the Person of my Husband have been inflicted in consequence of his Zeal and successful exertions against the common Enemy in the English Channell where he first hoisted the American Flag, I take the Liberty of calling the Attention of Congress to his distressed situation . . . To have lost a worthy and belov'd Husband in Battle fighting for the honour & Liberties of his Country would have been a light affliction. But to hear of a Person thus connected being chained to the Hold of a Ship, in vain looking back towards the belov'd Country for which he had fought, wasting his health and spirits in hopeless Grief, and at last compleating the measure of his sufferings by an ignominious Death under—Good God my heart shudders! At the thought. Forbid it Heaven, Forbid it Hon[or]able Gentlemen the Guardians of the Lives and Happiness of the good People of these States . . . the Delay of a single Hour may fix my Husband's fate for ever . . . the safety of your numerous officers, and soldiers, by Sea and Land is connected with that of my Husband . . .[7]

Anne presented the letter, accompanied by both her husband's note to her and a petition signed by eighty-one prominent Americans, among them naval officers Seth Harding and Thomas Read, and privateer owners like Mathew Irwin. Merchants, shipbuilders, and clergy added their names, along with congressmen, including the almighty Robert Morris.[8]

Faced with such a panoply of the influential, Congress acted with dispatch, referring the affair to a committee comprising Gouverneur Morris, William Whipple, and John Dickinson. They wasted no time deliberating, presenting their report to their colleagues that afternoon, along with a drafted letter to Commodore Collier, accusing him of treating Conyngham "in a manner contrary to the dictates of humanity and the practice of civilized nations" while demanding that Conyngham "be immediately released from his present rigorous and ignominious confinement." Congress also threatened that it would "cause to be confined in close and safe custody such, and so many persons as they think proper in order to abide the fate of the said Gustavus Conyngham." A post rider carried the letter to New York that day.[9]

Collier, deeming a personal response to the rebel government beneath him, had his secretary respond. The commodore, "not holding himself accountable for his conduct to any of His Majesty's subjects in this country"—meaning Congress—was "still less induced to answer demands when they are made in the uncivil way they appear to him in your letter of the 17th instant." Further, Conyngham had not been treated "contrary to the dictates of humanity," and

> As it is the practice of civilized nations to punish criminals in the usual course of justice, Gustavus Conyngham, whom you enquire after, stands in this predicament, and is therefore sent to England to receive that punishment from his injured country, which his crimes shall be found to deserve.[10]

Such haughty disregard of Conyngham's treatment, coming from the officer who ordered it, did not play well in Philadelphia, Paris, or Continental Army headquarters. Congress no sooner reviewed Collier's letter than it ordered that three captive British officers be placed in close confinement to show Collier they meant business. One of them, Lieutenant Christopher Hele of the recently captured HMS *Hotham* (and a favorite of Admiral Gambier), was in a Philadelphia jail. Earlier, Gambier had personally written Jay requesting that Hele be paroled, and Jay had agreed. Now Jay informed Gambier and Collier that Hele was receiving similar treatment to Conyngham's. For weeks Hele protested the drastic change in his luck, but Congress was not bluffing.[11]

From Passy, Benjamin Franklin wrote to David Hartley, a member of Parliament who knew Franklin before the war, assuring him that Conyngham was a Continental officer, adding

> I cannot believe that mere Resentment, occurred by [Conyngham's] uncommon success, will attempt to sacrifice a brave Man, who has always behaved as a generous Enemy, witness his treatment of his Prisoners taken in the *Harwich* Pacquet, and all that afterwards fell into his hands. I know I shall not offend you in recommending him warmly to your protection.[12]

Franklin also wrote Thomas Digges, a Maryland merchant living in London, to look into Conyngham's situation. From his headquarters, General Washington sent the simplest yet most threatening letter. Hang Conyngham, he promised Collier, and Washington would hang six British officers he held in custody.[13]

On July 24, an unfettered Gustavus Conyngham was brought out of Pendennis Castle. It was hot and humid, thanks to a balmy land breeze. Conyngham was taken aboard the tender *Fanny*, joined below deck with a group of impressed sailors, and bound for Plymouth. During the short passage, the *Fanny*'s captain gave Conyngham the same liberties the pressed men had as the tender sailed under constantly threatening skies. Once in Plymouth harbor, the reluctant tars found berths awaiting them on British warships. Conyngham would find his at Mill Prison.[14]

To his surprise, Conyngham was listed as "an exchangeable prisoner"—he was not yet aware of the diplomatic ruckus his treatment had caused. Back in Philadelphia, Lieutenant Hele's harsh confinement was taking its toll. He became so desperately ill that Dr. Benjamin Rush considered his recovery "doubtfull unless speedily indulged with a private Lodging." Once Congress learned that Conyngham was not to be executed, Hele was transferred and his parole again approved.

Conyngham arrived at Mill Prison with one goal in mind: escape.[15]

As grim as the news was for Conyngham and his family, 1779 had begun optimistically for the Continental Navy, although some of its captains were conspicuous by their absence on familiar quarterdecks. Boston's bickering couple, John Manley and Hector McNeill, now commanded privateers, as did John Barry. After the loss of the *Raleigh*, Barry was considered for command of the *Confederacy*, but she was denied him. Throughout 1779 and 1780, Barry led two privateers on several successful cruises, allowing him to make good money after three years of experiencing Congress's woeful track record in paying its naval officers.[16]

Command of the *Confederacy* went instead to Seth Harding, a Norwalk mariner whose political connections got him this command but whose capable service in the Connecticut Navy justified it. He terrorized British shipping. Governor Trumbull sent the forty-two-year-old with the hawk-like profile to Philadelphia to lobby for his own appointment. Harding informed Henry Laurens, then the president of Congress, that he was the right man for the job. He got it.[17]

One other new name appeared on the roster of Continental captains. Pierre Landais was a French naval officer whose nearly feminine facial features masked both a rampant ego and a neurotic temper. His family had sent its sons to sea for generations, and during the French and Indian War he had risen to command of a fireship. He had resigned from King Louis's navy in 1775 and latched onto Silas Deane while the American's star was ascendant in Paris, charming him into giving Landais command of an American supply ship whose passengers included Baron von Steuben. With a sheaf of recommendations from Deane under his arm, Landais sailed for Philadelphia. Having also won over John Adams and Arthur Lee in Paris, he turned his flattery on Sam Adams and Richard Henry Lee in Philadelphia. The Adams-Lee faction, green with envy over Ben Franklin and his popularity, saw Landais as a maritime Lafayette, and a useful pawn in their game playing with the elderly minister. Sam Adams was immediately impressed, calling Landais a "Master of his Business," and labored hard to get the Frenchman command of the recently built thirty-six-gun frigate *Alliance*, coincidentally docked in Boston harbor.[18]

For company, the *Alliance* had three other Continental ships in Boston: the frigates *Warren*, *Providence*, and *Boston* and the two French-built frigates *Deane* and *Queen of France*. They were idle, not because of winter weather, lack of guns, or a British blockade, but for lack of men.

The Eastern Navy Board was confronted with two extremes—six frigates in one harbor, but not enough hands on all the muster rolls combined to man two of them. "Every Ship here might sail in fourteen days if they could be manned," the board wrote to Congress, while pointing a collective finger at the culprits:

"The Conduct of the Privateers who are always seducing by every art the Men from the Public Service"—meaning the Continental Navy. They offered a simple solution: cease all privateering in Boston until the frigates were manned and out to sea; that would do the trick.[19]

But privateering was still a profitable investment among the politically connected, including more than a few congressmen themselves. Come up with another suggestion, the Marine Committee replied. One solution was no solution: enlisting rejects and deserters from the Continental Army. One officer wrote Washington suggesting that a deserter's death sentence be commuted to service aboard a Continental frigate, as "it might answer as good a purpose as to execute him." In Connecticut, Seth Harding, desperate to get the *Confederacy* to sea, began impressing French sailors fresh off a cartel. Upon learning of this, Boston captains began taking French sailors off the docks and into Continental frigates. Not wanting to alienate America's new and irreplaceable ally, Congress told Harding to put them back ashore, and sent the Navy Board the only solution that worked: a sailor's best friend, cash. The Eastern Navy Board was also besieged by shipwrights, merchants, carpenters, chandlers, and other creditors—all owed money. The navy was so far in arrears that board members James Warren, John Deshon, and William Vernon took out a $20,000 loan at their expense, mainly to save their reputations. Slowly, the muster rolls began adding names.[20]

The first of the frigates to depart Boston was the *Alliance*, bound for France and carrying the Marquis de Lafayette, on a mission from Washington to report to King Louis's court on the war's developments and personally entreat the king for manpower and money. The *Deane*, under Sam Nicholson, would be *Alliance*'s consort. Within three days of their departure from Boston, the ships parted company (Nicholson capturing two prizes en route to France).[21]

The new frigate's maiden voyage exposed Landais for what he really was. Once the Massachusetts coastline disappeared, he dropped his false modesty and charm to reveal his overbearing management style. It did not play well. In the fo'c'sle, a cabal of sailors plotted to take the ship, cast Landais adrift, put Lafayette in irons, and make for England. The *Alliance* was days away from reaching Brest when their mutiny broke out. It was barely suppressed, mainly thanks to Lafayette's courage and naked sword.[22]

The *Alliance* and the *Deane* had no sooner departed than the sloop *Providence* arrived at New Bedford. John Peck Rathbun had another successful cruise: five prizes that all reached port safely. But both ship and captain were in disrepair; the *Providence* needed careening and the captain was ill. William Ellery, Rathbun's champion in Congress, was saddened by Rathbun's leaving the sloop, and unhappier still when he learned the captain's replacement was Hoysted Hacker, "of whom," Ellery complained, "I have not the highest opinion."[23]

As the remaining captains in Boston tried every possible idea to lure New England tars away from privateers, geography once again played a part regarding where to send the frigates once they had enough manpower to be sent anywhere. Richard Henry Lee had been appointed head of the Marine Committee just when resentment among southern congressmen over the navy's New England influence reached a crescendo. Lee, who in 1776 had introduced the resolution "that these colonies are, and of a right ought to be, free and independent states," was determined to send as many Continental ships as he could southward, where their presence was sorely needed.

After the British abandoned Philadelphia, the focus of British war policy had shifted to the south. Loyalist privateers, based in New York, were voraciously preying on southern shipping. Merchantmen leaving the Virginia Capes had a better chance of being captured than they did of safely reaching their destination. Southern governors and congressmen made their opinions known: outside of Biddle and Rathbun, there had been scant success in southern waters these past two years. Lee was determined to change that.

On February 10, Lee sent a courier northward bearing orders to captains, agents, and the Navy Board to get the ships manned and sailing southward: America's southern trade was imperiled. By March 13 enough hands had been enlisted and the first cruise commenced with the *Warren* (John Hopkins), the *Queen of France* (Joseph Olney), and the *Ranger* (just in from Portsmouth and still under Thomas Simpson). With Hopkins in command, the Marine Committee ordered them to "Chastice the Insolence of those Small Cruisers upon the Coasts of Virginia and the Carolinas," and to cruise southern waters as long as their supplies lasted before returning to an American port.[24]

The ships headed south, reaching Cape Henry by April 6, when the *Ranger* took a small privateer of ten guns. Before sunrise the next morning—patrolling the same waters where Barry and the *Lexington* had captured the *Edward* exactly three years before—the *Warren*'s mastheader spotted ten ships to leeward. Suddenly, he hailed the quarterdeck again: nine ships to windward. With two fleets to choose from, Hopkins picked the ships to windward, giving him the weather gauge and a near 100 percent chance of overtaking them.

Conditions were ideal for the chase: "Pleasant gales and fair weather," Hopkins noted, ordering every inch of canvas raised. "Made all the Sail we could allow and aloft," Simpson recorded in his log. This was a rare sight thus far in the war: three American warships, sailing in unison to bag British and Loyalist merchantmen. Wind filled their sails, and the chase was on.

The fleet, escorted by two Tory privateers, did its utmost to outdistance their pursuers, but the *Warren*, the *Queen*, and the *Ranger* were like hawks. The *Warren*, one of the original thirteen frigates, was faster than her consorts, and Hopkins let her fly, leaving the other two ships in her wake. Ten hours later, the little squadron had bagged seven merchantmen and one privateer. They were carrying supplies for the British army, everything from flour barrels to "accoutrements" for a regiment of dragoons: a rich haul.[25]

After learning from the captured sailors that a host of British men-of-war were looking for him, Hopkins decided his cruise was finished. With so many captured ships requiring prize crews, he believed the best course for him was to disobey Congress's orders to cruise until his supplies were exhausted and return to Boston. In so doing he was bypassing the very waters Esek Hopkins had been sent in 1776 to protect and defend, only to return to a New England port. Like father, like son.[26]

Accordingly, Hopkins made for Boston with the *Queen of France* and five prizes, while the *Ranger* headed to Portsmouth with the others. Hopkins was greeted as rapturously as his father had been upon his return from New Providence. The family name was back in the headlines for the best of reasons, and Hopkins could not have been more proud of himself.[27]

Once the Navy Board heard that Hopkins's ships were in Nantasket Road they sent word that he not enter Boston harbor for two reasons: one, he still had enough supplies to return to sea; two, the board realized—if Hopkins did not—that once the frigates bumped against the docks, their sailors would make straight for the waterfront taverns and brothels, or worse yet, a privateer.

To the dismay of Warren, Deshon, and Vernon, the *Warren* entered the harbor, and their fears were immediately justified. The crew had signed on for one cruise, not for a specific duration. The cruise was over, and with it their service in the Continental Navy. The board next sent a letter to Olney aboard the *Queen of France*, ordering him to anchor in midstream, assuring him that anything he might need in the way of supplies would be delivered. But like Hopkins, Olney kept going, right into the harbor, where his men disembarked with the same alacrity shown by their brother sailors, late of the *Warren*.[28]

In Philadelphia, the Marine Committee was thrilled at the news of Hopkins's success, sending him hearty congratulations, along with the urgent wish that he and his men return to sea. Days later, word arrived from the Navy Board that Captains Hopkins and Olney were not entirely aboveboard. Sailing home, both convinced their men to allow the captains to act as their agents. Hopkins and Olney would receive not only their shares as captains but also a percentage of each sailor's money.

Further, Warren and Deshon suspected that the two captains had already bought out their crews' shares at a discounted rate. Sailors frequently did this with agents in order to be paid something immediately instead of everything later, after prize ships had been condemned and sold. With Congress's sorry history of payment, who could blame them? The board estimated that Hopkins and Olney would net $2,000 each as agents. If their suspicions were correct, they could make even more.

The Marine Committee's congratulatory letter was barely out of Hopkins's hands when another letter from the committee arrived, ordering that a court of inquiry be convened to investigate Hopkins's disregard of orders from the committee and the board, as well as his questionable meddling with the sailors' pay. The board suspended both Hopkins and Olney for conduct that they accurately described as "dishonorable," especially considering the financial burdens the three board members had just taken on to get the ships manned and out to sea, only to have them return so soon. In Philadelphia, the whole affair showed Congress that the current system of running the navy was a failure.

Changes were required, but for now the only ones made were with captains; Hopkins and Olney were dismissed from the navy. As the reader may have guessed, both became privateers. To replace Olney aboard the *Queen of France*, the Marine Committee wisely chose the recovered Captain Rathbun. To walk the quarterdeck of the *Warren*, they chose the *Trumbull*'s idle captain, Dudley Saltonstall. In so doing, they set in motion the navy's greatest disaster.[29]

Fortunately, other New England captains earned their share of success while avoiding such tawdry behavior. Even Hoysted Hacker got a chance to show his mettle. After taking over the sloop *Providence* from Rathbun, Hacker was ordered to accompany the frigate *Providence* (Abraham Whipple) and the *Boston* (Samuel Tucker) out to sea under Whipple's command to cruise New England waters for ten days, then head south as far as Virginia. They left Boston on April 13, but Whipple soon returned, so violently ill that the Navy Board feared he could no longer serve. Tucker and Hacker made the cruise without him. They were beset by fog one day, strong gales the next—the yin and yang of an Atlantic spring—and soon lost sight of each other. Tucker made for the Delaware Bay, while Hacker sailed to Sandy Hook.[30]

The *Providence* was "off the Hook" on May 7 when she was spotted by the British brig *Diligent*, twelve guns, and part of Commodore Collier's fleet. Her captain felt she was more than a match for the sloop and closed in, looking to attack the *Providence* on the larboard side where her long boom might become a hindrance to her fighting capability. For years she had served Jones and Rathbun well; now the little ship's sailing prowess took Hacker to victory. Seeing the enemy's intentions, Hacker, running with the wind, wisely and unexpectedly jibed. The *Providence*'s boom suddenly swung from one side to the other, her great sail filling with the wind, still coming off her stern. Now her boom would not be a factor in the coming fight.

Hacker had been unlucky through much of the war—and he would be again—but this was his day. Running up his colors, Hacker unleashed two broadsides before the *Diligent*, now luffing in the wind while changing *her* course, could return fire. Soon her sails and rigging were in tatters and her masts in danger of toppling. Hacker lost four killed and ten wounded, but the toll on the brig was significantly higher, and her captain struck his colors.

Hacker brought the *Diligent* into New Bedford, where he received orders to sail the waters off Martha's Vineyard. With news of Hopkins and Olney fresh in his mind, Hacker obeyed. The *Diligent* was sold at the handsome price of $26,000 and taken into the Continental Navy. Hacker was given the option of commanding the brig or the sloop; he stayed put.[31]

While Hacker patrolled Martha's Vineyard, Samuel Tucker was in Philadelphia. Coming up the Delaware, he passed the *Confederacy*, moored off Chester, twenty miles below Philadelphia.

Few ships in the age of sail could match the *Confederacy* for looks and construction. She was 155 feet long with a 37-foot beam. Along her bow were two carved red foxes; her figurehead was a bearded, menacing warrior. The frigate's stern was adorned with detailed filigree around the cabin windows. She was one of the few American frigates that had sweeps, allowing her to row out of danger when becalmed. The officers' berths and wardrooms were spacious; she even had a great room with an unheard-of eight-foot ceiling—perfect for hosting French admirals or diplomats. And she had teeth: thirty-six guns in all. All she needed was a large enough crew to properly man her and fight the enemy.[32]

After mooring the *Boston* nearby, Tucker was accompanied by Seth Harding on a coach ride to Philadelphia to report on their needs. Tucker had made no captures heading south, while Harding arrived under a cloud of suspicion that he was another James Nicholson, perfectly happy to have a beautiful frigate to command and content that he lacked the manpower to fight. He wanted a chance to lay those rumors to rest.[33]

With "The Confidence we repose in your Courage and Good Conduct," the Marine Committee sent Tucker and Harding on a three-week cruise, short but eminently successful both politically and financially. After safely convoying merchantmen southward, the frigates captured three prizes between them, including the *Pole*, a Loyalist privateer of twenty-six guns with a formidable reputation as a fighter.

Years later, Tucker became fond of relating his encounter with the *Pole*: how the *Boston* approached the privateer flying British colors when her captain, John Maddock, hailed him. Maddock was cruising for the *Boston* and "that rascal Tucker" and asked Tucker if he had seen him. "I know of him," Tucker replied. "They say he is a hard customer." The two captains spoke over the water a while longer while Tucker muttered orders from his quarterdeck to get the frigate in optimum readiness for what he had in mind next.

Suddenly the *Pole*'s mastheader cried down to Maddock, "That is surely Tucker!" As if on cue, Tucker hailed Maddock again: the time for talking was over. "Fight or strike your flag," Tucker suggested. Maddock struck his colors.[34]

Tucker and Harding were escorting their prizes up the Delaware when they encountered Sam Nicholson and the *Deane*. As the ships headed upriver a packet approached with fresh orders: Harding was to moor the *Confederacy* off Chester again to await further instructions, while Tucker and Nicholson were to make for the Virginia Capes and destroy British shipping. If none were found, they were to cruise the Atlantic for transports and British merchantmen, then return to Boston in September.[35]

This run of good fortune for the navy was not over yet. A story of blind luck—literally blind luck—awaited Captains Whipple, Rathbun, and Simpson. On June 18, their ships stood down Nantasket Roadstead on a cruise under the now healthy Whipple's command. The ships would have departed sooner but for Simpson's reluctance to leave Portsmouth for Boston. Simpson had taken the dismissal of Hopkins and Olney as a personal affront by both the Eastern Navy Board and the Marine Committee; ignorant of their scandalous behavior, he wanted to resign. Warren and Deshon responded immediately that if he must resign, he should at least sail the *Ranger* to Boston. Once he did so, and learned the facts behind the matter, he withdrew his resignation.[36]

As commodore, Whipple was to take the ships to Newfoundland and seize what transports and merchantmen he could find. En route, they took a couple of prizes, but nothing noteworthy. The passage was uneventful until July 18. A thick, damp fog hung over the American vessels that morning as they slowly inched their way across the water. Soon the Yankee tars could make out ship's bells and signal guns: they were not alone in this soup.

The captains instantly knew they were close by enemy sail—but were unaware whether they were merchantmen, men-of-war, or both. As morning lengthened, the fog began lifting. Once it did, the *Ranger*'s mastheader cried, "A sail, a sail on the lee bow; another there, and there!" Simpson's midshipmen took to the ratlines with their spyglasses—fifty—no, sixty sail lay ahead and beside them. They were surrounded by the Jamaica Fleet, five dozen ships in all, heading home to England and escorted by a squadron of British cruisers led by a sixty-four-gun ship-of-the-line.[37]

One of the *Ranger*'s hands was Andrew Sherburne, just fourteen, serving as a waiter to the bosun, Charles Roberts. Years later Sherburne recalled the trepidation the Americans initially felt over their precarious situation. If Whipple shared such worries, they were dispelled as he watched Rathbun bring the *Queen of France* alongside a large merchantman, the *Arethusa*. Having taken two forts with a single sloop, he was not cowed by such a vessel.

Taking his speaking trumpet, Rathbun hailed the *Arethusa*'s captain, inquiring if he had spotted any rebel privateers. They had, the man replied, but the Americans had been driven off. Rathbun invited him to come aboard for a visit. Ships in fleets of such size rarely knew their companions, and the captain had himself rowed to the *Queen*, where Rathbun offered him some tea and captivity, then sent a prize crew back with news of the captain's surrender. Next he sent the *Arethusa*'s boat along with his own to another merchantman, repeating his invitation, and getting the same results.

Soon another ship was alongside the *Queen of France*—the *Providence*. Now it was Whipple's turn to call across the water, ordering Rathbun to get under way and join the *Providence* in as subtle an escape as possible. Rathbun did not refuse his commodore—he merely pointed to his two prizes and asked permission to remain; the pickings were too easy to abandon; there were no signals between ships to alert the rest of the fleet of the danger they were in. Until a warship caught on to the act, the American foxes were in a very large—and thus far accommodating—British henhouse.

The man responsible for burning the *Gaspee* seven years before decided to join in the game. Soon Simpson followed suit. With pure bravado, the three ships sailed unobtrusively through the fleet chatting up captain after captain, taking ship after ship, manning them with skeleton prize crews and sending them homeward. The binge continued until evening, when the *Providence* captured a thirty-gun ship after a flurry of broadsides. But as the fleet was strewn across the Atlantic for miles, even this action did not give the Americans immediately away.[38]

Unbelievably, the Americans kept at it for three days, by which time the *Ranger* had separated from the frigates. At the end of the third day she was in hot pursuit of one last merchantman when two large sail came over the horizon, flying British colors and making straight for the *Ranger* and her prey. Simpson's concern soon turned to relief when he made out Whipple's signals from the *Warren*. With ten prizes accounted for, it was time to sail home before their incredible luck left them.[39]

No fewer than eight of the prizes reached Boston, where Whipple's squadron received a tremendous welcome as they docked on August 24. The holds of the captured ships were full of rum, sugar, and cotton; there were 113 cannons behind the gun ports. The total value of Whipple's haul topped a million dollars—not bad for two months' cruising. Whipple even had a ballad written in his honor:

> *Come listen and I'll tell you how first I went to sea,*
> *To fight against the British and win our liberty.*
> *We shipped with Captain Whipple who never knew a fear,*
> *The Captain of the* Providence, *the Yankee privateer.*[40]

On it went for six verses, adding color (in addition to erroneously calling the *Providence* a privateer) to what was as happy a tale of pluck as any in the war.[41]

On September 6, the *Deane* and *Boston*, accompanied by two of the thirteen prizes *they* had taken from the British that summer, including the *Thorn*, a sloop-of-war, sailed past Castle William, the fortress protecting Boston harbor, and docked at John Hancock's wharf—the designated refitting station for all Continental vessels. But the gaiety and joy over Whipple's arrival just two weeks earlier in Boston had turned dolorous; even Nicholson's and Tucker's great success could not overcome the disastrous news trickling in from Maine, at a place called Penobscot.[42]

Since the summer of 1778, John Paul Jones had been in France, watching the seasons change while his chances at fame and fortune dimmed. The notoriety he had achieved with the Whitehaven raid and victory over the *Drake* had lifted his spirits—and inflated his ego. Forgotten were the mishaps at Whitehaven and the near-comical kidnap attempt of the Earl of Selkirk. What the public remembered—as did Jones—was the panic he had put into play. In the weeks after his return to France, he had been congratulated by Benjamin Franklin, feted by Admiral d'Orvilliers, and taken under the wing of Louis Philippe Joseph, le Duc de Chartres, Grand Master of the French Masonic lodges. He even drew up his own coat of arms, ordering it engraved on a silver set he had purchased (perhaps inspired by Selkirk?).

Better yet, he learned from Franklin that *l'Indien*, the frigate he had been lusting for, was to be his. John Adams and Arthur Lee had been after Jones to turn the *Ranger* over to Simpson. With French Minister of Marine Antoine de Sartine's assurances that *l'Indien* would shortly be in Brest, Jones happily declared his independence from both Simpson and the *Ranger* on the Fourth of July: "I will with your approbation not only pardon the past, but leave [Simpson] to command the *Ranger*," he assured the commissioners, then accompanied them to a gala celebration of the Fourth at the Hôtel de Valentinois.[43]

While anxiously awaiting his frigate's arrival, Jones divided his time between learning French, happily flirting with the ladies (which made the strait-laced John Adams jealous), and bombarding Franklin and Sartine with new plans to finish off Whitehaven, destroy the fishery at Cameltown, and take the Irish linen fleet. All he needed was "three very fast Sailing Frigates" and who knows? He might even destroy the coal industry at Newcastle, sending all Britain to shivering in the coming winter. He even sent George Washington a present: a pair of giant epaulets. "Command me without reserve," he implored the general.[44]

But he did not get two more frigates; he did not even get *l'Indien*. The Dutch blamed slow construction, but the real reason was politics: they were not about to turn over such a warship to an American captain. Jones sought sympathy from the Comte d'Orvilliers only to find him preoccupied with his own disappointments. While Jones was in Paris, the admiral led his fleet in a battle against a British force under Admiral Keppel (HMS *Victory*, years later Nelson's command, was Keppel's flagship). After four days of angling for advantage, twenty-seven

French ships-of-the-line formed a line of battle against thirty British vessels. The fleets traded broadsides and then parted company. D'Orvilliers was taken to task for not maintaining the fight, but Jones's latest friend, de Chartres, took most of the blame once it was learned that he either misread or disobeyed d'Orvillier's signals.[45]

When Jones had left Brest for Paris weeks earlier he believed he had d'Orvilliers and other French officials in his pocket. Now his reception was cold, and he soon learned why. Ever since Simpson was released from jail, he informed anyone who lent an ear that Jones had been dismissed from the Continental service. The sale of the *Ranger*'s prizes, including the *Drake*, had gone badly; Jones was enraged to see the uniforms of the *Drake*'s officers—including that of her dead captain—on sale in waterfront shop windows. Further, the two hundred prisoners Jones had brought into port had yet to be exchanged for American captives in English prisons. He poured out his frustrations to Franklin's secretary, Edward Bancroft, interweaving with his travails a plan for attacking the British Isles, unaware that Bancroft relayed any useful information to the British Admiralty. Idle again, he told Bancroft, "If I had a Mistress here I have time enough on my hands to shew her Attention."[46]

If Jones had gotten his wish and *l'Indien* had been his, the war might have ended very differently for him. Had he put his plans into action, he would most assuredly have sailed into a trap, and rivaled Gustavus Conyngham as England's most famous prisoner. As before when Jones faced ennui, his petulant resentment rose to the surface. Returning to Paris, he learned that Abraham Whipple was at Brest with the *Providence* and asked him to arrange a court-martial for Simpson. To the prince of Nassau-Siegen, the nobleman sent to Amsterdam to bring *l'Indien* to France, Jones described himself as "cast off and Useless" and begged the prince to find him another ship. He referred to Arthur Lee as "the Wasp" and John Adams as "Mr. Roundface." Finally, he beseeched King Louis himself, blending flattery (calling *le Roi* "the Protector of the Rights of Human Nature") and umbrage ("I have been chained down to shameful activity for the Space of Five Months") with hope ("You will not . . . suffer me to remaining longer in this insupportable disgrace"). Even the attentions of Mme. de Chaumont did not alleviate his despair. Jones did not see himself as "on the beach" so much as marooned. Franklin, beset with his own sea of troubles, now saw Jones as a contentious boor.[47]

Ironically, it fell to Chaumont to rescue his wife's lover. At first the French power broker offered Jones his privateer, *l'Union*. Desperate though he was for a command, Jones declined. He wanted a navy vessel. Outside of that, he had but one specific at this time, telling Chaumont, "I wish to have no Connection with any Ship that does not Sail fast; for I intend to go in harm's way."[48]

By November he was near despair over getting a command, when he heard from an Irishman in l'Orient, James Moylan, who had established a good working relationship with American captains and the commissioners in Paris. Moylan had found a ship: the *Duc de Duras*, an armed former East Indiaman. She was twelve years old—positively ancient by contemporary standards . . . but she was a ship.[49]

Jones left Paris for l'Orient in December to inspect the *Duc*. He found her huge but certainly slow, opulent but rotten—a maritime Miss Havisham. The *Duc* had a poop deck and a captain's cabin below fit for an admiral, along with drawing and dining rooms to boot. She was 152' long with a 40' beam and 1,050 tonnage. With no frigates looming on Jones's horizon, he described her as "a good character for Sailing and working" to Chaumont, and entreated Sartine to buy her. Believing himself his own best salesman, he left for Paris to plead his case.[50]

Once the king was informed that the *Duc* was no longer fit to serve *les Companie des Indies*, he declared her fit for John Paul Jones. The captain officially took command on February 4, 1779.[51]

But the fates were not through tormenting Jones's mettle or ego. Before he left Paris to oversee the *Duc*'s refitting, he was subjected to one more embarrassment. Having endured the slings and arrows of Simpson, Lee, Adams, and the French court, the opposite sex now had its turn. Jones had gone to Passy to pay his respects to Mme. de Chaumont and Franklin. Once back in l'Orient, he received a letter from Franklin regarding his learning of a "mystery" in Jones's life. The captain immediately jumped to the conclusion that Franklin had learned of his killing "the Ringleader" in Tobago years ago, and sent a detailed explanation of the incident, including why he added "Jones" to his name.

Upon reading the letter, Franklin became perplexed; it was not that incident at all, he replied, but a recent one: a local priest had gone to Franklin and Mme. de Chaumont to report that Jones had attacked the wife of the hotel gardener. According to the clergyman, Jones had "attempted to ravish her," the priest titillating his listeners with details that Franklin found "not fit for me to write." The woman's grown sons planned to kill Jones, but he had already left for l'Orient.

Once Franklin investigated the allegation, his mood swung from worry to glee, "for the old Woman being one of the grossest, coarsest, dirtiest and ugliest that we may find in a thousand, Madame Chaumont said it gave a high Idea of the strength of Appetite and Courage of the Americans." While Franklin dismissed the incident as a tall tale, Jones could hear the laughter from his patron and his mistress—laughter directed at him, not with him. Knowing what he knew of Paris, he was sure the fictional escapade was common knowledge.

The humor eluded the captain, who poured himself into converting the French merchantman into an American warship. He had already given her a new name, inspired by Franklin's most popular writings, *Poor Richard's Almanack*. As Jones oversaw the piercing of gun ports and the lading of stores, painters were at work on the stern, scraping off *Duc de Duras* and adding the name *Bonhomme Richard*.[52]

In 1779, two Americans—one young, one younger—signed on ships commanded by two very different Continental Navy captains. Nathaniel Fanning, twenty-four, was already an experienced sailor. A Connecticut merchant's son, he had earlier gone to sea aboard a privateer, and been given a prize-master's duties on his second voyage.

His third voyage was not as lucky. He had signed on as a junior officer for the privateer *Angelica*'s maiden voyage out of Boston in May 1778. On his twenty-third birthday she was captured by HMS *Andromeda*, bound for Portsmouth, England, whose list of passengers included General Sir William Howe. Once aboard the British warship, Fanning and his shipmates were asked by the general if they would be interested in joining the Royal Navy. When all refused, Howe declared, "You are a set of rebels, and it is more than probable you will be hanged." Once the ship docked, Howe went off to meet with Lord North and his cousin King George; Fanning and the other Americans were sent to Forten Prison.

He found French as well as Americans imprisoned at Forten. For one full year he endured the rats, lice, foul water, and slop served as food, including bread laced with fine powdered glass. In June 1779 he and 120 others were exchanged for a like number of British prisoners. They arrived in Nantes, where they were welcomed by the townsfolk, singing their praises in French and treating them to a wondrous meal at l'Hôtel d'Orléans. From Nantes, Fanning made his way to l'Orient:

The town is not very large, and the dwelling houses are not so high nor so elegant . . . but the streets are pretty regular and well paved, and there is here an excellent dockyard and a long row of buildings which are founded upon the Key and make a fine appearance as one approaches the town from the sea.[53]

It was here that Fanning met John Paul Jones. The captain told him of his intent to cruise to America and offered him a midshipman's berth. Fanning learned from the ship's crew that Jones was to first cruise the English Channel, but "As there was no other opportunity of procuring a safe passage" home, Fanning signed on, not knowing that he was in for the battle of his life.[54]

While Fanning was coming to terms with Jones in l'Orient, the privateer *Delaware*, a twelve-gun brig, was departing Philadelphia for the West Indies. Aboard her was John Kessler, a seventeen-year-old landsman.

Born in Philadelphia to a German cabinetmaker and his wife, young John was apprenticed to a dry goods merchant at age eleven for five years. When war broke out, his master gave him permission to drill with a volunteer brigade who later marched to Perth Amboy, New Jersey, to meet Washington's army after the fall of New York, during which time his apprenticeship ended. He was next contracted out to serve a Philadelphia brewmeister, "rapidly instructed in the art of malting and brewing" when the Howe brothers came to call. After John and his master joined the fleeing patriots, the Redcoats feasted on what barrels they found at the brewery before destroying it.

Kessler next became a tobacconist's clerk. For years the youngster had watched friends go off privateering; by 1779 the lure of the sea and good money propelled him to the waterfront, where he signed the *Delaware*'s muster roll. His captain was John Barry. Like Kessler, Barry needed both a job and fast money.[55]

The *Delaware* had a successful maiden voyage, returning to Philadelphia with two handsome prizes. Once Kessler got his sea legs he proved a quick study, and Barry took a liking to the lad, raising him in the course of two voyages from clerk to steward to captain of marines. Returning up the Delaware from her second cruise, the brig sailed past the still shorthanded *Confederacy*, once again moored off Chester. Captain Harding was in Philadelphia, but he had left orders for his second-in-command, Lieutenant Stephen Gregory, to send a boarding party to each passing vessel, and press into service the hands necessary to provide a full crew for the frigate.

As the *Delaware* glided by, Gregory hailed her, ordering her captain to come to. Barry kept right on sailing. Gregory made a second hail, which Barry acknowledged, but still did not slow down. A third hail was accompanied by a warning shot. The *Delaware* maintained her course.

An enraged Gregory sent a longboat across the river manned with his toughest sailors and marines, only to watch as the brig's crew, brandishing pikes and cutlasses, cowed them at the gangway. They were heading back to the frigate when the brig's captain ordered his diminutive 4-pounders run out as he hailed Gregory: "I advise you to desist firing, this is the brig *Delaware*, and my name is John Barry." Now knowing who he was up against, Gregory did as he suggested.[56]

After this cruise Congress called Barry back to duty to oversee construction of the *America*, a ship-of-the-line being built in Portsmouth, New Hampshire. Kessler remained with the *Delaware*, now under the command of James Collins. A third voyage to St. Eustatius and Haiti went well; the fourth did not. Heading home, the brig was captured by a British frigate. The Americans were taken to Kingston, Jamaica, and locked in a small prison. Collins had a brother in Kingston who owned a small vessel. For months he and his men plotted their escape. On September 22, 1780, the day after Kessler's nineteenth birthday, they broke out, took over the little ship, and made for Port-au-Prince. Once there, Kessler recalled, "every one had to shift for himself," and he signed on another privateer bound for Salem, Massachusetts, wondering if he would ever be as lucky at sea as he had been under Barry's direction, not knowing that their courses would cross again, under much more dangerous conditions.[57]

As Jones was readying the *Bonhomme Richard*, Gustavus Conyngham was plotting his escape.

Mill Prison was perched on a spit of land by Mill Bay, just west of Plymouth, England. It was a rectangular structure with a large courtyard. There were high brick walls on the south and west; three long buildings—the first, a hospital—ran west to east, ending with the cook's house, a two-story structure, and finally the main entrance. All combined, they formed the north wall. Running north to south to form the east wall were the officers' quarters and the "long prison:" two-story buildings with an equally high wall between them on the east.[58]

By mid-July he had familiarized himself with his surroundings. Grim as conditions were, they were markedly better than those found in the New York harbor prison ships. Conyngham spent his first day confined in a guardhouse, then spent eight days in "the Black Hole," a dank, dark dungeon. What little air inside was foul. For company, he had some French prisoners. The Black Hole was primarily used for any prisoners caught escaping. Conyngham found it "a horrid room." He would know; over the next several months he would escape, only to be captured time and again.

There were several hundred prisoners at Mill, and by the time of Conyngham's arrival there were French and Spanish captives as well as Americans. The Europeans were not kept with the rebels, and were also better fed (at one point a proposal was made in Parliament to give equal status to the Americans, but it was voted down, forty-seven to fifteen). One Yankee tar described the rations as "3/4 lb. beef, 1 lb bread, 1 qt very ordinary beer, and a few greens per man for 24 hours. This is our allowance daily, except Saturday, when we have 6 oz cheese instead of beef." Conyngham's journal mentioned that "dogs, cats, rats even the Grass [was] eaten by prisoners," adding "this hard to be credited, but is a fact." Another prisoner recalled boiling snails and drinking the "broth" after downing the snails.[59]

Americans in Mill and Forten Prisons turned to the one man in Europe who could deliver salvation—Benjamin Franklin. He wrote endless letters to them and on their behalf, sending what money he could, usually through Thomas Digges, the Maryland merchant in London that Franklin had contacted once he learned of Conyngham's plight. Digges got some of Franklin's money to Conyngham and kept him abreast of the captain's situation.[60]

Peddlers visited the prison selling sundries at near impossible prices. The prisoners spent their time trying to earn money by making wood carvings, and writing family, friends, and congressmen, begging for cash or to use influence to be exchanged. They also set up their own code of laws: theft, for example, was punished by making the offender run a gauntlet, with each prisoner armed with a jagged rock or nettles to bruise and draw blood. Rarely were there repeat offenders.[61]

There were only four ways to leave Mill: death, exchange, escape, or joining the Royal Navy. While prisoners were forbidden newspapers, they learned of the latest events through coded letters or from blabbing guards. Jones's efforts to exchange Americans for the British tars from the *Drake* was soon common knowledge and raised hopes that a cartel might send some of Mill's captives home, or at least, to neutral Holland. But by the time of Conyngham's arrival the delay of such action had left many of the prisoners despondent of ever leaving Mill except by joining the King's Navy. Conyngham, using his rank as leverage, appealed to any doubting sailor's patriotism. He rallied, implored, and derided the tempted sailor, succeeding to such a great degree that even Franklin learned of it. So, unfortunately for the captain, did his captors, sending him to the Black Hole again. For Conyngham, there looked to be only one way out: escape.[62]

Two previously described attempts read like the stuff of legend. In one instance he mingled with a group of visitors and walked out of the prison, only to be captured when a woman recognized him before he got far enough to leave the crowd, and he was quickly apprehended. Another account told of how he donned a suit of dark clothes and a pair of wire-rimmed frames (minus the glass), giving him a marked resemblance to one of the prison doctors. With his nose buried in a book and imitating the physician's peculiar gait, he walked past the sentry at the gate and passed through, only to be spied by one of the prison's peddlers outside Plymouth. Conyngham left no such details in his own hand, only asides among his writings alluding to several attempts to break out.[63]

On August 23, on a windy, rainy evening, he broke out again; a prison log's entry simply reads, "Gustavus Conyngham, Philadelphia, ran away." He did not get far, as his journal describes a testy confrontation with a British militiaman at Mill the following day, by which time Conyngham and his fellow prisoners were aware of d'Orvillier's fleet having been near Plymouth.[64]

In the fall of '79, Conyngham hatched a plan to break out as many Americans as possible. Being on the coast, Plymouth's earth was as much sand as dirt. With at least one pair of eyes on the guards at all times, the men organized in shifts and spent nights tunneling their way under the floor of their cell, spreading the dirt discreetly along the courtyard during the day. Later, Conyngham would write Franklin how he was imprisoned "on suspicion of high treason on his majesties high seas"; now he and his large band "committed treason through his earth."[65]

In the dark of night on November 3, Conyngham pulled tufts of grass through the tunnel (according to one anecdote, he also poked his head up to find a guard in a tryst with a young Plymouth woman). Keeping as silent as possible, fifty sailors and three officers joined Conyngham in climbing through the small, circular hole. Conyngham had escaped, but he was not free—he was "at large." When—or more correctly, if—he safely got out of England, *then* he would be free.[66]

For more than three years, Boston had been free of British occupation. True, the town was still repairing the damage left by General Howe's Redcoats, British warships and Loyalist privateers still preyed upon the New England coastline, and many families waited daily for word of loved ones in the army or at sea, but the Lobsterbacks' immediate presence was gone. The focus of the war had moved to the south. Some semblance of routine, having been restored, was again the norm.

Imagine the surprise, then, when word reached Boston in June of 1779 that a force of more than 600 Redcoats from Halifax, Nova Scotia, led by Brigadier General Francis McLean, had landed on the Majabigwaduce Peninsula on the

Penobscot River in Maine Territory (commonly known as Bagaduce throughout New England and now called Castine). They had arrived in a convoy of transports and small warships under Captain Andrew Barkley.

Bagaduce is one mile long and two miles wide; a thin, wooded neck connects the peninsula to the mainland. McLean immediately put his men to work building a fort on the high bluff atop the peninsula that overlooked both Penobscot Bay to the left and the Penobscot River to the right, where a thick forest of trees and underbrush dropped straight down to the shore. Once the fort was completed and its guns were in place, Fort St. George would be nearly impregnable.

Before Barkley sailed for Halifax, he left three sloops-of-war to defend the waterways. They would be under Captain Henry Mowat, forever despised as "the firebrand that burned Falmouth."[67]

The fort was both a military and a political masterstroke. A military base at Penobscot placed British might just two hundred miles from Boston, making it easier to raid the New England coastline and strike quickly at those Yankee privateers preying on British shipping. It also gave the Admiralty convenient access to the territory's vast forests, whose timber was indispensable for construction and repairs of the king's ships—a resource they lacked in Nova Scotia. By taking the Penobscot, the shortage of lumber would still exist—but for the rebels.

Politically, the establishment at Penobscot solved the problem of what to do with the thousands of Loyalists who had fled their homes from Boston to as far south as Philadelphia and were virtually homeless, thanks to their fealty to George III. The British envisioned a new colony in the territory, to be named New Ireland.[68]

Patriots throughout New England reacted at first with alarm and then resolve. With Newport still in British hands, such a base put New England in general and Boston in particular between two pincers, dramatically increasing the odds against any merchantman leaving or returning to Boston safely. Mowat's very name conjured up the memories of Falmouth and the ease with which such raids could now be perpetuated along the New England coast. Something must be done.

Accordingly, both the Massachusetts General Court and the New Hampshire General Assembly ordered that a military force be sent to Penobscot to drive the Redcoats back to Halifax. Neither government believed there was enough time to wait for Congress to learn of their plight, deliberate and debate over what action to take or not take, and finally act. Therefore, the General Court called for both a land force and naval support. "To employ such armed vessels," it ordered the impressments of sailors as well as use of privateers, while the General Assembly agreed "to Joyn with those at Boston for the reduction of our Enemies."[69]

At first it seemed that the expedition would be assembled with the same speed at which the politicians had created it. Three Continental ships: the *Warren*, the sloop *Providence*, and Hacker's recent prize, the brig *Diligent*, would lead the fleet. From the Massachusetts State Navy came the brigs *Tyrannicide*, twenty guns; *Hazard*, eighteen; and *Active*, sixteen; while New Hampshire sent their thirty-gun ship, the *Hampden*. They would be accompanied by sixteen privateers along with twenty-one transports and supply ships. Command of the largest American fleet of the war—and for the next seventy years, for that matter—was given to the *Warren*'s captain, Dudley Saltonstall. Brigadier General Solomon Lovell would lead the land forces; the task of overseeing the artillery went to Lieutenant Colonel Paul Revere.[70]

Officers the venture had; sailors and soldiers it did not. As Continental Navy officers and marines prowled the waterfront streets, raiding the taverns and brothels to find "recruits," Lovell's goal of 1,500 militia fell far short in both numbers and ability. He settled for fewer than 900, most of whom were old men, boys, and invalids, some of whom had never fired a musket before.

Not everyone was rapt in patriotic determination. Marine Lieutenant John Trevett of the *Providence*, as brave as any man, sensed folly in the expedition. He had seen Saltonstall in action with Esek Hopkins's squadron, and was appalled at the makeup of Lovell's force. Trevett was sure that Tory spies would get information about the expedition to the British in New York, and perhaps even to the enemy at Penobscot before the Americans sailed from Boston. Believing that the expedition would be trapped once British reinforcements sailed into Penobscot Bay, Trevett asked and received a leave of absence, ostensibly to attend to family matters in Rhode Island.[71]

Carrying his orders to "Captivate, Kill or Destroy the Enemies whole Force both by Sea and Land," but "to conduct measures and preserve the greatest harmony" with Lovell, Saltonstall came aboard the *Warren* on July 19, and ordered his fleet to sail. When word reached Philadelphia that Massachusetts had, out of necessity, picked up both the responsibility and the tab for the enterprise, Congress joined New England in waiting and worrying. "I pray to God it may succeed," Congressman William Whipple wrote John Langdon in Portsmouth, but feared "the great delays" would give General McLean his greatest weapon: time.[72]

In 1775, John Adams had never been farther than fifteen miles out to sea from Boston, but he was the strongest advocate for the creation of the Continental Navy. Portrait by Charles Willson Peale.

Samuel Chase—as intimidating verbally as he was physically imposing—called John Adams's idea of a Continental Navy "the Maddest Idea in the world." Portrait by Charles Willson Peale.

In Paris, Benjamin Franklin championed Lambert Wickes, Gustavus Conyngham, and John Paul Jones in their successive raids along the British coastline—although he found John Barry difficult to deal with. Portrait by Joseph-Siffred Duplessis.

Only George Washington and Benjamin Franklin could match Robert Morris in holding the fragile new United States together. A financial genius, Morris saved the country from complete economic collapse and kept the Continental Navy sailing long after Congress had lost interest. Portrait by Charles Willson Peale.

National Archives

Tun Tavern, where John Adams, Stephen Hopkins, and other Continental congressmen discussed the formation of the navy during their meals. The Philadelphia waterfront establishment also hosted the first rendezvous for the Continental marines.

Independence Seaport Museum

With the Philadelphia waterfront buildings in the background, this engraving by W. Birch & Son of a frigate under construction gives us an idea of the hugeness of such an undertaking.

In some respects, Abraham Whipple began the fight against the Royal Navy when he led the Rhode Island mariners in burning HMS *Gaspee* in 1772. Portrait by Edward Savage.

Continental Navy ship *Columbus*, commanded by Abraham Whipple, bringing in a British brig. Note the upside-down British ensign—the telltale sign of a captured vessel. Painting by Nowland Van Powell.

When the Revolution began, John Barry was Robert Morris's top merchant captain. When the Revolution ended, the intrepid Barry was the Continental Navy's last captain. Portrait by Gilbert Stuart.

April 7, 1776: Continental brigantine *Lexington*, Captain John Barry, takes the Royal Navy sloop *Edward* off the Virginia coast. Painting by Nowland Van Powell.

The only officer to be called "Commander-in-Chief" of a naval force, Esek Hopkins failed to live up to the expectations of Congress and his own captains. Engraving by C. Corbutt.

Young, talented, and brave, Nicholas Biddle was easily the best of Commodore Hopkins's captains. Painting by Charles Willson Peale.

This portrait of John Paul Jones by J. M. Moreau captures the conflicting traits of the man: his ambition, his inner doubts, and his indomitable will. He was a skilled mariner and brave warrior, but his biggest enemy was often himself.

On Sunday, December 3, 1775, Lieutenant John Paul Jones raised the Grand Union flag aboard the Continental Navy flagship *Alfred*. The steeples of Christ Church and Independence Hall rise in the background. Painting by Nowland Van Powell.

The U.S. Navy has named destroyers after Gustavus Conyngham, the most successful of all Continental Navy captains, but he is almost forgotten now. Painting by V. Zveg.

Marine Captain Matthew Parke served under both John Paul Jones and John Barry. Artist unknown

The *Alliance* entering Boston harbor missing her mainyard after her battle with the *Atalanta* and *Trepassey*. Painted by Marine Captain Matthew Parke

Joshua Barney was just a teenager when he joined the Continental Navy— the beginning of more than forty years of maritime service to his country. Portrait by Charles Willson Peale.

Continental ships *Reprisal* and *Lexington*, their guns run out, spoiling for a fight. Painting by Nowland Van Powell.

The portrait of the quintessential frigate captain: Andrew Snape Hamond of the King's Navy. Painting attributed to both Thomas Lawrence and G. H. Phillips.

While serving in the Continental Navy, Lieutenant Richard Dale survived a lightning strike, imprisonment, and the Battle off Flamborough Head. He served with distinction under both Barry and Jones. Engraving by R. W. Dobson from a drawing by J. B. Longacre, after a painting by J. Wood.

On November 16, 1776, the brig *Andrew Doria* entered the harbor of St. Eustatius, where she received the first salute from a foreign government. Painting by Colonel Phillips Melville, USMC.

Arthur Lee's loathing of Benjamin Franklin sent him into mean-spirited machinations against Franklin's admirers, including John Paul Jones and Gustavus Conyngham. Painting by Charles Willson Peale.

Chosen Number One on Congress's infamous "Captains List" mainly for his southern roots, Marylander James Nicholson vexed Congress throughout the war for his unwillingness to confront the enemy—until he commanded the *Trumbull*.

Unlike Admiral Howe, Commodore Sir George Collier displayed a ruthless efficiency as commander of the Royal Navy, routing the American fleet at Penobscot and sending the Continental captain King George most despised to England to be hanged. Engraving by John James Hinchcliff.

As a longboat reaches the New Jersey shoreline, HMS *Augusta* blows up during the Battle for the Delaware—the largest British ship ever lost to the Americans in war. The besieged Fort Mifflin is in the background. Painting by James Hamilton.

How England—and the rest of Europe—imagined Gustavus Conyngham. He saw a similar drawing in the shopwindows of London.

A Dutch engraving of Gustavus Conyngham's *Surprise* capturing the royal packet *Prince of Orange*. With this capture, Conyngham started terrorizing British shipping, belying France's neutrality, and bedeviling George III. Engraving by H. Fokke.

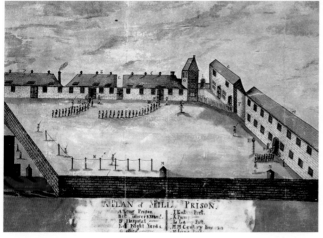

A contemporary drawing, later colored, of Mill Prison in Plymouth, England.

Under cover of darkness, John
Paul Jones leads his raiding
party into Whitehaven.
Painting by Colonel Charles
Waterhouse, USMC

After the Whitehaven
raid, British cartoonists
portrayed John Paul Jones
as the reincarnation of
Blackbeard the Pirate.

The Battle off Flamborough Head. The *Bonhomme Richard* and *Serapis* are in the foreground. To the right the *Alliance* unleashes a broadside at both ships while, to the left, the *Pallas* engages the *Countess of Scarborough*. Painting by William Elliot.

David Murray, 2nd Earl of Mansfield, Lord Stormont. King George's minister to France was convinced on a daily basis that King Louis's government was conspiring with the American rebels—and he was right. Painting by Sylvester Harding.

This early-nineteenth-century London engraving shows Commodore Collier's fleet blasting away at Saltonstall's ships on the last day of the ill-fated Penobscot Expedition.

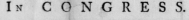

Gustavus Conyngham's captain's commission: signed by John Hancock, given to him by Benjamin Franklin, and taken from him by the French.

In fact, the Americans gave McLean two assets—the delay it took to get the forces ready, and the refusal of Saltonstall and Lovell to establish a working relationship. Neither one had a scintilla of experience in leading such a mission, nor did they have the ability. As Trevett foresaw, Tory spies got word to both New York and Penobscot about what was heading McLean's way. Preparations "not having been Conducted with that Secrecy the Nature thereof requir'd," as one legislator put it, virtually guaranteed that the British knew Saltonstall was sailing, before Saltonstall sailed.[73]

On July 18—the day before Saltonstall departed—McLean learned of the expedition. He put his men on round-the-clock details, felling trees to finish Fort St. George while Mowat sent his three sloops—the *Nautilus*, sixteen guns, and the *North* and *Albany*, fourteen guns each—north of the Penobscot with their port broadsides in a row. He anchored several transports behind them; they could be converted to fireships if the Americans took his sloops. Batteries were placed along the peninsula with an eye for maximum coverage and damage to an American attack by land or sea.[74]

British soldiers and sailors were attending to the defenses on the afternoon of July 25 when the first of Saltonstall's fleet was sighted. It made a magnificent sight: three dozen ships approaching the harbor, with the wind in their sails, looking every bit a formidable force, a mixture of battle-tested marines, seasoned salts along with green boys and old men, ready to do their duty.[75]

If only they had been better led.

Saltonstall acted immediately, sending nine warships directly at Mowat's sloops. Nine against three. Just as they were getting within range, Saltonstall pulled them back, and both sides spent the rest of the day peppering each other ineffectively. That night, Lovell sent a detachment to Bagaduce, establishing a foothold on the shoreline, but strong winds forced him to abort the operation, lest his first landing force become stranded. He and Saltonstall decided to pick up the attack the next day.[76]

That morning, Saltonstall sent the *Diligent* under Lieutenant Philip Brown to reconnoiter. Brown sailed back to Saltonstall with news: the fort was a fort in name only, what one marine sergeant called "a rough looking concern, built with logs and dirt" barely three feet high and far from finished. Furthermore, McLean's gun emplacements covered everything the eye could see except the west side of the peninsula—that wooded bluff, nearly four hundred feet, and nearly vertical to the shoreline.

Meanwhile Lovell sent 150 marines to Nautilus Island, just south of

Bagaduce. After a short but fierce battle, the British evacuated the island, leaving four cannons. The taking of Nautilus Island compelled Mowat to send his ships farther northward. So far, so good; the marines began building earthworks, preparing for the attack on the fort they were sure would take place the next day.

It did not. Watching from the *Warren*'s quarterdeck, Saltonstall grew increasingly wary about the offensive. Though Mowat was outnumbered, Saltonstall's experienced eye could see that his foe had set the table for an action that guaranteed American casualties. Mowat and McLean could be dislodged, but at what cost? As he swung his spyglass from Mowat's sloops down to Nautilus Island and up to McLean's high fort, Saltonstall's caution turned to intransigence.[77]

At a council of war in Saltonstall's cabin (one of many over the next seventeen days) the commodore and General Lovell, along with their senior officers, commenced hostilities against each other. Lovell wanted Saltonstall to move against Mowat to take the enemy's ships out of the coming assault on Fort St. George, while Saltonstall wanted Lovell's forces to capture the fort; he was not about to attack Mowat with McLean's guns bombarding his ships from on high. Saltonstall's ships would be moving, not sitting, ducks. The expedition was now a contest of wills, not between Americans and British but between Saltonstall, who seemed to care less about Lovell's militiamen and his own marines, and Lovell, who appeared to think Saltonstall's sailors and ships were expendable.

The commodore won, but at a price. The privateer captains were furious with him. They had been coerced into this enterprise. Used to swift raids and acting on their own volition, they chafed under Saltonstall's obstinate attitude, and presented a petition conveying their displeasure that foresaw the future:

> We think Delays in the present Case are extremely dangerous: as our Enemies are daily Fortifying and Strengthening themselves, & are stimulated so to doing in daily Expectation of Reinforcement . . . our desire of improving the Present Opportunity to go immediately into the Harbour, & Attack the Enemys Ships.[78]

One of the officers at this meeting went further, telling his commodore that the American warships would easily defeat Mowat and the hastily placed British batteries, only to be cut short by Saltonstall. "You seem to be d_ _n knowing about the Matter!" he exploded. "I am not going to risk my shipping in that d_ _ _ _d hole!"[79]

The decision was made to attack the fort first before taking on Mowat's sloops. Nearly 1,200 men, mostly militia but including 217 marines and 80 of Revere's artillerymen, would advance on the Bagaduce heights. The marines would attack on the right, while the militia would attack on the left. The landing would take place at midnight.[80]

The landing was, of course, delayed, but by three a.m. Saltonstall had his ships ready to unleash their broadsides at the woods below the fort to clear them of British skirmishers. At a prearranged signal between the commodore and the general, Saltonstall yelled, "Fire!" and a deafening barrage slammed into Bagaduce, followed by the sharp crack of timber as trees broke and fell below the bluff. Once again, Mowat sent his sloops farther upriver, just as Lovell's forces climbed into the longboats. With three lusty cheers, they headed to shore, as cannonballs screamed overhead.[81]

As they drew closer to shore each man could see for himself what lay before and above him. "The enemy had the most advantageous place I ever saw," Colonel Revere recalled. "A bank above three hundred feet high and so steep that no person could get up it but by pushing himself up by bushes and trees." Once the longboats reached the shore, the men had been ordered to form battle lines, but they came under immediate fire from the Redcoats above them. The only thing to do was head into the woods and begin the torturous ascent.[82]

The steepness of the heights prevented them from stopping to fire back at the British. Instead, they climbed hand over hand uphill, grasping first one branch or clump of bush and then another, methodically, courageously inching their way in the face of enemy fire. On the water, Saltonstall's gunners elevated their cannon, maintaining their bombardment of the peninsula.

The militia on the left was opposed by the British 82nd Regiment, comprised of lowland Scots. Dangerous as their climb was, they did not face the more experienced Highlanders of the 74th, who were doing their utmost to pin down the marines below them on the right. One volley of English muskets struck and killed Marine Captain John Welsh; Lieutenant William Hamilton lay severely wounded. Atop the bluff, Lieutenant John Moore, a fair-haired teenager, urged his men to maintain their relentless firing. From the corner of his eye, he saw rebels swarming over the bluff and the 82nd's soldiers scattering. Just after Moore ordered his men to fire another volley, he heard his captain yell "Retreat!" and the 74th also began running, with the exception of Moore's twenty men.

Thus abandoned, Moore carried on a rearguard action against the marines, backing off the bluff inch by inch, until he and his men looked to be surrounded. Then, with remarkable coolness, he finally ordered his men to retreat, leaving several dead comrades, while carrying off their wounded. "I was lucky to escape untouched," he reported (it was an early instance where Moore's courage came to the fore; he would later be knighted during the Napoleonic Wars).[83]

The American advance got within half a mile of the fort, but stopped at the woods' edge directly across from Fort St. George. Lovell ordered Revere to bring up some guns, a task that required the ships' carpenters to build a wooden road up the steep hill. Back at the shoreline, the proud Lovell took in what his men had done that day: "I dont think such a landing has been made since Wolfe," he wrote, comparing this assault to General Wolfe's climb and victory at the Plains of Abraham in the French and Indian War. Lovell's casualties were high: more than thirty killed and wounded.[84]

As Moore's men fell back to the fort that morning, Commodore Sir George Collier was issuing orders from the captain's cabin of the *Raisonable*. The report by Boston spies of the expedition had reached New York, and Collier was assembling a squadron to follow his ship-of-the-line and come to McLean's aid. Four frigates and a sloop went to sea six days later. Among the frigates was the *Galatea* and James Nicholson's old command, the *Virginia*.[85]

It took two days for Revere's hardy souls to haul several cannon to the top of the peninsula, but this delay did not matter, for Saltonstall still would not move. Both sides still fired the occasional round at each other, and one cannonball slammed into the *Warren*'s mainmast, confirming the commodore's fears that his ships would be decimated by British ordnance if they attacked Mowat. He would not advance until Lovell had taken the fort; Lovell would not attack until Saltonstall did.

July ended, August began. Each day the garrison at Fort St. George bolstered their defenses while the American commanders bickered. "What advantage would it do to go in and take the enemy's shipping?" Saltonstall haughtily and repeatedly inquired. The answer, of course, was everything. Only a few sorties took place over the next few days, resulting in more casualties among the militiamen.[86]

Reports of the attack on Bagaduce became exaggerated by the time they reached Philadelphia. Congress heard that a thousand Redcoats had surrendered, including Mowat." But more accurate reports began seeping in, and the Eastern Navy Board in Boston sent a dispatch to Saltonstall, urging him to stop playing Hamlet and attack. From Philadelphia, one congressman wrote General Gates: "I have now a Dread about that Expedition."[87]

Councils of war aboard the *Warren* had long grown pointless. At each meeting, Captain Titus Salter of the *Hampden* adamantly wanted to attack Mowat, but Saltonstall spurned him every time. Even Hacker bucked his commodore and proposed attack, only to get the usual nay. Morale among the sailors, marines, and militiamen was nonexistent.[88]

Saltonstall did see action, however. It occurred on August 7, when a longboat from the *Hazard* carrying Saltonstall and four of his captains went upriver to discover the whereabouts of Mowat's sloops. The boat was spotted, and Mowat sent eight longboats after them. The Americans made for the shore and scrambled into the woods. The British took the *Hazard*'s boat, but as Lovell recalled, Saltonstall's group "took to the Bush and escaped being made prisoners." Taking the long way through the woods, Saltonstall and company made it back to American lines.[89]

On the morning of Friday the thirteenth, Lovell took four hundred men through the woods to the back of the peninsula, and determined the fort would fall from an attack in the rear. He sent a courier to Saltonstall, requesting once again for assistance. To his utter amazement, Saltonstall gave the order Lovell had waited sixteen days to hear: "Weigh anchor."[90]

Aboard each warship, sailors had begun jumping to their bosun's orders to get under way when a lookout posted at the entrance of Penobscot Bay came aboard the *Warren*: a fleet of ships was approaching. Saltonstall sent word to Lovell. His courier hit the shoreline and then ran through the thickets towards the rear of the peninsula to tell Lovell the dire news. The advance was canceled. Attacked by chiggers, gnats, and mosquitoes, Lovell's men returned to their original position, where another message awaited the general: the approaching vessels were ships of force. It was Collier's squadron.[91]

The next morning, Lovell brought his men atop the bluff down to the shoreline. They had braved the elements and enemy fire; now, through no fault of their own, they were ordered to board the transports with the same alacrity with which they had stormed the heights. Aboard the *Warren*, Saltonstall met with his captains to prepare a defense of the transports: they would not engage, but fight a rearguard action as the entire fleet sailed upriver. Had the American sailors had a Lieutenant Moore to lead them, it might have worked. What they had was a fistful of privateer captains and Dudley Saltonstall.[92]

The commodore watched Collier's ships make straight for him with disciplined purpose. His plan to defend the transports required cooperation from the privateers, and for their captains to reach inside themselves—not for courage; they had that—but to fight as a squadron, a skill neither they nor Saltonstall possessed. The commodore signaled new orders: each ship was to fend for itself.[93]

"To give a description of this terrible Day is out of my Power," Lovell later wrote, calling what happened "the Great Mortification." It was a turkey shoot; calling it low comedy would be inappropriate considering the tragic loss of life. As Collier skillfully sailed his ships into battle, the Continental, state navy, and privateer vessels fled pell-mell, fouling the transports they were to protect, speeding past them instead as unerring British gunners did their duty, their shots shredding rigging, slamming into hulls, striking down sailor after sailor. Seeking safety, the American captains made for the streams and inlets, running aground.

As he and his men clambered ashore, Saltonstall ordered some hands to blow up the *Warren*. Other American captains followed suit. In between British cannonades (the American ships did not return fire), explosions rocked the air, as one American ship after another exploded. The sloop *Providence*, the last of Esek Hopkins's squadron, was soon afire, about a mile from the *Warren*. Those ships that were not burned or abandoned surrendered.[94]

The last American ship to get upriver was the ordnance brig carrying Paul Revere and most of his command, minus the ordnance. Once ashore, he tried to organize his men, but almost all ran frantically into the woods. Taking the few who remained upon one of the brig's boats, he rowed along the shoreline hoping to overtake them, only to give up the search at midnight.[95]

Lovell planned to make a stand on the fifteenth, but was persuaded otherwise. Fourteen ships were burned or blown up, the rest captured; more than five hundred Americans were dead, wounded, or prisoners. The only way home for the survivors was overland. Soon marines, sailors, and militiamen began the long, dispiriting trudge homeward.[96]

It took three weeks for the first stragglers to reach Boston, where they learned that a Continental Army regiment had been sent to assist them, only to turn back at Portsmouth when they learned of Collier's rout. Their defeat was already the talk of the town. Anger over the loss of men, ships, and artillery was mixed with panic. Numerous courts of inquiry were held. "It seems," one official wrote, "that our People were fascinated and charmed into their Destruction." The angry crowds in the streets, the merchants in the coffeehouses, and the politicians in New England and Philadelphia had one scapegoat in mind: Saltonstall.[97]

Other officers emerged from the investigations sullied but not bowed, including Lovell and Revere. The entire blame fell on Saltonstall. One Boston

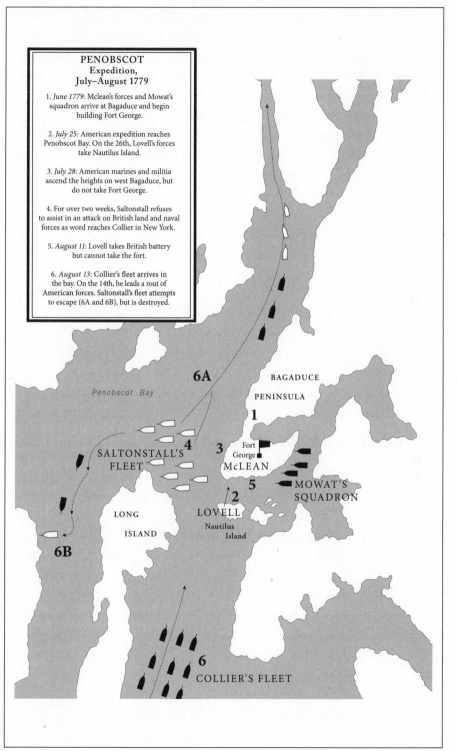

PENOBSCOT
Expedition,
July–August 1779

1. *June 1779*: Mclean's forces and Mowat's
squadron arrive at Bagaduce and begin
building Fort George.

2. *July 25*: American expedition reaches
Penobscot Bay. On the 26th, Lovell's forces
take Nautilus Island.

3. *July 28*: American marines and militia
ascend the heights on west Bagaduce, but
do not take Fort George.

4. For over two weeks, Saltonstall refuses
to assist in an attack on British land and naval
forces as word reaches Collier in New York.

5. *August 11*: Lovell takes British battery
but cannot take the fort.

6. *August 13*: Collier's fleet arrives in
the bay. On the 14th, he leads a rout of
American forces. Saltonstall's fleet attempts
to escape (6A and 6B), but is destroyed.

6A

BAGADUCE

Penobscot Bay

PENINSULA

1

4   **3**   Fort
George

SALTONSTALL'S
FLEET

McLEAN

5

2

MOWAT'S
SQUADRON

LONG

LOVELL
Nautilus
Island

ISLAND

6B

6

COLLIER'S FLEET

paper called him "A new fangled Commodore," adding that he had lost nothing "except the whole fleet." Saltonstall's court-martial was held upon the *Deane*, and he was summarily dismissed from the navy. The debacle cost Massachusetts seven million dollars, threatening to bankrupt the state and beginning a drawn-out argument over whether Congress should defray the enormous cost.[98]

Having led American forces into the worst defeat of the war, Saltonstall, the original captain of the *Alfred*, was finished. That very September, across the Atlantic, his former first lieutenant was about to fight the battle that would define the Continental Navy for centuries.

CHAPTER TEN

"DIAMOND CUT DIAMOND"

The Battle being thus begun was continued with
Unremitting Fury.

—JOHN PAUL JONES TO BENJAMIN FRANKLIN[1]

Captain Jones, an excellent sailor, they say, knows all the coasts thoroughly," an enthusiastic Marquis de Lafayette wrote a friend. The young general had every reason to look into Jones's background. Ever since the *Alliance* brought him to France, Lafayette had wanted to attack England and bring the horror of war to an enemy city: Liverpool, Bristol, and Bath were being considered. His plan required transports and a squadron to escort them. Benjamin Franklin suggested Jones in a meeting with Lafayette in March 1779. Giving Jones the command would make the venture a true Franco-American affair.[2]

Jones learned of this scheme just as he was beginning to convert the lumbering merchantman *Duc de Duras* into the lumbering warship *Bonhomme Richard*. He immediately shared Lafayette's passion for the enterprise, even promising Franklin that he would submerge his ever-present ego and submit to *le Général*'s leadership. "I shall expect you to point out my errors," he happily wrote Lafayette, while promising Franklin that his crew would be on their best behavior and refrain from another Selkirk-like foray against British citizens. Both Minister Sartine and Franklin gave their blessing to the partnership.[3]

The expedition was the answer to Jones's ambitious dream for himself: an entire squadron to command. In addition to the *Bonhomme Richard*, the Continental frigate *Alliance* and the French ships *Pallas*, *Vengeance*, and *Cerf* were placed under his leadership. Jones was ecstatic.[4]

Had this enterprise become reality (and succeeded), it would have rivaled Trenton and Yorktown. Alas, it was not to be: as enthusiasm and support grew, Louis XVI stepped in. Why not a mass invasion of England instead of a simple raid? Plans commenced to send 40,000 French soldiers to England, borne by an armada of French and Spanish ships. Lafayette's great scheme was quashed. Jones's disappointment was surprisingly small, however. He still had a squadron command, and Sartine planned to use it as a diversion, sending Jones around the British Isles before the grand invasion landed; all the more reason to hasten his ship's preparations.[5]

No drafts of the *Bonhomme Richard* exist, but a sister ship, *Duc de Penthièvre*, gives us an idea of her dimensions: 145 feet long, a 36-foot-8-inch beam, displacing about 900 tons. Thanks to the king, no expense was spared in refitting her. Historian Samuel Eliot Morison wrote that "Jones enjoyed fitting out more than anything except making love." For the next several weeks it became Jones's obsession. He wanted the old lady to look every bit as dangerous as he hoped her to be, painting her hull black—there would be no checkered look to his man-of-war.[6]

Jones's biggest difficulty was getting battle-worthy ordnance. He wanted the *Bonhomme Richard* to carry forty guns, and he pierced her bulwarks for that number. He visited several foundries, but found their guns defective. As spring turned to summer, however, Jones began to settle for what he could find, even from condemned stores. His new/old ship would mount six 18-pounders, twenty-eight 12-pounders, and six 9-pounders. He craved the 18-pounders, but would find them to be more dangerous to his crew than British guns. He also covered his rails with swivel guns and stored blunderbusses and shotguns below—they would come in handy. Day after day, ordnance, ammunition, rope, canvas, timber, and other stores were brought aboard, while carpenters, and rope men plied their trade under Jones's all-encompassing eye.[7]

If there was anything that took Jones's mind off his questionable guns it was his captains. The *Pallas*, a twenty-six-gun frigate, was commanded by Captain de Brûlot Cottineau de Kerloguen, a former privateersman who had proven his seamanship and courage in a fight with HMS *Brune*, one of the ships John Barry fought off Reedy Island in 1778. Lieutenant de Vaisseau Ricot commanded the twelve-gun brig *Vengeance*, while Enseigne de Vaisseau Varage commanded the eighteen-gun cutter *Cerf*. Each of them was also appointed a captain in the Continental Navy by Benjamin Franklin, still carrying the sheaf of commissions he used for Gustavus Conyngham. They did not appreciate being under an American's orders.

Then there was Pierre Landais. For such an observant sailor and warrior, Jones was often gullible in his judgments of people, and Landais proved this more than anyone. As he did with Deane, Franklin, and Lee, Landais flattered Jones while overstating his own maritime prowess. The combination worked at first. Jones declared Landais "a sensible, well-informed man." When Jones learned that the Frenchman's own officers wanted him removed from the *Alliance*, Jones defended him.[8]

The immense size of the *Bonhomme Richard* required a much larger crew than Jones had ever commanded. When his rendezvous ended he had more than 350 names or marks on his muster rolls, and an international cast of characters at that: not only Americans and Frenchmen but Scots, Irish, Swedes, Norwegians, and one Italian. They ranged in background from John Jordan, a sailor from East India (one of several blacks aboard), to Giusseppe Broricellia, a boy from Naples. The muster roll anglicized his name to Joseph Brussels. With so many countries represented, the fo'c'sle was a nautical Tower of Babel.[9]

Nor were these salts the salt of the earth. Monsieur de Grandville, Lorient's port captain, called Jones's French hands "wretches picked up on the street," while his English tars were mostly Royal Navy prisoners or deserters. Jones's officers, however, were mostly Americans, including Nathaniel Fanning.[10]

On May 13, John Adams arrived in Lorient, about to visit home after his first year as commissioner. Jones invited him to a dinner he was hosting for his officers at a local hotel, l'Epée Royale. Adams had been charmed by Landais when he first met him the year before; now he found the Frenchman "jealous of every thing and jealous of every Body," a far different man than he had observed at the Court of Versailles.[11]

Adams did find better company in Lawrence Brooke, ship's surgeon. Not yet twenty-one, Brooke came from a prominent Virginia family. He and his brother had been sent to Edinburgh by their father to continue their education: law for the brother and medicine for Lawrence—a vocation in which he showed great promise. But news of Lexington and Concord cut his education short, and the brothers escaped to France. Lawrence signed on as surgeon in April, becoming a favorite of Jones as much for his breeding as his medical skills.[12]

Table conversation turned to learning French. When the question was posed as to whether it could best be learned at the renowned Comédie Française or from a mistress, Adams answered, "Both at once"—a remark that he pointedly clarified later in his diary as what he had been told, not what he actually did. He also described his host for history:

> Eccentricities and Irregularities are to be expected from him—They are in his Character, they are visible in his Eyes. His voice is soft and still and small, his eye has keenness and Wildness and softness in it.[13]

Adams was peeved that Jones and his officers were in the captain's blue and white uniform and not the blue and red that Adams had designed. He was also miffed that Jones's marines were wearing red and white and not the green and white that Adams had directed, unaware that these marines *were* in uniform—that of l'Infanterie Irlandaise—an Irish regiment serving the French king.[14]

In June, Sartine sent Jones orders to escort several merchantmen into the Bay of Biscay. The captain felt the assignment beneath him, but with France having foot the bill for his ship's refitting and given him a squadron, Jones decided not to bite the hand that was feeding him. Instead, he used the mission as a shakedown cruise. Before departing, he sent a letter to Mme. de Chaumont. It was time to bid adieu to his patron's wife. He gave her the brush-off in a florid combination of sentiment ("My thoughts have done ample Justice to [your] Affectionate Friendship") and fare-thee-well ("I shall carry with me thro life the most Constant and Lively sense of your polite Attentions"). On June 19, the *Bonhomme Richard* led Jones's squadron and their convoy out of l'Orient, past Île de Groix, and into the bay.[15]

Months earlier, Jones had begged for a fast ship. Now he learned quickly that his flagship was painfully slow. He also found his subordinate, Landais, to be anything but subordinate. That night, a fierce storm struck the convoy. In the darkness, the *Bonhomme Richard* and *Alliance* ran into each other, damaging the flagship's bowsprit as it tore the rigging from the *Alliance*'s mizzenmast and toppled it. Jones suspected that Landais did not sheer off out of spite, while Landais stated that he had heard shouts coming from Jones's British sailors and believed they had mutinied and were attacking his frigate. Jones, being in his cabin when the accident occurred, decided to believe Landais, disciplining instead his own first lieutenant, Robert Robinson.[16]

For the next ten days British ships sailed over the horizon, only to change course when they saw the size of Jones's squadron. On one occasion Jones chased two British cruisers, but they easily left the *Bonhomme Richard* in their wake.

Still, Jones was determined to put a positive spin on his first days as commodore. Once back in l'Orient, he wrote to Franklin—not to complain as before (or beg for *l'Indien*) but to extol "the martial spirit of my crew."[17]

As the *Bonhomme Richard* and *Alliance* underwent repairs, Jones sought a worthy first lieutenant to replace Robinson. He found one: Richard Dale, the young man John Barry had brought into the Continental fold aboard the *Lexington*. Captured with Henry Johnson, the intrepid twenty-two-year-old had escaped Mill Prison, been recaptured, and escaped again, this time strolling out of the place wearing a Royal Navy uniform. Jones saw in Dale the same combination of grit and skill that Barry did. Dale would be the best officer Jones ever had.[18]

Jones also took steps regarding conditions in the fo'c'sle. The French and American hands were constantly fighting with each other, but that paled in comparison to the activities of the British sailors Jones had rescued from the l'Orient jail. Upon learning that they planned to mutiny, Jones seized the ringleader and sentenced him to 250 lashes—enough to kill a man (and 238 more than John Adams had declared the maximum punishment in the Continental Navy).

Jones replaced the British hands with Americans recently exchanged by the British, and also signed on several dozen Portuguese sailors, giving them permission to bring a statue of the Virgin Mary aboard.

The new hands were climbing the gangway just in time to witness punishment: a dozen sailors being flogged. Days before, these men had manned a longboat taking Jones to shore. Once he disembarked they did too—to get drunk at a wharf tavern. Jones was forced to return to ship on a fishing boat. Now that drunken detail took turns "tasting the cat." Jones would no longer tolerate the insolence and disobedience he had endured aboard the *Ranger*.[19]

Thirty days of stressful refitting, punishments, and re-manning sent an exhausted Jones to his cabin, but by early August he was himself again, awaiting new orders. They arrived in a coach carrying Jones's cuckolded patron M. de Chaumont. In a manner some historians believe was payback for Jones's peccadillo, Chaumont dealt with each captain in the squadron individually instead of with Jones alone as commodore. Chaumont intended that the captains reach "common Consent" regarding the capture of prizes during the forthcoming cruise, and that Chaumont, as a financier of the squadron, would act as agent for any and all prizes. This "concordat" was a hodgepodge of initiatives that Jones saw clearly as an attempt to undermine his already tenuous authority over the French captains. He duly sent a protest to Franklin, but not before he signed the concordat himself. On August 14, the squadron sailed, accompanied by two privateers, the *Monsieur* and the *Grand Ville*.[20]

After his cruise with the *Ranger*, Jones's mere name was sure to strike terror along the British coastline, and a squadron of this size guaranteed that the Royal Navy would bend every available sail in their desire to hunt Jones down. Sartine cautioned Jones against any Whitehaven-like raids, advising him to concentrate on taking prizes at sea, which would keep the British guessing about both his whereabouts and his destination.

This squadron was small potatoes to Sartine, who still intended it to serve as a decoy for the combined Franco-Spanish fleet under Admiral d'Orvilliers, now bearing down on England. Four British ships spotted the forty-five ships off the Scillies, a cluster of small islands off southeast England. To one English officer, the fleet looked "like a wood on the water."[21]

On August 17, the fleet was off Plymouth, raising hope in Mill Prison. While prisoners prayed that they were about to be rescued, Gustavus Conyngham wrote in his journal how the fearful townsfolk fled into the forts that evening. As alarm guns boomed into the night, the men of Plymouth threw up ditches and earthworks, anticipating the worst. "All in confusion," Conyngham happily noted.[22]

But poor planning and bad luck took the wind out of the fleet's sails and the will to fight out of d'Orvilliers. If no British force stood out to fight him, d'Orvilliers was supposed to establish a beachhead at Cornwall. He soon spotted a British fleet of thirty-eight ships. Their commander, Admiral Sir Charles Hardy, took d'Orvilliers on a two-day chase away from England.

D'Orvilliers had been at sea for weeks before he entered the channel, and he was already low on supplies. Epidemics of smallpox, typhus, and scurvy infected sailor and soldier. Thousands became ill; hundreds died—including d'Orvilliers's only son. The admiral sailed for Brest, where 7,000 Frenchmen were carted off to hospitals. There would be no invasion of England. Jones's mission was now the only act on the stage.[23]

"I had before me the most flattering prospect of rendering essential service to the common Cause of France & America," Jones wrote to Franklin before sailing, confident that his captains "would persue Glory in preference to Interest." The *Bonhomme Richard* was just passing Île de Groix when a topman fell off the main yard, hurtling sixty feet to his death and just missing Jones, who would have been killed himself on the spot, but the poor man only clipped Jones's tricorn hat. As Jones bent over to retrieve it, he ordered the body removed and buried on the island.[24]

Jones's optimism about his captains was tested four days later. On August 18, the *Monsieur* captured a small merchantman. What should have been a squadron prize was, in the privateer captain's eyes, his alone. When Jones discovered him looting the ship's hold of brandy and wine, he ordered the ship sent to l'Orient as a squadron prize. Privateers being privateers, the *Monsieur* slipped away, followed by the *Grand Ville* days later. Soon afterwards another prize, the brigantine *Mayflower*, carrying salt and butter, was also sent to l'Orient.

The squadron was becalmed off Cape Clear, the southernmost tip of Ireland, on the twenty-third, when the current and flood tide sent the *Bonhomme Richard* towards the rocks. Jones ordered out his barge to row his flagship to safety, placing it under command of the same man he had flogged for abandoning Jones for a l'Orient tavern. Fog set in and . . . let Jones explain: "Soon after Sunset the Villains who Towed the ship cut their Rope and Decamped with my Barge." While one of the 9-pounders was fired in an attempt to cow the deserters back to ship, a longboat was manned and sent off in pursuit. It, too, disappeared, never to return.[25]

"Hot Sultry Weather" greeted the becalmed squadron the next day, as Jones cruised the bay searching for the deserters. After two days he sent the *Cerf* closer to shore when a storm struck, and the cutter became the next to disappear (she eventually made for l'Orient). The tempest showed further evidence that the *Bonhomme Richard* was past her prime. Seams opened, and her old pumps required manning day and night. When a gun on the lower deck came loose from its tackle and bolts, it smashed into the hull, threatening to sink the ship by itself. To Midshipman Fanning, the old East Indiaman "appeared to have as many joints as a rattlesnake."[26]

Between weathering storms and looking for his missing vessels, Jones refused Landais's request to let the *Alliance* pursue a strange sail. On the twenty-fifth, the Frenchman's longboat bumped against the commodore's flagship, and Jones's *l'enfant terrible* came aboard.

Landais immediately abandoned any show of respect for the commodore, berating Jones for losing his boats and the *Cerf* before telling the Scotsman that he, the Frenchman, "was the only American in the squadron," having been made an honorary citizen of Massachusetts. Jones did his best to suppress his temper, but when Landais added that Jones's ineptitude caused the loss of the boats, he exploded. According to Landais, Jones called him a liar, but other witnesses disputed this.

Landais was an accomplished duelist, particularly good with the sword (he would later wound Captain de Cottineau in a duel), but Jones did not take the bait. However, in Landais's version, Jones agreed to meet him on the field of honor upon their return to France. From this moment on, Landais heeded neither Jones's signals nor his written orders.[27]

For the next week the squadron took numerous prizes. Jones used one "for the sake of Peace" to placate Landais, allowing the *Alliance*'s captain to place a prize crew on a ship the frigate had no part in capturing. Landais habitually disappeared from the squadron. Later, he would do worse.[28]

By the time Jones's squadron reached northern Scotland, they had made enough captures that the *Bonhomme Richard* had a large number of British prisoners below deck. But Jones's successes went hand in hand with increasing headaches. Starting with his freewheeling captains, the loss of his boats, the *Cerf* gone, and now the confounding, recurring question: where was Landais? Jones was averaging three hours of sleep a night. The pressure on him did not go unnoticed; Midshipman Fanning watched as Jones kicked a lieutenant down the hatchway, only to invite him to dinner half an hour later. "Thus it was with Jones," Fanning recalled. "Passionate to the highest degree one minute, and the next ready to make reconciliation."[29]

Jones did not know it, but those living on the British coastlines were not sleeping either. Once ashore in Ireland, the deserters from his boats spread the word that "the Pyrate Jones" was back. The Admiralty sent two frigates after him, making straight for Whitehaven, anticipating that Jones was heading back there to burn more shipping.[30]

September 14 began with cooperative winds and sunshine as the *Bonhomme Richard*, *Pallas*, and *Vengeance* came up the Firth of Forth, flying British colors. A cutter approached. Her captain, thinking the *Bonhomme Richard* to be the British warship *Romney*, hailed Jones, resplendent in his pseudo-British uniform, asking if he could spare any gunpowder. Jones said yes, inviting the cutter's pilot to come aboard.

"What is the news on the coast?" Jones inquired.

"Very great and bad news!" the pilot answered. "That rebel, Paul Jones, is expected to land every day."

Jones asked what the pilot thought of Jones and was told, "He is the greatest rebel and pirate that ever was and ought to be hanged."

"I am Paul Jones," the commodore replied.

As the unsuspecting pilot begged for his life, the bemused commodore said, "I won't harm a hair on your head, but you are my prisoner."[31]

Jones intended to take the port of Leith—the gateway to Edinburgh—and hold it for ransom or "reduce it to Ashes." The citizens of Leith knew who was coming and looked to their defenses. Drums beat and bagpipes blared as ragtag bands of Scotsmen gathered, carrying rusty flintlocks to defend their homeland (after Culloden the owning of firearms was prohibited in Scotland). Merchants piled their wares onto wagons, bankers carried bags of coins from their locked establishments, and villagers carried what goods they had on their backs, fleeing their homes. One old Presbyterian parson marched to the shore, planted a chair in the water, and beseeched God to turn the wind against the rebel ships.[32]

Jones made preparations for the landing, the French-Irish marines changing into the uniforms of their British counterparts. Jones composed a letter to the Provost of Leith, demanding a ransom of £200,000 or Jones would destroy the town. He signaled Captains Cottineau and Ricot to come aboard for a council of war. Now came their turn to oppose Jones.

By the time Jones overcame their objections to the raid, the prayers of the old Presbyterian minister were being answered. The wind changed, preventing Jones from getting ashore. He wanted to try again on the seventeenth, but by then the residents of Leith were convinced of the parson's influence with the Almighty: Jones's ships were within cannon shot of the town when a storm struck of such magnitude that one of the squadron's prizes sank, her crew just barely rescued.[33]

After the storm subsided, the squadron was off Newcastle, where Jones again met with his captains. He proposed sailing into the coal capital of the British Empire and burning the colliers in port, leaving much of England to face a very cold winter. Again, both captains were adamantly opposed. While Jones was seeking some headline-grabbing deed, "they saw the situation as most Perulous," and told him so. "If I Obstinately continued on the Coast of England two days longer we should all be Taken," he was assured by Cottineau. Both captains threatened to leave the squadron.

Jones considered raiding Newcastle alone but soon abandoned the idea; Cottineau might be right, after all. The *Pallas* and the *Vengeance* sailed on ahead, compelling Jones's old tub to catch up with them. Two more days of sailing southward netted the squadron a couple more prizes before the Frenchmen sailed over the horizon again.

On the morning of September 23, the *Bonhomme Richard*'s mastheader sighted the *Alliance* and the *Pallas*. The *Vengeance* also came into sight. The squadron of misfit captains was back under Jones's watchful eye.

His cruise had created widespread fear throughout Great Britain, but all Jones knew at the time was that he had sailed around the British isles with only a handful of prizes to show for it. In two weeks he was expected in Holland to escort another convoy of French merchantmen. Haggard and sleepless, he had fought more with his French captains than against the enemy. He believed his cruise to be a disappointing failure.

That afternoon the ships were sailing under "Pleasant Weather with [a] Moderate Brease of Wind." The *Bonhomme Richard* was pursuing a distant ship when the mastheader cried down to the quarterdeck. One sail after another was sighted—at least forty ships. Below deck, Lieutenant Dale heard the commotion and came up the hatchway to find Jones giving orders to make all sail. Dale asked the captured pilot from Leith if he knew the ships. "The Baltic fleet," he replied, "under company of the *Serapis* of 44 guns, and the *Countess of Scarborough* of twenty guns." The squadron gave chase.

The change in Jones's mood was remarkable. He sent Lieutenant Henry Lunt and thirty men in one of the captured pilot boats to pursue the ship discovered before the fleet's appearance. His squadron was sailing against the current and was impeded by the slackening SSW winds. By dusk, the ships were off Flamborough Head, just northeast of the town of Scarborough.[34]

Across the water Captain Richard Pearson of the *Serapis* had been studying the movements of the approaching ships. For the past eight days he had convoyed forty-four merchantmen bearing military stores from Scandinavia. Pearson was forty-eight years old, with thirty years at sea behind him. He was peculiarly handsome, with sharp features encircled by a round face and a high forehead with wide-set eyes. He had been well tested by the sea, wounded in battle—six years a captain in the King's Navy. His distinguished service was rewarded with the *Serapis*, a forty-four-gun frigate similar to the *Roebuck*: large, fast, and deadly.[35]

Pearson was not surprised to see Jones's squadron through his spyglass, having been forewarned of the rebel's presence in these waters by the bailiff of

Scarborough. The Baltic fleet was Pearson's responsibility, and he was determined to keep every ship out of Jones's clutches. He made two signals: one, for the merchantmen to stand in to shore; two, for the *Countess of Scarborough* to join the *Serapis* and make straight for Jones's squadron. Duty is duty.[36]

Flamborough Head juts out into the North Sea by the Yorkshire coast, easily recognizable from the water by its chalk white cliffs that rise four hundred feet from the shore. It is riddled with caves, once favorite hideouts for smugglers. Atop the cliffs, an equally white lighthouse, the oldest in England, still stands. In autumn, Flamborough Head is invaded by thousands of migratory birds. As the sun set this day, Scarborough's citizens made their way to the cliff tops to watch their navy take on an enemy squadron that included a rebel commanding a lumbering French merchantman and a volatile Frenchman in charge of a speedy Yankee-built frigate.

The sun would not witness the coming fight. It had begun sinking behind the cliffs just as the opposing ships made for each other and the pale moon began its ascent into the heavens. This would be a battle fought in moonlight.[37]

At five p.m. Jones ordered "Beat to Quarters," and the French-Irish marines under Colonel de Chamillard climbed the ratlines carrying their muskets. Once they reached the fighting tops, they hauled up their coehorns, a tub of water, and a basket of grenades. There was room on the *Bonhomme Richard*'s three tops for forty sailors and marines, a much larger contingent than was usually sent aloft. Three midshipmen were put in command, with Nathaniel Fanning in the maintop. Once the coehorns were raised, buckets of grog—enough for a double ration per marine—were brought aloft to calm nerves, deaden fear, and raise spirits.[38]

In the dimly lit cockpit, Surgeon Lawrence Brooke was making his preparations for the coming battle. With the help of the "Loblolly Boys"—the youngsters named for the gruel served in sick bay—he laid out a ten-foot-square platform of planks, covering it with an unused sail. Then he set out the tools of eighteenth-century triage:

> Instruments, needles and ligatures, lint, flour in a bowl, styptic, bandages, splints, compresses, pledges spread with yellow basilicon or some proper digestive . . . the medicine chest . . . wine, punch for grog, and vinegar aplenty . . . A bucket of water to put pongees in, another to receive blood from operations . . . Dry swabs to keep the platform dry . . . A water cask . . . to be dipped out as needed.[39]

Chamillard and twenty marines joined Jones on the poop deck. Dale commanded the gun deck. Boarding weapons were placed in tubs near the gunwales—not only cutlasses, pikes, and pistols, but the shotguns and blunderbusses Jones had wanted brought aboard at l'Orient for just such a night. From the moment he first saw the *Serapis* through his spyglass, Jones's battle plan was formed. If this were a single-ship encounter between the *Serapis* and the *Bonhomme Richard*, the frigate would outmaneuver the old East Indiaman at every tack. But Jones had four ships—more than enough to take both British men-of-war.[40]

The opposing ships were now a bit closer to each other. The squadron was on a port tack, heading west. Jones sent up a signal: a blue flag on the foremast, blue pendant at the main, and a blue and yellow flag atop the mizzenmast: *Form Line of Battle*.[41]

Not a captain obeyed.[42]

As the ships drew closer, Jones gave specific directions to the gun crews. The 18-pounders, manned by his best gunners, were to fire directly into the *Serapis*'s hull. Dale was to load the 12-pounders with double-shot and fire across the enemy deck to disable her masts and rigging. The 9-pounders on deck, under command of Purser Matthew Mease, were to do the same. Those manning the swivels along the rails were to join the marines aloft in taking out as many sailors on the *Serapis*'s deck as possible.[43]

The ships were now close enough to hear the orders of their opposing captains. The *Alliance* was in the lead, and would have been the first ship in Jones's squadron to encounter the *Serapis*—but Landais abruptly sheered off, leaving that honor to Jones. Taking a quick look behind him, Jones saw Cottineau do the same thing. The coming fight would begin, at least, as *Bonhomme Richard* versus *Serapis*.[44]

The two ships would soon be in hailing distance. Jones could see Pearson on his quarterdeck. Like the *Bonhomme Richard*, the *Serapis* had been flying St. George's colors—the white flag with the narrow red cross. Jones watched as the colors were lowered, and saw Pearson take a carpenter's maul and begin banging on a strip of wood too small to be a spar. It was a flagstaff; Pearson was nailing the red Royal Navy ensign, with the union in the canton, to the pole. Once done, Pearson raised it for friend and foe alike to see: there would be no lowering of his colors. Here was a captain equal to Jones in courage and determination, to be sure.[45]

Jones ordered his courses hauled up. Years later, Quarter-Gunner John Kilby remembered the deathly silence of the gun crews. "You may be sure," he wrote, "that our ship was as well prepared for action as it was in the power of man." Nevertheless, Jones wished he still had Lunt and his thirty men aboard. He would need them. Looking through his 18-pounder's gun port, Kilby saw the *Serapis* close in. Side lanterns ran along her gunwales, allowing Kilby to see every British tar on her deck. Also below with Kilby, young Joseph Brussels was given the assignment of "powder boy," to bring fresh powder horns on deck for the 12- and 9-pounders.[46]

From the maintop, Fanning waited as the *Serapis* tacked, bearing down to engage. The ships were well within hailing distance. For the rest of his life, Fanning recalled how "the moon was rising with majestic appearance, the weather being clear, the surface of the great deep perfectly smooth, even as in a mill pond": false serenity meeting desperate, quiet anxiety.[47]

It was Pearson who broke the silence. Taking his speaking trumpet, he cried across the water, "What ship is that?"

Jones had Sailing Master Samuel Stacey reply. "The *Princess Royal*," he shouted, hoping that Pearson would take the old French East Indiaman for a well-known British East Indiaman. Below, on the *Bonhomme Richard*'s gun deck, Kilby could hear everything being said.

"Where from?" the suspicious Pearson asked.

This time Jones answered, "I can't hear what you say," he replied. For a few seconds, all was quiet but the lapping of the water against the ships.

Breaking the silence, Pearson threatened, "Tell me instantly from whence you came and who you be, or I'll fire a broadside into you!"

Again, silence.

Then in a split second, the game playing ended, as did the peaceful night at sea under a harvest moon. With alacrity, Jones hauled down his false colors, raised the American flag, and ordered Dale to fire a broadside, just as Pearson gave the same order. "No man living could tell which ship fired first," Kilby wrote. The two simultaneous broadsides made for a deafening explosion.[48]

They were also deadly. Jones's doubts about the soundness of his 18-pounders were proven correct—two of them burst, killing several of the men manning them, burning and maiming several others from the blasts. Thrown free of their breeching rope and tackle, the guns ripped a gaping hole in the starboard hull just above the waterline. Add to this the casualties on the deck and the damage to the masts and rigging from Pearson's experienced gunners, and it seemed as if the devil himself was unleashing all hell aboard the *Bonhomme Richard*.[49]

But the Americans had struck hard at the *Serapis*. Jones's gunners were accurate, the 12- and 9-pounders striking their targets, ripping into the frigate's rigging and felling several sailors. From his quarterdeck, Pearson had his guns reloaded and fired, just as Jones was ordering aboard the *Bonhomme Richard*. Two more broadsides were exchanged; having seen that his 18-pounders were deadlier to his own men than to the enemy, Jones would not fire those on the port side in the engagement.[50]

Both captains now jockeyed their ships into a position that would put their foe at a disadvantage. Jones looked to get to windward of the *Serapis* and get the weather gauge to control the fight. But no matter what he tried, he could not gain an edge. From the maintop, Fanning saw "The *Serapis* out-sailing us *two feet to one*," outmaneuvering the *Bonhomme Richard* at every opportunity. Ten minutes into the fighting, Jones sent the *Bonhomme Richard* to windward, the old merchantman actually pulling ahead of the trim frigate—Jones could soon cross Pearson's bow, and fire at least one unanswered broadside into the *Serapis*.

But the instant Jones had waited for was the moment that Pearson anticipated. Being to windward, once the *Bonhomme Richard* moved ahead of the *Serapis*, Jones literally took the wind out of Pearson's sails. But Pearson turned the tables on Jones's advantage by backing his sails, sending his frigate *behind* the *Bonhomme Richard*. Jones's momentum now worked against him. Instead of his ship, it was the *Serapis* that "crossed the T" behind the *Bonhomme Richard*'s stern. Pearson was proving to be every bit the expert sailor Jones was; another British broadside smashed into the old ship's handsomely filigreed cabin windows and up into the poop deck.

Looking to keep control of the engagement, Pearson ever so delicately backed his sails again, slowing the *Serapis* and allowing him to fire two more unanswered broadsides. "Our men," Fanning recalled, "fell in all parts of the ship by the *scores*."[51]

Thus far, the captains were equal in courage and cunning, but the *Bonhomme Richard*, no match from the beginning for the *Serapis*, was now in disastrous shape. "I must confess," Jones later told Franklin, "That the Enemies Ship being much more Manageable than the *Bon Homme Richard* gained thereby several times an advantageous Situation in spite of my best endeavour to prevent it." These early broadsides caused extensive damage to her hull and rigging; she began taking in water.

Several of the 12-pounders had been directly hit by British cannonballs, killing and wounding the gun crews assigned them, blowing the guns off their carriages and rendering them as useless as the 18-pounders on the gun deck. When the fight began there were twenty-five marines on the poop deck with Jones, Chamillard, the helmsman, and other officers. Now there were three. Everywhere Jones looked he saw carnage and wreckage. Two thoughts raced through his mind: how to get the *Bonhomme Richard* close enough to board the *Serapis*—his only hope for a victory—and where in God's name was the *Alliance?*[52]

The scene below deck was even more harrowing. In the cockpit, Surgeon Brooke was overwhelmed by the numbers of wounded and burned men brought to him by the minute. To keep from slipping, he ordered one of the Loblolly Boys to pour sand on the blood-soaked floor. One of his first patients was John Jordan, the East Indian, his right leg pulverized by a British cannonball. Brooke reached for his saw.[53]

Ship's Carpenter John Gunnison hastened below with several hands carrying canvas and "plugs"—large wooden dowels. They approached each hole below the waterline, forcing the canvas against the inrushing water, and then hammering the plug in to secure—or at least slow—each leak. Once finished, they sloshed through the water to another opening, then another. Other hands manned the pumps in what looked like a futile effort to return the surging water back to the sea.[54]

By now over a thousand onlookers were swarming around the lighthouse on Flamborough Head, watching the battle beneath them. Lit from on high by the moon, the townsfolk of Scarborough could see the orange-yellow flash of the cannons; then, seconds later, they heard the echoing blast. Soon they were joined on the bluff by throngs from nearby Bridlington, all eyes on the macabre, otherworldly spectacle—horror from afar.[55]

Jones watched from the poop deck of the devastated *Bonhomme Richard* as Pearson sent the *Serapis* ahead this time to "cross the T" at Jones's bow. Until this very moment, everything had been going Pearson's way in the battle, including the wind.

No longer.

Without warning, the wind died. Pearson watched as the last wisp disappeared into his sails, leaving the *Serapis* off the *Bonhomme Richard*'s starboard bow. Being to windward of the frigate, Jones's ship got the final puff of breeze, giving him a split-second opportunity to turn the tables on Pearson. He immediately ordered Sailing Master Stacey, whom Fanning described as a *"true blooded Yankee,"* to "Lay the enemy's ship on board"—put their ship across the frigate's quarter, giving Jones a chance to board her. His officers rounded up a boarding party as the *Bonhomme Richard*'s bowsprit came across the *Serapis*'s mizzenmast. "Grappling hooks away!" Jones roared, and a score of lines flew across the air, the hooks digging into the frigate's bulwarks. In a flash, Pearson sent sailors carrying axes to cut the lines away, under cover of a volley from the British marines aloft.[56]

But attempting to board the *Serapis* now meant the Americans had to walk out single file along the bowsprit, making them easy targets for Pearson's marines. Within seconds Jones saw the folly of the attack. What grappling lines had not been severed by the British Jones's men now cut themselves, as Stacey backed the *Bonhomme Richard*'s sails. The ships separated. Wasting no time himself, Pearson let fly another broadside at the rebels. At such close range it was impossible to miss.

During all this, young Joseph Brussels had been running up and down the hatchway, carrying powder horns to the deck from the magazine and back again. A concussive blast struck nearby, and his powder horn fell to the deck. The boy reached down to pick it up, only to see his hand still gripped around it. The explosion had blown his arm off.

Joseph fell to the deck, unconscious. He was carried below, where Surgeon Brooke, using a device called a crow's beak to draw out the blood vessels from the wound, sutured the stump. An ointment of turpentine and egg yolk was applied before Brooke bandaged the area, leaving a channel open for the wound to drain. With no time to ponder the boy's age or condition, Brooke said, "Next." Young Brussels was carried away, while another poor wretch was laid before the surgeon.[57]

Another small puff of wind came Jones's way, and Stacey roared at the helmsman to change course. If the *Bonhomme Richard* could turn fast enough, she could cross the *Serapis*'s stern, letting her remaining starboard guns fire a devastating broadside into the defenseless frigate. But the old ship's rudder had been shot away, and instead of turning, she stalled, putting the *Serapis* on a collision course. In seconds she struck the *Bonhomme Richard* on her starboard side. With a jerk, the frigate's bowsprit enmeshed itself in the East Indiaman's mizzen shrouds and vang—the rope that set the spanker into position.[58]

The jolting contact took away the American colors flying at the ensign staff. Believing the rebels had struck, the British tars gave three cheers, only to be answered by a volley of small-arms fire from Jones's men. Kilby later recalled Jones crying, "Look at my mizzen peak!" while another ensign was run up.[59]

Entangled as they were, Jones and Pearson both took action—Jones to keep the ships in this deadly embrace, Pearson to escape it. Seeing the tide running out, Pearson ordered "drop anchor," hoping the combination of his secured ship and the moving current would pull the combatants apart and allow him to resume sailing around the crippled rebel ship and hammer her at will.[60]

But Jones was equally quick-thinking. Seeing the *Serapis*'s jib stay lying on his deck, Jones grabbed it and called Stacey to help him secure it to their mizzenmast. Straining to get the stiffened rope around the mast, Stacey began cursing. Jones cut him short. "Mr. Stacey, it is no time for swearing now, you may by the next moment be in eternity; but let us do our duty." Surrounded by death, Jones still found time to be both officer and gentleman. "Now," said Jones as they finished their task, "we'll hold her fast by this until one or the other sinks."[61]

For a second time, Jones called, "Grappling hooks away!" Once more, his sailors took the lines in hand, swinging the hooks over their heads once, twice, and then over to the *Serapis*. Clusters of men grabbed the lines; pulling sharply, they brought the ships closer, inch by inch. Again Pearson's men approached their bulwarks with axes raised, only to be cut down this time by Jones's marines in the fighting tops of the *Bonhomme Richard*.[62]

Now luck, so long against Jones in the fight, turned his way—along with the *Bonhomme Richard*. The *Serapis* could not break free, and the grappling hooks, the tied jib stay, the ship's anchor, and the current held Pearson's frigate in place while the *Bonhomme Richard* slowly but inevitably came 180 degrees around. As she did, the fluke of the *Serapis*'s spare anchor caught in the *Bonhomme Richard*'s quarter. With succinct eloquence, Pearson later reported that "we dropt alongside each other, head to stern." The ships were facing in opposite directions, unable to go anywhere.[63]

The battle was a little over an hour old. Despite skyrocketing casualties, neither side was close to victory. Jones's spur-of-the-moment stratagem had worked; now, like a punch-drunk boxer, he had his foe in a clinch he could maintain until a strong enough punch ended this butchery.

From the fighting tops Fanning and the others were firing "without inter-mission, with musketry, blunderbusses, coehorns, swivels, and pistols" into the enemy tops. In minutes they had wiped out all but one British marine, remaining in the foretop, bravely firing his musket, then ducking behind the mast to reload before firing again. Fanning ordered his men to hold their fire until he peeked out. Like a firing squad on high, they sent him falling to the deck. Small-arms fire came from both ships, Jones firing his pistol at a British officer on the *Serapis*'s quarterdeck.

Jones's ploy succeeded in negating the sailing advantage of the *Serapis*, but it also brought the enemy's mighty 18-pounders literally within inches of the *Bonhomme Richard*. Dale's gun crews—those whose cannons were still serviceable—joined their foe in a frantic scherzo of load and fire, load and fire. To work their cannons, the gun crews on both sides found themselves running their sponges and rammers through their enemy's gun ports. "The muzzles of our guns touched each other's sides," Pearson marveled.

That being the case, he kept his guns firing round after round into the *Bonhomme Richard*, taking out more rebel guns and battering holes below the waterline until she was perforated like a Swiss cheese. Jones's ship was no longer just taking on water; she was beginning to sink.[64]

Jones sent Carpenter John Gunnison to assess the damage below. He soon found himself in over six feet of water. The only sound that drowned out the roar of cannon and the inrushing seawater were the cries Gunnison heard coming from the British prisoners in the hold. Literally and figuratively in the dark, they were unaware of which way the battle was going; they only knew the hold was filling up with water. Locked inside, they were sure they were soon going to drown in a sinking ship. Gunnison went on deck to tell Jones his ship was sinking. Jones dismissed him: "Never mind," Kilby heard his captain tell the carpenter. "If she sinks, there are plenty of spars on deck and we shall not be drowned. Go back and do the best you can."[65]

Gunnison went for John Burbank, master-at-arms. Both went below to open the hold before it became a drowning pool. Scores of British prisoners clambered up the hatchway behind them, escaping the near certainty of drowning only to find themselves in the midst of a nightmare of cannon and musket fire. Before the escapees thought to mount an attack on their rebel captors, Jones sent them below again to man both the chain pumps and the hand pumps, relieving the sailors at that task and allowing them to rejoin the fight.[66]

By now the *Serapis*'s gunners had knocked out the last 12-pounder under Dale's command. This left Jones with only two starboard 9-pounders to return the enemy's broadside. Undaunted, he took a couple of men across the deck, where they freed another 9-pounder from her breeching rope and tackle, trundling it across the deck. The 9-pounders were under the command of Purser Mease, but now he fell with a serious head wound. In most sea fights, the captain never leaves the poop or quarterdeck, but this was no textbook battle. Jones manned this gun himself, directing each shot at the bright yellow mainmast of the *Serapis*.[67]

While British cannons slowly demolished the *Bonhomme Richard*'s hull, Jones's marines were firing volley after volley down at the *Serapis*'s sailors. Within half an hour, Fanning and the rest had all but cleared the enemy's deck; only the gun crews manning the forward guns were under cover and safe from the marines' marksmanship. As there was no breeze, smoke burned the eyes and choked the lungs of every man in the fight, officer and sailor alike. But they kept fighting.

With no wind, and water funneling into the *Bonhomme Richard*, another element came into play: fire. The sails of both ships, hanging limply in the air, were soon ablaze. In minutes both ships were burning, the *Serapis* in a dozen different places. The battle was halted so that bucket brigades could douse the fires with what Pearson called "the greatest difficulty and exertion imaginable."[68]

As both sides fought the flames and not each other, Jones found a moment's respite and sat on a hen coop—an image no novelist could imagine. Hearing distant gunfire, he turned his attention across the water, looking for the *Alliance*, *Pallas*, and *Vengeance*. He could make out another battle taking place between the *Pallas* and the *Countess of Scarborough*. As for his other two ships, Jones could only guess whether they were lurking somewhere in the darkness, chasing the Baltic fleet up the coast, or just plain gone.[69]

Once the fires on both ships were brought under control, the battle resumed. By this time Jones had all three 9-pounders loaded with bar-shot, firing at the *Serapis*'s mainmast, each shot slowly but surely weakening the massive pole. Within minutes, both ships were afire again. Suddenly, there was a broadside of grapeshot fired across the *Bonhomme Richard*'s decks, killing or wounding several of the men still on her poop deck. With the *Serapis* lashed lengthwise to his ship, Jones knew the barrage did not come from the frigate, and the *Countess* was embroiled in a fight of her own with the *Pallas*. Who had fired on him?

The broadside came from the *Alliance*. In the two hours since he had sheered out of Jones's way, Landais had stayed out of both fights; now he came in for the kill, apparently unconcerned as to whom he was killing. The same broadside that struck the *Bonhomme Richard* also hit the *Serapis*. "Don't fire into us!" Jones roared. "We are the *Bonhomme Richard*." Jones sent several men for lanterns and ordered them hung in the shrouds, along with two taken aloft to hang at the mizzen—the commodore's recognition signal at nighttime.

If Landais was deaf to Jones's cry, his second-in-command, Lieutenant James

Degge, was not. But when Degge told Landais of his error, the captain screamed, "Do you obey my orders! I know very well what to do." The *Alliance* sailed around the two deadlocked combatants, unleashing an even deadlier broadside. Among those struck down was young midshipman James Coram. "*Alliance* has wounded me," he gasped. Coram was wrong. *Alliance* had killed him. As shock and rage battled inside him, Jones watched the *Alliance* disappear into the darkness.[70]

He turned his attention back to his 9-pounders and winning what looked more and more to be an unwinnable fight, firing more rounds into the *Serapis*'s mainmast. His own mainmast had been a British target and was so damaged that she was held in place only by her shrouds and stays. Fanning feared that he and his men would soon be sent plummeting to the deck, or into the cold waters off Flamborough Head.

To make matters worse, the mainsail and standing rigging were burning. The bucket of water the marines had hauled aloft before the fighting had been consumed long before; the marines extinguished the flames with their jackets. With the *Serapis*'s tops cleared of her marines, and the spars of the two ships literally interlocked, Fanning ordered his marines to cross to the opposite mast—in this case, the *Serapis*'s foretop. Taking their muskets, coehorns, stinkpots, and grenades with them, they inched along the footropes until they were safely across.[71]

The situation below deck grew more perilous by the second. Water was pouring in so hard and fast that manning the pumps seemed futile to Gunnison, but the British prisoners kept to their task. Before returning to deck Gunnison found a friend, Gunner's Mate Henry Gardner, an Englishman. He, too, had eyes, and could see the ship was sinking. They climbed the port ladder together to find their captain.

They looked to the poop deck but did not see Jones or Dale. All they saw through the haze of stinging smoke were too many dead bodies to count—surely Jones and Dale were among them. Seeing no colors flying, they believed all was lost, and went forward to lower the commodore's pendant atop the main peak, crying loudly, "Quarter! Quarter!" Pearson heard them, and called for his speaking trumpet.[72]

But Jones heard them as well. Brandishing two pistols, he bolted from his gun, stepping over the dead without breaking his stride. "What dammed rascals are these?" he roared. "Shoot them! Kill them!"—an order he was giving as much to himself as anyone else within earshot.

Any initial surprise Gardner and Gunnison had in finding Jones alive was quickly replaced by sheer fear for their safety as he approached. They had called for quarter to save their lives from the British; now it looked like their own captain would shoot them dead.

And they would have been—at least Gunnison. Jones shot at the fleeing carpenter, but the pistol only clicked—he had forgotten to reload after firing it earlier. Enraged, Jones hurled it at Gunnison's head, striking him so hard he fell unconscious down the ladder leading to the ship's waist.

Just then Pearson hailed Jones: "Have you struck?" he asked. "Do you call for quarter?"[73]

Pearson's question silenced any fighting, as men from both sides listened for Jones's answer. From his post forward, Richard Dale also turned to hear his captain's reply.

Jones possessed two traits no one ever questioned: unflappable courage, and an actor's gift for the moment. Forty years later, Dale would remember Jones's reply for posterity: "I have not yet begun to fight." Others recalled Jones replying, "I may sink, but I'm damned if I'll strike"—an equally defiant phrase.[74]

Whatever defiant words Jones used, they did not cow Pearson, who cried, "Boarders away!" Two dozen of his toughest marines and sailors wielding cutlasses, pikes, and pistols clambered over the side, leaping across to the *Bonhomme Richard*'s bow. Pearson's 18-pounders resumed blasting away at what was left of the *Bonhomme Richard*'s hull.

Seizing a pike himself, Jones rushed forward to meet the enemy, but the intrepid Dale, leading thirty men, had already begun the counterattack. To Kilby, Dale fought "with bravery like that of Julius Caesar." Jones was soon among the phalanx of Dale's combatants in the bloody, hand-to-hand clash.

It was fierce but brief, thanks in great part to Fanning and the marines in the fighting tops, whose marksmanship was unerring throughout the night. They had obeyed Jones's orders to the deadliest letter. What boarders they missed were being dispatched by Jones, Dale, and their men. The attackers fell back. Feeling their way to the rail, trying not to trip over their own fallen shipmates, they returned to the *Serapis*. Jones returned to his 9-pounder and his dogged assault on the *Serapis*'s mainmast.[75]

Fanning and the others in the tops poured such a withering fire down on the deck of the *Serapis* that Pearson sent everyone below, while shots from his 18-pounders now passed clear through the *Bonhomme Richard*. "Only an old timber here and there kept the poop from crashing down on the gun deck," Jones later observed. By now half of the men on both sides were either killed or wounded; new fires sprang up above and below both decks. "The moon at this time, as though ashamed to behold this bloody scene any longer, retired behind a dark cloud," Fanning poetically and chillingly recalled.[76]

But Pearson was not yet ready to give up his ship. One of Jones's prisoners had succeeded in gaining entry to the *Serapis* through one of the empty gun ports. Finding Pearson, he begged him to hold out—the *Bonhomme Richard* was sinking.[77]

With British resistance now restricted to the gun deck, one daring man brought the battle to an end. William Hamilton, a Scotsman, was stationed in the maintop and had moved to the *Serapis*'s foretop with Fanning and the others. Now, carrying a leather bucket of grenades and a slow match in his other hand (or between his teeth), he crossed the footropes again, edging out along the spar. There was no enemy on deck to shoot at him—his balancing act alone was dangerous enough. Once he had a clear view of the *Serapis*'s deck and hatchway below him, he went to work, just as the moon rose above that black cloud.

Still manning his 9-pounder, Jones watched Hamilton's high-wire act, full of admiration for his fellow Scot. "As the flames from [the *Serapis*'s] railings and shrouds added to the light of the moon," Jones prosaically recalled, Hamilton stood over the frigate, a veritable Zeus, armed with grenades instead of thunderbolts. With methodical coolness, he lit a fuse; it would burn a few seconds before detonating. With perfect timing, Hamilton threw one at a cluster of British sailors, then another. The *Serapis* rocked with the explosions.

Hamilton threw one more. This grenade bounced down the hatchway to the gun deck, which was usually kept pristine, especially in battle. But this fight had been so frenetic that unspent cartridges littered the deck. No kindling could be more flammable or deadly. The grenade blew up, killing a score of men at the guns and igniting the cartridges. One blast followed another. Five of the nine starboard 18-pounders were blown off their carriages, and fire instantly swept through the gun deck. Those men not killed from the blasts climbed up the ladder screaming in pain, their skin and hair on fire, their lungs filled with smoke, while their shipmates blocked from the hatchway by the conflagration leapt through the gun ports into the sea.[78]

Ascending to his quarterdeck, Pearson assessed the situation. The *Serapis*'s quarter rails had been completely leveled with the deck. Everywhere he looked his ship was on fire; dead and wounded lay everywhere. Most of his starboard guns were destroyed. He could see, hear, and feel his mainmast totter, mangled by Jones's relentless barrage. "I fear," he believed, "the greatest part of the people

BONHOMME RICHARD against *SERAPIS*
off Flamborough Head, September 23, 1779

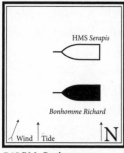

7:15 P.M.: Battle commences.

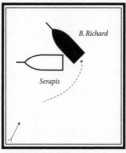

7:45 P.M.: With *Bonhomme Richard* on *Serapis*'s stern quarter, Jones attempts to board her.

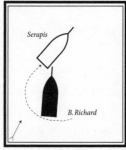

8:00 P.M.: Pearson tries to "cross the T" and rake *Bonhomme Richard* as the wind dies.

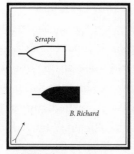

8:15 P.M.: Ships separate, exchanging broadsides.

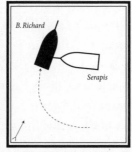

8:30 P.M.: *Bonhomme Richard* attempts to "cross the T" but is rammed by *Serapis*.

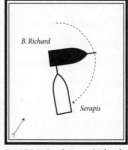

8:45 P.M.: *Bonhomme Richard* pivots on *Serapis*'s bowsprit.

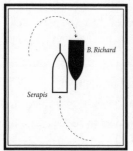

9:00 P.M.: Jones lashes *Serapis*'s forestay to his mizzenmast. Grappling hooks secure the ships together.

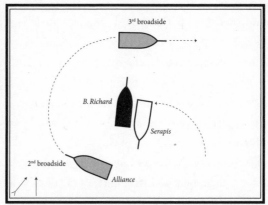

9:15 P.M.: Pearson drops anchor, swinging the ships around just as *Alliance* fires the first of several broadsides at both ships. Battle continues for two more hours.

will lose their lives." This madman who so willingly tethered his ship and his life to Pearson's frigate showed no sign of surrendering.

Then there was the *Alliance*—the undamaged, sound, thirty-six-gun frigate that had already hurt the *Serapis*. Even if Jones surrendered, Pearson could not possibly engage the *Alliance* "without our being able to bring a gun to bear on her." Pearson saw his situation "impracticable" without "the least prospect of success."[79]

Looking over to the *Bonhomme Richard*, he found Jones still at his 9-pounder. Taking his speaking trumpet one last time, Pearson called, "Sir, I have struck! I ask for quarter!"

Jones turned his attention towards the frigate's quarterdeck. Looking through the black smoke he found Pearson, his red flag still hanging above him. Months before, John Adams had marveled at Jones's "quiet voice"—he had obviously never witnessed Jones on deck. The commodore did not need his speaking trumpet now. "If you have struck," he retorted, "haul down your ensign!"

The sailors near Pearson stood stock-still. Having witnessed the marksmanship of the *Bonhomme Richard*'s marines, they were not about to move. Instead, Pearson, turning his back on Jones and the world, took charge one last time aboard his ship. The red flag he had nailed defiantly with his own hands was in tatters, shot through by musket fire and grapeshot. With as much dignity as he could muster, the brave captain of the *Serapis* ripped his colors, nail by nail, off the flagstaff.[80]

Seeing the flag in Pearson's hand, Jones cried, "Cease firing!" He ordered Dale to bring Pearson aboard the *Bonhomme Richard*. Dale leapt upon the gunwale, grabbed a line, and swung over the side, while Midshipman John Mayrant followed with a boarding party. Dale landed on the *Serapis*'s deck unscathed, but the battle of Flamborough Head was not yet over. As Mayrant came aboard the *Serapis*, one last skirmish began. A British tar stabbed Mayrant in the thigh with a pike—not everyone had heard Pearson ask for quarter.

Nor did the second-in-command, Lieutenant John Wright, climbing up the hatchway just as Dale addressed Pearson: "Sir, I have orders to send you on board the ship alongside."

Pearson was about to reply when Wright, sweat-stained and hoarse, asked Pearson if the rebels had struck. It was Dale who answered him: "No, sir, to the contrary; he has struck to us."

The shocked Wright accosted his captain. "Have you struck, sir?"

"Yes, I have," Pearson replied.

"I have nothing more to say," Wright responded. He turned his back on Pearson to return below when Dale informed him that he, too, was to come aboard the *Bonhomme Richard*. *Now* the battle was over.[81]

Pearson kept his shock at the human and physical wreckage he found aboard the *Bonhomme Richard* to himself until he made his report to the Admiralty three weeks later:

> I found her to be in the greatest distress; her counters and quarter on the lower deck entirely drove in, and the whole of her lower deck guns dismounted; she was also on fire in two places, and six or seven feet of water in her hold which kept increasing on them all night.[82]

Jones played the gallant host, exhibiting the traditional courtesies extended to the vanquished commander. Pearson, his handsome uniform smudged with soot, handed Jones his sword. Jones took it, complimenting Pearson on his gallantry and the hopes that King George would reward him handsomely for his devotion to duty. Then Pearson cleared his throat, and asked of the nationality of the crew—hoping against hope that the French-built ship was not manned by Frenchmen, which would only add to Pearson's mortification at losing his ship.

"Mostly Americans," Jones replied.

This was music to Pearson's ringing ears. The Americans were rebels, but at least of the same blood. "Then it was Diamond cut Diamond," he said. Jones invited him into his cabin for a glass of wine.[83]

It is not recorded whether, once the captains entered Jones's obliterated cabin, he found two unbroken wineglasses. On this night, above all others, the sharing of a glass of wine seems incongruous while two ships were burning and one of them was sinking.

Their formal pleasantries concluded, Jones and Pearson returned to battle the elements. Jones ordered Dale to cut loose the mizzen stay and grappling lines that had held the ships fast; he was to command the *Serapis* and follow the *Bonhomme Richard*. Returning to the frigate, Dale could not understand why she would not answer her helm, and sent a man below to see if her wheel ropes were cut away. Dale sat himself down on a binnacle—the box near the wheel that housed the compass. At this point, the sailing master of the *Serapis* came to the quarterdeck, informing the unknowing Dale that his prize was rocking at anchor.

Dale rose, only to collapse to the deck as if shot. During the fighting, a flying splinter had embedded itself in his leg, creating a deep wound he had been completely unaware of until this second. He was being helped back to the binnacle when he ordered a hand to cut the anchor cable. Suddenly, a sharp series of cracking sounds came from the waist. It was the mainmast. Jones's 9-pounders had done their work well; with one last loud snap, it toppled over the side. The *Serapis* was not going anywhere.[84]

Nor was the *Bonhomme Richard*. The rotten wood, pitch, and oakum that held her carcass together made a perfect torch for the fire that now threatened the powder magazine. Jones ordered his distress signal run up. Remarkably, the *Alliance*, *Pallas*, and *Vengeance* responded (along with Lieutenant Lunt's boat), sending their longboats over with more hands. But Jones could not wait for these men—according to Fanning, the fire was now "within the thickness of a pine board to the bulkhead" of the powder magazine. It would be the *Randolph* all over again, only doubly so: if the *Bonhomme Richard* blew up, being so close to the *Serapis*, Fanning was certain "we must have all gone to eternity together."[85]

British officers and sailors quickly boarded the *Bonhomme Richard*. Minutes earlier the crews were trying to kill each other; now they formed a long line, passing the half barrels of gunpowder hand over hand to the *Serapis*. They completed the task in minutes. Then Jones transferred the wounded to the other ships in the squadron, followed by his prisoners.[86]

Atop Flamborough Head, the spectators that had stood transfixed for three hours began to head home. But there was no rest for the weary combatants. Fires required fighting; pumps still needed manning, while aboard the other ships, surgeons and their assistants went from one grisly casualty to another.

The burn victims were in the worst shape; Fanning was aghast at the sight of men "burnt in such a shocking manner that the flesh of several of them dropped off their bones." When Surgeon Brooke came on deck to help transfer the wounded, Fanning found him "as bloody as a butcher." In addition to John Jordan and Joseph Brussels, Fanning saw literally scores who "had their legs and arms shot away."[87]

The casualties of the battle were as horrific as they were high. The percentage in a sea fight—dead and wounded combined—rarely exceeded 10 percent; it was 50 percent for both sides at Flamborough Head. Jones put it best: "A Person must have been an Eye Witness to form a just Idea of the tremendous Scenes of Carnage Wreck and Ruin which every where appeared," he wrote. "Humanity cannot but recoil from the Prospect of such finished Horror and lament War should be capable of producing Such fatal Consequences."[88]

The fires on the *Bonhomme Richard* were not put out until ten the next morning. Pumps were manned on both ships throughout the night, but while the *Serapis* was free of water in four hours, it became obvious to all that the *Bonhomme Richard* would not last the day; "the leak still gaining on us," Jones had entered in the ship's log as if he was being chased, not sunk.[89]

Morning came with fog. Jones could still see his squadron and his two prizes, but no sign at all of the Baltic fleet. Pearson's actions—and the dawdling of Landais and Ricot—had given it time to escape. Bone-weary as his men were, Jones knew he had not a moment to lose. British warships had been looking for him for weeks; at any instant they might sail over the horizon. While a new mainmast was being fished aboard the *Serapis*, other hands repaired her damaged bowsprit. Jones, meanwhile, summoned his captains to a council.

One can only imagine the reception Jones gave to Cottineau, Ricot, and especially Landais. At least Cottineau had acquitted himself in taking the *Countess*; Ricot, in his smaller ship, could be excused for his timidity—to a point. As for Landais, Jones had already made up his mind. Days later he would, in detail, make Franklin aware of the Frenchman's abhorrent behavior.[90]

After attempting to ascertain why the Baltic fleet was not pursued—especially by the *Alliance* and the *Vengeance*—Jones invited Cottineau "and other men of sense" to examine the squadron's wounded flagship. Officers and carpenters found it remarkable that the ship was still afloat. Fanning thought the massive hole through the ship's quarter and gun room was so wide "one might have drove in with a coach and six, at one side of the breach and out the other." All believed she should be abandoned except Jones, but by sunset he realized "It was Impossible to keep the *Bon Homme Richard* Afloat So as to reach a Port."[91]

For the past six months, Jones had had a true love-hate relationship with the *Bonhomme Richard*: glee at getting a command after his time "on the beach"; dismay that she was no *l'Indien* or *Alliance*; pride in his refitting of her; disgust with her sluggish sailing. More than anything, he wanted her to sail, or at least limp, into port with his prizes and consorts. It was not to be. The ancient East Indiaman had come through the most horrific of battles, and Jones was heartsick to leave her to her fate. He was not alone; years later, Fanning wrote, "It was even painful for me to quit this ship." She may not have been a fast ship, but she was a noble one.

Jones sent his men to recover their belongings, but almost all of the sea chests had been shot through so badly that the clothes inside were nothing more than rags, and even Jones lost some personal effects. The men transferred over to the *Serapis*. The frigate was some distance away from the sinking *Bonhomme Richard* when Jones thought of some valuable papers still in his cabin. He sent three men under Fanning across the water to retrieve them just when a gale blew up.

The closer Fanning's boat got to the *Bonhomme Richard*, the more he realized this dangerous errand was "a kind of forlorn Don Quixote undertaking." The boat was being sucked towards the sinking ship when Jones called for them to return, but Fanning could not hear him. He did not need to: he ordered the men to man the sweeps and row for their lives. They did not need to be told twice. They rowed back furiously, shipping water all the way.[92]

Jones watched the death throes of the *Bonhomme Richard* from the quarterdeck of the *Serapis*. Those of his crew still standing lined themselves along the rails, from the waist to the bow. "It was enough to bring tears to the most unthinking man," Kilby recalled. She lay with her head into the wind, her topsails backed against the masts, water running into her gun ports.

Fanning's men were still rowing to safety when the *Bonhomme Richard* "fetched a heavy pitch into a sea and a heavy roll, and disappeared instantaneously." Her bowsprit slid into the water, then her foremast, main, and finally the mizzen. At eleven a.m. on the twenty-fifth, Jones "saw with inexpressible Grief the last Glimpse of the *Bonhomme Richard*." Her service ended; her legend just beginning.[93]

By the time the *Bonhomme Richard* went to her watery grave, London had learned of Jones's victory. Eight of the king's cruisers were dispatched to Flamborough Head. The panic Jones had inspired with the *Ranger* paled in comparison to this cruise. Already in a state of alarm over the appearance of the Franco-Spanish fleet in August, Jones's latest exploits convinced the public that the Admiralty could not even keep order in her own yard, front or back. Jones's victory elicited more letters to the Earl of Sandwich than any other event in the war. Nary a one complimented him on the fine job he was doing as First Lord of the Admiralty.[94]

And the press had a field day. While the conservative *London Morning Packet and Advertiser* assured readers that the Royal Navy would soon catch Jones ("three frigates of force are cruising off Yarmouth"), the *Morning Post* took a different tack: "Paul Jones resembles a Jack o' Lantern, to mislead our mariners and terrify our coasts." The story of his throwing a pistol at Gunnison was embellished into a Blackbeard-like tale—shooting seven of his own men during the battle, even firing at an imaginary nephew, "damn his eyes"—all fiction, but lapped up by the terrified subjects of King George.[95]

Thus inspired, one illustrator drew Jones *as* Blackbeard, while another depicted him as a cross between a buccaneer and Nosferatu. It fell to the London *Evening Post* to remind readers of the burning and sacking of American homes by British troops, to present a more Whig-inspired spin on the Terror of England: "It appears that Jones's orders were not to burn any houses or towns. What an example of honour and greatness does America thus show to us!"[96]

Jones's squadron reached the Texel Island (the island harbor off Amsterdam we last visited with Gustavus Conyngham) on October 3. Once docked, he wrote a voluminous report of his cruise to Franklin. It was honest, thoughtful, even pointing out his failed attempts to outmaneuver the *Serapis* at Flamborough Head. But it was also clear that he was out for Landais's scalp. "Either Captain Landais or myself is highly Criminal and one or the other must be Punished." Jones was sure who that would be. The Frenchman, of course, also made his report—a somewhat different account.[97]

Jones was becoming exasperated with Pearson's disdain and snobbery. Since their departure from Flamborough Head, Pearson had shown no appreciation for Jones's chivalrous treatment of him. Jones had given him back his sword, let Pearson keep his cabin, taking a lieutenant's wardroom instead and, in a gesture that struck home for Jones after the Selkirk affair, made sure that Pearson's silver plate and other valuables were all accounted for after Jones saw to Pearson's comforts ashore. When Jones sent the trunks to his lodging, Pearson refused them, as they came from a rebel whom Pearson believed should have "a halter round his neck." Again, Jones turned the other cheek, giving the trunks to Cottineau to deliver. This time, Pearson accepted.[98]

Over the next two weeks the two engaged in polite but strained correspondence until Jones snapped at Pearson's overbearing pomposity. When Pearson pulled rank in one letter, Jones informed him there was no difference in "'Rank between your Service and Ours." However, Jones supposed "the difference must be thought very great in England"; how else could Jones reconcile the kindnesses he showed Pearson in contrast to the treatment of Gustavus Conyngham, who, Jones reminded Pearson, "bears a Senior rank in the service of America" but "is now Confined at Plymouth *in a Dungeon and in fetters!*" Jones insisted to Franklin that Pearson should only be exchanged for Conyngham. As before, Jones wanted his prisoners, about five hundred total, exchanged for American captives in England.[99]

Leaving the *Serapis* in Dale's capable hands, Jones took a coach to Amsterdam, where he was greeted like a conquering hero. Stepping out of the coach in his blue and white uniform, Jones was too mobbed to move. Charles-Guillaume-Frédéric

Dumas, the agent for the American commissioners in Paris, watched as merchants, sailors, bankers, and artisans joined the rapturous throng of women and children in congratulating the little commodore. While Jones maintained his reserve on the surface, he was bursting with happiness. Months earlier he had told Sartine "my desire for fame is infinite"; Dumas wrote Franklin that the crowd would have gladly kissed Jones's feet, had he asked them.[100]

Franklin replied, noting that Jones was not only the hero of the hour but the topic of practically every conversation at Versailles; a jealous John Adams wrote Abigail how the French "became as loud in favour of Monsieur Jones as of Monsieur Franklin." From Massachusetts, Mrs. Adams rued "that we had not such a commander" at Penobscot.[101]

Ironically, the failures at Penobscot and of the Franco-Spanish fleet helped elevate Jones's adventures to the heights of glory. One anonymous observer, thinking of the embarrassing tale of Jones and the gardener's wife, extended "Congratulations to the commodore" who "screwed the lady who works in the garden at Passy, and who is now screwing the English so nicely." Jones was feted and adored. Poems and ballads were written by friend and foe alike, while he, in turn, wrote a flattering ode (about himself) to Dumas's smitten teenage daughter.[102]

Such high paeans are usually countered with envious ripostes, and Jones's time in the sun was no different. Sir Joseph Yorke, the British ambassador to Holland, raised hackles with the Dutch government over Jones's very presence. The daily cheering of Jones every time he made an appearance at the coffeehouses and exchanges added fuel to his seething anger. Picking up where Lord Stormont left off, he insisted that the *Serapis* and the *Countess of Scarborough* be returned to Britain and Jones be turned over to British authorities.

Dutch authorities soon tired of him as well. They were still neutral in this war, and looked for a way to rid themselves of the man. When they learned that Dumas had written Jones that "a high degree of dirtiness and infection reigns aboard the *Serapis*," and heard rumors of rotting corpses still aboard the frigate, they began to pressure Jones to leave Holland.[103]

To complicate matters further, Jones was in an Amsterdam tavern when in walked Pierre Landais. The Frenchman repeated his earlier challenge, proposing a duel with "small swords." Jones, a bear for nerve, was not a fool. Looking Landais straight in the eye, Jones told him the matter would not be settled at sword's point but by a court of inquiry. Jones wanted Landais arrested, but the

Frenchman slipped out of town and headed to Paris. Jones returned to Texel Island.[104]

He did not board the *Serapis* a happy man. After chastising Dale for his laxity, he put the men to work scrubbing the ship clean and airing out the hammocks. He had a harder time restoring his men's faith in their captain. When he departed for Amsterdam they gave him three cheers. There were none for his return. The weather had turned colder, and most of the men were still wearing rags—the only clothes they had after Flamborough Head and the sinking of the *Bonhomme Richard.*

Many of the wounded were still aboard and still suffering. Seeing no help coming from Jones for these warriors, Surgeon Brooke, like many officers before him, changed his opinion of Jones, and not for the better. Desertions from the *Serapis* became more frequent. Among them was the intrepid William Hamilton, whose grenade throwing had ended the battle.

Jones's British prisoners went even further in their anger. Furious that his attempts to exchange them had failed thus far, they plotted to kill him on his return from Amsterdam. The plan was discovered and foiled, but the pressure put on the Dutch government by Sir Joseph Yorke was unrelenting. The squadron's prizes remained unsold; Jones's men received an "advance" of one ducat each—more insult than reward. British frigates lay off the Dutch coast, waiting for the day when Jones sailed. When the French ambassador, le Duc de la Vauguyon, informed Jones that the *Pallas* and the *Vengeance* would fly French flags instead of American colors—in an attempt to protect them from British threats of seizure—Jones knew he was finished at Texel Island.

Soon the fleur-de-lis was also flying over the *Serapis* and the *Countess of Scarborough.* As a sop to Jones, Vauguyon sent the *Countess* and the *Vengeance* to England as cartels, carrying 191 of Jones's prisoners for exchange. All that remained under Jones's command was the *Alliance.* His days as commodore were over.[105]

Late one night Jones led a gang of sailors aboard the *Serapis* and looted her of everything of value they could carry. Cutlasses, rum puncheons, hen coops, and all the leg irons (whether for future prisoners or mutinies Jones never disclosed) were carried to the *Alliance.* Cottineau took command of the *Serapis* the next day.[106]

Jones at least had a fine frigate to command—fine but filthy, thanks to Landais's slackness. An offer from Sartine to sail the *Alliance* as a privateer under a

French commission was spurned; Jones was fed up with French games. He also had had his fill of the rotten Dutch bread given his men, as well as the bullying of a Dutch captain whose ship-of-the-line was dispatched to Texel Island to coerce Jones into leaving. Jones icily let him know he would sail when his ship was ready.[107]

The transfer of Jones's threadbare crew to the *Alliance* padded the frigate's muster rolls but gave Jones a new headache. His men despised the Alliances, thanks to Landais's firing at them (and killing several) weeks before. Fights broke out continually. Jones wrote to both Franklin and Morris, begging them for orders to return to America. He continued to refit the *Alliance*, getting her cleaned and supplied, and re-stepping her masts while playing referee between the warring crews.[108]

Looming over all this activity was the fact that British cruisers were waiting for him as soon as he sailed. The Earl of Sandwich promised the captains, "If you can take Paul Jones you will be as high in the estimation of the public as if you had beat the combined fleet."[109]

One bright occurrence broke the tedium and tension: the arrival of another Continental officer, happy to find Jones still in Holland and eager to ship with him. "I have the pleasure to inform you," an elated Jones wrote Franklin, "that Captain Cunningham [*sic*] is now here with me."[110]

CHAPTER ELEVEN

"FRESH GALES AND DIRTY WEATHER"

We were bound to Philadelphia . . . but two revolts of the crew
have prevented . . . *Before God!* . . . You will find them out.

—PIERRE LANDAIS[1]

W hile Benjamin Franklin knew that Gustavus Conyngham had escaped, he was overjoyed to learn the captain was safe in Holland with
John Paul Jones. The commissioner had received an earlier letter from Thomas
Digges, telling him that Conyngham had tunneled out of Mill Prison with fifty
other prisoners confined to "the Black Hole."

Once they were past the prison walls, Conyngham dispersed them in small
groups to increase their chances of eluding British search parties. After ordering
them to make their way to English ports on the east coast and hopefully find
passage across the channel, he took three officers with him and made for London,
where the risk of being caught was offset by the sheer size of the city. Conyngham
had memorized Digges's address on Villars Street, in the Strand section of
central London. If anyone could get him off this island, it would be Franklin's
friend, the confidant of Yankee prisoners at the Mill.[2]

Hiding in woods, behind hedgerows, and under bridges during the day, they
walked towards London at night. Each day one of the three slipped into the
nearest village to buy food. (Conyngham stayed in hiding for fear of being recognized.) Remarkably, they reached London in less than a fortnight. On their way
to Digges's they saw broadsides about their escape in shop windows, depicting
Conyngham, who was five feet eight, as a giant, dressed like a seventeenth-century

pirate, brandishing a broadsword with several pistols stuffed in his canvas trousers. Eventually they found Digges's house. They waited until darkness to knock on the door.[3]

Digges whisked them in and provided food, shelter, and new clothes. A grateful Conyngham told him that he was responsible for their escape, having given another American sympathizer, the Reverend Robert Heath of Plymouth, the money that Conyngham used to get his group of four this far. The next morning, Digges made the rounds of the London docks, looking for a ship heading to Europe that the Americans could steal away on. Eventually he found a Dutch captain who agreed to take them to Rotterdam.[4]

On the evening of November 10, Digges got his charges past the British sentries and smuggled them aboard the Dutch vessel. Once in Holland, Conyngham sent word to Franklin of his arrival. "Irons, dungeons, hunger, the hangman's cart I have experienced," he wrote. Conyngham originally planned to go to Dunkirk, but upon hearing that Jones was at Texel Island he changed his mind. "I should at this time go with Capt. Jones," he continued, and "In a short time will be able to retaliate" against the "petty tyrants" of the British Empire.

Conyngham hoped—as did Jones—that the *Alliance* would be ordered home to America, but Jones had not yet received orders. As usual, the Scotsman was busy refitting the frigate and taking on victuals, including a tierce of rum (about forty-two gallons) and a pipe of gin (three times that amount). By Christmas, the *Alliance* had been careened, but Franklin denied Jones's request to have her bottom sheathed in copper. In the predawn hours of December 27, with a fresh breeze in her sails and a convoy of Dutch men-of-war and merchantmen for company, the *Alliance* left Texel Island. Jones would be on a cruise of his own initiative—once he eluded the British cruisers that had been waiting for him.[5]

He was in luck. A gale of sleet and snow had chased the British warships away. As the *Alliance* sped through the water, Jones forgot the travails of his last weeks in Holland, and the constant warring between Landais's men and his own. The *Alliance* was the finest ship in the Continental Navy, and she was all his to command. He planned to cruise the English Channel, boldly flying American colors. What British squadrons he encountered he would leave in *Alliance*'s wake; what single cruisers he met he would fight and take. As always, he anticipated prizes and glory.

He did not know his best days were behind him.

———

Naval action stateside, so promising before Penobscot, now went in fits and starts. Captains entered new chapters in their careers. After John Barry spent a year of successful privateering, Congress summoned him back to the navy, sending him to Portsmouth to oversee completion of the navy's most ambitious project, a seventy-four-gun ship-of-the-line, the *America*—the largest ship Congress would build for more than thirty years. After purchasing a horse for the commute to and from New Hampshire, Barry rode to Portsmouth.[6]

Barry's appointment and mission constituted both a plum assignment and a fool's errand. While the ship's keel had been laid two years before, there were only twenty-four carpenters assigned to the ship, but no money for them or for the timber, canvas, rigging, and guns needed to finish her (the Eastern Navy Board estimated the cost to exceed $500,000). Just seeing what was completed so far, Barry could imagine what a huge, beautiful ship she would be. But with no funds or manpower to finish her, Barry returned to Philadelphia and urged Congress to find the money to complete the construction. Instead, Congress bounced back Barry's request regarding compensation for his four-legged purchase (one legislator already bemoaned that "our Board and Horse keeping . . . cost us more than our pay"). Barry's mount was requisitioned. With no immediate prospect for resuming the *America*'s construction, Barry obtained another leave of absence and went back to privateering, commanding a brig called the *American*.[7]

The handsome frigate *Confederacy* was still moored in the Delaware River, but Seth Harding had finally pressed enough sailors to man her. Congress ordered Harding to take Conrad Gérard, the French minister to the United States, back to France. As Harding made final preparations, he was informed that John Jay and his family would also be sailing, Jay having been appointed minister to Spain. King Charles III had entered the war on the side of his nephew, Louis XVI—but only as an ally of France, not the United States. Congress hoped Jay might persuade Charles otherwise. The *Confederacy* departed on October 26 for Cádiz.[8]

For two weeks the frigate hummed blissfully through the Atlantic under ideal conditions, making nine knots with ease. But smooth sailing ended at dawn on November 7. Sailors on the morning watch were attending to their duties, several up in the rigging and one at the masthead. Suddenly they heard a sharp crack from one of the masts, followed by another, then another. Within three minutes, the foremast, mainmast, and mizzenmast came crashing down like giant dominoes, taking the bowsprit with them. The deck and rails were littered with timber, canvas, and rope; injured sailors were hopelessly entangled in it.

Every man aboard, from captain to cabin boy to diplomat, gazed slack-jawed upon the catastrophe.

Harding soon collected his wits and ordered some hands to clear the debris and get the injured below. Once the damage was assessed, he sent the carpenter, mates, and other tars to rigging new masts, all done while the *Confederacy* pitched on the rolling sea, threatening to founder. To make matters even worse, the wrenching of the ship upon being dismasted produced so much torque on the rudder that it was rendered useless. Now a solid, heavy weapon against the ship, it slammed into the stern as the frigate veered first one way, then another.

For nearly two weeks, officers and crew worked tirelessly against wind and water, securing smaller masts in place with shim and rigging while the carpenter came up with an ingenious solution for the rudder: an intricate configuration of eyebolts, chain, and rope attached to spars run out of the cabin gun ports, then connected through block and tackle to the capstan. The *Confederacy* was no longer a trim sailing wonder, but she was stable, and that was wonder enough.[9]

At this point Harding met with his officers, Jay, and Gérard to discuss possible destinations. The *Confederacy*, with her matériel depleted, could not survive a storm, and Harding believed they should make for Martinique: the hurricane season was over, and the chances of favorable weather increased if they headed south.

Gérard would have none of it. He insisted that they make for Cádiz, arguing that the South Atlantic conditions would be similar to those en route to Martinique. Cádiz was nearly the same distance, and the Azores and Canary Islands were along the way if they ran into more trouble. As much as Jay wanted to reach Spain and assume his new responsibilities, he sided with Harding: the risks were too great to disregard the expert opinions of captain and officers. Gérard was furious, and immediately "ceased to observe that cordiality and frankness" he had displayed thus far on the voyage.

The phrase "limped into port" has been used for centuries, but never was it more apt a description than when the *Confederacy* reached Martinique on December 18. Jay and Gérard booked passage on a French frigate two weeks later. Harding's clearheadedness and sailing skills had been sorely tested, and proved remarkable.[10]

Lieutenant Colonel Silas Talbot, who had captured the *Pigot* in 1778, returned to sea in 1779 as captain of the sloop *Argo*, carrying twelve 6-pounders. Using New London, Connecticut, as a base of operations, he made several successful cruises throughout 1779; among his prizes was the privateer *King George*, commanded by Loyalist Stanton Hazard. All of New England rejoiced that Hazard—as despised as James Wallace and Henry Mowat—was now a prisoner of war.

In another battle, against the privateer *Dragon*, everyone on the *Argo*'s quarterdeck except Talbot was either killed or wounded. When the *Argo* was returned to her original owner, Talbot believed his successes had earned him a better ship. His friend Congressman Henry Marchand got him a captain's commission in the Continental Navy but Marchand could not get him a Continental ship; even if he had, he could not guarantee a crew. "We cannot create Men," he stated rather obviously. Talbot turned to privateering, taking command of the nineteen-gun ship *General Washington* in Rhode Island. In 1780 she was taken by a British squadron. After weeks aboard the *Jersey* in the East River, Talbot, like Conyngham, was sent to England and Mill Prison.[11]

In Philadelphia, John Young, number 23 on the Captains List, was back from a cruise as captain of a letter of marque, the *Impertinent*, sailing in a squadron of privateers under John Barry's command. As the lone Continental captain in Philadelphia, and with all the captains ranked above him either on assignment, in disfavor, captured, or dead, Young was given command of the sloop-of-war under construction at the Southwark shipyard.

The ship, rising slowly on the stocks above the waterfront homes, was the latest creation from young Joshua Humphreys. Also known as a corvette—a ship with a flush deck and a single tier of guns—she was 94 feet long with a 29-foot beam and weighed about 300 tons. Completing her construction was a race against time, not so much with the coming winter weather but with the fact that Congress had no money. The sale of wines from captured enemy holds helped pay for her finishing touches. She slid off the ways into the Delaware as the *Saratoga*.[12]

Dudley Saltonstall's assumption of command for the Penobscot campaign left a vacancy aboard the frigate *Trumbull*. She had been freed from the confines of the Connecticut River by Elisha Hinman, who sailed her to New London. The good news was that she was finally to be fitted out, for a cruise. The bad news—on the surface, at least—was that James Nicholson, late of the *Virginia* and still top captain on that infernal list, was to take command.

Hinman took the news hard; he was eager to avenge his loss of the *Alfred* and remove any doubts about his capabilities. But Congress played the seniority card, denying his request to retain command as long as Nicholson was available and "considered a man of merit"—at least by Congress. Nicholson proceeded to New London to supervise the *Trumbull*'s fitting out and rendezvous. That took all winter.

As the 1770s came to an end and Americans entered their sixth year of war, Congress began centralizing the management of the navy. The Marine Committee was dissolved on October 28, replaced by a Board of Admiralty that would consist of three commissioners, along with two congressmen and a secretary—John Brown, Robert Morris's indispensable man. Leading the board was Francis Lewis, a New York merchant. He was joined by Congressman William Ellery of Rhode Island, a Marine Committee veteran. For months, they would be the sole members.[13]

Even with Penobscot, 1779 had been a decent year for the navy; thirteen ships had captured more than fifty prizes. But the Marine Committee was no longer considered an attractive assignment. The original thirteen frigates were all finished, and few ships had been built since. Starting in 1779, inflation began spiraling at a rate of 17 percent a month, making Continental paper money worthless. As the money in their pockets grew weaker, Philadelphians went from worry to anger, directing it at public figures like Robert Morris, who seemed to grow physically and financially fatter as the price of bread soared. One mob of militiamen, sailors, and unemployed dockworkers attacked the mansion of James Wilson, a signer of the Declaration of Independence with a well-deserved reputation as a war profiteer. A few of his friends, including Thomas Mifflin, defended "Fort Wilson" from the mob until Philadelphia's military governor, Benedict Arnold, sent a troop of cavalry to encircle the house, with sabers at the ready. The following day, John Barry arrived in town from a privateering cruise and offered to send his sailors to defend Wilson's mansion, but by then the mob had dispersed.[14]

News of Flamborough Head and Conyngham's escape reached the states at an opportune time, as another crushing defeat followed the Penobscot disaster—this time in British-held Savannah. While Jones's squadron was sailing around the British Isles, a small army led by General Benjamin Lincoln had landed in Georgia, along with Admiral d'Estaing's French fleet, whose transports carried more than 4,000 French regulars (including a black regiment that d'Estaing had recruited in Haiti). Flush with victories in which he had captured the islands of Grenada and Dominica, d'Estaing saw taking Savannah as a chance to atone for his earlier failures off New England.

However, while that attempt at a joint Franco-American venture had been disappointing, this campaign was disastrous. In a combined assault against British regular and Loyalist troops under General Augustine Prévost, more than 800 Frenchmen and Americans were lost, including cavalry legend General Casimir Pulaski. D'Estaing, twice wounded himself, was dispirited; his sailors were dropping with scurvy, and he sailed to Martinique and thence to France. Lincoln's battered army retreated to Charleston, thereby setting the stage for the next undertaking by the Continental Navy.[15]

News of another resounding defeat, coming on the heels of Penobscot, was bad enough. But d'Estaing's return to European waters also destroyed American hopes that the war was about to end victoriously. Soaring prices and plummeting morale made the coming winter bleak indeed. Washington's army had settled into its encampment at Morristown, New Jersey. While the winters at Valley Forge were grim, this winter, with its numbing cold and horrific blizzards, was the worst one that Washington's starved, ragged, unpaid soldiers would endure. "A wagon load of money," he wrote to John Jay, "will scarcely purchase a wagon load of provisions."[16]

Not that things were going better in Merry Olde England. Antiwar sentiment, fueled by Edmund Burke's speeches in Parliament, reached a fever pitch after Flamborough Head. Prime Minister Lord North, "miserable for ten years in obedience to your majesty's commands," begged George III to let him resign, and was refused. The size of the Royal Navy in America was now down to sixty ships, less than half of them ships-of-the-line or frigates. The First Lord of the Admiralty, the Earl of Sandwich, sent Vice Admiral Marriot Arbuthnot with four ships-of-the-line and 4,000 Redcoats for Clinton's army to New York. Arbuthnot assumed command of the fleet from Commodore Sir George Collier just as Collier was wrapping up his victory at Penobscot. The reinforcements had no sooner landed than they spread their epidemic of "jail fever" to Clinton's healthy troops. Soon thousands were in New York hospitals. By the fall of '79, both sides were tired of this war.[17]

But once Clinton learned that Lincoln's army was holed up in Charleston, he saw the great opportunity presented him. That summer, he had considered a southern invasion, and here was his chance. Washington was too encumbered with bad weather and no supplies to stir from Morristown; d'Estaing's fleet was not even in the hemisphere; and Savannah proved there was a substantial population of southern Loyalists, eager to rally again around Crown troops.

Capturing Charleston would give Clinton a southern port and a base of operations from which an army could strike into the Carolinas—even, perhaps, Virginia itself. Clinton had failed to take the city in 1776; a victory now could regenerate flagging support for the war back home, and wash away that earlier defeat. He informed Lord Germain that he was going to Charleston; Arbuthnot would take him there. After consolidating his remaining New York force with those in Newport, Clinton's 7,600 regulars and Hessians boarded the ships of the British fleet, departing Sandy Hook for Charleston.[18]

For once, Congress correctly anticipated a British move. Seeing such an invasion as not only possible but inevitable, it turned to the four Continental ships docked in Boston and Portsmouth. After their resounding success against the Jamaica Fleet in June, the frigates *Providence*, *Boston*, and *Queen of France*, and the sloop-of-war *Ranger* had returned to their home ports, fortunately too late to take part in the Penobscot disaster. By November they were all refitted and ready for duty. Their captains—Abraham Whipple, Samuel Tucker, John Peck Rathbun, and Thomas Simpson—were so eager to sail that they requested orders.

Days later, they got them: make for South Carolina. "The salvation of that State," their orders insisted, "depends on these vessels." So that he could better serve as commodore, Whipple was given a captain for the *Providence*, the luckless Hoysted Hacker.[19]

After three weeks of sailing through a series of storms, Whipple's squadron was off Bermuda when another vicious tempest struck. The *Providence*, *Boston*, and *Ranger* each lost a mast—but it was the *Queen of France* that gave Whipple the most concern. "If the gale had continued twelve hours longer she would have foundered," he wrote Congress. After capturing a brig, the ships sailed up Rebellion Road, docking in Charleston harbor on December 23. There, Rathbun and the other captains assessed the damage to the *Queen*, deeming her unseaworthy.[20]

Charleston sits on a peninsula, with the Ashley River to its west and the Cooper River to the east. To the south, Fort Johnson had been built on Jones Island. To the north, on Sullivan Island, sat Fort Moultrie. There were fewer fortifications on the peninsula north of Charleston. Since his arrival, General Lincoln had worked on strengthening the city's defenses. He had 2,000 Continental soldiers with him, and Governor Rutledge sent out a call for militiamen. However, rumors of a smallpox epidemic in the city kept them back.[21]

Whipple was ordered to place himself under Lincoln's command. Their first meeting was cordial. Like Whipple, Lincoln was a New Englander—a Massachusetts man. Both men were portly, but Whipple's dark, leathery features contrasted with Lincoln's shock of white hair and fair complexion. Over the coming months they would be significantly more cooperative than Saltonstall and Lovell were at Penobscot.[22]

On January 6, 1780, Whipple sent out Simpson and the *Ranger* along with the schooner *Eagle* to assist a Spanish ship that had run aground twenty miles above Charleston. They returned five days later with alarming news: the schooner had sighted a British transport carrying troops from New York. Word quickly spread throughout Charleston, and Lincoln ordered Whipple to send two more ships out, one north and the other south, to seek the whereabouts of the enemy fleet. Whipple took the *Providence* out himself, along with the *Ranger*.[23]

The cruise lasted just a week. While the *Providence* took a brig loaded down with New York Loyalists, both ships were chased back to Rebellion Road by British two-deckers. Once back in Charleston, Whipple met with Lincoln and Rutledge, delivering the long-feared news his prisoners had told him: 140 sail had departed New York in December, escorted by five ships-of-the-line and six frigates under Arbuthnot. Among them were the former Continental frigates *Virginia* and *Raleigh*.[24]

The British fleet arrived off South Carolina at the end of January after four weeks of stormy seas that scattered the transports for miles. One army officer, George Philip Hook, described the harrowing storms vividly: one transport leaked so badly her captain "was oblig'd to sink her." Hook was "in doubt whether we may gain our destin'd Port." Hundreds of horses suffered broken legs from the pitching of the ships and had to be destroyed. One transport was forced to dock in Bermuda; another, carrying Hessians, was blown so far off course she made for the nearest port for repairs—Cornwall, England. Nonetheless, the fleet arrived. On February 11, Arbuthnot landed 5,000 troops on Simmons Island.[25]

Rutledge placed the state navy, consisting of two ships, a brig, and several row alleys, under Whipple's command, and gave the commodore authority to press as many sailors as he might need—even giving him a warrant to conduct house searches along the waterfront for any reluctant recruits (Whipple wisely gave this task to a South Carolina officer). As part of his strategy, Lincoln wanted to use the ships as floating batteries, moored broadside to broadside to keep Arbuthnot's ships from easily entering the harbor. He asked Whipple and his captains to take soundings inside the bar.[26]

Their unanimous findings were not what Lincoln wanted to read or hear. If a strong wind blew from the east while the tide was coming in, it would be impossible for the American ships to safely ride at anchor with their broadsides ready. Furthermore, the combination of wind and tide would allow enemy ships to sail right past the anchored Americans, permitting them to sail close enough to shell both Fort Moultrie and Charleston itself.[27]

Lincoln was stunned. He had hoped the combination of the high sandbar and the massed firepower of the Continental warships would thwart any British offensive by water. He now questioned whether defending Charleston would be worth the cost in casualties, ships, and risk to civilian life and property. But Charlestonians, led by Lieutenant Governor Christopher Gadsden, would not hear otherwise. Gadsden had been an early advocate for the navy, had watched its ships serve at the whim of northern interests, and was not about to see four of the remaining vessels leave Charleston in the lurch. Whipple conducted another series of soundings, but they produced exactly the same result; his ships could not keep Arbuthnot's cruisers from coming into the harbor if nature did not cooperate.

Whipple recommended that the *Providence*, *Boston*, and *Ranger* move up the channel, join Fort Moultrie, and defend the city there. "The Channel is so narrow between the Fort," he argued, "that they may be moored so as to rake the Channel and prevent the enemy's troops being landed to annoy the Fort." Lincoln acquiesced. Whipple sent a detachment of marines and sailors to destroy the lighthouse. Seeing that Fort Johnson would be more of a hindrance than a defense in the coming battle, the marines leveled that as well. The *Queen of France* and the state navy vessels were sent up the Ashley River, past the Baker plantation that Nicholas Biddle loved to visit, with orders that Rathbun fire a gun three times at one-minute intervals when he sighted any British ships.[28]

Once the smallpox rumor proved false, Lincoln had about 5,000 Continentals and militiamen to defend Charleston. If Clinton sustained enough losses in his attack, the Americans might repeat their victory in '76, but few thought so: the British had taken both New York and Philadelphia by land and water and, if it came to a siege, it would be only a matter of time before Charleston fell.[29]

As if Whipple did not have enough to contend with, his men soon faced shortages of both trousers and rum. To address the former, he sent the ships' pursers ashore to impress any empty pairs of pants or bolts of cloth to stitch new ones. As to a solution for the latter, he put the men on half rations, then switched to an allowance of two quarts of beer a day, believing it "vastly better for health" than drinking large quantities of bad water. After sending Congress a report about the *Queen*'s deplorable condition, he received orders to fill her hold with rice and have Rathbun sail her to Philadelphia, where the market was good for selling rice. Only Congress.[30]

Any serious concerns over rum, beer, and rice were cast aside on March 4, when Arbuthnot's warships approached the bar. He ordered Andrew Snape Hamond and the other captains to remove their guns, water barrels, and other provisions. At high tide the depth was nineteen feet—just enough water to get the frigates across the bar. Hamond was particularly careful with his beloved *Roebuck*; having run her aground four years earlier in the Delaware, he did not want to make that mistake twice. For the next sixteen days, under peppering fire from the state navy vessels and Whipple's captured brig (now called the *General Lincoln* and commanded by Hoysted Hacker), British captains rearmed and re-supplied their ships. On March 20, the strong east wind Whipple had feared arrived with the rising tide, and Arbuthnot's ships crossed the bar. The British lion was in the henhouse.[31]

Samuel Tucker, with the other Continental captains in tow, proposed that a boom, consisting of chain, rope, expendable vessels, and enough anchors to secure them, be laid across the channel—it might prevent Arbuthnot's ships from getting any closer to Charleston. Lincoln and Whipple approved the idea, and for two weeks Yankee sailors, southern militiamen, Charleston citizens, and plantation slaves toiled to complete the obstruction. And each day Clinton's army inched closer to Charleston.[32]

At a council of war in Whipple's cabin, Lincoln interrogated the naval officers. Would the boom stop or at least delay the enemy? Would their ships and the guns of Fort Moultrie be a match for Arbuthnot's firepower? Was there anywhere on the Cooper River where the ships could hold back the British? The answer to each question was no. The captains recommended that the three Continental ships head farther upriver, and Lincoln reluctantly agreed.

Accordingly, Whipple sent the ships to Gadsden's wharf, where their guns were removed and placed at the shore batteries Lincoln had prepared. A host of ships in the harbor were freed from their moorings; led by the *Queen of France*, they were sunk in a long line from the Charleston docks across the Cooper River to Shute's Folly, with chevaux-de-frise anchored between them. Other ships and galleys were sunk at Hog Island Channel. Whipple's officers and crews were sent ashore to serve as artillerymen. The addition of these men to the shore defenses was more than offset on March 25, when 800 North Carolinians, their enlistment up, slipped out of Charleston, hoping to evade Clinton's army and get home. Four days later, Clinton's numbers also changed, with the addition of 1,400 troops from Savannah. He now commanded close to 10,000 men.[33]

The ring continued to tighten when, on April 9, with ideal conditions of wind and tide, Arbuthnot's frigates ran the gauntlet of fire from Fort Moultrie

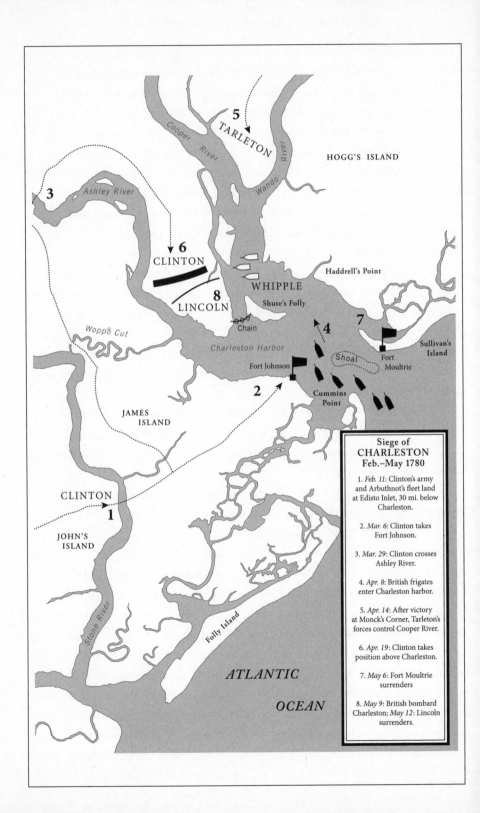

5
TARLETON

COOPER River

WANDO River

HOGG'S ISLAND

3
Ashley River

6
CLINTON

WHIPPLE

Haddrell's Point

8
LINCOLN

Shute's Folly

Chain

Woppo Cut

Charleston Harbor

4

7

Sullivan's
Island

Fort Johnson

Shoal

Fort
Moultrie

2

Cummins
Point

JAMES
ISLAND

CLINTON

1

JOHN'S
ISLAND

Stone River

Folly Island

ATLANTIC

OCEAN

Siege of
CHARLESTON
Feb.–May 1780

1. *Feb. 11*: Clinton's army
   and Arbuthnot's fleet land
   at Edisto Inlet, 30 mi. below
   Charleston.

2. *Mar. 6*: Clinton takes
   Fort Johnson.

3. *Mar. 29*: Clinton crosses
   Ashley River.

4. *Apr. 8*: British frigates
   enter Charleston harbor.

5. *Apr. 14*: After victory
   at Monck's Corner, Tarleton's
   forces control Cooper River.

6. *Apr. 19*: Clinton takes
   position above Charleston.

7. *May 6*: Fort Moultrie
   surrenders

8. *May 9*: British bombard
   Charleston; *May 12*: Lincoln
   surrenders.

and the shore batteries. Newspaperman Peter Timothy watched transfixed as the British warships came on: "They really make a most noble appearance, and I could not help admiring the Regularity and Intrepidity with which they approached . . . tis Pity they are not Friends!"

One by one, beginning with the *Roebuck*, the frigates took the heavy fire from the fort, returning it double-fold. Hamond's frigate, "after putting out Fire on both Side[s]," passed unharmed. One transport carrying naval stores, the *Acetus*, was damaged so badly by the American cannonade that she ran aground and had to be abandoned and burned. But the other ships got through with minimal damage and casualties—twenty-seven men killed and wounded.[34]

The next morning, Clinton and Arbuthnot sent a message to Rutledge and Lincoln. "Regretting the effusion of blood and the distress which must now commence," they warned "of the havock and devastation . . . from the formidable force surrounding them by land and sea." Save yourselves, they concluded, or face the consequences. Lincoln replied that "duty and inclination" dictated that the Americans decline this kind offer.[35]

If Lincoln had any lingering doubts about continuing resistance they were dismissed out of hand by Rutledge and Gadsden—Charleston would not surrender. Clinton's forces soon established a beachhead on Sullivan's Island, seizing the rebel batteries there. Thirty miles from Charleston, at Monck's Corner, Lieutenant Colonel Banastre Tarleton's cavalry, "the British Legion," routed five hundred mounted troops under General Isaac Huger. With most of their horses killed during the southbound passage, Tarleton's dragoons were forced to ride "tackies," the small but hardy horses native to the Carolinas, hardly dashing mounts for Tarleton's green-coated horsemen. After their victory they had plenty of suitable steeds. Charleston was now completely surrounded. Clinton began bombarding the town.[36]

For a month the Americans held out despite the intense shelling. The firing from Arbuthnot's ships was especially devastating; one British officer sneered, "Send twenty-four-pound shot into the stomachs of the women to see how they will deliver them." Fires broke out throughout the town from the ceaseless cannonade; one shot smashed a statue of William Pitt brandishing the Magna Carta. Again, Clinton called for Lincoln to surrender. Again Lincoln refused.[37]

Throughout the siege, Continental sailors manned their guns, returning fire as best they could. Along with Lincoln's quartermasters, Whipple's pursers kept watch over their rapidly dwindling supplies of food and ammunition. Fort

Moultrie fell on May 5; three days later, Lincoln was informed that there was enough food to last five more days. For the past month, Clinton had conducted the siege efficiently but not ruthlessly. Now he acted otherwise. On May 11, British guns poured hot shot into the city, setting hundreds of roofs afire. Clinton planned an all-out assault for the next morning, but it was unnecessary. Lincoln surrendered.[38]

The fall of Charleston was bad enough, but the surrender of Lincoln's 5,000 soldiers and sailors made it the greatest American defeat of the war. Clinton also captured 400 cannon, 5,000 muskets and pikes, and Arbuthnot gained three more ships for his fleet: the *Boston* (now the *Charlestown*), the *Ranger* (now called the *Halifax*), and the *Providence* (which kept her name). On May 15, Whipple, Tucker, Simpson, Rathbun, and Hacker petitioned Arbuthnot for paroles, promising to refrain from taking up arms until notified that they were exchanged for Royal Navy officers of suitable rank. Their request granted, they sailed for Philadelphia aboard the cartel *Friendship*.[39]

As crushing as Clinton's victory was to Washington and Congress, it was a tonic to the British, especially at home. Lord North's government had been in danger of toppling, due to a financial panic and increasing opposition to the war—both in Parliament and in the streets of London, where "King Mob" ran amok in the anti-Catholic Gordon Riots. King George had to send for Lord Amherst and his army to quell a riot that many feared could start a civil war. One Irish politician declared, "The English Military seem determined to conquer North America, if they beggar the nation."[40]

Clinton's triumph over the rebels did give heart to English Tories and American Loyalists. From New York, exiled Pennsylvanian Joseph Galloway believed that most Americans were ready to swear fealty to the king. Clinton and Arbuthnot soon returned to New York, leaving Cornwallis, Tarleton, and 8,000 Redcoats to continue the pacification of the south.[41]

Philadelphians were dealing with a smallpox outbreak when the *Friendship* docked on June 20. Within weeks, all of the sailors, marines, and officers found themselves exchanged except Whipple, as no British officer of similar rank was captured. He would remain "on the beach" for the remainder of the war, but he had no regrets, having "bent our whole force and strained every nerve for the defense of the town."

With the rapidly diminishing number of Continental vessels, Tucker, Rathbun, and Simpson also saw their naval careers come to an end. After Charleston, the navy was down to five ships: the frigates *Alliance, Confederacy, Deane,* and *Trumbull*, and the sloop-of-war *Saratoga*—the same exact number the navy had started with nearly five years earlier.[42]

As General Lincoln and Commodore Whipple surrendered Charleston and the last squadron of the Continental Navy, Captain number 1 was, for the first time since receiving his commission in 1776, sailing a frigate into the Atlantic.

Since September 1779, when Congress rewarded James Nicholson's farcical loss of the *Virginia* with command of the frigate *Trumbull*, the Maryland native had been in New London, getting his ship ready to sail. Frigate and captain were a perfect match—she had never been to sea, either. As with the *Virginia*, Nicholson took months to get to sea, much again to Congress's consternation. In fairness, Nicholson had parochial issues to deal with; like Barry and Jones, New Englanders considered him a "foreigner," a southerner being just as alien as the Irish Barry or the Scottish Jones.

By the spring of 1780, Nicholson had rounded up a crew of 199, most of whom he described as "green country lads" who did not know a keelson from a gunwale. He did have thirty seasoned marines under Captain Gilbert Saltonstall, Dudley's younger brother. Most of them were veterans of Penobscot.[43]

As the last stores were being loaded aboard the *Trumbull*, the Eastern Navy Board and the Board of Admiralty haggled over where to send the frigate. A proposed cruise to Hudson Bay, with Nicholson leading a squadron of privateers, was immediately refused by Congress, which had already seen how well privateers obeyed navy orders at Penobscot. No, the *Trumbull* would cruise alone until the end of June, then sail for Philadelphia, where a joint venture with the *Saratoga* was planned.[44]

In size, the *Trumbull* was similar to the *Virginia*: more than 125 feet long with a 34-foot beam. Designed for twenty-eight guns, she put to sea with thirty—twenty-four 12-pounders and six 6-pounders. Her sides were painted a burnished yellow. With so many landsmen aboard, Nicholson drilled them whenever their bouts of seasickness allowed. The *Trumbull* sailed smoothly enough, and by late May was 250 miles off Bermuda when Nicholson took his first prize as a Continental captain, the schooner *Queen Charlotte*. The capture was good for morale—most of Nicholson's "green-country lads" were still getting their sea legs, and taking the *Queen Charlotte* did much to steady their nerves.[45]

About ten a.m. on June 1, the *Trumbull*'s mastheader sighted a much larger sail. The ship was to windward, so Nicholson ordered the sails "handed"—taken in—"to keep ourselves undiscovered until she came nearer to us."[46]

Nicholson's ploy worked. Once the distant ship spotted the *Trumbull*, her captain, John Coulthard, changed course, making straight for the Americans. A half hour passed; as she closed in, Nicholson discerned she was not a frigate, but to his eye more "a French East-Indiaman cut down"—another *Bonhomme Richard*. He coolly kept his frigate into the wind. Few, if any, of the crew knew Nicholson had fought in the Royal Navy during the French and Indian War, nor had he shown his warrior side since joining the Continental Navy. He was about to.[47]

Seeing the ship shift her course to come up on the *Trumbull*'s stern, Nicholson called, "Make all Sail!" and brought the frigate through the wind to meet the approaching vessel. Coulthard changed course again, to come up on the *Trumbull*'s beam and see how many guns she carried. For another half hour the ships jockeyed for position, like two gunfighters each trying to put the sun in the other's eyes. Nicholson ordered his smaller sails taken in, hauled up his courses (the large sails set on the lower yards), and "hove the maintopsail to the mast" while clearing the decks for action. He ordered the guns loaded, but their ports closed—he did not want to show his teeth yet.[48]

The approaching ship was on the *Trumbull*'s beam when Nicholson's helmsman turned the frigate, allowing her main topsail to fill and letting Nicholson see both how this ship sailed and how many guns she carried. The oncoming vessel carried twenty-six 12-pounders and at least eight or ten 6-pounders on her quarterdeck and fo'c'sle. She was no British warship but a Liverpool privateer, the *Watt*. As the *Trumbull* picked up speed, Coulthard again took Nicholson's bait and tacked to pursue.

Nicholson spoke to his men. They were going to fight, he told them—a fight he knew they could win. His confident words gave them heart, and "they most chearfully agreed to fight her." After his "short exhortation," he sent Saltonstall's marines to the tops. From his quarterdeck, Coulthard watched them ascend the ratlines and noted how nimbly the *Trumbull* glided through the water, "she having a clean bottom and we foul," he later reported. A burgeoning hold from the *Watt*'s prizes also slowed her down. As to the *Trumbull*, "We took her for one of his Majesty's cruizing frigates," Coulthard recalled. But as the *Watt* edged away, Coulthard fired three shots at the Americans while he raised British colors.[49]

"Wear Ship!" Nicholson ordered his helmsman, and as the *Trumbull* came through the wind he ran British colors up the flagstaff as well "to get peacefully alongside her." But Coulthard was not gullible, and raised a private signal that any British warship in these waters would recognize. The game playing was at an end. The ships were about a hundred yards apart, and Coulthard's gunners had their slow matches lit, their hands cupping them until the order was given to fire.

Nicholson immediately lowered his false colors and ran up the Continental ensign just as the *Watt*'s first broadside slammed into the *Trumbull*. The ships sailed closer—about eighty yards of ocean were between them. "A fine close action commenced," Nicholson called it. The captains gave different orders to their gunners: Coulthard had his men firing on the up-roll, aiming for the *Trumbull*'s deck, rigging, and masts in order to disable her and take her as a prize; Nicholson's men fired on the down-roll, aiming for the *Watt*'s hull—to sink her.

For "five glasses"—two and a half hours—the ships hammered away at each other, sailing so close to each other that at one point the yardarms almost enlaced. At such short range, the gun crews could not miss. In one broadside, Lieutenant David Bill was struck by a piece of langrage—a case-shot with jagged pieces of iron, used by privateers particularly for its lethalness and its effectiveness at shredding rigging. It killed Bill instantly, taking off part of his head. Twice, wads discharged from the *Watt*'s guns set the *Trumbull* afire; once, the Americans returned the favor, forcing Coulthard's men to cut all the larboard netting away to stop the fire from spreading.[50]

The *Watt* carried more marines than the *Trumbull*, but the advantage in the fighting tops belonged to Saltonstall's seasoned men. Over the course of the engagement the privateer's men in the tops were either killed or driven below deck by the Americans' withering and accurate volleys. Standing by Nicholson, Saltonstall beheld a scene he never forgot: "It is beyond my power to give an adequate idea of the carnage, slaughter, havock, and destruction that ensued. Let your imagination do its best, it will fall short."[51]

Despite their limited practice, Nicholson's gunners were effective. A British tar came up a hatchway to the *Watt*'s quarterdeck, shouting to Coulthard that the privateer was "very leaky from a number of shot under water." American broadsides had destroyed all but one pump as well. But Coulthard's men were equally accurate and courageous. "My officers and men behaved like true sons of England," he would later report. They, too, were deadly accurate shots this day. "We were literally cut all to pieces," Saltonstall remembered, "not a shroud, stay, brace, bowling or any other of our rigging standing." Every mast, every spar of the *Trumbull* had been hit repeatedly.[52]

Throughout all this, Nicholson maintained his presence on the quarterdeck, urging his men to continue the fight and oblivious to the dangers around him. Now he ordered his gunners to direct their fire at the *Watt*'s deck, masts, and rigging. Soon "All our braces and rigging were shot away," Coulthard recounted, "and the two ships lay alongside of one another, right before the wind."[53]

Nicholson had every intention of finishing off the *Watt*. But then his first lieutenant approached, pointing out to the captain the tenuous condition of the frigate's masts and rigging. Reluctantly, Nicholson sheered off, hoping to quickly steady the masts and resume the fight. Coulthard, seeing his chance, hauled his wind. The *Watt* began slipping away.

Disregarding the peril to his masts and the fears of his officers that the *Watt* would capture them once any mast came down, Nicholson sent the *Trumbull* limping in pursuit. The painstakingly slow chase went on for eight hours, until the inevitable cracks were heard. From the deck, the exhausted Trumbulls watched as their maintop mast and mizzen top came crashing down. Only the wobbly foremast, "badly wounded and sprung," teetered in place. Before the maimed *Watt* slipped over the horizon, the Americans watched her mainmast go over the side.[54]

Nicholson, still anxious to renew the action, realized that further pursuit was both impractical and imprudent. Eight men were dead and thirty-one wounded—ten of whom died shortly afterwards. Saltonstall had eleven wounds himself—"from my shoulder to my hip; some with buck-shot, others with the splinters of the after quarter-deck gun. I had some shot through the brim of my hat," he wrote home, "but was not so disabled as to quit the quarterdeck till after the engagement." He later stayed with one of his lieutenants, Daniel Starr, "who was out of his head" after nearly being bisected by grapeshot. "I suppose his bowels was mortified," he reported, "as he was insensible to pain."[55]

Disappointed as he was in not taking the *Watt*, Nicholson was nevertheless proud of his men. "No people shewed more true spirit and gallantry than mine did," he wrote Congress. "Many of them [were] not clear of the sea-sickness, and I am well persuaded they suffered more in seeing the masts carried away than they did in the engagement." Of the *Watt*, he was equally effusive in his praise: "I give you my honour that was I to have a choice tomorrow, I would soon fight any two-and-thirty gun frigate [the British] have on the coast of America, than to fight that ship over again."[56]

Both ships reached their destined ports without meeting the enemy or stormy weather. The *Watt* received a hero's welcome in New York. Coulthard had lost thirteen killed and seventy-nine wounded. Combined with the *Trumbull's* losses, only the *Randolph-Yarmouth* and *Bonhomme Richard-Serapis* battles saw a higher percentage of casualties. The *Trumbull* slipped past British warships cruising off New Jersey and New York and reached Boston on June 14.[57]

For more than three years, sailors and politicians had questioned Nicholson's patriotism and courage behind his back (and Joshua Barney right to his face). Gilbert Saltonstall summed up the battle this way: "Upon the whole there has not been a more close, obstinate and bloody engagement since the war. I hope it wont be treason if I except even Paul Jones—all things considered [we] may dispute titles with him." On June 1, 1780, James Nicholson truly was the top captain in the Continental Navy.[58]

Admiral Arbuthnot's fleet was still sailing south through winter storms when, on January 16, John Paul Jones brought the frigate *Alliance* into La Coruña, Spain. When she left Holland on December 27, Jones promised his bickering crew that he would make straight for l'Orient and not take the circuitous route around the British Isles via the North Sea. He intended to sail straight down the English Channel.

He was, at least concerning his route, true to his word. Once the *Alliance* was out of Dutch waters, she sped past the very ships waiting to swoop down on her. In the predawn hours of the twenty-eighth, the mastheader sighted countless lanterns on the horizon. It was Admiral Hardy's fleet. At daylight, a couple of fifty-gun two-deckers stood for the *Alliance*. Jones was boldly flying American colors. While Midshipman Fanning thought, "Those John Englishman who now saw us thought we were pretty saucy fellows," Midshipman Kilby "saw little chance of escape."[59]

Jones thought otherwise. The *Alliance* was sailing under close-reefed topsails. Jones ordered out one reef. His topmen scrambled up the ratlines; climbing out and over the fighting tops, they continued their ascent until they reached the topmast spar. Walking along the footropes, they took out the reef. Jones ordered a second out, then a third. There was a strong blow, but Jones wanted the topsail yards "hauled up taut" to catch as much wind as possible. The *Alliance* immediately picked up speed, and began flying over the waves.

Lieutenant James Degge, Landais's second-in-command, warned Jones that such stress could snap the topmast. "She will either carry this sail or drag it," Jones calmly replied. The two-deckers receded into the distance. Running up to ten knots (it seemed like fourteen to young Kilby), the *Alliance* escaped the entire fleet. "In four hours we run every one of the ships hull down," Kilby bragged.[60]

The cruise did not meet Jones's expectations. "I encountered several ships but they all flew neutral flags," Jones reported, making only one capture, an English brig in which Jones placed a prize crew and sent her to France. His only other "prize" came after running down a Dutch brigantine, releasing her only after he swapped cooks—a petty act that later caused more diplomatic problems for Jones. On January 16, under "Fresh Gales and Dirty Weather," the *Alliance* reached La Coruña, Spain—a port that his fellow captain Gustavus Conyngham knew all too well.[61]

Having been promised landfall at l'Orient, the Alliances wanted no part of La Coruña at all. Jones passed l'Orient by because he had no prizes to triumphantly bring into port. Visiting Spanish dignitaries, whose long fingernails and ornamental finery contrasted with the crew's rags, were received in Jones's cabin. Had they gone below, they would have exposed themselves to the vermin feasting on the sailors and the multitude of rats running free. Four months had passed since Flamborough Head, and all the crew had to show for it was one ducat each, given them in Holland.

When roused to their duties on the morning of January 19, many refused to work. Jones sent his officers back into the fo'c'sle, waving their swords and driving the men on deck, where Jones waited for them. Instead of berating them, he "pledged his word and honor" that once in l'Orient he would get them paid. Since leaving Holland, Jones had been aware of a rumor in the fo'c'sle that a chest of money had been brought on board the *Alliance* before departure—and that Jones had kept the money for himself. He, too, he told them, was unpaid. After he issued a double allowance of grog to all, peace was restored—for the time being.[62]

After the *Alliance*'s yards were shortened (the ever-tinkering Jones believed her over-sparred), she was careened, resupplied, and "smoked"—fumigated of rats and lice by closing the hatches and ports while filling the decks with smoke pots—she sailed from La Coruña on January 28. One officer remained, with Jones's permission: Conyngham had learned that an American merchantman, the *Experiment*, was awaiting stores to take back to Philadelphia. Anxious to see his wife and family after his long imprisonment, Conyngham accepted the captain's offer to accompany him, with Jones's blessing.[63]

Once at sea, Jones called his officers into his cabin. They were still a contentious lot, Landais's men continually at odds with Jones's. Worst of all was Degge, who fought when he drank, and he drank too much (Fanning described the wardroom as a "wrangling, jangling . . . source of discord"). Once the men were assembled, Jones told them his plan to cruise the Bay of Biscay for prizes: he did not want to sail into l'Orient empty-handed.

In a rare show of agreement, the officers from both factions rebelled, telling Jones "his crew were then in a state bordering on mutiny." Jones became irate. "I aim to cruise as I please," he barked, before stamping his foot and dismissing them. For two weeks, he desperately sought a prize but took only a captured French bark so "Weak & Leaky" he had to sink her. The *Alliance* made l'Orient on February 11.[64]

The stress of the past six months was visible in Jones's face. Fanning wrote how the haggard captain nervously paced the quarterdeck, biting his lip when he was not talking to himself. "I am almost blind with sore eyes," Jones himself claimed. Before leaving La Coruña he accosted the bosun over an alleged affront, drew his sword, and threatened to run the man through. No one aboard the *Alliance* needed shore leave more than her captain.[65]

Once in France, Jones learned he was getting his earlier wish to sail to America. Franklin had amassed a huge shipment of uniform cloth and military supplies for Washington's army. Two diplomats, Arthur Lee and South Carolinian Ralph Izzard, were also going home. Ever the agitator, Lee insisted that the *Alliance*'s hold carry his latest bauble—a large coach. Jones refused.[66]

Jones was walking the dock streets of l'Orient one day when he accidentally encountered Philip Landais. The Frenchman immediately drew his sword, challenging Jones to a duel then and there. Jones turned his back and walked away, but Landais followed him up and down the waterfront, swinging his sword before him, spitting imprecations all the way. Jones found refuge in the room of an acquaintance, the Chevalier de Portigibaud, a young nobleman awaiting passage to America. Upon entering, Jones shouted, "Shut the door!" Portigibaud knew Jones was brave, but also sensible. Jones was no swordsman, and Landais had proven his talents with a blade too many times.[67]

Lee's frivolous demands and Landais's threats were not at the top of Jones's agenda—he had promised to get his men paid, and he wrote to everyone, including Franklin, Morris, and agent James Moylan, pleading their needs. To Edward Bancroft, Franklin's secretary and England's spy, Jones railed against "the shameful wrongs" his men were enduring. He returned to his old habit of seeing conspiracies where there were none, convincing himself that the cuckolded Chaumont was behind the delay. He decided to go to Paris and get the money himself. He also wanted to see if a hero's welcome awaited.[68]

He arrived in Paris to find his fame blooming with the spring flowers.

Though Sartine was indifferent to Jones at best, the rest of Paris lay at his feet. He was mobbed in the streets, cheered in the theater, and given a showstopping ovation at the opera. The renowned sculptor Houdon made a bust of him; royalty opened their salon doors; and the Lodge of the Nine Sisters—the greatest Masonic lodge of all—welcomed him as a member.

The climax of his triumphal stay came from King Louis, who presented him with a gold-hilted sword, engraved "To the valiant avenger of the sea." Louis wanted to make Jones a member of l'Ordre du Mérite Militaire with the rank of chevalier. In between his social obligations Jones pled his men's needs for money and clothing, and advocated his latest plans for another raid, perhaps commanding a ship-of-the-line or even a fleet. After receiving promises that a percentage of the back pay would be distributed, Jones turned his attention to the ladies.[69]

Although his sour relationship with both Mme. de Chaumont and her husband led him to find lodgings elsewhere, ladies of the court received him; countesses and courtesans pursued him. He gave them his poems and locks of his hair. He fell hardest for Charlotte-Marguerite de Bourbon, Madame la Comtesse de Lowendahl, married to an idle general. If American officers and politicians took mistresses to learn French (and other things), Charlotte saw Jones's advances as an opportunity to further her husband's career, and she found Jones an ardent suitor. Charlotte possessed a beautiful singing voice, and with each *chanson* he became more determined to win her heart.[70]

It fell to America's most famous Parisian flirt to bring Jones to his duty if not his senses. Franklin ordered him to return to l'Orient, load Washington's supplies aboard the *Alliance*, get Lee and Izzard aboard, and sail for America "with all possible Expedition." At the same time when Franklin recalled Jones to his responsibilities, Charlotte returned him to reality. While "touched by the feelings you have for me," she could not answer them "without deceiving a gentleman I live with." Jones departed Paris without her love—and without full pay for his sailors.[71]

When he arrived in port he found more trouble than he had anticipated—not from his men but from Landais. The Frenchman had been wooed by Arthur Lee to wrest command of the *Alliance* from Jones, a move that could accomplish three objectives for the ever-scheming Virginian. It was a slap at Jones, an embarrassment to Franklin, and a way to get Lee's coach and himself back to America sooner rather than later. Landais orchestrated a petition from his original officers to Franklin, demanding that the *Alliance* be returned to him.

Having reminded Jones of his duty, Franklin now reminded his officers of theirs: if they ran into the enemy at sea, Jones would fight, whereas Landais would run. The old minister also warned Jones of what he was returning to, appealing to his "prudence" in handling these two malcontents.[72]

By the time Jones arrived in l'Orient on June 9 the trap was set. Lee had emptied the *Alliance*'s hold of Washington's supplies and replaced them with his carriage and bags. Surprisingly, Jones did not argue, but went to find another American ship to carry them. On June 12, under brilliantly blue skies, Fanning watched as Landais, "to loud huzzahs," came aboard the *Alliance*. But rather than face another challenge at sword's point from Landais in front of the men, Jones decided to return to Paris. Let Sartine and Franklin remove Landais.[73]

Jones's round trip was made quickly for 1780—just eight days. He returned with orders from Louis XVI himself to retake command of the *Alliance*. The king also ordered l'Orient officials to run the long boom out across the harbor and, if need be, fire the fort's guns at the frigate should Landais attempt to leave port. All Jones had to do was have himself rowed out to the *Alliance* with French gendarmes to both back him up and bring Landais ashore, and then, after two long years' absence, Jones could sail home, where he would again be hailed the conquering hero.[74]

Jones's decision to keep fighting the *Serapis* after his own ship was literally wrecked had made him a legend; now came another decision that would alter his career. Everything was in place to return him to his quarterdeck. If he went aboard the *Alliance*, he went home. Furthermore, while it meant sailing with a troublesome crew, he was still captain of the finest ship he had yet commanded, and Landais, disgraced, would return to France, probably forever.

If Jones stayed, however, he might receive what he wanted more than a frigate—a ship-of-the-line or another squadron with which to raid England— but he would also be disobeying his orders. Jones's decision had ramifications for Washington's army, his standing with officials on both sides of the Atlantic, and his own future. What to do?

Jones's dilemma, difficult as it was, paled in comparison to Gustavus Conyngham's problems.

After several weeks in La Coruña, two months in Holland, and a year at Mill Prison, Conyngham was looking forward to getting home. The merchant ship carrying him, the *Experiment*, left the Spanish port shortly after Jones's departure aboard the *Alliance*. She slipped past the cruisers patrolling European waters and headed into the wintry Atlantic. If the weather gods smiled, and his luck held out, Conyngham would be reunited with his wife and family by springtime.[75]

It was not to be. One day the *Experiment*'s mastheader sighted several sails on the horizon. They immediately pursued the merchantman and overtook her. They were British men-of-war based in Newfoundland, then under the governorship of Admiral Richard Edwards. The *Experiment*'s captain surrendered; Conyngham was once again the king's prisoner. It was St. Patrick's Day.[76]

Admiral Edwards came from a navy family. He was a seasoned tar with reputation among the rebels for fair treatment of prisoners. But while Edwards did not abuse Conyngham as Collier had, he wasted no time in deciding what to do with him. After detaining Conyngham for only a short time in Nova Scotia, Edwards made arrangements to return him to England.[77]

News of Conyngham's recapture reached New York first, then Philadelphia; the report stating that Conyngham, guilty of "high treason," was being sent back to the "Mill prison Lodge." On the passage back to Plymouth, Conyngham caught a fever; by the time he reached Plymouth he was deathly ill.[78]

Such news struck Anne Conyngham especially hard. She was only twenty-four, with small children to care for. Beside herself with worry, Anne decided to do the unthinkable: she would go to France. She asked Gustavus's cousin, David Conyngham, to book passage on one of the Conyngham & Nesbitt ships. His partner, Jonathan Nesbitt, was conducting the company's affairs in l'Orient; once she arrived, he would see to her comforts. On the day of the ship's departure, Anne turned her children over to her family for care and climbed the gangplank, well aware that if the ship went down in a storm she might very well be making her children orphans.[79]

Being related to the firm's partner, Anne was certain to be well treated by the ship's crew. The sea would be another matter. This was no packet—the firm was in the business of transporting goods, not passengers. It is probable that the ship's captain gave her the best amenities aboard. As with any landsmen, Anne spent at least the first two weeks battling seasickness, her nausea worsened by the stench below deck as much as the pitching seas. There was an initial shock as she dealt firsthand with the abject conditions aboard. Abigail Adams, after her first voyage to France to be with her husband, wrote, "No Being in Nature was so dissagreable as a Lady at Sea." Anne learned this firsthand.[80]

While the sailors behaved as gentlemanly as possible, this was still an eighteenth-century ship. Anne had never been in the company of so many strangers—and all men to boot. More often than not they forgot their manners, slipping into their salty language in her presence. When Anne was on deck, she needed the arm of at least one tar to walk (Abigail Adams, ill for much of her first passage, was lashed to a chair when she came on deck.) Somehow, some way, Anne willed herself to get through this ordeal. Several weeks after leaving Philadelphia, the ship passed Île de Groix and reached l'Orient, where Jonathan Nesbitt met her at the wharf, took her in, and successfully talked her out of any idea of going on to Plymouth. "A Journey to England would be attended with many difficultys and disagreeable Circumstances," he said, and what would happen if Conyngham was exchanged while she was en route to Plymouth? Nesbitt sent word to Conyngham that Anne was in France, "determined to stay here until she hears further from you."[81]

Earlier, Anne had written Benjamin Franklin a missive similar to her heartfelt petition to Congress in 1779. Unaware that the commissioner was already arranging for money and assistance to her husband, while exhausting every diplomatic means to get her "dear Gusty" released, she begged Franklin to "Procure justice for him."[82]

Once more Franklin reached out to Thomas Digges and his other contacts to keep Conyngham in clothing, food, and cash—as well as looking in on his medical condition. The commissioner could not believe the captain's streak of bad luck. Franklin had hoped Conyngham would head for Dunkirk instead of sailing with Jones. Conyngham's presence there could have helped Franklin resolve the ongoing disputes regarding the pay—or lack of it—for those American sailors from the *Revenge* who had not sailed with Conyngham to Martinique in 1778. Now, with Conyngham back in prison, Franklin urged these men to return home, as that was where Conyngham's account books had been sent. In Philadelphia, Congress again resolved to hold an enemy officer in similar confines as Conyngham, until he was exchanged or paroled.[83]

Conyngham's health deteriorated to the point where he was transferred from the Black Hole to the hospital. It took him weeks to recover. Nesbitt tried to get him some money, but the "person in London employ'd to pay you"—Digges—"has constantly declared that he found it impossible." Upon learning that the British officer Congress ordered held "in close confinement" was released after complaining of a "slight indisposition," Nesbitt complained that "Americans in the power of the English are treated like Dogs or worse than Dogs." With his health shattered and no money for sustenance or to bribe the venal Mill Prison guards, things never looked so bleak for Gustavus Conyngham.[84]

Even in winter, the island of Martinique has its balmy days. But for Seth Harding, the beginning of 1780 was becoming his winter of discontent.

For weeks, Harding had overseen repairs aboard the battered *Confederacy*, dealing with the dawdling pace it was taking to get his frigate seaworthy. Both he and Congress's agent, William Bingham, worried that the long layover was having a deleterious effect on the *Confederacy*'s hull, lying so long in the warm salt water. There were other problems as well. Most of the crew was ill and others had deserted. Harding soon had international troubles with friend and foe alike regarding his men; the French admiral La Motte Picquet took the several dozen Frenchmen Harding had picked up in New England, taking thirty American hands for good measure.

While Marine captain Joseph Hardy saw this as "a good riddance of Lubbers," the loss of men was difficult for Harding, especially when his British sailors began making trouble. Most of them had been captured from British merchantmen. The arrival in March of a huge French fleet under Luc Urbain de Bouëxic, Comte de Guichen, was followed by rumors that a British fleet under the legendary Admiral Sir George Brydges Rodney was also approaching Martinique. Taking heart, the British tars erupted in mutiny, quelled by Harding's marines only after clapping them all in irons. Between French press gangs and British mutineers, Harding had just lost half his crew.[85]

Before the *Confederacy* put to sea, Harding accepted an offer from Guichen to join his fleet; the French were going to hunt for Rodney. At the last minute, Harding received a message from Bingham—Congress had finally sent orders for Harding to sail to Philadelphia. While Guichen's ships sailed into battle, the *Confederacy*'s hold was filled with sugar and cocoa. The *Confederacy* left St. Pierre escorting a convoy of merchantmen, firing a thirteen-gun salute to Guichen, who returned the compliment with eleven. Harding was well on his way when, on April 17, Guichen met Rodney off Martinique in a daylong battle that ended in a draw. It was the closest a Continental ship came to participating in a battle between the French and British navies.[86]

One day of sailing was all Harding needed to see that luck had not yet returned to the *Confederacy*. Smallpox broke out aboard ship and the new maintop mast sprung, forcing Harding to sail cautiously, bypassing potential prizes all the way north to Philadelphia. The frigate reached Cape Henlopen on April 25; Harding sent a junior lieutenant and six men in a longboat to retrieve a pilot. Instead, they deserted. It was two days before a pilot came aboard to take the *Confederacy* up the Delaware.[87]

In the split second when John Paul Jones decided to let Pierre Landais take the *Alliance* to sea, Jones had convinced himself that his decision was a sound one, both professionally and personally. His official reason for letting Landais go, he told Robert Morris, was "to prevent bloodshed between the allied subjects of France and America." In reality, Jones felt that the price of commanding the frigate was not worth the trouble of confronting the volatile Frenchman or the warring factions of officers and crew of the *Alliance* and the *Bonhomme Richard*. Something better had to be in the offing. All the new chevalier need do was let Franklin and Sartine know he was available. He waited in l'Orient for their reply.[88]

There may have been another reason for Jones to remain in France. After the Countess of Lowendahl dropped him, he was "on the rebound," engaged in a series of trysts with the Scottish-born wife of a French count, whom Jones called "Delia," after the title of a popular song. Whereas the Countess de Lowendahl's letters were a combination of enticing flirtation and cool rebuff, Delia's were unfettered by discretion ("I will love you beyond death") but rife with wild promises ("I have been told that neither you nor your crew have been paid . . . I have diamonds and all sorts of jewelry; I will easily find money").

Jones responded as always, with a burst of his poetry ("All Heav'n laments— but Juno shews / A jealous and superior woe"). However, in another, written in Latin, he seemed to show a different side of himself ("Give [show] your rear to men, your arrow to women"). Though Jones had been smitten with Dorothea Dandridge, and perhaps the Countess Lowendahl, he was not about to commit himself to Delia. But with a noblewoman at his feet, all he needed was Franklin's wise approval of his decision to tarry in France, and Sartine's gift of a ship-of-the-line or squadron, and everything would be perfect.[89]

In early July he heard from Franklin. "If you had staid on board where your Duty lay in stead of coming to Paris, you would not have lost your Ship," he chastised Jones. It was the letter of an exasperated father to a spoiled son, rebuking Jones for finding fault in everyone, including his friends ("You Complain of your friends who are in no fault. They spare you") and crew ("Give your officers and friends a little more praise than is their Due, and confess more fault than you can justly be charged with"). Do this, Franklin admonished, and perhaps "you will only become the sooner for it a Great Captain."[90]

The words stung. Franklin was truly a father figure for Jones. The captain had bewailed his lot to everyone of influence, especially to Franklin, these two years. Jones had endured the slings, arrows, snobbery, and other injustices of

Dudley Saltonstall, Esek Hopkins, John Langdon, and Pierre Landais. How, Franklin pointedly asked, was Jones any different from them?

And yet, in another letter, Franklin announced he had procured another frigate, the *Ariel*. Jones was to fill her hold with the supplies for Washington that Landais and Lee had abandoned on the docks of l'Orient. "You have *Ariel*, for heaven's sake load her as heavily as she can bear, and sail!" Franklin ordered. Despite Franklin's call for urgency, it took all summer for Jones to refit her, reducing her from twenty-six 9-pounders to sixteen, tinkering with her masts, taking on stores. His romance with Delia was interrupted by trysts with the elderly James Moylan's seventeen-year-old bride; in one instance his officers entertained the American agent aboard the *Ariel* while Jones was in Moylan's own boudoir.[91]

One more thing kept Jones from sailing to America: the money still owed him and the men of the *Bonhomme Richard*. The *Serapis* and the other ships had been sold, and Jones demanded to know from the minister of foreign affairs "with certainty in *what banker's hands in Paris* the money will be lodged." He despaired of any American getting his just due. Just before leaving port, he hosted a grand regalia for the officers of the French navy and l'Orient dignitaries, complete with food, wine, fireworks, a reenactment of Flamborough Head, and a tent aboard the *Ariel* that Jones had decorated to resemble a bordello. "Neither cash nor pains were spared," a frugal Fanning recollected years later, still unpaid for his services aboard the *Bonhomme Richard*.[92]

On October 7, the *Ariel*, with several passengers and too much weight in her hold, headed for the Bay of Biscay. That evening, "Wind fell very moderate and the Weather was very Serene," Richard Dale noted. It was the calm before the storm.

At two a.m. the wind returned, building slowly, steadily into an enormous gale. By daybreak the rain was coming sideways, pelting the crew while the wind whipped at their clothes. For three years, Jones had sailed the Bay of Biscay; he had experienced its storms before—but nothing like this. All day and into the night Jones and his men took the storm's blows, changing course, running under bare poles, manning the pumps. The crew was bone-weary, but there was no rest—all hands were needed to fight the storm.[93]

The *Ariel* was between l'Orient and Brest when the winds began driving her towards the treacherous Penmark Rocks. She was soon sailing on her beam ends. When it looked as if nature would win this battle, Jones sent his strongest hands to starboard to drop the best bow anchor, running out its cable to the bitter end.

The tempest was so strong that the anchor could not bite into the sea floor. Jones ordered his men to splice another cable to the first one. At the same time, he ordered the carpenter and his mates, axes in hand, to cut down the foremast. As it fell, the anchor grabbed sand; but in securing itself, the ship now threatened to break apart from the overwhelming pressure between the immovable anchor and the irresistible force of the storm. A series of harsh, grinding sounds came from below deck—the mainmast had unstepped itself. To Dale, it "reeled like a Man Drunk"; everyone aboard knew it would finish the job the storm had started, and destroy the *Ariel*.[94]

Jones now played the last card left him, sending the axmen to cut the loosened shrouds holding the mainmast. They were making their way across the slippery deck just as the gale pulled the chain plates securing the mast out from the bulwark. The mainmast immediately went over the side, taking the mizzenmast with it. Still, the movement of the ship "was so quick and violent," Fanning recalled, "that the most expert seamen on board could not stand upon their legs." For the next two days and nights the *Ariel* rode up and down the tempest's mountains and valleys, tethered by one anchor.[95]

Once the monstrous waves fell to bearable heights, Jones sent the carpenter and mates to jury-rig a foremast and yard, then bent a staysail and jib. Shortly after midnight on the eleventh, Jones had the anchor cable cut. Slowly, timidly, the *Ariel* inched its way back to l'Orient, most of the goods in her hold ruined, but all of her crew alive. Sailing along the coastline, Jones's men beheld one ship after another, wrecked against Penmark Rocks or the battered shore. The *Ariel* reached port on October 13.[96]

People crowding the waterfront thought they were looking at a ghost ship. The *Ariel* was believed lost, but here was Jones, successfully returning in his battered frigate. One passenger wrote Franklin that Jones gave all aboard "a delivery from death." Jones, with understated bravado, summed up the trial thusly: "Never before had a vessel been saved in such circumstances." It sounds like bragging, but both landsmen and old salts recognized what he had done. Years later, Fanning described him best: "He was an excellent seaman."[97]

While the *Ariel* underwent repairs, and praise was lavished on Jones for bringing in one of the few ships that made it into port after the great storm, he returned to his habit of angling for something better than what he had. But with French fleets in action against their ancient enemy, Sartine gave little or no thought to the captain's requests. Franklin, still nettled at Jones for letting the *Alliance* escape his command, was hobbled with the gout and in no mood to resume the role of mentor and savior. By mid-December the *Ariel* was repaired. With her hold full of gunpowder and secret dispatches in his sea chest, Jones bid adieu to Delia, Franklin, and dreams of another glorious raid.

Besides duty, Jones had yet another ulterior motive in returning to America. "My Friends here tell me the new 74 Gun Ship, called the *America* at Portsmouth will be reserved for me," he wrote Robert Morris.[98]

When the summer of 1780 came to an end there were four Continental ships in Philadelphia: the frigates *Confederacy, Trumbull,* and *Deane,* and the sloop-of-war *Saratoga.* The Board of Admiralty originally intended for them to sail as a squadron under James Nicholson, but the *Confederacy*'s repairs took too long for her to return to sea until the end of the year. Only the *Saratoga* was ready to sail.[99]

When completed that summer the *Saratoga* was 94 feet, 2 inches long with a 29-foot beam. Captain John Young had recently completed a successful cruise with other privateers under John Barry's command. The *Saratoga*'s second-in-command was Lieutenant Joshua Barney, who had been exchanged after being captured aboard the *Virginia.* He had recently married the young daughter of politician Gunning Bedford. Congress was happy to see Barney go. Ever since his arrival in Philadelphia he had assailed congressmen, demanding better pay for naval officers. For his top marine, Young enlisted Abraham Van Dyke, at sixty-one the oldest officer in the corps, but recommended highly by General Washington. Francis Lewis, de facto head of the Admiralty, knew Young from their days in New York before the war, and had been Young's champion and mentor in Congress.[100]

Having sent the *Trumbull* and *Deane* on an earlier cruise, Lewis hoped to send the *Saratoga* out with them upon their return. But as the dog days of August waned, he found another responsibility for Young: escort the *Mercury Packet* into the Atlantic. She was taking Congressman (and former president of Congress) Henry Laurens of South Carolina to Holland, in hopes that he would secure a loan of ten million dollars from the Dutch.[101]

The *Saratoga* and the *Mercury Packet* were standing down the Delaware when Congress received a dispatch from Washington, then in New York. Charles Henri-Louis d'Arsac, Admiral de Ternay, had arrived in Newport with seven ships-of-the-line and a small French army under General Jean Baptiste Rochambeau. Now Ternay suggested that a Continental ship sail to Santo Domingo and ask Admiral de Guichen to send four of his ships to reinforce Ternay's fleet. If Guichen sent them, Ternay told Washington, he "could transport your army to

Long Island the beginning of October, and finally decide the fate of America this year." What Ternay proposed was music to Washington's ears—a chance, at long last, to settle his old score with the British army in New York. Washington immediately agreed, and sent the request to Congress. On August 19, it sent a sealed dispatch to Henry Fisher, containing their orders and Washington's directives for Young to carry out Ternay's plan. With Rochambeau's troops and Ternay's strengthened fleet, Washington might end the war.[102]

But Ternay's brainstorm became one more "what if" of the war. By the time Congress's courier reached Fisher at Cape Henlopen, the *Saratoga* and the *Mercury Packet* were well out to sea. En route, Young also passed the incoming *Trumbull* and *Deane*, both short on water. The run of bad timing did not end there. Once at sea, Laurens asked Young to keep the packet company for a few more days. While the packet sailed quickly, the *Saratoga* plodded—her ballast was incorrectly stored. The *Mercury* constantly had to slow down to allow the *Saratoga* to catch up. Finally, Laurens was convinced that his ship was far enough from the British warships forever prowling the coast, and sent Young off on a short cruise.

Days later, the *Mercury Packet* was captured by the British frigate *Vestal*. Laurens weighted down his secret orders and threw them overboard, but the package did not sink. A British sailor picked it out of the water, and Laurens's new destination became the Tower of London. The *Saratoga* returned from her cruise too late to sail on Washington's mission.[103]

While the *Saratoga* was on her shakedown cruise, the Board of Admiralty was besieged with political tempests. Since Ternay's arrival in America, he had been after Washington to place the remaining Continental ships under French command, a proposition that both Francis Lewis and William Ellery opposed. After a series of requests for funds from the Eastern Navy Board, Lewis informed them that Congress was "entirely destitute of cash" regarding the dwindling navy. Some representatives wanted to sell the *Confederacy* and *Saratoga* just to continue financing the *Trumbull*, *Deane*, and *Alliance*, and let the unfinished ship-of-the-line *America* and the frigate *Bourbon* remain on their ways in New England.

To add to the board's woes, James Nicholson returned to being James Nicholson. As he sailed the sluggish frigate *Trumbull* up the Delaware, he beheld the larger, rakish frigate *Confederacy* for the first time. It was lust at first sight, and he made his craving known to Congress. After all, as "Senior officer in the American service . . . I think myself entitled to one of the largest Ships in the Navy but instead of that I have one of the smallest." He also returned to pressing sailors off incoming privateers.[104]

Last but not least, the board received the first detailed reports about the arrival of Landais and the *Alliance* in Boston. Once the frigate was in the Bay of Biscay, Landais put the officers from the *Bonhomme Richard*—including Marine Captain Mathew Parke—in irons. As the ship neared the Grand Banks, the American sailors requested permission to fish—fresh seafood being healthier than the spoiling meat stored below. Landais refused. One day, without explanation, he changed course repeatedly. When he threatened his puppetmaster, Arthur Lee, with a carving knife at dinner, even Lee had enough. Landais was practiced at subterfuge, but he was dealing with a master. Behind his back, Lee organized a mutiny, convincing Lieutenant Degge to wrest the ship from the Frenchman's command. Landais was confined to his cabin, and Degge sailed the frigate to Boston instead of Philadelphia.

The *Alliance*'s arrival gave everyone headaches. Washington was furious at the paltry supplies delivered as opposed to the larger amounts promised. Lee immediately made for Philadelphia, where he joyfully returned to savaging Franklin. For three days Landais refused to leave his cabin until his former marines carried him, kicking and screaming, down the gangplank and to the Navy Board's headquarters, where he haunted the hallways and slept on the floor. Abigail Adams wrote her husband John how "that poor vessel was the sport of more than wind and waves." In l'Orient, Jones also heard that "Captain Landais and the officers quarreled on the Passage, and they took from him the Command and carried him to Boston a Prisoner!" Concerned that his archenemy might be found innocent, Jones demanded to know who would be named to Landais's inquiry and who would lead it. "Who are the Men authorized to sit on that Court?—I have seen such Courts Chiefly composed of mere sailors & Fishermen."

A court of inquiry had to be appointed, and a captain had to be named for the *Alliance*. The trial would require a savvy leader who could navigate through the political chevaux-de-frise of an American mutiny against a French captain commanding an American frigate. The latter required an officer capable of restoring order and purpose to a ship with a history of bad luck, unhappy circumstances, and bad experiences under two very flamboyant commanders.

One man was the answer to both needs. The board sent for John Barry.[105]

CHAPTER TWELVE

✦ ✦ ✦

"SEND THAT SHIP TO SEA"

It will always give me Pain to know that the Public Service has
been delayed by private Bickerings and Animosities.

—ROBERT MORRIS[1]

O n February 11, 1781, the *Alliance* was standing down Nantasket Road
under John Barry's command, heading for l'Orient. At the same time,
the *Ariel* was nearing the Delaware Capes, having left l'Orient on December 18.
She reached Philadelphia exactly two months later.

John Paul Jones had sailed her south before taking the northeast trade winds.
In January, he was a hundred miles northeast of the West Indies when the *Ariel*'s
mastheader sighted a sail: the *Triumph*, a twenty-gun British privateer. Her
captain, John Pinder, immediately began giving chase. With the delayed but
valuable cargo of supplies for Washington in his hold, Jones sought to shake the
Triumph in the dead of night. But dawn found Pinder closing in, looking for a
fight, and Jones decided to accommodate him. After what Jones called a "brief
resistance," Pinder struck his colors.

The *Ariel*'s launch was lowered to bring Pinder aboard. The boat was
alongside the *Triumph* when Pinder quickly ordered "Make Sail!" and fled before
the wind. The weighted-down *Ariel* had no chance to catch the *Triumph*, and
Jones begrudgingly continued on his voyage to Philadelphia.[2]

Jones did not know it, but he had just fought his last battle in the Continental Navy. Barry did not know it, but for all his years of action, his greatest
adventures were just beginning.

Months earlier—on September 10, 1780—Barry mounted a horse and began the long ride from Philadelphia to Boston. The Board of Admiralty had given him command of the *Alliance*, but first, they wanted him to preside over the court-martial of her last captain, Pierre Landais.[3]

The twin assignments would be character building for the tall Irishman. At thirty-five, he had already spent a quarter of a century at sea, acquiring a reputation for courage, maritime skills, and as a captain who could be trusted by congressman and sailor alike. He did not seek this appointment. The past two years he had gone privateering and enjoyed it. His cruises were profitable for him as well as for the shipowners lucky enough to employ him.

Yet he was also burdened with the ramifications of his brother-in-law William Austin's activities. After fleeing Philadelphia for New York with the other Loyalists accompanying Clinton's army in 1778, Austin left an entanglement of financial woes in his wake for his brother, Isaac, and his sister, Sarah Barry, to settle. Because of Austin's treasonous actions, the Pennsylvania Assembly confiscated the family estate, seizing everything from the Arch Street Ferry and the family mansion to the square block of rental properties and slaves owned by the family, leaving only the family pew at Christ Church. Rumors that William was now an officer aboard Loyalist privateers did nothing to aid Barry, Sarah, and Isaac in their attempts to recover the family holdings. Now called back to duty, Barry asked Robert Morris to help clear the family's name and restore their fortune.[4]

Barry had company on his ride to Boston: his second-in-command, Hoysted Hacker, recently paroled after surrendering at Charleston; and Congressman William Ellery, who traveled as far as Rhode Island, where he was to seek both money and men for the *Alliance*. Barry and Hacker reached Boston on September 19, and reported to John Deshon and James Warren of the Eastern Navy Board. A short stroll down the waterfront gave the *Alliance*'s latest captain a chance to see his new command. She was beautiful to behold, but no one was aboard to greet him. The captain's cabin was in shambles. Practically everything, including the furniture, linen, and plate, were gone. Barry needed everything from a crew to dishware.[5]

Among his orders from Philadelphia was the news that James Nicholson had turned his covetous eyes on the *Alliance*. As senior captain, he believed the frigate should be his. But Barry's old friend John Brown defused the issue, citing that

Nicholson was at sea when the vacancy arose and that Barry's "popularity with Seamen" made his appointment an easy decision.[6]

Warren and Deshon had filled most of the officer vacancies, including assigning aged mariner Hezekiah Welch and young Patrick Fletcher as second and third lieutenants. Mathew Parke returned as captain of marines. But Barry's rendezvous for sailors was a failure for several reasons: privateers had a monopoly on sailors in Boston, Barry's last New England venture ended with the loss of the *Raleigh*, and he was still considered a "foreigner" by Boston standards. Besides, everyone believed the *Alliance* was "unlucky."

Barry was on deck one morning when a gaunt youngster came up the gangway. Barry instantly recognized him: it was John Kessler from the *Delaware*. After his escape from Jamaica, Kessler wound up in Salem, "an utter stranger, penniless and wretchedly clad." Upon hearing that Barry was in Boston, Kessler headed there, hoping for a berth. Happy to see a friendly face, Barry appointed him a midshipman on the spot.[7]

Although still occupied with recruiting sailors, Barry began Landais's court-martial on November 20. The court, including Hacker, Fletcher, and Sam Nicholson, conducted business behind the guarded doors to Barry's cabin, where his hot stove provided some warmth against the stiff winds along the Charles. For four weeks, accusations from Arthur Lee, Lieutenant Degge, and other witnesses were heard, often laced with profanity. While Barry at times joined in the laughter that some testimonies provoked, he maintained a steady hand over the daily proceedings, ensuring that the unstable Landais was treated courteously by the court. When the Frenchman requested two weeks to prepare his defense, Barry acquiesced.[8]

The trial resumed on January 2, 1781. After four days of Landais's melodramatic defense, including several theatrical outbursts, the court went into closed session. After a short deliberation, they found Landais guilty of everything: leaving Washington's badly needed supplies on the l'Orient dock, his aberrant behavior aboard ship, and his histrionics in the Navy Board hallways, where he had been sleeping for weeks, "courting persecution." Landais was broken, removed from ever serving in the navy again.[9]

Once this court-martial ended another began, reviewing Degge's conduct. He, too, was dismissed from the navy—a case in which the court sanctioned the mutiny but broke the officer leading it. For Barry, the biggest villain was a man the court could not touch: Arthur Lee, whose machinations Barry summed up as "repugnant." The trials over, he turned his full attention to his new orders from Congress and, indirectly, General Washington himself.[10]

The year 1780 had not been a good one for Washington. With Clinton's successful capture of Charleston, the land war shifted to the south. In August, General Gates's forces were shamefully routed by Cornwallis at Camden, South Carolina. To make matters worse, Washington learned in September of Benedict Arnold's attempt to turn West Point over to the English. Shocked to his soul, Washington called Arnold's betrayal "Treason of the blackest dye."

Now, as 1781 began, Washington watched his dreams of victory and independence unravel in his own camp. Having gone without new clothing and unpaid for a year, a thousand Pennsylvania soldiers mutinied at Morristown, New Jersey, Washington's winter base. He had two of the ringleaders shot. The winter of 1780–81 made the Valley Forge encampments look enchanting. In Philadelphia, Congress was out of money. "We are at the end of our tether," the general wrote.[11]

In an effort to rally support for the Cause, Thomas Paine wrote *The Crisis Extraordinary*, hoping this sequel to *The American Crisis* would succeed in creating a public groundswell to raise new taxes. Paine argued that if the rebellion was defeated, King George would waste no time in having his vanquished subjects pay for the war that subjugated them. After heated debate, Congress decided to ask France for 25 million livres. They chose Colonel John Laurens, one of Washington's dashing young aides, to go to France. Laurens, whose father, Henry, was still imprisoned in the Tower of London, took Paine and Lafayette's cousin, the Viscount de Noailles, along with him to Boston. The *Alliance* would carry them to France.[12]

The trio arrived on January 25, and Laurens presented Massachusetts governor John Hancock with instructions from Washington (ghosted by Laurens himself) to give every assistance in getting the *Alliance* to sea. In a meeting with Barry the following day, Laurens learned that Barry's crew thus far was an unattractive mix of poor sailors unfit for privateers and British prisoners. Some of Barry's Yankee hands recently engaged in a barroom brawl with some French tars. One American died from knife wounds, giving Barry one less name on the muster rolls.[13]

Initially, Barry did not want to sail at all, telling Laurens that the "ancient connexions" his British prisoners had to their homeland would come to the surface either when they sighted a Royal Navy ship or once the *Alliance* got closer to England. However, Laurens would not be dissuaded from his mission, more out of love for Washington than duty alone, and Barry reluctantly agreed to continue trying to round up enough hands.[14]

But no approach brought appreciable results. Another rendezvous also failed. When asked to provide soldiers to serve as marines, General Benjamin Lincoln, now commanding the land forces in Massachusetts, permitted Barry and Laurens to recruit only from the "invalid corps." Hancock let them approach guards from Castle William, but few volunteered. Barry, who had notably thwarted Seth Harding's attempt to impress his privateer sailors one year earlier, now asked the Massachusetts General Court for permission to use press gangs to round up hands. The court said no. When approached by prospective passengers, Barry would take only those who signed affidavits that they would fight if the *Alliance* was attacked. He and Laurens even knocked on sea captains' front doors, begging them to release hands—another fruitless idea.

Finally, on February 5, Laurens went before the Massachusetts General Court to appeal, with passionate eloquence, for a "sum of specie to raise volunteers" from Lincoln's Continental forces. His request was approved, and two days later, he wrote Congress that the *Alliance*, "barely in condition to go to sea," would sail that day for France.[15]

But only Barry's British sailors were more disgruntled than their Irish-born captain. Most of his 236 hands—about 75 percent of the number he needed—consisted of these British prisoners, army rejects, inveterate castle guards, and invalids. "*Alliance* is a fine ship," he reported, but "there was not ten men who could steer her." As best he could, he distributed his seasoned tars and British sailors equitably among the watches. Landsmen were usually whipped into shape with a rope's end; Barry feared that John Lewis, his bosun, would run out of rope.[16]

Once at sea, Barry found "there are no seamen aboard . . . but disaffected ones." He was heading into the Atlantic aboard the finest ship in the navy with the worst crew he would ever command.[17]

John Paul Jones had been absent from the United States for more than three years when the *Ariel* reached Philadelphia on February 18. The contents of his ship's hold—437 barrels of gunpowder, 146 chests of arms—were a help to Washington's army, but far short of the munitions and supplies promised months earlier: 1,000 pounds of gunpowder, 15,000 arms, and hundreds of bolts of uniform cloth. Congress, pressured by Jones's adversary Arthur Lee, handed the captain a forty-seven-question inquiry to learn why so much was guaranteed by the French and so little arrived. While some questions were easy lobs ("What prizes did you take when you commanded the *Ranger*?"), others were clearly Lee's handiwork ("Did any private property come in the *Ariel*?").[18]

If the Lee-Adams faction sought to trip Jones up (and in so doing, skewer Franklin), they were disappointed. Jones navigated his way through the questionnaire with a mariner's sure hand and a sea lawyer's guile (and maybe the help of Barry's confidant and amanuensis, John Brown). Tacking through them as he did, Jones steered to one answer whenever possible: Landais. Ignoring his own decision to disobey Franklin's orders to sail the *Alliance* home, he stressed the frigate's wretched condition, Landais's motley crew and dysfunctional officers, while Jones himself only wanted to "stop the savage burnings and wanton cruelties of the enemy."

Despite this attempt by Lee to undercut Franklin through Jones, Congress was still supportive of the top American in Paris. Barry's report on Landais's court-martial had readily been accepted by Congress, and Jones's answers only corroborated Barry's findings. Jones was not only exonerated but extolled for his "zeal, prudence, and . . . intrepidity." Even before Congress's findings were released, they had already tipped their hand. They approved the request of the Chevalier de la Luzerne, France's minister to America, that Jones be permitted to accept the gold sword and chevalier's rank bestowed upon him by King Louis.[19]

The captain was once again the hero of the hour; Luzerne gave a reception for Jones attended by congressmen and Philadelphia notables (even Washington sent a complimentary letter). When Congress passed the Articles of Confederation, Jones had the *Ariel* festooned with brilliantly lit decorations and fired a salute in its honor. Since his disobedient inaction at l'Orient, Jones had survived a tempest from Franklin, a tempest from God, and a tempest from Lee. All was going well—Jones just needed official command of the ship-of-the-line *America* and the title of "Admiral" to go with her. That spring, he began campaigning for both.[20]

Five days out of Boston, the *Alliance* was making good progress. To John Barry, the only threat to a safe passage thus far was still in the fo'c'sle, where those British prisoners he found necessary to take on kept to themselves—a perfectly natural occurrence, but one that only further aroused Barry's suspicions.[21]

His landsmen, invalid soldiers, and castle guards were just getting their sea legs when the *Alliance* was attacked on the night of February 16, two hundred miles southwest of Newfoundland—not by the British but by ice. It was a moonless night; Barry had turned in hours earlier but was awakened by a loud thud, followed by an unnatural lurch from the ship. Instantly alert, he came on deck to a situation more perilous than a fleet of enemy warships: icebergs dead ahead, to port, and to starboard, looming so high above the *Alliance* that they blocked out the sky. There was no way to gauge how wide, or how close, they were to the frigate's wooden hull. Barry called for all hands.

Thomas Paine, among the first on deck, could not believe his eyes. Laurens, given a cabin near the *Alliance*'s larboard gallery, soon joined him. The bergs were so immense that they robbed Barry of a "true wind"; his ship was a captive of the current. All the helmsman could do was steer, guessing as best he could what the men at the bowsprit could relay to him about the ice heading their way.

Barry summoned his leadman. Once by the rail, the man swung the weight in a circular motion. His shipmates heard the familiar *whoosh* above the lapping sound of the Atlantic before he cast out his line, long enough to descend twenty fathoms. The wax on the weight's bottom caught a berg, yanking the line through his hands, taking some skin from his palms and fingers before he could grab it again. Barry ordered the line heaved a second time. This attempt gave them the fathoms, but no bottom.[22]

By now the wind, coming from behind the *Alliance*, turned into a gale. Barry ordered his topmen aloft to take in every sail just as one was "torn in two from top to bottom." He sent other hands along the rails, armed with spars, bags of cork and canvas used as fenders, even rammers and sponges from the cannons, all to be used in an effort to keep the *Alliance* from any approaching mountain of ice. Barry told Paine, "Nothing could be done but to lay the Ship to and let her take her chance." Against such an adversary the formidable frigate was a fragile construction of wood.

Barry sent the crew off-watch below. Laurens and Count de Noailles joined them, but Paine remained on deck; nothing could keep him from seeing what might happen. "The Ice became every moment more formidable . . . the Sea, in whatever direction it could be Seen, appeared a tumultuous assemblage of floating rolling Rocks, which we could not avoid and against which there was no defence," he recalled. Yankee and Englishman alike, united by a common fear of nature's power, obeyed Barry's orders without question. Their only cause, for the present, was getting safely past this armada of ice.[23]

At eleven p.m., Laurens was just leaving his cabin—or perhaps, the adjoining head—when the ship struck a large iceberg by the gallery. The falling shards of jagged ice slammed through the gallery's roof and just missed killing him. As all hands watched fearfully, the berg passed the *Alliance* with no further damage.

For an excruciating five hours, the flotilla of bergs floated past the *Alliance*. At daybreak, the gale subsided. With unfettered joy, every man aboard watched as the last threatening mass glided by; Barry estimated the ship had sailed twenty miles through the ice. Paine spoke for everyone from captain to cabin boy when he wrote that the harrowing ordeal would not "be easily worn from our memories." Since her maiden voyage, the *Alliance* had been considered by superstitious salts to be an unlucky ship. Perhaps her luck turned that night.[24]

For several days, the *Alliance* made the most of "a glorious breeze." Only an inconsequential duel, fought between Paine and de Noailles for no documented reason, was noteworthy. (For Paine, his pen was mightier than any sword, and de Noailles did not share his countryman Landais's skills with a blade—both parties were unscathed.) But soon the British hands returned to their sullen ways above deck.[25]

Below deck, they were hatching a plot to take over the ship. Their ringleader was John Crawford, whom Barry, short of officers as well as crew, had made a quartermaster. With such responsibilities, Crawford freely roamed the decks, sounding out his fellow countrymen along the way to see who might fall in with his scheme.

Once he had enough willing conspirators, Crawford summoned them to the bowels of the fo'c'sle. Under the dim light of a couple of lanterns, he laid out a murderous plan. On a prearranged signal, the mutineers would seize what weapons they could, subdue the Americans, and kill every officer save one, spared on condition that he navigate the *Alliance* to England or Ireland. Before concluding his meeting, Crawford passed around a "Round Robin"—a paper on which each sailor signed or made his mark in a circular pattern, making each man equal in guilt.[26]

Barry had seen enough surly behavior to warrant extra precautions. He told his officers to keep a weather eye open for any sign of treachery and to keep him informed of any suspicious activity. He put the marines on round-the-clock patrol, moved every padlocked chest of arms aft, and posted a marine on each watch at the locked storehouse door.[27]

The *Alliance* was now off Belle Isle and entering the Bay of Biscay when two ships were sighted; after a quick chase, warning shots brought them to. One was a Scottish privateer, the *Alert*, from Glasgow; the other was her prize, the *Buona Compagnia*, a neutral ship from the Republic of Venice, her hold full of glass bottles, pepper, and indigo—along with her captain and crew.

Barry disregarded the lure of taking the Venetian without a second thought: as a neutral, she should not have been seized in the first place. He ordered captain and crew freed and "left at liberty to pursue [their] voyage." He did place a prize crew aboard the *Alert*, with orders to accompany the *Alliance* to France. Laurens and Paine were elated at Barry's statesmanlike common sense regarding the *Buona Compagnia*, Laurens calling it proof of "the determination of Congress to maintain the rights of neutral powers." Barry's action would later be gratefully acknowledged by the Venetian government.[28]

The *Alliance* picked up two more prizes before reaching l'Orient on March 8, just twenty-six days after leaving Boston—a fast passage, especially for wintertime. Three days later, Laurens and his companions were off to Passy to meet with Franklin and prepare their plea for more money. Laurens also carried a dispatch from Barry to Franklin.

With this letter, Barry began a two-year correspondence with Franklin. It was a detailed report of his passage, requesting that he be allowed to take the American sailors in l'Orient aboard the poorly manned *Alliance*, and permission to have his frigate's hull sheathed in copper. He anticipated a quick reply.[29]

He did not get one. After Barry was asked by American agent James Moylan to escort the French Indiaman *Marquis de Lafayette*—under charter of Franklin's grandnephew, Jonathan Williams, and carrying munitions and clothing for Washington—Barry sent another letter Franklin's way (Moylan, impressed with Barry's demeanor, invited him to stay at his home—an act of trust after Moylan had been cuckolded by Jones.)[30]

Mathew Parke had also written to Franklin, appealing for the money due the members of the *Alliance*'s crew who had also served—and were still unpaid— on the *Bonhomme Richard*. Parke informed Franklin that all of the Americans aboard the *Alliance* were "exceedingly happy in our present Commander"—a comment he did not believe fit Jones nor, obviously, Landais.[31]

Barry's impatience for an answer to his letters was temporarily forgotten due to breaches of conduct by three of his sailors: one for "Gitting Drunk Abusing the Officers & Dam[n]ing the Congress," the other two for merely "Gitting Drunk & Fighting." From his first day as a Continental captain Barry had rarely, if ever, let the cat-o'-nine-tails out of its red baize bag; this was the first documented entry of his taking such action. With substantial concern regarding his British hands, he decided to use the misconduct of the three miscreants as a chance to show what awaited them too if they got out of line.

The grating was placed at the gangway, and the bosun's mate did his duty. But instead of cowing the mutineers, the floggings only hardened their resolve. By now Crawford had decided they would strike once the *Alliance* returned to sea.[32]

Sometime after March 20 Franklin's letter arrived. Barry read and reread it: a pleasant, commiserating note that agreed with Barry about copper sheathing for the *Alliance* and that Barry's request for more American sailors was a grand idea. But it offered neither approval nor assistance.[33]

It is not known if Barry and Franklin ever met. Before the war, while Barry's career as a merchant captain was ascendant, Franklin was serving as the Philadelphia's agent in London. Their ensuing correspondence shows a sea captain looking for answers and a diplomat who rarely gave him any. Whereas Conyngham, Wickes, Sam Nicholson, and Jones all paid visits to Franklin in Paris, falling under both the city's spell and his own, Barry never did. Polite salutations were as friendly as they ever got with each other.

The captain was further encumbered with the *Marquis de Lafayette*. As far as Barry was concerned, her captain, one Monsieur de Galatheau, seemed intent on picking up where Landais had left off regarding Franco-American relations. In addition, Jonathan Williams informed Barry that he suspected de Galatheau was carrying a large quantity of smuggled goods along with Washington's supplies. Barry promised Williams that he would inspect the ship before anything was unloaded in Philadelphia.[34]

Days later, Barry was ready to sail when another letter arrived from Franklin, asking him to delay his departure until a courier reached l'Orient with Franklin's personal and official correspondence for Barry to take to Philadelphia. Citing the supplies for the army in the *Marquis de Lafayette*'s hold, Barry refused. Landais had left Washington's much-needed goods on the l'Orient dock the year before, and Barry did not want to let the general down. Someone else could carry Franklin's letters.[35]

The two ships were no sooner past Île de Groix when de Galatheau stopped obeying Barry's signals. This would never do; Barry ordered the *Alliance*'s pinnace lowered and was rowed over to the *Marquis*. Whether de Galatheau spoke English or Barry had his unsubtle orders translated, he did not depart the French ship until de Galatheau acknowledged—at least for now—who was in charge. After some small storms, the *Alliance* was homeward bound.[36]

The frigate was making eight knots in the black of night on March 29 when the watch heard a splash from the stern. "Man overboard!" came the cry, and all hands raced up the hatchway. As Barry turned the *Alliance* into the wind, all eyes scoured the dark water, looking for some sign of their shipmate. But the sea had swallowed him up. It began raining when Barry gave orders to make sail. "Lost a man over Board," Barry wrote in the log, "named Patrick Duggan." Barry was unaware the man was one of the mutiny's ringleaders.[37]

Duggan's fellow conspirators, however, were mightily spooked. They hastened below to the berth deck, where, hidden by some stored hammocks, they spat out their whispered fears that Duggan's death was a bad omen and the game was up. None admitted having any hand in his death, but more than a few wanted out, and told Crawford to destroy the round-robin; Crawford insisted that the mutiny be carried out, but tore up the incriminating paper round-robin before throwing it into the sea.[38]

The *Alliance* was sailing through the Bay of Biscay when, at dusk, one of the fo'c'sle hands—an American Indian from one of the New England tribes—asked to see Barry. Once in the captain's cabin, he revealed everything he knew of the plot to seize the ship. Sitting in his chair, Barry asked him question after question, pulling the story out of the man until he "Pointed out 3" leading the murderous plan: Crawford and two "Able Seamen," Patrick Shelden and William McEllany.[39]

Barry dismissed the sailor and called for his officers. In a low voice, he laid out his own ruthless plan to quell the mutiny before it could start. The ensuing discussion was carried on in the same hushed, desperate tones as the mutineers' meeting the night before, taking on the feel of a council of war. After determining who among the Yankee hands was capable of joining the marines in bearing arms—Barry could thank the stars he had those castle guards, after all—he sent his officers out to their tasks.

Once on deck Parke armed his marines, sending a detail below to arrest Crawford, Shelden, and McEllany and clap them in irons. Next, Parke assigned the marines in shifts to patrol the deck. Back in his cabin, Barry entered in his log that the three ringleaders were arrested for "~~Mutity~~ Mutiny," the crossed-out misspelling the only betrayal of his anxiety.

Neither American nor Briton slept well that evening, aware that whatever Barry planned for these three men—and God knew who else—would take place in the morning. Throughout the night, they heard his footsteps as he paced the quarterdeck, while the ship's bell tolled ominously with the change of each watch.[40]

At daybreak, Barry brought the *Alliance* into the wind as Bosun Lewis's shrill pipe summoned all hands. The crew scrambled up the hatchway. Hacker ordered them to assemble on the forecastle deck. Once it was filled, sailors took places along the rails. The marines stood at attention, their muskets loaded and bayonets fixed. As Barry descended the quarterdeck, he ordered Parke to bring up Crawford, Shelden, and McEllany. The sound of their clanking chains preceded them as they dragged themselves up the steps, while their British shipmates exchanged silent, worried glances.

After marines unshackled the three, everybody expected that Barry would call "hats off," and read what regulations the men had violated of the Articles of War. To everyone's surprise, he did not; instead, he called out all three names, telling them they were charged with mutiny and that their punishment would be lessened if they named their accomplices.[41]

Barry's offer went unanswered. For an interminable moment, the only sounds came from the *Alliance*, rocking "in irons" on the water, the wind whipping at the lifeless sails. Finally, Barry nodded to Lewis. As his mate took the cat-o'-nine-tails out, the Alliances noticed that the grating was not set up for a flogging.

Lewis and some others grabbed Crawford forcibly, stripping him of his shirt while they dragged him to the mizzen stay. Once there, they knotted small cords around Crawford's thumbs, securing them high enough on the stay that, no matter how hard he tried, he could not touch the deck. As he hung there, the bosun's mate began laying bloody stripes to Crawford's back, as Barry roared angrily at him to name names.

"Twelve stripes" was the maximum sentence in John Adams's Articles of War, but neither Barry nor the bosun's mate bothered to count how many times the cat whistled through the air. Crawford was in agony. As his back was being laid bare, the ligaments and tendons in his hands were pulling away from his bones. And he screamed, and he moaned.

But he did not talk.

Whether Crawford's will was fueled by hatred, courage, or both, Barry could see he was not breaking, and ordered Shelden and McEllany trussed up and whipped as well. At first, their resistance was equal to Crawford's, but eventually they broke, naming one accomplice after another (two of them flogged days earlier for "Gitting Drunk & Fighting"). By eleven a.m., eight more British tars were implicated, but the bosun's mate was so exhausted that Barry gave him a rest, then resumed the flogging until twenty-five more names were whispered or cried out. Barry knew he was violating the articles he had signed on to five years earlier, but this was not an issue of infractions. Lives were hanging in the balance, including his own.

By three o'clock, Barry was convinced that not a man jack aboard would give a split second's thought to a mutiny aboard *his* ship. He sent the ringleaders below, with orders that they remain in irons and on a diet of bread and water. Next, he approached the eight other scourged principals in the plot. "On their solemn declaration to conduct themselves well," they were returned to their duties—as best as they could perform them with their lacerated backs. The lucky unharmed twenty-five pledged the same. "Pleasant weather and Clear. The *Marquis* in Company" was how the *Alliance*'s log concluded that day.[42]

Once in the Atlantic, the *Alliance* and the *Marquis* pursued and captured two privateers, the *Mars* and the *Minerva*. Still suspicious of de Galatheau, Barry allowed him to place a prize crew from his hands aboard the *Minerva* and ordered their commanding officers to make straight for Philadelphia should the ships be separated. Over the next two weeks the vessels sailed through heavy squalls, in which Barry lost another man overboard. The storms also forced him to burn false fires so that the *Alliance* could be seen and followed by the three ships.[43]

His hunch about de Galatheau proved correct. First the *Minerva* disappeared one stormy day (de Galatheau had ordered her back to France); then, on April 25, the *Marquis* took advantage of the *Alliance*'s split foresail to shoot ahead of her, disappearing over the horizon. For days, Barry sailed his frigate back and forth, burning false fires and firing signal guns until, convinced of de Galatheau's duplicity, he sent the *Alliance* westward.[44]

At sunrise on May 2, the mastheader sighted two sail on the weather bow, and Barry gave orders to "make chace." By late afternoon, his bow chasers brought them both into the wind: a brig, the *Adventure*, and a snow, their holds carrying more than five hundred hogsheads of sugar. Even better, in Barry's eyes, were four new recruits: three sailors and a boy who preferred duties on the *Alliance*'s deck to the crowded confines of the *Alliance*'s hold.[45]

Barry's prisoners told him they were part of the Jamaica Fleet, "Ab't 65 sail convoyed by ten sail-of-the-line." Shortly after that, the *Alliance*'s mastheader spotted them all, heading west. Barry kept his distance, slipping away in the night, not knowing that the *Marquis* was not as lucky, having been taken after a three-hour battle with the ship-of-the-line *Egmont* and the frigate *Endymion* (the British towed the *Marquis* to Scotland, her goods assessed at £300,000 sterling).[46]

The *Alliance* had escaped the *Marquis*'s fate, but now horrific weather dogged her passage. "Ruff Seas" and severe gales beset the frigate on almost a daily basis. On May 16, the Alliances were battling another storm when a bolt of lightning split the main topmast in two, flying down the cleaved timber to the deck, where it struck at least a dozen sailors, burning the skin off them. Fighting fire, wind, and water, Barry sent for Surgeon Joseph Kendall. Finding "several much burnt," Kendall took them below to the orlop deck. Miraculously, they all recovered. "I thank God all of them have done well," Barry wrote.[47]

During repairs, Barry assessed his situation. It was grim at best. While a new topmast was stepped in and a new foremast was fished, there was no spar long enough to replace the main yard the lightning had destroyed. Barry was now frightfully short of hands: he had left l'Orient with 241 men, and had taken on eight more from his four prizes. But after three dozen were delegated to prize crews, two lost overboard, three mutineers in irons, twenty others at liberty but under suspicion, and fifty in sick bay from illness and injury, he had 138 hands—fewer than half of what he needed to adequately man the frigate. And there were more than 100 prisoners from his prizes locked in the hold.[48]

Small wonder, then, that when his maspeader spied two unescorted merchantmen just begging to be taken, Barry did nothing. Had he had even twenty more hands, he would have had two more prizes. Instead, he watched them sail unmolested to England, while the *Alliance* sailed as best she could for home.[49]

The frigate was about four hundred miles south of Nova Scotia on the evening of May 28, when the lookout again hailed the quarterdeck—two sail on the weather bow. Seeing the *Alliance*, the ships hauled their wind, tacking to sail parallel to her. Looking through his spyglass, Barry saw they were "an armed Ship & a Brig about 1 League distance." He ordered his helmsman to maintain his course and speed. Soon the "armed Ship" was flying signals that Barry could not understand. He already sensed that the ships were British; now he knew they were unafraid of his larger frigate's "superior force." The wind was slackening; what Barry would have given for one more storm, to shake these wolves.

His pursuers were the sloop-of-war *Atalanta*, Captain Sampson Edwards, sixteen 6-pounders, and the brig *Trepassey*, Acting Captain Smyth, fourteen 6-pounders. Edwards came from a distinguished naval family (his uncle Richard was the admiral so well thought of by New Englanders for his humane treatment of American prisoners). Only in his thirties, Edwards had fought the French at Pondicherry, the Spanish at Manila, and the Americans across the Atlantic.

While the *Alliance* had both ships outgunned by number and weight, Edwards believed the light winds more than evened the odds.[50]

As senior officer, it was Edwards's decision to fight or flee. The *Atalanta* and *Trepassey* maintained their course; as they got closer, Edwards saw that *Alliance* was "a large ship, but not a two decker." That made his choice easier. "Night coming on," he later reported. "We hauled our wind and sailed in sight of her all night."[51]

As the sun rose, Midshipman Kessler watched as the two ships hoisted their colors and beat to quarters. He was not surprised to see Barry do the same.

One witness to Philadelphia's lionization of John Paul Jones in the spring of '81 was neither impressed nor happy about the accolades bestowed upon the hero of the *Bonhomme Richard*.

Once Jones began angling for the ship-of-the-line *America* and to be the navy's first admiral, James Nicholson went to work to undermine him. Having already tried to wrest command of the *Confederacy* from Seth Harding and the *Alliance* from John Barry, he now turned his in malevolent focus on Jones. Nicholson had little else to do; lack of both funding and sailors kept him from taking the *Trumbull* to sea.[52]

As 1780 came to a close, the press gang practices of Nicholson and Harding were being applied to "any privateer or merchant vessel" in Philadelphia by the *Saratoga*'s captain, John Young. On December 7, he stopped a shallop heading down the Delaware. His boarding party found five deserters from the *Trumbull*. Young had them transferred to the *Saratoga*. Two days later, William Will, Philadelphia's high sheriff, was rowed out to the ship. Young met him at the gangway, where the sheriff demanded the return of the deserters, who had signed on with a squadron of privateers owned by influential local merchants. Young refused, and would not let Will come aboard. The indignant Will told Young he was under arrest, promising to return with a warrant for Young, a writ of habeas corpus for the deserters, and a boatload of deputies to back him up. Before leaving, Will added that Young's bond would be set at £500,000—roughly two and a half million dollars. Where there was a way to make the matter worse, there was Will.[53]

Young, in turn, went ashore to tell Francis Lewis of the Board of Admiralty, who saw this altercation as a tipping point for the navy. He went to Congress to seek support for Young and any other captain against any other such "litigious suits" that were also delaying Young's departure for a cruise ordered by Congress.

While the representatives did not act immediately or officially, they did order the Navy Board of the Middle Department to work round the clock to assist Young on his departure.

Days later, the *Saratoga* was ready to accompany the *Confederacy* and escort a fleet of merchantmen to Hispaniola, where Young and Harding would hopefully find Sam Nicholson and the *Deane*. After saying good-bye to his wife, Joanna, Young left Philadelphia on December 17, joining the *Confederacy* at Reedy Island.[54]

Had James Nicholson been one of the two captains, there might have been an issue over seniority. Young, commanding the smaller ship, actually outranked Harding in the larger one, but they sailed amicably together. After gunnery exercises—and pressing six hands off an incoming schooner—the two ships began their escort service.[55]

Once in Delaware Bay, the ships encountered high seas and stiff winds. Harding's pilot, not wanting the embarrassment of damaging one of the few remaining Continental frigates, proceeded so slowly that Young took the merchantmen out to the Atlantic alone. He had redistributed the *Saratoga*'s ballast after her shakedown cruise, and now she responded superbly, overtaking a Loyalist privateer off Cape Henlopen.

On January 9, 1781, the *Saratoga* was four hundred miles off St. Augustine when she encountered another letter of marque, the *Tonyn*, whose twenty 9-pounders were more than enough of a match for Young's vessel. But in a one-hour engagement, Young thoroughly outfought his opponent, and had another prize. Two days later he had a third, the brig *Douglass* from Madeira, her hold carrying three hundred pipes of the legendary wine from that island, meant for the British occupying force at Charleston. A happy Young sent her to Philadelphia, where each pipe sold for more than $300. After five years in the Continental Navy, Young was emerging as one of its finest captains. He arrived at Cap François, the northern point of Hispaniola (now Haiti), to find Harding and the *Confederacy* waiting for him.[56]

Cap François was an elegant city whose harbor had room for three hundred ships. It was called "the Paris of the Isles," rising above the waterfront and below two large mountains. Cap François had grown rich during the war, evidenced by the gentry, bedecked daily in garish tropical colors.[57]

The initial welcome given Young and Harding by Monsieur de Bellecombe, the island's governor, was soon replaced by indignation. An arranged salute by the *Saratoga*'s gunners went horribly awry. One gun burst, killing a sailor and maiming another, while another cannon contained a round of grapeshot, which killed a woman onshore. Seeking to defuse the incident, Young and Harding went to de Bellecombe, claiming the guns had been sabotaged by a British prisoner. To their relief, de Bellecombe let the matter pass. The life of one native woman would not cause a rift between the two allies.[58]

While the merchant captains filled their holds for the return voyage to Philadelphia, the *Confederacy* and *Saratoga* made a short but profitable cruise with a couple of prizes. They returned to find the *Deane* in port, after eight weeks of aimless sailing. The convoy departed Cap François on the Ides of March.

The ships were three days out of port when Young sent the *Saratoga* in pursuit of two ships. The seas were getting rough; as the *Saratoga* closed in, Young was forced to house his guns—the water was rushing into the gun ports. He soon overtook one, a snow bound for London. Young no sooner placed a prize crew aboard her under command of Midshipman Nathaniel Penfield than he sent the *Saratoga* flying after the second ship. The wind blew hard and it began to rain heavily. Penfield sent men aloft to reef in sail, hoping the little snow could ride out the storm. Peering through his spyglass, he saw his captain doggedly chasing the other vessel. Then both ships vanished over the horizon in the driving rain.[59]

While the *Deane* made it back to Boston in April, the star-crossed *Confederacy's* luck did not change. She was making for the Delaware Capes on April 14 with her contingent of merchantmen when a large sail was sighted. Harding signaled his charges to scatter, while he boldly gave orders to stand for the oncoming ship.

She was Andrew Snape Hamond's *Roebuck*, and she was not alone; accompanying her was the frigate *Orpheus*. Seeing the futility in fighting two large men-of-war, Harding struck his colors. After taking her, Hamond sent his frigate and the *Orpheus* after the merchantmen. For five years Hamond had prowled along Delaware Bay; he knew its waters as well as any American captain. Before the sun set, the two frigates had captured most of the merchantmen as well. Hamond triumphantly escorted his latest prizes into New York harbor, where the *Confederacy* was taken into the Royal Navy as the *Confederate*.[60]

Midshipman Penfield may have been the last American to see the *Saratoga* as she sped off in pursuit weeks earlier. The gale took her, John Young, and all hands to a watery grave. Tory newspapers reported Young had been killed in a battle with the HMS *Iris*, while others said that Young, like Conyngham and Talbot, had been sent to England. Both rumors proved false.[61]

For weeks, Joanna Young, wrapped in a shawl to ward off the early-morning waterfront chill, walked daily to the docks of Philadelphia, hoping against hope to see the *Saratoga* sailing upriver. Eventually she stopped going.[62]

"Ship ahoy! What ship is that?"

Since his days as a young merchant captain, John Barry had asked that question through his speaking trumpet. This time he was well aware that this vessel and her consort were British, and spoiling for a fight. But he always observed the traditions of hailing a ship during peace or war. According to Captain Sampson Edwards, the two ships were "two cable lengths away"; Barry guessed them to be "within pistol Shott."[63]

"*Atalanta*, Sloop of War, belonging to His Britannic Majesty," Edwards replied.

Barry watched as the other ship, the brig *Trepassey*, inched closer as well. The wind was dying by the minute; any sailor could see the spreading stillness across the ocean, now resembling a mirror—and still as glass.

"This is the Continental Frigate *Alliance*, John Barry. I advise you to haul down your colours," he said.

"I thank you, Sir," Edwards continued, hoping to pin Barry down to a conversation until the *Trepassey* was in position. "Perhaps I may, after a trial."

The brig was still drifting forward when the wind completely died. Sails were hanging limply against the masts when Barry put an end to this chatter. Nodding to his gun crews, he roared, "Fire!"

The *Alliance*'s starboard guns belched fire and smoke. Barry's gunners had honed their skills over this voyage, and the *Atalanta*'s port bulwark and hull were rocked and ripped by American round shot. Lieutenant Samuel Arden was standing next to Edwards when a cannonball took off his right arm. Edwards immediately sent him below, where the intrepid Arden had his stump cauterized so he could return to the fighting.[64]

Turning quickly to his helmsman, Barry yelled, "Wear Ship!" but there was no wind to turn through. Casting an eye at the *Atalanta*, Barry saw that Edwards was waiting for the *Trepassey* to come up. He also noticed a different activity aboard both enemy ships. British sailors had gone below. Soon long oars protruded from both vessels. The men had manned the sweeps. Barry could see what was coming: both ships would row into positions off the *Alliance*'s stern, where his guns could not hit them. No wonder Edwards had been so unafraid. Barry could only watch as the *Trepassey* rowed quickly towards the fight, Captain Smyth running out his guns at the same time.

But Smyth's men were pulling too hard at their oars. With no wind to turn into and slow herself, the *Trepassey* shot past the *Alliance*. As she glided by, Barry fired two broadsides into her. Iron and wooden splinters ripped into the rigging and hull, and several of her men fell dead, including Smyth. The second-in-command, Lieutenant King, took Smyth's place on the quarterdeck, ordering the men at the sweeps to row the brig out of *Alliance*'s range before taking position off the frigate's stern.

In a moment of pure courage, Edwards sent the *Atalanta* rowing in between the *Trepassey* and *Alliance* to give King enough time to escape Barry's guns. Another well-aimed rebel broadside slammed into the *Atalanta*, shuddering her masts and tearing her rigging.[65]

Within minutes, both British ships were on the *Alliance*'s stern quarters. Now the tide of battle turned swiftly and brutally, as fifteen British cannon fired at will into the American frigate in a perfect crossfire. If Barry tried to lower boats to row the *Alliance* out of range they would be blown out of the water. All he could do was what Jones did at Flamborough Head; he ordered his gunner, Benjamin Pierce, to disconnect a couple of 9-pounders from their ringbolts and set them where they could fire at the enemy, but where their recoil could be minimized.[66]

By now the fighting was an hour old. The three ships were literally yards away from one another, but without a wind the acrid smoke grew so thick that the men could hardly see their shipmates, let alone the enemy. Gunners aimed at the flash of enemy cannon. As he had aboard the *Bonhomme Richard*, Mathew Parke directed his green-coated marines in the *Alliance*'s fighting tops to pour fire into both enemy ships. They leveled their muskets towards the British masts that poked through the curtain of smoke, while their comrades fired their coehorns and lobbed grenadoes at the enemy.[67]

But the battle grew even more one-sided. British gunners switched to grapeshot and reduced their charges, slowing the speed of their projectiles so their shot tore longer splinters out of the *Alliance*'s bulwarks. Years later, Kessler recalled, "We could not bring one-half our guns nay oft times only guns out astern to bear on them." He fell with a leg wound. Barry's clerk, Fitch Pool, was struck by a splinter and taken below. Marine Lieutenant Samuel Pritchard was struck full force by a six-pound ball. Marine Sergeant David Brewer, son of one of Washington's colonels, was shot through the head; mutineer George Green was impaled on a long, jagged splinter.[68]

By three o'clock the smoke from the battle hung over the three ships like a deadly man-made shroud, while the still Atlantic mirrored every flash of cannon and musket fire. The heavy, humid air smelled of blood and gunpowder; every man on deck, from captain to powder boy, was soaked in his own sweat, many stained with soot and gore. Barry never left the quarterdeck, exhorting his men to keep fighting, passing along any encouragement, seemingly oblivious to the danger all around him. Each British broadside took more of his men out of the fight, but what of it? He was not about to quit.

Below deck, Surgeon Kendall and his Loblolly Boys were doing their best with the increasing numbers of wounded brought to them. Those who were lightly wounded were quickly patched up and sent back to the fighting; those too mangled by iron and wood were attended with the clinical but quick efficiency so long practiced in war. Sand was continually thrown on the deck to keep Kendall and his assistants from slipping in blood; if he ran out of his supply of laudanum, he doled out rum to dull the pain.

Kendall had just finished with one poor soul when word came from above deck: the captain was being carried below.[69]

Barry was directing the fight from the quarterdeck when he was struck in the left shoulder by a single grapeshot, knocking him prostrate. Momentarily stunned, he rose slowly to his feet, trying to clear his head just as the pain from the wound hit him. Hacker and Parke rushed to his side, but he waved his hand dismissively at them—he refused to go below, although his shoulder was bleeding profusely.

Strong and determined as Barry was, it was at most a few minutes before the loss of blood made him light-headed. His voice lost power, and he became unsteady. Once more his officers begged him to see the surgeon. This time he relented. Hacker called for Kessler and several hands to bear their captain below.[70]

Kendall was ready for Barry when he arrived. He removed the captain's coat and cut away his shirt, checking to see how much of it had gone into the body with the grapeshot. He ordered Kessler and the others to remain—holding Barry down, for what came next would be impossible for mere boys. After administering a dose of laudanum or a pannikin of rum, Kendall began his examination.[71]

The ball, about an inch and a half in diameter, was made of iron, not lead like a musket ball, so it did not deform, thereby minimizing any soft-tissue damage. Kendall had a probe among his instruments, but probably used his fingers instead. With the sounds of the battle coming from above, Kendall proceeded with his grisly work.[72]

Once he located the ball, Kendall inserted his retractors, widening the wound. Barry's sailors pressed down hard as he involuntarily writhed in pain. Removing the retractor, Kendall reached for his bullet forceps—a scissors-like instrument with cupped ends shaped for just this procedure. Once the forceps were widened around the ball, Kendall closed them. With methodical slowness, he removed them from inside Barry's shoulder. If the brachial artery had been hit, Kendall tied it off or cauterized it; if there were any bone fragments, he removed them along with any bits of Barry's shirt, and expelled any grumous blood from the wound.

After letting the wound bleed a bit, Kendall cleaned it, putting Barry, still flat on his back, in more agony (patients frequently lost consciousness or went into shock by this point). Kendall dressed the wound with lint dipped in oil.[73]

During Barry's surgery, Hoysted Hacker assumed command. He had just taken Barry's place on the quarterdeck when another broadside rocked the *Alliance*, the grapeshot missing him but instantly killing Quartermaster William Powell at the ship's wheel. Hacker ordered the gun crews manning the available 9-pounders to return fire when another broadside slammed into their frigate, carrying away the flag. Thinking the *Alliance* had surrendered, Edward's sailors manned their shrouds and gave three hoarse cheers.

They were wrong. In seconds, two American officers stepped over Powell's body. One took his place at the wheel, while the other seized the fallen ensign and hoisted it by the mizzen brail, near the very spot where Barry had the mutineers hung up and flogged. Seconds later, the *Alliance* returned fire, and the battle resumed.[74]

At this point Hacker wavered. There was no doubt he possessed courage, but he had eyes: the battle was being lost by the minute. From the quarterdeck he saw splintered bulwarks, perforated sails hanging limply, shredded rigging, and two deadly rows of guns, of no use at all. Blood, debris, and corpses were everywhere.

If there was a Jonah among the navy's captains, it was Hacker: he had lost the *Columbus* at Naragansett, the *Providence* at Penobscot, and the *General Lincoln* at Charleston, not from dereliction of duty but by seemingly forever being in the wrong place at the wrong time. After speaking with Parke, Hezekiah Welch, and the other officers, Hacker went below to tell his captain it was time to surrender, an act of courage in itself.[75]

He found Barry sitting up, with Kendall applying a bandage to his shoulder. The captain gave Hacker a dark look before asking what he was doing below. Taking a deep breath, Hacker updated Barry on "the shattered state of sails and rigging, the number of killed and wounded, and the disadvantages under which they labored, for the want of wind." Then Hacker asked "if the colours should be struck."[76]

Fueled by his agony, Barry's response was deafening. "No!" he roared. Then, to make sure Hacker fully understood his position on the subject, he angrily added, "If the ship cannot be fought without me, I will be carried on deck." As Barry simultaneously argued with Kendall while bellowing for his coat, Hacker rapidly returned to the quarterdeck, his question answered.

Where another man might have been angry or hurt by Barry's response, Hacker did not give it any thought—there was still a battle going on, and to be won, now at all costs. Kessler saw renewed resolve in Hacker's face as he "Made known to the crew the determination of their great commander." When he finished telling the crew they were not about to surrender, "one and all resolved to stick by him."[77]

Call it fate, call it luck, but just as Hacker revitalized the Alliances' fighting spirit, each man felt the wisp of a west wind on his sweaty face. Softly at first, it pulled the heavy haze of smoke apart. Kessler and the others inhaled their first clear breath in hours. As each man exhaled, he saw puffs of wind shake, then fill their shot-up sails. Immediately, Hacker ordered some of the men to man the braces, and ordered, "Hard a port." The battered *Alliance* answered her helm.[78]

The same soft breeze touched English cheeks, but its arrival meant something different aboard the *Atalanta* and the *Trepassey*. Edwards and King sent men back to the sweeps while their shipmates manned the braces, hoping to escape what the Americans had in store for them.[79]

After unleashing one broadside at the *Atalanta*—the Americans' first cannonade in three hours—Hacker swung the *Alliance* around to attack the *Trepassey*. When there was no wind, the closeness of the British ships to the *Alliance* was an acute advantage for them; now it became a death trap. Sixteen guns fired in unison at the *Trepassey*. Seconds later, King lowered his colors.

Barry was still "in a fit of Irish temper" about rejoining the battle when he felt his ship gently rock and then begin to sail. Kendall, having given up arguing, was helping Barry dress when they heard—and felt—the roar of the first broadside against the *Atalanta*. If Kendall thought it would change Barry's mind, he was wrong; he went back to re-rigging the captain for duty.[80]

Sampson Edwards, however, was not yet ready to give up. First and foremost he had to get the *Atalanta* away from the *Alliance*. The rebel frigate came around the *Trepassey*'s stern and was making straight for the *Atalanta*, now trying to break off the engagement and escape. But the earlier damage to her masts came

ALLIANCE against *ATALANTA* and *TREPASSEY* off Nova Scotia, May 28–29, 1781

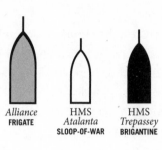

Alliance
FRIGATE

HMS Atalanta
SLOOP-OF-WAR

HMS Trepassey
BRIGANTINE

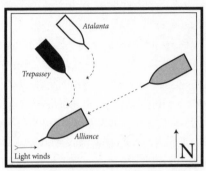

DUSK, MAY 28: *Atalanta* and *Trepassey* sight *Alliance* and change course to pursue.

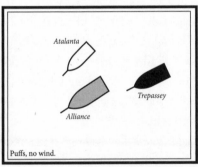

NOON, MAY 29: *Alliance* and *Trepassey* commence engagement just as light wind dies.

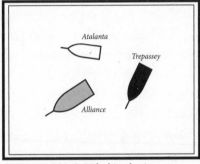

12:30–3:00 P.M.: British ships, having sweeps, row into position on *Alliance*'s stern quarters.

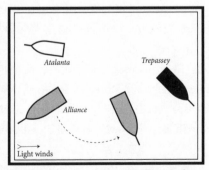

3:00 P.M.: Light breeze returns. *Alliance* sails into position to fire a broadside at *Trepassey*. She surrenders.

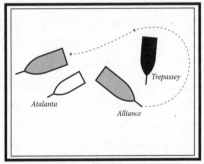

3:00–3:30 P.M.: Changing course, *Alliance* attacks *Atalanta* by sailing around *Trepassey*. *Atalanta* surrenders.

into play. The wind was growing stronger as the *Alliance* rushed up on the *Atalanta*'s starboard side, her 12-pounders run out, her gunners blowing on their fuses. Suddenly Edwards and his men heard one sharp crack, then another, as the battered fore and mizzen masts came crashing down, just as Hacker ordered the *Alliance*'s gunners to fire on the uproll. Edwards struck his colors, and called for quarter.[81]

Barry was being helped up the hatchway when there came a sudden silence after this last broadside. It was soon followed by raspy, joyous cheers from the Alliances. Now came their turn to leap into their shrouds, standing—exhausted, but standing—along the port rail. Hearing this, Barry ordered the men helping him to change course and make for his cabin.[82]

A short while later, Kessler brought Sampson Edwards to meet Barry, sitting in an easy chair. Edwards presented his sword, but Barry shook his head: "I return it to you Sir," he told Edwards. "You have merited it, and your King ought to give you a better Ship." He told Edwards to use his cabin as his own.[83]

Edwards explained to Barry that considering the lack of wind, he had been "confident that they would subdue the *Alliance*." Later, Barry confided to Kessler that if Edwards had known all of their disadvantages—the frigate's poor condition, the pitifully small crew, the large number of prisoners below, and the large contingent of British hands manning the *Alliance* in the first place—Edwards had more reason to flatter himself than he knew.[84]

Barry kept Edwards and King aboard the *Alliance* that evening. After assurances of "orderly conduct" from both officers regarding their men, he sent prize crews to each ship. Once the ships were repaired as best they could be, Barry loaded the *Trepassey* with all of his captured prisoners and sent her to Nova Scotia as a cartel, the men to be exchanged for a similar number of captured Americans. With jury-rigged masts, Barry turned the *Atalanta* over to Hezekiah Welch, with orders to make for Boston.

The *Alliance*, "Shattered in the most shocking manner," needed new masts, yards, sails, and rigging. Sure that she would never reach Philadelphia in such a state, Barry ordered Hacker to also make for Boston. Eight of her men were dead and twenty-one wounded; the combined British casualties were eleven killed and twenty-five wounded.[85]

On June 6, the overdue *Alliance* sailed up Nantasket Road. Bostonians believed her to be captured or lost at sea. Weeks earlier, Patrick Fletcher had brought the *Mars* into port, assuring one and all that the *Alliance*, the *Marquis de Lafayette*, and other prizes were not far behind him. (While one prize, the *Ad-*

venture, made it safely into port, the *Atalanta* was not so lucky. She was nearing Cape Cod when four British cruisers recaptured her, sending her to Halifax.) By June, most had feared the frigate was either captured or lost at sea, but here she was: no longer the beautiful, fast ship that stood down the Nantasket four months earlier, but battered and sluggish. Lacking a spar of sufficient size to replace her main yard, Barry simply sailed without one.[86]

First off the ship was her captain, carried on a stretcher by four sailors and taken to a house by the waterfront, with his clerk Fitch Pool and Kessler for company until they recovered from their wounds. Barry put Pool to work immediately. With his log beside him, the captain dictated letters to Congress, the Board of Admiralty, the Eastern Navy Board, and finally to Sarah. "I am amongst the wounded," he reported, but "shall be fit for duty before the Ship will be ready to Sail." Never a good patient, Barry put up with Kendall's harangues to rest, taking "one dram of bark every three hours" to ease his pain.[87]

News of Barry's voyage first appeared in Boston's *Continental Journal*, and was soon published in papers throughout the country. Congressmen praised both his victories and his diplomatic intervention on behalf of the *Buono Compagnia*, passing a resolution applauding his "utmost respect for the rights of neutral commerce"; even Franklin brought it to King Louis's attention. Only one representative, Maryland's Richard Potts, was dismissive of Barry's heroics, as he "was fortunate in capturing prizes but brought no Stores."

Happy as he was to be celebrated, he was happier to learn that Congress had granted him what Franklin could not: while both he and the *Alliance* were mending, she would be sheathed in copper. Better still, John Kessler, recovered from his leg wound, had been dispatched to Philadelphia to escort Sarah Barry to Boston. Weeks after her arrival, Barry was "in a fair way of recovery," and the *Alliance* at last had a copper-sheathed hull.[88]

On May 18, 1781, a Continental Navy officer made one of the more audacious escapes from Mill Prison. Weeks earlier, he had been clapped in double irons and confined in a solitary dungeon for thirty days for an attempted escape. Once released to general confinement, he complained that he had sprained his ankle. Now using crutches, he befriended one of the guards who had once served in America. On this sunny day, the officer hobbled past the guard. "Today?" he asked.

"Dinner," came the reply, meaning one p.m.—the regularly scheduled mealtime for everyone but a few sentries. Returning to his cell, the officer quickly donned a British uniform he had somehow obtained. Throwing his greatcoat back on, he took up his crutches and returned to the courtyard.

At a prearranged signal with some other prisoners, he approached a large, stout inmate while they distracted the nearby guards. Quickly the officer dropped his crutches, jumped on the big American's shoulders, and vaulted over the wall.

With more bravado than an entire fleet, the officer made his way to the home of an American sympathizer, took a small boat to the Channel Islands, bluffed his way past a British privateer, and boarded a ship bound for Holland. Eventually he made his way back to Philadelphia and was reunited with his young wife.

Gustavus Conyngham? No, Joshua Barney.[89]

Conyngham was still an inmate at Mill Prison when Barney made his breathtaking getaway. The captain's second stint as a prisoner was just as harsh as the first. Thomas Digges wrote Franklin that "there will be no hopes of liberating him his name being so offensive." This time around, in addition to Barney, Conyngham had John Manley for company.[90]

But nothing could deter Conyngham from escaping. Having earlier made attempts by disguise and tunneling, he now resorted to the most successful method: bribery. Another American prisoner neatly summed up the power of the pound: "A man who has money, has friends." The commandants at Mill and Forten Prisons were not fools; if they could not pay the guards enough to resist financial temptation, they would apply the same method the prisoners did, only outside the walls. They began offering five-pound notes to English citizens who turned in escapees.[91]

It worked. Luke Matthewman, John Barry's former lieutenant, was held captive at Forten Prison. In his memoirs he told of a mass escape, after which most of the fugitives were recaptured, thanks to the vigilance of Englishmen whom the prisoners scornfully labeled "five-pounders."[92]

At Mill, Conyngham tested the honor of each guard after watching their interaction with the prisoners. If he saw any degree of affability, he knew who to approach. Eventually his insight paid off. On June 4, 1781, Conyngham and three other sailors, with twenty pounds between them, convinced one sergeant and several guards that twenty pounds was enough for each to look the other way while they made their escape.

Twenty pounds worked for the four Americans, but not for the guards. They were arrested for dereliction of duty and abetting an escape. Once again, King George's most despised American was on the loose. Twelve days later, Conyngham was in Dunkirk, where he wrote Franklin, asking him to inform Anne of "her Gusty's" escape, not knowing if she was in Paris or l'Orient.[93]

A happy Franklin immediately replied, telling Conyngham that Anne was in l'Orient, before asking the captain, since he was finally in Dunkirk, to see who from the *Revenge*'s crew was in town. Franklin could not pay them without proof from Conyngham that they had served under him, three long years ago.

After a joyous reunion, the Conynghams headed to Paris, where Gustavus told Franklin he would happily return to fighting the British, "Should a Vessel be fitted out for America to my liking [and] with your Approbation." Too much time has passed for us to know how Anne felt about that.[94]

The perfect ship was found in Nantes by Franklin's nephew Jonathan Williams. "As a great number of our unhappy Countrymen are in the English prisons without any prospect of an Exchange for want of Prisoners to give in return," Jonathan Williams wrote his uncle, Benjamin Franklin, several American merchants in France wanted to "build & arm a stout privateer of 28 Guns" for Conyngham to command. "We choose him in preference," Williams recounted, "because his Name alone will make Sailors flock to his ship . . . and no American . . . will be more likely to be active in liberating his Countrymen." It was a win-win-win to Williams: Conyngham gets his command, future captures provide British prisoners to exchange, and profits from the sale of his prizes and their goods make the merchants richer.[95]

Williams selected Conyngham's old boss, Jonathan Nesbitt, to find a suitable ship if one could be bought quickly enough, and he found one—the *Layona*, waiting on the ways at l'Orient to be launched. That very day, the merchants began looking for guns and supplies while American sailors happily signed Conyngham's muster rolls.

But the French minister of marine had other plans for the *Layona*, scuttling Conyngham's hope of harassing the British one more time. A disappointed captain and a relieved wife took passage on the ship *Hannibal* for Philadelphia. She sailed only after Conyngham made arrangements for her crew to include ninety-five Americans recently escaped from British prisons.

This time Conyngham got home safely. Upon his arrival he visited Congress to get the six years of back pay due him. He was confident there would be no problem.[96]

Lack of funds and sailors had kept the *Trumbull* idle in the Delaware for more than a year, by which time even James Nicholson was running out of faults to find and feathers to ruffle. Instead, he focused his full attention on John Paul Jones.

Since Jones's arrival in Philadelphia, Nicholson had behaved like a petulant child over the Scotsman's success and ensuing adulation. But when he learned that some congressmen were considering Jones for an admiral's commission, he reached new heights of conspiratorial spitefulness. While Thomas Read was the only other Continental captain willing to join Nicholson in his plot to stop such a promotion (it was Read's wife who first learned of Jones's possible promotion from an indiscreet congressman), they had the Lee-Adams faction more than willing to assist. Nicholson "took my Hat and with very little Ceremony" called on Samuel Huntington, just finishing his term as president of Congress.

Nicholson coincidentally found Jones in the hallway, waiting to make his own pitch. Once alone with Huntington, Nicholson opened fire, beginning with Jones's junior status on the Captains List. At least five of the seventeen captains ranked above Jones were still in service (or at least, still alive). Elevating so low an officer was unfair to all of them, not just Captain number 1—that is, Nicholson himself. He then closed in for the kill, and "informed [Huntington] of what I had heard . . . Many things pretty severe of the Chevalier's private as well as Public Carrector to odious to mention."

Next, Nicholson visited the man he derisively called "Bob Morris the Financier," to lobby against Jones's getting the *America*. Nicholson adamantly insisted that it be offered to every captain ahead of Jones, realizing, as number 1, that it would only have to be offered once. Nicholson maintained a clear conscience regarding his malevolent offensive, as "The Chevalier ever since his arrival . . . has devoted his time, privately, by making personal application to members of congress to give him rank at the head of the navy."

Before departing on the *Trumbull*, he wrote a poison-pen letter to Barry, full of superficial praise for the Irishman's heroics, replete with his mean-spiritedness against Jones, but careful not to mention how hard Nicholson campaigned against Barry earlier:

> Your arrival and success came opportunily and I did not fail to make use of it I mean outdoors in the presence of Capt. Jones & some of his advocated Members, by observing that you had acquit yourself well, which they acknowledged. I then told them they could not do less than make you Admiral also. I had not a sentence of reply. It irritated the Chevalier so much that he was obliged to decamp.[97]

Nicholson and Read got half a loaf: Congress abandoned any promotion for Jones (in fact, the first admiral in an American navy was David Farragut in the Civil War). But "Bob Morris the Financier" was made of sterner stuff, and much savvier than Nicholson politically. Jones was made captain of the *America* by a unanimous decision of Congress. "I am convinced he will never get her to sea," Nicholson hissed to Barry, but Morris believed otherwise. "Send that ship to sea," he ordered.[98]

Nicholson's attempt to demolish Jones was suspended once the *Trumbull* was ready to sail. Like Barry, Jones, and Harding, Nicholson took on British prisoners for this cruise (fifty in all) to have enough hands to adequately man the frigate. After escorting twenty-eight merchantmen out to sea, Nicholson was to make for Havana, sell his hold of flour, and deliver Robert Morris's dispatches to the Spanish admiral in port.[99]

Among Nicholson's lieutenants were Alexander Murray and the resilient Richard Dale. After an earlier stint in the navy, Murray had served in the Continental Army before going privateering. Recently captured and exchanged, he was happy to be a Continental officer again. The fleet cleared the Delaware Capes on August 8, only to be immediately spotted by three British cruisers. Nicholson signaled the merchantmen to disperse before cracking on all sail himself. Two of the enemy ships gave chase.[100]

The *Trumbull* was making her getaway when a storm rolled over the horizon. Within minutes the gale was blowing hard, and the frigate lost both her foretop and main topgallant masts, the topsail yard puncturing the foresail before crashing onto the fo'c'sle. Nicholson had no choice but to "run before the wind," hoping to elude both the storm and his pursuers. As the Trumbulls did their best to clear away the wreckage, one British ship, far ahead of her consort, closed in on Nicholson's lame frigate.[101]

The enemy warship was the HMS *Iris*, formerly the Continental frigate *Hancock*—John Manley's old command. By daylight she had the *Trumbull* in range. From his quarterdeck, Nicholson cried "Beat to Quarters!" certain that he could rally this crew to duty just as he had before the engagement with the *Watt*. But in that battle he had "green country lads" who rose to the occasion; now Nicholson watched, stunned, as "three quarters of [the crew] ran below, [and] put out the lights"—not just his pressed British prisoners, but many Americans as well. It was the *Virginia* in reverse; Nicholson wanted to fight, but his men did not.

However, "with the remainder and a few brave officers we commenced an action," he later reported, adding that "at no time did I have more than forty men upon deck." Remarkably, he almost succeeded. For more than ninety minutes, his faithful officers and tars fought the fully manned *Iris* to a standstill. Finally, the second British ship sailed into the fight: the *General Monk*, eighteen guns. She had once been the Yankee privateer *General Washington*. Within minutes, the momentum of the battle shifted. Both Dale and Murray were among the wounded, and five others were dead. "Seeing no prospect of escaping in this unequal contest," Nicholson struck his colors. For the rest of his life, he never forgave the British and American sailors who "through treachery . . . and from cowardice betrayed me."

The *Trumbull* was so badly damaged that the *Iris* had to tow her to New York. Once she arrived, carpenters found her beams so rotten that they abandoned her. Nicholson and his officers were quickly paroled, his British sailors freed. His American hands were among the last Continental sailors turned over to the prison hulks on the East River. Some of them survived this nightmare; others did not.[102]

Historian William M. Fowler, Jr., cites the irony of the *Iris*'s capture of the *Trumbull*: "the first of the thirteen frigates built by Congress had captured the last." With the loss of the *Trumbull*, the *Confederacy*, and the *Saratoga*, the Continental Navy was down to the frigates *Alliance* and *Deane*. It was also about to have new management: a one-man committee named Robert Morris.[103]

As the days grew shorter that September, two seismic events were unfolding. One was the stuff of legend: in September, Admiral de Grasse's fleet and the combined armies of Generals Washington and Rochambeau bottled up General Lord Cornwallis's army in Yorktown. After a short siege, Cornwallis surrendered on October 19. While historians have written ever since how a British band played the popular tune "The World Turned Upside Down," it is interesting to note that it was also the melody to the song "When the King Enjoys His Own Again." As the war had more than a year remaining, perhaps it was that song's lyrics running through the Redcoats' heads.[104]

The other development, far less well-known but just as necessary for the American government's survival, was the consolidation of powers given to Robert Morris. He had been appointed superintendent of finance and given carte blanche to do what he deemed necessary to address the country's catastrophic economic mess. Though his detractors saw his appointment as the evil centralization of power, nearly everyone else saw Morris as the only man whose financial wizardry could keep both the economy and the government from total collapse.

In truth, he was effectively running the country, with the exception of the army. Morris had broad shoulders. He would need them.[105]

When news of Yorktown reached Philadelphia, Morris gained another title: Agent of Marine, similar in authority to England's First Lord of the Admiralty. In typical fashion, he plunged headfirst into the assignment. With just two frigates in action, the ships *America* and *Bourbon* still on the stocks, and no money to build any others, Congress had lost interest in the Continental Navy.[106]

Morris had not. He saw the navy as a means of maintaining commerce, still capable of escorting convoys, taking prizes, and thereby protecting and generating revenue. John Brown, his assistant since the Willing and Morris days, would be his right arm. Morris considered Brown "an honest, a modest, and a sensible Man"—just what he needed for this near-Sisyphean task. He sent Brown to Boston, where the *Alliance* and the *Deane* were docked. Brown, carrying a lengthy list of orders and ideas to get the two-ship navy ready, went right to work, making payments when required and cutting costs where necessary. Some egos were bruised in the process; when the Eastern Navy Board complained to Morris about Brown's actions, Morris unhesitatingly backed Brown up.[107]

No one was happier to see Brown than his old friend John Barry. His wife's nursing had gone a long way towards assuring Barry's recovery, although his shoulder would forever serve as a built-in barometer, alerting him of forthcoming squalls. In August, Barry breakfasted with John Paul Jones, who had stopped in Boston en route to Portsmouth and the *America*. Jones wanted to hear Barry's ideas about the *America*'s construction. They also discussed the *Alliance*, Landais, politics, and the war. Barry tactfully did not mention Nicholson's malicious letter. Later, when Jones learned of it, he wrote Barry, thanking him for his disregard of Nicholson's gossip.[108]

In August, another of Barry's prizes arrived in Boston along with the *Trepassey*, bearing 130 American sailors exchanged for Barry's prisoners. Barry's prizes were libeled and promptly sold, giving the Alliances some, if not all, of what was owed them.[109]

Boston merchant Henry Mitchell approached Barry with what he was sure was a viable "get rich quick" scheme. Barry's prize, the *Mars*, was for sale, and Mitchell wanted to convert her into a privateer, but Mitchell barely had half the asking price. Barry's name would certainly bring in other investors. Was Barry interested?

He was. Barry believed the *Mars* was so fast "he could not have catch'd her" but for her bearing down on the *Alliance* instead of running from her. He had enough for a one-sixteenth share. Soon Mitchell had enough backers. In Barry's honor, the *Mars* was renamed the *Wexford*, after Barry's Irish home.[110]

Mitchell also had the perfect captain in mind: the idle but able John Peck Rathbun. He had recently come to Boston hoping for a letter of marque, or even a lieutenant's berth aboard a Continental ship. Barry was familiar with his exploits, and Mitchell considered him "a Man of known Courage and conduct." As the *Wexford* was being refitted, Congress speedily approved the venture. Her owners ordered Rathbun to cruise in "the Chops of the Irish and English Channels." With 120 men, twenty guns, two sets of sails, and a hearty send-off from Barry and Mitchell, the *Wexford* headed out into the Atlantic in mid-August. Rathbun, whose boldness was well proven at Nassau and against the Jamaica Fleet, now hoped to repeat the successes of Wickes, Jones, and Conyngham. The British Isles beckoned.[111]

The *Wexford* proved to be every inch the fine vessel Barry described, easily crossing the Atlantic in six weeks. On September 27, she was less than a day's sail from Cape Clear in south Ireland. Rathbun always ran a happy ship, and his men anticipated swooping down on unsuspecting merchantmen in the channels, like a man-of-war bird after so many boobies.

At sunset, the *Wexford* was spotted by the mastheader of the British frigate *Recovery*, thirty-two guns. She was commanded by Lord Hervey, whose uncle was Earl of Bristol and Admiral of the Blue. Hervey wasted no time standing for the *Wexford*. Rathbun, seeing that his first sighted sail was not easy pickings but of superior force, swung his brig through the wind, showing her heels to the *Recovery*.[112]

Soon Rathbun discovered that the frigate not only had more guns but was also faster than his speedy brig. Shortly after noontime, Hervey's frigate overtook the *Wexford* and unleashed a broadside. Again, Rathbun changed course, sheering off in hopes of shaking his pursuer. The chase continued throughout the night.

Twenty-four hours after first sighting the *Wexford*, Hervey's frigate was ninety-eight miles off Cape Clear—Rathbun had made a circular retreat. The next morning, the *Recovery* was close enough for Hervey to bring his guns to bear when Rathbun surrendered. The *Recovery* escorted the *Wexford* into Cork harbor, and the Americans were taken to nearby Kinsale Prison.[113]

Rathbun and his men had wanted to see Ireland, but from the water, not from a prison cell. Over the next several weeks, seventeen of them died, while some escaped and eventually got back to America. An ailing Rathbun was not so lucky. On February 7, 1782, he was transferred to Mill Prison, his health broken.

Four months later another American sailor recorded in his journal that "Capt. Jno. Rathbun is dangerously ill."

On June 20, Rathbun, thirty-six years old, died, unaware that his young wife, Mary, only twenty-three, had passed away in April. His will requested he be "decently Interred." He was buried with other American and French sailors who did not survive George III's tender care.[114]

CHAPTER THIRTEEN

✯ ✯ ✯

SHUBAEL GARDNER

The King of G. Britain has acknowledged the Sovereignty of the
United States, but whether any thing more will follow from it . . . I
know not.

—JOHN ADAMS TO ROBERT MORRIS[1]

O n December 1, 1781, the brig *Somerset*, a 90-ton whaler, was docked at
Nantucket, Massachusetts. Her master, Thomas Brock, was overseeing
his crew's final efforts to ready the ship for sea. His sailors, from families that
had manned Nantucket ships for generations, included Uriah Bunker, Caleb
Coggerhale, Gideon Coffin, and Brock's second mate, Shubael Gardner, whose
earlier service in an armed vessel had gotten him disowned by the Nantucket
Society of Friends.[2]

Most of Nantucket's Quaker population proclaimed themselves neutral
during the Revolution, but many were loyal to King George. With their holds
packed tight with barrels of spermaceti and ambergris, whalers were a prized
target for men-of-war and privateers alike, and many a Nantucket vessel sailed
with a Royal Navy pass giving them both permission to sail and protection from
British warships or Loyalist privateers. The *Somerset*'s owner, John Ramsdell, obtained his pass from Robert Digby, the latest commander of the New York
squadron. It stipulated that the *Somerset* "shall not be found proceeding with her
Cargo to any other port than Nantucket or New York."

On New Year's Day, 1782, the men of the *Somerset* said good-bye to their
loved ones. They expected to return in the summer.[3]

Once John Paul Jones reached Portsmouth in September 1781, he set himself up as befitted a ship-of-the-line captain and chevalier. With his medal from King Louis pinned to his coat, he took the front room this time in the Widow Purcell's boardinghouse (playfully carving his initials in the window frame for posterity). Portsmouth gave him yet another hero's welcome—even his old nemesis from the *Ranger* days, John Langdon, seemed glad to see him.[4]

Langdon took Jones to his shipyard on Rising Castle Island to see the unfinished *America*, standing tall above the island. Jones could not wait to tell John Barry of his first impression of her, calling her "a Masterpiece" and asking Barry to send him what sheet copper remained after sheathing the *Alliance*. Once money ran out and work slowed, Jones changed his mind and accused Langdon of both stalling and shoddy workmanship.[5]

Jones spent Christmas in Portsmouth under the same snowy skies and foul humor he experienced in Boston in 1776. He always chafed at inactivity, but now it consumed him. He wrote Franklin that he would gladly shoulder a musket for Washington. Lafayette, recipient of a similar gloomy letter, sought to cheer Jones up, hoping he would soon sail the *America* with "plenty of Passion and *carte blanche*." Jones even wrote to Delia, stating that "absence will not diminish but *refine* the pure and spotless friendship that binds our souls together." He tried to take his mind off his ennui with parties in Portsmouth, but the town was no Boston or Philadelphia, and certainly no Paris; he informed old friend Hector McNeill that even Portsmouth's hair powder "is impregnated with luxurious mites."[6]

As 1782 began, Langdon and Jones were carping about each other to Robert Morris, who rebuked them both. He criticized Jones for not being on the "Terms of Cordiality" with a man of Langdon's stature, and upbraided Langdon for "the Coldness subsisting between you and the Chevalier." Put your enmity aside, he told them, and sent John Brown to Portsmouth to get them working together and investigate the *America*'s delay.[7]

For Jones, only Franklin's letter after Jones abandoned the *Alliance* cut deeper. "Nothing on my side shall be wanting," he promised Morris, and he was as good as his word. He enmeshed himself in work, held his ego in check, and kept a civil tongue with Langdon. Any supplies delivered to Rising Castle Island were gratefully appreciated. A shipment of green timber was delivered, but instead of throwing a tantrum Jones requested that Brown send enough oil and paint to prevent rot. When word reached Portsmouth that Marie Antoinette had given birth to a dauphin, Jones fired a twenty-one-gun salute from the 12-pounders Brown had sent him.[8]

But when $10,000 arrived from Morris, and Langdon hired only eight carpenters to work on the behemoth vessel, Jones snapped. He accused Langdon of corruption. A rumor soon reached Portsmouth that a British force was coming to put the *America* to the torch. Jones hired his own guards, joining them in round-the-clock patrols. Nobody—not Nicholson, Langdon, or the enemy—would keep him from getting his ship to sea.[9]

As Jones was enjoying a Christmas punch in Portsmouth, his friend John Barry was sailing the *Alliance* back to France. When he left Boston in October to escort his wife, Sarah, back to Philadelphia, there was no money to complete his ship's refitting, and only a hundred sailors on the muster rolls.[10]

His visit to Philadelphia gave Barry his first chance to meet with Morris since he had been named Agent of Marine. Morris wanted to engage crews for one-year terms, and offered new incentives to lure seasoned tars from privateers. His best idea was about pay: from now on, 100 percent of the sale of prizes would go to officers and crew, and not be split with Congress. Slops would be provided gratis, sign-on bonuses of up to ten dollars would be offered, and all wages were to be paid "punctually in Silver or Gold," instead of Continental scrip. Morris ordered Barry to take the *Alliance* and *Deane* on a joint cruise, signing on hands under these attractive terms.[11]

Barry sent Congress the transcripts from the trial of his three mutineers. John Crawford, Patrick Shelden, and William McEllany had been found guilty of mutiny and conspiracy, and the court's sentences were harsh: Crawford and Shelden were to wear a heavy halter around the neck and receive fifty lashes, while McEllany was "peculiarly Guilty" and sentenced to "be hanged by the neck on the starboard fore Yard Arm of the said Ship *Alliance*"—one of the first sailors in an American navy to receive a death sentence.[12]

Once back in Boston, Barry and Nicholson placed a broadside in the *Continental Journal*, the largest advertisement yet posted in an American paper:

> ALL able-bodied Seamen, ordinary Seamen, and Landsmen, Are hereby informed, that two fine fast sailing Continental Frigates AL-LIANCE and DEANE, the first commanded by JOHN BARRY, Esq.; and the other by SAMUEL NICHOLSON, Esq.; are bound in Concert

against the Enemy, and will sail soon, with every prospect of making a very advantageous Cruise.

In addition to Morris's new wages, the broadside promised an insurance policy of up to $200 compensation, free hospitalization and care, and half pay forever to anyone who became permanently disabled. This was the first time "universal coverage" was offered to sailors in the Americas since the Caribbean pirates, a century earlier.[13]

But the handsome offer brought no recruits because of "Propagated falsehoods" about Barry's character, spread by the *Alliance*'s departing officers, including Surgeon Kendall. Frustrated about the lack of pay, they fell to slanderous talk about Barry, who demanded an inquiry to publicly defend his reputation. The Navy Board determined that was not necessary. He returned to his task of appointing replacements and hiring hands.[14]

Barry's officers were scouring the waterfront, seeking recruits, on December 10 when Boston church bells began pealing, announcing the arrival of the Marquis de Lafayette, accompanied by aides and family, including Comte de Noailles.

After Yorktown, a disappointed Washington watched Admiral de Grasse's fleet sail south for the winter. With no follow-up campaign to lead, the general marched his troops back to New Jersey, resuming his place on the chessboard against General Clinton in New York. Most of the money John Laurens had brought back was spent, so Congress had decided to send the marquis for more. When Barry went to greet him, Lafayette handed over Barry's orders to take Lafayette's entourage to France.[15]

So be it. But for Barry, Morris's orders not only superceded any cruise with the *Deane*, but also belied the terms his men had agreed to. Furthermore, getting Lafayette safely to France was of such importance that Barry was "to avoid all Vessels, and keep in mind, as your sole object, to make a quiet and safe passage." No other passengers were to be permitted and, while laying in "the necessary Stores" for such a dignitary, Barry was "not to spend one Livre more than absolutely necessary." As a reward for his anticipated successful errand, the *Alliance* could go on a cruise after Lafayette was safely on a French dock, after hamstringing Barry stem to stern.[16]

"Few of the ships of the United States," Barry testily replied, were "sent on private service." Nor were they "to go out of their way but to keep clear of all Vessels whatever." He was known as a sailor's captain; even Congress had praised his "Popularity with Seamen." Now he was ordered to go back on his word to his recruits. Every hand that put name or mark to the recent muster rolls expected what Barry's broadside had promised. It was bad enough that Morris was breaking *his* word, but with these orders, he was breaking Barry's as well.[17]

When another rendezvous netted only seventeen "landsmen," Morris ordered Barry to take what hands he needed from Nicholson's crew—an order that Barry reluctantly carried out and Nicholson vehemently protested. But the *Alliance* was still short of hands, until Lafayette himself came to the rescue, taking thirty-seven "Sick and About Naked" French sailors off his country's ships that were moored in Boston. "I am at Last got on Board the *Alliance* in order to comply with your orders," Barry stiffly wrote Morris before sailing on Christmas Eve.[18]

To Barry's chagrin, the French mariners were the best hands aboard. Lafayette provided good company for Barry, who was charmed by the young nobleman's élan and dedication to the Cause. The two formed a fast friendship. "No Man feels for your Success more than I," the marquis told him. Lafayette wrote Washington that he enjoyed "A happy voyage."[19]

However, while Midshipman Kessler recorded that "Nothing of note passed on the passage," the American hands were grumbling over their orders to avoid a fight, openly wishing "the Marquis was [already] in France." When an easy prize was sighted, they turned to the quarterdeck, only to see that Barry's expression showed "the conflict in his mind between the calls of his duty & his inclination" to attack. When he ordered a change of course they grudgingly obeyed but openly complained. Instead of calling his men on their insubordination, Barry kept what Kessler called "a sullen silence," as if "propriety would have permitted" the captain to add, "*I* also wish the Marquis was in France."[20]

After a quick passage, the *Alliance* reached l'Orient on January 17, 1782. Almost immediately, Barry wished that he was anywhere but France. He wrote Franklin, asking the minister plenipotentiary's intercession in getting permission to take any American sailors now serving aboard French privateers. Franklin's reply offered no assistance, only a request that Barry take "Congress[']s] goods to Philadelphia." When Barry turned over his French sailors, he presented a bill for their slops. The *Intendant* for the French navy took the sailors, but not the bill. Barry's new friend Lafayette came through again, promising to assist in getting the shorthanded captain the men he needed. Days after Lafayette reached Paris, a French officer handed Barry a purse, filled with French coins, to pay for his French sailor's clothes—a gift from the marquis.[21]

With no help from Franklin and the French bureaucrats, Barry turned to

James Moylan and Consul Thomas Barclay to help him round up any American sailors in French ports. Hearing that Barry was in France, the recently paroled Monsieur de Galatheau wrote to him, demanding his "shares" of the *Alliance*'s prizes from their passage to America in 1781. Barry fired back, demanding to know what became of his prize *Minerva*, sent back to France by the Frenchman. His threat to make de Galatheau's statement public, with all details of their cruise, put an end to the Frenchman's perfidious claims.[22]

Having signed on some itinerant hands that he sardonically described as "half-built Gentlemen," Barry took the *Alliance* on a short but aimless cruise in February. Sailing through "nothing but Gales of wind," he sighted and chased sixteen ships, all neutrals. When he returned to l'Orient, he found new orders— not from Morris but from Franklin, telling him to go to Brest, take on a large supply of gunpowder that was waiting there along with Franklin's dispatches, and sail to America with the French fleet leaving in mid-March.[23]

An exasperated Barry was in no mood to obey. Still hampered by French officials and their refusal to release American sailors from French ships or French jails, he took out his frustrations in a series of letters to Franklin. As it was "out of my power to go to Brest" and still follow Morris's orders, Barry sent a courier there to get Franklin's dispatches, but would only wait "until the Return of this Post, which is stretching my Orders further than I wish for."[24]

Barry also received two letters that gave him pause. One was from Captain John Green, an old colleague from his Willing & Morris days, now languishing in Mill Prison. Green had heard that Barry was in France and asked his intercession in getting exchanged, and for "a little money as I want to buy some Cloth[e]s." Barry sent him some cash with a warm reply, telling Green he had visited "Mrs. Green and all your little ones" while in Philadelphia. The other letter, a request from one Alexander Thomas, asked for passage home. He was "not a Son of Marrs," so he could not fight, but he would need space for several trunks in the *Alliance*'s hold. Barry promised Thomas "you shan't go" home in the *Alliance*. "Take a passage in a Vessel without Guns," he advised, "and then you need not be under any Apprehension of being hurt."[25]

On March 15, the post carrying Franklin's dispatches arrived and Barry put to sea. Before leaving, he wrote a report to Morris, stating he had been "deprived of any Assistance" from Franklin, Moylan, or anyone else. Unbeknownst to Barry, a letter from Franklin to Morris was among the minister's dispatches, describing Barry's disregard for his orders and his refusal to take Congress's supplies. (Barry had, in fact, gotten his friend Thomas Truxton to take them home in his privateer.) Franklin signed off, calling Barry "a great man," but "influenced by small Matters."[26]

For Philadelphia merchants, the lack of Continental ships to defend their merchantmen compelled them to hire a Continental captain.

From 1781 into the spring of 1782, Loyalist raiders had taken a page out of John Barry's book, when he attacked British ships with surprising swiftness in the winter of '78. Using barges, shallops, and other small craft, they pounced on unescorted merchantmen on the Delaware. It did not matter if the ships were coming or going: their holds were always filled with valuable goods. On March 29, a band of Philadelphia merchants appealed to the state assembly, which swung into action—well, deliberation.

Nor could the financially strapped Congress help defend the waterway. Admiral Digby's blockade of northern ports was strangling rebel trade; the prowling British cruisers off the Delaware had little to prey on, thanks to these Loyalist letters of marque. The precipitous drop in trade gave Robert Morris fits, both publicly and personally. The new Bank of North America—his brainchild—stopped lending money, and the amount of his own fortune being lost to enemy raiders was so high that he feared merely mentioning the total would be "an appearance of ostentation."[27]

But while the public Morris could not help, the private Morris could and did. He engineered a loan from the Bank of North America to purchase and convert a small merchantman, the *Hyder Ally*, into a warship, arming her with four 9-pounders and twelve 6-pounders. Morris even found the perfect captain for the venture. "Lieut. Barney is just returned from Captivity," he noted, and had not yet left for Boston and a berth aboard the *Deane*. Joshua Barney's return to Philadelphia was circuitous: he had served on the *South Carolina* on her voyage from Texel Island to La Coruña, then with the privateer *Cicero* to Boston, finally by sleigh to Philadelphia.[28]

Anxious to get back in the fight, Barney signed on 110 men, including a contingent of backwoodsmen to serve as marines. By April 5 the guns were aboard, the bulwarks pierced, and orders delivered. Barney was to escort seven merchantmen down the Delaware and safely out to sea. As the ships approached the capes on April 7, they were spotted by three enemy ships, led by the frigate *Quebec*, which had helped take the *South Carolina* in December. Her captain sent his two consorts up the bay. They were both former American privateers: the *Fair American*, sixteen guns; and the *General Monk*, twenty guns—the former *General*

Washington commanded by Silas Talbot until his capture in 1780. The *General Monk* had been present when the *Trumbull* was taken.[29]

Barney immediately ordered the convoy back to Philadelphia. In seconds, the merchantmen were changing course, trying not to foul one another as they came through the wind, their captains desperate to avoid capture and get home. One captain hailed Barney; as the American ship was armed, he would not depart but "stick by him"—which he did, until he ran aground trying to avoid the traffic jam caused by his colleagues. The *Fair American* flew past the *Hyder Ally* to get to the fleeing merchantmen, firing a broadside at Barney's vessel for good measure as she passed.

Barney did not return fire. Instead, he sent the *Hyder Ally* after the *General Monk*, which appeared equally anxious to engage. Sizing up his foe, Barney saw she had enough firepower "to blow us into atoms." But he was not about to surrender.[30]

As the *General Monk* closed in, Barney ordered his helmsman and officers to pay attention: the next command he gave was to be obeyed "by the rule of contrary"—they were to do exactly the opposite of what he called for. Then he stood atop the binnacle—the box that held the compass beside the helm—so that everyone, including the enemy, could easily see him.[31]

The *General Monk* was within range and fired her bow chasers. Once the gun's report died, Barney, roaring in a voice the enemy could easily hear, ordered "Hard a-port your helm!" Hearing this, the *General*'s captain, Josias Rogers, also changed course, tacking to port—no different than when two daysailers approaching each other try to avoid a collision in a sailing race.

But as the *General Monk* turned to port, the *Hyder Ally* turned to starboard. In seconds, the two were afoul of each other, the *General Monk*'s jibboom enmeshed in the *Hyder Ally*'s fore rigging. Just before impact, Barney cried, "Fire!" A devastating broadside slammed into the *General*, just as Barney's frontier marines fired a withering volley across the water. Barney's next order was "Grappling hooks away," and the flying barbs further secured the *General Monk*. In seconds, Barney had neutralized her superior firepower, and she was not going anywhere.

For the next half hour, the *Hyder Ally*'s guns fired twenty broadsides into the *General Monk*, while Barney's marines put on a lethal show of frontier firepower, as well as ignorance of how to address their commander. As they were clearing the enemy tops of Loyalist marines, one American sang out, "Captain! Do you see that fellow with the white hat?" Before Barney could reply, the frontiersman shot the man dead. "Third fellow I've made hop," he continued, calmly ramming another musket ball down the barrel. Nor were Loyalist marines the only ones felled by American volleys. Rogers and all of his officers were soon dead or wounded on the *General Monk*'s quarterdeck.

Barney remained unharmed. Still standing on the binnacle, he turned to watch his cook angrily come after one of his men who had deserted his post, raising his meat cleaver to cut the man down. Just then, a Loyalist cannonball smashed into the binnacle, destroying the compass but only knocking Barney to the deck. The cook paused to see if Barney was hurt; finding the captain stunned but alive, he turned to find his cowardly colleague fighting the enemy with rediscovered nerve—or fear of the cleaver.[32]

One Loyalist sailor described the scene aboard his ship: "The deck full of killed and wounded . . . our rigging so much shot as to render it impossible to haul off." Minutes later, Rogers ordered a midshipman—the only unharmed officer aboard the *General Monk*—to strike the colors. Seeing this, the captain of the *Fair American* made for the capes, running aground in the process.[33]

Rogers had twelve killed and twenty-eight wounded; Barney four killed and eleven wounded. Remarkably, he was not one of them. In addition to his near miss atop the binnacle, he had one bullet hole through his hat and part of his coat shot off. As Barney began the short passage home he made another capture, a schooner with the oddest of names, the *Hook 'em Snivey*. He left the *Hyder Ally* at Chester, along with the wounded Captain Rogers, who was taken in and cared for by a lonely Quaker woman, who told passersby of her good deed for the next fifty years.[34]

Barney sailed the battered but still seaworthy *General Monk* into Philadelphia with the cheers of onlookers ringing in his ears. As a reward for his gallantry, the Pennsylvania Assembly presented him with a gold-hilted sword. Robert Morris provided an even better reward, persuading a reluctant Congress to purchase the *General Monk* for the Continental Navy (her copper-sheathed hull was a selling point). After renaming her once again the *General Washington*, Morris gave her to Barney, with orders to sail to Havana and fill her hold with what the United States needed most: money.[35]

What Barney did next is one of the overlooked accomplishments in the age of sail: a round trip to Cuba, complete with two battles with Loyalist privateers, several captures, and a safe return to Philadelphia with his hold full of Spanish milled dollars—all in thirty-five days. And he was not yet twenty-three years old.[36]

On his passage southward, Barney learned of a battle that dashed any hopes of a forthcoming end to the war.

Since Yorktown, British and French fleets had based themselves in the Caribbean and West Indies, taking each other's island colonies like so many checkers pieces. The British navy was operating without its curmudgeonly genius, Admiral Rodney, whose capture of St. Eustatius was followed by the seizure of 130 merchantmen from different countries, destruction of private property, and the expulsion of all Jews and French nationals on the island—measures so draconian they drew stinging rebukes from Edmund Burke in Parliament. Rodney sent Governor de Graaff, the Dutchman who first recognized the American flag flying atop the *Andrew Doria*, as a prisoner back to England.[37]

Rodney, who suffered daily from the gout, came down with a urinary tract infection that only added to his normally miserable countenance. His return to England for surgery in September 1781 meant that Admiral Graves, and not Rodney, would be Admiral de Grasse's opponent at the Chesapeake Capes. Rodney was under the surgeon's knife as the French and American pincers were closing in on Cornwallis by land and sea. Had Rodney been in command, things might have turned out very differently.[38]

But in April 1782, the sixty-four-year-old Rodney—still in pain and every bit as irascible—was again commanding a large fleet of His Majesty's ships. On April 12, Rodney and de Grasse sent their fleets against each other in the passage between the islands of Guadeloupe and Dominica, called the Saintes, in the war's last great sea battle between the British and the French. Rodney won, capturing de Grasse and his flagship, the *Ville de Paris*, for good measure. Casualties were high on both sides, but especially for the French. Even those ships that got away met with disaster. Aboard one, the crew broke into the rum and wine, knocking over a lit candle in the process. The small fire soon swelled into a conflagration that consumed the ship. All four hundred aboard were either burned to death, drowned, or eaten by sharks. Like Clinton's victory at Charleston, Rodney's triumph at the Saintes gave heart to American Loyalist and British Tory alike.[39]

After the Battle of the Saintes, and with Admiral Digby's stranglehold on northern ports, Robert Morris, John Brown, and Morris's friend Gouverneur Morris began soliciting ideas from politicians, naval officers, and merchants regarding what to do with America's diminished navy. After a long conversation with his friend John Maxwell Nesbitt of the Conyngham-Nesbitt firm, Morris presented a "State of American Commerce and Plan for Protecting It"—an appeal to both Congress and France to cooperate in guarding American merchantmen.[40]

It was long, detailed, and visionary. "The importance of American commerce, great as it is, will appear still greater when compared to the cheap and easy means of affording it protection," he argued. To rally support from southern as well as northern states, he stressed the importance of the tobacco trade, considering it equal in value to lumber, iron, and foodstuffs from New England and the middle states. He asked France to provide ships-of-the-line and frigates to patrol the American coastline and escort American merchantmen, and for Congress to build six frigates a year, until there were enough to do the job themselves. With the sale of American goods in France from merchantmen protected (at first) by French warships, Morris's plan would pay for itself.[41]

Congress did not see it Morris's way. With more than enough battles being fought over inflation, the army, and the infamous "Morris Notes" issued to prop up America's teetering treasury, the Agent of Marine dropped his bold idea. Only two other Americans carried equal burdens—Washington and Franklin. No others could fathom their stress, or their reluctance to complain about it. In a letter to Washington, Morris wrote of his "extreme Reluctance to wound your Mind with the Anxieties that distress my own." The first casualty of his abandoned dream for a renewed naval force was the largest Continental ship, and the most famous Continental captain.[42]

As John Barry was sailing the *Alliance* to France, Sam Nicholson was getting the *Deane* ready for sea.

Of the Nicholson brothers it was Samuel, the middle one, who saw the most action during the Revolution. Unlike his older brother, James, Sam was stocky, and more inclined to enjoy himself than to put on airs.

The *Deane* put to sea in March 1782 for a two-month cruise to the West Indies. To replace the men John Barry had taken for the *Alliance*, Nicholson signed on a dozen guards from Castle William.[43]

Throughout the war, Samuel had basked in the kind of success that James never knew. This cruise was another rewarding one, and he returned to Boston with the *Deane*'s hold crammed with goods taken from five different prizes. But Nicholson's winnings came at a price: the *Deane*'s hull was damaged from storms and fighting, and his sailors were fever-ridden. To John Brown, it looked like the frigate would be laid up for months with repairs and getting a new crew, but at least this Nicholson had done his job.[44]

Maybe it was the long layover, or bad luck, or just two navy officers who simply did not like each other. But the haughty aura that surrounded James

Nicholson now infected Sam. The high morale the crew displayed during their productive cruise was already tempered by rampant fever and the usual lack of pay, but now Lieutenant Michael Knies brought the festering ugly mood to a head.

It happened this way: on a fine June night, Knies was senior watch officer while Nicholson was ashore. According to Nicholson, Knies could be seen on deck from the captain's longboat on his return, smoking his pipe. Nobody had been stationed at the gangway to announce the captain's return. Nicholson hailed the *Deane* for a rope to secure the longboat. Knies ignored him and continued smoking. According to Knies, he did not hear Nicholson. After being berated by his captain and losing his shore leave, Knies wrote Morris that Nicholson had ridden him hard throughout the voyage with "a great variety of Insults and Injuries." Knies wanted a court of inquiry held to present his side. He considered Nicholson's conduct "a stretch of Arbitrary power unknown to the regulation of the American Navy."[45]

Nicholson was equally indignant, telling Morris "I never experienced such Treatment" at the hands of a junior officer. Knies then wrote Morris that Nicholson had "damned [him] for a Bugger" and threatened to throw him overboard. Whether Morris thought this whole affair a waste of his valuable time, or at least a distraction from his trying to save his country from financial implosion, we do not know, but he did order that a court of inquiry be convened. Words matter, and being called a sodomite was the ultimate insult in any navy.

The inquiry gave several idle Continental captains, including Abraham Whipple, Samuel Tucker, and Hoysted Hacker, something official to do. During the proceedings, the other junior officers confirmed Knies's accusations. To Nicholson's horror, he—and not Knies—was found guilty, not just of belittling his officers but also of leaving his ship without a sufficient number of men to guard his prisoners still aboard her. At Knies's subsequent court-martial in August, the lieutenant ably defended himself with a sea lawyer's skill.[46]

By this time, Morris had removed Nicholson from command of the *Deane*. He soon removed the name *Deane* from the frigate as well. For some time, Silas Deane's reputation and career had been in a downward spiral. The man who first championed American liberty at Versailles and gave aid and advice to Gustavus Conyngham, Lambert Wickes, and John Paul Jones had recently called for Congress to seek a rapprochement with George III. His letters had been found on a ship captured by the British and published in every Loyalist newspaper. To call one of the last Continental ships the *Deane* any longer was ridiculous; she was renamed the *Hague*, honoring Holland's recent loan to Congress, engineered by John Adams.[47]

Nicholson, distraught over the damage to his reputation from his officers and by being relieved, went to Philadelphia to plead his case to Morris, who agreed with him and voided the proceedings—an action taken too late to restore Nicholson's command. While Morris entertained Nicholson's request for a loan, the Agent of Marine had already replaced him with an astute choice for a ship docked in Boston: John Manley.[48]

If John Barry hoped that his return voyage from l'Orient would be better than his passage to France carrying the Marquis de Lafayette, he was disappointed.

The *Alliance* was still off the French coast on St. Patrick's Day when she encountered a series of storms, ripping the bowsprit from her rigging and bashing in two longboats. Once repairs were completed, Barry sent his frigate westward. Soon concerns about his crew returned, not about their poor mood but their poor health. As more gales forced Barry to sail southward, an outbreak of fever killed five sailors in thirty days. When the mastheader spotted a large fleet standing south, Barry, lacking enough men to fight, sent the *Alliance* northward without waiting to see the fleet's nationality. Those sailors healthy enough for duty returned to their foul humor: not only had they enlisted under the new, improved Continental pay scale and prize distribution, but they had determined to serve under the captain who captured six prizes the year before—and now, the marquis *was* in France.[49]

Barry sent the *Alliance* up the River Thames to the port of New London, Connecticut. In the fall of '81, the town and the ships in the harbor had been sacked and burned by Benedict Arnold's forces. Its citizens were still rebuilding when the *Alliance* came upriver.[50]

He found New London cold, damp, and utterly inhospitable. He requested a meeting with Thomas Mumford, the Continental agent, seeking supplies and money to pay his men, who were anxious to spend it in the waterfront taverns and brothels. Mumford sent his twelve-year-old son and nothing else. The Alliances had grown from surly to hostile. If Barry rode to Philadelphia to ask Morris for help, he would be leaving old Hezekiah Welch in command, an officer he deemed "superannuated" and lacking in authority. But, doubting that another officer could get from Morris what Barry needed, he decided to risk it.[51]

He was barely out of New London when a boat carrying beef for the frigate bumped against her. When Lieutenant Nicholas Gardner ordered hands to bring it aboard, they refused, cursing and shouting "Liberty and back allowance!" Gardner went to Welch and found him too fretful to take charge. Soon the other officers, led by Gardner and Mathew Parke, were armed and on deck. After their threatening presence at the hatchway stopped a rush up the ladder by the mutinous sailors below, they spent the day guarding the opening, ducking the occasional iron stand and plank thrown through the hatchway along with threats to rush the quarterdeck again, spoken between shouts of "Damn the officers." Gardner sent a midshipman to town, with orders to get mounted and ride like fury until he found Barry.[52]

As the afternoon sun began to bake the Alliances below deck, their tempers, ironically, began to cool. Those hands from the frigate's 1781 cruise began telling the tale of that year's attempted mutiny. Their chilling narrative, coupled with the fact that the men had no weapons, while their officers were waiting above with loaded firearms, did much to bring their tempers down to a simmer.

At dusk, two lathered horses, an exhausted midshipman, and one red-faced captain, his uniform soaked in sweat, approached the *Alliance*. Once at the hatchway, Barry ordered the Alliances on deck, one at a time. He reprimanded each sailor in a low voice that belied his anger, as he sized up what to do with each one by the man's manner and responses. After the last tar came on deck, Barry put sixteen in irons, sent others below to contemplate their actions, and ordered the rest to unload, in the dark of night, those barrels of beef, still on board that boat.[53]

Once Barry sent the ringleaders to the harbor guard ship, and those men too sick for duty ashore, he was given yet another diplomatic scenario to resolve—this one courtesy of Robert Morris. The French frigate *l'Emeraude*, under command of Chevalier Lieutenant Louis-Alexandre de Quémy, was off Connecticut. A dispatch arrived from Robert Morris, ordering Barry to assist de Quémy in a mission "of both secrecy and dispatch." Further, he was to obey de Quémy's signals and be "under the Orders" of the chevalier.[54]

Rumors circulated that the young chevalier was neither a captain nor even a lieutenant, but actually a midshipman in the French navy (he was a lieutenant). After Barry's years of service to his country, long absences from his wife, getting shot in battle, and being long unpaid, this turned out to be his breaking point. Serve under a junior officer, and a rumored midshipman to boot? And by orders from a man Barry considered more friend than boss? No more of this.

Words flew across the parchment as fast as Barry's quill could write them. He told Morris of his difficulties with Mumford, his mutinous crew, and that he would take de Quémy's orders, provided he was at least a captain. After all, Barry's rank was "all I have got for Serving my Country." He followed that with a tactful letter to de Quémy that the *Alliance*'s "Want of a Boatsprit" kept her from joining *l'Émeraude*. There was also the issue of hands: a rendezvous in New London netted exactly one sailor.[55]

As if a contentious crew, international issues over rank, and a perceived snub by Morris were not enough, Barry next heard from the New London Commissary that his brother-in-law, William Austin, was confined aboard the ship *Bonetta* off New York, with a host of other Loyalist prisoners taken at Yorktown. Having learned from the commissary that only Washington had the authority to release any prisoners, Barry wrote the general, asking for his intercession for his "Particular Friend" while omitting Austin's services under Benedict Arnold.[56]

When another letter arrived, this one from Governor Hancock about Ephraim Wales—a bullying Massachusetts sailor Barry had brought back from France—demanding that Barry release him to his family, Barry fired back at the man who signed his captain's commission. Wales was a thug, considered by Franklin "a public nuisance," and Barry would release him when he no longer needed him.[57]

Once he wrote the reply to Governor Hancock, Barry returned to the latest missives from de Quémy and Mumford. The French lieutenant's last letter dismissed the idea of their serving together; Mumford's consisted of promises of food, but no money or bowsprit. Instead of answering their letters, Barry wrote a straightforward one to Morris about his time in Connecticut ("I was never in such a Damb country in my life"), telling Morris he "wood not trust [Mumford] farther than I can see him," and that he would not serve under de Quémy if his rank was superior. Another letter to his friend John Brown was even more frank; after a litany of his woes in New London, he summed up his mood and situation in six words: "I serve the country for nothing." Then Barry went to Philadelphia.[58]

A visit to Philadelphia first meant a visit home. Barry found that his wife, Sarah, had "grown very fat"—a colonial euphemism for being pregnant. The war's impact, and the Austin family's financial and political troubles, was evident in her expression and carriage, putting every other issue Barry was dealing with in a far different perspective than he had brought with him from New London. A visit that evening from Brown, who was as good a friend to Sarah as to John, was a tonic for both of them—especially when Brown told Barry he could muster up a crew for the *Alliance* right there.[59]

Barry's visit with Morris the following day was equally pleasant. He greeted Barry warmly, showing him into his office. Barry noticed he was both heavier and, like Barry, grayer. The two spoke plainly with each other. Morris had already written Barry, apologizing for any miscommunication regarding de Quémy—of course Barry should never be subservient to a junior officer. As far as Barry's rank was concerned, Morris assured him, "It will always afford me particular pleasure to support it to the utmost of my power." Further, Barry was at liberty to ask for anything he needed, there or in New London, to get the *Alliance* back to sea. Relieved, Barry left for New London after celebrating his fifth anniversary and the seventh Fourth of July with Sarah, taking with him fifty seasoned sailors from a Philadelphia rendezvous—Brown was right, after all.[60]

En route to Connecticut, Barry paid a courtesy call on Washington at his headquarters on the Hudson. After reviewing Barry's voyage with Lafayette and the state of the American and French navies, Washington informed him that "Some Disputes" over prisoner exchanges made Austin's release unlikely.[61]

Once in New London, Barry was not surprised to see that Mumford had done nothing about refitting the *Alliance*, but that changed when Barry presented him Morris's orders. A pile of correspondence waited for him, including a letter forwarded from Boston but posted in County Wexford, telling Barry his parents were both dead. And, while no document exists, he also learned that if Sarah was indeed expecting, she had suffered a miscarriage. He immediately sent her a touching, loving letter, suggesting ever so gently that she not be depressed and withdrawn from life. "It is clever to visit ones friends now and then," he wrote, "besides it is helpful to good health." His personal world shattered, Barry returned to his duty.[62]

On July 27, Elisha Hinman, Seth Harding, and several other officers arrived in New London to take part in the three mutineers' court-martial. Found "Guilty of Mutiny and Sedition," they were sentenced to between twenty and ninety lashes. Punishment was carried out the next day. "I sail tomorrow with a Good Ship's Company," Barry wrote Morris on August 2. That hot, airless night, the crew slept aboard the *Alliance*, woken by the occasional mosquito or gnat that came to say good-bye. Barry's orders were to go on a prolonged cruise (thanks to the *Alliance*'s copper bottom). With his ship refitted, and a contingent of loyal and willing Pennsylvania sailors, he intended to do just that.[63]

To fill his muster rolls, Barry took two of the guilty mutineers back. Several other men also made their marks on the sheets: local slaves, whose owners were promised their wages and prize shares when the *Alliance* returned.[64]

Of all the ironies during the Revolutionary War at sea, the disparity regarding black men, both free and slave, American or British, stands out all too clearly.

After the *General Monk*'s colors fluttered to her deck, Joshua Barney sent a boarding party from the *Hyder Ally* to take command of his prize. They found two slaves, William Brown and Isaac Ball. Only five feet three, Brown was stocky and quite a fiddler. At five seven, Ball was slender, his face "marked with the smallpox." Both wore the ship's issued uniform of tow-linen shirts (made with rough, short fibers) and blue sailor jackets.

It is not known who owned them, or if their service aboard ship began when she was the *General Washington* or after she became the *General Monk*, but by this time they were, at the very least, fairly seasoned hands. But whether their owner was a patriot or a Loyalist had no bearing on their future. As slaves they were contraband of war. Once Barney brought the *General Monk* into Philadelphia they would be resold as slaves, and the proceeds of their sale would become part of the prize money shared by Barney and his men.

On April 9, Barney's prize nestled against other ships along the docks, flying the American flag atop the British ensign as was the victor's custom. Somehow, either that evening or early the next morning, Brown and Ball slipped off the *General Monk*. They crossed the Delaware to New Jersey, where (they hoped) it would be harder for the bounty hunters, who made their living capturing runaways, to find them (after the war, Lieutenant Luke Matthewman, who served under John Barry, among others, took on "the disagreeable business of transporting free Negroes from [New York] to their respective homes," and thus "incurred the appellation of Kidnapper.")[65]

They found refuge with one Whitehead Jones of Hog Point, Cumberland County. Three months later they left, perhaps upon learning that their hiding place had been discovered. Shortly thereafter, they were apprehended, still wearing their blue sailor jackets, and turned over to Nathan Johnson, the county jailer. Johnson posted a notice in the *Pennsylvania Gazette* that "Their masters (if any they have) are requested to come within four weeks" and "pay their charges," before Johnson sold them.[66]

When John Adams and Samuel Chase were debating the worth of "an American fleet," there was already an established presence of black sailors serving on both colonial and British ships. A U.S. Navy estimate states that 10 percent of the sailors who fought the British during the Revolution, be it in Continental or state navies and in privateers, were African Americans. One Royal

Navy admiral noted that black seamen shared "the same fate as the free-born white man."[67]

To an extent, this was true, but life at sea was not color-blind. Black sailors were commonly looked down upon by their white shipmates, although when a sailor needed assistance aloft in a storm, the only thing that mattered was the hand offered him and not its color. But a white sailor, whether enlisted or pressed into service, need not fear shore leave in American or West Indies ports, whereas a black seaman could be as easily shanghaied into slavery on land as shanghaied into service at sea. When the Howe brothers came to Head of Elk in 1777, two deserters from the *Isis*, a British two-decker, jumped ship and were captured by Maryland militiamen. After sharing information on the British plans for invading Philadelphia (if such low-ranking gentlemen had any knowledge), they told of how British tars bragged "they would make their Fortunes by selling them in the West Indies," and how these prisoners "were kicked and cuffed on every Occasion."[68]

Brown and Ball might have—might have—been better off had they been aboard the Loyalist privateer *Regulator*, captured by Sam Nicholson and the *Deane* on his recent cruise. The privateer's crew consisted of seventy slaves and five white officers. The *Regulator* was one of the five prizes Nicholson brought back to Boston. As with the *Hyder Ally* in Philadelphia, the Maryland-born Nicholson fully expected the slaves to be sold and the proceeds divvied up among officers and crew per Morris's latest percentages.

Imagine Nicholson's surprise when he learned that no such sale would take place. The Massachusetts Provisional Congress had barred the sale of slaves captured at sea, and there was nothing Nicholson could do about it (save take his frustrations out on Lieutenant Knies). The Massachusetts Court offered the slaves a choice: freedom in Massachusetts, or return to Bermuda. Sizing up their future, they chose Bermuda.[69]

Quite a few African American sailors jumped ship like Brown and Ball, including a couple of those who sailed with John Barry on the *Alliance*. When he returned from his final voyage of the war, Barry informed the Continental agent that the slaves among his crew had earned their masters "120 Livres each," but he had bad news for Congressman William Ellery about his slave, Caesar. Ellery had inquired as to Caesar's whereabouts. Barry claimed he had no idea that Caesar, who sailed through storms and fought a British frigate with free American shipmates, even had an owner. Barry had given Caesar "Liberty to go to N[ew] Port, and I dare Say he is there now." Caesar was not there.[70]

Names of African Americans are found on practically every surviving ship's muster roll. Suriname Wanton served aboard the *Cabot* in Esek Hopkins's first fleet. Cato Austin and Scipio Brown served in the Continental frigate *Boston*, Austin assigned to a starboard gun and Brown handling ammunition. John Martin, believed to be the first African American marine, was lost at sea. David Mitchell, a native of Bermuda and a slave, was captured while serving in a British ship. Held prisoner at Newbury, Massachusetts, he agreed to serve aboard the *Alliance* under Pierre Landais. Afterwards, he was given his freedom by the Massachusetts Council.[71]

One story that exemplifies both the lot of African Americans at sea during the war and their courage and patriotism is that of James Forten. Born free in Southwark near the Philadelphia shipyards in 1766, he learned to read and write at the African School run by the abolitionist Anthony Benezet. When his father died, James took on what work he could along the waterfront to help support his mother and sister. In 1781, he was a tall, strapping fifteen-year-old, and signed on the letter of marque *Royal Louis*, twenty-two guns, commanded by John Barry's friend Stephen Decatur, Sr.[72]

Though a "landsman," young Forten knew the sailor's lingo well enough, and once he got his sea legs he began mastering a sailor's duties. Decatur had a reputation for successful cruises, and this voyage of the *Royal Louis* was no exception. During one bloody engagement with the British sloop-of-war *Active*, Forten was the only man of his gun crew unharmed, and he won plaudits for his courage.[73]

Forten's second cruise was not so lucky. The *Royal Louis* had barely cleared the Delaware Capes when she was sighted and pursued by the warship *Amphion*, Captain John Bazeley, the man who captured the *Lexington* and fresh from participating in Arnold's raid on New London. Try as he might, Decatur could not shake free of her. The chase finally ended off the coast of Virginia, where Decatur struck his colors. The capture filled young James with dread—while his white shipmates faced the horror of the British prison ships, Forten knew "that rarely . . . were prisoners of his complexion exchanged; they were sent to the West Indies, and there doomed to a life of slavery."[74]

But Forten was lucky. Bazeley had his two sons aboard the *Amphion*, younger than Forten and not yet ready to begin service in the Royal Navy. Watching James's wizardry with marbles in a game with his son Henry, and learning that Forten was educated, Bazeley ordered him to serve as the boys' tutor. While his shipmates groused over the black Forten's good fortune, James was under orders, and carried them out so well that Bazeley summoned him to the captain's cabin shortly before the *Amphion* reached New York.

Impressed by Forten's intelligence and winning ways, the well-off Bazeley offered to send him to England with his sons to live at the family mansion. England had its prejudices, but a black man had a much better chance of making a future for himself in England than in a rebel country that was tolerant of slavery.

Forten's answer stunned Bazeley: "I have been taken prisoner for the liberties of my country, and never will prove a traitor to her interest." Bazeley could not change Forten's mind, and so he turned him over to the commandant of the *Jersey*, along with a letter urging that he be exchanged at the first opportunity. James willingly turned down the promise of a life in England, free from the possibility of slavery, and chose instead the evils that awaited captured rebel sailors aboard that reeking death trap of a prison ship. He was, after all, an American.[75]

Gustavus Conyngham had been back in Philadelphia for nearly a year when he took quill in hand to write to William Temple Franklin. Benjamin Franklin's grandson was serving as the minister's private secretary, and Conyngham knew he had Franklin's ear. Conyngham needed help that only Franklin could provide.[76]

The ship *Hannibal* docked in Philadelphia as the leaves were turning color and news of Yorktown was awaited with the city's collective bated breath. Conyngham wasted no time paying a visit to Robert Morris, hoping the Agent of Marine would have a Continental ship for him, or at least an officer's berth. Due to the diminished size of the navy, Morris had neither. Desperate to return to sea and further aggravate the British, Conyngham turned to the French for a commission, also with no results.[77]

He had even less luck in getting his back pay from Congress. The representatives were, on the surface, glad he was safe at home, but hoped he understood that they could not possibly dole out a captain's back pay unless they saw a captain's commission. Just having some accounts from his voyages commanding the *Surprise* and *Revenge* was not enough.

Conyngham had anticipated this response. Before departing France with Anne, he had asked Benjamin Franklin to help him prove his story. That was months ago. Now he wrote Temple. "I must request that you will speak to his Excellency," he pleaded, hoping that Franklin had found the commission that Comte de Vergennes had ordered seized, or would at least send Conyngham a certificate corroborating his claim. He also needed Franklin's assistance in getting all of his account books returned.

Weeks later, Conyngham received his answer from Franklin:

> I do hereby Certify to whom it may Concern that the Commissioners of the United States of America at the Court of France, Did issue on the first day of March One thousand seven hundred and seventy seven to Captain Gustavus Conyngham a Commission of Congress appointing him a Captain in the Navy of the said States and to Command a Vessel then fitting out at Dunkerque on their account to Cruise against their Enemies . . .

The affidavit went on, detailing what had occurred both to Conyngham and to his commission—exactly what he needed to present to Congress. Thus armed, he presented a proper memorial to Congress in October, asking for a new commission and reinstatement in the Continental Navy. Then he waited.[78]

What Pierre Landais could not do, and John Barry could only envision, John Paul Jones did. He oversaw the completion of the ship-of-the-line *America*.

She was titanic in length and breadth: 221 feet long with a 50-foot beam, displacing 2,000 tons. By September 1782 Jones had been in Portsmouth a solid year, but the fruits of his labors would soon be on tallowed ways, and in the Piscataqua River. "Will *America* ever be finished?" he had despairingly asked John Brown in the spring. As the days grew shorter and the New England breezes cooled perceptibly, she was nearly ready for launching. Jones wrote Gouverneur Morris, praising the ship's builder, William Hackett: "The workmanship is a piece of perfection," he crowed. Robert Morris sent word to both Jones and John Langdon, promising to send them enough money to get her launched that fall.[79]

On August 10, the French ship-of-the-line *Magnifique* was entering Boston harbor, a feckless pilot at the helm who underestimated the ship's draft. She ran aground so hard she was wrecked. Hearing this, Morris acted immediately with a solution that worked perfectly for everyone but Jones. "I have the honour to present to you the *America* . . . in the name of the United States for the Service of His most Christian Majesty," he wrote the Duc de la Luzerne. Morris's offer was both a token of gratitude for France's support and a way to get the giant ship off Congress's ledger.[80]

Jones despaired. While he was a good sport to Morris, calling his loss "a

Sacrifice I shall make with pleasure," he was bitter to everyone else, rhetorically asking Gouverneur Morris, "Are we in a condition to make presents?" adding it was like "offering to give a friend an empty Eggshell." On her first attempted launch, the *America* got stuck on the ways, but with the help of the anchor cables sent to Portsmouth from the *Magnifique*, the second attempt went flawlessly. Jones graciously turned her over to the French. James Nicholson was wrong: Jones did get the *America* to sea. Nicholson was also right: Jones never took her to sea.[81]

Morris thought he had a consolation prize for Jones: *l'Indien*, at long last, now called the *South Carolina* and leased by her owners to the South Carolina Navy.

She had sailed from Texel Island under Charlestonian Alexander Gillon, who possessed more diplomatic skills than nautical ones. Once she reached Philadelphia, Morris planned to give her to Jones, then send him on a cruise with the *Alliance* and *Hague* under Jones's command (imagine Barry's and Sam Nicholson's reaction to that!). She was larger than the American-built frigates, but as fast if not faster, carrying forty guns. The ship of Jones's dreams was in his home port—would she at last be his?[82]

But Gillon, learning of Morris's intentions, sent her back down the Delaware in November under command of his South Carolina colleague John Joyner, to keep her out of Morris's clutches. Foul weather kept her downriver until December 19. Once off the Delaware Capes she was chased and pursued by three of Admiral Digby's frigates for eighteen hours before they captured her and sailed her triumphantly into New York. For the third and last time, the frigate was taken from Jones.[83]

"If the War should continue I wish to have the most active part in it," Jones wrote. With rumors of peace reaching America, and the navy down to two frigates and a packet, Jones received permission to join a French fleet as the guest of Monsieur le Marquis de Vaudreuil, Lieutenant-Général des Armées Navales, about to embark on a cruise from Boston to the Caribbean. After purchasing horses and a sleigh for his wintry passage to Massachusetts, Jones left Philadelphia and the Continental Navy, but not before Morris wrote Elias Boudinot, president of Congress, that Jones

Is about to pursue a Knowledge of his Profession so as to become still more useful if ever he should be called to the Command of a Squadron or Fleet. I should do Injustice to my own Feelings as well as to my

Country if I did not most warmly recommend this Gentleman to the Notice of Congress whose Favour he has certainly merited by the most signal Services and Sacrifices.[84]

Before his departure, Morris gave Jones one more gift—his back pay of $20,705—a remarkable gesture, considering how many naval officers were due less but overdue longer. At Morris's suggestion, Jones invested $8,800 of it in the new Bank of North America, making him its largest stockholder when he left Philadelphia.[85]

After three years in prison, John Manley had finally been exchanged and returned to Boston. Still popular with both local politicians and sailors, Robert Morris hoped Manley's name alone might add more names to the *Hague*'s muster rolls.

On August 8, Morris sent orders for Manley to cruise the West Indies and, Morris hoped, "annoy the Enemies of the United States" once more. When Morris learned that two hundred transports were heading to America, he dropped another line to Manley suggesting they, too, would make good targets. On September 11, Manley ascended the *Hague*'s gangplank. The frigate was festively decorated, as a throng of Bostonians took to the waterfront to cheer their hero back to sea, complete with a thirteen-gun salute. Manley even delivered a short speech to his men and the crowd.[86]

The *Hague* made it to the West Indies, taking several prizes along the way. The last one, taken around New Year's Day, 1783, was the merchantman *Baille*, her hold packed tight with supplies. On January 9, Manley's frigate was spotted off Antigua by the HMS *Dolphin*, a forty-four-gun frigate. Soon the *Dolphin* had company: four ships-of-the-line, all anxious to join in the chase. For thirty-six hours Manley led them south, past Montserrat, hoping to find protection under the guns of the French fortresses along the eastern shore of Guadeloupe. Manley had already been captured twice; there would not be a third time.

Despite damage to his hull and masts from the enemy's long bow chasers, Manley made it, running aground on the reef off Grande Terre. Not wanting to give the French garrison gunnery practice, the British ships sailed off. "Without a man killed and only one slightly wounded," Manley got the *Hague* off the rocks and repaired. She sailed up Nantasket Road in May, by which time her crew was as tired of Manley's contentious attitudes as they had been with Sam Nicholson's.

His lieutenants, including Michael Knies, pressed charges against him, and Morris had him arrested.[87]

Navy veteran and historian Dr. William Morgan wrote that Manley, as one of the first captains in "Washington's Navy," had captured the first prize of note in the war, the brigantine *Nancy*. With the *Baille*, he also captured the last.[88]

On September 7, 1782, the *Alliance* was making for the Newfoundland Banks when her mastheader spotted a sail on the horizon. Taking up his spyglass, Captain John Barry determined her a prize worth pursuing, and gave chase. She proved no match for the fast *Alliance*, and was easily overtaken.

She was the Nantucket whaler *Somerset*, returning home after a profitable cruise, her hold full of barrels containing spermaceti and ambergris. Captain Thomas Brock objected: the *Somerset* was an American ship. His protest was soon contradicted once Barry perused Brock's papers and found Admiral Digby's pass protecting his ship from seizure by the Royal Navy and Loyalist letters of marque giving Digby's "permission to bring their Oyl to New York." That made her a prize—the third for this cruise. Barry placed a small crew aboard and sent her to Boston.[89]

More prizes meant fewer hands, but Barry was a veteran at sweet-talking captured Loyalists and convincing them of the error of their ways. Several of the Somersets signed on, including Second Mate Shubael Gardner. He was a rare find—a seasoned tar with gunnery experience. Barry made him a master's mate.[90]

Gardner was joining a crew far different from the ones Barry had taken with him on his previous voyages to France. "I have a good healthy ships Company, much beyond my expectation," he happily wrote John Brown. For John Kessler, it harked back to his first days with Barry, sailing the privateer *Delaware* in 1779. Barry was, at heart, a sailor's captain; the "Innocent mirth of the Seamen was his delight," Kessler later recalled. "Indiscriminate enjoyment of mirth & good cheer" was the norm aboard ship:

> It sometimes happened that when any one had neglected or done any-thing wrong & when asked by Capt'n Barry how he came to neglect it ... the person would begin to state, he thought so and so, Capt'n Barry would hastily say who gave you a right to think so, & which occasioned the crew among themselves to address their comrades with "who gives

you the right to think, don't you know that Capt'n Barry thinks for us all"—and on one of those times of play he heard it, and required and received an explanation with the greatest good humor.[91]

His cheerful demeanor was matched with unsurpassed skills as a mariner. "He knew how to perform all the duties of a Seaman from Stem to Stern," Kessler wrote, marveling how he could be awakened in the middle of the night during a storm or crisis and know exactly what to do: "His decisions on sudden emergencies was wondered at and admired." A sailor would look far and wide before he found a better commander.[92]

It had been a sweet five weeks for Barry and his men. Since leaving New London they had been blessed with both fortune and adventure. As soon as they left Connecticut waters, two prizes fell into their hands. First Barry sailed to Bermuda, a haven for Loyalist privateers, in hopes of freeing the American sailors imprisoned there, when he learned that the Jamaica Fleet—eighty-eight merchantmen in all—had recently passed the island on its northward course to Newfoundland before turning east towards England. Barry took off in pursuit. The Royal Navy's convoy, commanded by Admiral Graves, included nine ships-of-the-line, among them Admiral de Grasse's captured flagship, the *Ville de Paris*. Barry's plan was simple: get to the fleet and stay on its heels, avoid the ships-of-the-line, cut out as many prizes as possible, and don't get caught. He began sailing after them on September 8.[93]

To Barry's consternation, a vicious storm prevented the *Alliance* from making any headway towards the fleet. But on September 18, Barry learned how lucky he was. The *Alliance* captured a brig from the fleet, whose captain informed him that the storm he had safely sailed through was the tail end of a huge hurricane that had scattered the fleet for hundreds of miles. For two days, countless ships foundered. Two ships-of-the-line, including the *Ville de Paris*, went down with all hands. No fewer than thirteen merchantmen met the same fate. Graves's own flagship, the *Ramillies*, also went down, but most of her men were rescued and taken aboard the fleet's surviving ships.[94]

For days, the *Alliance* sailed through the wreckage of floating hogsheads, masts, and sailors' sea chests, the remains of much of the giant fleet and its mighty escorts, now at the bottom of the sea. The cruise became a combined prize-taking binge and rescue effort. One after another, the *Alliances* overtook merchantmen too damaged to sail effectively; some were literally floating derelicts, with the exception of the wealth in their holds. One captain told of watching a ship-of-the-line being torn apart plank by plank by the gales before the tempest's massive green waves swallowed her up.[95]

As before, Barry was a gracious host to his prisoners, including officers from the *Ramillies*, who thanked him for his kindnesses, a stark contrast to how American sailors were treated when captured. One asked Barry to "Accept my thanks for the genteel treatment we castaway dogs received on board the *Alliance*." With too many mouths to feed, while growing more shorthanded with each prize crew, Barry decided to make for France, taking four of his prizes in tow. After sailing through another storm that damaged the *Alliance*'s bowsprit, the five ships reached l'Orient on October 17.[96]

Coming into port, Barry saw no fewer than a dozen other prizes at anchor, taken by American and French privateers. With such a glut of ships, there would be no quick sale of his captures. Once ashore, he visited Consul Thomas Barclay to make arrangements for repairs, refitting, the sale of his prizes, and pay for his men. He found l'Orient abuzz with rumors that peace was at hand—which was welcome news at Versailles after the Battle of the Saintes, and recent reports that Russia was eyeing French holdings in the Crimea. Three days after Barry's arrival the *General Washington* sailed into l'Orient. Joshua Barney informed Barry he had secret dispatches to take immediately to Franklin.[97]

For months, peace negotiations had dragged on, slowed by the bickering between three principals—the American triumvirate of Franklin, Adams, and Jay, "the greatest quibblers I ever knew," one British diplomat groused. Barry was no warmonger, but he knew that peace rumors would drive down the sale of his prizes. He was also not eager to remain in l'Orient when news of actual peace arrived. Like the Philadelphia merchants who sent their ships hurriedly back to England to fatten their accounts before word of Lexington and Concord reached Parliament, Barry now wanted to escape France before peace put an end to his prize-taking. He gave Barney a slapdash note for Franklin, suggesting that Barney join Barry on another cruise that would "render Great Service"—or at least funds—"to the United States."[98]

He hoped to have his frigate ready and his prizes sold by the time Barney returned from Passy, but three things kept the *Alliance* from sailing. The first was Barclay's inability to get the prizes sold. The second was Barry himself. Without warning he was stricken with a "Bilious fever" that forced the giant Irishman to take refuge in a chamber above a waterfront tavern. No matter what Ship's Surgeon Joseph Geagan did to treat it, the fever would not spike, and Barry was confined to his room for weeks.[99]

Deathly ill, Barry did not see the third incident coming. Having deterred a mutiny by British sailors with the lash and one by American seamen with a tongue-lashing, Barry now faced a third, from his officers. While some, like Geagan, were new to the *Alliance*, others, like Mathew Parke, had served aboard her for years, with little or no pay to show for it. Parke paid a courtesy call to Barry's sickroom, informing him that six officers, fed up with Morris's promises of pay and having learned the officers aboard the *General Washington* had "rec'd considerable compensation," had left ship in Barry's absence and taken rooms in a dockside hostel. They demanded that Barry obtain notes they could discharge for payment.

Drawing himself up in his bed, Barry tried to reason with Parke, having "as Much reason to Complain as any of you." But while Barry refused to force Morris's hand, he promised that if wages were not paid the officers upon their return to America, he would join them "in any Petition or Remonstrance" Parke thought proper. Barry's offer was refused. With a hand trembling from his illness, Barry wrote orders to each of them: return to duty, or face arrest.[100]

By November's end he was well enough to return to his cabin and finish refitting the *Alliance*. Barney returned from Passy with orders to remain in l'Orient until negotiations were completed, then sail home with the momentous news of peace. Franklin had assured Barney "you will have an English passport"—proof to any British boarding party he might encounter that Great Britain now recognized the "band of rebels" as a sovereign nation. Barry wrote to Morris about "the Joyous news of peace" and that he would "run down the Coast of Guinea" before sailing to Martinique and from there, America.[101]

But what to do with disobedient officers who were still ashore? Barry's solution was simple and quick. Rather than send marines to return them to the ship and find enough officers in port to conduct a trial, Barry marooned them. He ordered Barclay not to pay the men; rather, let them "get to America as well as they Can," where "they will be Tried by a Court martial and merit their desserts." With just old Lieutenant Welch and young Marine Lieutenant Thomas Elwood remaining among the officers, he promoted several hands, young Kessler joining Shubael Gardner as a master's mate. With a cold, bitter wind filling her sails, the *Alliance* departed l'Orient for the last time on December 7 (soon afterwards, the preliminary peace accords were signed, "in as short a time as a marriage agreement," a sardonic John Adams noted).[102]

The *Alliance* sped south to Africa, then made her way without difficulty across the Atlantic. In just one month, her mastheader sighted Martinique, where Barry found orders awaiting him from Morris. He was to proceed to Havana and collect 100,000 Spanish milled dollars—about half a million dollars in U.S. currency—and bring it posthaste to Philadelphia. Congress was broke again.[103]

Before departing Martinique, Barry told the publisher of the local gazette that the preliminary articles of peace had been signed. The news island-hopped its way to the American coast, by which time the facts of Barry's report had been altered: "ARTICLES of PEACE were SIGNED on the 22nd day of December last!" the Boston *Evening Post* declared. The facts were wrong, but paper after paper attributed the good tidings to "Capt. Bary [*sic*] . . . an officer of credit."[104]

Barry did his own share of island hopping while heading to Cuba, with the occasional British cruiser for company until the *Alliance*'s superb sailing ability left them in her wake. At the Hôtel de la Coursonne in Cap François, Haiti, Barry met with Seth Harding. The former captain of the *Confederacy* had been recently paroled from the British prison in Jamaica, and needed passage home. Barry, needing senior officers, was happy to oblige. The *Alliance* resumed sailing on January 22, escorting two slow ships to Havana. They arrived at dusk on January 29.[105]

In the dim light of sunset Barry made out Spain's West Indies fleet, one long row of warships nestled under the mighty stone walls of Morro Castle, which guards Havana's harbor to this day. The following morning, after salutes were exchanged between the *Alliance* and the fortress, Barry's pinnace was rowed to the stone quay by the castle, both he and his sailors resplendent in their best attire.

To his pleasant surprise, he was greeted by his friends John Brown and John Green. Ever cautious, Morris had purchased yet another ship for the navy, fitted her with twenty guns and renamed her the *Duc de Lauzon*. Green, recently paroled from Mill Prison, was appointed captain, with orders to take Brown with him to Havana and bring back the cache of Spanish milled dollars in the event that Barry did not arrive.[106]

One last time, the best-laid plans for the Continental Navy ran into political shoals ashore. When Brown went to make arrangements for the transfer of the money, he was told that his country's credit was good for only $72,447—a far cry from what Morris expected. In fact, Brown was told by the banking official that, had Morris used *his* credit and not his country's, Brown would be taking home a substantially larger amount.[107]

Things got worse on the evening of February 1, when Barry hosted an ornate dinner for Don Luis Vizaga, the governor of Cuba; Don Josef Solano, admiral of the Spanish fleet; along with the American registrar, James Seagrove, Brown, and Green. The affair went swimmingly until Don Josef informed his host that the American ships were not going anywhere. The Spanish fleet was readying itself for a joint offensive with the French against British-held Jamaica. For the sake of secrecy, the port was closed until they departed.[108]

For more than a month, Barry petitioned both dons to let the two American ships go, but only the French ship-of-the-line *Triton*, also assigned to carry chests of money for her country, was allowed to depart. In the meantime, Barry made sure the Spanish knew he was in town. First, he careened the *Alliance*, with his men loudly hammering oakum into the frigate's copper seams. Next, he ran round-the-clock gunnery practice, exercising both his cannons and small arms as he paced under "the Havannah's Pleasant Weather." To keep his crew happy, he issued shore leave six sailors at a time, warning them that latecomers would be placed in irons, and further leave canceled for all.[109]

While Barry was entreating Don Luis to let his frigate go, Robert Morris was dealing with a thorny issue over one of Barry's prizes. Once word reached Nantucket that the whaler *Somerset* had been seized, her owner, John Ramsdell, fired off an angry complaint: just because Admiral Digby had given Captain Brock a pass protecting the *Somerset* from seizure by British ships did not mean she was not an American vessel. Morris turned the matter over to Congress.[110]

Finally, on March 5, with Morro Castle's guns firing endless salutes, the Spanish fleet left Havana. The following day, the *Alliance* and the *Duc de Lauzon*, escorting a number of American merchantmen, sailed for home. At first they followed the Spaniards, but Barry tired of their sluggish sailing and signaled the *Duc* to follow him to the Gulf of Florida, and then up the Gulf Stream and home. The *Duc*'s cargo was too valuable to risk.[111]

The ships were sailing past the Florida Keys, then called "the Martair's [Martyr's] Rocks," when Barry's mastheader sighted British ships bearing southeast. With the *Duc* weighted down with money chests, Barry ordered a course change—they, too, would head south, and make for the Spanish fleet. Green signaled back that he wanted to continue northward, but Barry overruled him.[112]

Their pursuers were the British frigates *Alarm*, Captain Charles Cotton, thirty-two guns, and the *Sybil*, Captain James Vashon, twenty-eight (a third, the eighteen-gun sloop *Tobago* under Captain George Markham, was right behind). Cotton signaled Vashon to make straight for the Americans, and he willingly obeyed. The *Sybil* was a French frigate captured at the Battle of the Saintes and awarded to Vashon for his bravery in that fight.[113]

For seven hours the British ships gave chase, with Barry reefing sail to let Green's lumbering vessel keep up with him. The *Sybil* was still ahead of the other enemy ships when she got within range of the *Duc*. It was now dark; Barry ordered the deck cleared for action. He planned to intercept the *Sybil* so the *Duc* could get away when the mastheaders on each ship saw lantern lights on the horizon: the Spanish fleet. Vashon sheered off, and the two American ships sailed into the welcoming arms of their Spanish allies.

To Barry's bemusement, sunrise showed them to be "8 or 10 Sloops and Scooners," with not a cannon among them. Nonetheless, the sardonic Barry reported, "they answered our ends," and the ships tacked to the westward, sailing between Florida and Grand Bahama Island. He signaled the *Duc*, ordering Brown and Green to come aboard. Once in his cabin he told them he was transferring the chests to the faster *Alliance*. While Brown saw the wisdom in this, Green became so furious that Barry suspected Green had more than his official cargo in his hold. For several hours, longboats and pinnaces rowed between the ships, as sailors moved the heavy chests to Barry's frigate. Then they were off again.[114]

At sunrise on March 10, the ships were four hundred miles off Cape Canaveral under light winds when Barry spotted the three sail bearing north by east. He knew exactly who they were. Suddenly the mastheader called down to him: there was another ship—a large sail—"Bearing SSW," and too far away to tell if she was British, French, or Spanish. Barry decided the two ships would again show their heels, and signaled Green to follow him on another race southward. Soon the *Alliance* was flying ahead of the *Duc*, and Barry signaled *Shift for Yourself*.[115]

By now every ship but the large sail in the far distance was flying its true colors. Signal flags went up from the *Duc*: Green wanted to speak with Barry. Irritated beyond words, he once again shortened sail. He did not want to abandon Green—he certainly did not want to abandon Brown—but his priority was the mission Morris had given him, the gold in his hold. Barry saw the *Alarm* closing in, the *Sybil* and *Tobago* close behind. "Beat to quarters," he ordered, and the Alliances jumped to their stations.

Shubael Gardner was responsible for the men manning the guns in the captain's cabin. Once there, they cut loose the guns, took out the tampions, and loaded them with iron shot, the slow fuses lit, ready in the gunners' hands. One of the powder boys came into the cabin, and began ladling out a ration of grog for each man. Gardner was a fighting Quaker; we do not know if he was a drinking one.[116]

Taking his speaking trumpet in hand, Barry demanded to know what Green was thinking. "They [are] Privateers," Green shouted, adding, "We could take them." For a second, Barry was dumbstruck. Then, "begging to differ," he pointed out the two ships in the lead were frigates, and told Green to do what was done in such a situation: heave his guns overboard to lighten the *Duc*, and "try them before the wind." Green might be in a disobedient mood, but as soon as Barry shouted his directions, the *Duc*'s crew started jettisoning all the guns overboard save her stern chasers. With flagrant disobedience, Green began sailing his ship next to the *Alliance* on her weather bow, putting the *Duc* in easy range of the *Alarm*'s guns.

Now the mastheader called Barry's attention to the distant ship. Through his spyglass Barry watched as she tacked and began standing straight at them. If she was British, he thought, she would have done this long ago; she had to be Spanish or French. After running up the Spanish fleet's signals for assistance, he changed course to save the *Duc de Lauzon*.[117]

The *Sybil* was just coming up to give the *Duc* a broadside when the *Alarm* bore away, crossing the *Duc*'s stern—not to "cross the T" but to depart. Barry was puzzled for an instant, then turned to see the large ship bearing down, now flying French colors. She was *le Triton*, the ship-of-the-line permitted to leave Havana days before Barry did. She was about an hour away, with these light winds.

Seeing that there was enough water between the *Sybil* and the *Duc*, Barry sent the *Alliance* between them in a risky pick play. He "ordered the courses hauled up and hard a Weather the helm." No sooner yelled than done; the helmsman turned the wheel, and the *Alliance* yawed through the wind so fast the crew felt the ship shudder from masthead to keelson. In a split second, she had righted herself. While Green took advantage of the maneuver to get the *Duc* away, Captain Vashon watched from his quarterdeck, well aware that a fight was seconds away. He had seen the *Alarm* sheer off but did not yet know why. He was a British captain; one did not reach that position if he had not conquered his fear. Like Barry, he was popular with his men. They were ready to fight for him.[118]

As he had done since that April day in '76 when he led the Lexingtons in their first battle, Barry grew quieter and calmer than the captain giving orders minutes earlier. Kessler watched as he "went from gun to gun, on the main deck cautioning against too much haste and not to fire until the Enemy was right abreast." Time seemed to stand still, but only minutes had passed since Barry sent his fast ship into harm's way. It was almost noon.[119]

The silence was broken by the *Sybil*'s bow gun, the round shot smashing into Barry's cabin, shattering the windowpane and sending shards of glass and splinters flying, wounding everyone inside, including Gardner. Vashon now tacked through the wind to fire a broadside from her port guns, but he fired before his gunners could take aim, and every shot missed the *Alliance*. The *Sybil* glided helplessly within "half a pistol Shott" of the *Alliance*, letting the Americans see the expression on their adversaries' faces. Barry "ordered the main top sail hove to the mast," slowing his ship down to take full advantage of what came next.

"Fire!" he ordered, and a devastating broadside from *Alliance*'s starboard guns ripped through the *Sybil*'s rigging, shredding the stuns'ls (studding sails) Vashon had not hauled in, killing a lieutenant and wounding several sailors. Seeing the damage to the *Sybil*'s sails and rigging, Barry ordered his helmsman to send the *Alliance* even closer. The next broadside was accompanied by the frigate's swivel guns, loaded with musket balls that flew like buckshot across the water. In the fighting tops, Lieutenant Elwood's marines poured a volley towards their British counterparts aloft.[120]

A second broadside from the *Sybil* wounded several Americans, but Vashon's frigate was too damaged to sail effectively. The *Alliance*'s guns answered with another broadside; aiming higher, the gunners took down the *Sybil*'s foretopmast. Below deck, Vashon's surgeon was overwhelmed with casualties.[121]

For another half hour, Vashon gamely maintained the fight, his stuns'ls dragging in the water while Barry's gunners turned their attention to the *Sybil*'s hull. With his sails and rigging cut to pieces, Vashon "hoisted a signal of distress" for the *Alarm* and *Tobago* to come to his aid. He changed course as best as he could and sheered off. Looking angrily towards the *Alarm*, he saw Captain Cotton's reply: *Break off the engagement.*[122]

Barry's blood was up, but not to the extent that he would make a foolhardy decision. His "Sails Spars and Rigging hurt a Little, but not so much they would all do again," he later reported. Much as he wanted to pursue the crippled *Sybil*, it would place the *Alliance*—and the treasure in her hold—at great risk, as long as she was the only ship in the fight against the three British ones. Where was that Frenchman?[123]

Later than sooner, *le Triton* came up. The Alliances could see her sixty-four guns run out. Barry hailed her captain: Had he seen *Alliance*'s signals? Why had he not entered the fight? The captain's answer was thin: he had half a million dollars aboard himself, feared that the *Alliance* and *Duc de Lauzon* were already captured and that Barry's signal was just an Englishman's trick. When the three ships finally made sail to pursue the British trio it was too late. *Le Triton* sailed poorly. At seven p.m., Barry lost sight of them, and watched angrily as *le Triton* also went on her way. He signaled Green, ordering him and Brown to come aboard the *Alliance*.[124]

Brown began the meeting praising Barry's actions, but Green was irate over Barry's perceived mistrust of his conduct. Barry, in turn, demanded an apology from Green, promising to report everything to Morris. Friends for years, they parted acrimoniously as Green, with a stunned Brown in tow, returned to his ship.[125]

The next day Barry sent two 9-pounders over to the *Duc* for her protection, and the two ships started for home. For several days, Barry shortened sail, uncertain if it was Green's ship or Green's black mood that kept the *Duc* lagging behind. After eight days they had sailed just four hundred miles, reaching Cape Hatteras on March 18. Barry had had enough: duty dictated that the *Alliance* proceed on her mission with all speed. After he gave orders to make all sail, the *Alliance* began flying homeward. In just twenty hours she was off Cape Henlopen. Home was just up the Delaware.

At six p.m. on the nineteenth, a welcome fog cloaked the *Alliance* as she entered Delaware Bay. But this time Barry was not alone in the mist: "I fell in with two British Cruisers," he noted, "one of them appeared to be a two-decker." Barry now used the fog to get away. After several more attempts he was convinced "the Coast was lined with Enemy Ships." A disappointed captain headed to sea just as the fog lifted, and the cruisers gave chase.[126]

If he could not fight the enemy he would out-sail them. With the wind on his side, Barry sent the *Alliance* northward at a speed her crew could hardly believe. A grinning Barry "hove the Logg myself" at one point to gauge the *Alliance*'s speed: "14 Knotts with a great deal of ease." For two straight days, the *Alliance* made two hundred miles.

Barry did not know it, but in taking the British on this jaunt, he had cleared the way for the *Duc de Lauzon*—minus the Spanish milled dollars—to stand up the Delaware and safely reach Philadelphia. Under clear spring skies on March 20, the *Alliance* dropped anchor at Newport, Rhode Island, nearly eleven years after Abraham Whipple and some Rhode Island sailors had burned the HMS *Gaspee* and set in motion the American Revolution.[127]

Three days later, a French sloop-of-war, the aptly named *Triomphe*, came up the Delaware. When she docked at Chester, a courier was found to carry the momentous news she brought from France. On February 3, King George had issued a "Proclamation of Cessation of Hostilities."[128]

The *Sybil* had suffered heavy casualties in her battle with the *Alliance*. While Vashon minimized his tally, other reports put his numbers as high as thirty-seven dead and forty wounded. A relieved Barry learned after the battle that just eleven Americans were wounded; only Shubael Gardner's looked to be fatal. He died of the wounds he received in Barry's cabin shortly afterwards, weeks after King George had called on his forces to cease fighting. Back in Philadelphia, Congress had determined that the *Somerset* had been wrongfully seized and her crew, including Gardner, should never have been taken.[129]

The following morning Bosun Lewis piped for all hands. They came on deck quickly but silently. Under sunny skies, some of Shubael Gardner's shipmates, including those who served with him aboard the *Somerset* and had known him for years, bore Gardner's shrouded body to the gangway, where they placed it on a plank and covered it with the Stars and Stripes. With their bare heads bowed, Captain Barry led the men in a recitation of John 11:25: "I am the resurrection and the life: he that believeth in me, though he were dead, yet shall he live . . ."

A pained stillness followed where the only sounds were the familiar creak of wood and the rustle of wind on canvas. Then, silently, sadly, Gardner's comrades tilted the plank and sent him into the sea.[130]

EPILOGUE

Over the Long List of Vessels Belonging to the United States
Taken and Destroyed, and Recollecting the Whole History of the
Rise and Progress of Our Navy, It Is Very Difficult to Avoid Tears.

—JOHN ADAMS TO SAMUEL HUNTINGTON, PRESIDENT OF CONGRESS[1]

News that peace accords had been signed had barely reached Robert
Morris's ears when he began reassessing what to do with the Continental Navy. As Agent of Marine he understood the need to grow a naval force
for protection of both commerce and coastline, but as Superintendent of Finance
he knew this was impossible. In 1782, Congress had cut the navy's budget by
90 percent. It was vain, he told Congress, to even consider a navy "Until revenues
can be obtained," adding that "Every good American must wish to see the United
States possessed of a powerful fleet," but the public mood and the country's poor
financial shape made this impossible. "The People," he dolefully concluded, "will
now give Money for Nothing."[2]

Morris had turned his attention further eastward. Knowing that the young
nation needed to broaden its business horizons, he decided to go around the
world—to China. With a group of investors he purchased a 400-ton merchantman, renamed her the *Empress of China*, and gave command of her to one of his
favorite captains—John Green.[3]

Over the coming months, Morris orchestrated the dismantling of the navy.
The *Hague* and the *Bourbon*—now launched but unrigged—were both sold to
two of Morris's business connections, transactions that many viewed as corrupt
at best. Morris had the *Duc de Lauzon* loaded with tobacco and sent to France,

where both the tobacco and the *Duc* were sold. Congress sold the *General Washington* in 1784; on her last voyage as a naval vessel, Joshua Barney took John Paul Jones back to Europe.

Once John Barry rid himself of the Spanish milled dollars, Morris ordered him to take the *Alliance* to Holland with a shipment of tobacco. He was leaving Rhode Island to start his mission when the ship's pilot struck a rock, damaging her so badly that he never left American waters. Congress spent a year debating whether or not to keep at least one ship for its navy, fueled in large part by a new enemy: the Barbary pirates. A Philadelphia merchantman, the *Betsey*, became the first in a long string of ships seized by the corsairs in the Mediterranean. Now that the United States was a sovereign nation, it no longer had the protection of the British navy or the tribute that England paid to the Barbary States. In the end, Congress sold the *Alliance* in 1785 to another Morris acquaintance, who paid for her with "Morris Notes."[4]

And Morris was not quite done with the *Alliance*. When her latest owner developed financial woes, Morris snatched her up and sent her to China (Richard Dale was first mate). By 1789 she was no longer seaworthy, and Morris had her "Broken up for her copper and iron." A skeleton crew beached her on the north end of Petty's Island. Over the next 120 years she slowly disappeared.[5]

The postwar years were trying for Continental naval officer and seaman alike. Sailors had already rioted in Philadelphia, "Clamorous for their Wages," as Robert Morris put it. The new country had its first recession after the war, and it hit sailors hard. Officers bombarded Congress and state governments with "Memorials": testaments enumerating their wartime services and sacrifices, each one concluding with a "prayer" that they be, at long last, paid. For years, they were not.[6]

Partisan politics began playing a part with these appeals, even if the petitioners had no political affiliations whatsoever. It only mattered who, or what side, presented the petition. When three survivors of Flamborough Head—amputees Joseph Brussels, John Jordan, and James McKenzie—appealed for a disability pension, Congress did not deliberate so much as bicker. Since this memorial was sponsored by Robert Morris, a sizable bloc of congressmen (mostly Arthur Lee's disciples) opposed it, merely because Morris supported it. Even William Ellery, long the navy's champion, voted against it. On September 15, the imposing Jordan hobbled in on crutches, appealing to Congress's sense of decency. Even with such a stirring appearance, their petition was passed by only three votes.[7]

Many a sailor suffered through the harsh winter of 1783–84. For eight years toasts were raised to their bravery, and naval captains could not find enough of them. Now gaunt and threadbare, they resembled ghostly specters, haunting the waterfront taverns and London Coffeehouse in the rain and snow looking for any berth, even on foreign ships.

John Barry found their condition unforgivable. He had already gone hat in hand to Morris to get a deathly ill but impoverished sailor financial assistance to go to a hospital, but Morris could do nothing. Now Barry, unpaid himself, took out a $200 loan from the Philadelphia Bank. His sympathetic friend John Brown did the same. Unable to pay the full worth of their shares, they offered the men a lesser amount in cash for the unpaid prize warrants. It was the first generous act the sailors had seen in months, and kept more than one mariner out of debtors' prison. Barry's $200 went quickly. Harassed by bill collectors himself, Barry was so hard up when the loan was called in that he asked his old rustling partner, Anthony Wayne, if *he* could loan him the $200. Wayne did not have any money either.[8]

Widows and orphans of naval personnel met with similar responses from Congress. Barry and John Paul Jones both took particular interest in the case of Joanna Young, whose husband, John, was lost with the *Saratoga*. When she learned that army widows were getting half-pay stipends from Congress, she applied for the same. Congress denied her request; after all, army officers were "subject to arduous duty without a prospect of booty," while naval officers, "in a less severe service," were "in a situation of realizing substantial riches"—prize shares—or what naval officers now called back pay. The Widow Young should seek assistance elsewhere.[9]

To be fair, Congress had little money and no will to raise more. In 1783, John Adams wrote Morris how he wished he were in Congress to "assist you in persuading our Country men to pay taxes and build ships." Eventually, the national government got around to some—not all—of navy veterans' pay. One example is that of the sailors from the *Bonhomme Richard*, who fought one of the fiercest battles in naval history. After some deliberation, Congress voted to pay them for their services—in 1848. If the soldiers and sailors of the American Revolution set the bar for devotion to duty and sacrifice for succeeding generations of Americans, so, too, did Congress—and the public—set the example of "support the troops"—as long as no taxes were required for the best weapons, decent wages, or the care of their widows and orphans.[10]

Some historians believe the Continental Navy was not worth the cost in money and lives for the results achieved, arguing that American privateers captured and destroyed far more British vessels than the navy did. But others disagree; the navy's fifty-seven ships captured much more than their share of enemy vessels, providing sorely needed revenue for Congress and arms and supplies desperately required for Washington's army.

The fact is, while John Adams's delight over the navy's birth was reduced to the thought of tears by war's end, the Continental Navy did succeed. Victories from Nova Scotia to the West Indies, coupled with the raids along the British Isles, boosted patriot morale, forced the Royal Navy to cruise and fight on two hemispheres, sent British insurance rates soaring, spread terror to sea towns throughout King George's realm, and fueled antiwar sentiment in Parliament and the British press. Their successes went a long way towards bringing France into the war.[11]

From Hopkins's fleet at the beginning to the lone frigate *Alliance* at the end, the roll call of Continental veterans—Jones, Barry, Biddle, Wickes, Conyngham, Rathbun, Parke, Trevett, Kessler, Fanning, Gardner, Jordan, and Brussels among them—set the bar for the United States Navy, born in 1794. As historian Gregory J. Urwin eloquently noted, these men—and their shipmates—left their new country a legacy of heroism. The enemy bloodied them and the sea took many of them, but the survivors, many wounded and worn down from their travails, returned from the sea to a home their sacrifices helped create. If, as some have written, the Civil War is America's *Iliad*, could the Continental Navy's saga be our *Odyssey*?

In 1787, John Paul Jones finally got his wish: the title of rear admiral. Thomas Jefferson, America's ambassador to France, helped him attain it.

The fact that it was with the Russian Navy was fine with both Jones and Congress. After four years of trips to Europe and back, hunting down the prize money for himself and his men from the *Bonhomme Richard*, Jones learned that Catherine, Tsarina of Russia, wanted to enlist his services. He would be given a fleet, and sent to fight the Turks in the Black Sea. Congress, which had awarded Jones with a gold medal, saw this as an opportunity for its best-known captain to master an admiral's responsibilities and battle tactics, and it would not cost a thing.

Jones arrived in Russia older than his forty years. His health was poor and he had not been to sea since commanding the *Ariel*. But after serving admirably in the Russian Navy, he fell victim to the intrigues of Catherine's court and was accused of raping a young girl. An inquiry found the youngster's story flimsy, and Jones did not stand trial.

It was a broken man who returned to western Europe. News of the scandal had beaten him there, and he found himself explaining the "dark Asiatic intrigue" to anyone who would listen to him. The writer Thomas Carlyle, seeing him in his old uniform, called him "the ghost of himself." America's new minister to France, Gouverneur Morris, was bored by the sight of him. Jones ached for another chance at fame, but no one would give it to him. He had pleaded with Jefferson, now secretary of state, to let him represent America to the Dey of Algiers in an effort to free those sailors captured by the Barbary pirates, but he received no answer.

On July 18, 1792, Gouverneur Morris received a "Message from Paul Jones that he is dying. I go thither and make his will." Morris found him alert but a ghastly color—Jones had jaundice. Later that evening Morris returned and found Jones dead, his body kneeling at his bedside. Days later, the dispatch he had been waiting for came from President Washington, asking Jones to lead a delegation to Algiers. Instead, his corpse was pickled in alcohol, sealed in a lead-lined coffin, and buried in a grave on the outskirts of Paris.[12]

John Barry spent the four years after the war trying procure payment for his men and himself. As captain of the *Alliance*, he was kept on Congress's payroll until the ship was sold. He and the Austins eventually reclaimed the family estate, and Barry bought his own, a plantation called Strawberry Hill, north of Philadelphia on the Delaware. From there he could look down on Petty's Island and watch the sad deterioration of the *Alliance*.

In 1787 he was given command of the merchantman *Asia*, and sailed her to China—but not before coming up with a solution to get the Constitution passed. After the Constitutional Convention that September, the Pennsylvania Assembly began debating its merits. When anti-Federalists did not show up for a vote to pass it, Barry led a crowd of sailors and wharf toughs to their boarding-house, shanghaied the two who were still there, and brought them back—guaranteeing a quorum and a vote. Benjamin Franklin, the president of the state's Supreme Executive Council, wanted to see the Constitution passed, but could not resist ordering Barry's old friend, Charles Biddle, now Pennsylvania Attorney General, to arrest the captain for manhandling state representatives. Biddle executed the order—while Barry was sailing to China.[13]

Barry "swallowed the anchor" after his return, but was called back to duty in 1794 when Congress created the United States Navy. President Washington gave him the first captain's commission. Now in his fifties and plagued by gout and asthma, Barry served honorably during the Quasi-War with France, wearing John Paul Jones's gold-hilted sword.

But while he captured a slew of prizes, he was openly derided as "old and infirm" by Benjamin Stoddert, the first secretary of the navy. Yet Barry made his flagship, the frigate *United States*, a floating naval academy, turning out officers who later distinguished themselves in the Barbary Wars and the War of 1812, including Stephen Decatur, Richard Somers, and Charles Stewart. He and Sarah never had children but raised two of his nephews as their own sons. Barry succumbed to asthma in 1803.[14]

The second captain of the new United States Navy was a Nicholson—Sam, not James. He had been honorably acquitted in his court-martial in 1783, and returned to his career as a merchant captain. Placed at number 2 on the new Captains List, he was the first commander of the frigate to be built in Boston, the *Constitution*. Throughout the challenges of getting her built, Nicholson drove Barry crazy with his correspondence, mostly dealing with the new uniforms.

Nicholson also had more misadventures than triumphs once he got the *Constitution* to sea. After seizing a British ship that had been captured by the French, he determined she was not a prize (she was) and released the French crew as well. He was also a victim of true tragedy, losing his son on another voyage. Relieved of command, he was made superintendent of the Charlestown Navy Yard. He died in 1811.[15]

His brother James had been in the ground seven years when Sam died. James Nicholson spent the last year of the war on a series of errands for Robert Morris, still angling for command of the *Bourbon*. After the war he settled in New York City and became a staunch Jeffersonian. He died in 1804.[16]

After the surrender of Charleston, Samuel Tucker turned to privateering, commanding the *Thorn*. He was captured in 1781 after an engagement with HMS *Hind* along the St. Lawrence River, and taken to Prince Edward Island as a prisoner. He escaped later that year, and wrote to the lieutenant governor, Andrew Snape Hamond, apologizing for breaking his word not to escape (Hamond's reply pretty much said "Think nothing of it"). After the war, he took up farming in the Territory of Maine. During the War of 1812, Tucker commanded a schooner, the *Increase*, and captured the Halifax privateer *Crown* in 1813, at the age of sixty-six. He died twenty years later.[17]

Unable to be paroled for a British officer of similar rank, Abraham Whipple also turned to farming. He served in the Rhode Island legislature, but soon his debts outpaced his worth, and he was forced to beg Congress for the money owed him just to keep his farm. "I have never been recompensed," he wrote in his memorial. Whipple moved to a small farm in Ohio, where he died in 1819.[18]

While a court-martial cleared Sam Nicholson of the charges made by the *Deane/Hague*'s officers, John Manley was found guilty in his, and forfeited his commission. It was an ignominious end for one of the earliest heroes in the war. He died in 1793.[19]

The Revolution was over, but Richard Dale's career was just beginning. After making voyages to China, Dale also became a captain in the new navy. By then he had married a cousin of Sarah Barry's and settled in Philadelphia. He took a squadron to the Mediterranean to battle the Barbary pirates. When he resigned, he went into the insurance business, becoming director of the Insurance Company of North America. He died in 1826. Among his possessions was Jones's sword, bequeathed to him by John Barry.

Silas Talbot was exchanged in 1781. After leaving Mill Prison he made his way to France and from there, back to America, only to learn that his wife had died. After a stint in the New York Assembly he was elected to Congress. His political future looked bright, but when Congress approved the building of six frigates for the new navy, the call of the sea became too hard to ignore. Old comrades like Hoysted Hacker asked him to help them attain a captain's commission, but Talbot was too busy getting his own. His was the third name on the new list. Talbot succeeded Nicholson as captain of the *Constitution* and commanded her through the end of the Quasi-War. His fellow captain, Thomas Truxton, considered him "a mere privateersman," but Talbot need not take a backseat to anyone in the service of his country. From Long Island to Fort Mifflin, from the *Argo* to the *Constitution*, Talbot did more than his share. He died in 1813 and is buried in Trinity churchyard in New York City.[20]

Inadvertently, Talbot kept Joshua Barney out of the United States Navy. Offered the fourth commission, Barney turned it down, believing that being ranked beneath Talbot (whose Continental commission came years after Barney's) was an insult. Instead, he accepted a captaincy in the French navy. When the Quasi-War broke out, he returned to America after resigning command of the French frigate *l'Insurgente*, which was later captured in the biggest engagement of the conflict by Thomas Truxton and the *Constellation*.[21]

For all Barney's heroics during the Revolution, it was his service during the

War of 1812 that he is best remembered for. He captured dozens of prizes as a privateer before accepting a captain's commission in the navy, and led a flotilla of gunboats and barges in a stubborn defense against a much larger British fleet on the Patuxent. Then he took his sailors and marines to defend the city of Washington at the Battle of Bladensburg, where he was wounded and captured by the British yet again, nearly forty years after his first stints as a prisoner. He died in Pittsburgh in 1818.[22]

After being removed from the Continental Navy, Pierre Landais moved to New York City, where he badgered Robert Morris and Congress for money. Ironically, it was John Paul Jones who interceded on Landais's behalf, in one last effort to make peace. No matter: in 1787, Jones was walking down a New York street when Landais saw him from behind. "I spit in your face!" he cried, once again challenging Jones to a duel. Jones demurred, later attesting that he was neither spat on nor challenged. Landais died at eighty-seven, and lies in the cemetery of St. Patrick's Cathedral.[23]

In 1797, newly elected president John Adams had been feted on a visit to Providence, Rhode Island, when he had one last visitor to his guestroom, "an old man bowed with infirmities." Moving stiffly with a cane, he shuffled into the room. It was Esek Hopkins.[24] The old commodore had come not just to pay his respects, but to thank the president for being his champion and friend when no one else thought or cared to do so. The seventy-nine-year-old Hopkins was truly, at the time, his country's ancient mariner—but because of his failures, he was their forgotten one as well. He was sixty when he was dismissed from the navy, and he never went to sea again. He died, practically unknown, in 1802, but will likely remain the only man given the title "Commander-in-Chief" of an American navy.[25]

After the *Ariel*, Nathaniel Fanning obtained a lieutenant's commission in the French navy and served on three privateers, making a host of captures and being captured two more times himself. Taken prisoner while commanding the privateer *Ranger* in late 1782, he was mistaken for being Irish by the captain, clapped in irons by a "one-eyed, surly" lieutenant (who had served under James Wallace aboard the *Rose*), and given a "half pound of wormy bread and one pint of water." Luckily for Fanning, he convinced the captain he was an American: the man had hung two of Fanning's Irish sailors earlier, calling them traitors to King George. Fanning was rescued by a French ship-of-the-line. Years later, Fanning joined the new United States Navy as a lieutenant. He died of yellow fever in 1805 while commanding a gunboat.[26]

Believing his taste for adventure satisfied, John Kessler ran a Boston grocery store and worked as a tax collector until a new career called him. He became a fur trader in Maine before returning to Philadelphia with his family, where he served as a constable. He retired in 1816 on a pension for injuries received while serving aboard the frigate *Alliance*, and died in 1840.[27]

On April 8, 1783, Captain John Bazeley of the *Amphion* came aboard the prison ship *Jersey*, where he read the king's proclamation ending hostilities. It took days to get the imprisoned sailors—many unable to walk and others dying—off the hulk. The *Jersey* was left to rot in the river. For the next hundred years, human bones washed up on the shores of Wallabout Bay. In 1873, the bones were buried with full military honors in a crypt at what is now Fort Greene Park in Brooklyn. The Prison Ship Martyrs Monument honors their sacrifice.[28]

Bazeley did not find young James Forten among the *Jersey*'s prisoners. He had been exchanged months earlier, and made it back to Philadelphia, to the great surprise of his mother, who had heard he was killed in battle. Apprenticed to a sailmaker, he later bought the business and patented a machine that revolutionized sail making. Forten became one of the richest men in Philadelphia. He was a staunch figure in the early-nineteenth-century abolitionist movement, living long enough to write articles for William Lloyd Garrison's *The Liberator*. When he died in 1841 his funeral was attended by thousands of Philadelphians. One newspaper heralded Forten as "earnest of his hatred of Slavery and love of liberty."[29]

Elizabeth Baker was not yet nineteen years old when her betrothed, Nicholas Biddle, was killed in 1778. It would be another nineteen years before she wed, her husband a Charleston gentleman named Isaac Holmes. Their marriage was childless. Elizabeth was only forty-eight years old when she died on Christmas Day, 1807.[30]

After being awarded a pension by Congress in 1783, Joseph Brussels, now a teenager, was taken under the wing of Henry Fisher, the head of the Delaware pilots. Fisher taught the boy about the Delaware River and Bay with knowledge that only a pilot could have. Brussels became a respected pilot, and married a friend of Fisher's daughter. He and his wife had a little girl. Life was good.

His wife died young, and Brussels turned his daughter over to the Fishers while he reenlisted in the navy. Brussels went to the Mediterranean under Commodore Richard Dale—his old lieutenant from the *Bonhomme Richard*. When the squadron was off the west coast of Italy, Dale gave Brussels shore leave. At that time Brussels had not seen his family in more than twenty years. There was an epidemic of fever in the city. Brussels caught it and died; his brothers buried him with his parents.

Years later, Fisher's daughter, Sarah Rodney, wrote to Brussels's daughter, telling her about her father's remarkable life, especially about his voyage aboard the *Bonhomme Richard*, and the "memorable Victory that will gild the Names of Paul Jones and R. Dale with their gallant crew as long as the pages of the Revolution will be read by unborn millions."[31]

On September 26, 1783, Gustavus Conyngham visited Robert Morris, accompanied by Colonel Walter Stewart, an acquaintance who offered his assistance in getting Conyngham his money and rank restored. Stewart's involvement in a plot to have Washington's officers mutiny over *their* back pay did not place him high in Morris's regard, but out of deference to Conyngham, Morris suggested the two present yet a more detailed memorial to Congress, and again include Franklin's certificate.[32]

On October 11, Conyngham's memorial was read in Congress, which turned it over to a three-man committee for review, consisting of Hugh Williamson, William Ellery, and Arthur Lee. After two days, another committee referred it back to Morris, believing that if Conyngham was telling the truth, then the Agent of Marine should pay him and restore his rank. Three months later, Lee convinced Williamson and Ellery to deny Conyngham's appeal: those commissions Franklin handed out in France, Lee claimed, were only temporary, and "not to give rank in the navy." Yet another captain, championed by Franklin or Deane, became a pawn in Lee's never-ending feuds with Franklin or Deane. Congress sided with Lee.[33]

The man who risked his life at sea for a living, faced cannon fire, a death sentence, abusive treatment in prison, and eating dirt as he tunneled his way to freedom, had finally met an obstacle he could not defeat: the Congress of the United States. But he would not give in: year after year, he presented a new memorial, a new petition, a new claim—all refused. He would have clearly won his case if he only had that commission, signed by John Hancock as Barry's and Jones's were—and with no mention of his captaincy being "temporary." It had to be lost—or destroyed—after the Reign of Terror took over France. As late as 1816, Conyngham made another effort, while admitting that one's "word in poloticks [is] like sending Coals to Newcastle."

Nor did he give up on his country. When Congress passed on his offer to serve the new navy in the Quasi-War, Conyngham commanded two privateers, the *America* and the *Maria*. After his beloved Anne died in 1811, he volunteered again for service in the War of 1812, but at sixty-five had no chance of getting a ship.

On November 29, 1819, a small notice was posted in a Philadelphia paper:

> Died on Saturday morning last [November 27] at one o'clock, in the 73rd year of his age, Captain Gustavus Conyngham, long a respectable inhabitant of this city.

> His connections and friends are respectfully invited to attend his Funeral . . .[34]

In the early 1900s, General Horace Porter, Civil War hero and Medal of Honor winner, was with a group of Frenchmen exploring a dark tunnel underneath a French laundry, some carrying picks and shovels. In the dim lantern light, they found what they had come for: a coffin. A couple of them opened the lid. As the lid was pried open, there was a perceptible whiff of alcohol. Moving away the straw and linen, they found themselves staring at the captain of the *Bonhomme Richard*. An ecstatic Porter wired home: "My six years' search for remains of Paul Jones has resulted in success."

Porter had no idea how successful his find would be, or how lucky it was that Theodore Roosevelt was president of the United States. Roosevelt had been enamored with the navy all his life, serving as assistant secretary of the navy in William McKinley's administration and using all his influence to get the Spanish-American War started. He wanted the American navy to be second to none, and saw Porter's discovery as a great public relations opportunity to sail his dream through Congress. After France gave Jones a funeral fit for a king, Roosevelt dispatched the USS *Brooklyn* and three other ships to bring the hero home.[35]

On April 24, 1906, another grand ceremony honored Jones at the United States Naval Academy in Annapolis. Politicians, American and French naval personnel, the academy's midshipmen, and thousands of spectators heard Roosevelt extol Jones's courage and example. A handsome tomb was built for him beneath the academy chapel; his crypt rests atop four carved dolphins. Among the items and paintings along the circular walkway is his gold-hilted sword.[36]

About the same time that Porter was searching for Jones, a catalogue announced the sale of autographs and documents collected by Charavay of Paris, including this item for sale:

143 Hancock (John), célèbre home d'État Americain, gouverneur du Massachusetts, signitaire de la Déclaration de l'Indépendance—Pièce sig. comme président du congrés; Baltimore, I mars 1777, 1 p. in-fol. Obl. Rare.

The catalog was mailed worldwide to renowned collectors, including Captain John S. Barnes (Ret.) of New York, a Civil War navy captain whose wife's family tree included William Bainbridge and John Barry. Barnes had been collecting Revolutionary War documents for years, and arranged for its purchase. Several weeks later the package arrived. Looking forward to adding a Hancock signature to his growing collection, Barnes got more than he bargained for. There was Hancock's signature, all right, but also a bit of Benjamin Franklin's handwriting as well.[37]

Gustavus Conyngham's commission had finally come home.

ACKNOWLEDGMENTS

As I write this I'm looking at a weather-beaten *Roget's Thesaurus*, given to me by Mother Mary Ephrem (later Sister Mary Rose) of the Sisters of the Holy Child Jesus upon my graduating eighth grade. It was hardly used for the first thirty-eight years, but it's been a lifesaver for the past eleven. Mother Ephrem was Katherine Hepburn in a habit—the kind of teacher you never forget, and hope that every student has at least once. A great lady.

Luckily there were more educators like her awaiting down the road, particularly Jim Hilty, recently retired after decades of service to Temple University. He is always available for questions, and his encouragement, advice, and example will forever be appreciated.

My interest in the Continental Navy began when I was a youngster and first saw where the Battle of Turtle Gut Inlet took place. I was taken there by Bob Starr, a World War II navy aviator, former North Wildwood lifeguard, and family friend. Bob personifies "the Greatest Generation": his great love of family and country is not worn on his sleeve, but found deep in his heart.

You would not be reading this if Bruce Franklin, the founder of Westholme Publishing, had not given me a chance with my first book on John Barry. Bruce's passion for history and his business acumen make for a wonderful combination, and I am grateful for both the opportunity he gave me and his friendship.

The stories of the Continental Navy have been told and retold every generation or so, but never more prolifically than by William Bell Clark. His books cover practically every character and event of the American Revolution, and he began the massive research that has thus far produced eleven volumes of *The Naval Documents of the American Revolution*, where so many of the firsthand narratives of the remarkable people in these pages can be found.

The experts who have followed in Mr. Clark's footsteps were once again generous with their time, knowledge, and suggestions. William Fowler of Northeastern University, Craig Symonds (Ret.) of the U.S. Naval Academy, and Dennis Conrad and Charles Brodine of the Naval Historical Center all provided valuable critiques and suggestions on parts of the text. James Nelson, a square-rigged sailor and exceptional writer, provided advice and encouragement. And I am very grateful to James Bradford of Texas A&M University, whose herculean accomplishment of harnessing the papers of John Paul Jones into a manageable and engaging resource was a huge help with this project, along with his time and kindness.

I am grateful for the assistance of two biographers of John Paul Jones: Rear Admiral Joseph E. Callo (Ret.), who also helped with support materials, and Evan Thomas, who shared his thoughts on what made this complex man tick. This book also greatly benefited from the informative works of Michael Palmer and the late Nathan Miller. The books that all these gentlemen have written are terrific reads, and served as sound sources.

When I first went to the local library as a boy and came back with Tom Fleming's first book, *Now We Are Enemies*, about the Battle of Bunker Hill, I had no idea I would have the opportunity to review ideas and discuss this project with Tom, whose name alone on the spines of his books stretches from the top to the bottom of a bookcase. And what a storyteller!

Source material came from stateside and Europe. In England, I was assisted by Roger Nixon, who unearthed Admiralty Records on many of the Royal Navy officers and ships in the preceding pages. Douglas McCarthy of the National Maritime Museum and Mathew Sheldon of the Royal Navy Museum took pains to answer various questions. French documents were translated by Dr. Maria G. Traub of Neumann University (my French has its limits), a *Chevalier dans l'Ordre des Palmes Académiques*, with a deep love of Franco-American history. Thanks once again to Dean King and John Hattendorf, whose *Sea of Words* and *Harbors and High Seas* were wonderful resources for terminology and geography.

I am also indebted to the following for their help: Bruce Gimelson of Garrison, New York; George Carpenter of Cold Spring Presbyterian Cemetery at Cold Spring, New Jersey; Gail E. Farr at the Philadelphia branch of the National Archives; Dr. David Winkler of the Naval Historical Center; J. J. Ahern at the University of Pennsylvania Archives; Sally Hastings at the Somers Point Historical Society; June Sheridan at the Atlantic County (NJ) Historical Society; John Mills of Princeton Battlefield State Park; John Anderies and Ann Upton at Haverford College; Nicole Joniec at the Library Company of Philadelphia; Heather Joyner of the John F. Kennedy Presidential Library and Museum; Adam Kane at the Lake Champlain Maritime Museum; George F. Nagle of the Afrolumens Project; Bill Troppman and Kim Szewczyk at Valley Forge National Historical Park; author Nancy Loane with the Friends of Valley Forge; Fran O'Brien with the Delaware River Port Authority; Beth Beatty, Executive Director at Fort Mifflin on the Delaware; Thomas Truxes and Anne Solari at Glucksman Irish House of NYU; Connie Cooper of the Delaware Historical Society; Professor Mark McIntire of Santa Barbara City College; Harvard College Library Reference Services; authors John Nagy, Glenn Williams, and Christian McBurney; the steadfast Ralph Day; Richard Latture, Eric Mills, and Liese Doherty of *Naval History Magazine*; Patricia Harty of *Irish America Magazine*; Jack Warren and Emily Schultz of the Society of the Cincinnati's Anderson House; Francis P. O'Neill at the Maryland Historical Society; Kim Burdick of the Duling-Kurtz House and George Washington Society in Wilmington, Delaware; Jennifer Patton of Fraunces Tavern; Arlynn Greenbaum of Authors Unlimited; Rear Admiral J. Robert Lunney, USN (Ret.), and Captain Liam Murphy, USN (Ret.), of the Navy League New York Council; and author and Captain John Rodgaard, USN (Ret).

John Kessler's papers were found and sent to me by Jonathan Stayer of the Pennsylvania State Archives. William Berret Kessler, Jr., a direct descendant of John Kessler, picked up John's trail where the documents left off.

I am also grateful to Martin Levitt, Sandra Duffy, and Valerie Lutz for their kindness and assistance at the American Philosophical Society in Philadelphia. The David Library of the American Revolution is a treasure trove of resources, ably manned by Meg McSweeney, Brian Graziano, and the ever-helpful Kathie Ludwig. Mary Jo Fairchild of the South Carolina Historical Society unearthed eyewitness accounts of the Siege of Charleston and what became of Elizabeth Baker. Anna J. Clutterbuck-Cook, Dan Hinchen, and Tracy Potter of the Massachusetts Historical Society found everything from Boston Tea Party tales through documents substantiating the "Odd Couple" relationship between John

Manley and Hector McNeill. Ted O'Reilly, Tammy Kiter, and Rob Delap at the New York Historical Society both helped with research and tracked down Gustavus Conyngham's commission. Carolyn Catona kept me on the straight and narrow in organizing research.

At Independence National Historical Park, Karie Diethorn and the resourceful Andrea Ashby were more than helpful with support illustrations, portraits, and long-out-of-print books both by and about many of the people in this book. Nick Noyes of the Rhode Island Historical Society helped track down diaries and letters pertaining to the Penobscot Expedition. At the Library of Congress, Bruce Kirby has been pointing me in the right direction for years. Jim Cheevers, Senior Curator at the US Naval Academy Museum, and Grant Walker came through with good suggestions and solutions in tracking down sources for both text and illustrations.

Christine B. Podmaniczky, Bethany Engel, and Jane Flitner of the Brandywine River Museum helped locate artwork and documents. Further help came from Lynette Pohlman, Allison Sheridan, and Adrienne Gannett at Iowa State University; Pam Overmann, Curator, Navy Art Collection, Naval History and Heritage Command; Joan C. Thomas at the US Marine Corps Museum, Quantico, Virginia; Frank Arre, Tiffany Gwynn, and John Royal at the Naval History & Heritage Command, Washington, DC; and Emma Lefley at the Royal Museums, Greenwich, England. Thanks go to Jenny Grehan and Eden Betz, daughter and granddaughter of the late Nowland Van Powell, in helping locate his remarkable paintings of the Continental Navy's ships.

Thanks are also due to Elizabeth Oldham at the Nantucket Historical Association for background information on Shubael Gardner. William Baehr provided documents from the Franklin Delano Roosevelt Presidential Library on Barry, Jones, and their fellow captains. At Christ Church in Philadelphia, Neil Ronk and Carol Smith provided church-related background on Captains Barry and Conyngham and Messrs. Franklin, Morris, and Hopkinson. Linnea Bass, Don Graves, Donald Hagist, John Houlding, and Jim Kochan reviewed naval ordnance, while Paul Kopperman and Laurence Todd were generous with their knowledge of eighteenth-century military medicine. Dr. Susan Klepp offered her expertise on women in colonial times, which helped flesh out the shortage of documents on Anne Hockley Conyngham, Sarah Austin Barry, and Elizabeth Baker Holmes.

Is there a finer view from a library than the one at Independence Seaport Museum? I don't think so. Nor have there been better hosts than John Brady,

Craig Bruns, Joshua Fox, and Megan Good. If I have another project there I'm bringing a sleeping bag. The same holds true for the Historical Society of Pennsylvania, thanks to Lee Arnold, Amanda Dean, Sarah Heim, Rob Medford, and Dan Rolph.

Few people possess the enthusiasm and dedication of Meghan Wren, Executive Director of the Bayshore Discovery Project, or have accomplished what she has in reawakening interest in the Delaware Bay and River. The best way to see those bodies of water is a trip upriver aboard the schooner *A. J. Meerwald*, captained by Meghan's husband, Jesse Briggs. I had the pleasure of my dear friend Gary Dunn's company on a trip to Port Penn and Reedy Island. And I will never be the sailor Larry Helmick is, but I appreciate the years of picking his brain on the subject while we're out on the water. Our friendship has even survived spinnakers—so far.

Years ago Megan Fraser introduced me to the Barry-Hayes Papers at Independence Seaport Museum. Now at UCLA, Megan is still a great sounding board, wise beyond her years. Michael Crawford, Senior Historian at the Naval History and Heritage Command, has answered every question and kept me from the shoals with his critiques and encouragement. Greg Urwin of Temple University read every word of the manuscript and served as both Henry Higgins and Father Confessor for this project. I am honored that all three of these experts are friends.

My daughter, Courtney—the real writer in our family—was there at every instance of a late-night call ("How would you say . . ."), and always spot-on with her suggestions. The elegant maps and battle diagrams in this book were done by my son Ted, an award-winning artist whose work has supported articles in magazines and newspapers around the world.

The cover painting for this book is by the renowned Patrick O'Brien. Once I learned that his painting would grace the book's cover, I started praying that the text would live up to what Patrick's talents promised.

My thanks to all at New American Library/Penguin, especially Christina Brower, a calm voice no matter the crisis; Steve Meditz, whose talents in design are self-evident just by this cover alone; Loren Jaggers, a dedicated publicist with a keen sense of humor; and publisher Kara Welsh, for her belief in this book.

It has been a privilege to work with my editor, Brent Howard. His talent, patience, and guidance are resources any author would benefit by. He would make a great shepherd if he ever changes careers.

Besides being a terrific agent, Jim Donovan is a good friend. A fine writer and historian in his own right, he dedicated one of his books to his dad, simply stating: *He was a good man.* So is Jim.

On June 22, 2012, the sailing ship *Bounty*, a replica of the HMS *Bounty* built for the 1962 film *Mutiny on the Bounty*, sailed up the Delaware to participate in a "Tall Ships Weekend" at the Philadelphia waterfront. Once aboard, the first person I met was Claudene Christian. After a great "Cook's tour," I was told by Captain Robin Walbridge to come back in two days—I had permission to go aloft after the weekend festivities ended. With the assistance of Chief Mate John Svendsen and Second Mate Matt Sanders, I got to do just that. I remembered seeing the newsreel of the ship's launching as a boy, and had seen both the movie and the TNT version of *Treasure Island* years ago, so climbing this ship's ratlines was an extra pleasure. To learn of its tragic end, and the loss of Ms. Christian and Captain Walbridge, was sad news indeed. Their obvious love for what all of them were doing, and their hospitality to a complete stranger, will always be gratefully remembered.

Finally, there's Cyd—who read every word and edited every page. She is even open to another book—providing I write it in Portugal. Sailing through life with her is an honor.

To all of the above, my thanks. The merits of this book are shared among you; its errors are mine alone.

ENDNOTES

✷　✷　✷

List of Abbreviations

AFP	Adams Family Papers
APS	American Philosophical Society
AWP	Abraham Whipple Papers
BFP	Benjamin Franklin Papers
BHP	Barry-Hayes Papers
FDR	Franklin Delano Roosevelt Naval Collection
GWP	George Washington Papers
HCL	Haverford College Library
HSP	Historical Society of Pennsylvania
ISM	Independence Seaport Museum
JBP	John Barry Papers, Library of Congress
JPJP	John Paul Jones Papers, Library of Congress
JCC	Journals of the Continental Congress
LDC	Letters of Delegates to Congress
MCLB	Marine Committee Letter Book
NDAR	Naval Documents of the American Revolution
NRAR	Naval Records of the American Revolution
NYHS	New York Historical Society
NYPL	New York Public Library
PMHB	*Pennsylvania Magazine of History and Biography*
PRO	Public Records Office, Kew Gardens, England
RDC	Revolutionary Diplomatic Correspondence
RIHS	Rhode Island Historical Society
RMP	Robert Morris Papers
SCHS	South Carolina Historical Society
USNAM	United States Naval Academy Museum
UVL	University of Virginia Library

CHAPTER ONE ★ "REBELLIOUS FANATICKS"

1 Naval Documents of the American Revolution (NDAR), 1:77, Major Adam Stephens to Richard Henry Lee, 2/1/75.

2 Benjamin Woods Labaree, *The Boston Tea Party* (New York: Oxford University Press, 1964), 235.

3 William M. Fowler, Jr., *The Baron of Beacon Hill: A Biography of John Hancock* (Boston: Houghton Mifflin, 1980), 160; Benjamin L. Carp, *Defiance of the Patriots: The Boston Tea Party and the Making of America* (New Haven, CT: Yale University Press, 2012), 130–131; Bruce C. Lancaster, *The American Revolution* (Boston: Houghton, Mifflin, 1971), 68.

4 Library Company of Philadelphia, Tea Ship Broadside, 11/27/73; *Boston Gazette*, 10/25/73; *Pennsylvania Gazette*, 11/10/73; Tinkcom, "The Revolutionary City," 108.

5 *Boston Gazette*, 12/20/73; Carp, 130; Labaree, 144.

6 Labaree, 145.

7 *Boston Gazette*, 12/20/73; Carp, 130, 139.

8 *South Carolina Gazette*, 11/21/74; NDAR, 1:628–669, John Adams to Elbridge Gerry, 6/7/75; Lancaster, 70; Franklin Delano Roosevelt Library, FDR Collection, John Adams to Elbridge Gerry, 6/7/75 (approx.).

9 Benjamin Pinkas, "The Vindication of John Adams: *Rex v. Corbet* and the Battle for the Heritage of the American Revolution, 1760–1816," *Tempus: The Harvard College History Review* 11:1–13; John F. Kennedy, *Profiles in Courage* (Inaugural ed.; New York: Harper and Row, 1961), 235–236.

10 L. H. Butterfield, ed., *Adams Family Correspondence*, 1:107.

11 Interview with William Ward, retired director of education, Independence Seaport Museum, Philadelphia, April 2004; Gary B. Nash, *First City* (Philadelphia: University of Pennsylvania Press, 2002), 31.

12 David McCullough, John Adams (New York: Simon and Schuster, 2001), 82.

13 Joseph E. Illich, *Colonial Pennsylvania—A History* (New York: Charles Scribner's Sons, 1976), 281.

14 McCullough, 22–23.

15 Historical Society of Pennsylvania ("HSP"), Christopher Marshall Diaries, 5/6/75; *Pennsylvania Evening Post*, 5/6/75.

16 Frederick Wagner, *Robert Morris: Audacious Patriot* (New York: Dodd, Mead, 1973), 26; John Kessler, "Life of John Kessler" (Pennsylvania Archives, John Kessler Papers), 1.

17   Deborah Mathias Gough, *Christ Church, Philadelphia: The Nation's Church in a Changing City* (Philadelphia: University of Pennsylvania Press, 1995), 137, 142.

18   Independence Hall Collections, Information for Independence Hall; HABS Drawing 9.

19   McCullough, 178.

20   NDAR, 1:628–629, John Adams to Elbridge Gerry, 6/7/75.

21   Ibid., 1:964, John Adams to James Warren, 7/24//75.

22   McCullough, 95.

23   NDAR, 1:916, Journals of the Continental Congress, 7/18/75.

24   Ibid., 1:205–6, Samuel Graves to Philip Stephens, 4/22/75.

25   Ibid., 1:372, Graves to Lord Dunmore, 5/20/75.

26   Ibid., 1:503, Journal of His Majesty's Sloop *Falcon*, John Linzee, commanding, 5/22/75; 819, Mercy Warren to John Adams, 7/5/75; Massachusetts *Spy*, 5/24/75.

27   Ibid., 1:337, General Thomas Gage to Vice Admiral Samuel Graves, 5/15/75; 655–656, Pilot Nathaniel Godfrey's Report of Action between the Schooner *Margaretta* and the Rebels of Machias, 6/11/75; Nathan Miller, *Sea of Glory: The Naval History of the American Revolution* (Charleston: Nautical and Aviation Publishing Company, 1974), 30.

28   NDAR, 1:676–677, James Lyons, Chairman of the Machias Committee, to the Massachusetts Provincial Congress, 6/14/75.

29   Ibid., Miller, 32.

30   Ibid., 655–56, "Pilot Nathaniel Godfrey's Report of Action between the Schooner *Margueretta* and the Rebels at Machias," 6/11/75.

31   Ibid.; Miller, 31–35.

32   NDAR, 1:997, Vice Admiral Samuel Graves to Philip Stephens, 7/28/75; NDAR, 1:1108, Lieutenant John Knight, R.N. to Vice Admiral Samuel Graves, 8/10/75.

33   Ibid., 1:737–738, Walter Livingston to Robert Livingston, Jr., 6/21/75; 818, George Washington in Account with the United States, 7/5/75; Butterfield, *Adams Family Correspondence*, Portia (Abigail Adams) to John Adams, 7/16/75; Lancaster, 100.

34   Ibid., 1057–1058, George Washington to Nicholas Cooke, Deputy Governor of Rhode Island, 8/4/75; Papers of the Continental Congress, 7/14/75.

35   Ibid., 851, George Washington to Richard Henry Lee, 7/10/75; Miller, 60–61; Walter Isaacson, *Benjamin Franklin: An American Life* (New York: Simon and Schuster, 2003), 302.

36   Ibid., 1114–1115, George Washington to a Committee of the General Court of Massachusetts Bay, 8/11/75.

37   D. Appleton: *Cyclopedia of American Biography* (New York, Appleton, 1900); George Athan Billias, *General John Glover and His Marblehead Mariners* (New York: Holt, Rinehart and Winston, 1960), 21.

38   NDAR, 1:1287–1289, George Washington's Instructions for Captain Nicholas Broughton, 9/2/75.

39   Ibid., 2:36, Captain Nicholas Broughton to George Washington, 9/17/75.

40   Ibid., 2:36, 2:56–57, Captain Nicholas Broughton to George Washington, 9/9/75; 169 Washington to John Langdon, 9/21/75; Miller, 62–63.

41   Ibid., 436, George Washington to Nicholas Cooke, 10/13/75; 1082, Washington to Colonel Joseph Reed, 11/20/75; Miller, 67–69; William M. Fowler, Jr., *Rebels Under Sail: The American Navy During the Revolution* (New York: Scribner's, 1976), 28–43.

42   NDAR, 1:47, Disposition of the Squadron under Vice Admiral Samuel Graves, 1/1/75; pp. 255–256; Some of the Principal Inhabitants of Falmouth to Lieutenant Henry Mowat, R.N., 5/2/75; p. 1 Major General John Burgoyne to Lord George Germain, 8/10/75; Miller, 22–27.

43   Ibid., 2:324–326, Vice Admiral Samuel Graves to Lieutenant Henry Mowat, H.M. Armed Vessel *Canceaux*, 10/6/75.

44   HSP, Christopher Marshall Diaries, 8–10/75; James C. Bradford, ed., *Command under Sail: Makers of the American Naval Tradition* (Annapolis, MD: Naval Institute Press, 1985): William M. Fowler, Jr., "Esek Hopkins: Commander-in-Chief of the Continental Navy," 5.

45   NDAR, 1:517, Portia (Abigail Adams) to John Adams, 5/24/75.

46   Ibid., 1:894–895, Portia to John Adams, 7/10/75.

47   Denise Kiernan and Joseph D'Agnese, *Signing Their Lives Away: The Fame and Misfortune of the Men Who Signed the Declaration of Independence* (Philadelphia: Quirk Books, 2009), "Samuel Chase," 155–159.

48   Miller, 18–20; Fowler, *Rebels*, 101.

49   John F. Millar, *American Ships of the Colonial and Revolutionary Periods* (New York: Norton, 1978), 35–36; *Pennsylvania Packet*, 6/19/75.

50   NDAR, 1:1236, Journal of the Rhode Island Assembly, 8/26/75.

51   Ibid., 1:1163–1164, Minutes of the Pennsylvania Committee of Safety, 7/6/75; 2:234–235, Diary of John Adams, 9/28/75.

52   Ibid., 2:149, Permit by George Washington to Procure Powder from the West Indies, 9/19/75.

53   Ibid., 1:1221–1225, actions of the ship *Asia* and various eyewitness accounts.

54   Thomas Fleming, *Liberty* (New York: Viking, 1997), 159–160.

55   Journals of the Continental Congress ("JCC"), 10/3/75.

56   JCC, 10/5/75; *Pennsylvania Journal,* 10/11/75; Miller, 45.

57   NDAR, 2:307–311; JCC, 10/5/75; John Adams' Notes of Debates in the Continental Congress, 10/5/75.

58   JCC, 10/6/75.

59   HSP, Christopher Marshall Diaries, 10/7/75.

60   NDAR, 2:331, Journal of the HMS *Rose,* Captain James Wallace, 10/7/75; ibid., 2:337, Journal of the HM Sloop *Swan,* Captain James Ayscough, 10/7/75; ibid., 2:376, George Benson to Nicholas Brown, 10/9/75; *Newport Mercury,* 10/9/75.

61   Butterfield, *Diary and Autobiography of John Adams,* 2:183, 9/25/75.

62   JCC, 10/7/75.

63   NDAR, 2:393, Thomas Jefferson to Francis Eppes, 10/10/75.

64   Ibid., 2:426, John Adams to James Warren, 10/12/75; ibid., 2:427, Outline for Proposal for Procuring Powder, 10/12/75.

65   Ibid., 2:301, George Washington to John Hancock, 10/5/75.

66   JCC, 10/13/75.

67   NDAR, 2:443, John Adams to James Warren, 10/13/75.

68   Ibid., Letter from Rev. Jacob Bailey, 10/13/75.

69   Ibid., 2:471, Lieutenant Henry Mowat, R.N., to the People of Falmouth, 10/16/75; ibid., 2:487–488, Letter from Rev. Jacob Bailey, 10/17/75; ibid., 2:489, Master's Log of H.M. Armed Vessel *Canceaux,* 10/17/75.

70   Ibid., 2:500–502, Letter from Reverend Jacob Bailey, 10/18/75; Narrative of Daniel Tucker of Falmouth, 10/18/75; Master's Log of H.M. Armed Vessel *Canceaux,* 10/18/75; ibid., 2:513–516, Lieutenant Henry Mowat, R.N., to Vice Admiral Samuel Graves, 10/19/75; ibid., 2:590–591, Pearson Jones' Certificate Concerning the Burning of Falmouth, 10/24/75.

71   Ibid., 2:590–591, George Washington to John Hancock, 10/24/75; Pearson Jones Certificate etc.

72   Ibid., 2:554–557, John Adams' Notes of Debate in the Continental Congress, 10/21/75; JCC, 10/30/75.

73   Ibid., 2:896–897, John Adams to Elbridge Gerry, 11/5/75; Adams to James Warren, 11/5/75.

74   Charles R. Smith, *Marines in the Revolution: A History of the Continental Marines in the American Revolution 1775–1783* (Washington, D.C.: History and Museums Division, Headquarters, US Marine Corps, 1975), 11, 88.

75   Butterfield, *Diary and Autobiography of John Adams*, 3:349–351.

76   NDAR, 2:907–909, Stephen Hopkins to Esek Hopkins, 11/6/75.

77   Fowler, *Rebels*, 59; Miller, 55.

78   Independence Seaport Museum (ISM), Barry-Hayes Papers (BHP), John Barry Memorial to Congress, 1785; Samuel Eliot Morison, *John Paul Jones: A Sailor's Biography* (Annapolis, MD: Naval Institute Press, 1989), 60; HSP, Joshua Humphreys Collection, Letterbook.

79   NDAR, 2:1093–1094, Minutes of the Pennsylvania Committee of Safety, 11/21/75; 3:471, Lord Stormont to Count de Vergennes, 1/2/76; 3:507, M. d'Anglemont to Gabriel de Sartine, 1/14/76; Robert Weeden Neeser, ed., *Letters and Papers Relating to the Cruises of Gustavus Conyngham* (New York, 1915), pps xxix, 159.

80   Butterfield, *Diary and Autobiography of John Adams*, 3:350, 12/6/75.

81   NDAR, 2:1255, Journal of John Trevett, 12/3/75; JCC, 12/2/75.

82   HSP, Joshua Humphreys Shipyard Accounts, December 1775; Pennsylvania *Gazette*, 1/4/76; JCC, 12/13/75.

83   HSP, Miscellaneous Collection, "First Commission in the Continental Marine Corps," 11/28/75; Smith, 12–14.

84   HSP, Christopher Marshall Diaries, 12/3/75.

85   Morison, 49–53; Thomas, 34–40; Noland Van Powell, *The American Navies of the Revolutionary War* (New York: G. P. Putnam's Sons, 1974), 28.

86   Butterfield, *Diary and Autobiography of John Adams*, 3:348–350.

CHAPTER TWO ★ "IF THE REBELS SHOULD PAY US A VISIT . . ."

1   NDAR, 3:1263–1364, Autobiography of Joshua Barney.

2   John F. Watson, *Annals of Philadelphia*, vol. 1 (Philadelphia: Edwin Stuart, 1887). Hereafter cited as Watson's *Annals*.

3   NDAR, 3:266, "Letter from Philadelphia," 12/27/75; Fowler, *Rebels Under Sail*, 248.

4   JCC, 11/28/75.

5   HSP, Christopher Marshall Diaries, December 1775–January 1776; NDAR, 3:636–638, Naval Committee to Commodore Esek Hopkins, 1/5/76. No American naval officer was awarded the rank of admiral until the Civil War.

6   Alverda S. Beck, *The Correspondence of Esek Hopkins, Commander-in-Chief of the United States Navy 1775–1777* (Providence: Rhode Island Historical Society, 1932), 12–13; Bradford, *Command Under Sail*; Fowler, "Esek Hopkins: Commander-in-Chief of the Continental Navy," 4–5; William Bell Clark, *Captain Dauntless: The Story of Nicholas Biddle of the Continental Navy* (Baton Rouge: Louisiana State University Press, 1949), 88.

7   NDAR, 3:213–214, Silas Deane to Elizabeth Deane, 12/27/75; NDAR, 3:641–642, Minutes of the Pennsylvania Committee of Safety, 1/5/76.

8   JCC, 12/22/75; PA Archives, Colonial Records, 1:425–426, Minutes of the Pennsylvania Committee of Safety, 12/11/75.

9   NDAR, 3:259, Dr. Benjamin Rush to Owen Biddle, 12/26/75; ibid., 3:615, Intelligence from Philadelphia, Transmitted by Captain Hyde Parker, Jr., R.N.; ibid., 3:721, Gilbert Barkly to Sir Gray Cooper 1/10/76. The *Providence* joined the squadron later.

10   *Pennsylvania Evening Post*, 1/8, 1/13, 1/18, and 1/20/76.

11   NDAR, 2:1251, Major General William Howe to Lord Dartmouth, 12/3/75; ibid., 3:209, John Hancock to George Washington, 12/22/75; ibid., 3:1193, Washington to Colonel Joseph Reed, 2/10/76; ibid., 3:1234–1236, Francis Lightfoot Lee to Landon Carter, 2/12/76; King, Hattendorf, and Estes, *Sea of Words*, 255–256; Miller, 71.

12   University of Virginia Library, Lord Dunmore's Proclamation.

13   *Virginia Gazette*, 12/30/75; Thomas Fleming, *Liberty!* (New York: Viking, 1997), 160–163.

14   NDAR, 2:258–260, Common Hall of the Borough of Norfolk to Lord Dunmore, 9/20/75; and Lord Dunmore to the Town Hall of the Borough of Norfolk, 9/30/75.

15   *Pennsylvania Gazette*, 12/22/75, 1/17/76; NDAR, 3:617–619, Lord Dunmore to Lord Dartmouth, 1/4/76.

16   NDAR, 3:636–637, Naval Committee to Commodore Esek Hopkins, 1/5/76.

17   Ibid., 3:637–638, Naval Committee to Commodore Esek Hopkins, 1/5/76.

18   Ibid., 2:678–679, Edmund Burke to Charles O'Hara, 8/17/75; ibid., 3:371–372, Richard Champion to Willing, Morris, and Co., 11/17/75; Miller, 135.

19   NDAR, 3:366–367, Rear Admiral George Brydges Rodney to Lord George Germain, 11/12/75 and Lord Germain to the Lord Commissioners, Admiralty, 11/13/75; Miller, 138–140.

20   Miller, 140–143; NDAR, 3:460–461, Lord Sandwich to Lord George Germain, 12/28/75; NDAR, 4:1081–1083, Lord George Germain to George III and Instructions to the Commanders of Ships and vessels in the British Navy, 5/2/76; David Syrett, *The Royal Navy in European Waters During the American Revolutionary War* (Columbia: University of South Carolina Press, 1998), 2–3.

21   Ibid., 2:250, General Thomas Gage to Vice Admiral Samuel Graves, 9/30/75; ibid., 2:983–984, Graves to Captain James Wallace, 11/11/75; ibid., 3, Graves to Vice Admiral Molyneux Shuldham, 1/15/76.

22   NDAR, 3, Continental Naval Committee to Commodore Esek Hopkins, 1/18/76; King, Hattendorf, and Estes *Sea of Words*, 144.

23   NDAR, 2:1163–1164, Caesar Rodney to Thomas Rodney, 11/27/75; HSP, Minutes, Meetings of the Committee of Safety, 9/20/75; John W. Jackson, *The Delaware Bay and River Defenses of Philadelphia 1775–1777* (Philadelphia: Philadelphia Maritime Museum, 1977), 7.

24   LOC, John Barry Collection, ship's log, *Industry*, 11/4–10/71.

25   NDAR, 2:220, Henry Fisher and Delaware Bay Pilots to the Pennsylvania Committee of Safety, 9/27/75; ibid., 2:484, Pennsylvania Committee of Safety to Henry Fisher, 11/28/75. Fisher's papers at the Delaware Historical Society are a remarkable read of a pilot's lot during the war.

26   *Portfolio Magazine* 2 (1809), "Biographical Memoirs of the Late Captain Nicholas Biddle"; Clark, *Captain Dauntless*, 98–99; Miller, 97–98.

27   Roger Knight, *The Pursuit of Victory: The Life and Adventures of Horatio Nelson* (New York: Basic Books, 2005), 449; Michael J. Crawford, ed., *The Autobiography of a Yankee Mariner: Christopher Prince and the American Revolution* (Dulles, VA: Brassey's, 2002), 15.

28   Wilbur, *Patriots and Pirates*, 15–24.

29   Ibid., 51; Morison, 95.

30   Ibid.

31   Miller, 86–87; King, *Sea of Words*, 189, 290–291.

32   King, *Sea of Words*, 99, 248, 393–394; Miller, 89.

33   Miller, 91.

34   LOC, John Paul Jones Papers ("JPJP"), Jones to Joseph Hewes, 5/19/76.

35 Wilbur, 70–71, 74, 90; Morison, 63–64; Barbara Tuchman, *The First Salute* (New York: Knopf, 1988), 118.

36 NDAR, 3:1287–1289, Commodore Esek Hopkins' Signals for the First Continental Fleet, 2/14/76.

37 Ibid., 3:1306–1307, Biddle to Lydia McFunn, 2/14/76.

38 Ibid., 3:1287–1289, Hopkins's signals.

39 HSP, Nicholas Biddle Papers, Commodore Esek Hopkins to Captain Nicholas Biddle, 2/14/76.

40 Ibid., Captain Nicholas Biddle to his Brother James Biddle, 2/15/76; NDAR, 3:637–638, Congress's orders to Hopkins, 1/5/76.

41 Ibid.

42 Van Powell, 30; PA Archives, 1st Series, 769–770, Henry Fisher to the Pennsylvania Committee of Safety, 6/7/76.

43 NDAR, 5:639–640, John Paul Jones to David Tillinghast, 6/20/76; Morison, 64, 75; Thomas, 48; Fowler, *Rebels*, 94, 101–103, 245.

44 NDAR, 4:1458–1459, Court Martial of John Hazard, Commander of the Sloop *Providence*, 5/9/76; ibid., 3:718–720, portrait and Naval Committee to Captain William Stone, 1/10/876; ibid., 3:1263–1264, Autobiography of Joshua Barney, 10/23/75–2/13/76.

45 Louis A. Norton, *Joshua Barney: Hero of the War of 1812* (Annapolis, MD: Naval Institute Press, 2000), 96; NDAR, 3:302, Command Officers of the Continental Fleet, 12/30/75; ibid., 3:888–891, Articles of Enlistment for the Continental Navy, 1/20/76; Morison, 67.

46 James S Biddle, ed., *Autobiography of Charles Biddle* (Philadelphia, 1883), 241–242, "Memorandum of Mrs. Mary Biddle"; Christ Church Marriage Records; William Bell Clark, *Captain Dauntless: The Story of Nicholas Biddle of the Continental Navy* (Baton Rouge: Louisiana State University Press, 1949), 5–7.

47 *Pennsylvania Gazette*, 3/10/63; Charles Biddle Autobiography; Clark, 7.

48 Charles Wilson Peale portrait of Nicholas Biddle; "Portfolio Biography," Clark, 35; King, *Sea of Words*, 341.

49 American Philosophical Society ("APS"), Benjamin Franklin Papers ("BFP"), Joseph Galloway to Benjamin Franklin, 4/23/71; Clark, 36. HSP, Biddle Papers, Nicholas Biddle to Lydia McFunn, 10/20/72; Edward Biddle memoir; Clark, 51.

50 *London Public Advertiser*, 5/24/73; Constantine John Phipps, *A Voyage Towards the*

North Pole Undertaken by his Majesty's Command, 1773 (London, 1775); Clark, 53–54; Knight, 28–32.

51   HSP, Nicholas Biddle Letters, Biddle to Lydia McFunn, 10/18/73; Phipp's Journal; Knight, 30–32; *London Gazeteer and New Daily Advertiser*, 3/19/74; Clark, 65–69.

52   JCC, 7/25/75, 8/1/75, and 12/22/75; NDAR, 1:992, John Adams to James Warren, 7/27/75; ibid., 1:1031–1032, Minutes of the Pennsylvania Committee of Safety, 8/1/75; Commission of Nicholas Biddle as Captain in the Pennsylvania Navy, 8/1/75; Clark, 75.

53   JCC, 11/28/75.

54   NDAR, 4:134, Journal, *Andrew Doria*, 2/19–31/76.

55   Ibid., 133–134, "Journal Prepared for the King of France by John Paul Jones," 735–76, Commodore Esek Hopkins to John Hancock, 4/9/76.

56   Beck, ed., *The Letter Book of Esek Hopkins*, 46–48; King, 396.

57   *Pennsylvania Magazine of History and Biography* ("PMHB") 49:361–66, Thomas Atwood to Lord Dartmouth, 3/22/76.

58   Ibid.; Morison, 68.

59   *Pennsylvania Gazette*, 4/17/76; NDAR, 4:748–752, "Extract of a Letter from the Captain of Marines [Samuel Nicholas] on Board the Ship *Alfred*, Dated at New–London, April 10, 1776."

60   NDAR, 7:48–51, Governor Montfort Browne to Lord George Germain, 11/5/76.

61   PMHB, XVIX:361–366, Thomas Atwood to Lord Dartmouth, 3/22/76; NDAR, 4:173–175, Journal of H.M. Schooner *St. John*, Lieutenant William Gray, 3/2–4/76.

62   NDAR, 4:249–250, Lieutenant William Grant to Vice Admiral Molyneux Shuldham, 3/8/76.

63   Ibid., 4:175, Journal of Lieutenant John Trevett, 3/4/76.

64   Beck, 50; NDAR, 4:711–712, Hopkins to Governor John Trumbull, 4/8/76; ibid., 4:735–736, Hopkins to Hancock, 4/8/76; Morison, 69.

65   NDAR, 4:373, *Andrew Doria* journal, 3/6–16/76; *Portfolio Magazine*; Clark, 106.

66   NDAR, 4:711–712, Hopkins to Governor John Trumbull, 4/8/76.

67   Ibid., 4: 375, Quarters Stations for the Continental Schooner *Wasp*, 3/16/76; PMHB, XLIX:366, Governor Montford Browne to Lord Dartmouth, 3/17/76.

68   NDAR, 4:403, Commodore Esek Hopkins' Sailing Orders from New Providence, 3/18/76; ibid., 4:516 and 543, *Andrew Doria* Journal, 3/25 and 3/27/76; ibid.,

4:532–533, Journal of the Continental Ship *Wasp*, Captain William Hallock, 3/26/76.

69   Ibid., 4:56, Captain Andrew Snape Hamond, R.N., to Captain Alexander Graeme, R.N., 2/23/76; ibid., 4:662 and 669, *Andrew Doria* Journal, 4/4 and 4/5/76; University of Virginia Library (UVL), Hamond Letter Book, Hamond to Lord Dunmore, 3/14/76; Clark, 109; King, *Sea of Words*, 365.

70   NDAR, 4:669, *Andrew Doria* Journal, 4/5/76; ibid., 4:669–670, Prisoners taken in H.M. Bomb Brig *Bolton*, 4/5/76.

71   HSP, Joshua Humphreys Papers and Correspondence, January–March 1776; Independence Seaport Museum (ISM), Barry-Hayes Papers (BHP), Memorial to Congress, 1785.

72   NDAR, 4:152, Journal of the H.M.S. *Liverpool*, Captain Henry Bellew, 3/3/76; ibid., 4:271–272, Journal of H.M Sloop *Otter*, 3/4–9/76; ibid., 4:310–311, Charles Carroll of Carrollton to Charles Carroll, Sr., 3/12/76; ibid., 4:355–356, William Lux to Daniel of St. Thomas Jenifer, 3/15/76; ISM, BHP, Memorial to Pennsylvania State Assembly, 1783; Memorial to Congress, 1785; NYHS, Barnes Collection, NY5–31, Certification affidavit, John Hancock, 9/26/76.

73   NDAR, 4:399–400, Extract of a Letter from Philadelphia dated 18th March 1776; ibid., 4:510, Henry Fisher to the Pennsylvania Committee of Safety, 3/25/76; HSP, Joshua Humphreys Papers, Wharton & Humphreys Ship Yard Accounts, 1773–1795; Millar, 174–176.

74   HSP, Wharton-Humphreys Charge Book; Woodhouse Collection, "Commissioners of the Continental Navy in Account with the Brigantine *Lexington*, 3/28/76; Christopher Marshall Diaries, 3/28/76; PA Archives, Colonial Records, 10:524–528; *Magazine of American History* 2, part 1 (1878), "Narrative of Luke Matthewman"; Clark, *Gallant John Barry*, 74–75.

75   PA State Archives, State Papers, 1:113–115, Henry Fisher to PA Committee of Safety, 4/1/76; UVL, No. 4, Hamond Papers, Narrative of Captain Andrew Snape Hamond (Hamond's Narrative), 3/28/76; HSP, Whipple to Bartlett, 3/28/76; NDAR, 4:595–597, Journal of the H.M.S. *Roebuck*, Captain Andrew Snape Hamond (*Roebuck* Journal), 3/25–31/76; ibid., 4:671, Henry Fisher to the Pennsylvania Committee of Safety, 4/5/76; King, *Sea of Words*, 229.

76   NDAR, 4:671, Fisher to Committee of Safety, 4/1/76; *Pennsylvania Gazette*, 4/17/76; NYHS, Commodore John Barry Papers, Continental Marine Committee to John Barry, 4/8/76; *New York Journal*, 4/11/76.

77   UVL, Hamond, No. 4, Hamond Narrative, 4/7/76.

78   NDAR, 4:448–449, "Disposition of His Majesty's Ships and Vessels in North America under the Command of Rear [Vice] Admiral Shuldham"; ibid., 4:679–681, *Andrew Doria* Journal, 4/6/76; Journal of John Paul Jones; Journal of H.M.S. *Glasgow*, Captain Tyringham Howe, 4/5–6/76; LOC, John Paul Jones Papers

("JPJ"), Jones to Joseph Hewes, 5/19/76; Miller, 113; Morison, 70–71; Beck, 43, Signals; 49–51, Hopkins to Cooke, 4/8/76.

CHAPTER THREE ★ "I FEAR NOTHING"

1   *Pennsylvania Evening Post*, 4/11/76.

2   Beck, 43.

3   NDAR, 5:27–28, Captain Nicholas Biddle to James Biddle, 5/10/76.

4   Ibid., 5:679–681: *Andrew Doria* Journal, 4/6/76; Journal of John Paul Jones, Journal of HMS *Glasgow* and Remarks, Captain Tyringham Howe, 4/5–4/6/76.

5   *Pennsylvania Gazette*, 4/17/76.

6   LOC, JPJ, Jones to Joseph Hewes, 4/14/76; Morison, 72–73.

7   NDAR, 5:680–681, *Glasgow* Journal and Remarks.

8   Ibid., 5:735–736, Commodore Esek Hopkins to John Hancock, 4/9/76; ibid., 5:819, George Washington to Commodore Esek Hopkins, 4/14/76; ibid., 5:860–861, Hopkins to Governor Nicholas Cooke, 4/17/76.

9   UVL, Hamond Papers, Hamond to Captain Henry Bellew, 4/8/76.

10   *Pennsylvania Evening Post*, 4/11/76; London *Public Advertiser*, 8/17/76; US Customs Office, Philadelphia, Admiralty Court Transcripts, "Condemnation Proceedings Against the British Tender *Edward*, 4/30/76.

11   HSP, Biddle Papers, List of People on Board the *Andrew Doria*; NDAR, 4:710, Gordon Saltonstall to George Washington, 4/8/76; ibid., 4:711–712, Commodore Esek Hopkins to Governor Jonathan Trumbull, 4/8/76; ibid., 4:735–736, Hopkins to John Hancock, 4/9/76.

12   NDAR, 4:819, Washington to Hopkins, 4/14/76; ibid., 4:868–869, Hancock to Hopkins, 4/17/76; ibid., 4:1252, Washington to Hopkins, 4/25/76; Miller, 117; Morison, 75.

13   HSP, Biddle Papers, Nicholas Biddle to Lydia McFunn, 4/26/76.

14   NDAR, 4:1296, John Adams to Abigail Adams, 4/28/76.

15   Ibid., 4:716–719, Round Robin of the Crew of the Continental Brig *Cabot*, 4/8/76.

16   LOC, JPJ, Jones to Joseph Hewes, 4/14/76; HSP, Biddle Papers, Nicholas Biddle to Charles Biddle, 5/2/76.

17   Ibid.; NDAR, 4:1328–1329, Captain Abraham Whipple to Commodore Esek Hopkins, 4/30/76; ibid., 4:1360, Crew of the Continental Sloop *Providence* to Commodore Esek Hopkins, 5/1/76.

18   NYHS, MSS Collection, Continental Marine Committee to Captain John Barry, 4/11/76; HSP, Christopher Marshall Diaries, 4/11/76; JCC, 3/28/76 and 4/13/76; *Pennsylvania Gazette*, 5/8/76.

19   HSP, Biddle Papers, Nicholas Biddle to Charles Biddle, 5/2/76; LOC, JPJ, Jones to Hewes, 4/14/76; NDAR, 4:1252: Washington to Hopkins, 4/25/76; ibid., 4:1358, Hopkins to Washington, 5/1/76.

20   David Cordingly, *Under the Black Flag* (New York, Harcourt Brace, 1995), 95–96; HSP, Biddle Papers, Nicholas Biddle to James Biddle, 5/10/76; A List of People on Board the *Andrew Doria* 10th May.

21   NDAR, 4:1419–1422, Proceedings of Court-Martial of Abraham Whipple, Commander of the *Columbus*, 5/6/76.

22   Ibid., 4:1458–1459, Court-Martial of John Hazard, Commander of the Sloop *Providence*, 5/8/76; ibid., 5:64–65, Hazard to Hopkins, 5/12/76 (approx.).

23   NDAR, 5:27, Commodore Esek Hopkins to Lieutenant John Paul Jones, 5/10/76; ibid., 5:639–640, Jones to Daniel Tillinghast, 6/20/76.

24   Ibid., 5:1264–1231, Hamond to Lord Dunmore, 4/26/76; ibid., 5:1441–1442, William Whipple to John Langdon, 5/7/76; HSP, Christopher Marshall Diaries, 5/5/76.

25   NDAR, 8:738–740, Muster Rolls for the Continental Navy Brig *Lexington*, 5/21/76; PA Archives, "Petition of a Slave to the Pennsylvania Committee of Safety," date unknown.

26   BFP, Richard Bache to Benjamin Franklin, 5/7/76; *Pennsylvania Evening Post*, 5/7/76; PA Archives, Henry Fisher Papers, Fisher to the Committee of Safety, 5/7/76; *Pennsylvania Evening Packet*, 5/27/76.

27   NDAR, 4:1415, 1447–1448, Narrative of Captain Andrew Snape Hamond, 5/5 and 5/7/76; ibid., 4:1447–1448, Journal of the HMS *Liverpool*, Captain Henry Bellew, 5/5–5/7/76; PA Archives, PA Colonial Records 10:556–559, Minutes of the Pennsylvania Committee of Safety, 5/7/76, Haverford College Library (HCL), Charles Roberts Collection, Robert Morris to John Barry, 5/8/76.

28   HSP, Etting Papers, Captain Henry Bellew to John Hancock, 5/8/76.

29   Biddle, *Autobiography*, 84–88.

30   Ibid.; NDAR, 4:1470, *Roebuck* Journal, 5/8/76.

31   NDAR, 4:1470–1471, *Roebuck* and *Liverpool* Journals, 5/8/76; ibid., 5:655–670, Deposition of John Emmes, A Delaware Pilot; *Pennsylvania Evening Post*, 6/29/76.

32   Ibid.

33   PA Archives, 1st Series, IV, 748, Colonel Samuel Miles to the Pennsylvania Committee of Safety, 5/8/76; NDAR, 4:1467, Joshua Barney Autobiography, 5/7–8/76.

34   NDAR, 4:1467–1469, Hamond to Bellew, 5/8/76; ibid., 4:1471, and 5:19, *Liverpool Journal*, 5/8/76 and 5/9/76; *Pennsylvania Evening Packet*, 6/29/76.

35   NDAR, 4:1465, Thomas Read to the Pennsylvania Committee of Safety, 5/8/76; PA Archives, 1st Series, 4:747–748, Thomas Read to the Committee of Safety, 5/8–9/76, three letters; ibid., 4:750, Barry to Robert Morris; JCC, 5/9/76.

36   NDAR, 5:15–16, Hamond's Narrative, 5/5–9/76; 5:17–20, Barney's Autobiography, 5/9/76; *Roebuck* Journal, 5/9/76; *Liverpool Journal*, 5/9/76; ibid., 5:655–670, Deposition of John Emmes, A Delaware Pilot.

37   HSP, Etting Autograph Collection, Captain Walter Stewart to John Hancock, 5/12/76; Purdie's *Virginia Gazette*, 5/24/76; JCC, 5/29/76.

38   NDAR, 5:34–35, Hancock to Washington, 5/10/76; ibid., 5:67, John Adams to Abigail Adams, 5/12/76; HSP, Christopher Marshall Diaries, 5/11/76; Charles Biddle Autobiography, 84.

39   PA Archives, Colonial Series 10:563–566, Marine Committee to Hopkins, 5/10/76; NDAR, 4:1358–1360, Hopkins to Hancock, 5/1/76.

40   HSP, Biddle Papers, Nicholas to James, 5/10/76; NDAR, 5:46, Journal of the HMS *Cerberus*, Captain John Symons, 5/11/76; ibid., 5:63, Hopkins to Biddle, 5/12/76; Hopkins to Elisha Hinman, 5/12/76.

41   NDAR, 5:182–183, *Andrew Doria* Journal and footnote; Clark, *Captain Dauntless*, 123–124.

42   HSP, Biddle Papers, Nicholas to Charles, 6/16/76; NDAR, 5:688, Dixon and Hunter's *Virginia Gazette*, 6/22/76.

43   NDAR, 5:473, Journal of Lieutenant Trevett, 5/29–6/11/76; *Pennsylvania Evening Post*, 7/2/76; Clark, *Captain Dauntless*, 129–130.

44   NDAR, 5:626, Captain Charles Pond to George Washington, 6/19/76.

45   Ibid., 5:492–493, *Cerberus* Journal, 6/12/76; Newport *Mercury*, 7/29/76; ibid., 5:975–976, Vice Admiral Molyneux Shuldham to Philip Stephens, 7/8/76; *Pennsylvania Evening Post*, 4/29/77; *Portfolio Magazine*, Nicholas Biddle Biography.

46   HSP, Biddle Papers, Nicholas to Charles, 6/16/76.

47   NDAR, 5:600, *Cerberus* Journal, 6/18/76; ibid., 5:638, Hopkins to General Nathanael Greene, 6/20/76; ibid., 5:1304, Nathanael Shaw, Jr., to John Hancock, 7/31/76.

48   Ibid., 5:424–426, Esek Hopkins to Stephen Hopkins, 6/8/76; ibid., 5:529–530,

Hancock to Esek Hopkins, 6/14/76; ibid., 5:599–600, Hopkins to Biddle, 6/18/76; LOC, GWP, Hancock to Washington, 6/19/76.

49   Ibid., 277–278, *Liverpool Journal*, 5/27/76; ibid., 5:457–458, Bellew to Shuldham, 6/10/76; *Constitutional Gazette*, 6/22/76; US Coast Guard Geodetic Survey, Coast Chart No. 24, *Delaware Entrance*, W. W. Duffield, Superintendent, 1895.

50   LOC, William Bell Clark Papers, *Kingfisher* Journal, 6/28/76; PRO, Admiralty, 52/479, *Orpheus* Journal, 6/28/76; Maryland Historical Society, Scharf Collection, Lambert Wickes to Samuel Wickes, 7/2/76.

51   LOC, Clark Papers, *Kingfisher* Journal, 6/29/76; PRO Admiralty, 51/479, *Orpheus* Journal, 6/29/76; Elizabeth Montgomery, *Reminiscences of Wilmington, Delaware* (Wilmington: Johnston and Borgia, 1872), 176–181; Maryland Historical Society, Lambert Wickes to Samuel Wickes, 7/2/76; *Pennsylvania Ledger*, 7/6/76; *Pennsylvania Evening Post*, 7/11/76; *Connecticut Courant*, 7/15/76.

52   JCC, 7/2/76; HSP, Dreer Collection, Marine Committee to John Barry, 7/2/76.

53   JCC, 5/10/76; NDAR, 5: 893, Washington to Hancock, 7/3/76; David Mc-Cullough, *1776* (New York: Simon and Schuster, 2005), 138; Fowler, *The Baron of Beacon Hill*, 208–210.

54   NDAR, 5:864–866, Major General Charles Lee to George Washington, 7/1/76; ibid., 5:927, John Wells' Account of the British Attack on Charleston, 6/29–7/4/76; ibid., 5:928–929, Journal of the HMS *Experiment*, 7/2–7/4/76; ibid., 5:997–1002, Commodore Sir Peter Parker to Philip Stephens, 7/9/76.

55   HSP, Dreer Collection, Marine Committee to John Barry, 7/2/76; HSP, Joshua Humphreys Collection and NDAR, 5:1018–1020, Dimensions of the Ships *Randolph* and *Delaware*, 7/10/76; ibid., 5:951, Hancock to Washington, 7/6/76.

56   JCC, 8/12/76 (including footnotes); NDAR, 6, Autobiography of John Adams, 8/12/76; ibid., 6:195–198, Thomas Jefferson's Notes on Commodore Esek Hopkins' Defense, 8/12/83 [*sic* 1776]; JCC, 8/16/76.

57   NDAR, 5:768–769, Governor Nicholas Cooke to General Artemas Ward, 6/27/76; ibid., 5:788, Biddle to Hopkins, 6/28/76; ibid., 6:1011–1012, Trial and Condemnation of the British Prize Sloop *Betsey* in the Pennsylvania Admiralty Court, 9/26/76; *Portfolio Magazine* 7 (June 1814), "Memoir of Richard Dale"; King, *Sea of Words*, 130.

58   Painting of Jones by Cecilia Beaux, Sculpture by Houdon, U.S. Naval Academy Museum.

59   Thomas, 14–15; Morison, 22–23; Lincoln Lorenz, *John Paul Jones: Fighter for Freedom and Glory* (Annapolis, MD: Naval Institute Press, 1943), 18.

60   Thomas, 21–22; Morison, 33–35; William Loren Katz, *Eyewitness: A Living Docu-*

mentary of the African American Contribution to American History (New York: Touchstone, 1995), 44.

61   LOC, JPJP, Jones' letter to his mother and sisters, 9/24/72; Morison, 38–40; Thomas, 24–25.

62   Ibid., Jones to Robert Morris, 9/4/76; Morison, 42; Thomas, 28–29.

63   LOC, JPJP, Jones to John Leacock, 4/15/73; Jones to Robert Morris, 9/4/76; Jones to Benjamin Franklin, 3/6/79; Morison, 43–45; Thomas, 30–32.

64   LOC, JPJP, John Read to Jones, 2/28/78; Thomas, 40–41.

65   LOC, JPJP, Jones to Franklin, 3/6/79; Morison, 51–53; Thomas, 39–41.

66   NDAR, 6:85–86, Marine Committee to John Paul Jones, 8/6/76; 209, Marine Committee to Jones and William Hallock, 8/16/76; McCullough, *1776*, 138–139; Charles Rappleye, *Robert Morris: Financier of the American Revolution* (New York: Simon and Schuster, 2010), 49, 137.

67   LOC, JPJP, Lieutenant Alpheus Rice to Jones, 9/9/76; NDAR, 6:684–685, Jones to Marine Committee, 9/4/76; 1371–1377, Muster Roll, *Providence*, from May 10, 1776.

68   Morison, 57; Thomas, 56–57; King, *Sea of Words*, 105.

69   NDAR, 6:684–685, Jones to Marine Committee, 9/4/76; LOC, JPJP, Jones to Morris, 9/4/76.

CHAPTER FOUR ★ "THAT REBEL IS MY BROTHER"

1   NDAR, 7:601–602, Governor Craister Greathead to Governor Johannes de Graaf, 12/23/76.

2   Ibid., 6:684–685, Jones to Marine Committee, 9/4/76; LOC, JPJP, Jones to Morris, 9/4/76.

3   NDAR, 6: Appendix, 1499–1511, David Bushnell and the Submarine *Turtle*; Bushnell to Ezra Stiles, 10/16/87.

4   Ibid.; Miller, 160.

5   Ibid., 1499–1500, Washington to Thomas Jefferson, 9/26/85.

6   Ibid., 1507–1511, Ezra Lee to David Humphreys, 2/20/1815.

7   Ibid., Miller, 160–62.

8   NDAR, 6:349–350, Minutes of the Council of War on the Evacuation of Long

Island, 8/29/76; ibid., 6:372, Journal of Captain Henry Duncan, R.N., 8/29/76; ibid., 6:874–875, Major General Nathanael Green to Governor Nicholas Cooke, 9/17/76.

9 Ibid., 6:1228–1230, Major General John Burgoyne to Captain Charles Douglas, R.N., 10/12/76; ibid., 6:1235–1237, Brigadier General Benedict Arnold to Major General Horatio Gates, 10/12/76. For further reading, the author recommends James Nelson's *Benedict Arnold's Navy*.

10 Ibid., 782, Journal of Lieutenant Stephen Kemble, 9/11/76; ibid., 6:928–931, Diary of Frederick Mackenzie, 9/21–22/76; Journal, H.M.S. *Rose*, Captain James Wallace, 9/21/76.

11 Franklin Delano Roosevelt Library (FDR), Captain Isaiah Robinson to Lieutenant Joshua Barney, 9/8/76; NDAR, 6:782, Autobiography of Joshua Barney, 7/5–9/11/76; ibid., 6:948–949, Hopkins to the Continental Marine Committee, 9/22/76; ibid., 6:1304, Hopkins to Daniel Tillinghast, 10/17/76; *Pennsylvania Packet*, 9/10/76; *New England Chronicle*, 9/12/76; *Independent Chronicle*, 10/3/76. *Connecticut Courant*, 10/18/76.

12 NDAR, 6:11–12, John Almon's *Remembrancer*, 1776; ibid., 6:76–77, William Bingham to Silas Deane, 8/5/76; ibid., 6:142–143, Vice Admiral James Young to Philip Stephens, 8/11/76; ibid., 6:583–584, Gabriel de Sartine to M. d'Argout, 8/11/76.

13 HSP, Biddle Papers, Lydia McFunn to Nicholas Biddle, 7/12/76; *Providence Gazette*, 9/7/76; NDAR, 6:770, Esek Hopkins to Marine Committee, 9/10/76; ibid., 6:790, *Cerberus* Journal, 9/11–12/76; *Newport Mercury*, 9/16/76; *Pennsylvania Journal*, 9/18/76; *Pennsylvania Packet*, 9/24/76; *Portfolio* Biography; Clark, *Captain Dauntless*, 146–149.

14 NDAR, 6:1047–1050, Jones to Marine Committee, 9/30/76.

15 Ibid.

16 JCC, 8/26/76; LOC, JPJP, Minutes of the Continental Marine Committee, 9/5/76; Uniforms recommended by a Group of Continental Navy Captains, 2/27/77.

17 JCC, 10/10/76; Morison, 118–119.

18 NDAR, 6:1166-68, Vice Admiral Clark Gayton to Philip Stephens, 10/8/76; Charles Biddle, *Autobiography*, 98.

19 NDAR, 6:1362, Hopkins to Jones, 10/22/76; ibid., 7:11–12, William Hooper to Joseph Hewes, 11/1/76; HSP, Gratz Collection, Hooper to Hewes, 11/16/76.

20 LOC, JPJP, Jones to Morris, 10/17 and 10/30/76; NDAR, 6:1457, Jones to Marine Committee, 10/30/76.

21 Miller, 183; NDAR 6:41–42, Caesar Rodney to Thomas Rodney, 8/3/76; King, *Harbors and High Seas*, 144.

22 NDAR, 6:1400–1403; Committee of Secret Correspondence to Captain Lambert Wickes, 10/24/76; ibid., 6:1403–1405, Committee of Secret Correspondence to Silas Deane, 10/24/76; ibid., 6:1405–1407, Committee of Secret Correspondence to the American Commissioners in France, 10/24/76; Stacy Schiff, *A Great Improvisation: Franklin, France, and the Birth of America* (New York: Henry Holt, 2005), 8–12; Fleming, *Liberty!*, 229–232.

23 NDAR, 6:622–624, Silas Deane to the Secret Committee of Correspondence of the Continental Congress, 10/1/76.

24 Ibid., 6:1400–1403; Committee of Secret Correspondence to Captain Lambert Wickes, 10/24/76.

25 Ibid., 6:1086–1087, Committee of Secret Correspondence Memorandum, 10/10/76; ibid., 7:7, Journal of Ambrose Serle, 11/1/76; William Temple Franklin, *Memoirs of the Life and Writings of Benjamin Franklin* (Philadelphia, 1818), 1:309; William Bell Clark, *Lambert Wickes: Sea Raider and Diplomat* (New Haven, CT: Yale University Press, 1932), 95.

26 HSP, Christopher Marshall Diaries, 11/1–12/31/76; HSP, Customs House Records, 12/19/74; HSP, Joshua Humphreys Collection, "Dimensions of the Randolph Frigate"; Van Powell, 44–45.

27 NDAR, 7:8, Howe to Stephens, 11/1/76; ibid., 7:78–79, Ambrose Serle to Lord Dartmouth, 11/7/76; ibid., 7:552–557, Howe to Parker, 12/22/76; UVL, Hamond Papers, Vice Admiral Richard Lord Howe to Vice Admiral Molyneux Shuldham; 11/25/76; *Connecticut Courant*, 12/20/76; PA Archives, 1st Series 5:100–101, Henry Fisher to Pennsylvania Committee of Safety, 12/11/76; McCullough, *1776*, 258.

28 JCC, 11/30/76; NDAR, 7:475–476, Morris to Hancock, 12/13/76; ibid., 7:476–477, Morris to Biddle, 12/13/76; ibid., 7:404–405, George Washington to John Cadwalader, 12/7/76; ibid., 7:534, Morris to the Committee of Safety, 12/20/76; ibid., 7:543, Cadwalader to the Pennsylvania Committee of Safety, 12/21/76.

29 NDAR, 7:450–451, Samuel Chase to James Nicholson, 12/11/76; ibid., 7:477, Nicholson to Lieutenant Henry Auchenleck, 12/13/76.

30 HSP, Christopher Marshall Diaries, 12/11/76; Tinkcom, "The Revolutionary City," 129; NDAR, 7:528–533, Morris to Deane, 12/20/76.

31 JCC, 12/12/76; NDAR, 7:475–76, Morris to Hancock, 12/13/76.

32 Ibid, 12/7, 12/12, and 12/13/76.

33 HSP, Biddle Family Papers and Bank of North America Papers, Morris to Biddle, 12/13/76; NDAR, 7:482–483, Marine Committee (Robert Morris) to William Bingham, 12/14/76; ibid., 7:1040, Morris to Hancock, 1/26/77.

34 NDAR, 7:504–505, Morris to Hancock, 12/17/76; HSP, BFP, Christianna McMullen to Biddle, 12/19/76.

35   NDA, 7:534–535, Journal of the H.M.S. *Pearl*, Captain Thomas Wilkinson, 12/20/76; UVL, Hamond Letter Book, Hamond to Vice Admiral Richard Lord Howe, 1/1/77.

36   NDAR, 7:544–545, Morris to Hancock, 12/21/76.

37   NDAR, 7:601–602, Greathead to de Graaf, 12/26/76.

38   Ibid., 7:374–376, Morris to Hancock, 12/23/76; ibid., 7:614–615, Lieutenant William Jones, RN, to Vice Admiral Richard Lord Howe, 12/27/76.

39   APS, BFP, Franklin to Silas Deane, 12/4/76; Franklin to the Committee of Secret Correspondence, 12/8/76; Wickes to Committee, 12/13/76; Clark, *Lambert Wickes*, 98–99; Schiff, 16.

40   NDAR, 7:595–596, Washington to Morris, 12/25/76.

41   Ibid., 7:905–906, John Bradford to the Secret Committee of the Continental Congress, 1/9/77; McCullough, 274; David Hackett Fischer, *Washington's Crossing* (New York: Oxford University Press, 2004), 216.

42   NDAR, 7:854, Journal of Ambrose Searle, 1/3/77; ibid., 7:932, Master's Log of H.M.S. *Roebuck*, 1/11/77; UVL, Hamond Papers, Narrative of Andrew Snape Hamond, 11/25–12/31/76.

43   NDAR, 7:600–601, Morris to Hancock, 12/26/76.

44   PA Archives, Second Series, 1:20; Flexner, *George Washington*, 97; Fischer, *Washington's Crossing*, 327–334; Miller, 219; Fleming, *Liberty*, 224.

45   UVL, Hamond Papers, Hamond's Narrative, 11/25/76–1/10/77.

46   NDAR, 7:614, Captain James Nicholson to Samuel Purviance, Jr., 12/27/76; *Continental Journal*, 1/16/77.

47   Ibid., Hancock to Morris, 1/2/77; NDAR, 7:862–863, Congressional Committee in Philadelphia to George Washington, 1/5/77.

48   NDAR, 7:629, Hamond to Morris, 12/30/76; ibid., 7:933, Morris to Pennsylvania Council of Safety, PA Archives, 1st Series 5:152–153, Henry Fisher to Pennsylvania Council of Safety, 1/1/77.

49   HSP, Biddle Papers, Margaret Tarras to Nicholas Biddle, 8/7/76.

50   *Pennsylvania Evening Post*, 1/9/77.

51   NDAR, 7:852–853, "A State of the Mutual Exchange of Prisoners, Etc.," 12/22/76; ibid., 7:876–877, Morris to Washington, 1/7/77.

52   NDAR, 6:1079, Commodore Hopkins to Reverend Samuel Hopkins, 10/1/76.

53   NDAR, 7:828, Master's Log, HMS *Diamond*, 1/1/77; ibid., 7:845–846, Brigadier

General William West to Governor Nicholas Cooke, 1/2/77; ibid., 7:923–996, Commodore Sir Peter Parker to Vice Admiral Richard, Lord Howe, 1/11/77; ibid., 8:98–99, Hopkins to William Ellery, 3/13/77.

54 NDAR, 6:1362 Hopkins to Jones, 10/22/76; LOC, JPJP, Jones to Captain Hoysted Hacker, 11/1/76; Provisions Aboard the Continental Ship *Alfred*.

55 NDAR, 7:16–17, Jones to Hopkins (and notes), 11/2/76.

56 LOC JPJP, Jones to the Marine Committee, 11/12/76; Jones to Robert Smith, 11/12/76.

57 Ibid.

58 NDAR, 7:183–184, Jones to Marine Committee, 11/16/76; ibid., 7:935–937, Jones to Marine Committee, 1/12/77; LOC, JPJP, Jones to Robert Morris, 1/12/77; Jones to Joseph Hewes, 1/12/77; *New York Gazette*, 10/26/76; Morison, 108.

59 LOC, JPJP, Jones's Orders to Prize Masters, 11/25/76.

60 NDAR, 7:416–417, Master's Log of the H.M.S. *Milford*, 12/8–9/76; ibid., 7:935–937, 923–927, Commodore Sir Peter Parker to Vice Admiral Richard Lord Howe, 1/11/77; LOC, JPJP, Jones' Notes on the *Alfred*'s Cruise, 12/7–8/76; Jones to Marine Committee, 1/12/77.

61 NDAR, 7:416–417, Master's Log of H.M.S. *Milford*, 12/9/76; ibid., 8:56, Hopkins to Marine Committee, 3/8/77.

62 NDAR, 7:935–937, Jones to Marine Committee, 1/12/77.

63 Ibid., 6:357, Owners of the Privateer *Eagle* to William Ellery; ibid., 7:983, Daniel Tillinghast to Jones, 1/17/77.

64 LOC, JPJP, Jones to Morris, 10/27/76 and 2/10/77; Jones to Hewes, 1/12/77; Millar, 152–154.

65 NDAR, 7: 510, Hopkins to Jones, 12/18/76; 1153–54, Jones to Robert Morris, 2/10/77.

66 NDAR, 7: 972–973, Congressional Committee in Philadelphia to John Hancock, 1/16/77; 7:1318–1319, Hopkins to Robert Morris, 2/28/77; 7:1319–1320, Hopkins to the Marine Committee, 2/28/77; Thomas, 78.

67 LOC, JPJP, Morris to Jones, 2/5/77; Hopkins to Jones, 2/11/77; Jones to President of Congress, 12/7/79; NDAR, 7:1315–1316, Hopkins to Jones, 2/28/77; 7:1318–1319, Hopkins to Morris, 2/28/77; 7:1319–1320, Hopkins to Marine Committee, 2/28/77; Thomas, 81.

68 NDAR, 7:1166–1167, Officers of the Continental Frigate *Warren* to Robert Treat Paine, 2/11/77.

69   Ibid., 8:189–192, Examination of Marine Lieutenant John Grannis by a Subcommittee of the Continental Marine Committee, 3/26/77.

70   JCC, Hancock to Hopkins, 3/29/77.

CHAPTER FIVE ★ "HEAVEN HAS SUCCEEDED OUR ADVENTURES"

1   NDAR, 8:838–839, Silas Deane to Conrad Alexandre Gérard, 5/11/77.

2   Neeser, xxix; D. H. Conyngham, "Reminiscences," *Proceedings and Collections of the Wyoming Historical Society* 8 (1904); Helen Augur, *The Secret War of Independence* (New York: Duell, Sloan and Pearce, 1955), 81–84.

3   Brian Dyde, *A History of Antigua* (London and Oxford: Macmillan Education, 2000), 140; Carleton Mitchell, *Isles of the Caribees* (Washington, DC: National Geographic Society, 1986), 124; Fowler, *Rebels*, 124.

4   HSP, Logbook: "Society for the Relief etc.," 1765–1773; Cadwalader Collection, Tonnage records, 1765–1775; PMHB, Clark, "The Sea Captains Club," 44–48.

5   Neeser, 159, "Attestation of Gustavus Conyngham."

6   Miller, 180, 285–286.

7   NDAR, 3:471, Lord Stormont to Count de Vergennes, 1/12/76; ibid., 3:507, M. de Anglemont to Gabriel de Sartine, 1/14/76.

8   NDAR, 6:1070, Willing, Morris & Co. to the Maryland Committee of Safety, 9/30/76; Hayes, "Gustavus Conyngham," 17–18; Neeser, 206–207, "Memorial of Gustavus Conyngham to Congress," 207–208, "Certificate Issued by Benjamin Franklin," 8/7/82.

9   NDAR, 6:1070, Willing & Morris to the Maryland Committee of Safety, 9/30/76.

10   HSP, PMHB, 22, "Narrative of Gustavus Conyngham," 486; NDAR, 4:1054, Philip Stephens to William Eden, 4/19/76; Neeser, 9–10; Miller, 291; Fowler, 124.

11   *Freeman's Journal*, 3/22/77.

12   NYHS, Barnes Collection, Papers of Gustavus Conyngham, Continental Navy Commission of Gustavus Conyngham, 3/1/77.

13   NDAR, 8:502–503, Lord Stormont to Lord Weymouth, 1/1/77; American Commissioners in France to the Secret Committee of the Continental Congress, 2/6/77.

14   JCC, 12/10/76; NDAR, 7:790–791, Wickes to the Committee of Secret Correspondence, 12/13/76; ibid., 8:525, Wickes to the American Commissioners in France, 1/14/77; ibid., 8:842, George Lupton (aka James Van Zandt) to William Eden, 5/13/77.

15   JCC, 12/10/76; King, 144, 239.

16   NDAR, 8:827–28, Deposition of John Beach, Prize Master of the *Prince of Orange*, 5/6/77; King, 123; Hayes, 20.

17   Ibid.; Fowler, 125; Miller, 291; Hayes, 20.

18   NDAR, 7:877–878, Congressional Committee in Philadelphia to John Hancock, 1/7/77.

19   Ibid.; JCC, 8/7/76 and 10/10/76; NDAR, 6:219, Washington to Richard Howe, 8/17/76; ibid., 6:235, Richard Howe to Washington, 8/19/76; Clark, *Captain Dauntless*, 168–169.

20   *Pennsylvania Evening Post*, 1/21/77.

21   NDAR, 6:602, Deane to Morris, 9/17/76; ibid., 7:1052, Morris to the Committee of Secret Correspondence and Morris to Biddle, 1/28/77.

22   Ibid., Morris to Biddle, 1/30/77; Morris to Elisha Hinman, 2/15/77.

23   Clark, 170–172.

24   HSP, Wodehouse Collection, Ship's papers 1776–1783, Account of the Frigate *Randolph*, 1/2/77; Clark, 172–173.

25   NDAR, 7:1064, Morris to Biddle, 1/30/77; Clark, *Captain Dauntless*, 173; Miller, 218–220.

26   PMHB, 29, "Journal of Captain John Ferdinand Dalziel Smyth, of the Queen's Rangers," 166–167; Clark, 177–178.

27   NDAR, 8:702–703, John Lloyd to Ralph Izard, 3/22/77; *New York Gazette*, 2/24/77; Clark, 176.

28   HSP, Biddle Family Papers, Nicholas Biddle to James Biddle, 3/11/77.

29   NDAR, 7:1210–1212, Morris to Biddle, 2/15/77; ibid., 7:1212, Morris to Warner, 2/15/77; ibid., 8:224, Morris to William Bingham, 3/12/77.

30   NDAR, 9:864–865, Officers of the Continental Navy Frigate *Randolph* to Captain Nicholas Biddle, 9/1/77.

31   HSP, Nicholas Biddle to James Biddle, 3/11/77; NDAR, 7:1318–1319, Hopkins to Morris, 2/28/77; Hopkins to Continental Marine Committee, 2/28/77; Clark, 177.

32   Miller, 105.

33   Clark, Appendix B, 259–261, Partial Muster Roll of the Frigate *Randolph*, October, 1776–March 7, 1778; HSP, Biddle to Biddle, 3/11/77; Miller, 103–105.

34   Ibid.

35   Ibid., Miller, 224.

36   NDAR, 8:439–442, Marine Committee to Biddle, 4/26/77.

37   Ibid., 8:89, footnote; HSP Biddle Papers, Nicholas Biddle to James Biddle, 3/10/77.

38   ISM, Joshua Humphreys Collection, Designs and Drafts of various ships, 1776–1794; Fowler, 222–223; Miller, 204–210.

39   Miller, 205–209; Millar, 12–27.

40   Ibid.

41   NYHS, John Barry Papers, Barry to James McHenry, 8/10/96.

42   NDAR, 8:482, Major General Benedict Arnold to Governor Jonathan Trumbull, 4/30/77; *Connecticut Journal*, 4/30/77.

43   NDAR, 7:1032–1033, Hancock to Morris, 1/24/77; ibid., 8:296–298, Continental Marine Committee to Captain James Nicholson, 4/8/77; ibid., 8:336, Col. Mordecai Gist to Colonel John Stone, 4/13/77.

44   Ibid., 8:421, Governor Thomas Johnson to Captain James Nicholson, 4/24/77.

45   Ibid., 8:430–431, Maryland Council to John Hancock, 4/25/77; JCC, 4/29/77, 5/1/77.

46   Ibid., 1050, Order of the Maryland Council, 5/31/77.

47   Ibid., 183, "Journal kept by the Officers of the Continental Navy Brig *Cabot*, Captain Joseph Olney, 3/23–24/77; 302–303, John Bradford to the Continental Marine Committee, 4/9/77; 357, Olney to Manley, 4/17/77; *Providence Gazette*, 4/26/77.

48   *London Chronicle*, 5/6/77.

49   PMHB, "Narrative etc.," 480–481; NDAR, 8:827–828, Deposition of John Beach, Prize Master of *Prince of Orange*; London *Public Advertiser*, 5/9/77; *London Chronicle*, 5/8/77; King, 324.

50   NDAR, 8:828–829, Lords Commissioners, Admiralty, to Captain Samuel Warren, R.N., 5/7/77; ibid., 8:838–839, Silas Deane to Conrad Alexandre Gérard, 5/11/77; ibid., 8:846–847, Lord Stormont to Lord Weymouth, 5/14/77 (two letters); London *Public Advertiser*, 5/14/77.

51   London *Public Advertiser*, 5/15/77.

52   Ibid.; *Pennsylvania Evening Packet*, 8/5/77; NDAR, 8:842, George Lupton (James Van Zandt) to William Eden, 5/13/77.

53   NDAR, 8:844, George III to Lord North, 5/14/77.

54   Miller, 289–290; Schiff, 73; Augur, 169.

55   APS, BFP, Wickes to Franklin, 1/14/77; NDAR, 8:546–547, American Commissioners in France to Samuel Nicholson, 1/26/77.

56   Auckland Manuscripts, King's College, Cambridge, England, Samuel Nicholson to Joseph Hynson, 2/2/77, from Clark, *Lambert Wickes*, 162.

57   Ibid.

58   Beck, *Letterbook of Esek Hopkins*, 44–45, "Copy of Manifesto Sent Onshore at New Providence," 3/3/76; Clark, *Wickes*, 163; NDAR, 8:631, Plan to Capture Joseph Hynson's Sloop, 3/3/77.

59   Clark, *Lambert Wickes*, 163; Miller, 289; Augur, 171.

60   Ibid.

61   NDAR, 8:728–730, "Statement Concerning the Employment of Lieut. Col. Edward Smith with Regard to Captain Hynson and a Sketch of the Information Obtained," 3/31/77; Isabella Cleghorn to Joseph Hynson, 2/13/77, from Clark, *Lambert Wickes*, 168–169.

62   Ibid.

63   NDAR, 10:981, Silas Deane to Jonathan Williams, Jr., 11/8/77; Memorandum by King George III, 4/6/77, from Clark, *Lambert Wickes*, 175.

64   LOC, JPJP, Jones to Morris, 4/7/77; "A Plan for the Regulation, and Equipment of the Navy, Drawn up at the Request of the Honorable the President of Congress," 4/7/77; Thomas, 82–83.

65   Woody Holton, *Abigail Adams* (New York: Free Press, 2009), 108–110; Thomas, 82; Fowler, *The Baron of Beacon Hill*, 206–208.

66   Samuel Cooper to Elbridge Gerry, 3/24/77, from Morgan, 75–76.

67   NDAR, 3:840–841, Brigadier General Benedict Arnold to Captain Hector McNeill, 1/18/76; ibid., 5:231, Major Philip Schuyler to George Washington, 5/24/76; Gardner W. Allen, *Captain Hector McNeill of the Continental Navy* (Boston: Massachusetts Historical Society, 1922), 6–7.

68   MHS, Hector McNeill Letter Book, 5/21/77, McNeill to Marine Committee, 5/21/77; Journal of Captain McNeill, 5/21/77.

69   King, 62–67; From the Coast Guard Manual, quoted from Miller, 221–222.

70   MHS, Benjamin Crowninshield, "A Journal of Our Intended Cruse in the Good Ship *Boston* Bound out a Cruse by God's Parmission, Hector McNeill Esq'r Commander," 5/29/77; LOC, John Bradford Letter Book, Bradford to Marine Committee, 6/19/77.

71   NDAR, 8:1040, Manley to McNeill, 5/29/77; ibid., 9:39–40, McNeill Journal, 6/6/77.

72 MHS, McNeill Journal, 5/30/77; McNeill Letter Book, McNeill to Captain Thomas Thompson, 7/21/77.

73 NDAR, 9:8–9, McNeill Journal, 6/3/77.

74 Ibid., 47, McNeill Journal, 6/7/77, 85–87, Deposition of Nathaniel Oakes, Quartermaster, H.M.S. *Fox*, 6/11/77; 87–88, Deposition of Captain Thomas Hardy, 6/11/77; LOC, William Jennison's Journal, 6/7/77.

75 Ibid., 51 and 76, McNeill Journal, 6/8–9/77.

76 HSP, Gratz Collection, Manley to McNeill, 6/27/77; NDAR, 9:224, Patrick Conner's Journal, Navy Frigate *Boston*, 7/6/77.

77 Ibid., LOC, Jennison's Journal, 7/7/77; MHS, Crowninshield's Journal, 7/6–7/77; NDAR, 9:227, Journal of the H.M.S. *Rainbow*, Captain Sir George Collier, 7/6–7/77; ibid., 9:227–228, Journal of M.M. Brig *Victor*, Lieutenant Michael Hyndman, 7/6–7/77; ibid., 9:228–229, Journal of H.M.S. *Flora*, Captain John Brisbane, 7/7/77.

78 NDAR, 9:239, *Rainbow* and *Victor* Journals, 7/8/77.

79 Ibid., 9:273–274, "Extract of a Letter from Sir George Collier to the Viscount Howe, dated the 12th of July 1777."

80 MHS, Crowninshield's Journal, 7/8/77; NDAR, 10:485–487, Muster Roll of the Continental Navy Frigate *Boston*, 11/14/77; Zachary B. Freidenberg, *Medicine Under Sail* (Annapolis, MD: Naval Institute Press, 2002), 17–18; C. Keith Wilbur, MD, *Revolutionary Medicine* (Guilford, CT: Globe Pequot Press, 1973), 62–63; NDAR, 6: Appendix, 1483–1489, Maurice B. Gordon, "Naval and Maritime Medicine during the Revolution."

81 MHS, Crowninshield's Journal, 7/8/77; with thanks to Laurence Todd and Dr. Paul Koppermann for sharing their knowledge of medical procedures of this era.

82 NDAR, 9:297–298; Thompson to McNeill, 7/19/77; MHS, McNeill Letter Book, McNeill to Thompson, 7/21/77.

CHAPTER SIX ⋆ "THE GANG OF PYRATES"

1 NDAR, 9:597–98, 8/23/77.

2 Watson's *Annals*, Vol. 2, "Occurences of the War of Independence," 295.

3 Gregory Keen, "The Descendants of Jöran Kyn," *PMHB* 4:486; HSP, Christ Church Marriage Records, 7/7/77; with thanks to Dr. Susan Klepp regarding Sarah's wedding dress!

4 *Pennsylvania Evening Post*, 7/29/77; NDAR, 9:821–822, John Dorsius to Continental Marine Committee, 8/26/77; Clark, *Captain Dauntless*, 187–191.

5   LOC, JPJP, Lieutenant William Grinnell to Jones, 1/17/77.

6   Henry Louis Gates, "Phillis Wheatley" (Jefferson Lectures, National Endowment for the Humanities); Vincent Carretta, *Phillis Wheatley: Biography of a Genius in Bondage* (Athens and London: University of Georgis Press, 2011), 11–23.

7   LOC, JPJP, Jones to McNeill, est. Summer 1777; Thomas, 84–85; Morison, 143–44.

8   Ibid., Jones to the American Commissioners in France, 6/3/77; NDAR, 8:937–938, Secret Committee of the Continental Congress to Jones, 5/9/77.

9   JCC, 6/14/77.

10   LOC, JPJP, Jones to Marine Committee, 7/21 and 8/30/77; Morison, 134–135; Van Powell, 90; Millar, 232–235.

11   NDAR, 9:208, *Ranger* Broadside; LOC, JPJP, Jones to Marine Committee, 7/21/77; Jones to John Langdon, 9/11/77; Jones to Morris, 7/28/77; Jones to McNeill, 8/24/77; Jones to John Brown, 10/31/77; NDAR, 10:367, JPJ Expense Account.

12   NDAR, 8:745–746, John Barton & Co. to Lord Stormont, 4/5/77.

13   NDAR, 8:641–642, Wickes to American Commissioners, 3/5/77; ibid., 8:786–787, American Commissioners to Captain Henry Johnson, 4/21/77.

14   APS, BFP, Wickes to American Commissioners, 4/15/77 and 4/25/77; NDAR, 8:791–792, Johnson to American Commissioners, 4/25/77.

15   NDAR, 8:862–863, Wickes to Nicholson, 5/23/77; APS, BFP, Franklin to Du Longpuy & Douglas, 6/23/77.

16   Ibid., 9:443–444, Captain George Bowyer, R.N., to Philip Stephens, 6/29/77; ibid., Wickes to American Commissioners, 6/28/77; Millar, 114–115; Clark, *Lambert Wickes*, 222–223.

17   APS, BFP, Wickes to American Commissioners, 6/28/77; Nicholson to American Commissioners, 6/28/77.

18   Liverpool *General Advertiser*, 7/4/77.

19   King, *Harbors, etc.*, 211.

20   APS, BFP, Wickes to American Commissioners, 6/28/77; Nicholson to American Commissioners, 6/28/77; NDAR, 9:443–444, Bowyer to Stephens, 6/29/77.

21   Ibid.; NDAR, 9:443–444, Bowyer to Stephens, 6/29/77.

22   NDAR, 9:443–444, Bowyer to Stephens, 6/29/77.

23   Ibid., 474–475, Wickes to Johnson, 7/8/77.

24   Ibid.; Miller, 295.

25   APS, BFP, Nicholson to American Commissioners, 6/28/77; NDAR, 9:436, Nicholson to Jonathan Williams, Jr., 6/28/77; ibid., 9:461, Williams to Robert Morris, 7/8/77.

26   Hayes, 28.

27   NDAR, 9:462–463, Weymouth to Stormont, 7/4/77.

28   Ibid., 9:472, Lord Mayor of Dublin to Richard Heron, 7/7/77; ibid., 9:478–481, Stormont to Weymouth, 7/9/77; ibid., 9:493–494, Stormont to Weymouth, 7/12/77; Augur, 185.

29   APS, BFP, Vergennes to Franklin and Deane, 7/16/77; Miller, 296.

30   NDAR, 9:510–511, American Commissioners to Vergennes, 7/17/77; ibid., 9:531–532, Weymouth to Stormont; 7/25/77; ibid., 9:540–542, Stormont to Weymouth, 7/30/77.

31   NDAR, 9:466–467, Frazer to Weymouth, 7/5/77.

32   Ibid., 9:411–414, Stormont to Weymouth, 6/19/77; ibid., 9:398–399, Lieutenant William Hills, R.N., to Philip Stephens, 6/14/77; ibid., 404–405, "A.B." to Edward Stanley, Custom House, London, 6/17/77; London Chronicle, 6/17/77.

33   London Packet, 6/25–27/77; NDAR, 9:409–410, Lords Commanders, Admiralty, to Commanders of Four Cruisers, 6/19/77; ibid., 9:411–414, Stormont to Weymouth, 6/19/77; ibid., 9:424, Frazer to Weymouth, 6/23/77.

34   Neeser, 53–54, M. de Gourlande to Vergennes, 7/1/77; ibid., 59–61, Carmichael to American Commissioners, 7/10/77; London Chronicle, 7/5/77; NDAR, 9:461, Frazer to Weymouth, 7/3/77.

35   Ibid., 63–66, M. de Gourlande to Vergennes, 7/12/77; William Caldwell to Conyngham, 7/15/77.

36   Neeser, 66–69, Stormont to Weymouth, 7/16/77; de Gourlande to Vergennes, 7/20/77.

37   PMHB, "Narrative," 480.

38   Neeser, 3; Hayes, 30.

39   NDAR, 9:517, Conyngham to Benjamin Bailey, 7/21/77; ibid., 9:534–535, Captain Francis Richards, R.N., to Philip Stephens, 7/26/77; Hayes, 30.

40   NDAR, 9:522, "An Agreement Made between Benjamin Bailey and Francis Mulligan," 7/23/77; ibid., 9:522, Lieutenant John Moore, R.N., to Philip Stephens, 7/26/77.

41   NDAR, 9:601, Conyngham to Deane, 8/24/77; ibid., 9:562, Lloyd's Evening Post, 8/11/77; Fowler, 127; Hayes, 32.

42 NDAR, 9:601, Conyngham to Deane, 8/24/77.

43 Ibid., 9:615–616, Herman Katencamp to Lord Weymouth, 8/30/77.

44 Ibid.; Hayes, 32.

45 MHS, McNeill to Marine Committee, 8/25/77; McNeill to Marine Committee, 9/9/77.

46 NDAR, 9:165, Captain John David to Governor Thomas Johnson, 6/24/77; ibid., 9:197, Samuel Purviance, Jr., to Robert Morris, 7/1/77; ibid., 9:225–226, Journal of HMS *Thames*, Captain Tyringham Howe, 7/2–7/6/77.

47 JCC, 7/24/77; *Pennsylvania Evening Post*, 7/10/77.

48 State Historical Society of Wisconsin, William Bell Clark Estate, Central Navy Board to John Barry and Thomas Read, 7/31/77.

49 HSP, William Howe's Proclamation, 8/27/77; NDAR, 9:56–57, Vice Admiral Richard, Lord Howe's Standing Orders to the Fleet, 6/8/77; Watson's *Annals*, 2:283; Fleming, 237–238; McCullough, 176; Lancaster, 173.

50 LOC, GWP, Washington to Hancock, 9/23/77; UVL, Narrative of Andrew Snape Hamond, 9/1–913/77; McCullough, 172–173; Ron Chernow, *Washington: A Life* (New York: Penguin, 2010), 99; Thomas A. Doerflinger, *A Vigorous Spirit of Enterprise* (Chapel Hill: University of North Caroline Press, 1986) 210.

51 ISM, BHP, Memorial to Congress, 1785; Barry's memorial to Congress, 1785, copied in Cark, *Gallant John Barry*, plate. David Library of the American Revolution ("DLAR") (copy), and PRO, 12/40/56, "The Memorial of William Austin, late of the City of Philadelphia," April 1786.

52 Watson's *Annals*, 2:282–283.

53 DLAR (copy), and PRO, 12/40/56, "The Memorial of William Austin, late of the City of Philadelphia," April 1786; PMHB, 6:41, "Journal of John Montresor."

54 *Pennsylvania Evening Post*, 9/27/77.

55 PMHB, Montresor, 42; NDAR, 9: 973–974, Diary of Francis Dowman, Royal Artillery, 9/26/77.

56 Ibid., 42–43.

57 ISM, BHP, Memorial to the Pennsylvania Assembly, 1783; Memorial to Congress, 1785; Clark, *Gallant John Barry*, 124.

58 NDAR, 9:974–975, Lieutenant Colonel William Smith to George Washington, 9/27/77; Jackson, *The Delaware Bay etc.*, 18.

59 *Liverpool Journal*, 9/30/77; NDAR, 10:487, Major General Nathanael Greene to George Washington, 11/14; ibid., 10:489–492, 503, de Fleury Journal, 11/14–

15/77; PMHB, Montresor's Journal, 44–57 and 195–197, entries for 10/11–11/30/77.

60 NDAR, 10:501–503, Dowman's Diary, 11/15/77; Miller, 251.

61 NDAR, 10:568–569, PMHB, Montresor Journal, 193; Miller, 251; Van Powell, 64.

62 LOC, GWP, Washington to Navy Board, 10/27/77; ISM, BHP, Barry to Congress, 1/10/78.

63 Crawford, ed., *Autobiography of a Yankee Mariner*, 104.

64 ISM, BHP, Barry to Congress, 1/10/78.

65 Ibid., JCC, 12/30/77; LDC, Morris to Marine Committee, 12/19/77.

66 NDAR, 9:583–587, Howe to Stephens, 11/23/77; ibid., 11:1038–1039, Stephens to Lord Howe, 2/24/78.

67 APS, BFP, Nicholson to American Commissioners, 8/11/77; NDAR, 9:863–866, Biddle to Morris, 9/1/77 (and footnote).

68 Ibid.; Biddle, *Autobiography*, 100–101; Clark, *Captain Dauntless*, 199.

69 NDAR, 9:863–866, Biddle to Morris, 9/1/77; PA Archives, Series 4, 552, "Certificate of Service of John McPherson"; Biddle, *Autobiography*, 103; *South Carolina and American General Gazette*, 9/11/77; Clark, 202.

70 HSP, Biddle Papers, Nicholas Biddle to James Biddle, 11/22/77; *Pennsylvania Evening Post*, 11/20/77; Clark, *Captain Dauntless*, 207.

71 NDAR, 9:919–920, Biddle to Morris, 9/12/77.

72 NDAR, 9:41–42, Journal of the NY Council of Safety, 6/6/77.

73 NDAR, 10:47, Journal of the HM Galley *Dependence*, Lieutenant James Clark, 10/6/77; ibid., 10:73, Colonel Hugh Hughes to Major General Horatio Gates, 10/8/77.

74 MHS, McNeill Letter Book, McNeill to Marine Committee, 8/25/77; NDAR, 9:891–892, Warren to J. Adams, 9/7/77; ibid., 9:922–923, Continental Navy Board of the Eastern Department to the President of Congress, 9/13/77.

75 *Providence Gazette*, 6/14/77; NDAR, 9:22, Journal of H.M.S. *Orpheus*, Captain Charles Hudson, 6/5/77; ibid., 9:133–136, John Bradford to Leonard Jarvis, 6/18/77 and footnote, Trevett's Journal; LOC, John Bradford Letter Books, Vol. 1, Bradford to Jarvis, 6/26/77.

76 NDAR, 9:854–855, Trevett's Journal, 6/1–8/31/77.

77 Ibid.; *New York Gazette*, 8/18/77.

78 Trevett's Journal, quoted from Morgan, 81–82.

79   LOC, JPJP, Jones to John Brown, 10/31/77; NDAR, 9:208, *Ranger* Broadside.

80   LOC, JPJP, John Wendell to Jones, 10/29/77; Jones to Wendell, 12/11/77; Thomas, 91.

81   Ibid., Jones to Brown, 10/31/77; Bradford Letter Book, Bradford to Jarvis, 6/18/77; Thomas, 90–92; Morison, 143–144.

82   Ibid.; MHS, Commodore George Henry Preble, USN, *Diary of Ezra Green*.

83   NDAR, 8:472–475, Continental Marine Committee to Captain Thomas Thompson, 4/29/77; ibid., 9:828–829, William Whipple to Robert Morris, 8/28/77; HSP, Gratz Collection, Whipple to Dr. A. R. Cutter, 8/31/77.

84   NDAR, 9:895–896, Thompson to Langdon, 9/8/77.

85   NDAR, 9:877, Journal of H.M. Sloop *Druid*, Captain Peter Carteret, 9/4/77; ibid., 9:877–888, Lieutenant's Journal of H.M. Sloop *Druid*, Lieutenant John Bourchier, 9/4/77; Journal of H.M. Sloop *Weazle*, Captain Charles Hope, 9/4/77; ibid., 9:881–882, Journal of H.M.S. *Camel*, Captain William Finch, 9/5/77; ibid., 9:882 and 888–889, Bourchier's Journal, 9/5/77 and 9/6/77; ibid., 9:895–896, Thompson to Langdon, 9/8/77.

86   NDAR, 9:895–996, Thompson to Langdon, 9/8/77.

87   APS, BFP, Wickes to American Commissioners, 7/23/77, 8/7/77, 8/15/77; Nicholson to American Commissioners, 8/11/77, 8/15/77.

88   NDAR, 9:528–530, Deposition of William and James Newell and John Harrison, 7/25/77.

89   NDAR, 9:640, Wickes to Johnson, 9/14/77.

90   APS, BFP, Nicholson to American Commissioners, 9/21/77.

91   NDAR, 9:669–671, Deposition of Captain Henry Johnson, Continental Navy Brig *Lexington*, 9/30/77; ibid., 9:673, Captain John Elliot, R.N., to Philip Stephens, 9/30/77.

92   NDAR, 9:651–652, Journal of H.M. Cutter *Alert*, Lieutenant John Bazeley, 9/19–20/77; ibid., 9:669–671, Johnson's Deposition.

93   Ibid., 9:659, Elliot to Stephens, 9/25/77; ibid., 9:662, Stephens to Elliott, 9/26/77; ibid., 9:663, Journal of Samuel Cutler, 9/26/77, Elliott to Stephens, 9/26/77.

94   London *Daily Advertiser*, 9/30/77; NDAR, 9:668–669, Sir Hugh Paliser to Lord Sandwich, 9/29/77.

95   NDAR, 10:942–945, William McCreery to John Adams, 10/10/77.

96   *Pennsylvania Packet*, 2/11/78; *Dunlap's Maryland Gazette*, 2/3/78; King, *Sea of Words*, 290–291.

97   NDAR, 10:180, Brigadier General Henry Watson Powell to Brigadier General Allan MacLean, 10/16/77; ibid., 10:339–340, Jones to Marine Committee, 10/29/77.

98   NDAR, 10:355–356, Massachusetts Council to Captain John Harris, 10/30/77; LOC, JPJP, Jones to Hewes, 10/30/77.

99   LOC, JPJP, Jones to Morris and Jones to Hewes, 10/30/77; Morison, 145.

100   MHS, Ezra Green Diary, 11/16–22/77; HSP, Dreer, Jones to William Whipple, 12/11/77; LOC, JPJP, Jones to Morris, 12/11/77; King, *Sea of Words*, 105.

101   *Freeman's Journal*, 4/14/78; MHS, Green's Diary, 11/29/77; APS, BFP, Jones to American Commissioners, 12/4/77; NDAR, 10: Appendix A, Log of the Continental Navy Ship *Ranger*, Captain John Paul Jones, 11/29–12/4/77.

102   NDAR, 10:1045, 1062, Journal of Dr. Jonathan Haskins, 11/28 and 12/3/77; Schiff, 110–111.

CHAPTER SEVEN ★ "UNDER THE VAULT OF HEAVEN"

1   NDAR, 10:1175–1177, Engagement Between Continental Navy Frigate *Randolph* and H.M.S. *Yarmouth*.

2   Ibid., 10:957–962, "Memoir on French Naval Strategy," January 1778; Susan Mary Alsop, *Yankees at the Court: The First Americans in Paris* (New York; Doubleday, 1982), 34–37.

3   NDAR, 10:1083–1085, Jones to Marine Committee, 12/22/77; LOC, JPJP, John Wendell to Jones, 10/29/77; HSP, Dreer, Jones to William Whipple, 12/11/77.

4   LOC, JPJP, American Commissioners to Jones, 12/17/77; Jones to John Young, 11/18/78; William Bell Clark, *The First Saratoga: Being the Saga of John Young and His Ship-of-War* (Baton Rouge: Louisiana State University Press, 1953), 14–16; NDAR, 10:1058, American Commissioners to Jones, 12/2/77; ibid., 10:1109–1110, Young to American Commissioners, 12/16/77.

5   Schiff, 119.

6   Ibid., 45–47; Thomas, 96–97.

7   LOC, JPJP, Thompson to Jones, 12/26/77; Thomas, 103.

8   Thomas, 102; Morison, 154.

9   McCullough, 190 and 201; Schiff, 61; Thomas, 97.

10   NDAR, 11:977–979, Stormont to Weymouth, 2/6/78.

11   LOC, JPJP, Simpson to Jones, 12/23/77 and 12/26/77; Jones to American Commissioners, 6/78; NDAR, 10: Appendices, Log of the Continental Navy Ship *Ranger*, 12/17/77–1/1/78.

12   APS, BFP. American Commissioners to Jones, 1/15/78. Historians differ on whether Jones actually had an affair with Mme. de Chaumont. Samuel Eliot Morison believes he did, while Evan Thomas thinks otherwise, given that Jones was drawn to attractive, younger women, while Mme. de Chaumont was . . . somewhat older than Jones, and her days as a young beauty were a bit . . . behind her.

13   Ibid., 1/16/78; NDAR, 11:919, Arthur Lee to Jones (with PS from Franklin and Deane), 1/17/78; LOC, JPJP, Captain Mathew Parke to Jones, 2/19/78.

14   NDAR, 11:1130–1132, Gabriel de Sartine to Comte d'Estaing, 3/26/78; Morison, 159–160; Thomas, 107.

15   NDAR, 11:1187, *Ranger*'s log, 2/14/78.

16   PMHB, 4:485–486, "Descendants of Jöran Kyn."

17   LDC, Morris to Marine Committee, 12/19/77.

18   PA Archives, Series II, 3:154, President Wharton of the Supreme Executive Council to Colonel Henry Haller; RG 27, AO 12/40/56, "Memorial of William Austin," 4/3/86; *Pennsylvania Packet*, 10/3/78; JCC, 12/30/77.

19   Emelin Knox Parker, "A Biographical Sketch of John Brown," *Historical Society of Pennsylvania* (Carlisle, 1918; revised 1928, 1935), 3; JCC 1/10/78; LDC, Morris to Marine Committee, 12/19/77.

20   NDAR, 11:172–174, de Fleury to John Laurens, 1/20/78; Watson's *Annals*, 2:336.

21   JCC, 1/29/78; LDC, Marine Committee to Barry, 1/29/78; Marine Committee to Middle Navy Board, 1/29/78.

22   Matthewman, "Narrative of Luke Matthewman," 178; LDC, Marine Committee to Barry, 3/11/78; NDAR, 11:200–201, William Bradford to President Thomas Wharton, Jr., 1/24/78.

23   Ibid.; ISM, BHP, Barry's Memorial to Congress, 1785.

24   LOC, GWP, Wayne to Washington, 2/25/78.

25   Ibid.; Wayne to Barry, 2/23/78; Matthewman, 178.

26   LOC, GWP, Wayne to Washington, 2/25/78; Barry to Washington. 2/26/78; NDAR, 11:420–421, *Roebuck* Journal, 2/24/78; ibid., 11:440, Master's Journal of H.M. Galley *Cornwallis*, Lt. Thomas Spry, 2/26/78.

27   *Pennsylvania Gazette*, 3/18/78; LOC, GWP, "Articles of Surrender for the British

Schooner" *Alert*, 3/7/78; Barry to Washington, 3/9/78; Smallwood to Washington, 3/9/78; NDAR, 11:803–805, "Extract of a Letter from Captain James Ferguson to the Viscount Howe, dated *Brune* at Sea the 27th March 1778."

28   NDAR, 11:559–560, Journal of HMS *Experiment*, Captain Sir James Wallace, 3/9/78; PMHB, Montresor Journal, 196–197.

29   LOC, GWP, Barry to Washington, 3/9/78; LDC, Marine Committee to Barry, 3/11/78.

30   Ibid.

31   Ibid.

32   NDAR, 11:559–560, Journal of HMS *Experiment*, Captain Sir James Wallace, 3/9/78; ibid., 11:560, Journal of HM Sloop *Dispatch*, Commander Christopher Mason, 3/9/78; ibid., 11:803–805, Ferguson to Howe, 3/27/78; LOC, GWP, Smallwood to Washington, 3/16/78; Matthewman, 178.

33   *Pennsylvania Gazette*, 3/18/78; LDC, Marine Committee Letter Book, Marine Committee to Barry, 3/26/78; LOC, GWP, Washington to Barry, 3/12/78.

34   LDC, Miscellaneous Papers, Marine Committee Letter Book, 1/13/78; *New Jersey Gazette*, 5/13/78; *Pennsylvania Packet*, 6/16/78; Excerpt of a manuscript by James Read, quoted in Gurn, *Commodore John Barry*, 97; LOC, GWP, Washington to Philemon Dickenson, 5/13/78.

35   DLAR (copy), and PRO, 12/40/56, "The Memorial of William Austin, late of the City of Philadelphia," April 1786.

36   PRO, 331/1017, Captain's Journal, HMS *Experiment*.

37   APS, BFP, Continental Navy Board of the Eastern Department to American Commissioners, 2/2/78; McCullough, 172, 174.

38   NDAR, 11:311–312, Continental Navy Board of the Eastern Department to Captain Samuel Tucker, 2/10/78 (two letters).

39   MHS, AFP, Diary of John Adams (D/JA 47), 3, 2/13/78.

40   Ibid., also 22–23.

41   Ibid., 5–7; NDAR, 11:353, Journal of the Continental Navy Frigate *Boston*, Captain Samuel Tucker, 2/16/78.

42   NDAR, 11:373–374 and 394–395, *Boston* Journal, 2/19–21/78.

43   MHS, Adams Diary, 8–9.

44   NDAR, 11:382, 383, 402, 405, 416, 425; Journal of Marine Lieutenant William Jennison, 2/20–25/78, *Boston* Journal, 2/20–25/78.

45   MHS, AFP, Adams's Diary, 11–12, 2/26/78.

46   Ibid., 12–16, 2/27–3/3/78.

47   Ibid., 19–20, 3/7/78.

48   NDAR, 11, 1078, *Boston* Journal, 3/11/78; Miller, 320.

49   McCullough, 186.

50   NDAR, 11:1079–1080, Tucker to Lieutenant Hezekiah Welch, 3/11/78.

51   Ibid., 11:1085 and 1120, *Boston* Journal, 3/14 and 3/26/78; MHS, AFP, Adams Diary, 22–26, 3/14–27/78.

52   Ibid., 11:1141, 3/31/78; Adams Diary; Morgan, 133.

53   NDAR, 10:865–866, Conyngham to Deane, 10/3/77; ibid., 10:878–879, Lord Grantham to Lord Weymouth, 10/6/77; ibid., 10:890, 10/8/77, Herman Katencamp to Weymouth, 10/8/77.

54   Ibid., 10:903–904, Conde de Floridablanca to Lord Grantham, 10/12/77.

55   Neeser, 106–107, Lagoanere & Co. to Pierre Lapierre and to Alexorde Caterelo, 9/19/77; Hayes, 36.

56   APS, BFP, Conyngham to American Commissioners, 1/4/78.

57   NDAR, 11:904-05, James Gardoqui to Arthur Lee, 1/10/78; ibid., 11:918, Lee to Conyngham, 1/16/78; ibid., 11:926, Deane to Conyngham, 926–28, 1/21/78; Hayes, 36.

58   NDAR, 11:1013, de Floridablanca to Francisco de Escarano, 2/16/78; ibid., 11:1019–1023, Agreements Concerning Wages and Prize Money of Continental Navy Cutter *Revenge*'s Crew, 2/14–18/78.

59   Ibid., 11:956–957, Conyngham to Lee, 1/31/78; ibid., 11:967, Conyngham to Deane, 2/5/78.

60   Ibid., 11:1038, Conyngham to Beach, 2/23/78; APS, BFP, Hodge to Deane, 3/31/78.

61   Ibid., 1091–92, Charles Murray to Robert Walpole, 3/16/78; HSP, Papers of Benjamin Franklin, "Ships from America Enter'd in the Bay of Cadiz since the 9th July 1777"; "Prises Made by the Sloop Privateer [*sic*] Capt. Gust. Cunningham from the 6th to the 20th March 1778."

62   NDAR, 11:1125, Joseph Hardy to Lord Weymouth, 3/27/78; *London Chronicle*, 5/5–7/78.

63   Neeser, 5–6; Hayes, 38.

64   Ibid.; PMHB, 482–483.

65   Ibid., 133, 138–139.

66   Neeser, 152; Franklin to Ferdinand Grand, 10/14/78, from Augur, 301; Fowler, 129; Miller, 301.

67   NDAR, 10:253–254, and 425, Marine Committee to Nicholson, 10/23/77 and 11/6/77; ibid., 10:714–715, Marine Committee to the Continental Navy Board of the Middle department, 12/12/77; Miller, 316.

68   NDAR, 10:379–380, Captain Hyde Parker, Jr., to Vice Admiral Viscount Howe, 11/2/77.

69   Ibid., 11:652, 757, and 764, Marine Committee to Nicholson, 12/2, 12/19, and 12/20/77.

70   Ibid., 11:119, Samuel and Robert Purviance to Governor Thomas Johnson, Jr., 1/14/78; ibid., 11:189, Samuel and Robert Purviance to President of Congress, 1/22/78; ibid., 11:222–224, Marine Committee to Nicholson, 1/28/78.

71   Ibid., 11: 509–510, Marine Committee to Nicholson, 3/4/78.

72   Ibid., 848, Captain Benjamin Caldwell, R.N., to Captain Richard Onslow, R.N., 3/31/78; ibid., 11:848–849, Journal of H.M.S. *Emerald*, Captain Benjamin Caldwell, 3/31/78; ibid., 11:849, Journal of H.M.S. *Richmond*, Captain John Lewis Gidoin, 3/31/78; Journal of H.M. Sloop *Senegal*, Commander Anthony J. P. Mollow, 3/31/78.

73   Ibid., Miller, 317–318.

74   The South Carolina and American *General Gazette*, 12/25/77; NDAR, 11:1169, Journal of Marine Captain John Trevett November–December 1777.

75   U.S. Naval *Proceedings*, November 1970, 40–43, Frank H. Rathbun, "Rathbun's Raid on Nassau."

76   NDAR, 11:1169–1170, Trevett's Journal.

77   Ibid.

78   Ibid., 245–252, Trevett's Journal, 1/1–31/78; ibid., 11:395–396, 2/18–21/78; 472.

79   Ibid., 472, Trevett's Journal, 3/78; 655, Bradford to Rathbun, 3/16/78.

80   NDAR, 11:113–114, Journal of the South Carolina Navy Board, 1/13/78; A Letter to Mr. John Stevenson, 1/13/78; A Letter to Captn. Nicholas Biddle, Esq., 1/13/78; ibid., 11:136–137, Brigadier General Moultrie's Account of the Burning of Charleston, 1/15/78.

81   Ibid.

82   Will of Nicholas Biddle, quoted in Clark, *Captain Dauntless*, 224–225.

83   NDAR, 11:136–137, Moultrie's Account, etc.; Charles Biddle, *Autobiography*, 105.

84   Ibid., 360–361, John Lewis Gervais to President of Congress, 2/16/78; ibid., 837–

838, President Rawlins Lowndes to President of Congress, 3/30/78; Biddle, *Autobiography*, 105; Clark, 232.

85   Ibid., 337–42, Captain Robert Fanshawe, R.N., to Vice Admiral Viscount Howe, 2/13/78.

86   Ibid., 850, Moultrie on the Fitting Out of the *Randolph*'s Squadron and her Loss, January–March 1778; *Portfolio* Biography; Clark, 236.

87   NDAR, 11:543–544, Journal of the H.M.S. *Yarmouth*, Captain Nicholas Vincent, 3/7/78.

88   Ibid.

89   Biddle, *Autobiography*, 108–109; NDAR, 11, 1175, Eyewitness Account of Engagement Between Continental Navy Frigate *Randolph* and H.M.S. *Yarmouth*, 8/21/1801.

90   Ibid.; King, *Sea of Words*, 14–15; Clark, 240; Miller, 311.

91   NDAR, 11:543–544, *Yarmouth* Journal, Biddle, 107; Miller, 311–312; Clark, 240–241.

92   Ibid.; also 11:850, Moultrie, 1–3/78.

93   Ibid., 11:1176, Engagement Between Continental Navy Frigate *Randolph* and H.M.S. *Yarmouth*.

94   Biddle, *Autobiography*, 108–109; *Pennsylvania Packet*, 3/29/78.

95   Ibid.

96   NDAR, 11:683–684, Vincent to Vice Admiral James Young, 3/17/78.

97   Biddle, *Autobiography*, 107–109; NDAR, 11:1175, Eyewitness Account of Engagement Between Continental Navy Frigate *Randolph* and H.M.S. *Yarmouth*, 8/21/1801.

98   NDAR, 11:623, *Yarmouth* Journal, 3/12/78; ibid., 11:683–684, Vincent to Vice Admiral James Young, 3/17/78.

99   Ibid., New York *Gazette and the Weekly Mercury*, 4/20/78; Clark, 245.

100   Ibid., 666–667, Deposition of Alexander Robinson, Hans Workman, and John Carew, 3/17/78; ibid., 11:1175, Eyewitness Account of Engagement Between Continental Navy Frigate *Randolph* and H.M.S. *Yarmouth*, 8/21/1801. The late Nathan Miller pointed out in his excellent *Sea of Glory* (313) that the rescued sailors, ironically, added to the bonuses paid to their rescuers. The Admiralty paid a five-pound bounty for any sailor on a captured or destroyed American ship. The deposition of the sailors, attesting that there were 305 men aboard, increased the *Yarmouth*'s bonus by £1,525.

101 Ibid., 11:837–838, Lowndes to President of Congress, 3/30/78; Biddle, *Autobiography*, 108–110; LDC, Marine Committee Letter Book, Marine Committee to John Bradford, 4/28/78; *Pennsylvania Packet*, 7/25/78.

102 AP, BFP, Thompson to American Commissioners, 12/29/77.

103 NDAR, 11:575, Journal of H.M.S. *Ariadne*, Captain Thomas Pringle, 3/9/78; Journal of H.M. Sloop *Ceres*, James Dacres, 3/9/78.

104 Ibid., Captain Thomas Pringle, R.N., to Vice Admiral James Young, 3/18/78; Fowler, 134.

105 LDC, Marine Committee Letter Book (MCLB), Marine Committee to Eastern Navy Board, 5/8/78; ISM, BHP, John Brown to Barry, 5/21/78.

106 NDAR, 11:355–356, Memoir of Elias Ware, 2/16/78.

107 Ibid., 11:614–615, Continental Navy Board of the Eastern Department to Captain Hoysteed [*sic*] Hacker, 3/12/78; ibid., 11:786–787, William Vernon of the Continental Navy Board to the Eastern Department, 3/25/78; ibid., 11:813–817, Journals of H.M.S. *Maidstone*, Captain Alan Gardiner, H.M.S. *Sphinx*, Captain Alexander Graeme, H.M.S. *Nonsuch*, Captain Walter Griffith, 3/28/78.

108 Ibid., 11:1046–1047, Jones to Deane, 2/26/78; ibid., 11:1188–1190, *Ranger* Journal, 2/20–25/78; Clark, *The First Saratoga*, 16.

109 APS, BFP, John Bondfield to American Commissioners, 7/4/78; LOC, JPJP, Thomas Bell to Jones, 11/2/78; Miller, 322.

CHAPTER EIGHT ★ "HER TEETH WERE TOO MANY"

1 APS, BFP, Jones to Deane, 3/25/78.

2 United States Naval Academy Museum (USNAM), John Paul Jones Letter Book, Jones to Gourlade and Moylan, 3/5 and 3/9/78.

3 NDAR, 11:1084, Minute of Cabinet, 3/14/78; ibid., 11:1120–1123, Louis XVI to Comte d'Estaing, 3/27/78; ibid., 11:1129–1130, Louis XVI to the Continental Congress, 3/28/78; USNAM, Jones Letter Book, Jones to Ross, 3/25/78.

4 Ibid., 11:1065–1066, Earl of Sandwich to Lord North, 3/6/78; 11:1069–1073, Lord George Germain to Lieutenant General Sir Henry Clinton, 3/8/78.

5 Ibid., 11:1117–1118, Jones to Deane, 3/25/78; ibid., 11:1119, Jones to John Ross, 3/25/78; LOC, JPJP, Jones to Ross, 4/8/78.

6 MHS, Ezra Green Diary, 4/10–15/78; LOC, JPJP, *Ranger* log, 4/15/78.

7 LOC, JPJP, Statement of Lieutenant Jean Meijer, 4/14/80; Morison, 140; Thomas, 114–115.

8   MHS, Green Diary, 4/15-17/78; LOC, JPJP, Jones to American Commissioners, 5/27/78.

9   Ibid.; LOC, JPJP, Jones to American Commissioners, 5/27/78.

10 Ibid., 4/19/78.

11 Ibid., 4/21/78; LOC, JPJP, Meijer's Statement, 4/14/80; Jones to American Commissioners, 5/27/78.

12 Ibid.; Morison, 172.

13 LOC, JPJP, Jones to the American Commissioners, circa 6/78; Jones to the President of Congress, 12/7/79.

14 MHS, Green Diary, 4/23–24/78; Thomas, 121–123; Wilbur, 70 and 75.

15 LOC, JPJP, Jones to American Commissioners, 5/27/78. Meijer's Statement, 4/14/80.

16 Ibid.; Morison, 174–175; Thomas 121–123.

17 Ibid.

18 Ibid.

19 MHS, Green Diary, 4/24/78.

20 LOC, JPJP, Jones to American Commissioners, 5/27/78; *Ranger* log, 4/24/78.

21 Ibid.

22 Morison, 178–179; Thomas, 124–125; Dennis M. Conrad, "John Paul Jones," from *Sea Raiders of the American Revolution*, 63.

23 Ibid.; Thomas, 124–125.

24 LOC, JPJP, Jones to Lady Selkirk, 5/8/78; Selkirk to Jones, 6/9/78; Jones to American Commissioners, 5/27/78.

25 LOC, JPJP, Jones to Lady Selkirk, 5/8/78; Gawalt, 19; Thomas, 126.

26 Ibid., Lady Selkirk to Lord Selkirk, 4/24/78; De Koven, 309–311; Gawalt, 19.

27 Ibid, Earl of Selkirk to Jones, 6/9/78; MHS, Green Diary, 4/24/78 (and footnote).

28 LOC, JPJP, Jones to American Commissioners, 5/27/78; MHS, Green Diary, 4/24/78 (and footnote).

29 Ibid.; MHS, Green Diary, 4/24/78; *Pennsylvania Packet*, 7/14/78; Gawalt, 20; Thomas, 129.

30 Morison, 200.

31   LOC, JPJP, Jones to American Commissioners, 5/9/78 and 5/27/78; Jones to John Black & Co., 5/28/78; *Pennsylvania Packet*, 7/14/78; MHS, Green Diary, 4/24/78; Gawalt, 20; Morison, 197; Thomas, 131–132.

32   LOC, JPJP, Jones to Simpson, 4/27/78; Jones to American Commissioners, 5/27/78; MHS, Green Diary, 5/7/78.

33   LOC, JPJP, Jones to American Commissioners, 5/9/78.

34   Ibid., Lee to Jones, 5/17/78.

35   LOC, JPJP, Jones to Lady Selkirk, 5/8/78.

36   Ibid., Earl of Selkirk to Jones, 6/9/78.

37   *London Public Advertiser*, 5/2/78; *London Morning Chronicle*, 5/9/78; Fowler, 141–142; Thomas, 134.

38   De Koven, 1:324; Thomas, 140.

39   NDAR, 11:31–35, Howe to Stephens, 1/5/78; ibid., 11:36–40, "Disposition of His Majesty's Ships and Vessels employed in North America under Command of the Vice Admiral the Viscount Howe," 1/5/78; Syrett, *American Waters*, 93; Miller, 331.

40   Syrett, 93–96.

41   Miller, 327–331.

42   Ron Chernow, *Washington: A Life* (New York: Penguin, 2010), 348; Miller, 331–337; Syrett, 99–103.

43   Chernow, 348–349; Miller, 348–350; Syrett, 105–107.

44   NDAR, 9:131, Marine Committee to John Deshon, 6/17/77; ibid., 10:441–447, Accounts of the Naval Brigantine *Resistance*, 11/9/77; ibid., 10:754–755, Josiah Waters to Nathaniel Shaw, Jr., 12/19/77; Morgan, 118–119.

45   HSP, Gratz, Samuel Chew to William Bingham, 1/15/78; NDAR, 11:319, Lieutenant William Leeds to William Bingham, 2/10/78; ibid., 11:623–624, Governor Thomas Shirley to Lord Germain, 3/12/78; *Boston Independent Chronicle*, 4/23/78; LDC, Marine Committee to John Bradford, 4/28/78.

46   LDC, Marine Committee to John Bradford, 4/28/78; JCC, 7/5/78; Morgan, 119.

47   JCC, 7/5/78; *Naval Records*, 310, Letters–of–Marque, *General Greene*, 3/12/80; Morgan, 120.

48   LDC, Marine Committee to Eastern Navy Board, 4/6/78; ibid., 5/9/78 (footnote); Samuel Adams to James Warren. 7/27/78; Morgan, 147–149.

49   Ibid.; Marine Committee to the Eastern Navy Board, 11/22/77; Miller, 81, 83; Morgan, 140–141.

50   Ibid., Marine Committee to John Bradford, 8/12/78; Ibid.

51   LOC, Bradford Letter Book, Bradford to Marine Committee, 9/2/78; JCC, 9/23/78; Smith, 175.

52   Ibid; JCC, 9/23/78.

53   FDR Library, Barry to Morris, 9/3/78; Fowler, *The Baron of Beacon Hill*, 235–237.

54   ISM, BHP, John Brown to Barry, 5/21/78; LDC, Marine Committee to the Eastern Navy Board, 5/30/78; Samuel Adams to James Warren, 6/1/78.

55   LDC, Marine Committee to Eastern Navy Board, 6/19/78; MHS, Samuel Adams Papers, Warren to Samuel Adams, 7/5/78; Samuel Adams to James Warren, 7/26/78.

56   Chappelle, 69 and 71; Millar, 228–229, 253; Van Powell, 94.

57   *London Public Advertiser*, 11/27/78; PRO, 32/441, Deposition of David Phipps; Smith, 174.

58   ISM, BHP, Barry to Eastern Navy Board, 9/17/78; Barry's Defense of the *Raleigh*, 10/78; LDC, Marine Committee to Barry, 8/24 and 8/28/78; Marine Committee to Eastern Navy Board, 9/17/78; FDR Library, Barry to Morris, 9/21/78.

59   ISM, Barry's Defense of the *Raleigh*; New Hampshire *Gazette*, 5/2/76.

60   Ibid.; PRO, Admiralty, 51/107, Captain's Journal, *Unicorn*, 9/25/78.

61   Ibid.

62   Ibid., Chappelle, 76; King, *Sea of Words*, 355.

63   Ibid.; PRO, *Unicorn* Journal, 9/27/78.

64   Ibid.; PRO, HCA 22/436/10, Deposition of David Phipps, 10/16/78. PRO, Admiralty, 331/1017, Captain's Journal, *Experiment*, 9/27/78; King, 396.

65   Ibid.; *Experiment* Journal, 9/27/78; Pennsylvania *Evening Post*, 10/19/78.

66   Ibid.

67   Pennsylvania *Evening Post*, 10/19/78.

68   Ibid.; ISM, BHP, Defense of the *Raleigh*.

69   PRO, HCA 22/436/10, Deposition of David Phipps, 10/16/78; *Unicorn* Journal, 9/28/78; ISM, BHP, Barry's Defense of the *Raleigh*.

70   ISM, Barry's Defense of the *Raleigh*. A look at accounts from both sides would place American dead at about fifteen.

71   Ibid.; *Pennsylvania Packet*, 10/22/78 and 11/10/78. Naval historian Craig Symonds finds that Barry's believing that Wallace gave up the chase was a monumental error

in judgment, as was giving a young midshipman the responsibility of torching a valuable frigate.

72   Miller, 271–275; Morgan, 136–140; NDAR, 5:437–441, John Adams to James Warren, "To Build a Fireship," 6/9/76.

73   Allen, chapter 9, 32–33.

74   Ibid., 35; King, 219.

75   JCC, 11/18/78; LDC, Henry Laurens to Silas Talbot, 11/17/78; LOC, GWP, Washington to Sullivan, 11/3/78; Miller, 272–273; Morgan, 140.

76   Miller, 195; NDAR, 7:1091.

77   NDAR, 5:360–361, Committee of Secret Correspondence to William Bingham, 6/3/76; ibid., 5:361–362, Willing, Morris & Co. to Bingham, 6/3/76 and 1205–06, 7/24/76; HSP, Gratz, Robert Morris to Bingham, 12/4/76.

78   Neeser, 150–151, Bingham to Conyngham, 11/29/78; ibid., 152–153, Account of Prizes Taken in the *Surprize* [*sic*] by Capt. Gust. Conyngham.

79   Ibid.; Neeser, 151, Bingham to Conyngham, 11/29/78; *Boston Gazette*, 2/15/79; Hayes, 38.

80   HSP, Gratz, Account of Sale of the Brig *Countess of Alaron*, taken by the Ship *Revenge* October 15, 1778; Hayes, 39; Syrett, 115.

81   *Boston Gazette*, 2/15/79; PMHB, "Narrative," 485.

82   JCC, 12/26/78; 1/4/79.

83   LDC, Committee of Foreign Affairs to William Bingham, 1/29/79; Neeser, 155–156, Marine Committee to Messrs. Jackson, Tracey & Tracey, 3/10/79; 216–223, "Observations on the Report of Benjamin Walker Esq., etc." (no date).

84   LDC, Marine Committee to Joseph Reed, 3/12/79.

85   Neeser, 158–159, Attestation of Gustavus Conyngham (no date).

86   LDC, Marine Committee to the American Commissioners, 4/27/79.

87   Neeser, xlvii–xlix, Introduction; 158–160, "Attestation."

88   Ibid.; PMHB, "Narrative," 487.

89   Ibid.; PMHB, "Narrative," 487; Fowler, 131; King, 48.

CHAPTER NINE ✶ "IN HARM'S WAY"

1   Neeser, 162, "Minutes from Gustavus Conyngham of his Treatment and Remarks," 4/27/79.

2   Ibid., 176, Conyngham to Anne Conyngham, no date (approx. 6/79).

3   Ibid., 174, Notice in *The Rembrancer*; King, *Harbors, etc.*, 210.

4   Ibid., 163.

5   Ibid., 164–167.

6   LDC, Marine Committee to John Beatty, 6/2/79; 7/5/79.

7   Neeser, 179–180, Anne Conyngham to the President of Congress, 7/17/79.

8   Ibid., 176–178, "Petition of a Number of Inhabitants of Philadelphia," 7/14/79.

9   JCC, 7/17/79.

10   *Pennsylvania Gazette*, 8/4/79; Neeser, 182–183, Sir George Collier to the Secretary of Congress, 7/24/79.

11   LDC, John Jay to Christopher Hele, 2/16/79; John Fell's Diary, 3/8/79; Marine Committee to John Beatty, 8/27/79.

12   APS, BFP, Franklin to David Hartley, 8/20/79.

13   Allen, 2:377; Brands, 528; PA Archives, 5:401, Washington to Collier.

14   Neeser, 168–169.

15   Ibid., also 174; APS, BFP, Hartley to Franklin, 9/1/79; LDC, Marine Committee to Thomas Bradford, 9/28/79; JCC, Memorial of Christopher Hele (read in Congress), 12/13/79.

16   *Pennsylvania Gazette*, 3/17/79, 8/11/79; LDC, Marine Committee to Eastern Navy Board, 10/25/78; NYHS, JBP 5–141; Clark Estate, "Shipping Order, Brigantine *Delaware*," 1779; HCL, Charles Roberts Autograph Collection, Barry to Matthew Irwin, 7/16/79; ISM, BHP, Barry Memorial to Congress, 1785.

17   LDC, Marine Committee to John Trumbull, 4/20/78; 9/25/78; Marine Committee to Seth Harding, 2/19/79; Trumbull to Marine Committee, 4/3/78, quoted from Morgan, 142–143; JCC, 9/25/78; James L. Howard, *Seth Harding, Mariner* (New Haven, CT: Yale University Press, 1930), 66.

18   *Memorial to Justify Peter Landais' Conduct During the Late War* (Boston: Peter Eades, 1784); LDC, Sam Adams to James Warren, 6/1/78 and 9/12/78; Marine Committee to Eastern Navy Board, 6/18/78.

19   NYPL, Letter Book, Eastern Navy Board, 1778–1779, Eastern Navy Board to Marine Committee, 12/9/78 and 1/16/79; Morgan, 151.

20   LDC, Marine Committee to Eastern Navy Board, 1/26 and 2/5/79; Morgan, 152; Miller, 409.

21   *Boston Post*, 2/6/79.

22   Miller, 374–375; Thomas, 161.

23   LDC, Ellery to Vernon, 3/23/79; Morgan, 154.

24   LDC, Marine Committee to Joseph Olney; Seth Harding; Commissioners, Navy Board, Boston; and to Governor Jonathan Trumbull, all 2/10/78; Morgan, 157; Miller, 410.

25   *Ranger* log, 4/6–7/79; Morgan, 157; Van Powell, 116.

26   *Pennsylvania Gazette*, 4/28/79; *Boston Gazette*, 4/19–26/79.

27   Ibid.; *Boston Gazette*, 4/19–26/79; Morgan, 158.

28   Allen, 2:374; Morgan, 158.

29   LDC, Marine Committee to Eastern Navy Board, 5/20, 5/26, and 6/21/79; Charles Henry Lincoln, *Naval Records of the American Revolution, 1775–1788* (Washington, D.C.: Government Printing Office, Library of Congress, 1906); "Letters of Marque," 350 (*Independence*, Rhode Island, 6/3/81), 466 (*Success*, 4/24/81).

30   LDC, Marine Committee to Eastern Navy Board, 3/26/79; *Pennsylvania Packet*, 5/25/79; John H. Sheppard, *The Life of Samuel Tucker, Commodore in the American Revolution* (Boston: Alfred Mudge and Son, 1868), 58.

31   *Pennsylvania Packet*, 5/25/79; *Maryland Journal*, 6/1/79; Allen, 375; Morgan, 162–163.

32   Chappelle, 89–91; Van Powell, 102; Miller, 97–98.

33   LDC, Marine Committee to Eastern Navy Board, 3/26/79; to Seth Harding 4/17, 4/27, and 6/2/79; Morgan, 161.

34   *Pennsylvania Gazette*, 6/16/79; *Boston Gazette*, 7/5/79; P.C.F. Smith, 59; Sheppard, 108–110.

35   LDC, Marine Committee to Samuel Nicholson, 6/15/79; to Seth Harding, 6/15/79.

36   NYPL, Eastern Navy Board Letter Book, Board to Simpson, 6/8/79; Morgan, 166.

37   Lieutenant Horace S. Mazet, USMCR, "The Navy's Forgotten Hero," *Proceedings*, March 1937, 351.

38   Ibid., 351–352; Andrew Sherburne, *Memoirs of Andrew Sherburne, A Pensioner of the Navy of the Revolution* (Providence, 1831, n.p.), 21–24; Smith, 204.

39   Ibid.; Sherburne, 21–24.

40   Fowler, 102.

41   LDC, Marine Committee to Abraham Whipple, 9/11/79; to Eastern Navy Board, 8/24 and 9/7/79; *Boston Gazette*, 9/27/79.

42   *Pennsylvania Gazette*, 9/22/79.

43   APS, BFP, Franklin to Jones, 6/1/78; LOC, JPJP, Jones to Morris, 11/13/78; Jones to Chaumont, 11/18/78; Jones to de Sartine, 7/5/78, American Commissioners to Jones, 5/17 and 6/3/78; Jones to American Commissioners, 7/4/78.

44   LOC, JPJP, Jones to de Sartine, and American Commissioners, 7/5/78; Jones to Washington, 7/5/78.

45   Syrett, 41–46; Thomas, 147; Morison, 213.

46   LOC, JPJP, Jones to Bancroft, 8/21/78.

47   Ibid., Hector McNeill to Jones, 9/4/78; Jones to Whipple, 8/18/78; Jones to Nassau–Siegen, 8/24/78; Jones to Louis XVI, 10/19/78; Thomas, 145–150; Morison, 217–219.

48   Ibid., Jones to de Chaumont, 11/16/78.

49   Ibid., Jones to James Moylan, 7/7/78; Moylan to Jones, 11/3/78.

50   Ibid., Jones to de Chaumont, 12/11/78; Millar, 73–75.

51   Ibid. Thomas, 152; Morison, 214.

52   LOC, JPJP, Franklin to Jones, 3/14/79.

53   Nathaniel Fanning, *Fanning's Narrative: The Memoirs of Nathaniel Fanning, an Officer of the American Navy 1778–1783* (New York, 1806, 1808, reprinted William Abbatt, 1913), 4–23.

54   Ibid.

55   PA Archives, "Life of John Kessler," 1–3.

56   Ibid., 2–4; HCL, Roberts Collection, Barry to Matthew Irwin, 7/16/79, *Pennsylvania Packet*, 6/5/79.

57   PA Archives, Kessler, 3.

58   Neeser, 170, Minutes, etc.; Francis Abell, *Prisoners of War in Britain, 1756 to 1815* (New York: Oxford University Press, 1914), ch. 17, p. 9.

59   Allen, 2:642–644; PMHB, 22, "Narrative of Gustavus Conyngham," 487; Sherburne, 91.

60   Neeser, 183, Franklin to Digges, 8/20/79; 190, Conyngham to Franklin, 11/18/79; APS, BFP, Digges to Franklin, 9/6 and 9/20/79; Brands, 586–587.

61   Abell, ch. 17, p. 9.

62   APS, BFP, Digges to Franklin, 10/12/79.

63   These accounts appear in Eleanor Coleman's *Gustavus Conyngham, U.S.N. Pirate*

or Privateer [*sic*], *1747–1819* (Lanham, MD: University Press of America, 1982), 126–127; David F. Winkler, "Conyngham's Great Escape," *Sea Power*, October 2003, 48.

64   Neeser, 172–173, "Minutes"; 184, "List of American Prisoners committed to Old Mill Prison, England, during the War," 8/23/79.

65   Neeser, 193–194, Conyngham to Franklin, 12/22/79.

66   Ibid., 190, Conyngham to Franklin, 11/18/79; Coleman, 127.

67   C. Smith, 205; *Pennsylvania Gazette*, 8/18/79.

68   *Boston Evening Post*, 7/10/79; Keith Scott, "New Hampshire in the Penobscot Expedition," *American Neptune* 8 (July 1947): 200; Fowler, 103–104; Morgan, 169; Miller, 412.

69   Quoted from Fowler, 105; quoted from Scott, 201.

70   NYPL, ENB Letter Book, Eastern Navy Board to Marine Committee, 6/30/79; William Fowler, "Boston as a Navy Base, 1776–1783," *America Neptune*, January 1982, 33; MHS, Paul Revere's Diary of the Penobscot Expedition, 7/21–8/19/79; Morgan, 168. NYHS, Papers Relating to the Penobscot Expedition.

71   C. Smith, 207 and appendix C, "Diary of John Trevett, Captain of Marines," 335.

72   LDC, William Whipple to John Langdon, 8/3/79.

73   Ibid., Nathaniel Peabody to Josiah Bartlett, 7/20/79.

74   *The Magazine of History with Notes and Queries Comprising the Journal of the Siege of Penobscot* (New York: William Abbatt, 1910); Maine Historical Society Collections, 1270, John Calef's Journal, 7/18/79; Fowler, *Rebels*, 106–107; Scott, 207.

75   Abbatt, 305-06, Calef's Journal, 7/25/79.

76   *Boston Gazette*, 8/9/79; C. Smith, 208.

77   Abbatt, 306–307, Calef's Journal, 7/26/79; Fowler, 107; Miller, 414, C. Smith, 210.

78   Lieutenants and Masters to Dudley Saltonstall, 7/27/79, quoted from C. Smith, 211.

79   Maine Historical Society, Colonel Brewer's Account of the Expedition; Miller, 415.

80   Allen, 2:425.

81   Ibid.

82   *The Original Journal of General Solomon Lovell, Kept During the Penobscot Expedition, 1779* (Weymouth Historical Society, Boston, Wright and Potter Printing Company), 99, Lovell's Journal, 7/28/79; Major General Sir J. F. Maurice, K.C.B., *The Diary of Sir John Moore*, Vol. I (London, Edward Arnold, 1904), 9-10; C. Smith, 211–212.

83   Ibid.

84   Lovell, *Journal*, 99, 7/28/79; *Boston Gazette*, 8/9/79.

85   Allen, 2:432.

86   Lieutenant George Little's Deposition, 9/25/79, quoted from Morgan, 172.

87   *Pennsylvania Gazette*, 8/18/79; Penobscot Papers, Eastern Navy Board to Saltonstall, 8/12/79; LDC, James Lovell to General Gates, 8/9/79; Morgan, 172–173.

88   Chester B. Kevitt, *General Simon Lovell and the Penobscot Expedition, 1779* (Weymouth, Massachusetts; Weymouth Historical Commission, 1976), 94-96, Hacker's Plan of Attack, 8/8/79; Scott, 207; Morgan, 172.

89   Lovell, *Journal*, 101–102, 8/7/79.

90   Ibid., 8/13/79.

91   Ibid.

92   Kevitt, 108-109, A Council aboard the *Warren*, 8/14/79; Morgan, 170; Moran, 175.

93   Fowler, 108–109; Allen, 432.

94   Lovell, *Journal*, 104–105, 8/14/79; Abbatt, 316–18, Calef's Journal, 8/14/79; C. Smith, 214.

95   MHS, Revere Family Papers, Microfilm Edition, Paul Revere's Diary, 8/14/79; *Pennsylvania Gazette*, 8/25/79; Allen, 432–433.

96   Miller, 416.

97   *Pennsylvania Gazette*, 10/6/79; *Providence Gazette*, 1/22/80.

98   *Boston Gazette*, 12/27/79; Allen, 437; Fowler, 109.

CHAPTER TEN ★ "DIAMOND CUT DIAMOND"

1   LOC, JPJP, Jones to Franklin, 10/3/79.

2   Quoted from Thomas, 158; Bradford, 28; Morison, 230.

3   LOC, JPJP, Lafayette to Jones, 3/31/79 and 4/27/79; Franklin to Jones, 4/27 and 28/79; Jones to Lafayette, 5/1/79.

4   JPJP, Jones to Franklin, 5/26/79.

5   Ibid., Franklin to Jones, 6/2/79; Syrett, *The Royal Navy in European Waters*, 70–71.

6   Callo, 66; Van Powell, 74; Jean Boudriot, *John Paul Jones and the Bonhomme Richard:*

A Reconstruction of the Ship and an Account of the Battle with H.M.S. Serapis (Annapolis, Maryland: Naval Institute Press, 1987), 7–15.

7   Morison, 228–229; Thomas, 157; Millar, 73; Van Powell, 74.

8   LOC, JPJP, Jones to Franklin, 5/14/79; Landais to Jones, 5/27/79; Thomas, 161; Morison, 232–233.

9   HSP, Society Collection, Sarah Rodney to Sarah B. Garrette, 8/4/1825; Report on a Pension for Mrs. Joseph Brussels to Hon. Charles Ingersoll, 1/13/1843; MHS, Henry Knox to John Nicholson, Esq., 7/8/90; LOC, JPJHP, Muster Rolls, *Bonhomme Richard*; Kilby's Journal, 28; Thomas, 165.

10   LOC, JPJP, Jones to Sartine, 8/11/79; Morison, 235–239.

11   Butterfield, Adams Papers 2:368.

12   Fanning, 53–54, footnote, Letter from Charles W. Stewart.

13   Quoted from Thomas, 162–163; Morison, 243–244.

14   C. Smith, 224–225.

15   LOC, JPJP, Jones to Franklin, 7/1/79; Jones to Mme de Chaumont, 6/13/79; Callo, 2–73; Thomas, 164–165.

16   Ibid., Thomas, 164–165; Morison, 236–137.

17   Ibid.

18   LOC, JPJP, Jones to Richard Dale, 5/25/79; Dale to Jones, 5/27/79; Morison, 246–247.

19   "Narrative of John Kilby," 28 (*Scribner's* Magazine 38 [July–December, 1908]); Fanning, 21–22; Kilby, 28; Thomas, 165; Morison, 249.

20   LOC, JPJP, Jones to Sartine, 8/11/79; Concordat of the Captains of the Fleet, 8/13/79; Jones to Franklin, 10/3/79.

21   Quoted in Syrett, *European Waters*, 74–75; King, *Harbors, etc*, 192.

22   Ibid., 114–115; Neeser, 172, "Attestation of Gustavus Conyngham," 8/7–8/20/79.

23   Miller, 406–407.

24   LOC, JPJP, Jones to Franklin, 10/3/79; Kilby's Narrative, 29.

25   Ibid.; Ship's log, *Bonhomme Richard*, 8/24/79; Kilby, 29.

26   Ship's log, *Bonhomme Richard*, 8/24–25/79; Fanning, 25; Thomas, 171.

27   LOC, JPJP, Landais Memorial, 29; HSP, Dreer, Letter of Matthew Mease, 11/13/79.

28   Ibid., Jones to Landais, 9/5/79; Landais to Jones, 9/2 and 9/5/79.

29   Ibid., Jones to Franklin, 10/3/79, Fanning, 26–27.

30   Ibid.; *London Evening Post*, 9/6/79; Morison, 254–256.

31   Kilby, 30.

32   Ship's log, *Bonhomme Richard*, 9/17/79; LOC, JPJP, Jones to Franklin, 10/3/79; Fanning, 29; Kilby, 30; Thomas, 175.

33   Ibid.; LOC, JPJP, Jones to Franklin, 10/3/79.

34   LOC, JPJP, Jones to Franklin, 10/3/79; Ship's log, *Bonhomme Richard*, 9/23/79; Callo, appendix B, "Commodore Richard Dale's Account of the Battle off Flamborough Head," 205; Morison, 268–269.

35   Conrad, 49; Thomas, 178.

36   Callo, Appendix C, "Captain Richard Pearson's Report of the battle off Flamborough Head," from Sherburne's *Life and Character of John Paul Jones*, 209.

37   Callo, Dale's Account, 205–206; Pearson's Report, 210; Kilby, 31; Fanning, 32.

38   Fanning, 34–36.

39   Freidenburg, *Medicine Under Sail*, 17–18; Wilbur, *Revolutionary Medicine, 1700–1800*, 62–63; King, *Sea of Words*, 129.

40   LOC, JPJP, Jones to Franklin, 10/3/79; Gerard W. Gawalt, ed., *John Paul Jones's Memoir of the American Revolution Presented to King Louis XVI of France* (Washington, D.C.: Library of Congress, 1979), 33–34.

41   LOC, JPJP, Ship's Log, *Bonhomme Richard*, 9/24/79; Morison, 273.

42   Naval Historian Dennis Conrad believes Cottineau and Landais might have been confused by Jones's changing course.

43   Jones's Memorial to King Louis XVI ("Jones's Memorial"); Fanning, 36; Thomas, 181.

44   LOC, JPJP, Jones to Franklin, 10/3/79; HSP, Misc. Collection, Matthew Mease's Certification of Captain Landais' Rude Behavior, 11/13/79.

45   Fanning, 33; Thomas, 182

46   Kilby, 31; HSP, Sarah Rodney to Sarah Garrette, 8/4/25.

47   Fanning, 36.

48   Ibid., 37; Kilby, 31; Callo, Dale's Account, 205; Pearson's Report, 210; Thomas, 183.

49   Ibid.; LOC, JPJP, Jones to Franklin, 10/3/79.

50   LOC, JPJP, Jones to Franklin, 10/3/79.

51   Fanning, 37; Callo, Dale, 206, and Pearson, 210; Kilby, 31; Morison, 274; Thomas, 184.

52   LOC, JPJP, Jones to Franklin, 10/3/79.

53   MHS, Henry Knox to John Nicholson, Esq., 7/8/90.

54   Fanning, 36; Kilby, 31.

55   Ibid., 55; *London Morning Post*, 10/1/79; Morison, 282; Thomas, 186.

56   Fanning, 37–38; Kilby, 31.

57   Dr. Paul Kopperman, e-mail, 10/3/13; Ranby, John, *The Method of Treating Gunshot Wounds*, 2nd ed. (London: Robert Horsefield, 1760), 21, 34–35.

58   Callo, Dale's Account, 206; Thomas, 188; King, 387.

59   Kilby, 31.

60   Callo, Dale's Account, 206; Pearson's Report, 210.

61   Fanning, 38; Kilby, 31.

62   Kilby, 31.

63   Fanning, 38; Callo, Pearson's Report, 210.

64   Ibid.; LOC, JPJP, Jones to Franklin, 10/3/79; Fanning, 41; Thomas, 191.

65   Kilby, 31–32.

66   Ibid.; LOC, JPJP, Jones to Franklin, 10/3/79; Conrad, 44.

67   Ibid.; HSP, Mease Certification.

68   Fanning, 39–40; Callo, Pearson's Report, 210.

69   *London Public Advertiser*, 10/30/79; LOC, JPJP, Jones to Franklin, 10/3/79; Gawalt, 34–35; Thomas, 190.

70   Historians have long debated whether Landais intentionally fired into the *Bonhomme Richard* or not. While it was dark, the ships could be easily distinguished by their build, and the fact that the hull of the *Serapis* was checkered black and yellow, while the *Bonhomme Richard*'s was all black. Samuel Eliot Morison was convinced that the firing was no accident, while Thomas J. Schaeper believes it was. Contrast this with the action of Captain Thomas Piercy of the *Countess of Scarborough*, who came across the *Bonhomme Richard*'s stern earlier in the battle and held his fire, lest his gunners also hit the *Serapis*. Kilby, 32; Fanning, 42–43; LOC, JPJP, Jones to Franklin, 10/3/79; Proofs Respecting the Conduct of Peter Landais, October–November 1779; HSP, Mease's Certificate, 11/13/79; PRO, 2305, Pearson's Report (enclosure); and thanks again to Dr. Dennis Conrad.

71   Fanning, 40, 50–51.

72   Ibid., 41; LOC, JPJP, Jones to Franklin, 10/3/79.

73   Fanning, 41; Conrad, 45; Thomas, 191.

74   There are other attestations that Jones's answer was both longer and more jocular. He himself wrote to King Louis that he said, "*Je ne songe point à me rendre; mais je suis determiné à vous faire demander quartier*"—"I have not yet thought of surrendering, but I am determined to make you ask for quarter." By its sheer length alone, this one is a stretch. Other accounts include the equally long "Ay, ay, we'll do that [strike] when we can fight no longer, but we shall see yours [colors] come down first: you must know, that Yankees do not haul down their colors till they are fairly beaten"; as well as "I may sink, but I'll be damned if I'll strike." The most honest account comes from Jones himself; writing to Franklin after the battle, he merely states that he replied to Pearson's question "in the most determined negative." For his part, Pearson claimed to never have heard Jones's reply. Let the reader decide. But, as John Ford put it in *The Man Who Shot Liberty Valance*, "When the legend becomes fact, print the legend." Callo, Dale's Account, 205; Pearson's Report, 210; Fanning, 42; Morison, 289–292; Thomas, 192; Conrad, 47; Jean Boudriot, *John Paul Jones and the* Bonhomme Richard (Annapolis, Naval Institute Press, 1987), Chapter IV, "The battle," by Peter Reaveley, 82.

75   LOC, JPJP, Jones to Franklin, 10/3/79; Fanning, 42; Kilby, 33, Gawalt, 35; Callo, Dale's Account, 206; Pearson's Report, 210; Thomas, 192.

76   Fanning, 42, Gawalt, 35–36.

77   Callo, Dale's Account, 206.

78   Fanning, 43; Kilby, 32; Callo, Dale's Account, 207; Pearson's Report, 210; Gawalt, 37.

79   Callo, Pearson's Report, 210–211; Fanning, 43–44; Kilby, 32; Gawalt, 37–38.

80   Fanning, 43–44; Kilby, 32, Callo, Dale's Account, 207; Thomas, 194.

81   Callo, Dale's Account, 207.

82   Ibid, 211; Kilby, 32–33; Conrad, 49; Morison, 288; Thomas, 196.

83   Kilby, 32.

84   Callo, Dale's Account, 207–208; Pearson's Report, 211.

85   Fanning, 50.

86   LOC, JPJP, Jones to Franklin, 10/3/79; Fanning, 45–47.

87   Ibid.; Fanning, 45–47.

88   LOC, JPJP, Jones to Franklin, 10/3/79; Fanning, 50–51.

89   LOC, JPJP, Jones to Franklin, 10/3/79; Fanning, 45–47; Ship's log, *Serapis*, 9/24/79.

90   Ibid.

91   Ibid.; Fanning, 49–50.

92   Fanning, 50–51.

93   Ibid.; Kilby, 33; LOC, JPJP, Jones to Franklin, 10/3/79.

94   Syrett, 80, and footnote 129.

95   *London Sunday Post*, 9/30/79; *London Morning Post*, 10/1/79.

96   *London Evening Post*, 9/28/79; Callo, 98.

97   John H. Barnes, ed., *The Logs of the Serapis–Alliance–Ariel under the Command of John Paul Jones, 1779–1780* (New York: Naval History Society, 1911), ship's log, *Serapis*, 10/3/79; LOC, JPJP, Jones to Franklin, 10/3/79; Jones to Morris, 10/13/79.

98   Fanning, 44, 57–58.

99   Ibid.; LOC, JPJP, Jones to Pearson, 10/20/79; Jones to Franklin, 10/11/79.

100 *London Evening Post*, 10/12/79.

101 Quoted from Morison, 301; quoted from Thomas, 203.

102 LOC, JPJP, Charles Dumas to Jones, 10/10/79; Thomas, 203.

103 LOC, JPJP, Dumas to Jones, 10/18/79; Fanning, 59.

104 Fanning, 57; Thomas, 207.

105 Fanning, 61; Kilby, 34; Gawalt, 74; Morison, 315.

106 Ibid., 61, 66; Ship's log, *Serapis*, 11/20/79.

107 LOC, JPJP, Jones to Duc de la Vauguyon, 11/11/79; Jones to John de Neufville, 11/26/79; Jones to Vauguyon, 12/13/79; Fanning, 66.

108 Ibid., Jones to Franklin, 12/13/79; Jones to Morris, 10/13/79; Kilby, 35; Morison, 314.

109 Quoted from Thomas, 208.

110 Neeser, 191, Jones to Franklin, 11/29/79.

CHAPTER ELEVEN ✶ "FRESH GALES AND DIRTY WEATHER"

1   Quoted from Tim McGrath, *John Barry: An American Hero in the Age of Sail* (Yardley, PA: Westholme Publishing, 2010), 213.

2   APS, BFP, Digges to Conyngham, 11/10/79; Neeser, 190; Conyngham to Franklin, 11/18/79; *London Chronicle*, 11/21–23/80; PMHB, vol. 77, William Bell Clark, "In Defense of Thomas Digges," 405.

3   David F. Winkler, "Conyngham's Great Escape," *Sea Power* Magazine, October 2003, 48.

4   Ibid.; Clark, 405–406.

5   Ship's Log, *Alliance*, 12/16–27/79; King, 369; Fanning, 66–67; Gawalt, 44.

6   LDC, MCLB, Marine Committee to Barry, 11/6/79.

7   Ibid.; Marine Committee to Eastern Navy Board, 11/6/79; Board of Admiralty to John Langdon, 12/20 and 28/79; Samuel Adams Papers, 11:2194–2197, John Warner to Adams, 7/15/78; NYHS, Barry Papers, "Received of Captain John Barry one Continental horse Pack saddle," 9/19/80; ISM, BHP, Barry Memorial to Congress, 1785.

8   McCullough, 230–231.

9   JCC, Jay to President of Congress, 12/22/79; Harding to the President of Congress, 12/30/79; King, 394; Morgan, 182–183.

10   Ibid.; *Boston Gazette*, 2/21/80; Morgan, 184–185.

11   LDC, Henry Marchand to Horatio Gates, 8/24/79; Morgan. 179–181; Fowler, 48–51, 54–57; Allen, 631.

12   HSP, Joshua Humphreys Papers, Correspondence 1775–1831, Navy Board of the Middle District to Humphreys, 7/1/79; JCC, 12/3, 12/8/79 and 3/21/80; Chappelle, 86; Millar, 257–258; Clark, *The First Saratoga*, 4, 24.

13   MCLB, Francis Lewis to Samuel Huntington, 12/18/79 and 3/21/80.

14   James Wilson to Robert Morris, quoted in Gurn, 127; Doerflinger, 255–258; Tinkcom, 147.

15   Fleming, 298; Lancaster, 281–282; Syrett, *American Waters*, 131.

16   Quoted from Chernow, *George Washington: A Life*, 366; Fleming, 299.

17   Quoted from Fleming, 290; Syrett, *American Waters*, 128–129; Allen, 488.

18   Syrett, 133–134; Lancaster, 283.

19   LDC, MCLB, Marine Committee to Eastern Navy Board, 11/10/79.

20   Quoted from Morgan, 190.

21   Ibid.; C. Smith, 245.

22   Miller, 421.

23   LOC, Jennison Journal, 1/17/80; RIHS, Abraham Whipple Papers (AWP), Benjamin Lincoln to Abraham Whipple, 1/17/80; Smith, 354.

24   *Boston Independent Chronicle*, 4/6/80; *Pennsylvania Gazette*, 3/15/80; Morgan, 193.

25   *Pennsylvania Gazette*, 3/15/80; William L. Clements Library, University of Michigan, Orderly Book Collection, George Philip Hooke, "Orderly Book, 17th Grs." (George Philip Hooke Journal), 1/6–16/80; Pennsylvania *Gazette*, 3/22/80; Syrett, 134–137.

26   *South Carolina Gazette*, 2/4/80; Morgan, 193–194.

27   RIHS, AWP, Continental captains to Whipple, 2/1/80; Ibid.; Ibid.

28   RIHS, AWP, Whipple to Tucker and Simpson, 2/13/80; Smith, 354–355. LOC, Jennison's Journal, 3/5/80.

29   Ibid., Whipple to Lincoln, 2/13 and 22/80; Morgan, 195–196.

30   LDC, MCLB, Board of Admiralty to Lincoln, 2/22/80; Whipple, 2/22/80; Rathburne [*sic*], 2/22/80.

31   Quoted in Allen, 495; *Pennsylvania Gazette*, 5/24/80.

32   South Carolina Historical Society (SCHS), Peter Timothy's Journal of Observations, 26 March–8 April 1780 (SCHS 37–22–01), 3/26/80; Clements Library, Hoyle's Journal, 2/11–14/80; Smith, 354; Morgan, 197.

33   SCHS, Timothy Journal, 3/29/80; LOC, Jennison Journal, 3/25/80; RIHS, Whipple Letter Book, Lincoln to Whipple, 3/10/80; Pennsylvania *Gazette*, 4/5/80; Syrett, 137; Smith, 248.

34   Ibid.; 4/8–9/80; Ibid., 4/8–10/80; Pennsylvania *Gazette*, 4/27/80; Ralfe, vol. 1, "Admiral Arbuthnot," 132; Smith, 248.

35   *Pennsylvania Gazette*, 5/16/80; LOC, Jennison's Journal, 4/10/80.

36   Ibid., 5/3/80; Hooke's Journal, 4/13/80; Lancaster, 283; Fleming, 300.

37   Ibid., 5/17/80; Miller, 423; Syrett, 138–139.

38   LOC, Jennison's Journal, 4/15–5/12/80; Allen, 497; Ralfe, 132–133.

39   RHIS, Whipple Letter Book, Petition of Captains to Admiral Arbuthnot, 5/15/80; *Pennsylvania Gazette*, 6/28/80; Smith, 249–250.

40   *Pennsylvania Gazette*, 5/3/80; Fleming, 300–304.

41   Ibid.; 7/19/80; Fleming, 305.

42   Ibid., 6/28/80; Mazet, 353–354; Miller, 423.

43   LDC, MCLB, Marine Committee to James Nicholson, 5/12 and 10/6/79; Board of Admiralty to Nicholson, 4/7, 4/17, and 5/21/80.

44   Ibid., Board of Admiralty to Nicholson 4/17/80; to Eastern Navy Board, 5/12 and 1/8/80.

45   HSP, Court of Admiralty Papers, Libel of James Nicholson against the Schooner *Queen Charlotte*, 5/27/80; Chappelle, 74; Millar, 284; Van Powell, 114.

46   Account of James Nicholson regarding *Trumbull* vs. *Watt*, from Allmon, *The Remembrancer*, 225–227, quoted from Allen, 499.

47   Ibid.

48   Ibid.; King, 139.

49   *Massachusetts Spy*, 8/17/80; *Boston Gazette*, 6/5, 19 and 7/24, 28/80; Boston *Independent Chronicle*, 7/6, 9/7/80; Allen, 505–506.

50   Ibid.; *Boston Gazette*, 6/5, 19 and 7/24, 28/80.

51   Boston *Independent Chronicle*, 7/6/80.

52   Quoted from Allen, 500–502.

53   Quoted from Allen, 505–506.

54   Allen, 504.

55   Quoted from Smith, 251.

56   *Boston Gazette*, 7/5/80; Allen, 501–502.

57   *Pennsylvania Gazette*, 8/23/80.

58   Gilbert Saltonstall to Gurdon Saltonstall, 6/19/80, *Records and Papers of the New London County Historical Society*, 1:4, 53–56.

59   Fanning's Narrative, 67; Kilby's Narrative, 34.

60   Ibid.; Kilby, 34; Ship's log, *Alliance*, 12/27–29/80.

61   Ship's Log, *Alliance*, 12/29/79–1/16/80; Morison, 322.

62   Ship's Log, *Alliance*, 1/19/80; Fanning, 71; Kilby, 35.

63   Ibid., 1/19–28/80; Neeser, 197, George Hooper to Conyngham, 7/13/80; 198, Jonathan Nesbitt to Conyngham, 7/26/80.

64   Ibid., 1/28–2/11/80; Fanning, 72.

65   Kilby, 35; LOC, JPJP, Jones to Gourlande and Moylan, 2/10/80.

66   LOC, JPJP, Lee to Jones, 2/20/80; Jones to Lee, 2/28/80; Thomas, 213.

67   Thomas, 224–225.

68   LOC, JPJP, Jones to Bancroft, 4/10/80; Jones to Sartine, 9/13/78; Morison, 327.

69   Ibid., Michelle de Bonneuil to Jones, 5/10/80; Jones to Sartine, 5/25/and 30/80; Sartine to Jones, 6/16/80; Jones to Dumas, 9/8/80; Gawalt, 47–50; Fanning, 78; Thomas, 220.

70   Ibid., Mme. de St. Julien to Jones, 5/17/and 18/80; Countess de Lowendahl to Jones, 6/7/80; Jones to Countess de Lowendahl, 7/7/80.

71   Ibid., Countess de Lowendahl to Jones, 6/7/80; APS, BFP, Franklin to Jones, 6/1/80.

72   Ibid., Officers of the *Alliance* to Franklin, 5/31/80; Franklin to Officer of the *Alliance*, 6/7/80; Franklin to Jones, 6/12/80.

73   Ship's Log, *Alliance*, 6/12/80; Kilby, 36; Fanning, 74–75.

74   LOC, JPJP, "Steps taken to Prevent the *Alliance* from Leaving Port," 6/6/80; Ship's Log, *Alliance*, 6/20/80; Fanning, 76; Kilby, 36.

75   Ship's Log, *Alliance*, 1/28/80; Neeser, 1. Some accounts of the *Experiment* call her a "tartan"—a small lateen-rigged, single-sail Mediterranean vessel—she was likely similar to a bark, with her first two masts square rigged and her third fore-and-aft rigged (King, 90, 364).

76   PMHB, Conyngham's Narrative, 487.

77   Ibid.; Ralfe, vol. 2, Sampson Edwards, 362; Ferguson, 193–194.

78   Ibid.

79   Neeser, 198–199, Nesbitt to Conyngham, 7/26/80; 200–201, Nesbitt to Conyngham, 1/24/81.

80   Woody Hilton, *Abigail Adams* (New York: Free Press, 2009), 193.

81   Holton, 194–195; Neeser, 200–203, Nesbitt to Conyngham, 1/24/81; Nesbitt to Conyngham, 5/2/81.

82   Quoted from Sheldon S. Cohen, *Yankee Sailors in British Gaols* (Newark: University of Delaware Press, 1995), 160–161.

83   Neeser, 204–205, Franklin to Agent Coffin, 3/23/81; JCC, 6/11/81.

84   Neeser, 200–201, Nesbitt to Conyngham, 1/24/81.

85   LDC, MCLB, Harding to Board of Admiralty, 12/30/79, 2/4 and 18/80; HSP, Gratz Collection, Joseph Hardy to William Bingham, 1/29/80.

86   LDC, MCLB, Board of Admiralty to Curson and Gouverneur, 3/4/80; Morgan, 203–205; Smith, 253; Tuchman, 173–176.

87 Ibid., Board of Admiralty to Harding, 5/2/80; Morgan, 203; Smith, 252.

88 LOC, JPJP, Jones to Morris, 6/27/80; Jones to Bancroft, 6/27/80; Jones to Ship's Company of *Alliance*, 7/3/80.

89 Ibid., "Delia" to Jones letters, June–July 1780 (dates estimated); John Paul Jones Poems.

90 Ibid., Franklin to Jones, 7/5/80.

91 Ibid., Jones to Dale, 9/9/80; Ship's Log, *Ariel*, 7/10–9/16/80; Fanning, 101.

92 Ibid.; Fanning, 88–89.

93 LOC, JPJP, Declaration of the Officers of the *Ariel*, 10/13/80; Ship's Log, *Ariel*, 10/8/80.

94 Ibid.; Gawalt, 53–54; Ship's Log, *Ariel*, 10/9/80; King, *Harbors and High Seas*, 206, and *Sea of Words*, 103.

95 Fanning, 79–81; LOC, JPJP, Declaration of the Officers of the *Ariel*; 10/13/80; Gawalt, 54.

96 Ship's Log, *Ariel*, 10/11–13/80; Gawalt, 54.

97 APS, BFP, Samuel Wharton to Franklin, 10/14/80; Gawalt, 54; Fanning, 105.

98 HSP, Etting Papers, Jones to Morris, 11/5/80.

99 LDC, MCLB, Board of Admiralty to Nathaniel Shaw, Jr., 5/22/80; Clark, 30.

100 HCL, Charles Roberts Autograph Collection, Barry to Matthew Irwin, 7/16/79; JCC, 5/27/80; Barney, 82–85; Chappelle, 86; Millar, 257–258; Smith, 253; Clark, 37.

101 JCC, 7/7 and 19/80; MCLB, Board of Admiralty to Young, 8/11 and 14/80; to Henry Laurens, 8/11/80; to William Pickles, 8/11/80.

102 LDC, MCLB, Board of Admiralty to Henry Fisher, 8/19/80; to John Young, 8/19/80; to M. de Carabasse, 8/19/80; Tuchman, 190; Clark, 55–56.

103 Ibid., Board of Admiralty to Captain William Pickles, 8/11/80; to John Young, 9/14/80; Clark, 59–60.

104 Ibid., Board of Admiralty to Eastern Navy Board, 9/12/80; to James Nicholson, 9/14/80; Nicholson to President of Congress, 10/21/80.

105 LOC, GWP, Washington to Jefferson, 9/11/80; De Koven, 141–143; National Archives, MSS, Barry's Report on the Landais Court-Martial; MCLB, Board of Admiralty to Barry, 9/5/80; to Eastern Navy Board, 9/5/80.

CHAPTER TWELVE ✫ "SEND THAT SHIP TO SEA"

1   RMP, 4:257, Morris to the Navy Board of the Eastern Department, 2/16/82.

2   Gawalt, 54–55; Barnes, *Logs*, Appendix F, 134, "The Continuation and End of the Voyage of the *Ariel* to the United States."

3   LDC, MCLB, Board of Admiralty to Barry, 9/5/80.

4   PA Archives, Series II, 154, and Colonial Records, 12:80; *Pennsylvania Packet*, 6/3 and 10/8/78; *Pennsylvania Gazette*, 4/10/79.

5   National Archives, MSS, Barry's Report on the Landais Court Martial; Clark, *Gallant John Barry*, 192.

6   JCC, 11/13/80.

7   LOC, Barry Collection, Muster Roll, *Alliance*, 1781; PA Archives, "Life of John Kessler," 4.

8   National Archives, MSS, Papers of the Continental Congress, 2:193; Landais' *Memorial*; Clark, *Gallant John Barry*, 194.

9   Ibid., "Barry's Summing Up of the Landais Court Martial."

10   Ibid.; Fowler, 237; Miller, 439.

11   Chernow, 389–391.

12   Ibid.; LDC, Madison to Jones, 12/12/80; Brands, 589; Keane, 203–204.

13   RDC, Laurens to President of Congress, 2/4/81; NDAR, 11:559, John Laurens to Henry Laurens, 3/11/78.

14   RDC, Laurens to the president of Congress, 2/4/81; Clark, 197.

15   Ibid.; also Laurens to President of Congress, 2/6/81.

16   HCL, Charles Roberts Autograph Collection, Account of Expenses for *Alliance*, 2/9/81; APS, BFP, Barry to Franklin, 3/13/81; Clark, 200.

17   Ibid.; Miller, 458.

18   LOC, JPJP, Board of Admiralty to Jones, 2/20/81; Jones to John Brown, 3/13/81.

19   LDC, Report of the Board of Admiralty, 3/28/81; Gawalt, 56–57.

20   Ibid.; *Pennsylvania Evening Post*, 3/5/81; Morison, 375; Thomas, 248.

21   NYHS, Thomas Paine to James Hutchinson, 3/11/81; John Keane: *Tom Paine: A Political Life* (New York: Grove Press, 1995), 208.

22   Ibid.; King, 229. My thanks to author and mariner James Nelson for his expertise.

23   Ibid.

24   Ibid.; RDC, Laurens to President of Congress, 3/10/81; e-mail from Jim Nelson, 2/25/08; Keane, 208; Clark, 201.

25   Kessler, "Rough Sketch," 5; Keane, 209; Clark, 201.

26   Ibid.

27   Ibid.; Miller, 458.

28   RDC, Laurens to President of Congress, 3/11/81; NYHS, Barnes Collection, *Alliance* Letter Book, 3/4/81; ISM, BHP, Barry to Franklin, 3/10/81; Ship's log, *Alliance*, 3/6–9/81.

29   APS, BFP, Barry to Franklin, 3/10/81 and 3/13/81.

30   NYHS, Barnes Collection, *Alliance* Letter Book, 8/1/82.

31   APS, BFP, Parke to Franklin, 3/13/81.

32   ISM, BHP, *Alliance* log, 3/13/81; NDAR, 2: appendix: "Rules and Regulations of the Navy of the United Colonies"; PA Archives, Kessler, "Rough Sketch," 5.

33   APS, BFP, Franklin to Barry, 3/19/81.

34   Ibid., Barry to Franklin, 3/23/81; JCC 7/15/82.

35   Ibid., Barry to Franklin, 3/27/81.

36   JCC, 7/15/82; ISM, BFP, *Alliance* log, 3/29/81; Captain William Robeson Letter, from Griffin, 170–171.

37   ISM, BFP, *Alliance* log, 3/29/81.

38   PA Archives, Kessler, 5.

39   Ibid.; LOC, JBC, Muster Roll, *Alliance*, 3/29/81.

40   Ibid.; ISM, BHP, *Alliance* log, 3/31/81.

41   Ibid.; ISM, BHP, *Alliance* log, 3/31/81; Miller, 474.

42   PA Archives, Kessler, 5–6; ISM, BHP, *Alliance* log, 3/31/81; Boston Newspapers, vol. 4, 6/14/81.

43   ISM, BHP, *Alliance* log, 4/2–3/81; PA Archives, Kessler, 6–7

44   Ibid., 4/25–29/81; LDC, Barry to Congress, 6/6/81 and 7/15/82.

45   Ibid., 5/2/81; PA Archives, Kessler, 7; Boston Newspapers, vol. 4, 6/14/81.

46   Griffin, 142, 174; Clark, 217–218.

47   LDC, Barry to Congress, 6/6/81; PA Archives, Kessler, 7.

48   Ibid.; Kessler, 10.

49   Ibid.; Kessler.

50   Ralfe, *Naval Biography*, 2:362; *London Daily Intelligencer*, 8/6/81.

51   *London Daily Intelligencer*, 8/6/81.

52   Charles Henry Lincoln, *Naval Records of the American Revolution* ("NRAR"), Washington: Government Printing Office, 1906), 175, Memorial of James Nicholson and others, 4/28/81; 176, Congress to Board of Admiralty, 5/5/81.

53   Ibid., Board of Admiralty to Congress, 12/9/80; Clark, *The First Saratoga*, 114–115.

54   Howard, Appendix, Hardy Journal, 260–261, 12/19/80; Clark, 119.

55   Ibid., 261, 12/20/80.

56   *Dunlap's Pennsylvania Packet*, or the *General Advertiser*, 2/14 and 2/27/81. LDC, John Gibson to President of Congress, 4/17/81; Clark, 125–129.

57   Howard, 156, 266–267, Hardy's Journal, 1/8/81; Tuchman, 231.

58   Ibid.; Tuchman, 231; Clark, 134.

59   *Pennsylvania Gazette*, 3/28/81; *Pennsylvania Journal and Weekly Advertiser*, 3/28/81; *New York Gazette and Weekly Mercury*, 4/23/81; Clark, 137, and 154–157, appendix B, "Muster Roll of the *Saratoga*"; RMP, 3:204, Diary, 11/19/81.

60   *Pennsylvania Gazette*, 5/2/81; *New York Gazette and Weekly Mercury*, 4/23 and 4/30/81; Clark, 142; Van Powell, 104.

61   *New York Gazette and Weekly Mercury*, 5/5/81; Clark, 144.

62   LDC, Francis Lewis to President of Congress, 7/12/81; Joanna Young to Congress, 2/23/85; Clark, 143.

63   *London Chronicle*, 8/6/81; LDC, Barry to Eastern Naval Board, 6/6/81.

64   Ibid.; PA Archives, Kessler, 8; Allen, 551.

65   Ibid.; Kessler.

66   ISM, BHP, *Alliance* Muster Roll, 3/29/81; Kessler, 8.

67   Kessler, 8; Brown and Kessler, *The Portfolio Magazine*, "The Life of Commodore Barry," 7–8; Miller, 95.

68   Ibid.; ISM, BHP, *Alliance* Muster Roll, 3/29/81; Clark, 223.

69   Freidenburg, 18; Wilbur, 49.

70 Barry to Congress, 6/6/81, from Griffin, 145; Kessler, "Rough Sketch," 8; Clark, 224.

71 Kessler, 8; Wilbur, 34; King, 54; NDAR, 6:1488.

72 Dr. Paul Kopperman, e-mail, 10/18/2005; Laurence Todd, Detached Hospital, BB BAR, e-mail, 10/18/2005. One military surgeon of the era insisted on using his finger, hating "to thrust a pair of long forceps the Lord knows where, with scarce probability of any success." From John Ranby, *The Method of Treating Gunshot Wounds*, 2nd ed. (London: Robert Horsfield, 1760).

73 Ibid.; Wilbur, 34.

74 Kessler, 8; LOC, JBC, *Alliance* Muster Roll, 3/29/81.

75 Ibid., 8–9; Brown and Kessler, 9–10.

76 Ibid.; Brown and Kessler, 9–10; Clark, 224.

77 Kessler, "Rough Sketch," 8–10.

78 Ibid.; Brown and Kessler, 9–10.

79 Ibid.; Allen, 552.

80 Brown and Kessler, 9–10.

81 *London Chronicle*, 8/6/81.

82 Brown and Kessler, 9–10.

83 Ibid.

84 Ibid.

85 Ibid.; LDC, Barry to Congress, 6/6/81; Barry to Eastern Navy Board, 6/6/81.

86 *Pennsylvania Gazette*, 6/27/81; LOC, Bradford Letter Book, Bradford to Board of Admiralty, 6/14/81; Clark, 227; Allen, 555; see Marine Captain Mathew Parke's painting of the *Alliance* entering Boston harbor.

87 *Pennsylvania Packet*, 5/26/81; Kessler, 11; LOC, JBC, from the pages of the Pension Office; Wilbur, 34; Laurence Todd e-mail, 10/18/2005; Boston Newspapers, vol. 4, *Continental Journal*, 6/14/81.

88 *Continental Journal*, 6/14/81; *Pennsylvania Gazette*, 6/27/81; HCL, Roberts Collection, Francis Lewis to Barry, 7/3/81; APS, BFP, Congressional resolution, 6/26/81; LDC, Franklin to Thomas McKean, 11/5/81; ISM, BHP, Brown to Barry, 6/26/81; RMP, 1:308; Brown and Kessler, 9; LDC, Richard Potts to Thomas Sim Lee, 7/3/81.

89 Barney, 89–99, Cohen, 185–187.

90   APS, BFP, Digges to Franklin, 4/14 and 8/18/80; PMHB, 22:414–415.

91   Matthewman's "Narrative."

92   Ibid.; Cohen, 186.

93   APS, BFP, Conyngham to Franklin, 6/16/81; Neeser, PMHB, 22:487–488.

94   Ibid., Franklin to Conyngham, 6/20/81; Conyngham to Franklin, 6/21 and 7/4/81.

95   Ibid., Williams to Franklin, 7/21/81.

96   Neeser, Memorial of Gustavus Conyngham to Congress; Hayes, 41.

97   NRAR, 181, Memorial of Nicholson to Congress, 5/31/81; De Koven, 2:212–214, Nicholson to Barry, 6/24/81; Morison, 377; Thomas, 249–250; Callo, 134.

98   Ibid.; NRAR, 180, Committee Report to Congress, 6/29/81; 181, Jones's Memorial to Congress, 7/17/81; RMP, 4:458–459, Morris to Langdon, 3/26/82.

99   RMP, 3:5, Morris to president of Congress, 10/1/81; *Pennsylvania Gazette*, 9/27/81; Fowler, 113.

100   *Continental Journal*, 9/13/81; *Pennsylvania Packet*, 9/27/81; Fowler, 113.

101   Ibid.; *Pennsylvania Packet*, 9/27/81; Allen, 556–557.

102   Ibid.; *Boston Independent Chronicle*, 8/30/81; RMP, 3:202, Morris to President of Congress, 11/17/81.

103   Fowler, 113–114.

104   Fleming, 334.

105   Rappleye, 227.

106   Michael J, Crawford, PhD: "Naval Administration under Robert Morris" (2000).

107   RMP, 4:451–452, Morris to the Navy Board of the Eastern Department, 3/25/82.

108   LOC, JPJP, Jones to Barry, 9/7/81.

109   Naval Historical Center, Early History Branch, Boston Newspapers 2:85; RMP, 2:193–194; JCC, 7/15/81 and 8/5/82; Clark, 233.

110   ISM, BHP, Henry Mitchell to John Brown, 9/4/81; Clark, 233.

111   Ibid.; Amalia Atkinson, "Captain Rathbun's Last Voyage," *New England Historical and Genealogical Register*, no. 115, July 1961, 165.

112   Ibid.; Tuchman, 127.

113   Ibid., 166; *Newport Mercury*, 4/2/82.

114   Ibid.; *Newport Mercury*, 4/17/82; *Providence Gazette*, 10/19/82.

CHAPTER THIRTEEN ★ SHUBAEL GARDNER

1   RMP, 3:20–21, John Adams to Morris, 11/6/82.

2   ISM, BHP, "Admiral Digby ['s] Permission to a Whale Brig Capt[ured] by the *Alliance*, 7 of Sept. 1782"; *Historic Nantucket*, July, 1963, Emil Frederick Guba, "Revolutionary War Service Roll," 5–17.

3   Ibid.; *Massachusetts Review* 18, no. 3 (Autumn 1977), George Rogers Taylor, "Nantucket Oil Merchants the American Revolution," 584–585, 590–591; Alexander Starbuck, *History of Nantucket* (Rutland, VT: Tuttle, 1969; 1st ed., Boston: Goodspeed, 1924), 210, 211n.

4   LDC, Huntington to Jones, 6/27/81; Gawalt, 60; Thomas, 250; Callo, 135; Morison, 381.

5   LOC, JPJP, Jones to Barry, 9/7/81; Jones to Brown, 12/9/81.

6   Ibid., Lafayette to Jones, 12/22/81; Jones to "Delia," 12/25/81; Jones to McNeill, 3/21/82; Thomas, 251–252.

7   RMP, 4:101, Morris to Brown, 1/23/82; to Langdon, 3/18/82; to Jones, 3/18/82; to Brown, 3/25/82.

8   Ibid., 458–459, Morris to Jones, 3/26/82; to Langdon, 3/26/82; Morison, 386–387. One of Morris's visitors in Philadelphia that spring was Dr. James Craik, the army's chief surgeon, Washington's personal physician, and the son of William Craik, Jones's laird (4:553, Diary, 4/10/82).

9   LOC, JPJP, Jones to Brown, 4/21/82; Jones to Measach Ware, 6/1/82; Gawalt, 61; Morison, 387; Thomas, 253.

10   RMP, 4:18, Morris to the Governor of Massachusetts, 8/4/81; Barry to Congress, 7/25/81, from Griffin, 148; PA Archives, Kessler, "Rough Sketch," 11; Clark, 191, 238.

11   HSP, Dreer, Morris to Brown, 9/19/81, *Continental Journal*, 11/1/81; Clark, 239.

12   RMP, 3:260–263, Morris to Barry 11/27/81 and enclosure, "Sentence of the Court-Martial on Three Men from the *Alliance*," 6/28/81.

13   *Continental Journal*, 11/1/81; Clark, 239.

14   RMP, 4:556–557, Morris to Joseph Kendall, 4/10/82; LOC, JBP, *Alliance* muster roll, 5/17/82; Barry to Eastern Navy Board, from Clark, 239.

15   HSP, Dreer, Morris to Brown, 11/27/81; PA Archives, Brown and Kessler, 11; RMP, 3:260–263, Morris to Barry, 11/27/81; Flexner, 168.

16   RMP, 3:260–263, Morris to Barry, 11/27/81.

17   Ibid., 3:429, Barry to Morris, 12/22/81, and 4:202, Barry to Morris, 2/10/82; JCC, 11/13/80.

18 LOC, JBP, *Alliance* Letter Book, Barry to Morris, 12/22/81.

19 Ibid., GWP, Lafayette to Washington, 2/18/82; APS, BFP, Barry to Franklin, 1/31/82.

20 Kessler, 12.

21 APS, BFP, Barry to Franklin, 1/17 and 1/31/82; Franklin to Barry, 1/24/82.

22 FDR, Captain de Galatheau to Barry, 2/2/82; LOC, JBP, Barry to de Galatheau, 2/9/82; JCC, 7/15/82; LDC, Charles Thompson to Barry, 7/16/82.

23 LOC, JBP, Barry to Morris, 1/30 and 2/10/82; Barry to Brown, 2/10/82; APS, BFP, Barry to Franklin, 2/27/82.

24 Ibid., Barry to Franklin, 2/29/82; APS, BFP, Barry to Franklin, 2/27/82.

25 ISM, John Green Collection, Green to Barry, 2/10/82; Barry to Green, 3/13/82; NYHS, Barnes Collection, Alexander Thomas to Barry, 3/5/82; Barry to Thomas, 3/8/82.

26 LOC, JBP, Barry to Morris, 1/20/82; RMP, 4:380–381, Franklin to Morris, 3/9/82. Barry had, in fact, arranged for the supplies to go in his friend Thomas Truxton's privateer.

27 RMP, 5:269, Morris to Richard Butler, 7/18/82; Rappleye, 300.

28 Ibid., 5:283, Diary, 2/21/82; Barney, 109–111.

29 Barney, 112–113; Miller, 276; Allen, 588; Fowler, *Silas Talbot*, 55–56.

30 Ibid.; Miller, 278.

31 Ibid., 114–116; King, 96.

32 Ibid., 114–116.

33 Ibid., 115–117; *London Chronicle*, 9/10/82.

34 Ibid., 118, 308.

35 Ibid., 118; RMP, 5:178–179, Diary, 5/15/82; 195–196; Morris to Robert Smith, 5/16/82; 197–198, to José Solano, 5/16/82.

36 RMP, 6:396, Diary, 9/19/82; Barney, 128–131.

37 Tuchman, 97.

38 Ibid., 237.

39 Ibid., 293–295; Syrett, 224; Miller, 508–514. For a captivating read on the Battle of the Saintes, see Nathan Miller's *Sea of Glory*.

40 RMP, 4:100–102, Morris to Brown, 1/23/82.

41   RMP, 5:145–157, "State of American Commerce and Plan for Protecting It," 5/10/82; Rappleye, 301.

42   Ibid., 6:345, Morris to Washington, 9/9/82; ibid., 290–291.

43   RMP, 4:214, Morris to Samuel Nicholson, 2/11/82; to John Brown, 3/25/82; *Boston Independent Chronicle*, 1/24/82.

44   Ibid., 5:349, Michael Knies to Morris, 6/5/82; J. Philip London, "The Challenging Life of a Patriot Captain," *Naval History* Magazine, October 2012, 49.

45   Ibid., Knies to Morris, 6/9/82; Ibid.

46   Ibid, 349, footnote 1; 487–488, Warrant Appointing a Court of Inquiry on Samuel Nicholson, 6/26/82; 6:204, Warrant Appointing a Court-Martial for the Trial of Michael Knies, 8/14/82; 616–617, Determination on the Court of Inquiry on Samuel Nicholson, 10/17/82; London, 49.

47   Fowler, *Rebels Under Sail*, 217; Rappleye, 274–275.

48   RMP, 5:75–79, John Jay to Morris, 4/28/82; (and footnote 10); London, 49–50.

49   LOC, JBP, Barry to Morris, 5/12/82; Barry to Brown, 5/16/82; Kessler "Rough Sketch," 13.

50   Allen, 570–571.

51   HSP, Proceedings of the Court-Martial Aboard the *Alliance*, 7/27/82; LOC, JBP, *Alliance* Letter Book, Barry to Mumford, no date; RMP, 5:254–255, Morris to Mumford, 5/24/82.

52   Ibid.

53   Ibid.

54   LOC, JBP, Barry to de Quémy, 5/29/82; RMP, 5:248–250, Morris to Barry, 5/24/82.

55   Ibid., Barry to Morris, 6/24/82; Barry to de Quémy, 5/29/82.

56   LOC, JBP, Barry to Washington, 5/30/82; HSP, PMHB, vol. 4, Keen, 485–486.

57   HCL, Roberts Collection, Hancock to Barry, 6/3/82; HSP, Connarroe Papers, Barry to Hancock, 6/6/82.

58   LOC, JBP, de Quémy to Barry, 5/29/82; Barry to Morris, 6/5/82; Manuscript Division of the U.S. Naval Academy Museum, no. 167, Barry to Brown, 6/4/82.

59   LOC, JBP, Brown to Barry, 6/10 and 6/20/82; with thanks to Susan Klepp, Temple University Department of History.

60   RMP, 5:448 Morris to Barry, 6/19/82; JBP, Barry to Brown, 7/22/82; Barry to Morris, 8/2/82. Morris had also defended Barry to Franklin. In his reply to Frank-

lin's letter questioning Barry's priorities, Morris insisted that Barry's orders "were such that was right not to stay longer in France, and therefore I must pray you to excuse his Inattention to your Requests"—RMP, 4:244.

61   LOC, GWP, Washington to Barry, 6/12/82; Flexner, 169.

62   Ibid., JBP, Tracy to Barry, 6/10/82; Barry to Tracy, 7/12/82; Barry to Sarah Barry, quoted from Griffin, 175.

63   Ibid.; also Barry to Brown, 8/4/82; HSP, Proceedings from the Court-Martial on Board *Alliance*, 7/27/82.

64   Ibid., Barry to Morris, 8/2/82; LOC, *Alliance* Letter Book, Barry to William Ellery, 4/4/82; Barry to Howland and Coit, 4/8/82.

65   *Pennsylvania Gazette*, 9/4/82; Matthewman's "Narrative"; e-mail from George Nagle/Afrolumens Project, 3/21/12.

66   Ibid.

67   Lt. Col. Michael Lee Lanning (Ret.), *Defenders of Liberty: African Americans in the Revolutionary War* (Kensington, NY: Citadel Press, 2000), 178; W. Jeffrey Bolster, *Black Jacks: African American Seamen in the Age of Sail* (Cambridge, MA: Harvard University Press, 1997), 30–31.

68   NDAR 9:889, Benjamin Rumsey to Governor Thomas Johnson, 9/6/77.

69   Bolster, 30–31, 153–155, 273 (footnote no. 50); RMP, Morris to President of Congress, 6/10/82.

70   LOC, JBP, *Alliance* Letter Book, Barry to William Ellery, 4/4/83.

71   Thomas Truxton Moebs, *Black Soldiers, Black Sailors, Black Ink: Research Guide on African-Americans in U.S. Military History, 1526–1900* (Chesapeake Bay: Moebs Publishing Co., 1994), 257, 259–260, 266.

72   Julie Winch, *A Gentleman of Color: The Life of James Forten* (New York: Oxford University Press, 2002), 28–29, 36–34: Lincoln, 449, Bonds of the Letters of Marque, *Royal Louis*, 7/23/81.

73   Ibid., 39–40; *Pennsylvania Packet*, 8/23/81.

74   Quoted from Winch, 43.

75   Quoted from Winch, 43–46; Lanning, 19–20. Winch's biography on Forten is a marvelous account of his adventures and accomplishments.

76   HSP, MSS Collection, Franklin Papers, Conyngham to W. T. Franklin, 6/8/82; Schiff, xiii.

77   Ibid.; PMHB, 22:488; Hayes, 41.

78   Neeser, 206–207, "Memorial of Gustavus Conyngham to Congress, October 1782"; 207–208, Certificate Issued by Benjamin Franklin, 8/7/82.

79   Millar, 48–49; LOC, JPJP, Jones to Brown, 4/21/82; Jones to Gouverneur Morris, 7/17/82; RMP, 6:178–179, Morris to Jones and Morris to Langdon, 8/13/82.

80   Ibid., 313, Morris to Chevalier de la Luzerne, 9/4/82.

81   Ibid., 6:17, Morris to Jones, 11/5/82; Gawalt, 63–65; Morison, 389–391.

82   Ibid., 5:515, Diary, 10/7/82; Van Powell, 120; Millar, 263–265.

83   *Pennsylvania Packet*, 12/31/82; *Boston Independent Chronicle*, 11/29/82; Allen, 585–586.

84   LOC, JPJP, Expense Report, 1781–82; Jones to Morris, 11/29/82; Morris to Jones, 12/5/82; Thomas, 255, Morison, 393–395.

85   RMP, 6:184–185, Diary, 12/9/82.

86   RMP, 5:75–77, John Jay to Morris, 4/28/82; ibid., 6:154–155, Morris to Manley, 8/8/82; 176–177, Circular to John Barry and John Manley, 8/13/82; *Boston Independent Chronicle*, 9/26/82; *Pennsylvania Packet*, 10/8/82.

87   *Boston Gazette*, 1/27, 2/3, and 3/3/83; Allen, 608–609; RMP, 8:266–267, Morris to Manley, 7/10/83; 844–445, Confirmation of the Sentence of John Manley, 12/17/83; Morgan, 213–215.

88   Morgan, 213–215.

89   ISM, BHP, "Admiral Digby['s] Permission to a Whale Brig Capt[ured] by the *Alliance*, 7 of Sept. 1782"; Kessler, "Rough Sketch," 14; *Pennsylvania Packet*, 12/17/82.

90   Ibid.

91   JBP, Barry to Brown, 8/4 and 8/10/82; PA Archives, Brown and Kessler, 20.

92   Ibid., 19.

93   Ibid., 19; Kessler, 13–14; NYHS, Barnes Collection, "Samuel Tuft's Statement," 8/23/82; "Statement of Manassah Short," 8/12/82; *Pennsylvania Packet*, 12/17/82.

94   LOC, JBP, Barry to Morris, 10/18/82; *Pennsylvania Packet*, 12/17/82; Tuchman, 293; Clark, 274; Miller, 517.

95   Ibid.; LDC, Virginia Delegates to Benjamin Harrison, 12/17/82.

96   Ibid.; also John Black to Barry, 10/25/82; Kessler, 15; King, 197.

97   Ibid., *Alliance* Letter Book, Barry to Lafayette, 10/28/82; RMP, 7:203–204, Franklin to Morris, 12/14/82; Clark, 278–279; Brands, 614–615.

98   Ibid., Barry to Franklin, 10/31/82; Mary Guinta, ed., *The Emerging Nation: A Documentary History of the Foreign Relations of the United States Under the Articles of Confederation*, 3 vols. (Washington, D.C.: National Historical Publicatons and Records Commission, 1996), 1:547, Lord Shelburne to Richard Oswald, 9/3/82.

99   Ibid.; various correspondence, November 1782.

100   Ibid., Ship's Officers of *Alliance* to Barry, 11/17 and 11/19/82; Barry to Ship's Officers, 11/19/82; Barry to Mathew Parke, 11/24 and 11/25/82; Barry to Patrick Fletcher, 11/25/82; Clark, 281.

101   Ibid., Barry to Thomas Barclay, 12/14/82; Barry to Morris, 12/7/82; ibid., 285–286.

102   Ibid., *Alliance* Muster book, 12/8/82; Barry to Henry Johnson, 11/29/82; Barry to Barclay, 12/14/82; HSP, Dreer Collection, Barry to Brown, 12/7/82; quoted from Schiff, 326. One man in Brest wanted to get to Lorient in time but could not: Henry Johnson, late of Mill Prison and former captain of the *Lexington* (HCL, Charles Roberts Autograph Collection, Johnson to Barry, 10/16/82).

103   Ibid., Barry to Morris, 1/22/83.

104   *Pennsylvania Journal*, 2/26/83, "Extract from the Martinique *Gazette*," 1/15/83; *Pennsylvania Gazette*, 2/12/83.

105   ISM, BHP, ship's log, *Alliance*, 1/1–1/22/83; Howard, 156.

106   ISM, John Green Papers, Extracts, Robert Morris's Diary, 8/13, 8/14, 11/27/82; Morris to Thomas Randall & Co., 10/17/82; Morris to Green, 11/27/82; HCL, Charles Roberts Collection, Barry to Morris, 2/13/83.

107   RMP, 7:467–468, Barry to Morris, 3/20/83.

108   ISM, BHP, Ship's Log, *Alliance*, 2/1/83; HSP, Society Collection, James Seagrove to Brown, 3/6/83; LOC, JBP, *Alliance* Letter Book, Barry to Morris, 3/20/83; Clark, 293.

109   Ibid., 2/6–3/5/83; ISM, John Green Papers, Barry to the Governor of Havana, 2/15/83; Howard, 159.

110   RMP, 7:424, Diary and Notes, 2/11/83.

111   ISM, Ship's Log, *Alliance*, ibid., 3/5–6/83; also "Barry's Account of Proceedings on the *Alliance* and *Duc de Luzon* [*sic*]," 3/20/83.

112   Ibid.

113   PRO, Admiralty, 51/875, *Sybil* Journal, 3/7/83; James Ralfe, *The Naval Biography of Great Britain*, vol. 3, "Historical Memoirs of James Vashon," 187–190.

114   ISM, BHP, Ship's Log, *Alliance*, 3/7–9/83; "Barry's Report," 3/20/83.

115   Ibid., 3/10/83; Ibid.

116   Ibid.; LOC, JBP, "List of Officers and Men on board the Continental Frigate *Alliance*," 12/8/82.

117   Ibid.; Kessler, "Rough Sketch," 16.

118   Ralfe, 190–191; PRO, *Sybil* Journal, 3/10/83.

119   Kessler, 17; Clark, 301.

120   Ibid.; PRO, *Sybil* Journal, 3/10/83; ISM, BHP, "Barry's Account"; Wilbur, 50.

121   PRO, *Sybil* Journal, 3/10/83.

122   Ibid.; Brown and Kessler, 10; ISM, BHP, Ship's Log, *Alliance*, 3/11/83; "Barry's Report."

123   ISM, BHP, "Barry's Report"; Howard, 160.

124   PRO, *Sybil* Journal, 3/10/83; LOC, BHP, Letter Book, *Alliance*, Barry to Morris, 3/20/83; ISM, BHP, "Barry's Report"; Brown and Kessler, 10.

125   LOC, JBP, Letter Book, *Alliance*, Barry to Morris, 3/20/83; ISM, BHP, "Barry's Report."

126   Ibid.

127   Ibid.; RMP, 7:618, Diary, 3/21/83; Barry to Brown, 4/19/83, quoted from Griffin, 247–248.

128   *Pennsylvania Gazette*, 3/26/83; JCC, LDC, Boudinot to Pritchard, 3/23/83.

129   PRO, *Sybil* Journal, 3/10/83; HSP, Seagrove to Brown, 4/24/83; RMP, 7:424, Diary and Notes, 2/11/83.

130   *Boston Continental Journal*, 3/27/83.

EPILOGUE

1   Quoted from Fowler, 262–263; Revolutionary Diplomatic Correspondence ("RDC"), Adams to Huntington, 7/6/80.

2   RMP, 8:264, Morris to Boudinot, 7/10/83; 325, "Report to the Congress on the State of Vessels of the United States," 7/22/83; Rappleye, 371–372.

3   Ibid., 857–865, appendix 1, Early Records of Robert Morris's Involvement in American Trade with China.

4   Ibid., 16, Morris to Thomas Read, 5/8/83; 264, Morris to Boudinot, 7/10/83; 326, nn. 3 and 4; 9:194, Morris to Thomas Mifflin, 3/19/84; Fowler, *Jack Tars and Commodores*, 4–9; Griffin, 258; *Pennsylvania Gazette*, 9/21/85; JCC, 10/21/85.

5   Charles Lyon Chandler, "Early Shipping in Pennsylvania, 1683–1812," in *Phila-*

delphia: Port of History (Philadelphia: Philadelphia Maritime Museum, 1976), 26; Watson's *Annals*, 2:339; Wagner, 108.

6   RMP, 5:544, Diary, 7/8/82; Examples of Memorials are from ISM, BHP, "Barry's Memorial to the Pennsylvania Assembly," 1783; RMP, 8:247–249, "Report to Congress on the Memorial of John Jordan, James McKenzie, and Joseph Brussel," 7/5/83.

7   Ibid., "Report to Congress on the Memorial of John Jordan, James McKenzie, and Joseph Brussel," 7/5/83; Rappleye, 366–367.

8   NYHS, Barnes Collection, Barry to Barclay, 11/28/83; Barry to Anthony Wayne, 3/10/84; Wayne to Barry (no date); RMP, 8:835, Diary, 12/23/83; from Griffin, 256: "An Account of Monies paid to the Officers and Crew of the Frigate *Alliance*, and also of the net profits on sundry shares purchased for the account of Captain John Barry and John Brown," 1/12/85.

9   LOC, William Bell Clark Papers, Petition of Joanna Young, 2/23/85.

10   Quoted from Rappleye, 377; Thomas, 213.

11   J. R. Dull: "Was the Continental Navy a Mistake?" *The American Neptune*, XLIV (1984), 167–176; William S. Dudley and Michael Palmer: "No Mistake About It: A Response to Jonathan R. Dull," *The American Neptune*, XLV (1985), 244–248.

12   FDR, "Jones's Appointment as Commissioner by Washington," 6/1/92; quoted from Thomas, 300, 301, 305; Adam Goodheart, "Home Is the Sailor," *Smithsonian Magazine*, April 2006, 32–38. For more details on Jones's experiences in Russia, see the previously recommended books by Evan Thomas, Admiral Joseph Callo (Ret.), and Samuel Eliot Morison.

13   *Pennsylvania Gazette*, 2/4 and 2/5/84; 10/10 and 11/19/87; Philadelphia City Archives, Settlement Papers, Strawberry Hill, 1785; LOC, JBC, *Asia* Letter Book; Biddle, *Autobiography*, 219;

14   ISM, BHP, Henry Knox to Barry, 6/5/94; Naval Documents of the Quasi-War, 3:176–77, Benjamin Stoddert to John Adams, 5/15/99; 13–32, Stoddert to Alexander Hamilton, 5/3/99; Griffin, 412.

15   Samuel Nicholson to Barry, 6/14/93, from Griffin, 293; HSP, Barry to Nicholson, 9/4/97; NYHS, JBP, Nicholson to Barry, 1/24/99; London, 50–51.

16   RMP, 4:234, Diary, 2/14/82; 296, Morris to Jonathan Trumbull, 2/23/82; 5:10–11, Morris to Nicholson, 4/16/82; 131, Morris to Nicholson, 5/8/82; 6:3–4, Diary, 7/22/82; 388, Morris to Nicholson, 9/17/82.

17   Allen, 625; Philip C. F. Smith, 78–82, 88–90.

18   Mazet, 353–354.

19   RMP, 8:265–266, Morris to John Manley and notes, 7/10/83.

20   Fowler, *Jack Tars and Commodores*, 22; and *Silas Talbot: Captain of "Old Ironsides,"* 100–1, 219–21—recommended for those interested in Talbot's heroics.

21   Barney, 182–86; HSP, Gratz, Truxton to Stoddert, 2/9/99.

22   Ibid., 250–74, 296.

23   RMP, 5:47–48, Morris to John Hanson, 4/24/82; 7:350–357, Morris to Landais, 1/21/83; 680, 4/7/83; Thomas, 265.

24   Fowler, "Esek Hopkins," from Bradford, *Command under Sail*, 3.

25   Ibid., 15; Miller, 215–17.

26   *Fanning's Narrative*, 134–229 (quote from 194); *Dictionary of American Fighting Naval Ships* (USS *Fanning*).

27   PA Archives, "Papers of John Kessler," Mount Laurel Cemetery Records.

28   Winch, 51; Swain, ed., *Recollections, etc.*, xxxiv–xxxv.

29   *Provincial Freeman*, 8/15/1857; Winch, 3, 51; Bolster, 160.

30   Joseph LaRoche Rivers: *Some South Carolina Families* (Charleston, Published by the Author, 2005–2006), 3, 77.

31   HSP, Society Collection, Mrs. Sarah Rodney to Mrs. Sarah B. Garrette, 8/4/1825.

32   RMP, 8:554 (and footnote), Diary, 9/26/83; Rappleye, 301, 347–348; Chernow, 434.

33   Ibid., JCC, 10/11/83 and 10/13/83;

34   Neeser, 212, "Account Presented by Gustavus Conyngham," 11/1/91; 213, Alexander Hamilton to Conyngham, 7/5/93; 213–214, Conyngham's Petition to Congress, 12/8/94; 214–215, Petition of Gustavus Conyngham to Congress, 12/96/97; 216–223, "Observations on the Report of Benjamin Walker . . . on the Subject of Capt. Gustavus Conyngham's claim against the United States," no date; HSP, Gratz Collection, Letter from Conyngham to Unknown, 10/5/16; *Poulson's Advertiser*, 11/29/19.

35   Goodheart, 34–38.

36   Ibid.; Thomas, 4–5.

37   Neeser, xxii–xxiii.

BIBLIOGRAPHY

Manuscripts and Collections

Adams Family Collection, 1776–1914. Library of Congress (LOC), Washington, D.C.

Adams Papers, 1639–1889. Library of Congress, Washington, D.C.

John Adams Papers. Massachusetts Historical Society.

Samuel Adams Papers. Library of Congress, Washington, D.C.

Admiralty Records: Ships' Logs and Captains' Journals. Public Record Office ("PRO"), Kew Gardens.

American Danish Colonies Papers, 1776–84. Library of Congress, Washington, D.C.

Baptismal, Marriage, and Church Records. Archdiocese of Philadelphia, Philadelphia.

Barnes Collection. New York Historical Society ("NYHS"), New York.

John Barry Papers ("JBP"). Library of Congress, Washington, D.C.

John Barry Papers. Manuscripts and Archives Division. New York Public Library ("NYPL"), Astor, Lenox, and Tilden Foundations, New York.

The Barry Collection and Other Historical Americana. American Art Association/Anderson Galleries, Inc., New York, 1939.

Barry-Hayes Papers ("BHP"). Independence Seaport Museum ("ISM"),
    Philadelphia.
Thomas Bee Papers, 1783–1812. Library of Congress, Washington, D.C.
Biddle Family Papers. Historical Society of Philadelphia.
William Bingham Papers, 1776–1779. Library of Congress, Washington, D.C.
Elias Boudinot Papers, 1776–83. Force Transcripts. Library of Congress,
    Washington, D.C.
John Bradford Letterbooks, 1776–82. Library of Congress, Washington, D.C.
Cadwalader Collection. Historical Society of Pennsylvania, Philadelphia.
Census Records, City of Philadelphia 1790–1830. National Archives, Washington, D.C.
City of Philadelphia, Marriage Records, Manumissions, Real Estate Transactions,
    Tax Records. City of Philadelphia Records, Philadelphia.
William Bell Clark Collection, 1770–1950. Library of Congress,
    Washington, D.C.
Sir Henry Clinton Papers, 1780–92. Library of Congress, Washington, D.C.
Continental Congress, Miscellany, 1775–95. Library of Congress,
    Washington, D.C.
Correspondence of Continental Congress. Library of Congress, Washington, D.C.
Correspondence of Marine Committee. Library of Congress, Washington, D.C.
Correspondence of United States Congress. Library of Congress,
    Washington, D.C.
Tench Coxe Papers. Historical Society of Pennsylvania, Philadelphia.
Richard Dale Papers. Library of Congress, Washington, D.C.
Richard Dale Papers. Operational Archives Branch, Naval Historical Center,
    Washington, D.C.
Silas Deane Letterbooks, 1777–84, Force Transcripts. Library of Congress,
    Washington, D.C.
Charles W. F. Dumas Papers, 1775–93. Library of Congress, Washington, D.C.
Dreer Collection. Historical Society of Pennsylvania, Philadelphia.
Sol Feinstone Collection of the American Revolution, 1741–1862. David Library of
    the American Revolution, Washington Crossing, PA.
Henry Fisher Papers. Richard Rodney Collection, Delaware Historical Society,
    Wilmington.
Benjamin Franklin Papers ("BFP"). American Philosophical Society ("APS"),
    Philadelphia.
Joseph Galloway Papers, 1779–1785, Force Transcripts. Library of Congress,
    Washington, D.C.

Captain John Green Papers, Independence Seaport Museum, Philadelphia.

Papers of the Hamond Family. Special Collections Department, University of Virginia Library, Charlottesville, VA.

Hamond Naval Papers, 1766–1825. Library of Congress, Washington, D.C.

John Hancock Papers, 1774–1776. Library of Congress, Washington, D.C.

Harwood Family Papers, 1767–1940. Library of Congress, Washington, D.C.

Jean Holker Papers, 1777–1822. Library of Congress, Washington, D.C.

Francis Hopkinson Collection, 1759–65. Library of Congress, Washington, D.C.

Joshua Humphreys Collection and Correspondence. Historical Society of Pennsylvania, Philadelphia.

Humphreys Shipyard Records, 1772–1840. Independence Seaport Museum, Philadelphia.

Independence Hall Collection, 1652–1845. Library of Congress, Washington, D.C.

Mathew Irwin Papers, 1769–84. Library of Congress, Washington, D.C.

John Paul Jones Papers, 1775–88 ("JPJP"), Force Manuscripts. Library of Congress, Washington, D.C.

John Paul Jones Papers, 1776–92. Library of Congress, Washington, D.C.

John Paul Jones Papers, 1777–1817. Library of Congress, Washington, D.C.

John Kessler Papers. Pennsylvania Archives, Harrisburg.

Christopher Marshall Papers 1774–ca. 1971. Historical Society of Pennsylvania, Philadelphia.

Hector McNeill Papers, 1765–1821; and Letterbook, 1777. Massachusetts Historical Society, Boston, MA..

Robert Morris Papers. Library of Congress, Washington, D.C.

William Penn Papers. Historical Society of Pennsylvania, Philadelphia.

Pennsylvania Vice-Admiralty Court, 1735–76. Library of Congress, Washington, D.C.

Penobscot Expedition Papers, 1778–1779. Massachusetts Historical Society, Boston, MA.

Philadelphia Customs House and Tonnage Duty Books. Historical Society of Pennsylvania, Philadelphia.

Franklin Delano Roosevelt Naval Collection ("FDR"). Franklin Delano Roosevelt Library, Hyde Park, NY.

Benjamin Rush Papers, Correspondence, Ledgers, and Account Books. The Stouffer Collection. Historical Society of Pennsylvania, Philadelphia. Library Company of Philadelphia, Pennsylvania.

Navy Board of the Eastern Department Letter Book, 1778–1779, New York Public
    Library (NYPL), New York, NY.
Nathaniel Shaw Papers, 1775–82. Library of Congress, Washington, D.C.
South Carolina Collection, 1780–82. Library of Congress, Washington, D.C.
Samuel Tucker Papers, 1777–81. Library of Congress, Washington, D.C.
Nicholas Van Dyke Papers, 1780–93. Library of Congress, Washington, D.C.
George Washington Papers. Library of Congress, Washington, D.C.

Journals, Diaries, Etc.

Diary of James Allen, Esq. of Philadelphia. Historical Society of Pennsylvania,
    Philadelphia.
Anonymous American Prisoners, 1777–1779. Library of Congress, Washington,
    D.C.
John Calef's Journal, Penobscot Expedition, 1779, 1849. Maine Historical Society,
    Special Collections, transcribed by Joseph Williamson.
Elizabeth Sandwith Drinker Diaries, 1758–1807. Historical Society of
    Pennsylvania, Philadelphia.
George Philip Hooke, "Orderly Book, 17th Grs." (George Philip Hooke Journal,
    1779–1780). William L. Clements Library, University of Michigan, Orderly
    Book Collection, 1764–1815. Ann Arbor.
Christopher Marshall Diaries. Historical Society of Pennsylvania.
Robert Morton Diary, 1777–1778. Independence Seaport Museum, Philadelphia.
Peter Timothy. Journal of Observations During the Siege of Charleston. South
    Carolina Historical Society.

Miscellaneous Manuscripts

Bonhomme Richard: Photostat List of Officers, 1779. Library of Congress,
    Washington, D.C.
Gustavus Conyngham. Account of the sale of the Prize Snow *Fanny*, 1778. Library
    of Congress, Washington, D.C.
George Gefferina. Conduct of Vice-Admiral Graves in North America in 1774,
    1775, and January 1776 [transcript], 1777.

Peter (Pierre) Landais. Photostats of Accounts and Letters, 1782–85. Library of
   Congress, Washington, D.C.
United States Navy. Miscellany, 1776–1909. Library of Congress,
   Washington, D.C.
———. Prizes and Captures, 1775–1776. Library of Congress, Washington, D.C.

Books and Compilations

Adams, Charles Francis. *The Works of John Adams.* Vols. 8–10. Boston: Little,
   Brown, 1853.
Adams, John. *Diary and Autobiography of John Adams.* Ed. H. Butterfield. Vols. 1–4.
   Cambridge, MA: Belknap, 1961.
Adams, Russell B., ed. *The Revolutionaries.* New York: Time–Life Books, 1996.
Alberts, Robert C. *The Golden Voyage: The Life and Times of William Bingham,
   1752–1804.* Boston: Houghton Mifflin, 1969.
Allen, Gardner W. *A Naval History of the American Revolution.* Boston: Houghton
   Mifflin, 1913.
———. *Captain Hector McNeill of the Continental Navy.* Boston: Harvard University
   Press, 1922.
Almon, J., ed. *The Rembrancer, or Impartial Repository of Public Events.* London,
   1776–1783.
Alsop, Susan Mary. *Yankees at the Court: The First Americans in Paris.* Garden City,
   NY: Doubleday, 1982.
Appleton, D. *Appleton's Cyclopedia of American Biography.* New York: D. Appleton,
   1900.
Augur, Helen. *The Secret War of Independence.* New York: Duell Little, 1955.
Barney, Mary, ed. *Biographical Memoir of the Late Commander Joshua Barney.*
   Boston: Gray and Bowen, 1832.
Barnes, John S., ed. *The Logs of the* Serapis, Alliance, *and* Ariel. New York: Naval
   History Society, 1896.
Bartlett, John Russell, ed. *Records of the State of Rhode Island and Providence
   Plantations in New England.* Vol. 8. Providence: Cooke, Jackson and Co., 1863.
Beck, Alverda S., ed. *The Correspondence of Esek Hopkins, Commander-in-Chief of the
   United States Navy . . . in the Library of the Rhode Island Historical Society.*
   Providence: Rhode Island Historical Society, 1933.
———. *The Letter Book of Esek Hopkins, Commander-in-Chief of the United States*

Navy, 1775–1777 . . . in the Library of the Rhode Island Historical Society. Providence: Rhode Island Historical Society, 1932.

Biddle, James S., ed. *Autobiography of Charles Biddle, Vice-President of the Supreme Executive Council of Pennsylvania, 1745–1821.* Philadelphia: E. Claxton and Co., 1883.

Billias, George Athan. *General John Glover and His Marblehead Mariners.* New York: Holt, Rhinehart & Winston, 1960.

Bolster, W. Jeffrey. *Black Jacks: African American Seamen in the Age of Sail.* Cambridge, MA: Harvard University Press, 1997.

Boudriot, Jean. *John Paul Jones and the* Bonhomme Richard. Annapolis, MD: Naval Institute Press, 1987.

Bowen–Hassell, E. Gordon, Dennis M. Conrad, and Mark L. Hayes. *Sea Raiders of the American Revolution: The Continental Navy in European Waters.* Washington, D.C.: Department of the Navy, 2003.

Bradford, James C. *John Paul Jones and the American Navy.* New York: Rosen Publishing Group, 2002.

———. *Command Under Sail: Makers of the American Naval Tradition, 1775–1850.* Annapolis, MD: Naval Institute Press, 1985.

Brands, H. W. *The First American: The Life and Times of Benjamin Franklin.* New York: Anchor Books, 2000.

Breen, T. H. *The Marketplace of Revolution.* New York: Oxford University Press, 2004.

Brodie, Faun M. *Thomas Jefferson: An Intimate History.* New York: Norton, 1974.

Brodsky, Alyn. *Benjamin Rush: Patriot and Physician.* New York: St. Martin's, 2004.

Brown, John Howard. *American Naval Heroes, 1775–1812–1861–1898.* Edited by Gertrude Battles Lane. Boston: Brown and Co., 1899.

Butterfield, Lyman Henry, ed. *Diary and Autobiography of John Adams.* Vol. 3. Cambridge, MA: Harvard University Press, 1961.

———. *Letters of Benjamin Rush.* Vol. 2. Princeton, NJ: Princeton University Press, 1951.

Callo, Joseph. *John Paul Jones: America's First Sea Warrior.* Annapolis, MD: Naval Institute Press, 2006.

Campbell, Charles F. *The Intolerable Hulks: British Shipboard Confinement, 1776–1857.* Bowie, MD: Heritage Books, 1994.

Carp, Benjamin L. *Defiance of the Patriots: The Boston Tea Party and the Making of America.* New Haven, CT: Yale University Press, 2010.

Carretta, Vincent. *Phillis Wheatley: Biography of a Genius in Bondage.* Athens: University of Georgia Press, 2011.

Carse, Robert. *Ports of Call.* New York: Charles Scribner's Sons, 1967.

Catanzariti, John, and E. James Ferguson, eds. *The Papers of Robert Morris.* Vols. 1–8 ("RMP"). Pittsburgh: University of Pittsburgh Press, 1984.

Chandler, Charles Lyon. "Early Shipping in Pennsylvania, 1683–1812." In *Philadelphia: Port of History.* Philadelphia: Philadelphia Maritime Museum, 1976.

Chappelle, Howard I. *The American Sailing Navy.* New York: Bonanza, 1949.

Chernow, Ron. *Alexander Hamilton.* New York: Penguin, 2004.

———. *Washington: A Life.* New York: Penguin, 2010.

Churchill, Winston S. *The Age of Revolution.* Vol. 3. New York: Dodd, Mead, 1957.

Clark, William Bell. *Ben Franklin's Privateers: A Naval Epic of the American Revolution.* Baton Rouge: Louisiana State University Press, 1956.

———. *Captain Dauntless: The Story of Nicholas Biddle of the Continental Navy.* Baton Rouge: Louisiana State University Press, 1949.

———. *The First Saratoga: Being the Saga of John Young and His Sloop-of-War.* Baton Rouge: Louisiana State University Press, 1953.

———. *Gallant John Barry.* New York: Macmillan, 1938.

———. *George Washington's Navy: Being an Account of His Excellency's Fleet in New England Waters.* Baton Rouge: Louisiana State University Press, 1960.

———. *Lambert Wickes, Sea Raider and Diplomat.* New Haven, CT: Macmillan, 1932.

Clark, William Bell, William James Morgan, and Michael J. Crawford, eds. *Naval Documents of the American Revolution.* Vols. 1–11 ("NDAR"). Annapolis, MD: U.S. Navy, 1964–2007.

Coggins, Jack. *Ships and Seamen of the American Revolution: Vessels, Crews, Weapons, Gear, Naval Tactics, and Actions of the War for Independence.* Harrisburg, PA: Stackpole Books, 1969.

Cohen, Sheldon S. *Commodore Abraham Whipple of the Continental Navy: Privateer, Patriot, Pioneer.* Gainesville: University Press of Florida, 2010.

———. *Yankee Sailors in British Gaols: Prisoners of War at Forton and Mill 1777–1783.* Newark, DE: University of Delaware Press, 1995.

Coleman, Eleanor S. *Captain Gustavus Conyngham, U.S.N., Pirate or Privateer, 1747–1819.* Washington, D.C.: University Press of America, 1982.

Coletta, Paolo, ed. *American Secretaries of the Navy.* Vol. 1. Annapolis, MD: Naval Institute Press, 1980.

Connolly, S. J. *Religion, Law, and Power: The Making of Protestant Ireland, 1660–1760.* Oxford, UK: Oxford University Press, 1992.

Cook, Fred J. *What Manner of Men: Forgotten Heroes of the American Revolution.* New York: William Morrow, 1959.

Cooper, James Fenimore. *History of the Navy of the United States of America.* Vols. 1–2. Philadelphia: Lea and Blanchard, 1840.

Cordingly, David. *Under the Black Flag.* New York: Harcourt Brace, 1995.

———. *Women Sailors and Sailors' Women: An Untold Maritime History.* New York: Random House, 2001.

Corner, George W., ed. *The Autobiography of Benjamin Rush: His "Travels Through Life" Together with His Commonplace Book for 1789–1813.* Westport, CT: Greenwood Press, 1970.

Crane, Elaine Forman, ed. *The Diary of Elizabeth Drinker.* Vols. 2–3. Boston: Northeastern University Press, 1991.

Crawford, Michael J., ed. *The Autobiography of a Yankee Mariner: Christopher Prince and the American Revolution.* Dulles, VA: Brassey's, 2002.

Dann, John C. *Revolution Remembered: Eyewitness Accounts of the War for Independence.* Chicago: University of Chicago Press, 1980.

Daughan, George C. *If by Sea: The Forging of the American Navy—From the American Revolution to the War of 1812.* New York: Basic Books, 2008.

Davis, Allen F., and Mark H. Haller, ed. *The Peoples of Philadelphia: A History of Ethnic Groups and Lower-Class Life.* Philadelphia: Temple University Press, 1973.

De Koven, Mrs. Reginald (Anna). *The Life and Letters of John Paul Jones.* Vols. 1–2. New York: Charles Scribner's Sons, 1913.

Doerflinger, Thomas M. *A Vigorous Spirit of Enterprise.* Chapel Hill: University of North Carolina Press, 1986.

Dorson, Richard M., ed. *Patriots of the American Revolution.* New York: Gramercy Books, 1953.

Dring, Thomas. *Recollections of Life Aboard the Prison Ship Jersey in 1782.* Edited by David Swain. Yardley, PA: Westholme, 2010.

Dudley, William S., and Michael J. Crawford, eds. *The Early Republic and the Sea.* Dulles, VA: Brassey's, 2001.

Dull, Jonathan R. *A Diplomatic History of the American Revolution.* New Haven, CT: Yale University Press, 1985.

———. *The French Navy and American Independence: A Study of Arms and Diplomacy, 1774–1787.* Princeton, NJ: Princeton University Press, 1975.

Ellis, Joseph J. *American Sphinx: The Character of Thomas Jefferson.* New York: Knopf, 1998.

——. *Founding Brothers.* New York: Knopf, 2000.

——. *His Excellency, George Washington.* New York: Knopf, 2004.

Engle, Eloise, and Arnold S. Scott. *America's Maritime Heritage.* Annapolis, MD: Naval Institute Press, 1975.

Fairburn, William Armstrong. *Merchant Sail.* Vol. 1. Center Lowell, ME: Fairburn Marine Educational Foundation, 1945.

Fanning, Nathaniel. *Fanning's Narrative: Being the Memoirs of Nathaniel Fanning, an Officer of the American Navy 1778–1783.* New York: 1806, 1808, Reprinted by William Abbatt, 1913.

Ferguson, Eugene S. *Truxton of the Constellation.* Annapolis, MD: Naval Institute Press, 1956.

Fischer, David Hackett. *Paul Revere's Ride.* New York: Oxford University Press, 1994.

——. *Washington's Crossing.* New York: Oxford University Press, 2004.

Fleming, Thomas. *Liberty.* New York: Viking, 1997.

——. *Now We Are Enemies: The Story of Bunker Hill.* New York: St. Martin's, 1960.

Flexner, James Thomas. *Washington: The Indispensable Man.* New York: Little, Brown, 1969.

Footner, Hulbert. *Sailor of Fortune: The Life and Adventures of Commodore Barney, USN.* New York: Harper and Brothers, 1940.

Ford, Worthington C., ed. *The Journals of the Continental Congress* ("JCC"). 34 vols. Washington, D.C.: U.S. Government Printing Office, 1904–1937.

Fowler, William M., Jr. *The Baron of Beacon Hill: A Biography of John Hancock.* Boston: Houghton Mifflin, 1980.

——. *A Gentlemanly and Honorable Profession: The Creation of the U.S. Naval Officer Corps, 1794–1815.* Annapolis, MD: Naval Institute Press, 1991.

——. *Jack Tars and Commodores: The American Navy, 1783–1815.* Boston: Houghton Mifflin, 1984.

——. *Rebels Under Sail: The American Navy During the Revolution.* New York: Scribner's, 1976.

——. *Silas Talbot: Captain of Old Ironsides.* Mystic, CT: Mystic Seaport Museum, 1995.

Fraser, Robert, Esq. *Statistical Survey of the County of Wexford.* Dublin: Graiseberry and Campbell, 1807.

Freidenberg, Zachary B. *Medicine Under Sail.* Annapolis, MD: Naval Institute Press, 2002.

Frey, Sylvia R. *Water from the Rock: Black Resistance in a Revolutionary Age.* Princeton, NJ: Princeton University Press, 1991.

Gawalt, Gerard W., ed. *John Paul Jones' Memoir of the American Revolution Presented to King Louis XVI of France.* Washington, D.C.: Library of Congress, 1979.

Gilje, Paul E. *Liberty on the Waterfront: American Maritime Culture in the Age of Revolution.* Philadelphia: University of Pennsylvania Press, 2004.

Gilkerson, William. *The Ships of John Paul Jones.* Annapolis, MD: Naval Institute Press, 1987.

Gillespie, Joanna Bowen. *The Life and Times of Martha Laurens Ramsay.* Columbia: University of South Carolina Press, 2001.

Giunta, Mary, ed. *The Emerging Nation: A Documentary History of the Foreign Relations of the United States Under the Articles of Confederation, 1780–1789.* Vols. 1–3. Washington, D.C.: National Historical Publications and Records Commission, 1996.

Goodrich, Reverend Charles A. *Lives of the Signers to the Declaration of Independence.* New York: William Reed & Co., 1856.

Gough, Deborah Matthias. *Christ Church, Philadelphia.* Philadelphia: University of Pennsylvania Press, 1995.

Green, Ezra, *Diary of Ezra Green, M.D.* Edited by George Henry Preble and Walter C. Green. Boston, 1875.

Griffin, Martin I. J. *The History of Commodore John Barry.* Philadelphia: American Catholic Historical Society, 1897.

Griffiths, George, ed. *Chronicles of the County Wexford to the Year 1777.* Enniscorthy, 1902.

Gurn, Joseph. *Commodore John Barry.* New York: P. J. Kennedy and Sons, 1933.

Hastings, George Everett. *The Life and Works of Francis Hopkinson.* Chicago: University of Chicago Press, 1926.

Hawke, David Freeman. *Everyday Life in Early America.* New York: Harper and Row, 1988.

Henkel, S. V., ed. *The Confidential Correspondence of Robert Morris: The Great Financier of the Revolution and Signer of the Declaration of the Independence.* Philadelphia: S. V. Henkel, 1917.

Hill, Frederic Stanhope. *Twenty-six Historic Ships.* New York: G. P. Putnam's Sons, 1903.

Howard, James L. *Seth Harding, Mariner.* New Haven, CT: Yale University Press, 1930.

Howe, Admiral Lord. *Reflections on a Pamphlet Entitled "A Letter to the Right Honble. Lord Vict. H—E."* Edited by Gerald Saxon Brown. Ann Arbor: University of Michigan Press, 1959.

Illich, Joseph E. *Colonial Pennsylvania—A History.* New York: Charles Scribner's Sons, 1976.

Ireland, Bernard. *Naval Warfare in the Age of Sail: War at Sea, 1756–1815.* New York: Norton, 2000.

Isaacson, Walter. *Benjamin Franklin: An American Life.* New York: Simon and Schuster, 2003.

Jackson, Donald, and Dorothy Twohig, eds. *The Diaries of George Washington.* Vol. 6. Charlottesville: University Press of Virginia, 1979.

Jackson, John W. *The Delaware Bay and River Defenses of Philadelphia, 1775–1777.* Philadelphia: Philadelphia Maritime Museum, 1977.

———. *The Pennsylvania Navy, 1775–1781: The Defense of the Delaware.* New Brunswick, NJ: Rutgers University Press, 1974.

———. *With the British Army in Philadelphia.* San Rafael, CA: Presidio Press, 1974.

James, William M. *The British Navy in Adversity: A Study of the War of American Independence.* London: Longmans, Green, 1926.

Jefferson, Thomas. *Writings.* New York: Library of America, 1984.

Jones, Charles Henry. *Captain Gustavus Conyngham: A Sketch of the Services He Rendered to the Cause of American Independence.* Philadelphia: Pennsylvania Society of Sons of the Revolution, 1903.

Katz, William Loren. *Eyewitness: A Living Documentary of the African-American Contribution to American History.* New York: Touchstone, 1995.

Keane, John. *Tom Paine: A Political Life.* New York: Grove Press, 1995.

Kennedy, John F. *Profiles in Courage.* New York: Inaugural Edition, Harper and Row, 1961.

Kevitt, Chester B. *General Solomon Lovell and the Penobscot Expedition 1779.* Weymouth, MA: Weymouth Historical Commission, 1976.

Kiernan, Denise, and Joseph D'Agnese. *Signing Their Lives Away: The Fame and Misfortune of the Men Who Signed the Declaration of Independence.* Philadelphia: Quick Books, 2009.

King, Dean, and John B. Hattendorf. *Harbors and High Seas.* New York: Henry Holt, 1996.

———, John B. Hattendorf, and J. Worth Estes. *A Sea of Words.* New York: Henry Holt, 1995.

Klepp, Susan E., and Billy G. Smith, eds. *The Infortunate: The Voyage and Adventures of William Moraley and Indentured Servant.* University Park: Pennsylvania State University Press, 1992.

Knight, Roger. *The Pursuit of Victory: The Life and Achievement of Horatio Nelson.* New York: Basic Books, 2005.

Knox, Dudley W., Capt., ed. *Naval Documents Related to the Quasi-War Between the United States and France.* Vols. 1–7. Washington, D.C.: U.S. Government Printing Office, 1935–37.

———. *Naval Documents Related to the United States Wars with the Barbary Powers.* Vols. 1–3. Washington, D.C.: U.S. Government Printing Office, 1939.

———. *The Naval Genius of George Washington.* Boston: Houghton Mifflin, 1932.

Labaree, Benjamin Woods. *The Boston Tea Party.* New York: Oxford University Press, 1964.

Lacour–Gayet, Georges. *La Marine Militaire de la France sous le règne de Louis XVI.* Paris: H. Champion, 1905.

Lafayette, Marquis de. *Lafayette in the Age of Revolution: Selected Letters and Papers,* Vols. 2–3. Edited by Stanley J. Idzerda. Ithaca, NY: Cornell University Press, 1979, 1980.

Lancaster, Bruce C. *The American Revolution.* Boston: Houghton Mifflin, 1971.

Landais, Pierre. *Memorial to Justify Peter Landais' Conduct During the Late War.* Boston: Edes, 1784.

Lanning, Lt. Col. Michael Lee (Ret.). *Defenders of Liberty: African Americans in the Revolutionary War.* New York: Citadel Press, 2000.

Lavery, Brian. *The Arming and Fitting of English Ships of War, 1600–1815.* London: Conway Maritime Press, 1987.

Lewis, Charles L. *Admiral de Grasse and American Independence.* Annapolis, MD: Naval Institute Press, 1945.

Lincoln, Charles Henry, ed. *Naval Records of the American Revolution, 1775–1788.* Washington, D.C.: Government Printing Office, 1906.

Log of the Bonhomme Richard. Mystic, CT: Marine Historical Association, 1936.

Lorenz, Lincoln. *John Paul Jones: Fighter for Freedom and Glory.* Annapolis, MD: Naval Institute Press, 1943.

Mahan, Alfred Thayer. *The Influence of Sea Power upon History, 1660–1783.* New York: Dover, 1987.

Marryat, Frederick. *Mr. Midshipman Easy.* New York: Henry Holt, 1998.

———. *Peter Simple.* London: Dent, 1970.

Maurice, Sir John Frederick, K. C. B. *The Diary of Sir John Moore,* Vol. I. London: Edward Arnold, 1904.

McCullough, David. *John Adams*. New York: Simon and Schuster, 2001.

———. *1776*. New York: Simon and Schuster, 2005.

McGrath, Tim. *John Barry: An American Hero in the Age of Sail*. Yardley, PA: Westholme Publishing, 2010.

Melville, Herman. *White Jacket*. New York: New American Library, 1979.

Metzger, Charles H. *The Prisoner in the American Revolution*. Chicago: Loyola University Press, 1971.

Millar, John F. *American Ships of the Colonial and Revolutionary Periods*. New York: Norton, 1978.

Miller, Nathan. *Sea of Glory: The Naval History of the American Revolution*. Charleston, SC: Nautical and Publishing Co. of America, 1974.

Mitchell, Carleton. *Isles of the Caribbees*. Washington, D.C.: National Geographic Society, 1986.

Moebs, Thomas Truxton. *Black Soldiers, Black Sailor, Black Ink: Research Guide on African-Americans in U.S. Military History 1526–1900*. Chesapeake Bay: Moebs Publishing Company, 1994.

Montgomery, Elizabeth. *Reminiscences of Wilmington, Delaware*. Wilmington, DE: Johnston and Bogia, 1872.

Morgan, William James. *Captains to the Northward: Captains of the Continental Navy*. Barre, MA: Barre Gazette, 1959.

Morison, Samuel Eliot. *John Paul Jones: A Sailor's Biography*. Annapolis, MD: Naval Institute Press, 1989.

Morris, Robert. *The Confidential Correspondence of Robert Morris*. Philadelphia: Kessinger Publishing, 1917.

Nagy, John A. *Rebellion in the Ranks: Mutinies of the American Revolution*. Yardley, PA: Westholme Publishing, 2008.

Nash, Gary B. *First City*. Philadelphia: University of Pennsylvania Press, 2002.

———. *The Forgotten Fifth: African Americans in the Age of Revolution*. Cambridge, MA: Harvard University Press, 2006.

Neeser, Robert Wilden, ed. *Letters and Papers Related to the Cruises of Gustavus Conyngham: A Captain of the Continental Navy*. New York: Printed for the Naval Historical Society by the DeVinne Press, 1915.

Nelson, James L. *Benedict Arnold's Navy: The Ragtag Fleet That Lost the Battle of Lake Champlain but Won the American Revolution*. New York: McGraw Hill, 2006.

———. *George Washington's Secret Navy: How the American Revolution Went to Sea*. New York: McGraw Hill, 2008

Norton, Louis Arthur. *Joshua Barney: Hero of the Revolution and 1812*. Annapolis, MD: Naval Institute Press, 2000.

O'Connor, Raymond G. *Origins of the American Navy: Sea Power in the Colonies and the New Nation*. Lanham, MD: University Press of America, 1994.

O'Neill, Richard, ed. *Patrick O'Brian's Navy*. London: Salamander Books, 2003.

Palmer, Michael A. *Command at Sea: Naval Command and Control Since the Sixteenth Century*. Cambridge, MA: Harvard University Press, 2005.

Paullin, Charles Oscar. *The Navy of the American Revolution: Its Administration, Its Policy, and Its Achievements*. Cleveland: Burrows, 1906.

———. *Out-Letters of the Continental Marine Committee and Board of Admiralty*. Vols. 1–2. New York: Devinne Press, 1914.

Peckham, Howard H. *The War for Independence: A Military History*. Chicago: University of Chicago Press, 1958.

Phipps, Constantine John. *A Voyage Towards the North Pole Undertaken by His Majesty's Command, 1773*. London: W. Bowyer and J. Nichols for J. Nourse, Bookseller to His Majesty, in the Strand, 1774.

Peterson, Robert A. *Patriots, Pirates, and Pineys*. Medford, NJ: Plexus, 1998.

Pope, Dudley. *Life in Nelson's Navy*. London: Chatham, 1981.

Quarles, Benjamin. *The Negro in the American Revolution*. New York: Norton, 1973.

Rappleye, Charles. *Robert Morris: Financier of the American Revolution*. New York: Simon and Schuster, 2010.

Ralfe, James. *Naval Biography of Great Britain*. Vols. 2–3. Boston: Gregg Press, 1972.

Ranby, John. *The Method of Treating Gunshot Wounds*. 2nd ed. London: Robert Horsfield, 1760.

Randall, William Sterne. *George Washington: A Life*. New York: Henry Holt, 1997.

Rediker. Marcus. *Between the Devil and the Deep Blue Sea: Merchant Seamen, Pirates, and the Anglo-American Maritime World, 1700–1750*. Cambridge, UK: Cambridge University Press, 1987.

Rivers, Joseph LaRoche. *Some South Carolina Families*. Charleston, Published by the Author, 2005–2006.

Ross, J. E., ed. *Radical Adventurer: The Diaries of Robert Morris, 1772–1774*. Bath, UK: Adams and Dart, 1971.

Sands, John O. *Yorktown's Captive Fleet*. Charlottesville: University Press of Virginia, 1983.

Sandwich, John Montague, 4th Earl. *The Private Papers of John, Earl of Sandwich, First Lord of the Admiralty, 1777–1782*. Edited by G. R. Barnes and J. H. Owen. London: Navy Records Society, 1932–38.

Sawtelle, Joseph G., ed. *John Paul Jones and the* Ranger. Portsmouth, NH: Peter Randall, 1994.

Scharf, J. Thomas, and Thompson Westcott, eds. *The History of Philadelphia.* Vols. 1–2. Philadelphia: Everts and Co., 1884.

Schiff, Stacy. *A Great Improvisation: Franklin, France, and the Birth of America.* New York: Henry Holt, 2005.

Seitz, Don C. *Paul Jones: His Exploits in English Seas During 1778–1780.* New York: Dutton, 1917.

Sherburne, John Henry. *Life and Character of John Paul Jones.* New York: Wilder and Campbell, 1825.

Smelser, Marshall. *The Congress Founds the Navy.* Notre Dame, IN: University of Notre Dame Press, 1959.

Smith, Charles R. *Marines in the Revolution: A History of the Continental Marines in the American Revolution, 1775–1783.* Illustrated by Charles H. Waterhouse, USMCR. Washington, D.C.: U.S. Marine Corps, History and Museums Division, 1975.

Smith, Paul H., ed. *Letters of Delegates to Congress, 1774–1789* ("LDC"). 26 vols. Washington, D.C.: U.S. Government Printing Office, 1976–2000.

Smith, Philip Chadwick Foster. *The Empress of China.* Philadelphia: Philadelphia Maritime Museum, 1984.

———. *Fired by Manley Zeal: A Naval Fiasco of the American Revolution.* Salem, MA: Peabody Museum of Salem, 1977.

Starbuck, Alexander. *History of Nantucket.* Rutland, VT: Tuttler, 1969; 1st ed., Boston: Godspeed, 1924.

State Papers and Publick Documents of the United States: From the Accession of George Washington to the Presidency, Exhibiting a Complete View of Our Foreign Relations Since That Time 1789–1796. Boston: T. H. Wait and Sons, 1815.

Stout, Neil R. *The Royal Navy in America, 1760–1775: A Study of Enforcement of British Colonial Policy in the Era of the American Revolution.* Annapolis, MD: Naval Institute Press, 1973.

Symonds, Craig L. *Decision at Sea: Five Naval Battles That Shaped American History.* New York: Oxford University Press, 2005.

———. *Historical Atlas of the U.S. Navy.* William J. Klipson, Cartographer. Annapolis, MD: Naval Institute Press, 1995.

———. *Navalists and Anti-Navalists: The Naval Policy Debate in the United State, 1785–1827.* Newark, DE: University of Delaware Press, 1980.

Syrett, David. *The Royal Navy in American Waters, 1775–1783*. Aldershot, Eng.: Scolar Press, 1989.

———. *The Royal Navy in European Waters During the American Revolutionary War*. Charleston: University of South Carolina Press, 1998.

———. *Shipping and the American War, 1775–83: A Study of British Transport Organization*. London: University of London, Athlone Press, 1970.

Taaffe, Stephen R. *The Philadelphia Campaign, 1777–1778*. Lawrence: University Press of Kansas, 2003.

Taillemite, Étienne. *Archives de la Marine, Série B*. Paris: Imprimerie Nationale, 1969.

Thomas, Evan. *John Paul Jones*. New York: Simon and Schuster, 2003.

Tuchman, Barbara. *The First Salute*. New York: Knopf, 1988.

Tyler, David Bradley. *The Bay and River Delaware: An Illustrated History*. Cambridge: Cornell Maritime Press, 1955.

Urwin, Gregory J. *The U.S. Cavalry: An Illustrated History*. Oklahoma City: University of Oklahoma Press, 1983.

———. *The U.S. Infantry: An Illustrated History*. Oklahoma City: University of Oklahoma Press, 1988.

U.S. Naval History Division. *The American Revolution, 1775–1783: An Atlas of 18th Century Maps and Charts: Theaters of Operations*. Compiled by W. Bart Greenwood. Washington, D.C.: Government Printing Office, 1972.

Van Powell, Noland. *The American Navies of the Revolutionary War*. New York: G. P. Putnam's Sons, 1974.

Wagner, Frederick. *Robert Morris: Audacious Patriot*. New York: Dodd, Mead, 1973.

Watson, John F. *Annals of Philadelphia Peoples*, Vols. 1 and 2. Philadelphia: Edwin Stuart, 1887.

Weigley, Russell, ed. *Philadelphia: A 300-Year History*. New York: Norton, 1982.

Wharton, Francis, ed. *The Revolutionary Diplomatic Correspondence of the United States* ("RDC"). 6 vols. Washington, D.C.: Government Printing Office, 1889.

Wheeler, George A. *History of Castine, Penobscot, and Brooksville, Maine*. Bangor: Burns and Robinson, 1875.

Whinyates, Colonel F. A., ed. *The Services of Lieut.-Colonel Francis Dowman, R.A. in France, North America, and the West Indies. Between the Years 1758 and 1784*. Woolwich: Royal Artillery Institution, 1898.

Wilbur, C. Keith, M.D. *Pirates and Patriots of the Revolution*. Guilford, CT: Globe Pequot Press, 1973.

———. *Revolutionary Medicine 1700–1800*. Guilford, CT: Globe Pequot Press, 1973.

Winch, Julie. *A Gentleman of Color: The Life of James Forten*. New York: Oxford University Press, 2002.

Wolf, Stephanie Grauman. *As Various as Their Land*. New York: Knopf, 1988.

Wood, Virginia Steel. *Live Oaking: Southern Timber for Tall Ships*. Boston: Northeastern University Press, 1981.

Young, Eleanor. *Robert Morris: Forgotten Patriot*. New York: Macmillan, 1950.

Zacks, Richard. *The Pirate Hunter*. New York: Hyperion, 2002.

Articles and Presentations

Alberts, Robert C. "Business of the Highest Magnitude." *American Heritage Magazine* 22, no. 2 (February 1971).

Allen, Jane E. "Lying at the Port of Philadelphia Vessel Types 1725–75." *American Neptune* 53, no. 3 (Summer 1993).

Anderson, William Gary. "John Adams and the Creation of the American Navy." Ph.D. diss., State University of New York at Stony Brook, May 1975.

Atkinson, Amalia. "Captain Rathbun's Last Voyage." *New England Historical and Genealogical Register* 115 (July 1961).

Barnett, Richard C. "The View from Below Deck: The British Navy, 1777–1781." *American Neptune*, April 1978.

Baugh, Daniel A. "The Politics of British Naval Failure, 1775–1777." *American Neptune*, July 1982.

Baurmeister, Carl. "Letters of Major Baurmeister During the Philadelphia Campaign, 1777–1778." *Pennsylvania Magazine of History and Biography* 60 (1935).

Bolander, Louis H. "The Frigate *Alliance*, the Favorite Ship of the American Revolution." *U.S. Naval Institute Proceedings*, July 1928.

———. "The Log of the Ranger." *U.S. Naval Institute Proceedings*, February 1936.

Bradford, James C. "The Navies of the American Revolution." In *Peace and War: Interpretations of American Naval History*, edited by Kenneth J. Hagan. 2nd ed. Westport, CT: Greenwood, 1984. Print.

Breen, Kenneth C. "A Reinforcement Reduced? Rodney's Flawed Appraisal of French Plans, West Indies, 1781." In *New Interpretations in Naval History: Selected Papers from the Ninth Naval History Symposium*, edited by

William R. Roberts and Jack Sweetman. Annapolis, MD: Naval Institute Press, 1991.

Brewington, Marion V. "American Naval Guns, 1775–1785." *American Neptune* 3 (1943): 11–18, 148–158. Print.

———. "The Designs of Our First Frigates." *American Neptune* 8 (1948): 11–25. Print.

———. "Maritime Philadelphia 1609–1837." *Pennsylvania Magazine of History and Biography* 63 (1938). Print.

———. "Signal Systems and Ship Identification." *American Neptune*, July 1943.

Bronner, Edwin H. "Village into Town, 1701–1746," in *Philadelphia: A 300-Year History*, edited by Russell Weigley. New York: Norton, 1982.

Brown, John, and John Kessler. "American Biography: The Life of Commodore Barry." *Portfolio Magazine* (July 1813).

Bruns, Craig. "William Rush, Ship Carver." A research document of Rush's works assembled by Craig Bruns with contributions by Daniel N. Train and John Brown. Independence Seaport Museum, Philadelphia, 2000.

Buell, Augustus C. "Narrative of John Kilby." *Scribner's*, July 1905.

Callo, Rear Admiral Joseph F., U.S. Naval Reserve (Retired). "A New Look at John Paul Jones." *U.S. Naval Institute Proceedings*, May 2013.

Chandler, Charles Lyon. "Early Shipping in Pennsylvania, 1683–1812." In *Philadelphia: Port of History*. Philadelphia: Philadelphia Maritime Museum, 1976.

Clark, William Bell. "A Forgotten Investment of John Paul Jones." *Pennsylvania Magazine of History and Biography* 77 (1952).

———. "Letters of Captain Nicholas Biddle." *Pennsylvania Magazine of History and Biography* 74 (1950).

———. "James Josiah, Master Mariner." *Pennsylvania Magazine of History and Biography* 79 (1954).

———. "The Sea Captains Club." *Pennsylvania Magazine of History and Biography* 81 (1956).

Conyngham, D. H. "Reminiscence." Proceedings and Collections of the Wyoming Historical Society 8 (1904).

Cooper, James Fenimore. "Sketches of Naval Men: John Barry." *Graham's Magazine*, 1839.

Craig, Michelle L. "Grounds for Debate? The Place of the Caribbean Provisions Trade in Philadelphia's Pre-Revolutionary Economy." *Pennsylvania Magazine of History and Biography* 129 (April 2004).

Crawford, Michael J. "Naval Administration under Robert Morris." Paper presented at the conference "Founding Financier Robert Morris," New York, April 7, 2000.

———. "The Privateering Debate in Revolutionary America." *Northern Mariner* 21, no. 3 (July 2011).

Dale, Richard. "Biographical Memoir of Richard Dale." *Portfolio Magazine* 3, no. 6 (June 1814).

Dudley, William S., and Michael A. Palmer. "No Mistake About It: A Response to Jonathan R. Dull." *American Neptune*, XLV (1985).

Dull, Jonathan R. "Was the Continental Navy a Mistake?" *American Neptune*, XLIV (1984).

Egnal, Marc. "The Changing Structure of Philadelphia's Trade with the British West Indies, 1759–1775." *Pennsylvania Magazine of History and Biography* 99 (1974).

Eller, Ernest M. "Sea Power in the American Revolution." *U.S. Naval Proceedings* 62 (June 1936).

Everett, Barbara. "John Barry, Fighting Irishman." *American History Illustrated* 12, no. 8 (December 1977).

"Extracts from the Diary of Jacob Hiltzheimer, of Philadelphia 1768–1798." *Pennsylvania Magazine of History and Biography* 16 (1892).

Feldman, Clayton A. "Continental Navy Brigantine Lexington (1776–1777): Deriving New Plans from Original Data." *Nautical Research Journal* 49, no. 2 (2004).

Fowler, William M., Jr. "The Business of War: Boston as a Naval Base, 1776–1783." *American Neptune*, January 1982.

———. "Esek Hopkins: Commander-in-Chief of the Continental Navy." In *Command Under Sail: Makers of the Naval Tradition 1775–1850*, edited by James C. Bradford. Annapolis, MD: Naval Institute Press, 1985.

———. "James Nicholson and the Continental Frigate *Virginia*." *American Neptune*, April 1973.

Fraser, Megan Hahn. "Barry-Hayes Papers Overview." Independence Seaport Museum, 2006.

———. "Guide to the Barry–Hayes Papers." Independence Seaport Museum, 2003–2004.

Gates, Henry Louis, Jr. "The Trials of Phillis Wheatley." Thomas Jefferson Lecture in the Humanities, delivered at the Library of Congress, 2002.

Goodheart, Adam. "Home Is the Sailor . . ." *Smithsonian* Magazine, April 2006.

Goold, Nathan. "Colonel Jonathan Mitchell's Cumberland County Regiment." Paper presented to the Maine Historical Society, October 27, 1898.

———. "Captain Henry Mowat's 'Relation,' and Biographical and Topographical Notes." *The Magazine of History with Notes and Queries*, Extra Number – No. 11 (New York: William Abbatt, 1910).

Grant, Captain Patrick, U.S. Navy (Ret.). "The Resurrection of John Paul Jones." *Naval History*, February 2012.

Guba, Emil Frederick. "Revolutionary War Service Roll." *Historic Nantucket*, July 1963.

Hayes, Frederick H. "John Adams and American Sea Power." *American Neptune*, January 1965.

Hildeburn, Charles R. "Francis Hopkinson." *Pennsylvania Magazine of History and Biography* 2 (1877).

Humphreys, Col. Henry H. "Who Built the First United States Navy?" *Pennsylvania Magazine of History and Biography* 40 (1915).

"John Paul Jones at Bethlehem, Penna., 1783." *Pennsylvania Magazine of History and Biography* 39 (1915).

Keen, Gregory. "The Descendants of Jöran Kyn: The Founder of Upland." *Pennsylvania Magazine of History and Biography* 4 (1879).

London, Dr. J. Phillip. "The Challenging Life of a Patriot Captain." *Naval History*, October, 2012.

Mahan, Alfred Thayer. "John Paul Jones in the Revolution." *Scribner's*, July 1898.

"Captain Hector McNeill." *Massachusetts Historical Society Proceedings* 55 (November 1921). Massachusetts Historical Society.

Matthewman, Luke. "Narrative of Lieutenant Luke Matthewman." *Magazine of American History* 2, part 1 (1878).

Mazet, Lieutenant Horace S. "The Navy's Forgotten Hero." *U.S. Naval Institute Proceedings*, March 1937.

McCusker, John J. "The American Invasion of Nassau in the Bahamas." *American Neptune*, July 1965.

———, comp. "Ships Registered at the Port of Philadelphia before 1776: A Computerized Listing." *Pennsylvania Magazine of History* 23 (1898).

McGrath, Tim. "His Brother's Keeper." *Irish America* Magazine, April–May 2011.

———. "I Passed Philadelphia in Two Small Boats." *Naval History*, June 2009.

———. "Two Captains at Breakfast." *Naval History*, August 2013.

Merritt, Jane T. "Tea Trade, Consumption, and the Republican Paradox in Pre-

Revolutionary Philadelphia." *Pennsylvania Magazine of History and Biography* 129 (April 2004).

Miller, Richard G. "The Federal City, 1783–1800." In *Philadelphia: A 300-Year History*, edited by Russell F. Weigley, 155–207. New York: Norton, 1982.

Montrésor, John. "Journal of Captain John Montrésor." *Pennsylvania Magazine of History and Biography* 6 (1881).

Morgan, William James. "American Privateering in America's War for Independence, 1775–1783." *American Neptune*, July 1976.

———. "John Barry: A Most Fervent Patriot." In *Command Under Sail: Makers of the Naval Tradition 1775–1850*, edited by James C. Bradford. Annapolis, MD: Naval Institute Press, 1985.

Morris, Richard B. "The Revolution's Caine Mutiny." *American Heritage*, April 1960.

Niderost, Eric. "Capital in Crisis." *American History Magazine* 39, no. 3 (August 2004).

Norton, Louis Arthur. *"Alliance*: The Last Continental Navy Frigate. *Naval History*, August 2008.

———."The Continental Brig *Andrew (Andrea) Doria*." *American Neptune*, Winter 2001.

———. "The Penobscot Expedition: A Tale of Two Indicted Patriots." *Northern Mariner* 16, no. 4 (October 2006).

———. "A Victory 'By the Rule of Contrary.'" *Naval History*, April 2004.

Parker, Emelin Knox. "A Biographical Sketch of John Brown." In *Historical Society of Pennsylvania*. Carlisle, PA, 1918 (rev. 1928, 1935).

Parramore, Thomas C. "The Great Escape from Forten Gaol: An Incident of the Revolution." *North Carolina Historical Review* 45 (October 1968).

Paullin, Charles Oscar. "The Conditions of the Continental Naval Service." *U.S. Naval Institute Proceedings* 32 (March 1906).

Pennypacker, Hon. Samuel. "Anthony Wayne." *Pennsylvania Magazine of History and Biography* 32 (1908).

Pinkas, Benjamin. "The Vindication of John Adams: Rex v. Corbet and the Battle for the Heritage of the American Revolution, 1760–1816," *Tempus: The Harvard College History Review* 11:1–13

Poirier, Noel B. "Raids Target Western England." *Naval History*, August 2003.

Porter, General Horace. "The Recovery of the Body of John Paul Jones." *Century*, September 1905.

Quilley, Geoff. "The Image of the Ordinary Seaman in the 18th Century," National Maritime Museum, Greenwich, England, website.

Rafferty, Celestine. "The Barry Hayes Papers: A Presentation for the Wexford County Library." Wexford, 2002.

Rankin, Hugh F. "The Naval Flag of the American Revolution." *William and Mary Quarterly* 2 (1954): 229–353.

Rathbun, Frank H. "Rathbun's Raid on Nassau." *U.S. Naval Institute Proceedings,* November 1970.

Roach, Hannah Benner. "Taxables in Chestnut, Walnut, and Lower Delaware Wards." *Pennsylvania Genealogical Magazine* 22 (1961–62).

———. "Taxables in the City of Philadelphia, 1756." *Pennsylvania Genealogical Magazine* 22 (1961–62).

Rogers, George C., Jr. "The Charleston Tea Party: the Significance of December 3, 1773." *South Carolina Historical Magazine* 75, no. 3 (July 1974).

Salvucci, Linda. "Merchants and Diplomats: Philadelphia's Early Trade with Cuba." Historical Society of Pennsylvania website.

Scheina, Robert L. "A Matter of Definition: A New Jersey Navy, 1777–1783." *American Neptune* 39 (July 1979): 209–217.

Scott, Kenneth. "New Hampshire's Part in the Penobscot Expedition." *American Neptune* 8 (July 1947).

"Ship Registers for the Port of Philadelphia 1726–1775." *Pennsylvania Magazine of History and Biography* 28 (1904).

Smelser, Marshall, and Steven T. Preiss. "The Fleetless Nation." *American Secretaries of the Navy.* Vol. 1. Annapolis, MD: Naval Institute Press, 1980.

Taylor, George Rogers. "Nantucket Oil Merchants of the American Revolution." *Massachusetts Review* 18, no.3 (Autumn 1977).

Thayer, Theodore, "Town into City, 1746–1765." In Russell Weigley, ed., *Philadelphia: A 300-Year History.* New York: Norton, 1982.

Tinkcom, Harry M. "The Revolutionary City, 1765–1800." In Russell Weigley, ed., *Philadelphia: A 300-Year History.* New York: Norton, 1982.

Urwin, George J. "When Freedom Wore a Redcoat." *American History,* Summer 2008.

Warner, Oliver. "The Action Off Flamborough Head." *American Heritage,* August 1963.

Newspapers

American Daily Advertiser (Philadelphia)

Boston Evening Post

Boston Independent Chronicle 1778–1783

Boston Newspapers
Boston Packet
Connecticut Courant (Hartford)
Continental Journal (Boston)
Dudley's Maryland Gazette (Annapolis)
Dunlap's Pennsylvania Packet and General Advertiser
Liverpool Journal
London Chronicle
London Daily Intelligencer
London General Evening Post
London Morning Chronicle
London Public Advertiser 1775–1782
Maryland Gazette
Massachusetts Spy (Worcester)
National Gazette (Philadelphia)
New Hampshire Gazette (Portsmouth)
New Jersey Gazette (Bridgeton)
New London Courant-Gazette
New York Journal (New York)
Pennsylvania Chronicle (Philadelphia) 1775
Pennsylvania Evening Packet (Philadelphia)
Pennsylvania Evening Post (Philadelphia)
Pennsylvania Gazette (Philadelphia) 1765–1803
Pennsylvania Journal (Philadelphia)
Pennsylvania Ledger (Philadelphia)
Pennsylvania Packet (Philadelphia) 1765–1785
Philadelphia Advertiser
Philadelphia Aurora
Philadelphia Daily Advertiser
Philadelphia Gazette
Philadelphia Independent Gazette
Pittsburgh Sunday Dispatch
Porcupine's Gazette (Philadelphia)
South Carolina Gazette and Daily Advertiser
Weekly Mercury (Philadelphia)
Worcester Gazette

Maps, Charts, and Atlases

The American Revolution, 1175–1783: An Atlas of Eighteenth-Century Maps and Charts. Washington, DC: Naval History Division Department of the Navy, 1972.

Symonds, Craig L. *The Historical Atlas of the U.S. Navy*. Annapolis, MD: Naval Institute Press, 1995.

Delaware River to the Atlantic Ocean (G 3792.D44): J. Luffman, 1814.

Delaware River Estuary (Rare G 3824.P5; 2F6 S3 1777a.F58, .F583, .F585): Francois de Fleury.

Delaware River Estuary, etc. (Rare G 3832 .D4 P5 1794): Joshua Fisher.

Cape Sable to Cape Hatteras (G 3321 .P5 1882 US) U.S. Coast Guard Geodetic Survey.

The Island of Cuba (Rare G 4920 1775 .J4): Thomas Jefferys.

Penobscot Bay, Maine (G 3732 P.5 1887 US).

West Indies Maps to 1800 (Rare G 4390 1762 .A2).

National Charts—Caribbean Area (Rare G 4901 .P5 1824 >B5): Edmund Blunt.

National Geographic Family Reference Atlas of the World. Washington, DC: National Geographic, 2002.

The N. American Pilot for Newfoundland, etc. (Rare Bk. G 1106 N6 1788 Vol. 1): Thomas Jefferys.

Mud Island with the Operations for Reducing It: Dickey, Weissman, Chandler, Hoyt (copy).

An Accurate Map of the West Indies with the Adjacent Coast (ca. 1762): ISM, copy.

Coast Chart No. 124, Delaware Entrance (United States Coast and Geodetic Survey): William Duffield, Superintendent, ca. 1895.

INDEX

★ ★ ★

CANADA

Quebec

Newfoundland

NOVA SCOTIA

Halifax

COLONIES

Boston

THIRTEEN

Newport

New York

Philadelphia

THE

Charleston

Bermuda

FLORIDA

The Bahamas

Gulf Of Mexico

Havana

CUBA

Haiti

Santo Domingo

Jamaica

Puerto Rico

Antigua

Caribbean Sea

Guadeloupe

Dominica

Martinique

St. Lucie

Barbados

St. Vincent

Grenada

SOUTH AMERICA